The Louisiana Purchase Collection
PAUL E. HOFFMAN, EDITOR

Published with the assistance of the V. Ray Cardozier Fund,
an endowment created to support publication of scholarly books

INTERIM

W. C. C. Claiborne Letter Book, 1804–1805

APPOINTMENT

Edited with Biographical Sketches by

JARED WILLIAM BRADLEY

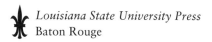

Louisiana State University Press
Baton Rouge

Designer: Amanda McDonald Scallan
Typeface: Sabon
Typesetter: Coghill Composition Co., Inc.
Printer and binder: Thomson-Shore, Inc.

Library of Congress Cataloging-in-Publication Data:

Claiborne, William C. C. (William Charles Cole), 1775–1817.
    Interim appointment : W. C. C. Claiborne letter book, 1804–1805 / edited with biographical sketches by Jared William Bradley.
        p. cm. — (The Louisiana Purchase collection)
Includes biographical references and index.
    ISBN 0-8071-2684-5 (hardcover : alk. paper)
    1. Claiborne, William C. C. (William Charles Cole), 1775–1817—Correspondence. 2. Governors—Louisiana—Correspondence. 3. Louisiana—Politics and government—1803–1865—Sources. 4. Louisiana—Social conditions—19th century—Sources. 5. Louisiana—Ethnic relations—Sources. 6. New Orleans (La.)—Politics and government—19th century—Sources. 7. New Orleans (La.)—Social conditions—19th century—Sources. 8. New Orleans (La.)—Biography. I. Bradley, Jared William, 1931– II. Title. III. Series.
    F374.C56 2001
    976.3′04′092—dc21

2001004234

To Yvonne Wolston Bradley

CONTENTS

LIST OF LETTERS, ADDRESSES, PROCLAMATIONS, CERTIFICATES, CIRCULARS, ETC.

LIST OF BIOGRAPHICAL SKETCHES

ACKNOWLEDGMENTS

These letters and the studies of some of Governor Claiborne's associates would still be reposing as scattered dry facts on the shelves of repositories were it not for the assistance of librarians, special collections staff members, and local researchers from the United States, England, Ireland, Scotland, and Spain. Their assistance is gratefully acknowledged with heartfelt thanks.

Foremost among the repository staffs to whom I am indebted is that of the Louisiana and Lower Mississippi Valley Collections of the Hill Memorial Library, the Louisiana State University Libraries. Faye Phillips, assistant dean of libraries for special collections, rendered assistance with a smile and such cheerfulness that she invariably lifted my sometimes flagging spirits. Much the same may be said of Judy Bolton, head, public services for special collections. The care that Mrs. Bolton and staff members working with her demonstrated toward materials in their charge also was shown in the invariably courteous assistance they rendered. Particularly helpful during the later months of research were Ann Collins; Amy Baptist; Charles Thomas; Emily Robison; Linda Schneider, coordinator of the Louisiana Newspaper Project; Anne Smith; and other staff members whose names I do not know. Elaine Smyth, curator of rare books and the E. A. McIlhenny Natural History Collection, and Christina Riquelmy, cataloguer of rare books in special collections, shared their expertise on bookbinding, which was of great help in my efforts to determine the origins of the paper and the binding of the Claiborne letter book.

At key points in my research, Myrtle S. "Smittie" Bolner, head of reference, and Barbara Witkopf, reference librarian, in the Troy H. Middleton

Library, the Louisiana State University Libraries, provided assistance in identifying and locating elusive research materials.

I also am indebted to the busy staff members of the Louisiana Department of the New Orleans Public Library, particularly Colin B. Hamer, Jr., now retired; Irene Wainwright; and Wayne B. Everard, curator of the New Orleans City Archives, which are housed in the department. Wilbur E. Meneray, assistant university librarian for special collections, and the staffs of the Louisiana Department and Special Collections of the Howard-Tilton Memorial Library, Tulane University, assisted my search for important pieces of information that helped to provide insights regarding several of the personalities and developments in early territorial New Orleans and Louisiana. The Special Collections of Loyola University Library, New Orleans, first made available to researchers microfilm of the *Audiencia de Santo Domingo* papers from the Archives of the Indies years ago under the administration of Dr. Bobs M. Tusa and most recently during construction of the new university library. Alice Daly Forsyth, now deceased, functioned as archivist and researcher with the St. Louis Cathedral Archives, New Orleans, in providing invaluable information from the marriage, birth, and death records of the archdiocese when I first began this project more than twenty years ago. Sally K. Reeves, archivist, the New Orleans Notarial Archives, assisted with those valuable records. Mrs. Pamela D. Arceneaux, librarian in the Reference Department, the Historic New Orleans Collection, shared her knowledge of obscure sources. Edith Atkinson, now retired, and her successors, Virginia Smith and Judith Smith, as head of the Louisiana Division, the State Library of Louisiana, all provided assistance along the way, as did Pat Leeper, also now retired, and Marc Wellman. Gary Ferguson, assistant head, Reference, and Nora Jenkins, also in Reference in the State Library of Louisiana, on several occasions assisted when time seemed to be flying and the task weighed heavily. Valuable information was found in several other Louisiana repositories: the Louisiana State Museum Library, New Orleans; the microform collection of the Edith Garland Dupré Library, the University of Louisiana, Lafayette; the Louisiana State Archives and Records Service Library, Baton Rouge; and the East Baton Rouge Parish Clerk of Court's Office.

Several libraries and special collections in Pennsylvania made available materials that were crucial to the study of early Louisiana and some of the personalities associated with its history and development. Jennifer Ambrose, research services librarian, the Historical Society of Pennsylvania, assisted with my inquiries to that repository and the Library Company of

Philadelphia. Rita Dockery, assistant manuscripts librarian, the American Philosophical Society, was most helpful. John Ward Willson Loose, secretary, the Lancaster County Bicentennial Commission, Inc., and Florence I. Gallagher, the Lancaster County Historical Society, provided pertinent pieces that helped to shed light on the life of George T. Ross. Barbara Gill, library director, the Berks County Historical Society, Reading, confirmed that there was little information on the early years of Benjamin Morgan in that county. Two local researchers who greatly aided my research in the Philadelphia area were Helen M. Rietheimer and Susan S. Koelble.

The staffs in libraries and special collections of several other states assisted in locating materials essential to understanding Louisiana's development in the early and middle years of American history. These include Elizabeth Wills, staff genealogist, the Kentucky Historical Society. Susan Fint, a local researcher in Frankfort, was of great help with my requests for information from early Kentucky state documents and newspapers. Richard A. Shrader, reference archivist, the Southern Historical Collection, the Wilson Library, the University of North Carolina, Chapel Hill, helped to unravel confusion created by years of interruption in my research. William R. Erwin, Jr., senior reference librarian, the Rare Book, Manuscript, and Special Collections Library, Duke University, provided similar invaluable assistance. Scattered pieces of the lives of some of Louisiana's early figures were found to make sense with the assistance of Suzanne Porter, curator, History of Medicine Collection, Duke University Medical Center; Dennis Northcott, assistant archivist, the Missouri Historical Society; Joanne J. Brooks, the Virginia Historical Society; William C. Luebke, the Virginia State Library and Archives; Kenneth S. Carlson, the Rhode Island State Archives; and Faye Simkin, executive officer, Local History and Genealogy Department, New York Public Library.

Clark Evans, reference specialist, the Rare Book and Special Collections Division of the Library of Congress, assisted in locating and making available vital information on political developments in early territorial Louisiana.

Beyond the borders of the United States, the staffs of four repositories in Great Britain assisted in locating and providing pertinent biographical information on several key figures in early territorial Louisiana: John Wood, Reader Services Department, the Public Record Office, London; W. W. Bream, librarian, and his successor, Adrian Blunt, deputy librarian, the Honourable Society of the Inner Temple Library, London; Robert D. Mills, assistant librarian, and his successor, Jonathan N. Armstrong, librarian, the

King's Inns Library, Dublin; and Jo Currie, assistant librarian, Special Collections, Edinburgh University Library. I owe special thanks to Mary (Mrs. Henry Z.) Pain. Her collection of information on the life of Lewis Kerr in the British Public Record Office and other repositories in London was invaluable and shall always be gratefully remembered.

D. Gail Saunders, archivist, Public Records Office, Nassau, The Bahamas, with the able assistance of John Wood, Reader Services Department, of that repository, provided information on the life and notable career of Lewis Kerr in the West Indies after his departure from New Orleans in 1809.

Before work on this project actually began, I received several partial reels of microfilm from the Archivo General de Indias, Seville, for use in another research project. I am indebted to unknown staff members of the Archivo for their prescient selection within the broad guidelines that I long ago provided. Information from one of the *legajos* (bundles or files) on those reels proved useful in this study.

Thanks also to Dr. Lucia G. Harrison, Foreign Languages Department, Louisiana State University, for assistance in translating a long and complex Spanish language document that illuminated an important facet of Dr. John Watkins's life and career in colonial Louisiana under Spain. Thanks, too, to Margaret Fisher Dalrymple, who now lives in Nevada, and Professor Jane Lucas DeGrummond, now deceased, whose interest in my research over the years spurred my resolve to complete it.

Finally, my wife Yvonne receives special thanks for her support and encouragement through the years. Her assistance in proofing the electronically produced copy of the letter book with the original manuscript made that tedious task seem less difficult. The thought patterns exhibited in the phrasing of the letters, she said, was a little like reading a regency novel.

Every effort has been made to eliminate errors. Unfortunately, some may remain. For these, I accept full responsibility.

THE LETTER BOOK

PREFACE TO THE LETTERS

This letter book of William Charles Cole Claiborne, Louisiana's first governor—provisional, territorial, and state—has been the property of the Archives and Manuscripts Department of Louisiana State University, and its successor, the Louisiana and Lower Mississippi Valley Collections, since sometime in the mid 1930s. The letters, dated October 3, 1804, through May 4, 1805,[1] cover portions of Claiborne's first two years as governor of Orleans Territory, the lower portion of the Louisiana Purchase land that became the state of Louisiana in 1812. One letter from Secretary of State James Madison to Governor Claiborne is dated earlier, August 28, 1804.

The contents of the bound volume provide a mystery: Why were these letters not included in the six-volume *Official Letter Books of W. C. C. Claiborne, 1801–1816*, edited by Dunbar Rowland and published by the Mississippi State Department of Archives and History in 1917? Where was this volume of letters when Rowland was preparing his edition of the Claiborne letters? Did Rowland know of its existence? Why was the letter book not made available for inclusion in his study? Finally, who possessed this letter book in the years before it became the property of the Louisiana State University archives?

The acquisition record of the Louisiana and Lower Mississippi Valley Collections is silent on how the library became the owner. The frontispiece

1. This information is inscribed by hand on four separate lines of the title page of the letter book. The inscription, with its sectioning indicated here by slashes, reads: "Journal / From 3d October 1805 / to / May 4th 1805[.]" The cursive letter *J* in "Journal" is about three times the size of the other letters in the word and in design might be considered a variant of Vivaldi script.

of the letter book is inscribed in pencil, "Property of John L. Henning, Lake Charles, LA, 1916." Several letters in the manuscript have been initialed "A. H." in pencil.[2] My attempts in the spring of 1976 to contact Mr. Henning in Lake Charles brought referral to his widow, who by then lived in San Antonio, Texas, with her daughter.

The interview of Mrs. Henning on an evening in June 1976 provided an answer to the question of who previously owned the letter book. Mrs. Henning said the letter book came into her family when her husband, John, bought it from Colonel C. C. Claiborne in 1916. Mrs. Henning described Colonel Claiborne as a "friend of my husband . . . cronies, you know, great friends." She said the colonel needed money toward the end of his life and decided to sell the letter book. Years later, in 1936 or 1937, during some of the darkest days of the 1930s Depression, Mrs. Henning sold the letter book to James A. McMillen, director of the Louisiana State University Library.[3]

Mrs. Henning said her husband met Colonel Claiborne through the Louisiana Historical Society.[4] C. C. Claiborne was William Charles Cole Claiborne IV, a great-grandson of Governor Claiborne and his second wife, Clarisse Duralde. C. C. Claiborne's parents were William C. C. Claiborne III and Jeanne Robelet.[5]

The letter book in appearance is age-darkened vellum over stiff board binding. The original blond color of the vellum suggests calfskin polished with alum, the kind of cover used by Irish scribes from the seventh to the ninth centuries and later elsewhere in Europe.[6] The fact that vellum remained popular in Europe, but less so in England,[7] along with other circumstantial evidence, suggests the ledger may have been manufactured on the continent, perhaps in France.

2. One entry in the original manuscript is written on a letter to James Madison, April 22, 1805, Letter No. 205 in this compilation.

3. Interview of Mrs. John L. Henning by Jared W. Bradley, San Antonio, Texas, June 18, 1976. Tape and transcription property of Jared W. Bradley. Hereinafter cited as Interview of Mrs. John L. Henning, June 18, 1976.

4. Ibid.

5. Stanley Clisby Arthur and George C. H. de Kernion, *Old Families of Louisiana* (1931; Baton Rouge: Claitor's, 1971), 148.

6. Matt T. Roberts and Don Etherington, *Bookbinding and the Conservation of Books: A Dictionary of Descriptive Terminology* (Washington, D.C.: Library of Congress, 1982), 277; and Geoffrey Ashall Glaister, *Glaister's Glossary of the Book*, 2nd ed., completely rev. (Berkeley: University of California Press, 1979), 499.

7. Philip Gaskell, *A New Introduction to Bibliography* (New York: Oxford University Press, 1972), 152.

Early in the provenance of the letter book, someone with an unsteady hand wrote in ink on the cover the partially visible title "original letter book." These words have been rendered even less legible by the pasting of a partially accurate description of the contents on the cover. The description, in capital block letters, began to wear off before the letter book became the property of the university archives department.

The ledger measures 35.7 centimeters high by 24.1 centimeters wide by 4.5 centimeters thick. Its once-sturdy binding suggests that the letter book may have been specially requested, and it may have been bought from Mc-Neil & Montgomery and Pezerban much as were the stationery and candles paid for by Claiborne in the fall of 1804.[8] The pages of the letter book are unlined and originally were not numbered. The Louisiana State University Archives and Manuscript Department numbered the 327 (consecutive) pages of the letter book. It is not known whether the blank pages of the bound book were gathered and bound by a stationer in New Orleans, or if the book in its entirety was shipped to an outlet there.

Several pages of the letters have watermarks. One of the clearer watermarks appears to be the initials "C S" placed within a circle.[9] The most frequent watermark found on pages throughout the manuscript appears to

8. McNeil & Montgomery and Pezerban, two or more separate businesses, were paid $52.75 for "Stationary and candles for the use of the office" in the fall of 1804. See Letter No. 200, W. C. C. Claiborne Disbursements during Temporary Government, Fourth Quarter 1804, entry nos. "3 & 4."

McNeil may have been the Joseph McNeil who is listed as residing at 75 Rue Royale South in *New Orleans in 1805: A Directory and Census, Together with Resolutions Authorizing Same Now Printed for the First Time from the Original Manuscript* (New Orleans: Pelican Gallery, 1936), 75. It may have been this same Joseph McNeil who was appointed with Benjamin Morgan and others by Governor Claiborne in May 1811 to serve as one of the commissioners to establish the Bank of Orleans. See By William C. C. Claiborne Governor of the Territory of Orleans [May 3, 1811], in *Official Letter Books of W. C. C. Claiborne, 1801–1816*, ed. Dunbar Rowland, vol. 5 (1917; New York: AMS Press, 1972), 230–1 (hereinafter cited as CLB with volume and page numbers).

Montgomery may be the William Montgomery listed as residing at 19 Levee South (*New Orleans in 1805*, 65). No business establishment containing the names McNeil & Montgomery has been found among the listings in any of the city directories for early territorial New Orleans. It is possible William Montgomery and W. W. Montgomery are the same person. W. W. Montgomery is identified as a businessman from Philadelphia who attended the banquet honoring George T. Ross following his dismissal as sheriff by Claiborne in March 1807. See the biographical sketch of Ross.

9. William C. C. Claiborne Letter Book, 1804–1805, [8], Louisiana and Lower Mississippi Valley Collections, Louisiana State University Libraries. Pagination by the department.

read "Annovay," suggesting the paper may have been made in Annonay, one of the three papermaking centers in seventeenth- and eighteenth-century France.[10] Another watermark that appears in the paper is clusters of grape-like rings, which was a frequently used watermark of early papermakers.[11]

The paper on which the letters are written has some foxing, water stains, and minor tears on a very few pages, but generally is in good condition. The paper tears are a reflection of the onset of brittleness and deterioration. The original sturdy cotton cord binding is now very loose, but otherwise, the overall condition of the volume is good. Careful examination of the letter book reveals that two whole pages appear to have been ripped out of the bound volume. The torn place in the manuscript occurs at a point where the paper was gathered and bound, so it is not readily visible to the unsuspecting viewer.[12] The removal of these pages may partly account for the loose binding. The letter, or letters, removed fall between those to Casa Calvo, dated November 9, 1804, and to Ferdinand Leigh Claiborne, dated November 12, 1804.[13] Mrs. Henning said the pages were not missing until after she retrieved the manuscript from a depository in Texas. She had temporarily placed the letter book with the depository for its staff to consider adding the manuscript to their collection. Mrs. Henning said that when she arrived to reclaim her manuscript she found it in use and the user writing something in it. Forty years later, Mrs. Henning was still upset over the missing pages and the defacement of the manuscript.[14]

The chief mar in the quality of the manuscript now is the information entered in pencil by a different hand at a later date. The original letters are written in ink. The information entered later was written in the margins and/or at the beginning of about a half dozen letters. These pencil entries are in the nature of a précis of the contents of the several letters near where the entries have been written. The comments are not included in this study because they clearly are not part of the original letters.

10. These markings most easily may be seen in ibid., [4] and [6]. Early papermaking centers of Europe are identified in W. A. Churchill, *Watermarks in Paper in Holland, England, France, etc., in the XVII and XVIII Centuries and Their Interconnection* (1935; Nieuwkoop, The Netherlands: B. DeGraff, 1985), 8, 28.

11. Claiborne Letter Book, 1804–1805, [212].

12. The paper appears to have been gathered in quarto. However, the quarto occasionally appears to have had another page or pages sewn into the volume. This observation and the sturdy binding would tend to support the belief the letter book was a special order item.

13. Claiborne Letter Book, 1804–1805, [62]–[63].

14. Interview of Mrs. John L. Henning, June 18, 1976.

There are no incomplete letters and except for an occasional strike-through of words and letters in a few of the communications, they are quite legible. A number of different hands wrote the letters, reflecting the fact that Governor Claiborne relied on more than the two secretaries—James Workman and Thomas Seilles Kennedy—known to have worked for him during the six months from October 3, 1804, through May 4, 1805. It may have been Workman who used the English or Continental spelling for some words, such as "honour" for honor, "controul" for control, and "Superieur" for superior. Workman was employed as clerk for Claiborne in September and October 1804.[15] The man who pleased Claiborne most with his services as secretary was Thomas S. Kennedy. He worked as clerk for the governor from July through September 1804 and again from November 19, 1804, into May 1805.[16]

The intent in editing the letters was not to produce a facsimile, but to retain with accuracy as much of their original flavor as possible. For this reason, the headings, salutations, and closings used by the governor have been kept. The headings are fairly standardized. Located in the upper right-hand corner of each letter in the letter book, the heading identifies the place of writing, most often New Orleans, followed immediately on the same line by the date of each letter. As an aid to readers, the editor has given each letter an additional heading that identifies the recipient and/or the sender.

The original paragraphing of each letter also has been retained. All the letters begin a few spaces in from the left edge of the unlined paper and gradually stagger downward toward the left margin. Because this is not a true indentation, this spacing is not treated as paragraphing in the edited transcription. When indentations are clearly present, they have been transcribed as such in the edited letters. The governor's amanuenses would sometimes indent the first word of the opening sentence after the salutation. In such cases, the indentation is reflected in the edited letters. Subsequent paragraphs in all the letters were obviously indented, and this sectioning also is reflected in the transcribed letters.

The salutation most often used by the governor was "Dear Sir." Occasionally, the governor's secretary would abbreviate this salutation to "DSir." In a few letters, the governor began his letter with "Sir." The "Sir"

15. See Letter No. 200, W. C. C. Claiborne Disbursements During Temporary Government, Fourth Quarter 1804, entry 5; and Letter No. 202, W. C. C. Claiborne Disbursements During Temporary Government, Third Quarter 1804, entry 5.

16. See For Sundry Disbursements during the Temporary Government, CLB, 3: 90; and Gov. Claiborne to Albert Gallatin, August 17, 1805, ibid., 172.

seems to have been used to vary the salutation, command attention, or, in some cases, convey displeasure. Whatever the salutation, it is duplicated in the transcription of each letter.

The addition of punctuation marks to the edited manuscript has been kept to a minimum. These marks have been supplied only where they are essential to clarify the meaning of a sentence, or to establish an abbreviation. Added punctuation marks are set in brackets. The deviation from this practice occurs with the abbreviations Mr., Messrs., Sr. (sister) and St. (saint). Periods following these abbreviations sometimes were omitted by the secretary but have been entered consistently here. When a word was not decipherable or was omitted, but a guess could be made about what it should or might be, the word was placed in brackets and included in the text simply for ease of reading. Illegible words and passages have been identified as such in the transcription. Questionable words or seemingly jumbled meanings have been followed by a bracketed question mark ([?]). When the meaning of an occasional word or passage eluded comprehension, its interpretation has been left to the reader's knowledge or imagination to determine what may have been meant by the governor and/or his secretary. Accounts and other financial information are transcribed exactly as written.

Explanations are provided in footnotes. Any previous publication of a letter, and the differences between the earlier published version and the draft found here, are usually noted in the first footnote. Over half of the 218 letters in this volume have never been published. Of course, they have been available to researchers who journeyed to the Louisiana State University archives facility to use them or, since 1957, the microfilm of them.

Certain decorative markings entered by the governor's secretaries at the ends of several letters have not been retained. These marks are of two kinds: large, hand-drawn brackets ({}), or several dashes above the sentence line interrupted by quotation-like hash marks. The brackets were used by the scribe to link two or three lines identifying the name and title of the recipient of a letter. They were drawn to the right of the ends of those lines identifying a recipient or applied at the end of the formal closing, such as "Your most obt[.] Hmble[.] Svt[.]" The few times the decorative dash and quotation marks were used, they were placed by the amanuensis beneath the last line identifying the name and title of the recipient.

The letters are published here in the same sequence they were entered in the letter book. The original letters are not numbered. They are numbered here from 1 through 218 for ease of reference and access.

INTRODUCTION

American and other nationals were arriving almost daily in New Orleans in 1804–1805 when the letters contained in this book were being written.[1] How much the population had grown since the acquisition of Louisiana by the United States is not known, nor is there an accurate count of the people living in lower Louisiana,[2] the Orleans Territory that President Jefferson appointed W. C. C. Claiborne to govern.[3] The chief deterrents to potential resi-

1. Letter No. 16, To James Madison, October 16, 1804, tells how a number of friendly planters above New Orleans probably saved "several Americans" from death from the yellow fever epidemic then raging in the city by detaining them as their guests. In addition to the Americans who were moving into the Orleans Territory, more than one thousand refugees from Santo Domingo settled in New Orleans in 1803–1804. Several hundred more had arrived between 1791 and 1802. Paul F. LaChance, "The 1809 Immigration of Saint-Domingue Refugees to New Orleans: Reception, Integration and Impact," *Louisiana History* 29, no. 2 (spring 1988), 110 n. 5.

2. The population of the "island of New-Orleans" with its "opposite margin" and adjacent settlements was 55,000, according to *Appendix to an Account of Louisiana, Being an Abstract of Documents, in the Offices of the Departments of State, and of the Treasury* (Philadelphia: John Conrad, 1803), Appendix VI, p. xc. The population of New Orleans, from the same source, was 8,056, including 700 white persons "not domiciled" (Appendix V, p. lxxxix). Nearly two years later, the population of New Orleans was said to be 6,119. *New Orleans in 1805: A Directory and Census, Together with Resolutions Authorizing Same, Now Printed for the First Time from the Original Manuscript.* (New Orleans: The Pelican Gallery, 1936), 31–83. Both these population counts must be taken as estimates because they are known to be incomplete and inaccurate.

3. Claiborne and General James Wilkinson were authorized to receive Louisiana jointly or separately from the representative of the French government, but Claiborne alone was to exercise governing authority over the newly acquired land. The Secretary of State to Governor

dents were the "common chronic and debilitating maladies" that occurred in conjunction with "a variety of unidentifiable hot weather 'fevers and fluxes.'" One of these was malaria, but the most feared was yellow fever, which made its first appearance in New Orleans in 1796 and returned annually thereafter with varying, but often deadly, virulence to those either not acclimated or not aware of how to protect themselves.[4]

The influx of newcomers, whether American, French, or some other nationality, could be overemphasized, but it is clear they added to the social instability created by the uncertainties introduced when the governments for New Orleans and lower Louisiana, the future Territory of Orleans, were changed. Newcomers to New Orleans in 1804 and 1805 found the residents lived much as they had before the Louisiana Purchase. The mostly French and some Spanish settlers, who began to move into the colony after the Treaty of Paris, 1763, by which Spain acquired Louisiana, had settled in scattered pockets along the rivers and bayous of lower Louisiana. However, the largest number of residents lived in New Orleans. There the settlers, with a smattering of English businessmen who somehow escaped Governor Alexander O'Reilly's September 2, 1769, order excluding all English merchants from trade and residence in Louisiana, stretched along the east bank of the Mississippi River for "nearly a mile . . . from the gate of France on the south, to that of Chapitoulas above."[5]

The houses facing the Mississippi and for "a square or two backwards" by 1803 were built mostly of brick with slate or tile roofs, a requirement instituted in 1795 by the Spanish after the disastrous fire of 1794 in which a significant portion of the town was destroyed.[6] Many of the twelve to

---

Claiborne, October 31, 1803, Clarence E. Carter, comp. and ed., *The Territorial Papers of the United States,* vol. 9, *The Territory of Orleans, 1803–1812* (Washington, D.C.: U.S. Government Printing Office, 1940), 91–2 (hereinafter cited as TP, 9 with page range). Claiborne subsequently was appointed governor of lower Louisiana and was continued in this position by President Jefferson. See Letter No. 1, To James Madison, October 3, 1804, and the references in note 2.

4. Jo Ann Carrigan, *The Saffron Scourge: A History of Yellow Fever in Louisiana, 1796–1905* (Lafayette: Center for Louisiana Studies, University of Southwestern Louisiana, 1994), 13–4. Carrigan also points out that early in the history of Louisiana the "sickly season" was "regularly" described as the summer and fall.

5. *An Account of Louisiana, Being an Abstract of Documents, in the Offices of the Departments of State, and of the Treasury* (Philadelphia: John Conrad, 1803), 18.

6. Minter Wood, "Life in New Orleans in the Spanish Period," *Louisiana Historical Quarterly* 22, no. 1 (January 1939), 646, 696. Illustrations 45 and 46 in Samuel Wilson, Jr., *The Vieux Carré, New Orleans: Its Plan, Its Growth, Its Architecture* ([New Orleans: Bureau of Governmental Research, 1968] 48) are plans showing the part of New Orleans destroyed by

fourteen hundred houses in the town were two stories. Generally, those beyond the first two streets paralleling the river were built of wood with shin-
gle roofs.[7] Often the timber used in the construction came from the
abundant stands of cypress, oak, and pine trees nearby.[8]

All the homes and businesses in the town were located as closely as possible to the Mississippi River because its bank offered the highest point in the
low-lying topography between the river, on one side, and Lakes Pontchartrain and Borgne and the Gulf of Mexico on the other. This, perforce, created a settlement that was "little more than a third of a mile in breadth from
the river."[9] Close beyond the width of the town lay the swamp and marsh
that held the lakes and gulf at bay except during excessive rains or the hurricane season.

A large and growing upriver suburb lay just beyond the poorly built and
decaying defenses that had been erected around the town in 1792. The dilapidated defenses had been hurriedly built on the heels of reports received
by Governor Don Francisco Luis Hector, Baron de Carondelet de Noyelles,
that an American army was being assembled in South Carolina to seize New
Orleans.[10] The suburb, Faubourg Ste. Marie (St. Mary), comprised homes
and businesses of newer arrivals in the city, many of whom were Americans.
The rapid development of this suburb beyond the ramparts of the original
city was a reflection of the growing importance of New Orleans as an outlet
for produce from throughout the Mississippi Valley, a growth that began in
the last decade of the eighteenth century.[11]

The Louisiana Purchase was agreed to in Paris on April 30, 1803, but
changes in the lives of Louisianians generally and residents of New Orleans
in particular did not begin until the fall of 1803, after the arrival of the offi-

---

the fire of December 8, 1794. An illustration of the plan showing the boundaries of the great
conflagration of New Orleans on the 21st of March 1788 is found in Edwin Adams Davis,
Louisiana: A Narrative History, 3rd ed. (Baton Rouge: Claitor's, 1971), facing p. 124.

   7. *Account of Louisiana,* 18.

   8. Ibid., 17; and John G. Clark, *New Orleans, 1718–1812: An Economic History* (Baton
Rouge: Louisiana State University Press, 1970), 28–9, 42, 52, 53, 57, 137, 177, 192, 193, 201,
231.

   9. *Account of Louisiana,* 18.

   10. Ibid., tells about the decaying fortifications, as does Wilson, *Vieux Carré,* 57–8. Ibid.,
45–6, also tells of Carondelet's defensive preparations for the city in 1792. Additional information on other Carondelet defensive preparations may be found in the brief sketch of the history
and early development of Fort St. Philip and the biographical sketch of John Watkins, both in
the Biographical Sketches portion of this study.

   11. Clark, *New Orleans,* 201.

cials involved in the transfers of the colony from Spain to France to the United States.[12] Actual changes in the governmental arrangements that would impact the lives of residents did not begin until after the governments established for Louisiana began to take shape under Governor Claiborne. Some weeks later the problems facing the American governor began to emerge. Those problems may be categorized broadly as diplomatic, political, and social, along with wrenching personal losses in the deaths of his wife, daughter, and brother-in-law in the fall of 1804.

The diplomatic problems that Claiborne faced in New Orleans were catapulted to the forefront by chauvinism, perhaps the leading characteristic of the age of colonial expansion that helped to create the colony of Louisiana. Sometimes these problems assumed the form of subtle psychological warfare; at other times, the diplomatic problems appeared as challenges to local law enforcement. On several occasions before, during, and after the transfers of Louisiana, the challenges to public order threatened to explode in a clash of arms. Initially the tensions were between Pierre Clément de Laussat, the French representative of the Republic of France, and Sebastián Calvo de la Puerta y O'Farrill, the Marqués de Casa Calvo, who was ordered to New Orleans to represent the Spanish government in the transfer of Louisiana. After departure of the French officials and their very small military contingent, tensions arose between the lingering Spanish officers and the Americans. The tensions, however, were never restricted solely to these opposing groups.

Governor Claiborne reported that many of the Frenchmen who made common cause were not those that he labeled the "Ancient Louisianians." The problems arose, Claiborne said, from the "intrigues of certain late emigrants from France, and Some of the satellites of the Spanish Government." This group, the governor advised Secretary of State James Madison, often "indulged in illiberal abuse of Americans, who otherwise would probably have remained neutral" in the tense relations that developed between Laussat and Casa Calvo.[13]

The tensions between the French and Spanish sometimes involved other nationalities whose ships docked in New Orleans. One such incident was the hot-tempered altercation between a Frenchman and an Englishman late in the second week of October 1804. This quarrel culminated in a near riot

12. Alexander DeConde, *This Affair of Louisiana* (New York: Charles Scribner's Sons, 1976), 171.

13. Letter No. 18, To James Madison, October 19, 1804.

in which several Americans rescued the Englishman after he had fired his pistol at his angry pursuers. Two of the principals in this public brawl were confined to jail for three days and then released on a twelve-month peace bond.[14]

The simmering tension between the French and Spanish officials was potentially more serious because of the international consequences. It appears at one point to have involved Governor Claiborne, who went so far as to draft a letter apparently intended for, but never sent to, Casa Calvo.[15] The tension was kept from boiling over through the restraint exercised by both Laussat and Casa Calvo, and a display of all the pomp and glitz the arrogant representatives of France and Spain could muster in the remote frontier river port.

Social festivities occurred for several days before and after the transfer of Louisiana from Spain to France, but on November 30, 1803, Casa Calvo, with the aging Juan Manuel de Salcedo, the governor of Spanish Louisiana, officially transferred ownership of Louisiana to France.[16] Three weeks later, on December 20, 1803, Laussat formally transferred ownership of Louisiana to Governor Claiborne.[17] Even after the transfer, Laussat continued to agitate in behalf of French ownership of Louisiana. On the one hand, he advised his government that something should be done to keep alive the resentment of the former French colonists toward the United States.[18] To certain Creoles, Laussat privately intimated that the transfer of Louisiana was a trick and in time the colony would be returned to France.[19] Early in 1804, Claiborne reported that Laussat was appealing to the pride of the French Creoles as a means of keeping them loyal to France.[20]

14. Ibid.

15. See Letter No. 159, To [never sent], March 19, 1805.

16. These events took place in the Place d'Armes (Jackson Square) in front of St. Louis Cathedral and in the social center of the town, the public ballroom built in 1792 at Chartres (Condé) and Dumaine Streets. A firsthand account of them was left by Pierre Clément de Laussat in his *Memoirs of My Life to My Son During the Years 1803 and After . . .* , trans. Sister Agnes-Josephine Pastwa, ed. Robert D. Bush (Baton Rouge: Louisiana State University Press, 1978), 78–81.

17. Ibid., 87–91; and DeConde, *This Affair of Louisiana,* 205–6.

18. Charles Gayarré, *History of Louisiana,* 5th ed., vol. 4 (1903; New Orleans: Pelican, 1965), 12.

19. François-Xavier Martin, *The History of Louisiana, from the Earliest Period* (1882; New Orleans: Pelican, 1963), 322.

20. *Official Letter Books of W. C. C. Claiborne, 1801–1816,* ed. Dunbar Rowland, vol. 1 (1917; New York: AMS Press, 1972), 330 (hereinafter cited as CLB with volume and page numbers).

Frictions began to develop between the Spanish officials, who lingered in New Orleans, and their American hosts after the departure of Laussat from New Orleans on April 21, 1804. These problems for Americans, like those for the departing French, stemmed from continued Spanish resentment over the loss of Louisiana. This hostility first was expressed to Secretary of State Madison at the seat of the U.S. government in September 1803 by Carlos Martínez de Yrujo, the Spanish minister plenipotentiary to the United States. The peevish king of Spain, whose covert objective was to protect Spain's gold- and silver-rich colony, New Spain (Mexico), had the Marqués de Yrujo notify Madison that the United States had no right to Louisiana because France had promised never to alienate the province.[21] This resentful attitude soon began to show itself in the conduct of the Spanish officials in New Orleans and along the northern shores of the Gulf of Mexico. It was demonstrated in the bold attempts of the Marqués de Casa Calvo and the former intendant, Juan Ventura Morales, to undermine and usurp the authority of Claiborne and United States ownership of the former Spanish colony. Claiborne's problems in this area may be traced in other sources, but the sense of immediacy in the threat posed by the activities of these two Spanish officials and their manipulative followers is captured here in several letters as few other sources reveal it.

A major incident that created quite a stir in the town involved a hitherto unknown American citizen, David Bannister Morgan, and Captain Manuel García y Muñis, commander of the fleet of small ships transporting three hundred Spanish troops from Baton Rouge to Pensacola in the fall of 1804. García was the officer who usually brought the payroll, the *situado* silver, from New Spain (Mexico) for all the Spanish officials in the Floridas and Louisiana.[22] Morgan, originally from upstate New York, had been authorized by the Spanish to do survey work north of Lake Pontchartrain along the Tchefuncte River. For reasons never explained, he was seized and his survey equipment confiscated, and he was held prisoner on one of the Spanish ships anchored several miles off Bayou St. John in Lake Pontchartrain. Somehow, Morgan escaped and swam to shore at the American fort located at the entrance to Bayou St. John, where he claimed protection from his

---

21. Dumas Malone, *Jefferson and His Time*, vol. 4, *Jefferson the President, First Term, 1801–1805* (Boston: Little, Brown, 1970), 321–3; and DeConde, *This Affair of Louisiana*, 193–4, 201–3.

22. Additional information on García's earlier career in the Mississippi Valley may be found in Abraham P. Nasatir, *Spanish War Vessels on the Mississippi, 1792–1796* (New Haven, Conn.: Yale University Press, 1968), 103 n. 29.

Spanish pursuers.[23] Three days later, Morgan, in an attempt to regain possession of his surveying instruments, caused a warrant to be issued for the arrest of Captain García.

The warrant for García's arrest was served where he and Spanish troops often were garrisoned during their stays in New Orleans: at the home of Vicente Folch y Juan, Spanish governor of West Florida. García refused to surrender when the warrant was served. At first it appeared this confrontation might result in an open clash of military arms between the Spanish guards at Folch's house and the U.S. Army soldiers called in to assist in García's arrest. In response to the arrest of García, Casa Calvo sent his representative to Governor Claiborne with a formal protest. The agent presented Casa Calvo's letter with an oral demand for "an immediate answer" and release of García, asserting that the marqués "'would not be answerable for the consequences and Revolution that might ensue'" if Claiborne's answer was not forthcoming.[24] Later the same evening, Claiborne reported, a "Mob of more than 200 Men" assembled in front of Casa Calvo's house evincing "a disposition for mischief," but dispersed at the request of Lewis Kerr, the *alguacil mayor* (sheriff).[25]

It is difficult for modern Americans to comprehend how contemptuously many European government officials regarded the young and almost defenseless United States. The Marqués de Casa Calvo believed the American experiment with republican government would fail. Indeed, in his attempts to undermine development of support for the United States among Louisianians, Casa Calvo used the arguments of some Federalists and other critics of the Jefferson administration that the nation would collapse in anarchy, or that it would again become a part of the British Empire.[26] With such thinking, Casa Calvo persuaded himself the lands beyond the Mississippi River could be reclaimed by Spain. The marqués encouraged circulation of this rumor with the caveat that not only was all the Louisiana Purchase land west of the Mississippi River going to be returned to Spain, but he also suggested the land west of the Mississippi would be exchanged for East and West Florida, portions of which the United States claimed as part of the Louisiana Purchase.[27] The effect of this and similar anti-American dissimu-

23. To James Madison, November 23, 1804, CLB, 3: 14, states the ships were anchored six miles offshore.

24. Letter No. 57, To Casa Calvo, November 18, 1804.

25. To James Madison, November 23, 1804, CLB, 3: 15–6.

26. See the biographical sketch of Casa Calvo.

27. See Letters No. 78 and 197, To James Madison, December 11, 1804, and April 21, 1805, respectively.

lations was to discourage uninformed native Louisianians from supporting the United States and the government Claiborne was trying to organize in the Orleans Territory.

Casa Calvo's efforts to undermine U.S. ownership of Louisiana was tailored to support the objections of some Louisianians to the provisions of the law providing for the creation of the Territory of Orleans. How much the marqués's activities inhibited or lessened the attachment of Louisianians to the United States cannot be quantified because no evidence has been found. Thus, the effect of his psychological warfare, aided and abetted by such pro-Spanish supporters as the Catholic priest Antoine de Sedella, Louis Brognier de Clouet, and others, can only be estimated. However, there is no doubt it did have an impact on public stability. Fortunately, Casa Calvo's attempts had no long-lasting effects, chiefly because, as John Watkins pointed out, "Many of the old Inhabitants . . . are already as good Americans as any in the U. States."[28]

The high-water mark for those Louisianians who were unhappy with U.S. rule occurred with the presentation of a memorial, or testimonial, to Congress voicing their criticism of the government established for them and asking that certain changes be made in it. The memorial was presented to Congress by three of the more unhappy Louisianians, Pierre Sauvé, Jean Noël Destréhan and Pierre Derbigny, whereas the most pro-French of Louisianians, Etienne de Boré, headed the committee that orchestrated complaints from New Orleans.[29] Claiborne sent a copy of this memorial to Nathaniel Macon, Speaker of the U.S. House of Representatives, in January 1805 with a request that it be laid before the whole House.[30] It is not known whether this action brought about the decision of the House in the spring of 1805 to reconsider the question of a government for the Orleans Territory.[31] Nonetheless, the memorialists were not granted any of the important demands they made.[32] Claiborne had no direct role in the decisions made by the Jefferson administration, but he was left to soothe the unhappy memorialists and their supporters.

An even greater problem facing Governor Claiborne was how to recon-

---

28. John Watkins to Secretary Graham, September 6, 1805, enclosed in Secretary Graham to the Secretary of State, September 9, 1805, TP, 9: 504.

29. Marietta Marie LeBreton, *A History of the Territory of Orleans, 1803–1812* (Ann Arbor, Mich.: University Microfilms, 1973), 145–50.

30. Letter No. 111, To Nathaniel Macon, January 21, 1805.

31. LeBreton, *Territory of Orleans,* 148.

32. Ibid., 149.

cile the fundamental philosophical differences between the Jefferson administration's objectives and the desire of the business community in New Orleans to expand the flow of goods through its port. The historical view of this conflict of interests has been clouded because it has been reduced to a clash of personalities: Jefferson and Claiborne on one side, Edward Livingston and a few little-known men on the other.[33]

The lifeblood of New Orleans, of course, was commerce. New Orleans businessmen desperately wanted and needed a bank, but Jefferson, supported by Claiborne, steadfastly opposed establishment of such an institution in New Orleans.[34] The orientation of New Orleans toward business also was reflected in the desire of the business community for a system of law that would facilitate commerce. Cast against this background, the real political problems of Claiborne began with the publicly printed refusal by Evan Jones to serve on the territorial council.[35]

Evan Jones was a native American originally from New York, a wealthy and prominent businessman who had lived in New Orleans and along the Gulf Coast since the 1760s. He had served as U.S. consul in New Orleans immediately before the Louisiana Purchase.[36] Jones's public refusal to serve on the territorial council was an unexpected setback to Claiborne's efforts to organize a government for the Territory of Orleans as soon as possible. The governor had hoped to have all the council members appointed in October and to summon them into session on November 12, 1804. However, it was not until the end of November that Claiborne obtained the acceptance of eight men to serve on the twelve-man council, enough to have a quorum if one of the councilors could not attend.[37] It is perhaps a coincidence, but public criticism of Claiborne started in October 1804, shortly after Evan Jones declined to serve on the territorial council. The criticisms began with an anonymous publication attributed to Pierre Derbigny, who formerly had served as translator in the governor's office.[38]

---

33. A good example of the reliance on personalities to develop the history of this period is William B. Hatcher, *Edward Livingston: Jeffersonian Republican and Jacksonian Democrat* (Baton Rouge: Louisiana State University Press, 1940). Business interests are dealt with chiefly as extensions of personality conflicts and only a limited number of specific businesses are touched on.

34. Letters No. 99 and 123, To James Madison, January 5, 1805, and January 13, 1805, respectively.

35. Letter No. 4, From Evan Jones, October 8, 1804.

36. See the biographical sketch of Evan Jones.

37. LeBreton, *Territory of Orleans*, 108–9, 113, 132–4.

38. Letter No. 16, To James Madison, October 16, 1804.

Claiborne's ability to find men who would serve in the new American government was boosted by the strong public support of Julien de Lalande Poydras, generally believed to be the richest man in Louisiana. He willingly agreed to serve on the territorial council, saying that it was a duty to serve and added that the people of Louisiana "must be initiated in the sacred Duties of Freemen and the Practices of Liberty."[39]

The letters contained in this volume also reveal that Claiborne often had to deal with issues brought to him by residents who were ignorant of the law, or who chose not to understand how representative government, particularly the U.S. government, worked. Included here are such matters as the elopement of Mlle. Orso and Lt. Doyle in April 1804;[40] the incident on the street outside of Casa Calvo's house between the marqués's Spanish guard and the American George T. Ross on the evening of December 5, 1804, which led to removal of the guard;[41] the robbery of Casa Calvo's residence, in which nearly $700 was stolen and misleading evidence in the form of a U.S. bayonet and ramrod were found near the scene;[42] and the case of Pedro Villamil, whose slaves had been sold by Juan Ventura Morales and his mistress, Mrs. Villamil, to Francis Hulin.[43]

There were other events that set Claiborne's responsibilities as governor of Orleans Territory apart from those of earlier and later frontier governors. Among these were the problem of slaves being brought into Louisiana for and from neighboring Spanish West Florida;[44] the retrieval of runaway Natchitoches slaves from Spanish Texas;[45] the operation off the mouth of the Mississippi River of English privateers who stopped and boarded commercial vessels, particularly U.S. ships, to seize goods and passengers who the privateers said were English citizens;[46] and the attempts by the French and

39. Letter No. 40, To James Madison, November 5, 1804.

40. Letter No. 114, To James Madison, January 26, 1805, p. 3; and Letters No. 115–20, Certificates [Depositions] of George King, Lt. William Murry, James W. Lanier, and John Watkins, all dated January 23, 1805; and John W. Gurley, January 24, 1805; and Lt. Joseph Taylor, January 25, 1805.

41. Letters No. 75 and 98, From George Thompson Ross, December 6, 1804, and To James Madison, January 5, 1805, respectively.

42. Letter No. 100, To Casa Calvo, January 5, 1805.

43. Letter No. 107, From Casa Calvo, July 26, 1804, pp. 1–3; and Letter No. 108, To Casa Calvo, September 5, 1804.

44. Letter No. 26, To James Madison, October 28, 1804, and Letter No. 64, To Thomas Jefferson, November 25, 1804.

45. See Letter No. 28, To Casa Calvo, October 30, 1804; and Letter No. 39, To Edward Demaresque Turner, November 3, 1804, and the additional references given there in n. 3.

46. Letter No. 205, To James Madison, April 22, 1805.

British to use the Port of New Orleans as an asylum in the war raging between those two countries.[47]

Finally, these letters also reveal the personal grief Claiborne had to deal with on two separate occasions. The first occurred when his first wife, Eliza (Elizabeth) W. Lewis, and their three-year-old daughter, Cornelia Tennessee, died of yellow fever within hours of one another on September 26, 1804.[48] Six months later, while still recovering from this shock, Claiborne found it necessary to console his father-in-law, Colonel William Terrell Lewis, once more. This time Claiborne had the sad responsibility of reporting the death of Colonel Lewis's only son, Micajah G. Lewis. Micajah, a younger brother of Eliza, was serving as Claiborne's personal secretary when he was killed in a duel defending the reputation of his deceased sister and Governor Claiborne.[49]

These letters of Governor William C. C. Claiborne have been available for scholarly use since shortly after they were placed in the Louisiana State University archives. Until they were microfilmed sometime in the late 1950s, the chief obstacle to using them was getting to the university. Not surprisingly, many of the users have been graduate students there. Hopefully, through this publication these letters will find a wider audience.

47. Letters No. 36, 37, and 85, To Samuel Boyer Davis, November 3, 1804, and To James Madison, November 3, 1804, and December 23, 1804, respectively.

48. Letter No. 2, Claiborne's First Louisiana Inaugural Address, October 2, 1804, n. 3.

49. Letter No. 170, To William Terrell Lewis, March 23, 1805, particularly n. 2.

ABBREVIATIONS

AGI
Archivo General de Indias

CLB
Official Letter Books of W. C. C. Claiborne, 1801–1816, ed. Dunbar
Rowland (1917; New York: AMS Press, 1972) (with volume and page
numbers)

TP
Clarence E. Carter, comp. and ed., *The Territorial Papers of the United
States*, vol. 9, *The Territory of Orleans, 1803–1812* (Washington, D.C.:
U.S. Government Printing Office, 1940) (with volume and page numbers)

{ 1 }

TO JAMES MADISON
New Orleans October 3rd 1804[1]

Sir

Your letter of the 30th of August enclosing me a commission as Governor of the Territory of Orleans was duly received.[2] Will you be pleased to communicate to the President how Sensible I am of the Honour confer'd upon me; and how Solicitous I shall be to merit by my conduct a continuance of his Confidence.

On this Morning the oaths of office were administered to me by Mr. Pitot Mayor of this City, and a Copy of a Short address which I made on the occasion is herewith enclosed.[3] I shall in the course of four or five days issue a Proclamation convening the Legislative Council, and will do every thing in my power to organize the Government with Dispatch. Neither of the Judges have yet arrived.[4] Colonel Kirby I understand has been ill at Fort Stoddart, but is now on the recovery. Mr. Brown (the Secretary) is at Natchez, and does not propose adventuring into New Orleans until about the close of this month;[5] I think this a wise precaution, for the City is not yet free of that dreadful Scourge the yellow-fever.

Accept assurances of my Respect and Esteem

(Signed) *William C. C. Claiborne*

The Honble
James Madison
Secretary of State

1. This letter To James Madison is dated October 8, 1804, in CLB, 2: 349. The present tense of the letter suggests that its correct date should be October 2, 1804, the date it carries in TP, 9: 303. It is possible the letter may have been completed the day after the events described.

2. The letter from Madison, Letter No. 5, To Governor Claiborne, August 30, 1804, also may be found in James Madison, *Letters and Other Writings of James Madison, Fourth Presi-*

dent of the United States, vol. 2 (Philadelphia: J. B. Lippincott, 1865), 204. Governor Claiborne to the Secretary of State, September 27, 1804, TP, 9: 299, acknowledges receipt of the letter. The act creating the Territory of Orleans was signed into law by President Thomas Jefferson on March 26, 1804. See An Act for the Organization of Orleans Territory and the Louisiana District, TP, 9: 202–13. Because Claiborne's initial appointment in 1803 was temporary and it was generally known the president wanted someone else as governor of the populous lower portion of the Louisiana Purchase Territory, Jefferson enclosed in the Madison dispatch to Claiborne a letter, also dated August 30, 1804, explaining to Claiborne the delay in his appointment. See the President to Governor Claiborne, August 30, 1804, TP, 9: 281–2. This recess appointment in August continued the interim arrangement until Jefferson nominated Claiborne for permanent appointment as governor on January 17, 1806. See Commission of Governor Claiborne, December 12, 1804, ibid., 351 n. 81; and Commission of Governor Claiborne, January 17, 1806, ibid., 571.

3. Claiborne's First Louisiana Inaugural Address, October 2, 1804, Letter No. 2, immediately follows this letter. For a brief biographical sketch of Pitot, see pp. 255–7 of this study. Greater detail on the life of Pitot may be found in Henry C. Pitot, *James Pitot (1761–1831): A Documentary Study* (New Orleans: Bocage Books, 1968).

4. The judges referred to were the initial appointees to the territorial Superior (Supreme) Court, John B. Prevost of New York and Ephraim Kirby of Connecticut. Their appointments were announced in the *Union,* October 8, 1804, p. 1, c. 1, along with other appointments by President Jefferson. See also the President to Governor Claiborne, August 30, 1804, TP, 9: 282, and To Governor Claiborne, August 28, 1804, Madison, *Letters and Other Writings,* 2: 204.

5. James Brown of Kentucky, the Orleans Territory Secretary. See pp. 258–65 for a biographical sketch of his life.

{2}
CLAIBORNE'S FIRST LOUISIANA INAUGURAL ADDRESS[1]
A Speech delivered by the Governor,
previous to his being sworn into
office

Fellow Citizens,

The President of the United States having been pleased to appoint me Governor of that part of Louisiana which is constituted the "Territory of Orleans" I have attended in this Hall Fellow Citizens to take in your presence the oaths of office required by Law. In this additional and distinguished proof of Confidence from the chief Magistrate of our Common Country I find the strongest inducements to merit by my conduct a continuance of his *Approbation;*[2] to deserve *yours* also fellow Citizens is my Sincere desire and shall be the fondest object of my cares.

All the felicity which a recent Domestic calamity has left for me to seek, or enjoy, is, in contributing to the Happiness of those over whom I am

called to preside.[3] The importance of the Trust committed and the high responsibility attached thereto are forcibly impressed upon my mind: and have
excited the most anxious Solicitude—On entering however upon my arduous
duties, I anticipate with pleasure the powerful aid which I shall receive
from the Judicial and Legislative Authorities, and the kind indulgence and
Support which a generous people always extend to the Honest efforts of a
public officer. Past events Fellow Citizens guarrantee the fulfilment [*sic*] of
these expectations[.]—

—In the course of my late administration which from a variety of circumstances was accompanied with peculiar difficulties, I received from the officers, Civil and Military, a zealous co-operation in all measures for the public
good, and from the people in general an indulgence and Support which encouraged harmony and insured the Supremacy of the Law.

I am now ready to take and Subscribe the oaths of office required, and I
pray almighty God to visit with his favor the Magistrates and Legislators
of this Territory;— to enable them to preserve to her Citizens and their posterity the blessings of *peace, Liberty, Laws,* and thus to Soften ~~to Soften~~ those
evils which a wise Providence has annexed to this world to the condition of
Man.

(Signed) *William C. C. Claiborne*

New Orleans
October 2nd 1804

1. Printed as "The Inauguration of Governor Claiborne, October 2, 1804," in TP, 9:
303–4, with a brief account of the event reprinted from the *Louisiana Gazette,* October 5,
1804.

2. The emphasis that Claiborne gave this word reflects the concern he had discreetly expressed six months earlier to Ephraim Kirby about his future with the Jefferson administration.
In writing Kirby, Claiborne said, "I know not how long I may be detained here nor am I yet
advised of my future destination." W. C. C. Claiborne to Ephraim Kirby, March 8, 1804,
Ephraim Kirby Papers, Rare Book, Manuscript, and Special Collections Library, Duke University. Claiborne believed the president intended the Orleans Territory governorship for James
Monroe. Jefferson did offer the post to Monroe, but the president's first choice was Marie
Joseph Paul Yves Roch Gilbert Du Motier, Marquis de Lafayette. Dumas Malone, *Jefferson
and His Time,* vol. 4, *Jefferson the President, First Term, 1801–1805* (Boston: Little, Brown,
1970), 357–8.

3. Claiborne's wife, Eliza (Elizabeth) W. Lewis, and their three-year-old daughter, Cornelia
Tennessee, both died of yellow fever on the same date, September 26, 1804. Governor Claiborne to the Secretary of State, September 27, 1804, TP, 9: 299; *Union,* October 1, 1804, p.
1, cc. 1–2; and the *Louisiana Gazette,* September 28, 1804, p. 3, c. 3. Two weeks later, Claiborne, who also had been afflicted with the disease, wrote Ephraim Kirby that he was still in

a "very feeble state, and my spirits quite depressed." W. C. C. Claiborne to Ephraim Kirby, October 10, 1804, Ephraim Kirby Papers, Rare Book, Manuscript, and Special Collections Library, Duke University.

{3}

To Legislative Council Nominees[1]

New Orleans October 5th 1804
(Circulaire)
To each member of The Legislative
Council[2]

Sir,

I have the pleasure to inform you, that you are appointed by the President of the United States a Member of the Legislative Council for the Territory of Orleans. Your Commission is in my possession, and shall be delivered whenever it may be agreeable to you to attend and take before me the oaths of office required by law.

I flatter myself you will afford to your fellow Citizens, the benefit of your Services in the Council and request that you would inform me of your determination as early as may be convenient.—

I am Sir very Respectfully
Your Hble Sevt.
(Signed) *William C. C. Claiborne*

1. Also printed in the *Union,* October 8, 1804, p. 1, c. 1, and the *Louisiana Gazette,* October 12, 1804, p. 3, c. 1, with a copy of the Proclamation Convening the Territorial Council, dated October 9, 1804, Letter No. 12.

2. Sent to Joseph Deville Degoutin Bellechasse, Jean Etienne de Boré, Michel Cantrelle, Daniel Clark, Gaspard DeBuys, Robert Dow, Evan Jones, William Kenner, Benjamin Morgan, Julien L. Poydras, John Roman, John Watkins, and William Wyckoff. See Governor Claiborne to the President, December 2, 1804, TP, 9: 346. The newspaper stories identified John Roman as "J. Romain of Attacapas" and Wyckoff as "Mr. Wikoff of Appalousa." *Union,* October 8, 1804, p. 1, c. 1, and *Louisiana Gazette,* October 12, 1804, p. 3, c. 1.

{4}

To James Brown

New Orleans October 4th 1804

Dear Sir,

The President of the United States has transmitted to me the Commission by which you are appointed Secretary for The Territory of Orleans. I congratulate you on the occasion, and Sincerely hope the appointment may be agreeable to you. Altho your assistance would be of peculiar importance in organizing the new Government, I nevertheless do not wish to See you in New Orleans until about the last of this month.

The yellow fever has much abated, but is not yet extinguished. I think however that in two or three weeks you may approach the City in Safety.[1] Accept assurances of my respect and Esteem[.]

(Signed) William C. C. Claiborne

The Honble[.]
James Brown
now at Natchez

1. By the end of October, New Orleans occasionally experiences a frost and infrequently a freeze which, if it occurred, would have ended the threat of yellow fever by killing the mosquito carrier. Secretary Brown to the Secretary of State, October 26, 1804, TP, 9: 314, advised Madison he would be in New Orleans before November 5, but Claiborne was still expecting the territorial secretary on November 26, 1804.

{5}
FROM JAMES MADISON
Virginia August 28th 1804[1]

Sir,

I have received your favours of the 12th and 14th July. The continuance and conduct of the Spanish Officers at New Orleans justly excite attention. In every view it is desirable that those foreigners should be no longer in a Situation to affront the authority of the United States, or to mingle by their intrigues in the affairs of your Territory. The first of October will be an epoch which may be used for letting it be understood that their Stay So much beyond the right and the occasion for it is not Seen with approbation.

The mode and measure of the intimation are left by the President to your Discreet Judgment. With Morales there may be less need of very delicate management, especially if he perseveres in retaining a Title which having belonged to a Spanish officer purily [sic] Provincial in Louisiana, Seems to arraign the present Jurisdiction of the United States.[2] You will soon receive from Mr. Granger some Blank Commissions for officers within his Department.[3] The President wishes you to Sound the Marquis of Casa Calvo[4] on the Subject of a Link of the chain of Post Offices within the contested Territory, and by friendly explanations to obtain his concurrence in making such an establishments for mutual convenience by mutual consent; with an understanding, or if pressed[,] and express declaration, that the measure is neither to strengthen nor weaken the rights of either nation. Should a Post office within the Limits possessed by Spain not be acquiesced in, it is thought best that it be waved for the present, leaving to the Mail a mere passage to which it may be presumed no opposition will be made.[5] By the last communications from Madrid of June 12th it appears that the Spanish Government had imbibed the discontent expressed here by the Marquis D'Yrugo[6] at the Act of Congress Authorizing a Revenue District on the waters of the Mobile[7] &c and that it manifested a backwardness to ratify the convention, which had been ratified here, in the very terms in which it was concluded on there. A knowledge of this ill humor may be useful in the course of your transactions[,] particularly those with the Spanish functionaries.

> With Sentiments of the Highest
> Respect and Esteem I
> Remain Sir
> Your most obd
> Hble St
> (Signed) *James Madison*

Governor Claiborne
New Orleans—

1. Also published as To Governor Claiborne, August 28, 1804, in James Madison, *Letters and Other Writings of James Madison, Fourth President of the United States,* vol. 2 (Philadelphia: J. B. Lippincott, 1865), 203–4.

2. Juan Ventura Morales, intendant for the Province of West Florida. See pp. 495–8 in the Biographical Sketches.

3. Gideon Granger, postmaster general.

4. Sebastián Calvo de la Puerta y O'Farrill (sometimes spelled with an *e*, O'Farrell), the Marqués de Casa Calvo. Claiborne, Madison, and Jefferson consistently followed accepted international practice in addressing Casa Calvo in their correspondence as *marquis* rather than *marqués*. At this time Casa Calvo was commissioner of the king of Spain for the expedition to determine the boundaries of Louisiana. He was appointed to this post on August 20, 1804, but appears to have done little to fulfill the responsibilities of the office until October 1805, when he set out by boat and horse across southern and western Louisiana and east Texas. The United States never recognized Casa Calvo's appointment as boundary commissioner. See the Secretary of State to Governor Claiborne, November 18, 1805, and January 10, 1806, TP, 9: 533–4 and 564, respectively. For a biographical sketch of Casa Calvo, see pp. 484–94 herein.

5. Claiborne did not ask the Spanish for a postal route through West Florida until after receipt of President Jefferson's January 7, 1805, letter indicating that he wanted the route to run from Georgia to Fort Stoddart and from there to the Pearl River. Claiborne may have delayed making the request in the hope of improved relations with the nearby Spanish officials.

On the suggestion of Jefferson, Casa Calvo was approached first because of his apparent disposition to be useful to both the Spanish and U.S. governments. The President to Governor Claiborne, January 7, 1805, TP, 9: 363–4. However, the marqués held no official position in West Florida and permission had to be sought from the governor of the province, Vicente Folch y Juan. Captain Daniel Carmick, commander of the U.S. Marines stationed in New Orleans, was selected for the mission to obtain Folch's answer. The route was in use by early July 1805 before Carmick could return to New Orleans, but was not considered safe because of hazards to the riders and the hostility of the Spanish. See To the Post Master General, June 17, 1805; Daniel Carmick to Gov. Claiborne, July 4, 1805; To Thomas Jefferson, July 14, 1805; To James Madison, August 9, 1805; all in CLB, 3: 97–8, 113–4, 125–6, and 156–7, respectively.

6. Carlos Martinez de Yrujo (Irujo, d'Yrujo), Marqués de Casa Yrujo, Spanish minister plenipotentiary to the United States 1796–1807. At the beginning of his administration Jefferson was favorably disposed toward Yrujo, partially because Yrujo married Sarah ("Sally") McKean, daughter of Thomas McKean, the republican governor of Pennsylvania in 1799 and friend of Jefferson. Jefferson's attitude changed beginning with Yrujo's violent language to Madison over the Mobile Act. William S. Baker, "Washington After the Revolution, 1784–1799," *Pennsylvania Magazine of History and Biography* 21 (1897): 43; and Dumas Malone, *Jefferson and His Time*, vol. 4, *Jefferson the President, First Term, 1801–1805* (Boston: Little, Brown, 1970), 97.

7. The act objected to by the Spanish was the revenue law for Louisiana, or as it is traditionally known, the Mobile Act, which became law on February 24, 1804. The Spanish objected to two parts of the law: section four, which provided for the annexation to the Mississippi revenue district of all of the navigable streams that opened onto the Gulf of Mexico east of the Mississippi River; and section eleven, which authorized the president, at his discretion, to establish a separate revenue district for Mobile River and Mobile Bay. *United States Statutes at Large, 6th–12th Congress, 1799–1813*, vol. 2, *Public Acts* (Boston: Little, Brown, 1850), 251–4. On Yrujo's objections, see Malone, *Jefferson and His Time*, 4: 342–6.

{6}
To James Madison
New Orleans October 5th 1804[1]

Sir,

Your Letter Dated Virginia August the 28th reached me on the evening of the third Instant;—[2] a number of Spanish Officers are yet in Louisiana, and there is no doubt with me but they encourage the discontents which arise here. I shall take an early opportunity to intimate to the Marquis of Casa Calvo, that the continuance of these officers in our Territory "so much beyond the right and the occasion for it, is not Seen with approbation" [sic][3] and with respect to Mr. Morales I shall without reserve express my desire for his Speedy departure. I paid a visit to the Marquis on yesterday, and informed him that for the accommodation of the People of West Florida, I had no objection to authorize some discreet person of that District, to receive, open, and close the Mail of the United States. The Marquis seemed pleased with the proposition, and approved highly of a Colonel Fulton near Baton-Rouge whom I named as a proper person.[4]

I am myself of opinion that one Post office on the Mail Route passing through West Florida is Sufficient, nor do I think it Safe at this time to multiply the establishments in that quarter. I very much regret the late news from Madrid;— I had Sincerely wished that the President would have completed his negotiations with Spain in a manner consonant to his fondest wishes, and that the good understanding between the two nations would not for a moment [have] been disturbed. But if Spain Should prove unaccommodating perhaps a little time will occasion reflection and make her prudent: But should She be disposed to be unjust, the United States can readily maintain their rights, and if (which God forbid) a War Should ultimately ensue, perhaps there is no Nation upon Earth, on whom we ~~could make So Sensible~~ [*sic*] so promptly and easily make ~~an~~ Sensible impression, and command an advantageous peace.[5] I recently received dispatches from Natchitoches;— they announce that three Citizens of the United States had been killed (Supposed by Indians) in the vicinity of the Sabine River.

A small Tribe of Indians living in the District of Ouichita having Solicited of me a Flag of the United States, I have procured a common one made of Buntin, and Shall present it to them.

> I am Sir with the greatest
> Respect and Esteem
> Your very Hble Sevt
> (Signed) *William C. C. Claiborne*

The Honble
James Madison
Secretary
of State

1. Also printed as To James Madison, October 5, 1804, CLB, 2: 347–8.

2. It is clear from this letter that the stress of Claiborne's office was considerably compounded by his personal grief over the deaths of his wife and daughter. The governor appears to have forgotten that he privately acknowledged receipt of Madison's August 28 letter on September 27, 1804. See Governor Claiborne to the Secretary of State (Private), September 27, 1804, TP, 9: 299.

3. The quote is from the last sentence of the first paragraph of Letter No. 5, From Madison, August 28, 1804, which immediately precedes this one.

4. For a biographical sketch of Samuel Fulton, see pp. 476–83.

5. Claiborne's discreet reference to the use of force against the Spanish to obtain U.S. ownership of West Florida undoubtedly reflected the frontier influence of his residence in Tennessee and Mississippi, but it also reflected exposure to Thomas Jefferson's attitude toward Spain as secretary of state in 1793. On the latter, see Randolph C. Downs, "Indian Affairs in the Southwest Territory, 1790–1796," *Tennessee Historical Magazine* 2nd ser., 2 (1937), 253–4.

{7}

To Mother Superior

New Orleans October 6th 1804
To the Superior of the Convent of St[.]
Ursula[1]

Holy Sister,

Accept my Sincere thanks for your congratulations on my appointment to the Government of this Territory; and for your kind condolence on the Domestic Calamity which I have lately experienced.[2] Rest assured that you Sister and the very respectable Community over whom you preside, Shall continue to receive all the protection which my authority can afford.[3]

> I have the Honour to be with
> respectful attachment!
> Your most Obt Sevt
> (Signed) *William C. C. Claiborne*

1. Ursuline Convent, the school for girls.

2. Claiborne is referring to the deaths of his wife, the former Elizabeth ("Eliza") W. Lewis, and three-year-old daughter, Cornelia Tennessee, on the same day, September 26, 1804.

3. The letter of the mother superior, Thérèse Farjon de St. Francis Xavier, has not been found, but it is clear from Claiborne's response that his installation as governor was used as the occasion by her to seek accommodation with the United States government in Louisiana. Undoubtedly, the nun's letter reflected her concern for financial security, which had been provided by the Spanish government. At this period in the history of the Catholic Church in Louisiana, parishioners were opposed to financial support of the church and usually provided very little financial assistance. It was for this reason that sixteen of the Ursuline nuns, including the preceding mother superior, Sr. Monica Ramos, sailed for Havana on May 29, 1803. They must have created quite a sight as they were escorted by Fr. Thomas Hassett, the canon of St. Louis Cathedral, and others to the boat that was to take them to Havana. Underlying Mother Thérèse's concern for the ten Ursuline nuns who remained and the nonreligious charges left in her care was her fear of the effects of the change in culture and attitudes of the new government. Under the government being created in Louisiana by Pierre Clément Laussat, the French colonial prefect, there would be no provision for the upkeep of the nuns. It also was well known the United States government was not pledged to any church and that most of the incoming Americans followed no church at all. Roger Baudier, *The Catholic Church in Louisiana* (1939; New Orleans: Louisiana Library Association, 1972), 251–2.

{8}
To James Pitot and the City Council
New Orleans October 6th 1804
To the Mayor and Municipality[1]

Gentlemen,

I approve highly of the monthly meetings of Physicians proposed by the Committee of Health;[2] and shall not fail to attend at the first meeting that takes place. I request however that the Committee would be So obliging as to appoint one of their own members to deliver an address appropriate to the occasion. So little knowledge have I of Medical Subjects, that I must decline the Honour which the Committee would wish to confer on me.

> I remain Gentlemen with great
> Respect
> and esteem your most obt Hble Svt
> (Signed) *William C. C. Claiborne*

1. For a brief sketch of the creation and membership of the "Municipal," or city council, see pp. 589–90.

2. The origins of this committee, subsequently referred to as *Comité Medical,* are set forth in John Duffy, ed., *The Rudolph Matas History of Medicine,* vol. 1 (Baton Rouge: Louisiana State University Press, 1958), 326–30; and Gordon E. Gilson, *Louisiana State Board of Health: The Formative Years* (New Orleans: n.p., 1967), particularly, 15–20.

{9}
To Casa Calvo
New Orleans October 6th 1804

Sir,

In answer to your Excellencys Letter of the 24th ultimo I have the Honour to observe that the whole of my Judicial Authority ceased on the first of this month, and that the dispute concerning the property of the Schooner Nancy[1] must be determined by the Tribunals of The Territory. Should any Subject of His Catholic Majesty Sustain an injury in consequence of a Suit commenced in one of the courts of this Territory, there is no doubt but Such compensation will be decreed him as Justice and the Law shall prescribe.—

> I have the Honour to be with
> Sentiments of Esteem and
> Respect your Excellencys
> most obt Hble Svt

(Signed) William C. C. Claiborne

His Excellency
The Marquis of
Casa Calvo

1. The Danish vessel out of Kingston, Jamaica, commanded by Captain Belhome. The property in question probably was slaves. See To William Cooper, May 19, 1804, CLB, 2: 151.

{10}

To Jean Baptiste Victor Castillon[1]

New Orleans October 8th 1804

Sir,

Your Letter mentioning the appointment of Doctor Blanket[2] as Physician to the Charitable Hospital of New Orleans has been received. Altho I have every disposition to respect the choice of Mrs. Castillon,[3] I presume She must have been uninformed that Doctor Blanket had not as yet complied with the Municipal regulations of this City respecting Practitioners of Medicine. If the Doctor has a Diploma of Doctor of Medicine from any regularly established University, there can be no objections to his holding that appointment;— but if he is not possessed of Such a credential, it is proper that he should undergo the examination prescribed by the Laws of our Country, before he can be admitted to Practice either in the Hospital or in Private Families.

I have the Honour to be Sir with
Sentiments
of Respect your most obdt Sevt
(Signed) William C. C. Claiborne

Mr. Castillon

1. Jean Baptiste Victor Castillon (sometimes spelled Chatillon) served as pharmacist for the San Carlos (St. Charles) Charity Hospital. *Premier 'Directory' de la Nouvelle-Orleans, 1807,* printed in *Le Diamant* 1, no. 14 (May 1, 1887), 46. It was as president of the "Marguilliers," the elected board of wardens of St. Louis Cathedral in 1806, that Castillon appealed to Napoleon for support in their contention that the Capuchin Father Antonio de Sedella, *Père Antoine,* was bishop of the Catholic Church in Louisiana. Marietta Marie LeBreton, *A History of the Territory of Orleans, 1803–1812* (Ann Arbor: University Microfilms, 1973), 321. Stanley Faye, ed. "The Schism of 1805 in New Orleans," *Louisiana Historical Quarterly* 22, no. 1 (January 1939), 98–141, prints the pertinent correspondence with a useful introduction. Castillon claimed to be the Spanish consul in New Orleans until 1807. Stanley Faye, "Consuls of Spain in New Orleans, 1804–1821," *Louisiana Historical Quarterly* 21, no. 3 (July 1938),

677–9. In the same year that Castillon sought to have Napoleon appoint *Père* Antoine head of the Catholic Church in Louisiana, he also was an unsuccessful candidate for a seat in the territorial house of representatives. See H. Molier to Governor Claiborne, January 21, 1806, TP, 9: 574, giving the election returns.

2. Jean-Baptiste Casimiro Blanquet Ducaila (1771–September 13, 1809) was born in Mandes, France. Powell A. Casey, "Masonic Lodges in New Orleans," *New Orleans Genesis* 20, no. 77 (January 1981), 7. Blanquet received his medical education at the College of Montpelier. Letter No. 17, To James Pitot and the City Council, October 18, 1804. Blanquet may have had some connection with Louisiana before 1803. Someone named Jean Baptiste Blanquet was in Louisiana in 1773 and 1786. See translations of French Document 47, dated only 1773, and Spanish Documents 1240 and 1442, dated March 7, and November 29, 1786, respectively, Louisiana State Museum Library MSS. If Blanquet was not in Louisiana before the transfer of the colony to the United States, he came to New Orleans as "health officer" and "professor of chemistry" in the entourage that accompanied Pierre Laussat, colonial prefect and commissioner of the French government in the transfer of Louisiana, to New Orleans in 1803. Pierre Clément de Laussat, *Memoirs of My Life to My Son During the Years 1803 and After. . .,* trans. Sister Agnes-Josephine Pastwa, ed. Robert D. Bush (Baton Rouge: Louisiana State University Press, 1978), 1, 41. Like many physicians of his time, Blanquet prepared most of the medicines that he dispensed. By 1808 he had established his own pharmacy to serve all comers, particularly "gentlemen planters at a distance." See the advertisement from the January 20, 1808, *Louisiana Courier,* printed in Duffy, *Matas History of Medicine,* 1: 343–4. Although Claiborne questioned the appointment of Blanquet to the hospital post, the hospital board overruled him and appointed Blanquet. Letter No. 179, Claiborne To Garrett Elliott Pendergrass [Pendergrast], March 31, 1805.

3. Mrs. Castillon (d. 1825 or 1827?) was the former Louise de la Ronde and the widow of Andrés Almonester y Roxas. She married Jean Baptiste Victor Castillon in mid-March 1804. Christina Vella provides numerous references to Louise in the biographical study of her daughter, *Intimate Enemies: The Two Worlds of the Baroness de Pontalba* (Baton Rouge: Louisiana State University Press, 1997). For a description of the charivari given the mature Castillons after their marriage, see John S. Kendall, "The Pontalba Buildings," *Louisiana Historical Quarterly* 19, no. 1 (January 1936), 127, 130. As the widow of Almonester, the founder of San Carlos Charity Hospital, Mrs. Castillon continued to exercise the prerogative granted by the Spanish crown to appoint the hospital medical and administrative staffs. See Letter No. 179, To Garrett Elliott Pendergass [Pendergrast], March 31, 1805, in which the governor states that he has little or no authority in appointments to the Charity Hospital in New Orleans. See also Jack D. L. Holmes, "Andrés Almonester y Roxas: Saint or Scoundrel?" *Louisiana Studies* 7, no. 1 (spring 1968), 54–5, 62.

{11}
To Territorial Council Members

A Circular, To each Member of The
Council
New Orleans October 9th 1804[1]

Sir,

I have the Honour to enclose you a Proclamation Convoking the Legislative Council; the Interest of the Territory rendered this call necessary, and I rely with confidence on your punctual attendance[.]

I am Sir very Respectfully
Your Hble Sevt
(Signed) *William C. C. Claiborne*

1. Also printed in the *Union*, October 8, 1804, p. 1, c. 1, and *Louisiana Gazette*, October 12, 1804, p. 3, c. 1. The individual notices of appointment in the *Louisiana Gazette* included a copy of the Proclamation Convening the Territorial Council. See Letter No. 12, October 9, 1804, which immediately follows. The council members were identified in the circular notices sent to each of them and in the newspapers. See Letter No. 3, To Legislative Council Nominees, October 5, 1804, n. 2.

{12}
Proclamation Convening the Territorial Council[1]

By His Excellency William C. C.
Claiborne
Governor of The Territory of Orleans
A Proclamation

Whereas the Interest of the Territory would in my opinion be promoted by an early Session of the Legislature thereof, I have thought proper to issue this my Proclamation hereby requiring each and every Member of the Legislative Council to meet in Council at the Hotel DeVille in the City of New Orleans on Monday the 12th of November next.—

Given at New Orleans this 9th Day of October
in the year of our Lord One thousand eight hundred and four, and of the Independence of the United States of America the twenty ninth.

In testimony whereof I have undersigned
my name and caused the Public Seal to be
hereunto affixed.—

(Signed) *William C. C. Claiborne*

SEAL

1. Also printed in the *Union,* October 8, 1804, p. 1, c. 1, and the *Louisiana Gazette,* October 12, 1804, p. 3, c. 1, with the circular sent to each territorial council nominee listed in Letter No. 3, To the Legislative Council Members, October 5, 1804, n. 2.

{13}
TO CASA CALVO
New Orleans October 9th 1804[1]

Sir,

It is now near ten Months since Louisiana was delivered to the United States, and yet the complete evacuation of the Province by the former Spanish authorities as Stipulated by Treaty has not taken place.[2]

I can therefore no longer refrain from observing to your Excellency, that the continuance in this Territory of so many Spanish officers "So much beyond the right and occasion for it is not Seen with approbation";[3] and I must particularly mention that the early departure of Mr. John Ventura Morales, who stiles [*sic*] himself Intendant and Contador of the Royal Armies would afford me Satisfaction[.]—

> I renew to your Excellency
> assurances
> of my respectful consideration
> (Signed) *William C. C. Claiborne*

The Marquis of
Casa Calvo

1. Also published as To Casa Calvo, but dated October 9, 1804, CLB, 2: 371, and with variations in the text. It also is in Spanish enclosed in Casa Calvo to Miguel Cayetano Soler, Secretario de Estado Y Despache Universal de Hacienda de España e Indias, October 14, 1804, AGI, *Papeles de Cuba,* legajo 179-B. No folio numbers are on the pages in this microfilm, which is owned by the author.

2. Under the terms of the "Treaty for the Cession of Louisiana," the French commissioner was to relinquish all military posts to the United States and all troops, French and Spanish, were to leave Louisiana within three months after ratification of the treaty. The treaty was ratified on May 22, 1803, by France and on October 21, 1803, by the United States. Ratifications were exchanged in Washington on the latter date. Therefore, French and Spanish troops should have completed evacuation of Louisiana by January 21, 1804. See Hunter Miller, ed., *Treaties and Other International Acts of the United States of America,* vol. 2 (Washington, D.C.: Government Printing Office, 1931), 498, 502. The French officials and military personnel left in March 1804. Nearly three hundred Spanish troops sailed for Pensacola in April 1804. However, Casa Calvo, Morales, a few minor Spanish officials, approximately a dozen Spanish officers, and a small number of enlisted men remained in New Orleans. Marietta

Marie LeBreton, *A History of the Territory of Orleans, 1803–1812* (Ann Arbor: University Microfilms, 1973), 70.

3. The quotation is from the first paragraph of Letter No. 5, Madison to Claiborne, August 28, 1804. Perspective on the difficulties with Morales and Casa Calvo is provided in the Biographical Sketches.

{14}
FROM EVAN JONES
New Orleans October 8th 1804[1]

Sir,

I did not receive 'till within this hour the Letter you did me the Honour to write me on the fifth Instant, from which I learn that the President of the United States has been pleased to appoint me a member of the Legislative Council for the Territory of Orleans; and that my Commission is in your hands &c.

As I have not the Honour of being personally known to the President, I cannot well imagine to whom I am indebted for the favorable idea that somebody must have surely given him of me. Such a mark of his good opinion is extremely flattering to me; and under other circumstances might be extremely acceptable; but in my present situation I do not feel myself at liberty to accept of the appointment. Conjointly with almost all the Inhabitants of Lower Louisiana I have Signed a Memorial to Congress, respectfully remonstrating against the act made for our Government and humbly praying for a repeal thereof.—[2] I cannot therefore with any consistency, accept of any office under a Law of which I have from the beginning so openly expressed by disapprobation, and which for the happiness of my fellow Citizens, & (forgive me if I add) for the honour of my native Country I So ardently wish to See annulled.

When calm reflection Shall have taken the place of passion and of party Spirit, I flatter myself that my Conduct on the present occasion will be approved—I was born an American—I glory in the name.— In defence of that happy land which gave me Birth my life and my fortune shall always be staked—but I cannot consent, for any consideration to do an act which I think Subversive of the rights and liberties of my fellow Citizens.—

> With great Respect I have the
> Honor to
> be Sir Your Excellency's most obt
> Sevt

(Signed) *Evan Jones*[3]

his Excellency
Governor Claiborne

1. Also published as From Evan Jones, October 8, 1804, CLB, 2: 350–1, with variations in the text and punctuation. Parts of the second and third paragraphs of this letter, with slight differences in phraseology, are quoted in Charles Gayarré, *History of Louisiana,* 5th ed., vol. 4 (1903; New Orleans: Pelican, 1965), 20. The complete letter was published in two New Orleans newspapers, the *Télégraphe* on October 10, 1804, and five days later reprinted in the *Union,* October 15, 1804, p. 1, cc. 3–4. The issue of the *Télégraphe* in which the letter was printed has not survived.

2. This second petition to Congress from Lower Louisiana grew out of the June 1, 1804, meeting of about twenty-five New Orleans residents. The petitioners objected to specific provisions of the Louisiana government act, which was adopted by both houses of Congress on March 23, 1804, and signed into law by President Jefferson three days later. *Annals of Congress: The Debates and Proceedings in the Congress of the United States, 1789–1824,* 8th Cong., 1st sess., 296–7; and *Journal of the House of Representatives of the United States,* vol. 4 (Washington, D.C.: Gales and Seaton, 1826), 690. The memorial, or petition, to which Jones refers in his letter is generally believed to have been the work of Edward Livingston, Evan Jones, and Daniel Clark. Marietta Marie LeBreton, *A History of the Territory of Orleans, 1803–1812* (Ann Arbor: University Microfilms, 1973), 118. There is no record that the first memorial ever was drafted. It was to have been written by John Watkins, John F. Merieult, and James Pitot. They were given this responsibility at the public meeting called by Benjamin Tupper, a Bostonian who had come to Louisiana via France, and presided over by Etienne de Boré, who was then mayor of New Orleans, on March 12, 1804. Ibid., 104–8.

3. See the biographical sketch of Evan Jones, pp. 374–88.

{15}
To Evan Jones
New Orleans October 9th 1804

Sir,
Your Letter of yesterday announcing your determination to decline Serving as a Member of the Legislative Council has been received, and Shall be forwarded to the Secretary of State by the next Mail.

(Signed) *William C. C. Claiborne*
Mr. Evan Jones

{16}
To James Madison
New Orleans October 16th 1804[1]

Sir,
I returned to this City on this Morning and find my health benefitted from my late (tho Short) excursion into the Country.[2] The Sugar Crops are very

promising, and the Labours of the Planter will be abundantly rewarded. The Citizens whom I visited appeared to enjoy Health and Contentment, and I was well pleased with their friendly Hospitality. I also observed with pleasure the Humanity of Several Planters who by detaining at their Houses several Americans destined for this City, have probably rescued them from sudden death.—

The Fever Still exists but it has greatly abated, and I think in a few days will entirely disappear. The enclosed Political Pamphlet[3] is circulating in this Territory; it is written with ingenuity, and is certainly well calculated to encrease [*sic*] the existing discontents. That a part of the Statements in this Pamphlet are true I will readily admit; but on Some occasions the writer has manifested an ignorance of facts, or a great want of Candor. The Writer is not correct in Stating that native Americans enjoyed all the Lucrative employments under my late administration;— I at present recollect but Six officers of that description. Mr. Derbigny[,] late Interpreter of the Government[4] was appointed Clerk of the Court of Pleas, Mr. Lewis Kerr[5] Sheriff for the City, and two ancient and two Modern Louisianians Notaries Public. But with respect to offices of Honour and Trust not lucrative, the Ancient Louisianians have enjoyed a very great proportion; I do not believe that a Single modern Louisianian, (except those of the Volunteer Corps) holds an appointment in the Militia, and among the Officers of the Volunteer Corps there are Several ancient Louisianians, and one of them is the Major commanding.

The Mayor of the City ~~and a Majority~~ and a Majority of the Municipality are ancient Louisianians, and every member (except one) speaks French correctly.— An equal number of the Court of Pleas are ancient Louisianians, and every member (except one) are Supposed to be well versed in the French Language. The native language of the Clerk of the Court is French, and I believe his precepts were generally issued in his native language. Among the various District commandants, I can at present recollect but three native Americans, and I may add that two of four Aids Du Camp who in my character as Commander in Chief of the Militia I have appointed are ancient Louisianians. I could make further details upon this Subject; but I deem it unnecessary. If I have discovered partiality in appointing to office it has been in favour of the ancient Louisianians and I believe candid men will acknowledge the fact.

But as the writer has taken great exception to the formation of the Volunteer Corps perhaps it may not be unnecessary to make one or two observations upon that Subject.— Previous to my arrival in New Orleans the Citizens of the United States residing in the City had associated for purpose of as-

sisting preservation of order, and offered their Services as a Volunteer Corps
to Mr. Laussat, and of which he readily accepted: When the Flag of their
Country was unfurled and Louisiana declared a part of the United States their
services (as might have been expected) were again offered, and that Governor who had rejected the Patriotic ~~offer~~ tender would have acted unworthily.
Several Companies were formed and I have understood that Some of the
ancient Militia were enrolled in the new Corps: But the Command of the Battalion was given by me, to an ancient Louisianian. Did this evidence impress partiality for native Americans? there [*sic*] were then also existing
circumstances which highly evinced the expediency of organizing the Volunteer Corps; but it is not necessary to State them. I recollect with pleasure
that on this occasion, my conduct has been approved by the Executive.

    With respect to the Body of the Militia their organization was delayed by
imperious circumstances. It is however now nearly completed and I owe to
Colonel Bellechase[6] (the Officer Commanding) many obligations for his able
assistance in this troublesome undertaking. As to the Flag presented to the
Volunteers, if it excited the jealousy of the old Corps, I presume that feeling
has now ceased, for on the Fourth day of July last, to the City Regiment
was presented a very beautiful Pavilion,[7] dissimilar from the first only by its
motto: That of the one being "The Orleans Volunteers" and of the other
"The Orleans Militia." I am charged with making unfortunate innovations
on the Spanish System of Jurisprudence, and with much of the confusion
which ensued. On my arrival in Louisiana I found a disorganized Government, and a dissatisfied people. The Colonial Prefect had abolished with
the exception of the District Commandancies all the former Spanish Tribunals. In lieu of the Cabildo I found a Municipality organized upon French
Principles, but composed of the most respectable Citizens in the Province. The
Seals were put upon the different Judicial Offices, and no regular Judiciary
in existence.[8] Had the *Prefect* organized Tribunals of Justice, the writer of the
Pamphlet would have been furnished with additional ground to eulogise
his Talents:[9] But if this had been done, perhaps the organization would have
been upon French Principles, and that like the Municipality, the Tribunals
would not have known the extent of their Powers. But the formation of a
Court System devolved upon the American administration: the necessity
for the establishment was obvious, and the clamour of the People of the people [*sic*] would not permit me to delay my measures.

    To have revived the Spanish Tribunals in their full extent was impossi-
ble;— to have done so in a partial manner, it would have been necessary
to have ~~established~~ abolished the Municipality and re-instated the *Cabildo;*
for between *that body* and the Judiciary there was an intimate Connexion,

they elected annually two persons as first and Second Alcaldes[10] for the City, and these Judicial officers were ex-officio members of the Cabildo, and in the absence of the Governor presided at its meetings. The destruction of the Municipality would have given umbrage to many of the Louisianians; it would no doubt have been gratifying tto the Spanish Commissioner and their friends; but would certainly have been mortifying to the Colonial Prefect and all those who approved his measure, and here let me add that at the moment of taking possession of the Province the friendly disposition of the Prefect was Supposed to be of importance to the Interest of my Country. I determined therefore to recognize the authorities and Laws as I found them, and to make such farther [sic] arrangements for the good of the Province, as might here after Suggest themselves to my own mind, or might be Suggested by others, and which my own judgment Should approve.

The Treaty has destined Louisiana for Some future period to be incorporated into the Union, and in the mean time the Inhabitants were to be Secured in "Their Liberty, Property and Religion." This clause of the Treaty rendered great innovation upon the Spanish Laws and Spanish Tribunals absolutely necessary. The criminal System of Jurisprudence could not be preserved for the Liberty of the Citizen could not be Secured thereby, nor did I Suppose that in their Civil Courts, there was as great Security for personal property as I could wish. The better therefore to comply with the Treaty, I determined to organize an Inferior Court in the City of New Orleans, upon Principles congenial to the wishes and Interest of the Peoples and Somewhat Similar to the Tribunals of the United States.[11] My ordinance however upon that Subject was not hastily adopted; the first draft was Submitted to the Consideration of the Municipality; they proposed Several amendments, which were adopted and the ordinance finally passed in a Shape which received (as I understood their entire approbation [sic]. The Municipality was also requested to give me the names of Such Citizens as were best calculated to act as Judges of the City Court; they recommended Several Gentlemen and all were Commissioned;— I have since added other Members to the Court, and my own acquaintance with the Citizens enabled me to make a Selection. I believe the Inferior Court was for Some time popular, but the certainty and expedition with which Debts were recovered, excited the Clamour of Debtors, and the great influx of American and French Lawyers wearied by their pleadings the Patience of the Court, and occasioned the disgust of Some of the Members. The writer of the Pamphlet has alluded to the Magnitude of my late Judicial Powers and Stated what is very correct my want of information as to the Spanish Laws, and also of the French Language. The Magnitude of those powers was always a Source of uneasiness to me, and I refused to exercise Judicial authority So long as the Interest of the People would permit.— But New Orleans is a great Commercial City.— Trade and Credit are inseparable, Debts were incurred and contracts entered into and disputes between Merchants and others daily arising. My favorite wish to exercise but little Individual authority could not be indulged, and I found myself compelled to open a Supreme Court, and to preside therein as the Sole Judge. I however tried but few original causes.—[12] No Gentleman who attended the Governors Court but witnessed the reluctance with which I took cognizance of Suits, and the desire I manifested to postpone Such as could be done without injury to the Parties. Altho' I will readily acknowledge my want of information of the Spanish Law; yet I profess to be acquainted with the Laws of Justice, and I verily believe none of my decisions are in violation thereof.— But the writer of the Pamphlet has not attacked my probity as a judge, and I feel a conscious conviction, that in that character the purity of my conduct and intentions will never be questioned.

But it is objected that the Supreme Court was not organized upon Spanish Principles; this was also impossible. An Officer called the Auditor was formerly Council to the Governor: All causes were committed to him, he reported a Statement of each case in writing together with his opinion thereon;— if this opinion was Sanctioned by the Governor the Auditor was responsible, but the Governor had authority (upon his own responsibility) to decree otherwise than was advised. The Auditor was appointed by the King and was allowed a liberal compensation. It was not in my power to have appointed Such an Officer.— It is objected that the proceedings of the Supreme Court were conducted in the English Language. This if indeed, *it* should be considered as improper, was unavoidable—for the Judge knew neither French nor Spanish. It certainly would have been a great convenience to have been acquainted with the French Language:— But I do not Suppose that for want of Such knowledge on my part the Public Sustained any injury. When in Court I always had an Interpreter of Talents at my Side, and when in my office I seldom was at a loss for an Interpreter: and of late my own knowledge of the French Language has been Sufficient to guard me *in Some measure* against a misinterpretation or misrepresentation of my Sentiments. The writer of the Pamphlet charges me with manifesting much indifference as to the admission into Louisiana of the Brigands— This Charge is as ungenerous as it is unfounded. Upon this Subject I have taken every precaution in my power, and it has really been a ~~Scene~~ Source of great trouble and anxiety to me.— The extract from my official Journal accompanying this Letter from Page No. 1 to Page No. 20 will acquaint you with various measures that have been taken to prevent the importation of dangerous Slaves—

A few distressed French Families who were exiled from Jamaica and Sought an assylum [*sic*] in Louisiana were permited to Land their faithful domestics upon giving Satisfactory proof that they had not been concerned in the troubles of St. Domingo, and I have never understood that this permission which humanity dictated was disagreeable to the Louisianians. Not many weeks Since, four or five English Gentlemen Emigrating to Louisiana were also permitted to Land their Domestics upon giving like assurances, and entering into Bonds not to Sell any of their Slaves above the age of eighteen years for a limitted [*sic*] time. It is not improbable but Some base Speculators may have taken advantage of these indulgencies, and introduced dangerous Negroes, and it is also very possible (and it is So reported) that Some Brigands may have escaped the vigilance of the officers at the Balize and Plaquemine by a passage in the night or concealment in the Holds of vessels. But on this account no blame should attach to me; Since however the first of October, the Act of Congress ~~in their particular~~ in this particular, has given to the Citizens additional Security. To conciliate public opinion and to promote harmony have been my fondest objects, but I have been less fortunate than I had anticipated. Unfortunate divisions certainly exist in Louisiana: But the Seeds of discontent were Sown previous to my arrival in the Province, and they have derived nourishment from causes which I could neither controul [*sic*] or counteract.

The news Paper Scribbling which has excited So much Sensibility I have Seen and Sincerely regreted; but it does not devolve on me to correct the licenciousness of the Press— Its Liberty I never will invade— Perhaps there are Some other Statements in the Pamphlet which I ought to notice; but I at present feel myself very unwell, and must therefore hasten to a conclusion. On taking a retrospective view of my late administration, I can charge my memory with no act that my conscience and judgment do not approve;— It is nevertheless probable that I may have committed many errors, for I was placed on a new Theatre and had a part to perform, which I did not well understand. Amidst however many difficulties I have caused the Laws in Mercy (& I hope in Justice too) to be administered. Amidst a contrariety of Interests, of prejudices, of designs and Intrigues the peace of Society has been maintained and the Liberty, Property and religion of the Citizens preserved.—

I pray you Sir to ~~accept~~ excuse the length of this letter, and to receive assurances of my great Respect and Sincere Esteem

(Signed) William C. C. Claiborne

The Honble
James Madison
Secretary of State

1. Also printed as To James Madison, October 16, 1804, in CLB, 2: 352–60, and James A. Robertson, ed. and trans., *Louisiana Under the Rule of Spain, France and the United States, 1785–1807,* vol. 2 (1911; Cleveland: Arthur H. Clark, 1969), 268–78, with variations in the text and punctuation, and a few of the emphasis marks found here below. A duplicate copy of this letter was mailed to Madison ten days later with a copy of Claiborne's response to the charges made against him. See Letter No. 20, To James Madison, October 22, 1804.

2. In a private letter to Madison on October 13, 1804, Claiborne notified the secretary of state that he left New Orleans because he felt very unwell. James Madison Papers, Series I, General Correspondence and Related Items, 1723–1859, Presidential Papers microfilm no. 2974, reel no. 8. Troy H. Middleton Library, Louisiana State University Libraries. Claiborne apparently continued to suffer from the debilitating effects of yellow fever that had made him sick and caused the deaths of his wife, Eliza Lewis, and their three-year-old daughter, Tennessee, almost three weeks earlier in September.

3. Most probably the pamphlet *Esquisse de la Situation Politique et Civile de la Louisiane depuis le 30 Novembre jusqu'à 1er Octobre 1804 par un Louisianais* (New Orleans, 1804), attributed to Pierre Derbigny by Claiborne in a private letter to Madison on October 22, 1804. James Madison Papers, microfilm 2974, reel no. 8.

4. According to the *Union,* December 27, 1803, p. 1, c. 1, Derbigny was appointed "French and Spanish Interpreter of the Government." No date for his appointment was given, but it is clear he was hired very early in the U.S. assumption of control of Louisiana. Letter No. 202, W. C. C. Claiborne Disbursements during Temporary Government, Third Quarter, 1804, December 31, 1804, entry nos. 1 and 3, reflects that Derbigny was employed in July, August, and September 1804 as interpreter. From the Marquis of Casa Calvo to Gov. Claiborne (translation), CLB, 2: 155–8, is undated, but its location between other correspondence dated in the fourth week of May 1804 suggests Derbigny had then been employed as interpreter for weeks if not months.

5. For a biographical sketch of Lewis Kerr, see pp. 415–37.

6. Joseph Deville Degoutin Bellechasse. See pp. 266–81 for a biographical sketch.

7. Tent.

8. George Dargo, *Jefferson's Louisiana: Politics and the Clash of Legal Traditions* (Cambridge: Harvard University Press, 1975), 105, states that Laussat, the colonial prefect, deliberately did not replace the abolished judicial system. Although Laussat's intentions are not certain, it is clear that his actions emanated as much from anti-American and anti-Spanish biases as from a pronounced pro-French attitude. On the former, see Pierre Clément de Laussat, *Memoirs of My Life to My Son During the Years 1803 and After. . .,* trans. Sister Agnes-Josephine Pastwa, ed. Robert D. Bush (Baton Rouge: Louisiana State University Press, 1978), 117 n. 21, and the index references to "Laussat." In several instances Laussat clearly perceived that his action would, rightly or wrongly, prevent certain Louisianians, or Frenchmen, from coming to trial for actual or suspected misdeeds. See ibid., 29–32, 74–6, and 82–4. A useful short study of Laussat is André Lafargue, "Pierre Clement Laussat: An Intimate Portrait," *Louisiana Historical Quarterly* 24, no. 1 (January 1941), 5–8.

9. These emphasis marks suggest that Claiborne almost immediately associated Derbigny with the authorship of the *Esquisse* pamphlet.

10. The writer most probably meant *alcalde,* a public office comparable to the office of

mayor. His assistant most probably was comparable to the office of president of the city council.

11. The extent to which Louisiana's laws were based on the civil law of France and/or Spain has attracted numerous writers. Dargo, *Jefferson's Louisiana*, is a recent work that sheds much light on this complex question. Kate Wallach, *Bibliographical History of Louisiana Civil Law Sources, Roman, French, and Spanish* (Baton Rouge: Louisiana State University Press, 1958), is an exhaustive bibliographic study of the subject.

12. I.e., cases.

{17}
To James Pitot and the City Council
New Orleans October 18th 1804
To the Mayor and Municipality

Gentlemen,

In answer to your Letter of the 8th Instant I have the Honour to observe, that the ordinance to which you allude ought not in my opinion to have any retrospective operation with respect to the Medical Gentlemen who had previously practiced in this City. Of this Class are the Doctors Blanket and Flood,[1] the former of whom Studied at the College of Montpelier, and came to this Country as Physician to the French Prefect Mr. Laussat; the latter also studied under an Eminent Medical Gentleman in Virginia, Practiced with Reputation in Alexandria, and possesses (I believe) the esteem and confidence of many of his Fellow Citizens in New Orleans.

As to the Medical claims of the other Gentlemen you mention, I am not perfectly informed. If there are any of them who did not practice here previous to your Regulation, it will devolve upon the Municipality to enforce obedience to their ordinance; perhaps this can best be done by prescribing a penalty for a violation thereof; and which penalty it will be the duty of the Civil Magistrates to cause to be inflicted when the occasion may require. My correspondence with Mr. Castillon relative to Doctor Blankets [*sic*] appointment as Surgeon to the Hospital has made me acquainted with that Gentlemans [*sic*] claims to confidence as a Medical Character[.][2]

> I am Gentlemen with Respect
> and Esteem your Hbe St
> (Signed) *William C. C. Claiborne*

1. Information on Jean Baptiste Casimiro Blanquet may be found in Letter No. 10, To Baptiste Victor Castillon, October 8, 1804, n. 2. A biographical sketch of Dr. William Flood may be found on pp. 557–9 herein.

2. The only other Claiborne-Castillon correspondence identified is Letter No. 10, To Jean
Baptiste Castillon, October 8, 1804.

{18}
To James Madison
New Orleans October 19th 1804[1]

Sir,

On the 17th Instant a Duel was to have been fought between a French Citizen
and a British subject who are temporarily residing in this City;— by Some
means however this affair of Honour did not take place—But on the Same
day the Frenchman was caned by the Englishman in the Street, and this
circumstance had very nearly produced on yesterday Some Serious effects:
Several of the warm Frenchmen espoused the cause of their friend who had
been caned the day previous, and determineding upon revenge, met his assail-
ant; an affray immediately ensued, the Englishman being assaulted, fired a
Pistol at the aggressor, retreated with haste, and called aloud for succour. Several Americans went to his assistance and relieved him from his angry pursuers.

The rioters were immediately brought before me, and with the advice and
consent of five of the Magistrates two of them were committed to Prison
for three days, and bound in a Recognizance to keep the Peace for twelve
months. The affair which in any other City in the United States would be
viewed as unimportant has excited much agitation here; Many Frenchmen, I
mean those who are not ancient Louisianians Seem to make a common
cause, and having indulged themselves in Some illiberal abuse of the Americans, many of them, who otherwise would probably have remained neutral,
are enlisted on the side of the Englishman.— In this State of things we thought
it best to keep the Principals in Jail for a few days, until the Public ferment
Should have Subsided. Neither of the Judges having arrived and it being esteemed doubtful how far the acts of Congress has recognized the late Tribunals of Louisiana, the criminal Jurisprudence is left in a very lax State. The
general opinion here is that the powers of the Court of pleas for this City
have ceased, and a few of the Members seem unwilling to act even as conser-
vators of the Peace.

Under these circumstances (however painful it is to me, to exceed in the
least the bounds of my authority) I find myself compelled from necessity to
take measures for the Public Tranquility— This City requires a Strict Police,
the Inhabitants are of various descriptions, *many highly respectable,* and
Some of them very degenerate— Great exertions have been made (and with

too much Success) to foment differences between the Native Americans, and the native Louisianians; every incident is laid hold of to widen the Breach, and to excite jealousy and confusion— The intrigues of certain late emigrants from France, and Some of the satellites of the Spanish Government, have tended considerably to heighten the discontents in that~~is~~ [*sic*] quarter. Every thing in my power has been done to counteract ~~to counteract~~ these Intrigues, but with little success. The fact is that the affections of many of the Louisianians for their Mother Country are warm, and others Seem attached to the Spanish Government.

I have to complain also of Some of the Native Americans, they are rash and very imprudent— The News-Paper Publications likewise add to my embarrassments.— They give inquietude to the Louisianians and trouble to me— The present State of things mortifies me excessively, but I hope that good order will be preserved, and harmony Soon restored. These objects Shall constitute my first and greatest cares.—

> I am with great Respect Sir
> Your very Hble Sevt.
> (Signed) *William C. C. Claiborne*

The Honble
James Madison
Secty of State

P.S. On yesterday about thirty Frenchmen Dined with their Countrymen in Prison. The enclosed lines were composed and Sung on the occasion.[2] I do not know that any Native Louisianians were of the Party. But I have understood there were Several, who under the Treaty claim to be Citizens of the United States.
(Initialed) W. C. C. C[.]

1. Also printed as To James Madison, October 20, 1804, CLB, 2: 367–9, with slight variations in the text and punctuation.
2. The lines were not with the manuscript.

{19}
TO JAMES MADISON
New Orleans October 20th 1804[1]

Sir,
I enclose you a Copy of a Letter which I addressed to the Marquis of Casa Calvo on the 9th Instant relating to the continuance of certain Spanish Of-

ficers in this Territory as also a translation of his answer. I am persuaded that these foreigners are not well disposed to the Interest of the United States, and I thought it ~~very~~ a duty to express my disapprobation to their residence here So much beyond the right and occasion for it. The Marquis tells me that the Auditor and Intendant are the only Officers remaining; but I nevertheless daily See persons in Spanish Uniforms, and Several others who were employed in the Custom House under the Spanish Government. It is possible that these persons may have been permitted to retire on Pensions, or to remain in this Territory in the enjoyment of their full pay.

I have also understood that the Spanish Monarch has not yet withdrawn his Patronage from the Priests in Louisiana, and particularly that the vicar general (Mr. Walsh)[2] is paid his Salary regularly by the Marquis. I do not vouch for the accuracy of this information, but I will make further enquiries and will communicate the result. If the information Should prove correct, it may merit the attention of Government. The influence of the Priests here is ~~in~~considerable [sic].

> I am Sir very Respectfully
> Your Hble Sevt
> (Signed) *William C. C. Claiborne*

The Secretary of
State

1. Also printed as To James Madison, October 10, 1804, CLB, 2: 369–70, with slight variations in the text and punctuation.

2. Father Patrick Walsh. On this Irish graduate of the College of Nobles in Salamanca, Spain, see Stanley Faye, ed., "The Schism of 1805 in New Orleans," *Louisiana Historical Quarterly* 22, no. 1 (January 1939), 99; Roger Baudier, *The Catholic Church in Louisiana* (1939; New Orleans: Louisiana Library Association, 1972), particularly 250; and Michael J. Curley, C.SS.R., *Church and State in the Spanish Floridas (1783–1822)* (Washington, D.C.: Catholic University Press of America, 1940), 192–4, 233, 246–7, 287, 294–9, 303–9.

{20}
To James Madison
New Orleans October 22nd 1804[1]

Sir,
I have the Honour to enclose you a list of the Christian names of the Gentlemen Commissioned by the President [to be] Members of the Legislative Council, as also the Christian Names of the Gentleman appointed Marshall.—

Three of the Councillors to Wit Messrs. Dow, Boré and Jones have declined Serving— Messrs. Watkins, Morgan and Debuys have accepted;[2] I have taken measures to inform the others of their appointments; but have not yet received their answers. I have issued a Proclamation convening the Council on the 12th of next month;— But very much fear I shall not be enabled to form a quorum. The opinion of Mr. Jones in relation to his inconsistency Seems to have been adopted by Mr. Boré and I fear may also be embraced by other Gentlemen named:— You will therefore See the necessity of the vacancies being early filled; I will venture to recommend Mr. George Mather, Eugene D'Orcier [*sic*] and William Donaldson as deserving the confidence of the President.

The enclosed Letters from the Commanding officer at Natchitoches will give you the news from that Quarter.[3] Governor Folch having quelled the Insurrection at Baton Rouge without the loss of blood, or ever Seeing an Insurgent, is about returning to Pensacola, and has Solicited my permission for the passage of himself and Suite by the way of New Orleans; this has been granted accompanied by assurances of my protection and friendly attention.[4]

> I am Sir very Respectfully
> Your Hble Sevt
> (Signed) *William C. C. Claiborne*

The Honble
James Madison
Secty of State

1. Also printed as To James Madison, October 22, 1804, in CLB, 2: 372, with variations in the text and punctuation.

2. Dr. John Watkins, Benjamin Morgan, and Gaspard Debuys (sometimes spelled with an *i*, DeBuis) accepted. Dr. Robert Dow declined to serve on the territorial council and served only briefly (July 9 to early August 1804) on the board of health created by the city council in June 1804. Ibid., To the Mayor and Municipality of New Orleans, June 6, 1804, and From Robert Dow, October 10, 1804, ibid., 194, 374, respectively; and John Duffy, ed., *The Rudolph Matas History of Medicine*, vol. 1 (Baton Rouge: Louisiana State University Press, 1958–62), 383–5. For more information on Dow, Morgan, and Watkins, see their biographical sketches herein.

3. Not present.

4. The insurrection referred to was the attempt by Reuben and Nathaniel Kemper to take West Florida for the United States. Details on the event may be found in Isaac J. Cox, *The West Florida Controversy, 1798–1813: A Study in American Diplomacy* (Baltimore: Johns Hopkins University Press, 1918), 151–68; and Governor Claiborne to the President, October 27, 1804, TP, 9: 315. For a biographical sketch of Vicente Folch y Juan, see pp. 499–532 herein.

{21}

To Vicente Folch y Juan
New Orleans October 22nd 1804

Sir,

I have the Honour to acknowledge the Receipt of your Excellencys ~~Letter~~ favour under date of the 16th Instant.

Your Excellency may be assured of my protection, as well for yourself as Suite, on your way to Pensacola, and I am the more pleased at your Route through this City Since it will afford me the Satisfaction of assuring you in person of my Sincere regard and great respect[.][1]

(Signed) *William C. C. Claiborne*

His Excellency
Governor Folch

1. Folch's request for permission to pass through New Orleans has not been found, but Claiborne advised Secretary Madison he granted the request with "assurances of my protection and friendly attention." Letter No. 20, To James Madison, October 22, 1804. Folch apparently spent thirty days in New Orleans on this occasion, during which Claiborne's entertainment of the West Florida governor and the Marqués de Casa Calvo included assisting Casa Calvo at a high mass on the feast of St. Carlos "with a view to testifying my respect for his *Catholic Majesty so long as my Country shall be in Peace with him.*" Governor Claiborne to the President, November 4, 1804, TP, 9: 319 (emphasis in the original). A biographical sketch of Folch y Juan appears on pp. 499–532 herein.

{22}

To the Mayor and Municipality
New Orleans October 23rd 1804
To the Mayor and Municipality

Gentlemen,

Mr. Workman[1] will deliver to you all the papers touching the Estate and Interest of a Colonel Maxant[2] Deceased together with thirty Seven Dollars and Five Bitts which were forwarded to me by the Marquis of Casa Calvo Some time Since, and of which ~~and of which~~ I advised you in my Letter of the ———. [3] These Documents &c ought previous to this time, to have been transmitted to you—But the delay proceeded from the inattention of a young Gentleman who formerly wrote in my office.[4]

I request that the Papers may be deposited in the Office of the Secretary of the Municipality and the money with the City Treasurer for the inspection and use of the Persons concerned.

I am Sir with Respect and
Esteem your Obdt Sevt
(Signed) *William C. C. Claiborne*

1. James Workman was employed as clerk in Claiborne's office in October 1804. See Letter No. 200, W. C. C. Claiborne Disbursements during Temporary Government, Fourth Quarter, entry no. 5. A biographical sketch of Workman is on pp. 389–414 herein.

2. Gilbert Antoine de St. Maxent (March or April 1727–August 8, 1794) had been the principal merchant in lower Louisiana and a partner of Pierre Laclède Liguest, who founded the trading post that became St. Louis. St. Maxent, whose name is misspelled in this letter, was in high favor with the French and Spanish authorities because of his loyalty. Prior to its capture Maxent spent some forty-two days near Fort Bute below Baton Rouge on Bayou Manchac, accumulating exact descriptions of the English forces there. During the American Revolution, he spent some $76,000 of his own money on behalf of Spain in the capture of Fort Bute, Baton Rouge, Natchez, Mobile, and Pensacola. He directed the capture of Mobile. To launch the proposed Spanish program of trade with the Indians, he used some $50,000 of his own money. Although he was later reimbursed on the orders of the king of Spain from the treasuries in Mexico, none of the ventures would have been successful without his assistance. In recognition of his services, the king of Spain appointed St. Maxent commandant of all the militia in the province of Louisiana; commissioner of Indian Affairs for Louisiana and West Florida; and lieutenant govenor-general of Louisiana and West Florida. Abraham P. Nasatir, *Spanish War Vessels on the Mississippi, 1792–1796* (New Haven: Yale University Press, 1968), 305 n.; James J. Coleman, Jr., *Gilbert Antoine de St. Maxent: The Spanish Frenchman of New Orleans* (New Orleans: Pelican, 1968); and "Genealogy and Personal History of Colonel Gilbert Antoine de St. Maxant" (typescript; New Orleans: Louisiana State Museum Library, s.d.). One of Maxent's daughters, Felicitas, married Bernardo de Gálvez. Louis Houck, ed., *The Spanish Regime in Missouri,* vol. 1 (1909; New York: Arno Press, 1971), 210 n. 6. The large collection of succession papers of Maxent's estate is on deposit with the Special Collections Department, Howard-Tilton Memorial Library, Tulane University, and on microfilm in the Louisiana Department of the New Orleans Public Library.

3. Claiborne may have meant his letter of July 21, 1804, to Casa Calvo. See To the Marquis of Casa Calvo, July 21, 1804, CLB, 2: 259–60, and From the Marquis of Casa Calvo to Gov. Claiborne, September 2, 1804, ibid., 317–8.

4. This may be a reference to Joseph Briggs, son of Isaac Briggs, who was Claiborne's secretary from about June 6, 1804, until Briggs's death from yellow fever on September 16, 1804. See An Ordinance, June 6, 1804, ibid., 195, in which Briggs is listed as "Secty. Pro tem.," and To James Madison, September 17, 1804, ibid., 337, in which the Governor states that his "private Secretary Mr. Briggs died on yesterday."

{23}
To Casa Calvo
New Orleans October 25th 1804

Sir,

The Cessation of my Judicial Powers which took place on the first instant prevents me from exercising any official authority in the affair of the Ne-

groes claimed by Don Pedro Villamil;— I regret this circumstance extremely
as the Interest of his Catholic Majesty may be afflicted by the delay; and
as it may Serve to retard the departure of Don Juan Ventura Morales. I am
in daily expectation of the arrival of some of the Judges of the Superiour
[*sic*] Court, who I doubt not will make such a decision on this business as
will give your Excellency perfect Satisfaction.

The Same reasons which precludes me from acting in the case of the Negroes will operate with respect to the House (if indeed there Should be conflicting claims, and which I presume exist, or there could be no objection to
the Sale.[1] If in my Character as Governor of the Territory of Orleans, I can
render your Excellency any service, I pray you to be assured of the pleasure
which I should feel in affording them.

> I have the Honour to be Sir with
> Great Respect your Excellency's
> Most Obdt Sevt
> (Signed) *William C. C. Claiborne*

The Marquis
of
Casa Calvo

1. The closing parenthesis symbol was not in the original. For details in this case, see Letter
No. 102, To James Madison, January 19, 1805; Letter No. 103, the enclosed Certificate (deposition) of John Watkins; and Letter No. 104, the Certificate (deposition) of Thomas Seilles Kennedy, both of which were given on January 18, 1805.

{24}
To James Madison
New Orleans October 26th 1804[1]

Sir,
I enclose you a Duplicate of my Letter of the 16th Inst.[2] which presents you
with my reply to certain charges contained in a Pamphlet which has heretofore been forwarded to you. Perhaps this Publication will not receive any
credit to the Northward; But as the attention of the American Citizens is
turned to Louisiana, and from our great distance from the Seat of Government, and other causes, events in this quarter are too apt to be misrepresented. I thought it prudent not to remain Silent under accusations made
against me, even by an anonymous writer.

Altho there has been much discontent manifested in New Orleans and its

Vicinity, yet I do not believe that the disaffection is of a Serious nature, or that it is extensive. That Some difficulty Should attend the introduction of American Government and Laws was to have been expected: On every change of Dominion, discontents more or less invariably ensue, and when we take into view the various and rapid transitions, and transfers, which have taken place in this territory, we may indeed felicitate ourselves on the great Share of good order which has been preserved.

The most arbitrary Governments find advocates, and the most unprincipled Despot is seldom without Friends. When Despotism Reigns, (Silence produced by Fear, is received as the test of contentment, and a tame Submission to injustice, as proof of the Public Sanction.[3] Had an administration rigid, coercive and unjust been introduced into the Ceded Territory, under the Authority of the United States, I am persuaded there would have been less murmuring, and a delusive appearance of Popular approbation: But under a mild and just Government, which admits of freedom of Speech, and of opinion, the man indeed, must be little acquainted with human nature, who would expect to find in Louisiana union in expression and Sentiment— I know not whether any ~~will~~ [?] or what exception may be taken at the Seat of Government to my administration— But I can conscientiously Say that my conduct throughout, has been directed by the purest motives of Honest Patriotism, and that my measures were rendered necessary by existing circumstances, or Strong considerations of Political expediency.

> I have the Honour to be Sir
> with great Respect and
> Esteem your most obdt Hbl St
> (Signed) *William C. C. Claiborne*
>
> The Secty
> of State

1. Also published as To James Madison, October 26, 1804, CLB, 2: 375–6, with variations in text and punctuation.
2. See Letter No. 16, To James Madison, October 16, 1804.
3. No closing parenthesis in original.

{25}
To James Madison
New Orleans October 27th 1804[1]

Sir,

In my Letter of the 16th Instant[2] I mentioned only Six offices that might properly be considered as lucrative; perhaps to those I ought to have added the

Attorney General for the Province, the Physicians of the Port of New Orleans, the Secretary to the Municipality, and three Vendue Masters or Auctioneers, all of whom are Commissioned by the Governor, altho their emoluments are supposed to be very inconsiderable.

The Attorney General is a native American, as is also the *Physician* of the Port but *this* Gentleman has resided in Louisiana for some time and is married to a creole of the Country.[3] The Secretary to the Municipality is a native Frenchman, and I believe an ancient Louisianian. One of the auctioneers is a native of Ireland, a Citizen of the United States and had been an Inhabitant of this City for Several years; another is a native of France, a Citizen of the United States and resided in this City on my arrival; and the third (lately appointed) is a native of the United States and the Son of a Frenchman. With respect to the appointments of Honour and Trust not enumerated in my Letter of the 16 Instant, I may Mention the members of the Board of Health consisting of nine Members of whom two only are Modern Louisianians.[4]

My object has been to avail the public of the Services of the well informed and deserving Citizens, and as there are many native Americans of this description residing in Louisiana, it ought not to be a matter of Surprise that Some of them Should have received Offices. The Ancient Louisianians hold as many appointments as their numbers and qualifications entitle them to and therefore they ought not Complain.—

> I am Sir with great Respect
> and Esteem your most
> Obdt Sevt.
> (Signed) *William C. C. Claiborne*

The Secretary
of State

1. Also printed as To James Madison, October 27, 1804, CLB, 2: 377–8.

2. See Letter No. 16, To James Madison, October 16, 1804.

3. The port physician at this time was Dr. John Watkins, whose wife was Eulalie Trudeau, the daughter of the former lieutenant governor of upper Spanish Louisiana, 1792–1799, Zenon Trudeau. The emphases shown are in the original.

4. The two "Modern Louisianians" referred to probably were Dr. John Watkins and Dr. William Flood, both of whom were married to native Louisianians. See their biographical sketches herein, pp. 299–371 and 557–9, respectively.

{26}
To James Madison
New Orleans October 28th 1804[1]

Sir,

On yesterday I was informed by a Mr. Dubourgh and a respectable Merchant of this City, that a vessel of his with forty Negroes on Board had entered the Mississippi Since the first of October, that these negroes belonged to his Father and another Inhabitant of Louisiana.[2] That owing to contrary winds and bad weather this vessel was prevented entering the Mississippi until Subsequent to the first of October. Mr. Dubourgh prayed that the Negroes might be permitted to Land and pledged himself that they should be forthcoming on the arrival of the Judges in the Territory, and that he would await a Judicial decision. I did not know well how to act on the occasion. it would Seem [*sic*] as if it was more particularly the duty of the District Attorney to notice and bring before the Court persons who had violated the Law: But as neither of the Judges or the Attorney General have arrived, I esteemed it my Province to take measures to enforce the observance of the Law; but on the present occasion as the importer was himself the informer, I permitted him to Land the Negroes upon giving me on oath their names and number and Satisfactory assurances that they Should be forthcoming on the arrival of the Judges.

Mr. Dubourgh showed a permission which he had procured from the Spanish Governor Grand Pré, to introduce into the Settlement of Baton Rouge Sixty negroes, and intima~~midated an~~ [*sic*] an intention to avail himself of Said permission. If Negroe Vessels are permitted to pass up to Baton Rouge, the Law prohibiting the African Trade in This Territory will in effect be a nullity, and I pray your instructions whether or not I am to oppose their passage. I have understood that Several African Vessels were sent out in time to return previous to the first of October, but from Some cause they have not arrived, and their delay is a Source of anxiety to the persons concerned.

I am Sir very Respectfully
your most obdt Sevt—
(Signed) *William C. C. Claiborne*

The Honble
James Madison
Secty of State

1. Also printed as To James Madison, October 28, 1804, in CLB, 2: 346–7, with variations in punctuation.

2. This was probably Peter F. DuBourg, Jr., son of the DuBourg in the firm of DeBuys and DuBourg.

{27}
TO JAMES MADISON
New Orleans October 29th 1804[1]

Sir,

On last Evening Mr. Prevost (one of the Judges) arrived in this City and will proceed I believe immediately to organize the Supreme Court. In the course of my efforts to introduce the American System of Jurisprudence in to the Ceded Territory, I experienced many difficulties, and excited Some dissatisfaction among the people;— I Sincerely wish that the Judges may find their duties agreeable, and that the happiest result may attend their exertions for the Public good. But I fear the Trial by Jury, the admission of Attorneys, the introduction of oral testimony &c will illy comport with the for~~mor~~mer [*sic*] habits of the people; and that the Court (as I have been) will be accused by the designing few of making injurious innovations on the Spanish Law.

I do not know that I shall be enabled to form a Council on the 12th of November—Messrs. Watkins, Morgan, and Kenner will Serve, Messrs[.] Jones[,] Boré and Dow have declined, and I fear the Situation of Colonel Bellechasse's private affairs will not permit his acceptance. Of the determination of the other Gentlemen named I am not yet advised— I hope however that the President will early forward the names of Such Gentlemen as he would wish to Supply the existing vacancies.[2] I am very desirous to form a Council. The good the Territory requires many Legislative acts, but I am fearful that a party Spirit which Seems to have acquired a great ascendency over certain Individuals will occasion much temporary embarrassment. It was unfortunate that Messrs. Boré, Jones, and Clark were appointed Councillors, they are the great Supporters of the Memorial, and will not only decline Serving in the Council, but will induce others to do so likewise.

I have the Honor to be Sir
with great Respect and Esteem your
most obdt
and very Hble St
(Signed) *William C. C. Claiborne*

The Honble
James Madison
Secty of State

1. Also published as Governor Claiborne to the Secretary of State, October 29, 1804, in TP, 9: 317–8, with variations in punctuation and a postscript not found here.

2. The territorial courts could not function without authority from the legislative council. Under the provisions of the act creating the Orleans Territory on March 26, 1804, the legislative council was not granted such authority until October 1, 1804. See An Act for the Organization of Orleans Territory and the Louisiana District in TP, 9: 213, Section 16. Because only five of Jefferson's thirteen appointees to the council accepted appointment, Claiborne used the blank commissions sent by the president to appoint four men to the council to make a quorum, thereby enabling the body to meet. Marietta Marie LeBreton, *A History of the Territory of Orleans, 1803–1812* (Ann Arbor: University Microfilms, 1973), 108–9, 113, 133–4.

{28}

To Casa Calvo

New Orleans October 30th 1804[1]

Sir,

I have received recent dispatches from Natchitoches which announce the desertion of nine Slaves (the property of Citizens of the United States) to Nacogdoches and the arrest of many others who had formed a determination to desert and repair to that Post in full expectation of receiving protection from the Spanish Government. The Inhabitants of the District of Natchitoches manifest on this occasion much inquietude, and entertain just apprehensions for the Safety of their property.[2] The causes which have led to these unpleasant occurrences I have heretofore communicated to your Excellency and the assurances which were given me, that no existing Decree of ~~your~~ [*sic*] His Catholic Majesty promised freedom and protection to Negroes escaping from the Service of their Masters, and that your Excellency had addressed a Letter ~~from~~ to the Commandant of Nacogdoches upon the Subject, induced me to hope that the fears of the Inhabitants of Natchitoches would prove groundless.— But these fears are now realized, and I must again request the interference of your Excellency. If protection be afforded by the Commandant of Nacogdoches to a Single slave deserting the Service of his Master, the consequences which will ensue may readily be anticipated, consequences which will be injurious to the Citizens of the United States and may tend to distrust that good understanding between our *two* Nations, which it is *their* mutual Interest to cherish and preserve[.][3]

> I pray your Excellency to be assured
> of my
> great Respect and high
> Consideration!

(Signed) *William C. C. Claiborne*

The Marquis of Casa Calvo

1. Also printed as To Casa Calvo, October 30, 1804, CLB, 2: 382–3, with variations in punctuation and emphasis marks not on this copy.

2. For additional information on this situation, see Edward D. Turner to Governor Claiborne, July 30, 1804, in TP, 9: 271–3, with its enclosure, Petition to Edward Turner by Inhabitants of the District of Natchitoches, July 29, 1804, pp. 273–4; Edward D. Turner, to Governor Claiborne, November 21, 1804, ibid., 334–7; and Letter No. 36, To Samuel Boyer Davis, November 3, 1804. The several essays by Isaac J. Cox shed much light on the border situation in the Natchitoches area. See Cox, "The Louisiana-Texas Frontier, I," *Quarterly of the Texas State Historical Association* 10, no. 1 (July 1906), 1–75; "The Louisiana-Texas Frontier, II," *Southwestern Historical Quarterly* 17, no. 1 (July 1913), 1–42; and "The Louisiana-Texas Frontier, III," ibid., no. 2 (October 1913), 140–87.

3. Emphasis in the original.

{29}

To Casa Calvo

New Orleans October 31st 1804[1]

Sir,

Communications from Several Commandants on the Frontier of Louisiana State, that late attempts have been made by Some Subjects of His Catholic Majesty residing in the Province of Taxus [Texas] to alienate the affections of certain Indian Tribes from my Country, and to excite them to the Commission of outrages. Persuaded that this conduct is not authorized by the officers of Spain and that his [sic] Catholic Majesty would hear with regret, that any of his Subjects Should be instrumental in involving a neighbouring and friendly power in the horrors of Savage Warfare, I have made you Sir this Communication, and I doubt not but your Excellency will address a Letter on the Subject to the Governor of Taxus, and impress upon that officer the propriety of restraining the People within his Government from all acts of aggression or injury towards the Citizens of the United States. I take this occasion to renew to your Excellency the assurances of my great Respect and Sincere Esteem

(Signed) *William C. C. Claiborne*

His Excellency
the Marquis of
Casa Calvo

1. Also printed as To Casa Calvo, October 31, 1804, in CLB, 2: 383–4, with variations in punctuation and emphasis marks not on this copy.

{30}

TO THE MAYOR AND CITY COUNCIL

New-Orleans November 1st 1804
To the Mayor and Municipality

Gentlemen,

I have received both your Letters of this day.[1] With respect to the Breach of faith, and violation of the Public Security committed by Mr. Petavin[2] I have taken the best measures in my power to prevent the Mischief which his misconduct might occasion.

As to the accused Negroes and Negresses Sent hither by Mr. Cantrelle,[3] there is no doubt but the Superior Court will do Speedy Justice. Should all or any of them be convicted, I shall take care that the punishment to which they Shall be Sentenced, be inflicted in Such a manner, and at Such ~~pla~~ places, as may best Serve to terrify those who may be inclined to commit Similar enormities.

> I am gentlemen with Respect and
> Esteem your very Hble Sevt
>
> (Signed) *William C. C. Claiborne*

1. Not present.

2. Probably Joseph Antoine Peytavin, who had imported some Negro slaves and sold them after having promised Claiborne that he would not. See Letter No. 31, To Joseph Antoine Peytavin, November 1, 1804. For a biographical sketch of Peytavin, see pp. 585–6 herein.

3. Michel Cantrelle, Commandant of the Acadian, or German Coast, the name given that area of settlement along the east bank of the Mississippi River above New Orleans stretching from present-day St. Charles through St. John the Baptist, St. James, and Ascension parishes. On at least one occasion, Daniel Clark spelled the Cantrelle surname "Cantarelle." See Characterization of New Orleans Residents, July 1, 1804, TP, 9: 255, no. 88. For a biographical sketch of Cantrelle, see pp. 570–4 herein.

{31}

TO JOSEPH ANTOINE PEYTAVIN

New Orleans November 1st 1804

To Mr. Petavin Sir,

I am informed that in violation of your promise to me relative to the Slaves you lately imported from Jamaica, you have Sold Some of them, and dispatched others into the Interior of the Country, and created thereby considerable alarm among the good Citizens;—[1] I now acquaint you, that if you do not immediately Send out of this Territory Such of your Negroe men lately

imported as may be of bad characters, I shall be obliged to take Such measures, as will be highly disagreeable to me, and may prove troublesome to
you—

> I am Sir your very
> Hble Svt
> (Signed) *William C. C. Claiborne*

1. For information related to this matter, see Letter No. 30, To the Mayor and City Council, November 1, 1804, immediately preceding this letter. For biographical information on Peytavin, see pp. 585–6.

{32}
TO THOMAS BUTLER
New Orleans November 1st 1804[1]

Sir,

Late accounts from Natchitoches represent that Settlement as being in a State
of inquietude and alarm. This has arisen from Some unpleasant movements
among the Slaves: the desertion of nine Negroe Men who carried off Twenty
Horses and other plundered property to Nacogdoches and the arrest of
many others, who had formed a design to repair to that Post in hopes of receiving protection, and a report which I fear is not without foundation, that
attempts have recently been made by Subjects of His Catholic Majesty to excite certain Indian Tribes West of the Mississippi to wage War against the
United States.[2]

In this state of things, I have deemed it my duty to Suggest to you the propriety of Sending a Small reinforcement to Natchitoches. It is at present a
Barrier Post on our most exposed Frontier, and liable to Sudden attacks by
Indians. I am inclined to think that a Small detachment from the Troops now
in Atakapas and Opelousas, might with propriety be ordered to Natchitoches.
A Subaltern officer and twelve or fifteen men detained at Atakapas will in
my opinion be Sufficient to aid the Civil authority in the ~~formation maint~~
maintenance of good order. The Command of the Regular Forces in that
quarter being intrusted to you, I have addressed you this Letter, in full confidence that a reinforcement will be ordered to Natchitoches, provided it can
be done without *injury to the Service,* and *of this* you are the Judge.[3]

> I am Sir with great Respect and
> Esteem your obdt Sevt
> (Signed) *William C. C. Claiborne*

Colonel Butler

1. Also printed as To Col. Butler, November 1, 1804, CLB, 2: 384, with variations in the text and punctuation; with emphasis not found in this copy; and without the last sentence.

2. For correspondence related to this subject, see Letters No. 28 and 29, both To Casa Calvo, dated October 30, 1804, and October 31, 1804, respectively.

3. The letter mailed to Colonel Butler did not contain the last sentence found here. The omission of this sentence before the letter was mailed reflects Claiborne's keen awareness of the friction between General Wilkinson and Lieutenant Colonel Constant Freeman in matters of military authority, and the governor's desire to avoid a similar problem with Butler.

{33}
To Daniel Clark
New Orleans November 2nd 1804

Sir,

By the last Mail I received your Letter of the 19th Ultimo Dated at Bayou Sarah, and which I answered by the returning Post.— Having heard however of your arrival in this City, and of course Supposing that my late Letter had passed you on your way down, I now have the honour to acquaint you that the communication of the 5th of October without Signature, but directed in my hand writing, which you mentioned to have received was forwarded by my orders;— the omission of my Signature I assure you Sir was not the effect of design, but proceeded from inadvertency in a great press of Business—[1]

I am Sir very Respectfully
Your Hbl St
(Signed) *William C. C. Claiborne*

Daniel Clark
Esq—

1. The tension between Claiborne and Clark is apparent from the subject and tone of Claiborne's letter. The wealthy and imperious Clark thought Claiborne was a fool and told the governor this in February 1804. See Nolan B. Harmon, *The Famous Case of Myra Clark Gaines* (Baton Rouge: Louisiana State University Press, 1946), 59. The return of Clark to New Orleans noted here by Claiborne was an oblique reference to Clark's personal drive throughout Orleans Territory in the summer and fall of 1804 to obtain signatures to the Orleans Memorial, which called on Congress to give Louisianians representative government. See Governor Claiborne to the Secretary of State, October 13, 1804, TP, 9: 310. Clark described his activities in support of the memorial in a letter to General Wilkinson on October 10, 1804. See Records of the Office of the Secretary of War, Letters Received, Unregistered Series, 1789–1860, record group 107, document F 25, microcopy 222, reel no. 1, 1789–1804. The memorial is generally believed to have been written by Edward Livingston with the aid of Daniel Clark and Evan Jones. See Governor Claiborne to the Secretary of State, July 13, 1804, TP, 9: 261; and Mari-

etta Marie LeBreton, *A History of the Territory of Orleans, 1803–1812* (Ann Arbor: University Microfilms, 1973), 118, 120 n. 58.

{34}
To Constant Freeman
New Orleans November 2nd 1804[1]

Sir,

Colonel Butler being absent from the City, I pray you Sir to issue orders to Captain Nicolls[2] not to permit a British Vessel[3] now in the Mississippi with near two Hundred French Prisoners on Board to pass Plaquemine;[4] to cause the said Vessel to Anchor opposite the Fort and to permit no person on Board, to Land until he receives further orders.

This Vessel has been taken at Sea by the Prisoners and brought into the River Mississippi. As the orders upon this occasion require dispatch, I hasten to address you this Letter.

I am Sir very Respectfully
Your most obdt &
very Hble St
(Signed) *William C. C. Claiborne*

To Colonel
Freeman

1. Lieutenant Colonel Constant Freeman was the second highest ranking army officer in New Orleans at this time. He became commanding officer after the death of Colonel Thomas Butler and held the post until June 1807. A brief biographical sketch of Freeman appears on pp. 564–6.

2. Captain Abimael Youngs Nicoll replaced Captain Henry L. Cooper in command of the fort at Plaquemine in July 1804. See To Capt. Nicoll, July 25, 1804, CLB, 2: 262–3; and James Wilkinson to the Secretary of War, January 3, 1803 [1804], TP, 9: 151. A short biographical sketch of Nicoll may be found on p. 569 herein.

3. The bark *Hero,* which was commanded by Captain John Calver. Additional information on this troublesome ship may be traced through the indices of both CLB and TP, 9. Because of the loose application of the terms "bark" and "brig" after 1720, it is quite possible that the corsair *Hero* described as a brig and attacked by Captain Manuel García y Muñis in September 1799 is the same ship. On the terminology, see Howard I. Chapelle, *The History of the American Sailing Navy: The Ships and Their Development* (New York: Bonanza Books, 1949), 11–2, 15.

4. By referring to the military fortification below New Orleans simply as Plaquemine, Claiborne followed the Spanish practice. See, for example, the instructions of Governor Carondelet to Don Antonio de St. Maxent, the first commandant at the installation in 1793, in which Carondelet referred to the location alternately as "Placaminas" (Plaquemine) and Fort San Felipe. *The Favrot Papers, 1793–1796,* vol. 4, transcription by the Louisiana Historical Records

Survey (New Orleans, 1941), 46–8. The fort, of course, was Fort St. Philip, or as it was formally titled in Spanish, *Fuerte San Felipe de Placaminas*. A sketch of its history through the
War of 1812 appears on pp. 604–7 herein.

{35}
To Abimael Youngs Nicoll
New Orleans November 3. [*sic*] 1804[1]

Sir,

On yesterday Colonel Freeman at my request, issued orders to prevent the
passage of a vessel by Plaquemine lately entering the Mississippi, with a
number of Frenchmen on Board who were late Prisoners of War to the British
Government, and who captured Said Vessel from the Crew, on her passage
to Some Port in great [*sic*] Britain.

Captain Davis[2] who will hand you this Letter, carries my orders for the
immediate [word here blotted out with original ink, undecipherable] departure of Said Vessel, unless indeed She Should be in Distress, and in that case
She may be permitted to obtain the necessary Supplies, and forthwith retire
with all possible dispatch. I hope you will be careful to prevent any person
on board from landing or passing up the River. I tender you my thanks for
your past vigilance, and am persuaded that on the present occasion, your
good conduct will entitle you Still further to the confidence of Sir

Your most obdt &
very Hble St
(Signed) *William C. C. Claiborne*

To Captain Nicolls [*sic*]
Plaquemine

PS I will thank you to receive Captain Davis with friendly attention, and
to forward him on his return as far as Gentilly's,[3] where he will procure a
Horse

W. C. C. C[.]

1. Published as To Capt. Nicoll, Commanding at Plaquemeine [*sic*], November 3, 1804,
CLB, 2: 380, with differences in text and punctuation, and with emphasis not found here.

2. Samuel Boyer Davis arrived in New Orleans in 1799 as captain of the sixteen-gun frig-
ate *General Washington*, formerly the British ship *General Monk*. Information on his life and
association with Daniel Clark may be found through the index references in Nolan B. Harmon,
The Famous Case of Myra Clark Gaines (Baton Rouge: Louisiana State University Press,
1946).

3. This ridge of land northeast of early New Orleans was known into the nineteenth cen-

tury as the Gentilly Ridge. It subsequently was incorporated as part of New Orleans and is known today simply as Gentilly.

{36}
To Samuel Boyer Davis
New Orleans November 3rd 1804[1]

Sir,

I have received information that a Vessel[2] with near two Hundred Frenchmen on Board, Said to have been Prisoners of War to the Government of great [*sic*] Britain, has entered the Mississippi with a design of coming to this Port. It is further represented that the Said Vessel on her passage from Jamaica to Some Port in great [*sic*] Britain was taken by the French on Board and brought into the Mississippi.—

    If this Statement be correct no refuge or Shelter can be given in any Port in this Territory to the Said Vessel, and She must depart as Soon as possible— You will therefore proceed immediately to Plaquemine, where you will find that Vessel detained, and ascertain how far the Statement made to me be true. If you find that the Vessel is a Prize, or that She was captured in the manner described, you will hand the Letter herein enclosed to the person who Shall appear to have command of Said Vessel, and urge his immediate departure;— On your return you will be pleased to make me a particular Report upon the Subject of your mission, wishing you a continuance of your Health and agreeable Journey— I remain Sir with the greatest Respect and Esteem your most obdt Hble St

(Signed) *William C. C. Claiborne*

Capt Davis

    1. Also printed as To Capt. Saml. Davis, November 3, 1804, CLB, 2: 379–80, with variations in text and punctuation.
    2. See Letter No. 34, To Constant Freeman, November 2, 1804, n. 2, for related correspondence.

{37}
To James Madison
New Orleans November 3rd 1804[1]

Sir,

On yesterday I received a Letter from the Deputy Collector,[2] of which the enclosure No. 1 is a Copy, informing of the arrival in the Mississippi of a

Vessel with a number of Frenchmen on Board, who had captured Said Vessel on the High Seas. I determined that under the Treaty it would be improper to permit this Vessel to find an Assylum here, and I was further convinced, that the Sudden arrival of So many Frenchmen in this City (whose habits and Situation are not probably calculated to render them useful Members of Society) might disturb the Harmony of our community— With a view therefore to the Speedy departure of Said Vessel and her Captors, I have taken certain measures of which the enclosures Nos. 2. 3. 4 & 5 will particularly inform you.[3] I have done on this occasion what prudence Suggested, and my Judgment Sanctioned, and Sincerely hope my conduct will be approved by the President.

> I am Sir with great respect and Esteem
> Your most obdt & very Hble St
>
> (Signed) *William C. C. Claiborne*

The Honble
James Madison
Secty of State

1. Printed as To James Madison, November 3, 1804, CLB, 2: 378–9, with variations in text.

2. Andrew Porter, Jr., whose appointments as port surveyor and inspector were confirmed March 1, 1805. See Hore Browse Trist to the Secretary of the Treasury, April 1, 1804; Hatch Dent to James H. McCulloch, July 14, 1804; Recommendation of Andrew Porter, Jr., as Port Inspector, November 22, 1804; and postscript at the end of Governor Claiborne to the President, November 25, 1804; all in TP, 9: 218–9, 267, 337, and 341, respectively. Porter's letter was not present. See also James Brown to the Secretary of the Treasury, October 30, 1805, ibid., 517, and Thomas Jefferson, Esq., President of the U. States [*sic*], October 16, 1805, CLB, 3: 204.

3. Not present, but see Letter No. 34, To Constant Freeman, November 2, 1804; Letter No. 35, To Abimael Youngs Nicoll, November 3, 1804; and Letter No. 36, To Captain Samuel Boyer Davis, November 3, 1804.

{38}
To James Madison
New Orleans November 3rd 1804[1]

Sir,
I enclose for your perusal Several Letters, which I have lately received from Natchitoches, together with Copies of Several communications Nos. 1. 2.

3 and 4 which inconsequence thereof I have made to the Marquis of Casa Calvo, Colonel Butler and to Captain Turner the Commandant at Natchitoches[.][2]

It will certainly require great prudence and caution to preserve Peace on the Frontiers, and to maintain a good understanding with our Spanish and Indian neighbors;— on my part nothing Shall be omitted to insure tranquility, but if the Spanish authorities are unfriendly disposed, I fear Some troubles may ensue. When the Marquis's answers to my communications are received they Shall be transmitted to you.

> I am Sir very Respectfully
> Your most obedient
> and very Hble Svt
> (Signed) *William C. C. Claiborne*

The Secty
of State

1. Printed as To James Madison, 3rd November 1804, CLB, 2: 381–2, with variations in the text and punctuation, and with emphasis not found in this copy.
2. The four letters most probably were: Letter No. 28, To Casa Calvo, October 30, 1804; Letter No. 29, To Casa Calvo, October 31, 1804; Letter No. 32, To Thomas Butler, November 1, 1804; and Letter No. 39, To Edward Demaresque Turner, November 3, 1804. For more on Turner, see pp. 567–8.

{39}
To Edward Demaresque Turner
New Orleans November 3rd 1804[1]

Sir,

Your Several Letters of the 16th and 17th Instant have been received,[2] and Shall be forwarded to the President of the United States. The aspect of affairs in your District is not Such as I could wish, but it is in times of ~~Some~~ [?] difficulty that the prudence and Judgment of an officer are put to the Test, and I am certain that you will prove yourself worthy the Trust committed to you.

It is expected that you will establish and enforce a Strict Police among the Slaves. The Patroles at night will be continued, and I am persuaded that you will give Such protection to the Inhabitants of your District as your means will permit. The Marquis of Casa Calvo censures the conduct of the

Commandant at Nacogdoches, and will probably again write to that officer. I hope ~~that~~ the Negroes that have deserted to Nacogdoches, instead of being protected, will be arrested and restored to their masters. If this conduct Should be observed by the Spanish authorities, the Negroe property in your District will be Secure, and no further Symptoms of insubordination among that class of people, will probably be manifested. But if contrary to this just expectation, an assylum Should be afforded in the Province of Taxus [Texas] to Slaves escaping from the Service of their masters, I must request you in that case to ascertain the number and estimated value of the Negroes escaped, the period of their departure, and the name or names of their owner or owners, and to inform me thereof as Soon as may be convenient.[3]

If the public mind in your District should not previous to the Receipt of this Letter be quieted by the return of the Negroes, I beg you to assure the Citizens that the affair is now with their Government, that their Interests will be attended to, and in due time full redress will be obtained. But acts of aggression on their part against the Subjects of Spain are forbidden, and you are enjoined to ~~position~~ [?] prevent any attempts of the kind. With respect to the Indian Tribes you will continue (I hope) to do every thing in your power to engage their good will and friendship towards the United States; you may furnish Rations to such Honest and Well disposed Indians as may visit the Post, but presents to them generally I am not authorized to make.

I however will take upon myself the responsibility, and permit you to make to the Chief of the Caddoes and his principal men presents not exceeding in value 200$. I shall intimate to Colonel Butler the propriety of Sending a reinforcement to Natchitoches, and it is not improbable but Such arrangements may be made, as will Shortly render your force more respectable[.]

I am Sir very Respectfully
Your Hble St
(Signed) *William C. C. Claiborne*

Captn Turner—

---

1. Also printed as To Capt. Turner, November 3, 1804, CLB, 2: 389–90, with variations in text and punctuation, and emphasis marks not on this copy.

2. Not present.

3. For related letters, see Letter No. 28, To Casa Calvo, October 30, 1804, as well as Letter No. 38, To James Madison, November 3, 1804.

{40}

To James Madison
November 5th 1804[1]

Sir,

Since my last Letter Mr. Cantrelle and Mr. Clark have also declined accepting
their commissions as Members of the Legislative Council. There is no
doubt but Some of the promoters of the Memorial have taken those means
to embarrass the local Government, and to force Congress to accede to
their wishes; but Such imprudencies Seem to me illy calculated to benefit their
cause. I have the pleasure however to inform you that Mr. Julien Poydrass
[*sic*] of Point Coupeé [*sic*] the wealthiest and most influential Man in the Territory accepts his appointment.[2] Mr. Poydrass in his Letter to me upon the
Subject Says "My answer to your Letter of the 5th of October shall be Sincere; The President of the United States appointed me a Councillor, I conceive it a duty to accept— If those who have great Interest in the Country
should decline Serving it when called upon, their conduct would be unwarrantable; I could offer many plausible excuses, Such as Age, insufficiency of Talents, Self Interest &c &c &c;— But in doing So I Should not act the part
of a patriot— A beginning must be made; we must be initiated in the Sacred
duties of freemen, and practices of liberty— I shall endeavor to meet you
in Council on the 12th November[.]"

The acceptance of Mr. Poydrass is a fortunate occurrence, and his conduct
and reasoning form a happy contrast to the part acted by Messrs. Jones[,]
Clark and others— There are three Gentlemen named from whom I have not
yet received answers; their acceptance will enable me to form a Council,
but I very much fear one, or perhaps two may decline, and in either event a
Legislature cannot be organized, until the President Shall have forwarded
me the names of other Gentlemen— If a Council is not formed on the 12th
Instant, I fear the people will experience much inconvenience, and of which
when fully apprized, they will probably confide less in the discretion, Patriotism or wisdom of the present influencial [*sic*] characters. I had no idea that
any Citizen named a Councillor, would decline Serving from party motives,
until after I had received the nominations of the President, and I early communicated to you my fears, that the Sentiments conveyed by Mr. Jones in his
letter to me would be embraced by others, and that it was doubtful whether
a Council would be formed— In consequence of this information I indulge a
hope that I Shall Soon receive from the President the names of Several Gentlemen as Successors to those who may have declined.

The Supreme Court was organized on this morning— Judge Prevost (the only Judge in the City) delivered a Sensible charge to the Jury and everything was well conducted.

> I am Sir very Respectfully
> Your Hbl St
> (Signed) *William C. C. Claiborne*

The Secty of State

1. Also published as To James Madison, November 5, 1804, CLB, 2: 390–2, with variations in punctuation and text.
2. Julien Lalande Poydras (April 3, 1746–June 23, 1824) was born near Nantes, France. While serving in the French Navy, he was taken prisoner by the British in 1760, but escaped. He reached Santo Domingo in 1768 and came to Louisiana in 1774. With his native shrewdness, reputation for honesty, and knowledge of the English language, learned while a prisoner in England, Poydras progressed from peddler to plantation owner. By the time of the Louisiana Purchase, Poydras was believed to be the wealthiest man in Louisiana. Spurred by the appointment to the territorial legislative council, Poydras thereafter showed interest in public office. He served as civil commandant (judge) in the Pointe Coupée District, 1804–1807; member of the territorial legislative council, 1804–1807; first president of the territorial legislative council, 1804; president of the ill-fated first bank in New Orleans, the Louisiana Bank, 1804; Orleans Territory delegate to Congress, 1809–1811; president of the first Louisiana constitutional convention, 1811; state senator, 1812–1813, 1819–1824; and president of the first state senate, 1812. Poydras also was a poet and philanthropist. His will bequeathed more than $100,000 to charitable enterprises, among them the Poydras Female Orphan Asylum, the Poydras Academy, and the Poydras Dowry Fund. The fullest treatment of Poydras's life is Mary Flower Pugh Russell, "The Life of Julien Poydras" (master's thesis, Louisiana State University, 1940). Also useful is Frances P. Zink, *Julien Poydras: Statesman, Philanthropist, Educator* (Lafayette: University of Southwestern Louisiana, 1968). Sam Mims, *Trail of the Pack Peddler* (Homer, La.: Guardian-Journal, 1968), provides insight on Poydras's life, but often is factually unreliable. The likeness of Poydras used in the Zink study is reproduced in *Louisiana Historical Society Publications* 6 (1912), facing p. 73. Quite useful is *A Dictionary of Louisiana Biography,* s.v. "Poydras, Julien de Lalande."

{41}
TO THE COMMANDANT AT POINTE COUPÉE[1]
New Orleans November 8th [1804][2]

Sir,
In consequence of the representations[3] to me from the Inhabitants of your District, and my Sincere desire to give all possible protection and Security to my fellow Citizens, I shall take measures to detach to Point Coupeé [*sic*] a Subaltern officer and twenty-five men—[4] The officer will also be fur-

nished with one Hundred Muskets to distribute to the Militia, in the event that any danger should exist on his arrival.

There is no doubt with me but the reports from Nacogdoches have occasioned the late unpleasant movements among the Negroes at Point Coupeé [*sic*] and while I flatter myself that the mischief is arested [*sic*] by a timely discovery, I nevertheless advise and direct you to observe on your part the utmost vigilance, and to give orders as usual for Strong Patroles at night. You will cause the Militia in your District to be immediately organized— Every Male full person between the ages of 16 and fifty will be considered as Subject to Militia Service, and I look with confidence to my fellow Citizens for a faithful discharge of Public duty. Captain Liblong [LeBlanc ?] will take Rank in the Militia in your District as Captain, and I desire you will notify my wishes to him, and urge his immediate attention to the Service. If any thing interesting Should arise you will be pleased to communicate the Same to me by express.

I am Sir very Respectfully
Your most obt Sevt—
(Signed) *William C. C. Claiborne*

To the Commandant
at Point [*sic*] Coupée

1. There was no military commandant at Pointe Coupée. Julien Poydras was the civil commandant (judge). Reference to Poydras's acceptance of the appointment may be found in To Julien Poydrass [*sic*], April 6, 1804, CLB, 2: 82–3.

2. The failure to record the year in which this letter was written reflects the unsettled state of affairs in Claiborne's personal and public life at this time following the deaths, on September 26, 1804, of both his wife, Eliza, and three-year-old daughter, Cornelia Tennessee, from yellow fever. See Letter No. 2, Claiborne's First Louisiana Inaugural Address, n. 3, and the sources cited therein. Earlier in the month, on September 16, Claiborne wrote Jefferson that Joseph Briggs, his private secretary, had died of yellow fever. In the same letter Claiborne also reported that his brother-in-law, Micajah G. Lewis, was so ill with yellow fever that he was expected to die "in the course of the day." Governor Claiborne to the President, September 18, 1804, TP, 9: 298. Claiborne, too, suffered from the effects of the disease, so much so that he requested a four- or five-month leave of absence in early October. Governor Claiborne to the President, October 5, 1804, ibid., 307. The petition, without the list of signers, also is printed in James Robertson, ed. and trans., *Louisiana Under the Rule of Spain, France and the United States, 1785–1807*, vol. 2 (1910–1911; Freeport, N.Y.: Books for Libraries Press, 1969), 300–1.

3. The "representations" referred to were the signatures of more than one hundred inhabitants of Pointe Coupée on the petition delivered by Dr. Ebenezer Cooley to Claiborne in early November 1804. Petition to Governor Claiborne by Inhabitants of Pointe Coupée, November 9, 1804, TP, 9: 326–7.

4. A detachment of thirty enlisted men under the command of Lieutenant John Cleves Symmes (or Syms) was sent to Pointe Coupée. Symmes and the detachment apparently remained there until General Wilkinson closed the post in December 1806. See Charles Morgan to the Secretary of War, September 1, 1807, and Governor Claiborne to the Secretary of War, March 9, 1808, ibid., 762 and 776, respectively.

{42}
To Thomas Butler
New Orleans November 8th 1804[1]

Sir,
A Spirit of Insubordination among the Negroes at Point Coupeé [sic] has occasioned considerable alarm in that District, and the Citizens have asked a Supply of arms for the use of the Militia, and a Small regular force to Serve as a rallying point in case of danger. I am myself impressed with an opinion that the prompt marching of a Small detachment of Troops to Point Coupeé [sic], may avert Mischief and give Security to private property. I therefore think it my duty to Solicit you to detach a Subaltern and 25 or 30 men to Point Coupeé [sic] with all possible expedition, and that the officer commanding the detachment Should be furnished with a hundred Stand of arms to distribute to the Militia in case the danger on his arrival Should be imminent.

> I am Sir with great Respect
> and Esteem
> Your very Humble Sevt
> (Signed) *William C. C. Claiborne*

Colonel Butler

1. Also published as To Col. Butler, November 8, 1804, CLB, 3: 5, with variations in the text and punctuation.

{43}
To Casa Calvo
New Orleans November 8th 1804[1]

Sir,
I have this moment been informed that the news of protection being offered at Nacogdoches to Slaves escaping from the Service of their masters was in circulation among the Negroes at Point Coupeé [sic], and had produced a general Spirit of Insubordination. I communicate to your Excellency this further information, in order ~~Solicit~~ to justify my Solicitude for prompt and

effectual interference. I fear Sir that nothing but the immediate arrest and return of the Negroes who have escaped to Nacogdoches, will prevent much injury to the Territory of Orleans, and perhaps the destruction of many of her Citizens[.]

The Letters received from your Excellency on yesterday are now in the hands of my interpreter, translations will be furnished me in the course of this day, and if answers are required they shall be returned on tomorrow.

I offer to your Excellency assurances
of my Respect and Esteem
(Signed) *William C. C. Claiborne*

The Marquis
of
Casa Calvo

1. Also published as To Casa Calvo, November 8, 1804, CLB, 3: 5–6, with slight variations in the text and punctuation.

{44}
To James Madison
New Orleans November 8th 1804[1]

Sir,

I enclose you a Petition[2] from the Inhabitants of Point Coupeé [*sic*] which was this day presented to me by two Gentlemen[3], who mentioned to me that the news from Nacogdoches was in circulation among the Negroes in that Settlement, and had produced in their opinion that Spirit of insubordination which existed. In consequence of the petition I have requested Colonel Butler by Letter No. 1 to detach a Subaltern command to Point Coupeé [*sic*], and have also made communications to the Marquis of Casa Calvo, and the Several District commandants of which Nos. 2. 3 & 4 are Copies.[4]

Our Troops here are too few in numbers to admit of Detachments to the various Posts where they would be Serviceable, and most earnestly advise that the regular force in Louisiana be augmented with all possible dispatch. A revenue Cutter and Gun-Boat would also be highly useful in this quarter, and tend greatly to the Security of the revenue.

I am Sir very Respectfully
Your Hble Sevt
(Signed) *William C. C. Claiborne*

The Secty
of State

P.S[.] I am well aware that the Marquis has no control over the officers in the Province of Taxus [Texas]. But my Letters to him will command *answers,* and it is probable, that in *them* may be discovered the real views of the Spanish Court.

W. C. C. C—

1. Also published as To James Madison, CLB, 2: 394, without the emphasis marks found in the postscript of this copy.

2. Not present, but see Petition to Governor Claiborne by Inhabitants of Pointe Coupée, November 9, 1804, TP, 9: 326–7, for the petition with the list of signatories, and James Robertson, ed. and trans., *Louisiana Under the Rule of Spain, France and the United States, 1785–1807,* vol. 2 (1910–1911; Freeport, N.Y.: Books for Libraries Press, 1969), 300–1, for a copy of the petition without the list of signers.

3. The man deputed to present the petition was Dr. Ebenezer Cooley. Petition to Governor Claiborne by Inhabitants of Pointe Coupée, November 9, 1804, TP, 9: 326. Although he is not identified, the man who most likely accompanied Cooley was Julien Poydras, the civil commandant for the Pointe Coupée district.

4. Not present, but for a letter similar to the one sent to the commandant at Pointe Coupée, see To Edw. Turner, November 8, 1804, CLB, 3: 6–7.

{45}

FROM JOHN BISHOP PREVOST[1]

New Orleans November 8th 1804

Sir,

The room designated for the Sessions of the Supreme Court is So incompletely furnished that I must request the interference of your Excellency to direct Such additional chairs[,] Tables[,] &c to be provided as may be necessary for the convenience of the Court, its officers and the Jury. I have been obliged to procure a Seal for which no provision is made, I beg leave also to Submit the propriety of making this a public charge. It is with regret that I trouble your Excellency on this occasion, but from the State of the Territory at this moment there can be no other power to make the Provisions which is [*sic*] essential to the administration of Justice.

> I have the Honour to be Sir
> with great respect
> Your Excellencys most obdt Sevt
> (Signed) *J. B. Prevost*

Gov. Claiborne

1. John B. Prevost wrote Secretary Madison in August 1803, asking for an appointment in Orleans. See J. B. Prevost to the President, July 30, 1804, TP, 9: 269 n. 34. He was nomi-

nated for judge of the superior court for the Orleans district on November 30, 1804, and his appointment was confirmed by the Senate on December 11, 1804. An earlier recess appointment said his commission formally began on August 18, 1804, in conformance with the act of March 26, 1804. However, the forms confirming the earlier appointment date were never filed and had to be reaccomplished. Commission of Judge Prevost, December 11, 1804, and June 10, 1805, both in TP, 9: 350 n. 78, and 455, respectively. Prevost arrived in New Orleans to assume his judicial duties on October 28, 1804. Governor Claiborne to the Secretary of State, October 29, 1804, ibid., 9: 317.

{46}

To Casa Calvo

New Orleans November 9th 1804[1]

Sir,

The answers of your Excellency to my communications of the 30th and 31st Ultimo I have had the pleasure to receive. I persuade myself that the Letters you have addressed to the Commanding General of Inland Provinces and the Commandant at Nacogdoches, will impress upon the officers the propriety of adopting on their part that line of conduct which is calculated to Strengthen, rather than weaken the ties of friendship between our two nations.

It is not impossible but the French Inhabitants may have manifested a want of caution in communicating the intelligence from Nacogdoches, but I am inclined to think that the Commandant at that Post has been excessively imprudent, unless indeed his conduct was prescribed by his Superiors, and this from your Letters I have no reason to Suppose. The property of the Citizens of Natchitoches under whatever Government acquired, must now be Secured to them by the United States, the complaints of the Citizens have therefore very properly been directed to me, and altho I flatter myself that your representations to His Catholic Majesty will induce that Sovereign to apply a just and prompt corrective, I nevertheless think it my duty to lay the whole affair before the President of the United States, and if your Excellency is in possession of the Royal Decree which has occasioned the unpleasant occurrences at Natchitoches I shall esteem it a favor to be furnished with a copy. The return of the Negroes who have Sought refuge in His Catholic Majesty's Dominions upon the conditions you have prescribed I cannot approve of, inasmuch as I am firmly convinced their unconditional surrender can alone, put an end to the growing evil of which the Citizens at Natchitoches complain.— I wish it however to be understood, that I am not an advocate for the punishment of those fugitives, but I am desirous that their lenient treatment should depend upon the clemency of their masters, or the Humane interposition of the Territorial Government.—

> I render to your Excellency
> assurances of my High
> and Respectful consideration
> (Signed) *William C. C. Claiborne*

The Marquis
of
Casa Calvo

1. Also published as To Casa Calvo, November 9, 1804, CLB, 3: 8–9, with variations in the text and punctuation.

{47}
To Ferdinand Leigh Claiborne[1]
New Orleans November 12th 1804

Sir,

I enclose you a Packet for Captain Turner which I pray you to forward by the first safe conveyance and if one Should not offer in a few days you will be pleased to forward the Packet by express.

> I am Sir very respectfully
> Your Hble Sevt
> (Signed) *William C. C. Claiborne*

Major Claiborne
Commandant
at Concordia

1. F. L. Claiborne was replaced as civil commandant of Concordia, opposite Natchez, by L. Wooldridge in January 1805. Governor Claiborne to Ferdinand L. Claiborne, January 29, 1805, TP, 9: 386–7. For biographical information, see Letter No. 165, To Ferdinand Leigh Claiborne, n. 1.

{48}
To Edward Demaresque Turner
New Orleans November 12th 1804

Sir,

I enclose you a Letter from the Marquis of Casa Calvo to the Governor of the Interior Provinces, and another to the Commandant at Nacogdoches, which I pray you to forward by the first Safe conveyance to Nacogdoches. These letters relate to the late desertion of the Negroes, and their early delivery may produce good effects. The Marquis in his correspondence with me upon the affairs in your District attributes the late movements among the Negroes, to the imprudence of the farmers at Natchitoches, and declares the conduct of the Commandant at Nacogdoches was marked with propriety. The Marquis States that the existence of the Decree was communicated by the Inhabitants of your vicinity to their negroes, by imprudently conversing upon the Subject, and that they had given to the Decree a construction which it did not deserve. If it is in your power to rescue your fellow Citizens from this charge, and attach the blame on the Commandant at Nacogdoches—I wish you do So. The Marquis has advised the immediate return of the Slaves, and I presume his advice will be pursued.

> I am Sir with Respect and
> Esteem your Hble Svt
> (Signed) *William C. C. Claiborne*

Capt Turner

{49}
To James Madison
New Orleans November 15th 1804

Sir,
I have the Honour to enclose you Several Documents relative to the Barque Hero from No. 1 to No.   . Inclusive as also a Copy of two Letters from me to Captain Nicolls marked   .[1]

Some of the Prisoners who have made their escape from the Hero and came up to this City have already proved themselves unworthy members of Society, and I am therefore the more desirous to prevent the Men now on Board that vessel from landing. I must confess Sir I did not know what were the most prudent measures to direct in relation to the Hero, ~~and~~ her passengers and Crew; but under existing circumstances, I thought it best that the Vessel and those on Board Should depart;— I suggested Some Port in the United States as proper for their destination under an impression that it would serve as an inducement to their departure, and that no where in the United States would the residence of these Strangers be as dangerous as in New Orleans. The arrest of a Spanish officer in this City by a writ issuing from the Office of the Supreme Court has occasioned much agitation here and greatly excited the displeasure of the Marquis of Casa Calvo and of Governor Folch;—[2] I will give you the particulars in my next Letter and in the mean time I pray you to be assured that the conduct of the constituted authorities has been correct.

I have not yet been able to form a Council, only five of the Gentlemen nominated by the President have accepted to Wit Messrs. Poydrass [sic], Watkins, Morgan, Wikoff and Kenner, the first four are now in the City and the fifth is every day expected. I hope in God that the next mail may furnish me with the names of Some Gentlemen as Successors to those who may decline. A Council is greatly wanted, and the Interest of the Territory Suffers much by the delay of Legislative interference. Party Spirit here is certainly Subsiding, and I am persuaded that the Inhabitants of the Country are becoming much better disposed to the United States. But in this City there are many disorderly and dangerous characters. Neither the Secretary Mr. Brown or Colonel Kirby have yet arrived. The latter Gentleman is reported to be dangerously ill at Fort Stoddart.

> I am Sir very Respectfully
> Your Hbl Set [sic]
> (Signed) *William C. C. Claiborne*

The Honble
James Madison
Secty of State

1. None of the letters referred to was present. The blank spaces occur in the original. See Letter No. 35, To Abimael Youngs Nicoll, November 3, 1804, for a related letter on the barque *Hero*.

2. The incident involved David Bannister Morgan, an American originally from upstate New York, and Manuel García y Muñis, the captain of the Spanish schooner that often brought the payroll from Mexico for the Spanish officials in West Florida and New Orleans. The ship that held Morgan captive stood off the mouth of Bayou St. John in Lake Pontchartrain. The complete story of García's arrest appeared in the *Louisiana Gazette*, November 23, 1804, p. 3, cc. 1–3.

{50}
FROM CASA CALVO
New Orleans November 16th 1804

Sir,

I was informed by the Governor of West Florida Don Vincent [sic] Folch that Don Manuel Garcia a Captain in the Kings Army and Commanding

the Squadron of Galleys in Said Province, being on his way through this City
with the Officers of his retinue was notwithstanding a Safe conduct he had
from your Excellency, has been arrested by two Constables who presented
him with an order to constituteider himself a Prisoner as a Security towards
the man named Morgan[1] who had brought an Action against him. The Said
Morgan has been detained in consequence of the orders from Governor
Folch, on board the Schooner Favorite of which Captain Garcia is Commander. Said Vessel being stationed in the Creek Chefoncte,[2] and I am authorized to think that in the present case your Excellency has been led into
Some error, and I hope you will be pleased as soon as you will be informed
that the detention of Said Morgan was ordered by Said Governor, in the Territory of his Catholic Majesty, and within the limits of the Province under
his command, to order the Judge whoever he may be, who issued Such order
of arrest to repeal the Same, and to put a stop to all the proceedings, because the affair ought not to be enquired into by the Government of the
United States, as the Spanish Governor on his Side is very careful not to
interfere in Such cases as belong to the American Jurisdiction, however far
they may relate to Spanish Subjects.

The good harmony established between both Nations and the regard to
be paid to the officers of a friendly power, require a Scrupulous preservation of the privileges introduced in the Society at large by the common Law
of Nations. I am therefore persuaded your Excellency will without delay,
attend to Such measures as may be the most effectual in promoting a further
progress of an affair. The Public consequences of which threaten to be very
serious, besides setting up a bad example for the future.

> May your Excellency live many years
> (Signed) *The Marquis of Casa Calvo*

Gov. Claiborne
I certify the above translation
Moreau Lisley [Lislet] Interpr &c

---

1. David Bannister Morgan.
2. The Tchefuncte River in St. Tammany Parish, southeast Louisiana. Before it disgorges
into Lake Pontchartrain on its northern shore, the river is joined by the smaller Bogue Falaya
River on the east. The city of Covington, Louisiana, is nestled between the confluence of the
two rivers, which continues with the name Tchefuncte on its way to the lake. See Edwin Adams
Davis, ed., *The Rivers and Bayous of Louisiana* (Baton Rouge: Louisiana Education Research
Association, 1968), 153, 159 (map), 165, 166, 170.

{51}
To Casa Calvo
New Orleans November 16th 1804[1]

Sir,

I have read with respectful attention your Excellencys Letter of this Evening, and in reply I have only to State that the Spanish Officer you allude to is in arrest in virtue of a process regularly issuing from the Superior Court of this Territory. Upon what grounds it may have been issued, or how far it may have been irregular it is not within my Province to enquire. The Powers of the Judiciary are derived immediately from the General Government of the United States. The Court is Independant [sic] and not Subject to my controul [sic]. If the arrest of the Officer be illegal, the Court will certainly direct his liberation on a proper application to that effect. I cannot perceive in this transaction any just cause for the agitation which has been discovered on the part of your Excellency and of Governor Folch. In a verbal message to me from your Excellency expressions are conveyed derogatory to the Government which I represent, as well as personally offensive to me, and I learn with regret that Governor Folch has used a language equally exceptionable.

Your Excellency can readily conceive my feelings on receiving Such communications. No threats of this nature you may be assured, can induce me to Swerve from my duty, and permit me to add that the power does not *exist* which can *Shake* the authority of *my Country over this Territory.*—[2]

I pray your Excellency to be assured
of my respectful consideration
(Signed) *William C. C. Claiborne*

His Excellency
The Marquis
of Casa Calvo

1. Also published as To Casa Calvo, November 10, 1804, CLB, 3: 22–3, with variations in punctuation and without the emphasis found here.
2. Emphasis in the original.

{52}
To Abimael Youngs Nicoll
New Orleans November 16th 1804[1]

Sir,

Your Letter relative to the Hero together with its several enclosures I have received. The Situation of the Sick and wounded on Board of that Vessel excites my commiseration, and I am certainly desirous to render them acts of kindness. Will you request the Surgeons mate of your Garrison to visit the Hero and administer such relief to the Sick and wounded, as may be in his power. He will be pleased to make his charge, and I will endeavour to obtain payment for him from the Ministers of those Nations near the United States, whose distressed Countrymen have unfortunately been thrown upon our Shores. If the Doctor Should Suppose that exercise on Shore would assist the convalescents, you may permit them occasionally to Land for that purpose, and I desire that every act of kindness may be extended to them. If the person having charge of the Vessel has the means of procuring fresh provisions and Rice for the Sick and wounded, you will be pleased to permit him to obtain the necessary Supplies;— but if he is without means, (that is if he has no Money) I will thank you to procure two dozen of fowls and two Barrels of Rice and present them to the Sick. For the expenses of the rice and fowls, you will draw upon me, and your Bills Shall immediately be paid;— as Soon as those Supplies are furnished and the Sick and wounded have received the necessary aid from the Physician of the Garrison, I would advise that the Bark Hero Should put to Sea, and proceed to Some of the Atlantic Ports in the United States or to the West Indies, but their departure need not for the present be pressed.—

Those on Board in whose Honour you can Confide, you may at your pleasure permit to Land for exercise.

> I am Sir very Respectfully
> Your humble Servant
> (Signed) *William C. C. Claiborne*

Capt Nicoll
Commanding
at Plaquemine

1. Published as To Capt. Nicholl [*sic*], November 16, 1804, CLB, 3: 12–3, with variations in the text and punctuation.

{53}
REPORT OF LEWIS KERR ON THE ARREST OF CAPTAIN MANUEL GARCÍA
[November 17, 1804][1]
A Report of the Sheriff to the Governor
on the Subject of Captain Garcia's
arrest[,] a Spanish Officer.

Sir,

In compliance with your Excellency's request, I have the Honour to Submit to you the following Statement of the circumstances attending the late arrest of Captain Don Manuel Garcia. On Friday last the fifteenth Instant I received from the office of the Superior Court, an order to hold to Bail Manuel Garcia at the Suit of David B Morgan in the Sum of Six hundred dollars and upwards (The Plaintiffs petition ([*sic*] a Copy of which was at the time ~~jinxxx~~ transmitted to me to be delivered to the Defendant) exhibited the particulars of Morgans [*sic*] claim, namely the value of a Negroe Some wearing apparel and other movables which he stated to belong to him and to be unjustly detained from him by the defendant.[2]

As I presume that your Excellency has required this communication with a view to its use where the leading circumstances of the transaction are unknown, it may not be improper here to mention that Morgan is a native Citizen of the United States, and has been for Some time past employed as a Surveyor in West Florida. Falling lately under the displeasure of the Government he was arrested, and he together with the property mentioned in his Petition was put on Board of a Spanish Galley Commanded by the Defendant bound I believe to Pensacola. At the entrance of the Bayou St. John where the Galley anchored on her way down the Lakes, Morgan made his escape and could not be retaken, being then within the Territories of the United States[.] On his arrival in this City he applied to the Spanish authorities, then on their passage by this route to Pensacola, for his property on Board of the Galley: But his application not being attended to, he Sued Garcia in the manner which I have stated. I had often before experienced Serious difficulties in the execution of Such process against Spanish Officers; long accustomed to extraordinary privileges, they always Submitted with reluctance to the equal operations of American Law and as there were a number of those officers in Town, I thought it prudent particularly at the present moment, to make arrangements for the vigorous Support of my authority.

Garcia being by Some means apprized of the process that had issued against him Secreted himself in the House of a Spanish officer in this City, and it required the utmost vigilance of my officers, as well as of the Plaintiff and his friends to discover him. His retreat being at length discovered, I sent an officer to Serve the process on him, and at the Same time a Message requesting him to meet me at my office. At first he consented, but refused to *go in custody,* and as my officer could not with propriety leave him he refused altogether. Having previously known Captain Garcia as a Gentleman of respectable Standing, I determined then to wait on him myself. But least any insult should be attempted I provided myself with a Small force which I left in the street when I entered the House. I then found that Captain Garcia's going to my office would have been but of little use, as he told me he was determined not to give Bail, alleging that Such were his orders from his

Superior officers. I remained Some time to reason with him, both in private
and in the presence of his friends; Several Gentlemen offered to Bail him, but
he refused every offer, and avowed his intention of not Submitting till compelled. He however requested me to await the arrival of Governor Folch,
whom he had Sent for and expected every minute. This I consented to. But
Governor Folch, as I was informed, being confined by indisposition, his Son
Lieutenant Folch arrived, as I understood with his orders, and in my presence directed Garcia not to give any Bail, nor to leave the House he was then
in, and to resist by force any attempts to remove him. By this time the
Room was crowded principally by Spaniards many of whom were armed. I
then told Captain Garcia, that after what I had heard, I must leave him in
the hands of my officers and was about to order in the force from the Streets,
when I was entreated to desist a few minutes longer, and assured that if I
would See Governor Claiborne, the Marquis of Casa Calvo, or Governor
Folch upon the Subject, the matter would be arranged, for that in virtue of
Governor Claibornes [sic] permission to the Spanish officers generally to pass
through this Territory from Baton Rouge to Pensacola, Captain Garcia was
protected by the Laws of Nations, and the good faith of the American Government from arrest. Being well aware that this Suggestion was dictated by
a mistaken notion of the powers of the Executive, I merely promised to report
Captain Garcia's plea, and giving orders that nothing further Should be
done till my return, I waited on Judge Prevost and related to him the circumstances of the case. His answer was Such as I expected, that as a ministerial
officer I had the process directed to me as my only guide, and could not refuse
to execute it but at my own peril. I then returned but hearing on my way
that a large concourse of people to the number of at least two hundred persons had assembled in and about the House, I took with me from the main
guard a further force consisting of a Lance-Corporal and three men. On my
arrival I ordered my officer to complete the arrest, and Sent in the Men to
Support ~~my~~ his authority. As they entered Some Swords were drawn in the
Room, but no violence was actually attempted.

   Being provoked at this threatened resistence, and now feeling it my duty
to arrest not only Captain Garcia, but at the Same time all those who men-
aced my authority, I suffered a parley to take place, while I searched, but in
vain, among the crowd for a Sufficient number of ~~Men~~ persons on whose
Support I could rely. I then determined to apply at the Barracks for a reinforcement, and during my absence Lieut Wilson of the United States
Army (the officer of the day) probably anxious for the Safety of the Men he
had dispatched under my command, arrived at the House with a few more

Soldiers. As he entered the Room the Swords which had been drawn were sheathed: He demanded the Prisoner, who immediately Surrendered himself and was conducted by him to the Main guard without any further tumult or opposition.

> I have the Honour to be Sir with
> Sincere respect your Excellency's
> faithful
> friend and obt Sevt
> (Signed) *"Louis Kerr,"* *Alguazil*
> *Mayor and Sheriff*

To His Excellency
Gov. Claiborne

1. No date was on this letter in the manuscript. The date entered here is derived from Governor Claiborne to the President, November 19, 1804, TP, 9: 334 n. 55, where it is noted that Kerr's report is one of the enclosures in Claiborne's November 19, 1804, letter to Secretary of State Madison.

2. David B. Morgan continued for years to seek a favorable settlement of his claim. Specifically, he tried to attach Governor Folch's property in East Florida. See William A. Patton to General D. B. Morgan, August 25, 1818, in Folder 1, William H. Seymour Papers, Louisiana and Lower Mississippi Valley Collections, Louisiana State University Libraries. Morgan steadfastly maintained that the Spanish held and never returned his papers and instruments, valued at two thousand dollars. David B. Morgan to David Rees, December 6, 1804. David Rees Papers, Special Collections Department, Howard-Tilton Memorial Library, Tulane University.

{54}

TO JAMES MADISON
New Orleans November 17th 1804[1]

Sir,

I enclose you two original Letters from the Marquis of Casa Calvo relating to the late news from Natchitoches and Point Coupeé [*sic*];— a Small Detachment of troops has been ordered to Point Coupeé [*sic*], and I believe every thing is now quiet at that place. I have received no late dispatches from Natchitoches: But I persuade myself that there also, the cause for alarm has in a measure ceased. If my communications have reached Washington regularly, you are furnished with Copies of the various Letters which I have addressed to the Marquis upon the Subject of the Royal Decree concerning Slaves.— It is a length of time Since I have been Honoured with a Letter from you.— My impressions are that the Post from Washington to this City, is not at this time a Safe conveyance for Official Letters, and I advise that Duplicates of Such of your dispatches as are of importance be forwarded by Water—

> I am Sir with Respect & Esteem
> Your most obt & Hbe St
> (Signed) *William C. C. Claiborne*

The Honble
James Madison
Secty of State

1. Also published as To James Madison, November 17, 1804, CLB, 3: 9–10, with variations in text and punctuation.

{55}
To Abimael Youngs Nicoll
November 17th 1804[1]

Sir,

If you Should find the Persons on Board the Hero, destitute of the means of procuring fresh Provisions, you will oblige me, if in addition to the Rice mentioned in my last Letter, you would purchase four or five dozen of fowls and present them to the Sick, and if you think proper you may also procure a Small quantity of fresh Beef for their use.

> I am Sir your very Hble St
> (Signed) *William C. C. Claiborne*

Captain
Nicoll Plaque—
mine

1. Also published as To Capt. Nicholl [*sic*], November 17, 1804, CLB, 3: 13, with variations in text and punctuation.

{56}
From Casa Calvo
New Orleans November 17th 1804

Sir,

Your Excellencys Answer which I received last night is not Such as I imagined it would be, and expected from the Justice[,] righteousness and wisdom belonging to the Government of the United States. Before establishing the reasons on which my assertion is founded, Your Excellency will permit me to inform you that the Character of the Commission to me entrusted by the King my Master, does not authorize my entering into any discussion with other persons, let them be ever So worthy of esteem, but the Head of the Government ~~of~~ himself, who has a right to correspond with the Courts or officers employed in his Territory, and ought to take thereupon the most Suitable measures which Sufficiently Shews [*sic*], that to your Excellency alone I must apply for obtaining the attention which I requested of you by my Letter of yesterday.

I must repeat to your Excellency, that Captain Don Manuel Garcia acted as to the detention of Morgan by the orders of the Governor of West Florida; that Morgans [*sic*] fault was committed in the Spanish Territories where the orders for putting him under arrest, and for Seizing his property were issued; I will Say moreover, that Morgan was actually Commissioned by our Lands Surveyor General, and therefore liable to our Laws and Constitution. The American Government in consequence should not have interfered in the cognizance of a case of this nature, under any pretence or motive whatever, otherwise it would imply a pretension to Superiority, which cannot be acknowledged, and is both repugnant to reason and in opposition with Sound Judgment;— I then expect your Excellency will find it convenient, to let me know the reasons why to the great astonishment and Scandal of the Public" [*sic*] violent proceedings were used against an Officer of His Catholic Majesty and a considerable number of armed men employed in wresting him from the House of another Spanish Officer where he had taken refuge, where the Constables went in to arrest him, which was effected, without his offering the least resistance and at a time when I was compromising that affair with your Excellency.—

The moderation which was manifested by the Spanish Government, respecting the detention of Pedro Villamil,[1] occasioned by a false charge laid against him by the man named Hulin, and also in the complaint made against Thomas Randall,[2] for infringement of the Privileges of my House, and likewise in the extraordinary proceedings held against Eustatius a Mulatto belonging to myself, and in many other instances wherein I requested what assistance was necessary to promote the Kings Interest, and to bring to a close the operations of my Government relative to its late administration of this Province; *all that* in my opinion called for a reciprocal conduct, and that before going on to Such a noisy and Scandalous measure, a previous communication had been granted to me, So as to avoid many disagreeable discussions, that your Excellency thoroughly informed of the causes of the affair, might have given, or caused the Judicial Courts of the Territory to give the convenient orders.

By the means of Such precautions your Excellency would have known long ago, that the affair is of the Sole ~~District~~ cognizance of the Governor of West-Florida and that Governor Folch ~~in xxxx xxx of some room for~~ if there be complaint on the Side of the United States is the only person answerable for it, and that the Same ought not be imputed to Captain Garcia, who only obeyed his Superior officer. How melancholy and much to be pitied would be the lot of a Government that Should tamely Suffer Such a Conduct! I am persuaded that all this derives from Some misunderstanding, and that your Excellency will be pleased, to take the Steps and measures which are dictated by a love of good order, and a natural desire of preserving good Harmony between two contiguous States: The interruption of which might bring on ir-remidiable [*sic*] evils— Your Excellency Should meanwhile be firmly per-suaded, that neither Governor Folch nor myself in our writings or Letters could ever mean the least injury, to your character or person, but only at-tempted to Vindicate the lawful rights and privileges of the Spanish nation.—

> May your Excellency enjoy many
> years
> (Signed) *The Marquis of Casa Calvo*

Gov. Claiborne

I do certify the above to be a true
translation
Moreau Lisly [*sic*]
Interpt To the Govt—

---

1. The relevant facts of this case involving Pedro Villamil, former steward of the Royal Hospital in New Orleans, some slaves (whose ownership was questioned), and the claims on them by Francis Hulin are set forth in To the Marquis of Casa Calvo, September 5, 1804, CLB, 2: 320–5. Hulin's first name is given in To Peter Pedisclaux [*sic*] Esquire Notary Public, ibid., 219. On Morales, see pp. 495–8 herein.

2. Thomas Randall (d. 1818) was born in England but was a merchant and justice of the peace in New Orleans. He wanted to be appointed an auctioneer, but Claiborne did not ap-point him to this office. See the postscript in Governor Claiborne to the Secretary of State, January 26, 1805, TP, 9: 382. The complaint against Randall was his entering Casa Calvo's home to arrest Blas Ciergo. See From the Marquis of Casa Calvo to Gov. Claiborne [September 2, 1804], CLB, 2: 317–8, and To Casa Calvo, November 18 and 22, 1804, ibid., 3: 19 and 22. Subsequently, Randall settled in Donaldsonville, where he became the town's first postmaster

(1808–1818). Sidney A. Marchand, *Across the Years: [Donaldsonville and Ascension Parish]* (Donaldsonville, La.: S. A. Marchand, 1949), 38.

{57}

To Casa Calvo
November 18th 1804[1]

Sir,

I am Honoured with your Excellencys Letter of Yesterday, and after a respectful attention to its contents I hasten to reply. Your Letter Commences with adverting to the Commission entrusted to you, by His Catholic Majesty; and afterwards you Seem more than once, to allude to Some of the privileges which you conceive yourself entitled to, in virtue of that Commission.

In answer, ~~to~~ your Excellency will I trust excuse my remarking, that whatever *Diplomatic Agency* it may have been the intention of your Sovereign to invest you with, that it is only through the Government ~~that~~ I serve, that I can be apprized of it. To the President of the United States, is constitutionally reserved the exclusive right of accrediting the Ambassadors, Ministers or Agents of foreign powers, and therefore altho' as Gentlemen of distinction and information, and High in the confidence of your Government, I Have with great pleasure corresponded with you on local Subjects, and the mutual Interests of this Territory and the Dominions of His Catholic Majesty, in our Vicinity, it never was my intention, nor *is it in my power,* to recognize your Excellency in any manner as a Diplomatic Character, or entitled to any privileges beyond those of a highly respected personage temporarily residing in this Territory.

To your corresponding with me on the subject of the arrest of Captain Don Manuel Garcia, I could not ~~possibly~~ have objections; But as this was altogether a Judicial Affair, and as I have already explained to your Excellency utterly beyond my controul, I indulged a hope that my explanations on that head would have been Satisfactory. The Judges Sir, of the Territory, are not named, nor, liable to be removed by me: To their Tribunals I can give no orders, and in their Councils even my advice would be unwarrantable, because an unconstitutional interference:— Willing however to Co-operate with your Excellency in any measures that may conduce to a reconciliation of our differences, I will communicate to the Attorney General (the only Officer through which the Executive can approach the Court) the reasons assigned by your Excellency to Shew the illegality of Captain Garcia's arrest, and will request him, the Attorney to adopt Such measures, [*sic*] as may be in his power to effect a Speedy examination and discussion of the question.

You ask Sir the reasons why Captain Garcia was arrested by an armed
force? to [*sic*] that I have only to answer that the *Laws of my Country are
Supreme,* and are to be obeyed respectfully and promptly by every Individual
of whatever nation he may be, while within the limits of their authority—
Had Captain Garcia Surrendered himself in the first instance to the Civil authority, the aid of the Military would not have been called in. To Save himself the disagreeable alternative of imprisonment, it was only necessary for
him to give Security for his appearance before the Court. He was Surrounded by his friends Several of whom offered themselves as his Bail, but he
refused their offers, Saying that Such were his orders, and in the presence
of the Civil officers (I am informed) he received from Governor Folch through
an officer a further ~~offer~~ order, in positive and energetic terms, not to give
Bail nor leave the House he was then in, unless compelled by a Superior force,
and to resist any attempt to remove him. The Civil authority thus opposed,
could not do otherwise than demand the assistance of the Military. Several
of Captain Garcia's friends, officers of the Spanish Army were armed, and
on the entrance of the Guard, Swords were actually drawn, but happily the
threatened resistance was not attempted. In your Excellencys conduct and
that of your friends in behalf of Don Pedro Villamil when arrested at the Suit
of Hulin, I must confess myself unable to discover those proofs of moderation which you Seem to rely on. Don Pedro Villamil was as Captain Garcia
now is, in the Custody of the Law, and in giving Security for his appearance
before the Tribunal by whose order he was arrested, he did only what the
Law made necessary to his enlargement. Nor can I understand how the affair of Mr. Randall to which you allude, or the punishment of your Servant
is connected with the Subject immediately before us, unless as violations of
Some Supposed Diplomatic Privilige, on the Subject of which I have already
expressed myself to your Excellency. I have complained of no injury either
to my character or person in the writings or Letters of your Excellency or of
Governor Folch.— By adverting to my last Letter, you will find, that the
offensive language was conveyed in verbal communications, & on this Subject, my impressions must remain the same, unless your Excellency will dis-
avow the following expressions used by a Gentleman who in Company with
your Secretary Don Andre Lopez Said to me— "that the Marquis requested
an immediate answer to his Letter, and the release of Captain Garcia, or he
would immediately depart the Country, and would not be answerable for
the consequences and Revolution that might ensue."

The language of Governor Folch to which I alluded, was his complaining
of injury and threatening "retaliation" and adding "that the people of this

Country would not see him injured";— these expressions were addressed to
a Gentleman who bore a verbal message from me to Governor Folch explaining to him in terms the most conciliatory and candid, that the arrest of
the Spanish officer was by virtue of the Judicial authority, and that the
Court would certainly direct his release, provided the arrest was illegal whenever the case was brought before it.—

But I am unwilling to enlarge on this Subject, having too much confidence
in the good Sense of your *Excellency* and of *Governor Folch* to apprehend,
that either on dispassionate reflection will be disposed to persist in, or to justify expressions of that unpleasant nature.

> I wish your Excellency a long life and
> beg leave to renew to you
> assurances of my respectful
> consideration.—
> (Signed) *William C. C. Claiborne*

His Excellency
The Marquis of
Casa Calvo

1. Also published as To Casa Calvo, November 18, 1804, CLB, 3: 16–20, with variations
in text, punctuation, and emphasis. This letter provides insight into the problems the Spanish
officials caused Claiborne as a result of Jefferson's cautious foreign policy in the old Southwest.

{58}
FROM CASA CALVO
New Orleans November 19th 1804

Sir,
I would have been completely gratified with the explanation contained in the
fifth paragraph of your Excellencys answer concerning the arrest of Captain
Don Manuel Garcia, were it not for the observations you thought proper to
quote, with respect to the public Capacity which I find myself invested with
for this place, these observations require on my part that I do Submit a few
others to your Excellency not unworthy of your attention, as they more
effectually assert the rights and priviliges, which may or ought to belong to
the Public Commission I am entrusted with.— Your Excellency will be notwithstanding at Liberty, to give the Same Such bounds as you please as I am
determined not to insist any more on this point. By the Commands of the
King my Master, I was appointed Commissary[1] to execute jointly with Briga-

dier General Don Manuel De Salcedo, both the remittance of Louisiana to the French Republic, and the evacuation of the Province, with orders to remain Hither until the former was completed, for the purpose of regulating the limits and other matters relative to the cession and evacuation; it is not unknown to your Excellency that it was by virtue of the Said Capacity that I did put Citizen Laussat, acting with Special powers on his side, ~~of~~ from the first Consul in possession of Louisiana, and that the upper inland Ports, were delivered into the Hands of the American Officers, by the result of respective orders issued and communicated agreeably by the aforesaid Prefect, and by myself;— it is on that ground that I go on now the same way which is but very natural, as long as the ends of my Commission is not yet accomplished. The President of the United States is not certainly a Stranger to these facts, as till now he never manifested any objection against my residence in this Territory, and as it appears Suitable for the Interest of His Catholic Majesty, that either myself or another person do represent him hither, and perform his orders in the important duties of my Commission. I do not aim to be considered by your Excellency, as a Plenipotentiary Minister, or an Ambassador ordinary, or Extraordinary, but what I do not cease to claim, are the immunities priviliges and regards, which belong and are due to a Public Minister, in my Capacity— My Commission respecting Louisiana is anterior to that of your Excellency's, and requires no further credentials, but the actual activity in which is placed a Public Minister, who continues his duty in a Territory given up, and whose limits are to be determined, in order to insure the Identity of the Cession. Your Excellency will thus become Sensible that I cannot depart myself in any manner from the Public Capacity with which I am entrusted, and that I must with Some concern see myself considered by your Excellency, under the mere particular relations which you are pleased to point out; and further refering to final decision of the contested point to our respective ~~Constituents~~ governments, I will dispense enumerating ~~among~~ many other reasons which could be added to the Support of the rights belonging to me, which *reserve* ought by no means to be viewed as a renunciation of the immunities inherent to my Commission.

I never expressed a desire either in my messages or written correspondence, that your Excellency should Commit any Such acts of Authority, as might exceed the Sphere of your powers, but as I must correspond with your Excellency alone, ~~it is to your Excellency alone,~~ it is to your Excellency that I did manifest what I repeat to you, that the Cognizance of that fact which took its origin from the orders of the Governor of West Florida, issued in his own Territory, cannot and ought not to be Submitted to the Trial of the

Courts of the United States, ~~and So much and So much~~ nor can the Said
Courts render Subaltern Spanish officers answerable for things which they
have done, in obedience to the orders of their Superior Officer. On that
indisputable ground was founded the Solicitude which I expressed to your
Excellency, without any pretension whatever to prescribe what I had no
right to do, which ways and means your Excellency Should adopt in the case,
the conclusion of which will Soon take place, if the proceedings[2] of the Attorney General have the Success to be expected.

I never concealed to myself likewise that the Laws of every State or Territory must be respected and obeyed exactly, but in the Same time I supposed,
that Some regard ought to be paid to a Safe conduct, delivered by your Excellency to Governor Folch, and to the officers of his retinue, and that previous to any proceedings against any of them, it was incumbent with the
kindness and mutual good correspondence, that at least timely application
should be made, either to Governor Folch or myself whereby Such Satisfaction would have been undoubtedly afforded as to avoid the noisy Conflict
that took place;— the implicit obedience prescribed by our Military regulations, and required from Subaltern Officers towards their Superiors was the
cause of the conduct of Captain Don Manuel Garcia, who hesitating the resolution he was to take declined giving Security and Submitting to any authority whatever, until he could consult his chief officer, and know what
determination your Excellency would adopt in Consequence of the Letter
he had directed to you. There was as I am informed no other resistance offered by the officers, than by standing ~~on Axxx Side~~[3] with their Swords or
Sabres in their Hands, without unsheathing, notwithstanding all contrary as-
sertions, and I Sincerely rejoice with your Excellency, that the intention was
not carried into effect.

The different Cases alluded to in my Letter of the 16th are indeed as your
Excellency observes a proof of my moderation, whilst I cannot help complaining of the infringement, not of the imaginary as your Excellency is
pleased to call them,, [sic] but of the real priviliges, which in my opinion
belong to my character of Commissary for His Catholic Majesty, for the regulating the limits and other affairs relative to, or connected with the delivery
of Louisiana[.] That is to Say. [sic] In the case of Villamil I did not complain
of the conciliatory Steps taken, but I do and will complain So far as to observe, that when Hulins declaration was proved to be a falsehood, the laws
of the United States did not cause him to be punished, and to give Satisfaction for the injury made to Villamil contrary to that impartial Justice which
I observed in the Same affair when I was exercising a Superior Jurisdiction.

But I do and will complain of not yet having obtained the Satisfaction, I think due to me for the violation of the immunities of my House by Thomas Randall notwithstanding my having represented the Same as it was expedient to do it. I do and will complain of the manner how my Coachman was punished whom I had on your first demand put in prison entirely at the disposal of your Excellency, without the Said Servant being to this day acquainted with the cause of his punishment, and I do not See with less concern the little Success that attended my endeavours for the recovery of the Kings Revenue and for enforcing the Judgments rendered during the Spanish administration, and in cases which originated in the Said Government.

With respect to what your Excellency mentions about the expressions and Style made use of in the Verbal message which I sent Your Excellency, I must beg reference to the very expressions which the Secretary Don Andre Lopez de Armesto, in compliance with his Sound judgment and prudence Shall have used in delivering to your Excellency, my letter of the 16th Instant which took place in the House of His Honour the Judge of the Superior Court of this Province, as he informs me, with an assurance that none of his words deserved the answer Your Excellency returned immediately, and contained no further meaning than the purport of my orders to him, that is to Say "that I could not help Such consequence as would happen in the present State of things, if I was obliged to leave the Territory in order to avoid displeasure and in order to avoid being ill-treated and undervalued" the expressions of the Under Lieutenant Don Estevan Folch were perhaps the effect of natural warmth ~~of temper~~ and Sensibility, but their meaning was the Same with those of the Secretary. Altho I was present myself to the message of the Attorney General, I took no part therein, and what Governor Folch Said there, could not be construed So as to convey any other idea, but that he conceived the Spanish Government was injured, and that it was giving room on his Side to a conduct towards the United States, that would be Similar to the treatment he experienced from them—

I am in hopes that Your Excellency upon examing [*sic*] with your usual attention, the plain account of our conduct, will know the reason and Justice with which I was Seeking for a reciprocity of good Offices between Allies and contiguous powers, whose aim is always to preserve their authority and prerogatives from encroachments, acknowledging on my part the kind expressions of Your Excellency and the very great trouble which you have taken, to avoid every disagreeable consequence, by means of your authority, and also by the Interest of the Attorney General—

May Your Excellency enjoy many years

(Signed) *The Marquis of Casa Calvo*

His Excellency
Gov. Claiborne

I do Certify the above translation
(Signed)
Moreau Lisly
Interpreter to the
Government

1. Derived from the medieval Latin, the word "commissary" was used here by Casa Calvo, or the translator in Claiborne's office, to convey one of the word's less frequent meanings. In this application the noun identifies a person to whom some duty is given by a superior authority. Twentieth-century use of the word commissary generally has meant a store where food and supplies may be obtained, usually on a military reservation.

2. After this word the handwriting in the manuscript changes. This is about the time that Thomas Seilles Kennedy became Claiborne's private secretary.

3. Words here crossed through and undecipherable in the manuscript.

{59}
To Casa Calvo
New Orleans November 20th 1804

Sir,
I have the pleasure to inform your Excellency that on last evening I received
Letters from the officer Commanding at Natchitoches which announced
the return of the Negroes who had escaped to Nacogdoches. It Seems that the
Spanish Commandant directed the arrest of the Negroes and caused them
to be delivered to the Citizens of Natchitoches who went in pursuit of them—
The issue of this affair is Such as I could wish, and is attributed by me to
the timely and proper interference of your Excellency[.]

Accept assurances of my
Respectful consideration
(Signed) *William C. C. Claiborne*

His Excellency
The Marquis of
Casa Calvo

{60}

TO CASA CALVO
New Orleans November 22nd 1804[1]

Sir,

I have the honour to acknowledge the receipt of your Excellencys Letter
of the 19th Instant and I learn with pleasure that you are at length convinced that the affair of Captain Garcia is placed on the only footing which
the existing Laws of this Country can admit of.

How far my permission for Governor Folch and Suite to pass by this route
to Pensacola entitles Captain Garcia to exemption from arrest, is matter
for the consideration of the Court, and on this question there is no doubt but
the decision will be a proper one. The Sentiments contained in my last Letter to your Excellency, concerning your claims to certain priviliges as the
Agent for a foreign power, were well considered before they were transmitted to you, and have not been Shaken by any of the arguments contained in
your Excellency's last Letter. The American Commissioners received this
Country from Mr. Laussat; with your Excellency they neither had nor could
have had ~~any thing to do~~ with propriety any official intercourse on the Subject. The transfer of the Country being completed, any difficulty in ascertaining the limits of the Ceded Territory which may arise must be the object of a
Separate mission or agency, if you are Commissioned in that behalf by your
Government, your powers must be accredited at least by the nomination
of an ~~new~~ American Commissioner to meet you on the Subject, before your
appointment can have any operation, or entitle you to any of the privileges
which may be attached to *it*. For these and other reasons that I have already
communicated, I Still feel myself compelled by duty to refuse any recognition of your Excellency as a privileged Character in this Territory; permit me
however to add that this refusal is not dictated by any kind of uneasiness at
your Excellencys Stay in this Country, or the most distant wish of rendering
your Situation among us as irksome to you. On the contrary during your
Excellencys Stay in this ~~Country~~ Territory I will reciprocate with great pleasure friendly offices, and I shall esteem it a duty to give you all the protection which the national amity of our respective Countries entitle you to and
our Laws admit of.

I observe in your Excellencys last letter but one Subject not before touched
upon during the present correspondence, namely your complaint of your unsuccessful endeavours to collect the arrears of the Kings Revenue;— I can recollect no interruption which your Excellency met with in this particular,

except a refusal on my part to carry into effect certain Judgments which your Excellency was pleased to say had been rendered against certain Individuals by the Spanish authorities.

An acquaintance with the Laws of the United States Sir, would be Sufficient to inform you that they will Suffer no Judgment to be executed but those rendered in their own Courts; that in those Courts foreign Judgments however respectable the Tribunals which rendered them are, only evidence, and require the confirmation of an American Judgment before any execution can flow therefrom; I have only therefore to add, that in all cases of this nature, as well as that of Mr. Randall, the Courts of this Territory are open to you, and are vested with the power (no longer in my hands) of redressing any grievances which you may have occasion to complain of—

> I pray your Excellency to accept assurances
> of my most respectful consideration
> (Signed) *William C. C. Claiborne*

His Excellency
The Marquis of
Casa Calvo

1. Also published as To Casa Calvo, November 22, 1804, CLB, 3: 20-2, with variations in the text and punctuation.

{61}
To James Madison
New Orleans November 23rd 1804[1]

Sir,

Within a few days events have occurred here which I conceive it my duty particularly to represent to you.— I have heretofore informed you of the arrival in this City of Governor Folch and Several other Spanish Officers on their return from Baton Rouge to Pensacola, and that their passage by this route was with my consent. Governor Folch and Suite have now departed, but during their Stay a fleet of Small Vessels with near two Hundred Troops on Board lay in the Lake about Six miles from the Bayou St. John;— a Supply of Provisions for the Troops was purchased in this Territory with my approbation, nor did I oppose a wish which was expressed by the Spanish officers generally to visit New Orleans— In this State of things every thing remained quiet for Several days, and frequent acts of Civility were exchanged between the officers of the United States and those of Spain.—²

On the 13th Instant an American of the name of Morgan who had been taken a prisoner by Governor Folch in West Florida (but with what offence charged I know not) made his escape from the Fleet; he was pursued and overtaken near Fort St. John. But upon declaring himself to be a Citizen of the United States, and claiming protection, a non-Commissioned officer commanding the Fort, would not permit his pursuers to take him, and he Morgan made his escape to this City.— This event did not Seem to excite the displeasure of Governor Folch, and not a word was Said upon the Subject.

Between the 12th and 14th Instants Several Frenchmen who had made their escape from the Barque Hero, whose care I have made you acquainted with reached this City, and it was soon reported that they had been enlisted in the Army of Spain by Governor Folch. Being in the vicinity of the Lodgings of the Marquis of Casa Calvo, when this information was received by me, I immediately determined to pay him a visit, and to mention the Subject Verbally. The object of my visit was promptly communicated, and I expressed my regret, that So direct an insult to the Sovereignty of my Country Should have been offered. The Marquis assured me that the report was not correct, he observed "that four or five individuals had offered their Services to Governor Folch, but were told that they were now on American ground, and he (the Governor) could not recruit them, if however they thought proper to visit Pensacola, and would there tender their Services, it was probable they might be enlisted." The Marquis added that the Subject would be mentioned particularly by him to Governor Folch, and assured me that no indignity or disrespect Should be offered to this Government.—

On the afternoon of the 16th Instant Mr. Morgan the person mentioned as effecting his escape near Fort St. John, Sued out a writ from the officer of the Supreme Court, and the particulars attending its execution you will find fully detailed in a Letter to me from the Alguazil Mayor herewith enclosed marked No. 1. I was early advised by a message from Governor Folch of the arrest of Captain Garcia and his release was required in terms not very delicate. The impropriety nay impossibility of an official interference on my part, was communicated in terms the most conciliatory to Governor Folch, but he was irritated and indulged himself in language intemperate and highly indelicate:— Shortly afterwards I received from the Marquis a *Letter* the original of which *no.* 2 is enclosed, and I returned an answer of which the enclosure no[.] 3 is a copy. When the Marquis's Letter was handed me I was informed of by the Bearer of it "that the Marquis requested an immediate

answer, and the release of Captain Garcia, or he would immediately leave
the Territory, and would not be answerable for the consequences and revolution that might Ensue."[3] The Gentleman delivering this message expressed
himself in English, and I desired him to inform the Marquis "that the Letter
would be answered when convenient, and if he wished to withdraw from
the Territory the customary passports should on application be furnished
him." In the course of the evening I was informed that ~~near~~ a mob of near
three Hundred men had assembled in front of the Marquis's House, and
evinced a disposition for mischief. I immediately requested Colonel Butler
to Strengthen the guards, and directed the Alguazil Mayor, to proceed to the
place of this assemblage and to Solicit (in my name) the people to repair
to their respective Homes. But previous to the arrival of the Alguazil Mayor,
many had retired, and the few which were then remaining immediately Separated at his request. Several Letters have Since passed between the Marquis
and myself upon this Subject copies of which are enclosed Nos. 4.5.6&7[.]

I was on a visit to Judge Pre[v]ost when I heard the particulars of the Spanish Officers arrest, and there continued until the verbal message between
the Marquis, Governor Folch and myself had passed. On my return to the
Government House, I found that many Americans had repaired there,
under an impression that a Serious riot would ensue. But throughout the
night the most perfect tranquility reigned, and I take pleasure in adding
that on this occasion, the great body of the Citizens manifested no disposition
unfriendly to good order or to the existing Government.

I am Sir with great respect and
Esteem
Your faithful friend
(Signed) *William C. C. Claiborne*

James Madison Esqr
Secy of State.
~~Thos Jefferson~~
~~President of the~~
~~United States~~

---

1. Also published as To James Madison, November 23, 1804, CLB, 3: 13–6, with variations in the text and punctuation.

2. According to returns prepared late in October 1804, there were 375 U.S. Army regulars
and 75 U.S. Marines stationed in New Orleans at this time, or almost double the number of
Spanish troops passing through the city. In addition, there were 67 U.S. Army regulars at Fort
Plaquemine, 19 at Ouachita, 14 at Attakapas, 47 at Opelousas, and 75 at Natchitoches. The

travel time between these outlying posts and New Orleans varied from twenty-four hours to three weeks. The number of U.S. Army regulars at Fort Adams, Mississippi Territory, the place from which troops and supplies could most quickly be dispatched in case of need, had dropped in November 1804 to 14. *American State Papers: Military Affairs,* vol. 1 (Washington, D.C.: Gales & Seaton, 1832), 177.

    3. The messenger was Estéban, one of the sons of Governor Folch.

{62}
To Casa Calvo
New Orleans Nov. 24th 1804

Sir,

Messrs Foni[1] and Watkins members of the Municipality are authorized to receive the Records and Papers belonging to the office of Mr. Ximines,[2] late Notary Public, and Such Documents appertaining to other offices as may be in a State of for delivery.

> I pray your Excellency to accept
> assurances of my respect and Esteem
> (Signed) *William C. C. Claiborne*

The Marquis
of Casa Calvo

    1. Probably Joseph Faurie, a prominent young commission merchant in New Orleans.

    2. Carlos Ximines, notary to the Spanish government in New Orleans, had been custodian of Spanish land records prior to his death. The odyssey of these valuable records may be traced in Claiborne to Richard Relf and [Blank], March 12, 1805; James Brown to the Secretary of the Treasury, December 11, 1805; The Secretary of State to Governor Claiborne, February 6, 1806; and James Brown to Governor Claiborne, March 19, 1806; all in TP, 9: 416, 546, 580, and 614, respectively. See also To James Brown, March 18, 1806, and Message to the Legislature, May 26, 1806, CLB, 3: 272 and 311–3, respectively.

{63}
To James Madison
New Orleans November 24th 1804

Sir,

    A Letter I have just received from Captain Turner the Commandant at Natchitoches informs of the return to that Post of certain Negroes that had escaped to Nacogdoches: The recent conduct of the Spanish Authorities on this occasion is Such as I could wish, and may in Some measure be attributed to the prompt interference of the Marquis of Casa Calvo.[1]

The News from Point Coupeé [*sic*] is also of a pleasant nature, the alarm has Subsided, and no Spirit of insubordination is now manifested. In relation to Slaves the Louisianians are a very timid people, and yet many of them are very Solicitous to add to their present numbers. The importation of Jamaica negroes is an object of uneasiness to Some Planters, and yet by these Same men the prohibition of the African trade is esteemed a great grievance. I am also advised by Captain Turner of the present favorable disposition of the Caddo Indians to the United States. He represents the contemplated meeting on the Sabine River as being likely to fall through; and that the Several small Tribes near our Frontiers are not enclined to listen to the War Talks of the Spaniards. I think it would be good policy to cultivate with care the friendship of these Indians. It may Serve to guard our frontier Settlements against the more warlike and numerous Tribes in the Interior of Louisiana. Perhaps a conference in the Spring with the Caddoes, and the Chiefs of Such other nations as would attend at Natchitoches might produce good effects.[2] It need not be made an expensive business. one [*sic*] thousand Dollars cost of goods might be sufficient to distribute among them.

Accept assurances of my great respect and Esteem!
(Signed) *William C. C. Claiborne*

The Honble
James Madison
Secretary of State

1. Claiborne was only partly correct on Casa Calvo's assistance. The Spanish officials in Texas went as far as they dared in thwarting Casa Calvo's interference in their jurisdiction. See Isaac J. Cox, "The Louisiana-Texas Frontier, II," *Southwestern Historical Quarterly* 17, no. 1 (July 1913), 40–2.

2. Contrary to standard practice, Congress made no provision for the administration of Indian affairs by the governor of the Orleans Territory in the 1804 act creating the territory. Relations with the Indian tribes in all of the Louisiana Purchase territory were brought under the March 30, 1802, law titled An Act to Regulate Trade and Intercourse with the Indian Tribes, and to Preserve Peace on the Frontiers. See also An Act for the Organization of Orleans Territory and the Louisiana District, March 26, 1804, Section 15, TP, 9: 213. Ultimately, the administration of Indian affairs was brought under the factory system. See Marietta Marie LeBreton, "A History of the Factory System Serving the Louisiana Indians, 1805–1825" (master's thesis, Louisiana State University, 1961). Claiborne's earlier interest in the Indian trade is delineated in Jared W. Bradley, "William C. C. Claiborne, the Old Southwest and the Development of American Indian Policy," *Tennessee Historical Quarterly* 33, no. 3 (fall 1974), 265–78.

The small Caddo tribe apparently had some influence over other tribes nearby in Orleans Territory, Upper Louisiana, and Texas. During the Spanish incursion near Natchitoches in August 1806, Claiborne sought to continue the friendly attitude of the Caddoes through personal contact and distribution of gifts. See Claiborne's address to the Grand Chief of the Caddo Nation, September 5, 1806, CLB, 4: 2–5; and The Secretary of War to John Sibley, December 13, 1804, TP, 9: 352–3 (provision for funds to buy gifts and their distribution by Dr. John Sibley, the Indian agent to the Caddoes). See also The Secretary of War to John Sibley, May 25, 1805, and October 17, 1805, ibid., 449–50 and 514–5.

{64}

To Thomas Jefferson

New Orleans November 25th 1804[1]

DSir, [*sic*]

My administration here from the time of my arrival in Louisiana to the ~~time~~ close of the late Provisional Government has already become an object of Some discussion. To this I can have no objection. I would rather Court it were I assured that the enquiry would be conducted with candor, but Some publications have appeared here upon the Subject, in which I do not think Justice has been rendered me. I am well assured that those publications will make their way to the Northward, and may perhaps make Some unfavorable impressions;— with a view therefore to my Justification and for your Satisfaction, I will take the liberty to animadvert in a few words ~~to~~ on the principle points to which objections have been raised. Many of the embarrassments I have experienced, may be attributed to the disorganized and Revolutionary State in which we received Louisiana from Laussat. That Minister demanded and possessed himself of the Province nearly a month before the arrival of the American Commissioners. I candidly confess Sir, that my early impressions were that Mr. Laussat had done Some good in the course of his Short career, and for the destruction of the Cabildo I had Supposed myself indebted to him. But I Soon found that the changes made were too radical and immediate, not to Subject both the American Government and the Citizens to inconvenience;— nearly all the ancient establishments of the Country were overthrown— The Cabildo dissolved, the Judiciary abolished, and nothing erected in their places but a municipality, or City Council, whose powers were undefined, and Seemed to be limited only by the will of their creator.[2] Instead of finding a regular Government to which the people were accustomed, and the general principles and forms of which, I could for awhile have adopted, I beheld a new order of things which no one perfectly understood. In this State ~~of things~~ I had to provide Some means for preserving

the peace of the Country, and protecting Individuals in their rights. A revival
of the Spanish Tribunals was thought of, but powerful objections presented. There were then two Strong parties in the Country, one Spanish and
the other French; the latter the most numerous and influential. To undo therefore all that Laussat had done, would not only have given offence to him, and
thereby embarrassed the unfinished negotiations then pending between us,
but would also have afforded matter of triumph to the Spanish Interest, and
probably kindled a flame among the French partizans that could not easily
be extinguished. I had also particular objections to the Spanish Tribunals;
they Seemed to me illy calculated for the Security of personal liberty, and
therefore altho ~~if I~~ had I found those Tribunals in existence, they would have
been recognized, Yet I was not Solicitous to revive them.

Under existing circumstances therefore and after mature deliberation, I determined to Steer as near as possible a middle course, I revived Some of the
Spanish offices and appointed Magistrates with powers resembling those of
the United States; I introduced Some new members into the Municipality,
~~and~~ defined its powers; &[3] vested the Judicial authority in a Court, which I
created for the purpose with a Jurisdiction extending to all Suits under
3000$ [*sic*]— Higher causes I took cognizance of myself. All those regulations
were not prescribed in a day. As occasion required, my plan was pursued,
and the Interest of the people kept Constantly in view; nor was I inattentive
to their wishes and opinions, as far as they could be collected from those
persons who I supposed would answer my enquiries with most candour. The
general clamor of the Citizens for a Court of Justice necessarily placed that
measure foremost on the List. The others followed gradually in Succession.
The proceedings of the Court which I erected have been the Subject of Some
animadvertion. To this I can only answer, that it was composed exclusively
of Citizens of the Territory a majority of whom were French, and I took
pains after consulting the Municipality, to Select the most respectable characters in the City and its vicinity— Ignorant of Law and unaccustomed to its
powers, these Gentlemen may have been *betrayed into* little irregularities, and
Sometimes perplexed by jarring Sentiments of right[4] or by indecision;— but
this I am assured of, that they were honest and upright in their intentions,
and rendered much service to the Country.

I have been accused of ~~betraying~~ bestowing the lucrative Offices of Government to Americans exclusively. This is not true. Few offices were given
to Americans, which could in my opinion, have been filled with propriety by
Frenchmen or ancient Louisianians. It would have been rank indeed for me
to have entrusted important duties and high trusts to men I knew not. Hence

let it not be a matter of Surprize that Some of my Countrymen, of whom my own knowledge, or whose established characters entitled them to confidence Should have experienced my patronage. Of those offices which I could Safely confide to Citizens indiscriminately, much the greater portion has been conferred on Frenchmen or native Louisianians.

The late admission of foreign negroes has also been a Subject of complaint against me. The Searcher of all hearts knows how little I desire to see another of that wretched race set his foot on the Shores of America, & how from my Heart I detest the rapacity that would transport them to us. But on this Point the People here were united as one man; there Seemed to me to be but one Sentiment throughout the Province, they must import more Slaves or the Country was ruined forever. The most respectable characters could not even in my presence, Suppress the agitation of their tempers, when a check to that trade was suggested;— under Such circumstances it was not for me without the authority of previous Law, or the instructions of my Government to prohibit the importation of Slaves;— to give Security to the Province and quietude to the Citizens, I gave *orders* for the exclusion of St. Domingo negroes, and took every precautionary measure to enforce *them.*— But I entertained little hopes of Success— nothing but a general exclusion could have counteracted the evasions and frauds that were Sometimes practiced by West India Slave traders. The organization of the Volunteer Corps and Some other of my official acts have been objected to. But my explanations on almost every measure of my late administration have been So general and particular in my official Letters to the Secretary of State that I deem it unnecessary to dilate further upon the Subject. In a Country like Louisiana where intrigue has, So long Sported, where interests exist, where the Citizens lately released from Despotic Sway, are not fully apprized of the nature nor do they Sufficiently estimate the value of a pure and free Government, I do really conceive myself peculiarly fortunate, in having drawn my late administration to So peaceful a close.—

> I have the Honor to be Sir
> with Sentiments of the
> Highest respect and Esteem
> (Signed) *William C. C. Claiborne*

Thomas Jefferson
President of the
U. States

~~The Honble~~
~~James Madison~~
~~Secty of State~~

1. Also published as Governor Claiborne to the President, November 25, 1804, TP, 9: 338–41, with variations in the text and punctuation; different emphasis marks; and a postscript not found here. After drafting this letter, Claiborne apparently debated whether to send it to Madison or Jefferson, but ultimately sent it to Jefferson. This letter, along with Letter No. 58, From Casa Calvo, November 19, 1804, provides genuine insight into the problems Claiborne faced in New Orleans.

2. Laussat expected to be the chief government official in Louisiana for six to eight years, but his appointment was cut short by the sale of Louisiana to the United States. He regarded the Municipality as his personal creation that would continue in existence after the Americans assumed control of Louisiana. Laussat's chauvinism was so great that it may have cost him appointment as ambassador to the United States. Pierre Clément de Laussat, *Memoirs of My Life to My Son During the Years 1803 and After . . .*, trans. Sister Agnes-Josephine Pastwa, ed. Robert D. Bush (Baton Rouge: Louisiana State University Press, 1978), 56–7, 75, 129 n. 32.

3. Here, the ampersand and the word "vested" are written above the line. The ampersand also appears to have been imposed over the personal pronoun "I," so that in the manuscript, the original wording appears to have read: "I touted" rather than "& vested" as it reads.

4. In the original manuscript a comma placed after the word "right" was lined out.

{65}
To James Madison
New Orleans November 26th 1804

Sir,

Your Letter of the 23rd of October with its several enclosures I have had the Honor to receive. The Captors of the Prize are Still in this City and Messrs. Amory & Callender Merchants are appointed Agents for the British Claimants. But in the absence of the District Judge no measure can be taken to hasten a Judicial decision. The Cargo of the Prize has been Stored, and it (together with the Vessel [*sic*] has been considered in the care of Mr. Kerr, who acted as Marshall during the temporary Government. To avoid an accumulation of expense on the Vessel and Cargo by continuing them in the care of Mr. Kerr, the Captors and *British agents* (I understand) will unite in petitioning me to place both Cargo and Vessel in possession of the latter upon their giving ample Security that the same shall be held Subject to a Judicial decision. The Cargo is said to be wasteing [*sic*], and the expense of storage &c daily encreasing. This Vessel and Cargo have really been Sources of great trouble to me. But I persuade myself that the arrival of the District Judge will Soon relieve me from further responsibility in this case.

Colonel Kirby[1] died at Fort Stoddart on the 20th Ultimo. The Death of a man So Honest, firm and enlightened, would at any time be a Public Loss, but at this particular period, it is to this Territory a Serious misfortune. Mr. James Brown is expected in this City in the course of the day; I consider this gentleman as a great acquisition to the local Government, and I hope to receive from him great aid in the discharge of my Executive duties.

I am this moment informed, that a Vessel with Military Stores for the Garrison at Fort Stoddart, had been stop't at the Town of Mobile and duties on the Cargo exacted;— The person having Charge of the Vessel not being furnished with money to pay the duties, the Stores are Still detained to the great inconvenience of our Garrison. Every thing is quiet in this City; and I believe throughout the Territory.

> I am Sir very Respectfully Your
> Most obdt Hble Sevt
> (Signed) *William C. C. Claiborne*

The Honble
James Madison
Secty of State

1. Ephraim Kirby (February 23, 1757–October 20, 1804) is usually referred to as being from Litchfield, Connecticut, but was born in Woodbury, Connecticut. His name became associated with Litchfield because he studied law there in the office of Reynold Marvin, former king's attorney; began to practice law there; and married Marvin's daughter. Although Kirby was a genuine hero of the Revolutionary War, having been wounded thirteen times and left for dead on the battlefield in Maryland, he is best remembered in American history as a lawyer and law reporter. He earned this niche with the publication of the first volume of what became the Massachusetts reports of the state supreme court in 1789. The work became a model for later such reports in the United States. Dunbar Rowland, *Courts, Judges and Lawyers of Mississippi, 1798–1935* (Jackson, Miss.: Hederman Brothers, 1935), 20. He was several times a candidate for governor of Massachusetts; had studied law at Yale; received an M.A. degree from Yale; and was appointed one of the land title commissioners for the district east of the Pearl River on July 12, 1803. Kirby was appointed territorial judge in Mississippi on April 6, 1804, but told Claiborne he would accept appointment as territorial judge in the Orleans Territory. To James Madison, January 10, 1804, CLB, 1: 332; and November 18, 1804, ibid., 2: 393. Like Claiborne, Kirby was a republican before he became a Jeffersonian Republican. He arrived in New Orleans on the evening of January 8, 1804, with William Nicholas. Both men were on their way to the Tombigbee District to fulfill their duties as U.S. commissioners to determine the boundaries of Louisiana. Notice of Kirby's death appeared in the *Union*, November 24, 1804, p. 1, c. 1.

There is no biography of Kirby. In addition to the sources cited above, see *Dictionary of American Biography*, s.v. "Kirby, Ephraim"; Ella Kent Barnard, "Isaac Briggs, 1763–1825," *Maryland Historical Magazine* 7, no. 4 (December 1912), 409–19; and Noble Cunningham, Jr., *The Jeffersonian Republicans in Power: Party Operations, 1801–1809* (Chapel Hill: University of North Carolina Press, 1963), 63, 125–6, 131, 245.

{66}

To Casa Calvo
New Orleans November 28th 1804

Sir,

The Letters of your Excellency relative to the claim of Don Joseph De Orne, against Madam Castillon together with the accompanying Documents, I have had the pleasure to receive.

All my Judicial powers having now ceased, it is indispensible that Don Joseph De Orne Should bring his Suit in the Supreme Court of this Territory, and on the Trial, he may give the Judgment of the Spanish Tribunal in evidence.[1]

The usual way of approaching the Court in Cases of this kind is by Petition, and to Save your Excellency any further trouble in this business, I shall Suggest the propriety of committing it to the care of an Advocate or Attorney at Law. I have returned to your Excellency the Documents which were transmitted to me.

> Accept assurances of my great
> Respect.
> ~~and Sincere Esteem~~
> (Signed) ~~Willliam~~ *William C. C.*
> *Claiborne*

His Excellency
The Marquis of
Casa Calvo

1. See To the Marquis of Casa Calvo, June 5, and September 10, 1804, CLB, 2: 193, and 328–9, respectively, for related letters. Casa Calvo attempted to use this dispute to get Claiborne to admit that Spanish law was still effective in Louisiana and thus to concede a point to the validity of Spain's continued claims to Louisiana. Claiborne's reply on how the common law–based legal system of the United States worked left Casa Calvo thoroughly vexed and confused. Biographical Sketches, "Casa Calvo," 484–94.

{67}

To James Pitot
New Orleans November 29th 1804
To the Mayor of The City of New
Orleans

Sir,

I have received your Letter of yesterday and with respectful attention noticed its contents. that [*sic*] any event Should tend to create disssention or excite Jealousy between the City Militia and regular troops is to me a Subject of regret. A good understanding has hitherto existed between them, and I hope it will not be Seriously disturbed by the late affair at the Principal.[1] The officer of the Main Guard to whose conduct exceptions have been taken has Solicited a Court of enquiry, and it will certainly be directed, provided the Municipality wish it, in the mean time measures have been taken to prevent an occurrence, Similar to the one which has given rise to the present correspondence.

With respect to the occupation of a Room in the Principal by the Supreme Court, I have to inform the Municipality, that it was done by my permission— The Key of the Room thus occupied, was delivered to me many weeks ago by the Marquis of Casa Calvo, and my impression was that, that apartment (as well as the lower Story of the Building) was national property, and more immediately under my controul. If however this impression was erroneous, the mistake can easily be remedied. I have no disposition to Trespass upon the rights of the Municipality or to appropriate (against the Will of that Body) City Property for public uses;— I trust however there will be no objections to the Sessions of the Supreme Court being Holden in the Room to which its furniture has been removed, or to the legislative Council occupying temporarily the apartment which was formerly appropriated for the use of the City Court; As the Council will probably meet in a day or two, you will oblige me if you will call a meeting of the Municipality, and communicate to me, how far it may meet their convenience to accommodate the Legislature in the way I have suggested.

> I have the Honor to be Sir
> very Respectfully your most
> obdt Hble St
> (Signed) *William C. C. Claiborne*

The Mayor
of
The City

1. The "Principal" was the City Hall. The cost of its construction had been borne by both the government of Spain and the City of New Orleans. The government of Spain claimed the first floor and used it for storage of weapons. The remainder of the building belonged to the city. See Letter No. 77, To James Madison, December 9, 1804.

{68}
TO JAMES PITOT
New Orleans November 30th 1804

Sir,

The regulations you have drawn up for the Theatre[1] meet my entire approbation, and I should be happy to see them published in your name as Mayor of the City. The care of the property of the City is by my ordinance committed to the Municipality, and I certainly feel no disposition to trespass upon that, or any other prerogative of the Municipality.

The apartment in the Principal to which (with my permission) the furniture of the Supreme Court has been removed, was formally appropriated by the Spanish Government as I have understood, as an arsenal.— The Key was delivered to me Some time Since by the Marquis of Casa Calvo, and I certainly considered that apartment as more immediately under my controul— But the enclosed Letter to you upon the Subject will explain my Sentiments more particularly, and to which I refer you. Having had cause to approve highly of your conduct as Mayor of New Orleans, and believing that your retiring from that office at the present period, would prove a public inconvenience, I must again express my unwillingness to receive your resignation.[2]

> I have the Honor to be
> Sir with Sentiments of Respect and
> Esteem
> Your most obdt St
> (Signed) *William C. C. Claiborne*

Jas. Pitot Esqr
Mayor of New
Orleans

1. Information on the Théâtre St. Pierre, or St. Peter Theatre, located at 716 St. Peter Street may be found in René J. LeGardeur, Jr., *The First New Orleans Theatre, 1792–1803* (New Orleans: Leeward Books, 1963), 38–42, 45, 49. John S. Kendall, *The Golden Age of New Orleans Theater* (Baton Rouge: Louisiana State University Press, 1952), is useful, but has very little information on this or any of the other theaters because so little has survived. Robert E. Bittner, "The Concert Life and the Musical Stage in New Orleans up to the Construction of the French Opera House" (master's thesis, Louisiana State University, 1953), 20–1, also is helpful.

2. The earliest indication that Pitot wished to give up his duties as mayor are in To James Pitot, September 1, 1804, CLB, 2: 316. Claiborne ultimately accepted Pitot's resignation in July 1805. See To James Pitot, July 24, 1805, ibid., 3: 136. See also the biographical sketches of James Pitot and John Watkins, pp. 255–7 and 299–371 herein.

{69}
From Robert [Abraham] R. Ellery
New Orleans December 4th 1804[1]

Sir,

Lieutenant William Wilson of the Regiment of Artillerists having called a Court of enquiry for the purpose of investigating his conduct, as the Officer Commanding the Main Guard, on the night of the 27th Ultimo. On this Morning the Court was regularly formed; and beg that Your Excellency will have the goodness to furnish them with a copy of the complaint presented to your Excellency against Lieutenant Wilson, with all the Papers connected with it, or that have any relation to his conduct on the Said night, in order that a full and complete investigation may be had[.]

We have the Honor to be Sir
With Respect your Excellencys
most obdt Sevt

(Signed) *Robert R. Ellery*
Recorder &c

Govr. Claiborne–

1. Ellery filed this request in his capacity as recorder for the court. He is identified in more than one letter as Robert R. Ellery, but his correct name is Abraham Redwood Ellery. A Federalist and former employee of Alexander Hamilton, Ellery entered the law profession after settling in New Orleans. What is known about his life and contributions to early Louisiana are set forth in pp. 539–45.

{70}
To Robert [Abraham] R. Ellery
New Orleans December 5th 1804

Sir,

I have the Honor to acknowledge the receipt of your Letter of yesterday, and to transmit you for the information of the Court, an Extract from the proceedings of the Municipality, as the only document in my possession that relates to the conduct of Lieutenant Wilson on the night of the 27th Ultimo.—

I am Sir with Sentiments of great
Respect your most obdt Hble St

(Signed) *William C. C. Claiborne*

Robert
~~Abraham~~ [*sic*] R[.] Ellery
Esquire

{71}
To Abimael Youngs Nicoll
New Orleans December 7th 1804

Sir,

Your Letter of the 4th Inst With its enclosures I have received. Captain John Callender[1] of the Hero has always been at liberty to procure provisions in this Territory for his Voyage, and for that purpose he may now be permitted (if he wishes it) to come up to this City with his Vessel. To the Sick and wounded both French and English, while the Vessel Should be detained at Plaquemine, I esteemed it an act of benevolence to furnish ~~with~~ fresh Provisions and Medical attendance— But the general Supplies required for a European Voyage I conceived myself under no obligations to procure. You will be pleased to take Duplicate receipts for the Supplies furnished the Sick and wounded.

I am Sir with Esteem
your Hbe St
(Signed) *William C. C. Claiborne*

Captain Nicolls [*sic*]
Commanding at
Plaquemine

1. The captain's name earlier was given as John Calver. See Letter No. 34, To Constant Freeman, November 2, 1804, n. 3, and the references cited therein.

{72}
To James Madison
New Orleans December 8th 1804[1]

Sir,

On the 4th Instant the Legislative Council formed a quorum, and on the following day I delivered to them an address of which the enclosure marked 1 is a copy.[2]

The Meeting of the Council has had a happy effect. It has checked a Spirit of anarchy that had made its appearance, and given to the good Citizens a Confidence in the Government. The answer of the Council to my address, you will find in the news-paper enclosed.[3]

> I am Sir very Respectfully
> Your Hbe St
> (Signed) *William C. C. Claiborne*

The Secty of State

    1. Also published as Governor Claiborne to the President, December 8, 1804, TP, 9: 348, with variations in punctuation and text, but without Claiborne's address and the legislative council's response by Julien Poydras.

    2. The governor's address, Letter No. 73, to the First Legislative Council of the Territory of Orleans [December 5, 1804], immediately follows.

    3. The newspaper clipping referred to was not found in the original manuscript, but there is a handwritten transcription of Julien Poydras's December 7, 1804, response for the council. Letter No. 74, From Julien Poydras, December 7, 1804, immediately follows Claiborne's address to the legislature.

{73}
Governor Claiborne[']s Speech to the First Legislative Council of the Territory of Orleans—[1]

Fellow Citizens of the Legislative Council!

Receive my Sincere congratulations on your present assemblage, and permit me to accompany an acknowledgment of the pleasure I feel on the occasion with an expression of my anxious Solicitude for the Honor and usefulness of your labors. When I revert to the important events which produced our present Political connexion, and look forward to the pleasing prospects of permanent aggrandizement: when I reflect upon our Union with the freest people upon Earth, and our dependence upon that just Government under whose auspices a young nation has So Soon become powerful, and amidst an unexampled advancement of Agriculture and extension of Commerce, enjoyed Liberty, Laws and uninterrupted peace, the Satisfaction with which I contemplate the future destinies of this Territory is equalled only by my admiration of the wisdom and virtue which have diffused Such political blessings and promise (under the favor of Heaven) their perpetuity. To you Gentlemen is first committed the important trust of giving Such Laws to this flourishing District, as local wants Shall Suggest, and the Interest of the Citizens may require. I trust important and arduous, but one of which Patriotism and Talents will insure a faithful and able discharge. I confidently look to you Gentlemen for these qualifications, and I doubt not but your Labors will be brought to a fortunate close. The obstacles however we have to Surmount, ought not to be concealed. To miscalculate them in any way might prove injurious. To esteem our duties too light to require extraordinary execution, would be to err in one extreme, to be dismayed by an apprehension of their gigantic weight would be equally unfortunate on the other. To know that they are within the compass of our powers and not much below them, is the happy mean which encourages exertion and insures Success. For my part I am deeply Sensible of the delicacy and importance of the Situation in which my present office places me. I enter upon it with a degree of Diffidence produced by existing circumstances, and the expectations of the Districts— My only Sources of confidence are in your wisdom and experience, and in an honest intention on my part to assist your Councils in every measure that may tend to promote the public good.

The Territory of Orleans, in Some points may be considered as a new Territory; but for the most part as one more than matured. much [*sic*] is to be created but more regenerated. Too great care, therefore, cannot be taken to draw the line of distinctions between those parts of the System, which require only to be Strengthened, and those that demand reform. Innovation in an impetuous or careless hand, often does injury, but when evils exist, the indolence or timidity that refuses to extirpate them partakes in the criminality of the Commission. Begin then Gentlemen the work with caution; but it is your province to prepare your Country for the political rank that awaits her.

The first object of your attention, I trust will be, to provide a system of Jurisprudence suited to the Interest, and as much as possible adapted to the habits of the ~~people~~ Citizens. This Subject Should indeed, receive the earliest attention, for until Some Judicial organization is directed by the Legislature, the Territory will remain exposed to great inconvenience. When the American Commissioners first arrived here, we found most of the former Spanish authorities abolished, and no Courts of Justice in existence; daily in expectation of Some fixed Government, and unwilling to exercise my temporary powers in matters of Such permanent importance, I made no Systematic attempts to organize Tribunals of Justice. To meet however the wishes of the people, and to promote what I thought their Interest, I established an inferior Court of limited Jurisdiction for the City of New Orleans, and in all cases of more moment the best exertions were used in the Court where I had the Honour to preside, to dispense Justice with an equal and impartial hand.— These and a Small Jurisdiction given to Commandants and Justices of the peace are the only arrangements of a Judicial nature which were made during the late Provisional Government. But they were not intended or calculated for permanency, and I persuade myself, that Such Legislative Provisions will Speedily be made as will give the Judicial authority a more convenient and wise direction.

On this Subject the Act of Congress under which your powers are derived, has marked the outlines of your duty. The number of Superior Judges, the extent of their Jurisdiction, the mode of trial and number of Sessions are prescribed. To finish the detail, and give motion to the System, to determine in what manner those Sessions Should be distributed this the [sic] Territory, the Forms of Practice to be observed, and above all, the laws which are to be administered, are objects of high consideration devolving upon the Legislature— In regard to the forms of practice, permit me to hope that they may be Simple and Short, as may be consistent with equity and public convenience. The tedious and expensive Routine of forms which often embarrasses the avenues of Justice, and Sometimes render it inaccessible, I trust are forever banished from this Country[.] A System of Criminal Jurisprudence is also matter for your consideration;— I think it probable, that on examination you will find the existing Code of Criminal Law imperfect, and not adapted to the present constitution of The [sic] Territory. On this Subject I cannot forebear recommending an energetic System. But by the Term energetic, I do not mean a Sanguinary or cruel System. Laws are not the weaker by being merciful; it is not the Severity but the celerity and certainty of punishment that repress crimes. While there is a hope of impunity Sons of rapine would brave even the axe or the wheel, who would tremble at detection, when followed by a prompt and certain, tho a light Suffering.

The establishment of inferior Courts of limited Jurisdiction throughout the Territory, and the powers and duties thereof will necessarily engage your attention, and in their arrangement your own Judgment and knowledge of the Country will be your surest guides. Before I finish my observations in relation to a Judiciary, allow me to give an opinion, that the laying out the Territory into Several Judicial Districts of Superior Jurisdiction might be attended with happy effects. The presence of the Supreme Judges would attach confidence and command respect; their charges to Jurors and their legal opinions, would disseminate information as to the principles and advantages of the American Government, and above all justice would be brought to the doors of our fellow Citizens; and might be obtained freely without price, and promptly without delay. Allow me also to embrace the present occasion to congratulate you on the introduction among us of the inestimable privilige of Trial by jury, a privilige [sic] revered throughout the United

States as the Barrier against oppression, and the Bulwark of freedom. Some inconveniences I am aware will attend its first introduction, but be assured it is well worth a temporary embarrassment. This mode of Trial is invaluable; and I trust will remain the pride and boast of every American.

As another object of Legislative care, I must request your attention to the Interest, convenience and comfort of this City. Having an extensive Trade and being the residence of many Citizens of mercantile reputation and enterprize, New Orleans already claims high rank. Happily Situated on the only effective outlet that connects the Western States and Territories with the Sea, it must become the grand deposit for the Surplus productions of the extensive countries which stretch from the Allegany mountains to the distant and yet unexplored Western Frontiers of Louisiana;— Countries rich beyond calculation in natural resources, and daily increasing in popula~~lations~~tion and improving in the arts. To this City as a Center the Missouri, the Ohio, the Mississippi and all their Tributary Streams will annually convey their treasures, and will ee'r [*sic*] long be the channels of an immense reverting Commerce.

New Orleans is moreover the only City or Town in this Territory; the only general market for the consumption or commercial transfer of property, either imported or produced from the Soil. The City therefore has great claims on your most affectionate Patronage. Altho not neglected heretofore and of late greatly benefitted by the care of the Municipality, yet much remains to be done to organize a more energetic police, to improve the Streets, to enforce cleanliness, and above all to take every measure with the merciful aid of almighty god [*sic*], to preserve the Health and promote the comfort of the Inhabitants and make charitable provision for the relief of Poverty and Sickness. How far therefore it may be expedient to enlarge the powers of the present municipality, or to vest the care of this City in a corporate body differently organized, is an enquiry worthy of your Serious deliberation. Having said this much of the welfare of the Commercial ~~part~~ Centre of the Territory, my reflections are naturally turned towards the Interest of Agriculture. On Agriculture as a Basis, rests all the real prosperity of a Country. The people who draw their wealth from the Soil they Inhabit are truly Independent. Among Such a people commerce makes her most liberal returns, and enterprize finds the most agreeable field for exertion. Commerce and agriculture are as intimately connected as the mother to the offspring to which She gives Birth and nourishes. The real Interest of the Merchant and Planter is the Same, and he is no friend to either who would wish to divide them. Permit me to remind you then that the Interest of the Territory would be benefitted by an early attention to our internal intercourse, particularly to our Rivers, Creeks, roads and Levies; and that Some liberality Judiciously applied to those interesting objects might be attended with beneficial effects. In adverting to your primary duties, I have yet to Suggest one, than which none can be more important or interesting; I mean Some general provision for the education of youth. If we revere Science for her own Sake, or for the innumerable benefits She confers on Society;— if we love our children and cherish the laudable ambition of being respected by our posterity, let not this great duty be overlooked. Permit me to hope then that under your Patronage, Seminaries of Learning will prosper, and the means of acquiring information, be placed within the reach of each growing family. Under a free Government, every Citizen has a Country, because he partakes of the Sovereignty and may fill the highest offices. Free America will always present flattering prospects for talents and merit. Let exertions then be made to rear up our Children in the Paths of Science and virtue, and to impress upon their tender hearts a love of civil and religious liberty. Among the Several States of the union an ingenuous emulation happily prevails, in encouraging Literature, and literary institutions, and Some of these are making rapid Strides towards rivaling the proudest establishments of Europe. In this Sentiment So favorable to the general good, you Gentlemen, I am certain will not hesitate to Join. I deem it unnecessary to trouble you with any detail of arrangements— I am however persuaded that parsimonious plans will ~~hardly ever~~ Seldom Succeed. My advice therefore is that your System be extensive and liberally Supported.

As connected with the education of youth every Constitutional encouragement should be given to ministers of the Gospel.— "*Religion* exalts a Nation while Sin is the reproach of any people." *It* prepares for those vicissitudes which So often chequer Human life— It deprives even misfortune of her victory— It invites to harmony and good will in this world, and affords a guarantee for happiness hereafter. Before I conclude Gentlemen I should be wanting in duty did I not Solicit your attention to the Militia of the Territory— In the age in which we live, as well as in almost every one that has preceded it, we find that neither moderation nor wisdom nor Justice can protect a people against the encroachments of Tyrannical power. The abundance of agriculture, the advantages of Legislation the usefulness of the arts, in a word any thing dear to a *free people* may be considered as insecure unless they are prepared to resist aggression— Hence we find that the Congress of the United States, and the Legislatures of the Several States, are particularly Solicitous to keep the Citizens armed and disciplined, and I persuade myself that a Policy So favorable to the general Safety will be pursued by this assembly. In all your arrangements for the public convenience, let me g advice [*sic*] a prudent economy;— extravagance in a Government leads inevitably to embarrassment, liberality but not profuseness, Economy but not parsimony should be your guide. In all your deliberations Gentlemen permit me to recommend a free, candid and dispassionate discussion, as the best means of evincing an Harmonious and useful Session.—

(Signed) *William Charles Cole Claiborne*

1. This heading is from the manuscript. The complete address was published in the *Louisiana Gazette*, December 7, 1804, p. 2, cc. 1–4, two days after Claiborne delivered it before the council. Charles Gayarré, *History of Louisiana*, 5th ed., vol. 4 (1903; New Orleans: Pelican, 1965), 34–5, quotes from the address.

{74}
FROM JULIEN POYDRAS
Answer of the Council to the
above address
Council Chamber Dec 7th 1804[1]

To His Excellency
Gov. Claiborne Sir,

We beg leave respectfully to Join our congratulations with yours on the first meeting of the Legislature of this Territory, and to return our thanks for your Excellent and comprehensive Speech. Our Union with a wise and free people, and our connexion with their first Government, under whose auspices they have So Soon become powerful; ~~who~~ have made Such rapid advances in Agriculture and commerce, and who have been in the continual enjoyment of Liberty of Laws and of uninterrupted peace, make us look forward to the pleasing prospect of permanent aggrandizement. Upon us has devolved the Honorable and important trust of first giving to this flourishing District, Such Laws as the wants and Interests of its Inhabitants may Suggest; and however great may be the obstacles we have to Surmount our Patriotism forbids us to Shrink from the attempt. Whatever Talents we possess, Shall be faithfully employed to insure as far as in us lies, an able and faithful discharge of that arduous task. Our anxious Solicitude for the effect of our labors is lessened by the hope of the aids we Shall derive from wisdom and experience of your Excellency, and our confidence in your willingness to assist in all measures which may tend to promote the public good.

Your advice, and our own inclinations will make us endeavour to avoid the evils resulting from impetuous ~~and~~ or careless innovation on the one hand, or from indolence or timidity on the other. A System of Jurisprudence suited to the Interests and as much as possible to the habits of the Citizens, will occupy our first attention; persuaded that without it the Territory remains Subject to great inconvenience. And altho your Excellency from a daily expectation of Some fixed Government found yourself under the necessity of delaying the organization of regular Tribunals of Justice, yet we are fully persuaded that according to existing circumstances, you acted for the best and with the purest intentions in establishing the temporary Courts which lately existed. We cannot omit this opportunity of testifying, that an authority almost without limit, was upon all occasions exercised by you with a moderation unexampled. Indeed when we reflect that you were obliged to exercise, at the Same instant, the Several duties of Governor, Intendant, chief Justice and Commander in chief, and consider also the interruption arising from the free access which ~~ever~~ our Citizens had to your person at all times, and upon all occasions, great or trivial we are more Surprised that So much has been done than that more has not been effected. No time will be lost on our part to give the Judicial authority a fit and convenient direction, to Shorten and Simplify the forms of practice, and So far as may be to prevent the delay of Justice. We will also endeavour in forming a System of criminal Jurisprudence, to avoid a too Sanguinary or cruel Scale of punishments, by tempering Severity with mercy. The establishment of inferior Tribunals, will be early attended to, and we entirely agree with your Excellency, in the advantages that will result from the laying out the Territory into Several Judicial Districts whereby Justice will be brought to the very doors of our fellow Citizens.

The City of New Orleans has great claims on the Patronage of the Legislature; and it will be our care to vest Such powers in a municipal body, as will enable it to organize a more energetic police, to preserve with the aid of God the Health of the Inhabitants and to effect the other desirable ends designated in your address. Our best attention will be directed to the establishment of Public Seminaries for the education of youth, and the advancement of learning and Science; and every constitutional encouragement Shall be given to the ministers of our Holy religion, which blunts the edge of misfortune, invites to Harmony and mutual good will in this world, and gives us the glorious promise of Happiness in the next.

Convinced that neither moderation nor wisdom nor Justice can always Secure to people the enjoyment of peace, our attention will be necessarily directed to the organization of the Militia of the Territory, and to devise Such measures as will best tend to keep our fellow Citizens armed and disciplined for the protection of our Laws and our government, and for the preservation of the blessings we enjoy under them.

In our Several arrangements we will never loose [*sic*] Sight of a prudent economy; and we entreat that your Excellency will from time to time favor us with Such communications and Suggestions as may enable us the better to execute our high and important trust.

> Julien Poydras
> President of the Council
> By the President

James Workman
Secretary

1. Poydras's response was published one week later in the *Louisiana Gazette,* December 14, 1804, p. 3, cc. 2–3, with his signature as president of the council and that of James Workman as secretary.

{75}
FROM GEORGE THOMPSON ROSS[1]

To His Excellency Governor Claiborne

I regret Sir that in consequence of an Insult offered me last Evening as an American I am compelled to trouble you with an information of it— As Mr. Lynd[2] and myself were in a conversation at the distance of a Square from the Marquis of Casa Calvo's residence, we were Hailed by a Spanish Soldier from the opposite corner, who after my informing him of his audacity in So doing, returned to the Marquis's Guard. I followed him with a desire of making him known to the officer of the Guard, but was refused every Species of Satisfaction by them.— The Soldier on my reproaching him for his insolence placed his hand to his Sword, but on finding I was also armed did not draw.[3] It is unnecessary for me to comment as I am well convinced of your Excellencys disposition to preserve the dignity of our characters.

> I am Respectfully your obdt Sevt
> (Signed) *Geo. T. Ross*

Thursday Morning
December 6th 1804

1. For a biographical sketch of George T. Ross, see pp. 447–60.

2. Dr. John Lynd. See pp. 560–3.

3. A similar and potentially uglier incident occurred during the daylight hours of February 3, 1804. See To James Madison, February 4, 1804, CLB, 1: 358–60; and James Robertson, ed. and trans., *Louisiana Under the Rule of Spain, France and the United States, 1785–1807*, vol. 2 (1910–1911; Freeport, N.Y.: Books for Libraries Press, 1969), 245–7. Two days after this incident, Claiborne wrote Casa Calvo to suggest that he station his guard "Somewhere within your own enclosure." See Letter No. 76, To Casa Calvo, December 8, 1804, which immediately follows.

{76}
To Casa Calvo
New Orleans December 8th 1804

Sir,

Several Citizens have complained to me, that when passing by your Excellencys House, they have been forced by your guard to abandon the Side way of the Street and from a representation lately made to me by a gentleman of respectability and of which a copy is enclosed, it appears that a Soldier of your Guard (at Some distance from your dwelling) has thought himself authorized to hail and Stop a Citizen. I deem it unnecessary to make any comments upon the above facts, but persuaded as I am of Your Excellency's disposition to prevent any occurrences that might tend to excite irritation— I will Suggest the propriety of your Excellencys Guard being withdrawn entirely from the Street, and Stationed Somewhere within your own enclosure.

> Accept assurances of my very
> Respectful
> Consideration
> (Signed) *William C. C. Claiborne*

His Excellency
The Marquis of
Casa Calvo

{77}
To James Madison
New Orleans December 9th 1804

Sir,

About five months ago a Spanish officer attached to the family of the Marquis of Casa Calvo presented me a Key which he Said was the Key of a large Room in the Principal (or City Hall) belonging formerly to the King of Spain, and which he Said had been heretofore occupied as an arsenal[.] The officer added that the Principal had been built at the joint expense of the King and City, that the former claimed the Lower Story, and the Room in which the arms had been placed— The Balance of the Building belonged to the City.

When Judge Prevost arrived he applied to me for an apartment to hold his Court in, when the key above alluded to and which had been So long in my possession was handed to the Sheriff who was directed to cause the necessary furniture to be procured and the Room put in order— Under my ordinance defining the powers of the Municipality, the care of the City Property was committed to that body, and they were taught to believe (by the intriguers) that the Principal in toto was the property of the City, and that the Governor appropriating any part thereof without previously consulting the Municipality, was a great contempt to that Body, the consequence was that a Letter upon the Subject was addressed to me by the Mayor of the City, which was answered with mildness and candour. The temporary agitation Subsided and without determining the question as to the right of the Property, the Municipality consented to accommodate the Court as well as the Legislative Council.

I have mentioned these occurrences in order to Show you to what miserable expedients the Intriguers here resort, in order to embarrass my administration, and to excite public discontent— But Sir the line of conduct I have prescribed for myself shall never be departed from; my acts Shall be the result of reflection and my best Judgment; I will continue to observe as much moderation as the Interest of my Country will permit, and while gentleness in the manner will be manifested, I Shall nevertheless be firm to my objects— I have heretofore had an arduous task, and there are yet many difficulties to encounter. But I persuade myself that in a little time the State of things here will be Such as I desire.

> I am Sir with great Esteem
> Your Hbe St
> (Signed) *William C. C. Claiborne*

The Honble
James Madison
Secretary of State

{78}

To James Madison
New Orleans December 11th 1804[1]

Sir,

The Mail of last Evening brought me your Communication of the 12th Ultimo. The late Insurrection at Baton Rouge (If indeed it can be called Such) has Subsided and I believe will not be renewed. The Insurgents were few in number and at no time exceeding thirty;— their place of rendezvous was within what is called West-Florida, and the part composed almost entirely of persons who resided in that District.

I have understood that a general amnesty (with the exception of Kemper and two others) has been granted by Governor Folch to the Insurgents, and that they have returned to their respective homes, those not included in the amnesty have retired to Pinckneyville, in the Mississippi Territory;[2] Should any future disturbances arise, your Letter of the 12th Ultimo will regulate my conduct. I read with pride and pleasure the Presidents ~~Letter~~ message to Congress. The prosperity of our Country is unexampled, and I pray almighty God, that nothing may intervene to mar the happy prospect before us. I had feared that the little misunderstanding which had arisen with Spain might assume a Shape not So favorable to the Pacific Policy which our national Interests So Strongly recommend.— But the remarks of the President with respect to our foreign relations generally have removed my fears, and I persuade myself, that in a Short time the Western and Eastern limits of Louisiana, as contended for by the United States, will be acknowledged, and East Florida acquired on terms the most Satisfactory.

The Presidents message has been translated into the French language, and I will take care to have it circulated among the people. It will tend to remove an impression which has heretofore tended greatly to embarrass the local administration, to wit, that the Country West of the Mississippi would certainly be receded to Spain, and perhaps the whole of Louisiana.[3] So general has been this impression, particularly as it relates to the Country West of Mississippi, that many Citizens have been fearful of accepting any employment under the American Government, or even manifesting a respect therefor; lest for a future day it might lessen them in the esteem of Spanish officers. This opinion as to a recession has been greatly encouraged by the Marquis of Casa Calvo, and Governor Folch, who are really So uninformed of the Strength of the United States, as to Suppose that the Spanish Mon-

arch could readily acquire and maintain possession of Louisiana, and I doubt
not but they have made Such representations to their Court.

> I have the Honor to be Sir
> with great Respect and Esteem
> your most Obdt Hbe St
> (Signed) *William C. C. Claiborne*

The Honble
James Madison
Secty of State

1. Published as To James Madison, December 11, 1804, in CLB, 3: 25–6, with slight variations in text and punctuation.
2. In addition to the Kemper brothers, Reuben and Nathan, the other men alluded to apparently were the sons of Arthur Cobb. See Letter No. 214, Pardon of William Cobb.
3. See Letter No. 197, Claiborne to Madison, April 21, 1805.

{79}
EXTRACT OF A LETTER FROM THE PRESIDENT OF THE UNITED STATES DATED WASHINGTON JULY 7TH 1804 TO GOVERNOR CLAIBORNE[1]

"The Position of New Orleans certainly destines it to be the greatest City
the World has ever Seen. There is no Spot on the Globe to which the produce of So great an extent of fertile Country must necessarily come. It is three
times greater than that on the Eastern Side of the Allegany which is to be
divided among the Sea-Port Towns of the Atlantic States. In the middle and
Northern parts of Europe where the Sun rarely Shines they may Safely
build Cities in Solid blocks without generating disease, but under the cloud-
less Skies of America where there is So constant an accumulation of Heat,
men cannot be piled on one another with impunity. Accordingly we find the
disease confined to the Solid Built parts of our Towns, and the parts on the
Water Side where there is most matter for putrefaction rarely extending into
the then Built parts of the Town and never into the Country. In these latter
places it cannot be communicated, in order to catch it you must go into the
local atmosphere where it prevails. Is not this then a Strong indication, that
we ought not contend with the Laws of nature; but Should decide at once—,
[*sic*] that all our Cities should be there built? You will perhaps remember
that in 1793 yourself, the present Governor Harrison and Some other young
Gentlemen, Dining with me in Philadelphia, the then late yellow fever being

the Subject of conversation, and its incommunicability in the Country, I observed that in Building Cities in the United States we Should take the chequer Board for our Plan, leaving the white Squares open and unbuilt forever
and planted with Trees. Harrison treasured this idea in his mind, and having to lay off a City two or three years ago on the Banks of *Ohio* opposite
Louisville, he laid it off on this Plan.

As It is probable that New Orleans must be Soon enlarged, I enclose you
the Same Plan for consideration. I have great confidence that however the
yellow fever may prevail in the old part of the Town, it would not be commu-
nicable in that part which Should be built on this Plan: Because this would
be all like the then built parts of our Towns where experience has taught us
that a person may carry it after catching it in its local region, but can never
communicate it out of that. Having very Sincerely at Heart, that the Prosperity of New Orleans Should be unchecked, and great faith founded as I think
in experience, of the effect of this mode of Building against a disorder which
is Such a Scourge to our close built cities, I could not deny myself the communication of the Plan, leaving to you to bring it into real existence if those
Interested Should think as favorably of it as I do, for beauty[,] pleasure and
convenience it will certainly be eminent" [*sic*]

1. The complete letter may be seen in *The Writings of Thomas Jefferson,* ed. Andrew A.
Lipscomb and Albert E. Bergh, vol. 11 (Washington, D.C.: Thomas Jefferson Memorial Association of the United States, 1904), 36–8 and 62–9.

{80}
To the Legislative Council
New Orleans December 14th 1804

Gentlemen of the Legislative Council!

The Malignant fever which lately prevailed among us may justly excite our
Sympathy and attention, not only on account of the many amiable persons
who were its immediate Victims, but with a prospective view to the future
increase and welfare of this City. The important event was foreseen and
contemplated by a fellow Citizen whose penetrating and Philosophic mind is
ever actively employed in Some Subject connected with the Happiness of
mankind. An extract of a Letter which pending the contagion I received from
the President of the United States, I now have the Honour to lay before the
Council. It embraces objects highly interesting to our Society, and worthy the
Serious consideration of the Legislature. The present inconsiderable extent of
New Orleans affords an opportunity for future improvement not possessed

by those Cities that have obtained their full growth. In prescribing therefore measures for the improvement and enlargement of New Orleans, I am persuaded that the Plan Suggested by the President will receive the respectful attention of the Legislative Council; the preference to which it is entitled as well on the Score of elegance and comfort as of Health, forcibly presents itself to my view.

(Signed) *William C. C. Claiborne*

{81}
To James Madison
New Orleans December 15th 1804[1]

Sir,

I have the pleasure to inform you, that the Council progresses in Business with great Harmony[,] care and industry and that the well disposed Citizens appear Satisfied. The enclosed Paper contains the address of Mr. Poidras [*sic*] on the opening of the Session.[2] His influence is considerable, and there is no doubt but his Sentiments will make a favorable impression. The Bark Hero whose Situation I informed you of some time Since not being in a situation to proceed to Sea was detained at Plaquemine for 16 or 18 days, during which time the Sick and wounded on Board as well French as Englishmen was by my order furnished with medical assistance and a Small quantity of Rice and Fresh Provisions. The Captain of the Hero required a large Supply of Stores to enable him to prosecute his Voyage to Europe, and to procure the Same I have lately permitted him to proceed with his Vessel to this Port.

I was unwilling that So many needy persons as were on Board the Hero, Should on a Sudden be introduced into this City; it was probable they would have proved troublesome in Society, for this therefore as well as other reasons I gave orders for the early departure of the Vessel, and that in the mean time She Should not be permitted to pass the Fort— Many of the Prisoners having Subsequently made their escape and dispersed throughout the Territory, and apprehending no inconvenience from the landing of those now on Board I have permitted the Hero to approach the City.

An account of the Supplies furnished, [*sic*] the Sick and wounded will in due time be forwarded to you. It is very inconsiderable, and I presume will readily be paid by the British Minister. I hope my conduct in this affair will be approved of. I was desirous that the Vessel Should Speedily depart, but She was without the necessary Sea Stores and I did not Suppose there would be a propriety in my furnishing any other Supplies than what was necessary for the comfort of the Sick and wounded during their Stay at Plaquemine and *that* humanity enjoined. The alarm which lately existed at Natchitoches has Subsided, and the farmers of Point Coupee [*sic*] at present consider themselves in a State of Security. The Militia of that Settlement is now completely organized, and the Small detachment of Regular Troops Stationed in the District will Serve as a rallying point in case of danger[.]

> I am Sir with Sincere Esteem your
> Hble St
> (Signed) *William C. C. Claiborne*

The Honble
James Madison
Secty of State

1. Also published as To James Madison, December 15, 1804, CLB, 3: 26–8, with variations in text and punctuation.
2. See Letter No. 74, From Julien Poydras, December 7, 1804.

{82}
TO MICHEL CANTRELLE
New Orleans December 17th 1804[1]

Sir,

I have appointed Mr. Tureau[2] Captain of Cavalry, and directed him to take the command (Subject to your orders) of the Militia of your District. The other Citizens proposed as Officers, I wish to do duty in the Grades to which they have been respectively recommended, but I have deemed it inexpedient at this time to Commission them, Since the Legislative Council is now in Session and may probably pass a Militia Law which might interfere with the proposed arrangement for your District.

> I am Sir very Respectfully
> Your Hble St
> (Signed) *William C. C. Claiborne*

Capt Cantrelle
Commandant &c.

1. For a biographical sketch of Cantrelle, see pp. 570–4.
2. Augustin Dominique Tureaud of the Acadia District (present-day St. James Parish). He was one of the exiles from St. Domingue. By his marriage to Elizabeth (Betsy) Bringier, daugh-

ter of Marius Pons Bringier, Tureaud allied himself with one of the influential planter families along the Mississippi River above New Orleans. Claiborne reappointed Tureaud captain of the cavalry again the following summer (August 25, 1805). Other public offices held by Tureaud were treasurer of the Acadia District (appointed May 15, 1805); auctioneer (appointed February 19, 1806); justice of the peace (appointed August 21, 1811); and judge (September 11, 1812). Register of Civil Appointments in the Territory of Orleans, enclosed in John Graham to the Secretary of State, February 13, 1806, TP, 9: 601, 632, 663, and 984, respectively. See also Lillian Bourgeois, *Cabanocey: The History, Customs, and Folklore of St. James Parish* (New Orleans: Pelican, 1957), 23, 29, 89.

{83}
To William Bayard Shields
New Orleans Dec 19th 1804[1]

DSir,

Your Letter of the 8th Instant has been duly received. The records of Grants issued in Natchez District do not appear to have been kept Separate and Distinct, they are included in the general Record of Land Lying in Louisiana. A transcript from the Record will be a work of time, and attended probably with a greater expense than $200. I however will examine particularly and write you further by the next mail.[2]

I am DSir [*sic*], with Respect
and Esteem
Your Hble St
(Signed) *William C. C. Claiborne*

Wm B Shields Esqr
Atty at Law
Washington
Mississippi Territory

1. Shields, like Claiborne, was a friend of Caesar A. Rodney, leader of the republicans in Delaware, friend of Jefferson, and member of Congress from Delaware, 1802–04. William C. C. Claiborne to Caesar A. Rodney, August 9, 1803, William C. C. Claiborne Collection, Historical Society of Pennsylvania. Born in Maryland in 1780, Shields received his legal education in Delaware. He arrived in the Mississippi Territory in the third week of August 1803 where he held appointment as United States agent to adjust land claims west of the Pearl River. Governor Claiborne to William B. Shields, February 4, 1805, TP, 9: 389 n. 48. See also To Wm. B. Shields, May 10, 1805, CLB, 3: 52. More detail on his career and life may be found in Dunbar Rowland, *Courts, Judges and Lawyers of Mississippi, 1798–1835* (Jackson, Miss.: Hederman Brothers, 1935), entry no. 162, 68–9. Before returning to live in Mississippi, Shields held the contract for the postmaster's job at the Opelousas post in 1807. The Postmaster General to David Parmelee, February 12, 1807, TP, 9: 707. After his return to Mississippi, Shields

was appointed attorney general of the territory by Governor David Holmes in 1809, rising to
a position of prominence in the legal profession of that state before his death on April 19,
1823. Governor Holmes to Joseph Johnson, September 21, 1809, TP, 6: 18, and Rowland,
Courts, Judges and Lawyers, entry no. 162, 68–9.

  2. See Letter No. 197, To James Madison, April 21, 1805. Some months passed before
Claiborne provided the followup on the Natchez District land titles. See the index references
in TP, 9: and CLB.

{84}

TO ALBERT GALLATIN

New Orleans Dec 20th 1804

Sir,

  Your Letter of the 5th of November with its enclosure I have received. The
records of Grants and Surveys of Land made under the Spanish Government in the Mississippi Territory have not been kept distinct from those of
Louisiana and will not admit of a Seperation [*sic*];— I however will make
arrangements to furnish Mr. Shields Such copies as are wanted for the purposes mentioned in his Letter.[1]

I am Sir with Respect
and Esteem your Obdt Sert
(Signed) *William C. C. Claiborne*

The Honble
Albert Gallatin
Secty of the
Treasury

  1. The Shields letter referred to has not been found.

{85}

TO JAMES MADISON

New Orleans Dec 23rd 1804[1]

Sir,

  The Bark Hero arrived in this ~~City~~ Harbour three days ago. The French
prisoners have all escaped. Some have gone into the Country for employment. A few remain in the City, and others have entered as Sailors on Board
of Merchant Vessels. The Situation of the Sick and wounded Englishmen
on Board the Hero is peculiarly distressing. They are *without Hospital Stores
of any kind, medical attendance, or any provision* except *a little Salt Beef,
or the means* of obtaining the necessary Supplies.[2] There being no British

Consul or Agent in this City, and those unfortunate Strangers having applied to me for Succour, I addressed on this day to Colonel Freeman a Letter of which the enclosed No. 1 is a Copy and received the answer No[.] 2.[3] During the detention of the Hero at Plaquemine, the Sick and wounded as well as French as Englishmen were furnished by my order with fresh provisions. The Captain of the Hero Speaks favorably of the Humane treatment of Captain Nicolls [sic], the officer Commanding at Plaquemine and of Doctor Williamson the Surgeon of the garrison to the Sick and wounded.

> I am Sir with great Respect
> your most obdt Servt
> (Signed) *William C. C. Claiborne*

The Honble
James Madison
Secty of State

PS. The account, for Supplies furnished the Sick and wounded at Plaquemine amounted to forty one Dollars, and which I have paid.
W. C. C. C[.]

1. Also published as To James Madison, December 23, 1804, CLB, 3: 28–9, with slight variations in the text, punctuation, and the postscript.
2. Emphasis in the original.
3. Neither enclosure no. 1 nor no. 2 was present. Claiborne's letter to Colonel Freeman (no. 2 mentioned here) is published as To Col. Freeman, December 23, 1804, CLB, 3: 29.

{86}
To Edward Demaresque Turner
New Orleans Dec 25th 1804[1]

Sir,
Your Letters of the 21st Ultimo, and of the 8th Instant have been duly received. The liberation of the Negroes implicated in the late plot (but who did not escape) meets my approbation, and if the Masters of those who did absolutely disert [sic], should be disposed to pardon them I Should approve their release from confinement. But unless their masters interfere you must detain them for Trial. In furnishing Indians who have visited your Post with rations and a Small Supply of Powder, Lead, and Tobacco you acted very proper, and I am certain that no exception will be taken by our Superiors. The friendly disposition of the Indians towards the United States Should be cultivated with great care, and your exertions in this particular are noticed

with pleasure. I will forward to you by the first opportunity three or four Small flags to be presented to the different Tribes, and you may assure them, that in due time ample provision will be made by their father the President of the United States to Supply them upon good terms with all the goods they may want.

The Military Movements in the Province of Taxus [Texas] do not excite anxiety; it is believed that the United States will amicably and Speedily adjust the difference which exists as to the limits of the Ceded Territory.— But if in this reasonable expectation we Should be disappointed, and a Serious dispute ensue, you will no doubt believe me correct in Saying that our Country has nothing to fear from the force of Spain. It is nevertheless of importance to cultivate an Honorable peace and a friendly intercourse with all the world— By that wise and pacific policy our Government has acquired respect abroad and confidence at home, accompanied with an increase of National Wealth and Happiness.—

> I am Sir very Respectfully
> Your &c
> (Signed) *William C. C. Claiborne*

Captain Turner
Natchitoches

1. Also published as To Edw. D. Turner, but dated December 28, 1804, CLB, 3: 32–3, and with variations in text and punctuation.

{87}
To Edward Demaresque Turner
New Orleans December 25th 1804[1]

Sir,
Your Letter of the 28th Ultimo is now before me. The arrest of the Spaniard charged with the murder of an American on the Road from Appelousas [sic] to Nacogdoches is an act for which the Spanish Commandant deserves credit. If the murder was committed without the acknowledged Jurisdiction of the United States we can take no cognizance of the offence, and therefore a Surrender of the person accused to the American Government would be useless. But if the Murder has been committed within ~~the~~ our acknowledged limits, and the murderer be Surrendered you will hold him in Safe keeping until the case can be enquired into by a competent Tribunal.

It is not however, my desire that you Should make a formal demand of the offender from the Commandant at Nacogdoches.

> I am Sir with great Respect
> Your most obd St
> (Signed) *William C. C. Claiborne*

Capt Turner
Commanding at
Natchitoches

1. Published as To Capt. Turner, but dated December 24, 1804, CLB, 3: 32. There also are variations in punctuation and emphasis not found in this copy.

{88}
To Constant Freeman
New Orleans December 29th 1804

Sir,
I am Honored with the Receipt of your Letter of the 28th Instant. During my Intercourse with the officers under your Command which has been general and friendly, I have observed no conduct on their part disrespectful to the constituted authorities of our Country, or Hostile to the measures of Government: On the contrary their Deportment as Gentlemen and officers appeared to me to be unexceptionable. Accept my best wishes—

> I am Sir with Respect and Esteem
> Your very Hble St
> (Signed) *William C. C. Claiborne*

Colol [*sic*] Freeman

{89}
To Casa Calvo
New Orleans December 29th 1804

Sir,
The answer which you was [*sic*] pleased to return to my Letter of the 8th Instant is not Satisfactory, and of which you would have been earlier notified, had not your late absence from the City and my own engagements prevented. I have no doubt but the orders you ~~gave~~ State were given to your guard, but Mr. Ross's Statement (of the accuracy of which I am well assured) is a proof that they have not been attended to. If it be inconvenient to withdraw

your guard entirely from the Street within your own enclosure, I must desire
that it be discontinued altogether. Several Citizens have complained of
being interrupted in passing the Streets by your guard, and therefore it is that
the longer continuance is not approved of.

Your person and property are under the Safeguard of the Law, and I am
persuaded ample protection will be afforded. Solicitous however to extend
to your Excellency every mark of attention during your temporary residence
in this City, as well on account of consideration of private regard, as from a
respect for that Sovereign in whose armies you hold Such distinguished Rank,
if your Excellency Should wish it you Shall be furnished with a guard from the
American Troops.

> I pray your Excellency to receive
> assurances of my Respectful
> Consideration
> (Signed) *William C. C. Claiborne*

His Excellency
The Marquis of
Casa Calvo

{90}
To James Madison
New Orleans December 31st 1804[1]

Sir,

I have never witnessed more good order than at present pervades this City,
and as far as I can learn the whole Territory. I discover also with great pleasure the existence of a friendly understanding between the Modern and the
ancient Louisianians. The winter amusements have commenced for Several
weeks, the two descriptions of Citizens meet frequently at the Theatre, Balls
and other places of public amusement, and pass their time in perfect harmony. A great anxiety exists here to learn the fate of the Memorial to Congress. The importation of Negroes continues to be a favorite object with the
Louisianians, and I believe the privilege of electing one Branch of the Legislature would give very general Satisfaction. Immediate admission into the
Union is not expected by the reflecting part of Society, nor do I think there
are many who wish it. I find in Some anonimous [*sic*] publication to the
northward, I have been represented as opposing the assemblage of the people

to Sign the Memorial, and that on one occasion the Troops were called out in order to intimidate the Citizens. These Statements are incorrect; I never did oppose the meeting of the people, but it is true, that in the then unsettled State of the Government I Saw with regret any manifestation of Public discontent, and the more So Since I suspected there were many designing men among us whose attachments were foreign that might labour to give an improper direction to the public deliberation. I remember to have been Strongly urged to Suppress by force the first meeting which took place in March last, and by Some of those who are now great advocates of the memorial— But I answered that "the people had a right peaceably to assemble together to remonstrate against grievances" and would not be prevented by me. In consequence Several Subsequent public meetings took place in this City without experiencing any interruption by me, or by my authority. The Troops were under arms on the first of July, and on that day there was a meeting of part of the memorialists;— But the Parade was altogether accidental.

It is usual to muster the Troops for Inspection on the last day of every month. On the last day of June this ceremony was prevented by Rain, and the following day it took place. The Inspection and muster were ordered by Colonel Freeman, and So little design was there in this Transaction, that neither Colonel Freeman or myself knew of the meeting of the memorialists until after the Troops were dismissed. I am not in the habit of noticing anonimous [*sic*] publications nor do I suppose much weight is attached to them at the Seat of Government.— But in this remote Territory events are So apt to be misrepresented, that I owe it to my own reputation to keep you advised almost of every occurrence.

> I am Sir very Respectfully
> Your obdt Sevt
> (Signed) *William C. C. Claiborne*

The Honble
James Madison
Secty of State

1. Also published as [To the Secretary of State], December 31, 1804, CLB, 3: 35–6, and in James Robertson, ed. and trans., *Louisiana Under the Rule of Spain, France, and the United States, 1785–1807*, vol. 2 (1910–1911; Freeport, N.Y.: Books for Libraries Press, 1969), 278–80, with variations in punctuation.

{91}
To Edward Demaresque Turner
New Orleans Dec 31st 1804

Sir,

I cannot by this Mail reply fully to your Letter of the 23rd of November. The Subject of it requires some consideration; and at present I am very much pressed with Business. I however See in your conduct in Madam Caperous [?] case, as well as on other occasions a Sincere disposition to conform your acts to the Principles of Justice. Present me respectfully to your Lady—

> I am Sir with great Esteem
> Your Hbe St
> (Signed) *William C. C. Claiborne*

Capt Turner
Natchitoches

{92}
To Albert Gallatin
New Orleans December 31st 1804

Sir,

You will receive herewith an account[1] and Vouchers for Sundry disbursements of a Contingent nature, made by me during the temporary Government of Louisiana amounting to 334$. In the course of a few days I Shall prepare a general Statement of my accounts and forward it to the Treasury.— This Statement has hitherto been delayed by insuperable difficulties— among others the Death of one[2] and the temporary absence of another Gentleman employed in my office are to be mentioned.

> I have the Honor to be very
> Respectfully
> Your obt Sert
> (Signed) *William C. C. Claiborne*

The Honble
Albert Gallatin
Secty of the Treasury

---

1. The account statement and vouchers were not present with this copy of Claiborne's letter, but the originals were returned to Claiborne at his request by Secretary Gallatin. See Letter

No. 198, From Albert Gallatin, February 25, 1805. It is clear from the postscript to Gallatin's letter enclosing the returned statement and receipts that no action was taken on them.

2. Claiborne was referring to Joseph Briggs, the son of Isaac Briggs, who died of yellow fever on September 16, 1804. See Governor Claiborne to the President, September 18, 1804; and Governor Claiborne to the Secretary of State, January 4, 1805, TP, 9: 298 and 361, respectively. Notice of young Briggs's death appeared in the *Union,* September 19, 1804, p. 1, c. 1.

{93}
To James Madison
New Orleans Dec 31st 1804[1]

Sir,

I enclose for your perusal three Letters which I have lately received from the officer Commanding at Natchitoches together with Copies of my answers thereto Marked Nos. 1 & 2[.][2]

You discover by these Letters that the late alarm at Natchitoches relative to the negroes has wholly Subsided, and also that the neighboring Tribes of Indians manifest the best dispositions towards the United States.

> I am Sir with Esteem and Respect
> Your obdt Sert
> (Signed) *William C. C. Claiborne*

The Honble
James Madison
Secty of State

1. Also published as [To the Secretary of State] December 31, 1804, CLB, 3: 30, with minor variations in text and punctuation marks.

2. The Turner letters were not present, but may be those of November 8 and 21 referred to by Claiborne in his letter to Turner dated December 28, 1804. See Edw. D. Turner, December 28, 1804, ibid., 32.

{94}
To James Madison
New Orleans Dec 31st 1804[1]

Sir,

I enclose you a resolution which has been proposed in the Legislative Council.[2] The guard alluded to Says the Marquis of Casa Calvo, consists of a Corporal and three Men, and is a part of a Guard assigned to accompany him on the Line of demarcation and that he is appointed a Commissioner of limits &c. The Marquis has been requested by me to discontinue his Guard and informed that his person and property were perfectly Secured by the municipal Laws; but nevertheless if he wished it he Should be furnished with a temporary Guard from the American Troops. My correspondence commenced with the Marquis on this Subject, the eighth of this Month, and to my last Letter an answer is not returned.

The resolution of the Council I consider as premature and improper. I do not think the Marquis is entitled to his guard; but really it is not an object of Serious concern[.] I know not what Negotiations may be pending and am unwilling to excite irritation on the part of the Spanish Agents. I will do nothing rashly. The Spanish Authorities might if they pleased, Subject the Americans to great inconvenience in West Florida.

> I am Sir very Respectfully
> Your Hble St
> (Signed) *William C. C. Claiborne*

The Honble
James Madison
Secty of State

P.S[.] A Copy of the Correspondence Shall be transmitted you by the next Mail.

W. C. C. C[.]

1. Also published as [To the Secretary of State] December 31, 1804, CLB, 3: 34, with the following phrase of the third sentence in paragraph one italicized: "*me to discontinue his guard.*" In addition, the postscript to Dunbar Rowland's edition of this letter carries a concluding sentence not found here. The sentence added to the postscript reads: "In a Letter of the 25th July last, I mentioned to you, the existence of the Marquis's Guard, & from your silence, I supposed you considered it, as unimportant."

2. The copy of the resolution was not in the manuscript, but is published as Resolution of the Legislative Council, December 31, 1804, TP, 9: 360–1. See also James Robertson, ed. and trans., *Louisiana Under the Rule of Spain, France and the United States, 1785–1807*, vol. 2 (1910–1911; Freeport, N.Y.: Books for Libraries Press, 1969), 246 n. 122.

{95}
To Casa Calvo
New Orleans Jany 4th 1804[1805]

Sir,

I have received your Excellency's Letter of the 2nd Inst. and notice with Satisfaction your disposition to conform to my requests. The existence of your Guard was not considered an object of Serious Concern, Since I was well assured that your Excellency would disapprove and repress any interference on their part with the Citizens. But as complaints were made I thought it would conduce to Harmony to have the guard withdrawn from the Streets. The *protection*[1] due your Excellency is prescribed by our Laws, and every officer of this Government will be happy to render it.

I tender your Excellency my best wishes accompanied with assurances of my respectful consideration[.]

(Signed) William C. C. Claiborne

His Excellency
The Marquis of
Casa Calvo

1. Emphasis in the original.

{96}

To Albert Gallatin

New Orleans January 5th 1805

Sir,

So great was the press of Business at the Date of my two last Letters of the 31st of December Ultimo, the one covering an amount for Sundry Disbursements prior to the first of October 1804, the other a Statement of Several incidental expences incurred by me under the Territory of Orleans during the last quarter, that copies of both of the Letters and amounts were neglected. Permit me therefore respectfully to Solicit that copies of each may be furnished me as early as convenient[.][1]

I have the Honor to be very
Respectfully your most obdt St
(Signed) *William C. C. Claiborne*

The Honble
Albert Gallatin
Secty of the Treasury

1. Claiborne apparently intended to have copies of the statement sent to Secretary of State Madison. See Claiborne to Madison, January 4, 1805, James Madison Papers, Series I, General Correspondence and Related Items, 1723–1859, reel no. 8, in which the governor referred to his large expenses as a result of sickness in his family.

{97}

TO CASA CALVO

New Orleans January 5th 1805

Sir,

Messrs. Lebreten D'orgenoy[1] and Watkins who were heretofore named to receive the Papers of certain Notarys Offices (which your Excellency informed me were ready for delivery) being too much occupied to attend to that Business, the Trust has been committed to Messrs[.] Carrick and Donaldson Members of the Municipality, who will attend as Such time and place as may be appointed.—

I pray your Excellency to receive assurances of my Respect and Esteem (Signed) *William C. C. Claiborne*

His Excellency
The Marquis of
Casa Calvo

1. Francis Joseph LeBreton D'Orgenois (Dorgenoy, D'Orgenoi, D'Orgenoy), a longtime resident of Louisiana who was appointed U.S. marshal for the District of Orleans by Claiborne in 1804. Claiborne appointed D'Orgenois because of his "Inflexible integrity" and because he was "American in sentiment." Although D'Orgenois was respected as a man of "sense and integrity," he angered some by his outspokenness about the Spanish government, which, given the problems with Casa Calvo, may have enhanced D'Orgenois's appeal for Claiborne. Governor Claiborne to the President, October 22, 1804; and The Secretary of State to Governor Claiborne, November 10, 1804, TP, 9: 311, 532–3, respectively. See also To James Madison, October 26, 1804, CLB, 2: 375. D'Orgenois appears to have followed Lewis Kerr as U.S. marshal after Kerr's appointment as sheriff. D'Orgenois served as marshal until May 30, 1809, resigning then because of his "advanced age and inability to discharge in person the duties of his office." To Robert Smith, May 30, 1809, ibid., 4: 373, and Governor Claiborne to Julien Poydras, June 4, 1809, TP, 9: 843. D'Orgenois may have come to the attention of Claiborne as a signer of the September 17, 1804, petition expressing concern that the incident at the home of Michel Fortier on the Acadian Coast on the morning of September 16, 1804, suggested the existence of a plot by the slaves that threatened the public similar to the one that "laid waste the French . . . Colony of San Domingo." Petition of the Inhabitants and Colonists of Louisiana to Governor Claiborne, September 17, 1804, TP, 9: 297 (translation). D'Orgenois also was one of several candidates for the vacated seat of Robert Avart in the territorial house of representatives in January 1806, but came in a poor second to Benjamin Morgan. Morgan received twenty-three votes to D'Orgenois's two. H. Molier to Governor Claiborne, January 21, 1806, TP, 9: 574. D'Orgenois also received appointment as a justice of the peace in 1811. Return of Civil Appointments made in the Territory of Orleans from the 1st Jany 1811 to the 31st Dec. of the Same Year, ibid., 984.

{98}
To James Madison
New Orleans January 5th 1805

Sir,

I now enclose you the Correspondence between the Marquis of Casa Calvo
and myself upon the Subject of his Guard. I had not considered this Guard
as an object of Serious concern, it was Small and for Some time did not Seem
to excite disquietude among the Citizens;— I was certainly impressed with
an opinion that the Marquis could not maintain his Guard as a matter of right,
but Since it had produced no mischief, and as the Marquis Seemed pleased
with the establishment, I thought it unworthy of my Serious attention, but of
late two or three complaints having been made by Citizens who had experienced Some interruption by the Spanish guard, I addressed to the Marquis my
Letter of the 8th Instant;— His answer of the 9th was not Satisfactory—
But owing to his absence from the City my reply was delayed until the 25th
Ultimo, and on that day Mr. Pollock Submitted his resolution to the Council. I am persuaded that Mr. P. was influenced by motives of Honest Patriotism, but I am inclined to think that he was advised to the measure by Some
one who wished to embarrass me here, and to injure me at the Seat of Government. The resolution gave to the Guard an importance it did not deserve,
and to the Subject generally a colouring which will make it misunderstood
every where but in this City— For no one unacquainted with the facts
would Suppose that these Spanish troops whom the proposed resolution ~~has~~
represented as So dangerous to the peace of the City and to the Sovereignty
of the United States, consisted only of a Corporal and Four men, posted at the
Lodging of the late Commissioner for the delivery of Louisiana to the
French Republic and who also claims to be a Commissioner of limits[.]

The resolution has been rejected by the Council, inasmuch as it related to
no object falling within their Province. The Marquis however, has as you
will See by his last letter discontinued his guard, and on this Score I presume
no further inquietude will exist.

> I am Sir with great Respect
> and Sincere Esteem your
> most obt Sevt
> (Signed) *William C. C. Claiborne*

The Honble
James Madison
Secty of State

{99}

To James Madison
New Orleans January 5th 1805

Sir,

Great exertions are now making to revive the Louisiana Bank, and I understand the probability is that the Capital required will in a few days be Subscribed. My own doubts as to the Solidity of the charter are known, as is also the opinion of Some of the Officers of Government, that it was in itself a nullity; but many Citizens Seem nevertheless determined to adventure[.]

I am Sir with great Respect
Your Hble St
(Signed) *William C. C. Claiborne*

The Honble
James Madison
Secretary of State

{100}

To Casa Calvo
New Orleans January 5th 1805

Sir,

In consequence of your Excellencys Letter to me of the 28th Ultimo Stating the recent Robbery of 680$ [*sic*] of the money of the King of Spain, a Strict examination has been made by the officers of this Garrison, in order to ascertain whether the Bayonet and Ramrod found near the apartment which had been forced open, were of the Arms of the United States; and the result of this examination So favorable to the innocence of the Soldiery you will find in the enclosed Letter to me from Colonel Freeman.

The City Magistrates are informed of the Robbery; and their Vigilance will be exercised to discover the Offenders.

I pray your Excellency to accept
assurances of my Respectful
consideration
(Signed) *William C. C. Claiborne*

His Excellency
The Marquis
of Casa Calvo

{101}

To Albert Gallatin

New Orleans January 6th 1805

Sir

I have understood that the incipient Capital of the Louisiana Bank is Subscribed, and the Stock Holders will meet on tomorrow for the purpose of choosing Directors.—

I had hoped that this measure would not have been carried into effect, Since it had been disapproved of at the Seat of Government. But the Spirit of adventure which for a length of time was Dormant, has been revived by the exertions of a few individuals, and it Seems the people are determined to put the Bank in motion.

I am Sir very Respectfully
Your Hbe St
(Signed) *William C. C. Claiborne*

The Honble

A. Gallatin
~~James Madison~~
Secty of ~~State~~ the Treasury

Insert two Letters to the
Secty of State under date of January
13 & 14, and which are found
immediately after Jany 28 to Captain
Turner, before you insert the
following [Letter of January 19,
1805, to Secretary of State James
Madison].[1]

1. This note and the changes specified to be made in the chronological arrangement of the letters appear to be in the hand of Governor Claiborne. Clearly, Claiborne wanted his January 13 and 14 letters to be followed by his January 19, 1805, letter to Secretary Madison and all three to precede his January 28, 1805, letter to Captain Edward Turner.

{102}

To James Madison

New Orleans January 19th 1805[1]

Sir,

I feel myself bound in Duty to myself and the Government I have the Honor to represent to forward to you the enclosed Papers[2] containing Some Severe Strictures on my late administration, general public Character and private manners, and I hope I shall be excused for offering Some observations on the principlepal matters of accusation.

I trust the executive will not readily believe, that the affairs of this Territory have been administered in the Slovenly and ridiculous manner exhibited by those Papers; and I feel it a justice due my own reputation to take the earliest opportunity of meeting the calumny in that quarter, when it Seems to be the object of the writer to injure me. I at first contemplated a publication of the documents that avert to my exculpation, but I was dissuaded from it by a conviction that those pieces would do me only a temporary injury here, and that the people would Soon be aware of the Characters and real objects of those who have So wantonly attacked me.

Under Such circumstances I thought a perfect Silence on my part would not only be the most dignified, but also the most, [*sic*] prudent conduct to pursue.— I have however determined thro your Department to convey to the Executive a few comments upon the Subject, as next to an approving conscience the approbation of the President is the first object of my Ambition, the most anxious wish of my Heart.— My accusers you will observe take great pains to impress the public with an opinion that my Government here commenced under the most favorable auspices— An assertion contradicted by every circumstance of the times: But on this point my former Letters to you were So explicit as to Supercede the necessity of entering into detail: I will therefore in general terms State, that when possession of Louisiana was received the aspect of affairs was not Such, as promised either a pleasing administration, or a happy result. The people were Split into parties, divided in their affections, and the Sport of foreign and Domestic intriguersguess. The functions of Government were nearly at a Stance, and much was wanting to produce System in and restore order to the different departments— Great changes were expected under the new order of things, and more was required to conciliate and attach the general Sentiment to the American Government, than my resources permitted, or the energies of any one man could accomplish.

The honest distrust which I entertained of my Talents, the Sincere diffidence with which I entered upon the duties of my office; my constant reluctance to exert any of the large discretionary powers entrusted to me, except when urged by imperious necessity, or the strong pressure of political expediency, and my anxious Solicitude for a Speedy termination of the provisional Government are all known to you.— I could not but be Sensible of the difficulty and peril of my Situation.— My Successor may perhaps— enter upon his Office with more pleasing prospects and I pray to God he may acquire many Laurels— But in being the first appointed to conciliate a people of different manners, languages and Nations, to introduce among them principles of Government and a System of administration altogether new to them, which few understood, and not many Sufficiently appreciated; I felt myself as one Sent on a forlorne hope risquing [sic] my political reputation in the Breach, when every arm raised against me would be raised with advantage—³ Fortune however So far favored me, as to have brought my provisional administration to a peaceful close— That I committed errors I readily admit, but I am not Sensible of having been betrayed into any material measure that I can reflect on with Self accusation— It is true I did not do So much as Some Seem to have expected, nor was my administration marked with any of those Strong traits which some would call energy but others more properly oppression. A charge of Tyranny on the one part, or imbecility on the other was equally an object of dread. I was Solicitous to Steer that course which a just and conciliatory Policy dictated, but I expected that by avoiding either extreme, I Should Subject myself to the imputation of its opposite, and it Seems I have not been disappointed.

The continuation of the Spanish Troops here after the expiration of the time limitted by the Treaty was a Subject of Serious uneasiness to me, and one on which the Commissioners from time to time expressed much Solicitude and urged frequently the immediate removal of those Troops. Our correspondence with Mr. Laussat I trust Sufficiently evinces our dispositions and exertions in that behalf.

To take any other measures to hasten the departure of those Troops would have been unauthorized on our part, and I doubt even had we had the Authority, whether we had the force necessary to carry any compulsory measures into effect. As to the Marquis of Casa Calvo's having retained a Centinel [sic] at his House, it never gave me any uneasiness, and indeed I knew not until lately that it was even considered as an object of Jealousy by any of our Citizens.— I however communicated the circumstance to you and conceiving from your Silence that you viewed it as I did, in a very un-

important light I did not interfere on the Subject 'till lately on a complaint
made against the Guard for an outrage on a Citizen, and the Centinel [*sic*]
was then discontinued at my request. Concerning the affair of Mr. Hulin, it
will be necessary for me to enter into Some explanation, as you are yet unacquainted with the circumstances of that contest, and the Statement exhibited in the enclosed paper has not wanted the aid of professional Skill to
render the writers [*sic*] cause as plausible as possible.

The enclosures Nos. 1.2.3 & 4 are Copies of Official Letters on the Subject
and the Certificates Nos[.] will go in explanation.—[4] These Documents will
place the Transaction in its true point of view.— I have only to add in further
illustration of the Subject, that between the Marquis and the Intendant
there Subsists not only a Political Rivalry, but even a personal hatred. Hulin
is a man little known, except as a Defendant of the Intendants. Villamil is
a violent partizan of the Marquis's, but his wife Madam Villamil is in the
opposite Interest, having been long Separated from her Husband, and enjoying
in a particular manner as is Said the *protection* and *intimacy* of the Intendant.
When the Subject was first mentioned to me by the Marquis, I was led to
understand that his intention was under the authority of the Government of
the Havana, to procure Testimony touching the Official conduct of the Intendant, not having the most distant idea that he intended to interfere in any
manner with the right of Mr. Hulin or Mr. Villamil to Property Still within
this Territory. It is true that I learned from the Marquis that Hulins [*sic*] Title
was a fraudulent one, and at his request I notified the notaries Public (before whom Bills of Sale for Slaves are taken) that Such Suggestion had been
made, in order that the property might not be alienated, until Villamil
might have an opportunity of Supporting his claim before a competent Tribunal.— Under a like impression that the Intendants [*sic*] Official Conduct
alone was the object of the Marquis's investigation, Mr. Randall at my request asked Mrs. Villamil to permit one of her Servants to attend at the
Marquis's House for half an hour, it was a request made by me to gratify a
wish of the Marquis, and Mrs. Villamil was at liberty to comply or not as
She pleased. As to the Story of the insolence of the Spanish Soldier Sent by
the Marquis to Mrs. Villamil, it is denied by the Marquis's Secretary, and
I am inclined to think it not correct.

Mr. Hulins [*sic*] Memorial quoted in the Paper was not presented to me
until about the last of July, or the beginning of August, not long before I
was taken with the yellow fever; and the memorial remained unread until
after my recovery.

Viewing this contest from the Beginning as one arising altogether out of the private animosities of two foreign Officers, in which neither I nor my Country was any wise interested, I was unwilling that my name or Authority Should be used on the occasion, and was also desirous that the affair might terminate without troubling our Government, or involving its Officers in the question.— But So Soon as I discovered that the Marquis proceeded to unauthorized lengths, and called upon me to carry into execution his Decrees between persons answerable only to the Territorial Tribunals, my conduct was immediately Such as a knowledge of the rights of my Country dictated;— that conduct is communicated in the correspondence, and I trust will be approved of:— you will observe that to the Marquis's last Letter I returned no answer; but my Silence may be attributed to the then pressure of my Domestic misfortunes, and the early approach of the period which limited my Judicial Powers.—

The injurious and ill founded allusion made to the influence of the Marquis over my conduct, deserves no notice. The truth is that nothing but a formal intercourse of Civilities ever Subsisted between us, and even that has been discontinued Since the affair of Don Manuel Garcia, in which tho' exclusively a Judicial proceeding, the Spaniards through ignorance of our Government have Supposed me to have been concerned.

It may perhaps be to you a matter of curiosity to know the nature and extent of the party, to which I am indebted for those unfriendly attacks. I have therefore no hesitation to tell you that they proceeded originally from the resentment of Mr. Daniel Clark, who conceiving himself entitled to the confidence of the President, and possibly Some distinguished situation in the administration here is mortified to find himself So entirely overlooked. To his party Mr. Edward Livingston, who as prudence ought to have Suggested probably at first intended no interference with the Politicks of the country, was too easily persuaded to attach himself, and his opposition to me and the acts of the Government I represent Speedily ensued. I easily discovered the Political views of these Gentlemen;— they want in my opinion to injure the Interest and character of our Government in this Country, and I therefore pursued Such a Line of conduct towards them and their measures as my duty required. I might I believe name another Gentleman late of New-York as attached to this party from whom I did not expect opposition;— But the party are few in number, and but for the standing which their Talents give them, could not be considered as formidable. For my part the plain and economical habits in which I have been educated and hitherto lived, united to an [two words blotted out][5] unsuspicious disposition, qualify me but badly for a personal competition with those whose manners have been formed on a model

better calculated for the etiquette of this City, and who from long practice are
more conversant with the arts of Intrigue. To what lengths the opposition
to me may be carried I know not— But I am inclined to think that nothing
will be left unsaid which can wound my feelings, and that my Public and
private character will be cruelly misrepresented. I pray you Sir to lay this Letter before the President of the United States and Should be much obliged
by your early communication to me of any Sentiment he may be pleased to
express.

I have the Honor to be Sir
very Respectfully your obdt St
(Signed) *William C. C. Claiborne*

The Honble
James Madison
Secty of State

P.S— In the Paper called the Union a piece
written in Broken English ridiculing the
Memorialists was published. This
production greatly irritated the ancient
Louisianians and my enemies told them that
it was with my knowledge and approbation,
as was every thing else which appeared in
that Paper. To Shew you what foundation
there was for these reports, I refer you to
the enclosed certificate from the Editor of the Union marked No ____ [6]
W. C. C. C—

1. Also published as Governor Claiborne to the Secretary of State, January 19, 1805, TP,
9: 371–5, with variations in punctuation and the text.

2. Not present.

3. See Letter No. 112, Claiborne to Madison, January 21, 1805, where Claiborne offered
a correction to the phraseology employed here to circumvent the apparent military simile.

4. The certificates and pertinent correspondence immediately follow this letter.

5. The letter as it was sent to Madison used only one word in the phrase: "united to a
candid and unsuspicious disposition." See Governor Claiborne to the Secretary of State, January 19, 1805, TP, 9: 374.

6. The enclosure, Letter No. 105, Certificate [Deposition] of John Kidder, January 18,
1805, is not marked. Claiborne described Kidder, the editor of the *Union* newspaper, as "a
man of neither Judg'ment or discretion" and the newspaper as of "no service to the Government here" in Claiborne to the Secretary of State, October 22, 1804, TP, 9: 313.

{103}
CERTIFICATE [DEPOSITION] OF JOHN WATKINS[1]
Here follows the Certificates and
Correspondence alluded to in the
above Letter—

The following is a Statement of what I recollect relative to the circumstances
of Hulins [*sic*] case, or the correspondence which took place between the
Governor and the Marquis of Casa Calvo upon that Subject. I well remember
that Shortly after the Governors [*sic*] illness and while he was Still low and
very feeble I found him at his Table writing. I censured him for attending to
Business So early, while his Health and even life was in So precarious a
State and requested him to retire to his chamber— He replied that the occasion was Such as to make it necessary for him to act, that by translations
of letters from the Marquis of Casa Calvo just received, he had learned that
the Marquis had attempted to use Judicial authority in Louisiana. He
added that information to this effect had been before given him, but that he
had discredited it in consequence the verbal explanations of the Marquis
and of Don André his Secretary. The Governor Seemed very much hurt on
the occasion, and regretted that the Translator for the Government had So
long delayed furnishing him with Translations. I further remember to have
been present at a conversation between the Governor and Mr. Derbigny
the Translator for the Government upon the Subject of the Marquis's Letters.
The Governor lamented the delay, and said that it had Subjected him to
embarrassment and censure, and that his Silence might have encouraged the
Marquis to a proceeding which was highly improper. Mr. Derbigny replyed
[*sic*] that he himself equally regretted the delay, that being uninformed of the
importance of the Letters they had been laid aside with many other Papers
for translation and forgotten or neglected by the Press of Business, otherwise
translations would have been earlier made. This transaction took place
Somewhere about the first of September 1804[.]

(Signed) *John Watkins*

New Orleans
Jany 18th 1805

1. Also printed in TP, 9: 377, but there dated January 21, 1805.

{104}
CERTIFICATE [DEPOSITION] OF THOMAS SEILLES KENNEDY[1]

The undersigned has for Some time past been employed in the Office of
Governor Claiborne—[2] To the best of his recollection he thinks that about

the last of July or the first of August in the year 1804 Mr. Edward Livingston handed a Petition to Governor Claiborne, and Said it was upon the Subject of the Marquis of Casa Calvo's improper interference about Some Slaves, and that after Some little conversation the particulars of which he does not recollect, the Governor Said he would take the Subject of the Petition into consideration— About the time this Petition was handed in Mrs. Claiborne was taken Sick and the Governor himself was complaining every day of being more or less indisposed, and was at last on the 9th day of August taken ill of the yellow fever— Early in September the translator for the Government Mr. Derbigny handed in translations of two letters from the Marquis of Casa Calvo which had been written in June— I heard the Governor regret exceedingly the delay of the translations saying in Substance that they were important Letters and ought to have been Sooner received, Since they confirmed certain improper proceedings of the Marquis in relation to Some Negroes, concerning which he heretofore heard Some reports, but did not credit them.

The Governor immediately Set about answering those Letters, he was then in a Low State of Health[.] I recollect advising him frequently not to attend to Business in his then debilitated Situation, but he replied, "the Letters of the Marquis are of Such a nature as to render an immediate answer necessary,["] I have also heard the Governor Say that the Marquis and the former Intendant Morales were at varience and that the Marquis was So Solicitous to prove the Malconduct of Morales that he had gone So far even, as to take the deposition of Slaves[.]

(Signed) *Thomas Seilles Kennedy*

New Orleans
Jany 18th 1805

1. Also published as Certificate of Thomas S. Kennedy, January 18, 1805, TP, 9: 375–6, with variations in punctuation.

2. A native of Maryland, Kennedy is sometimes referred to as Thomas, Thomas L., or Thomas S. His correct middle initial apparently is S., for Seilles, although it is spelled as Sirlles in one place in Dunbar Rowland's edition of the Claiborne letter books. See The United States To Wm. C. C. Claiborne. . . . For Sundry Disbursements during the Temporary Government, CLB, 3: 90, No. 5, for the incorrect spelling. The List of Civil and Military Officers, April 21, 1809, TP, 9: 836, Clerk of the City Court of New Orleans, identifies Kennedy as a native of Maryland. Thomas Seilles Kennedy began service as a clerk in Claiborne's office in July 1804 and continued to work for the governor until sometime in May 1805, when he was appointed clerk of court. The United States To Wm. C. C. Claiborne, CLB, 3: 90, No. 5; Governor Claiborne to the Secretary of State, February 21, 1805; and Register of Civil Appointments in the

Territory of Orleans, February 13, 1806, in John Graham to the Secretary of State, February 13, 1806, TP, 9: 395, 598. Claiborne described Kennedy's secretarial services in 1804 and 1805 as "indispensible" (*sic*) and "faithful." See Gov. Claiborne to Albert Gallatin, August 17, 1805, CLB, 3: 172. It apparently was Kennedy, with John Watkins and James Workman, who held Claiborne's office together when the governor and his family were ill with yellow fever in July, August, and September 1804. Kennedy was reappointed clerk of court in the spring of 1807 and again in 1809. A Register of Civil Appointments, June 30, 1807, Clerks, and List of Civil and Military Officers, April 21, 1809, Clerk of the City Court of New Orleans, TP, 9: 749, 836, respectively. During the War of 1812, Kennedy was commissioned by Claiborne to serve as a lieutenant in the First Regiment of the State Militia. Claiborne to Col. I. B. Labatut, January 5, 1812, CLB, 6: 29.

{105}
CERTIFICATE [DEPOSITION] OF JOHN KIDDER[1]

I certify that I was Editor of the Paper called the Union, when a piece in Broken English signed Serpent D'eau was published— I believe Governor Claiborne knew nothing of that piece until he Saw it in Print, for he immediately after expressed to me his great regret at the publication, Saying that every thing Should be avoided that might tend to irritate the Public mind. I further Certify that I never did consult Gov. Claiborne what I should or Should not publish— The Paper was conducted according to my own Judgment, and I know of no influence attempted by Governor Claiborne over the Press except a general wish, which he more than once expressed, that nothing might be published which could tend to divide or agitate the Citizens[.]

(Signed) *John Kidder*

New Orleans
Jany 18th 1805

1. Also published as Certificate of John Kidder, January 18, 1805, TP, 9: 376–7, with variations in punctuation.

{106}
FROM CASA CALVO
To His Excellency the Governor and
Intendant General of the Province of
Louisiana—[1]

Sir,

In the Judicial proceedings which I am making with your Excellency's knowledge for the purpose of Securing the Interest of the King my master in the cause prosecuted by the Royal finances against Don Pedro Villamil formerly Steward of the Royal Hospital, it appears that the Negroe and mulatto Slaves belonging to this Man have been fraudulently bought by Mr. Jolly his wife in the name of Francis Hulin, these people being afraid of the consequence of the verification are endeavouring to Sell the Slaves and Hulin has given to two of these a written permission to that effect which I have in my power consequently in order that Justice may not be frustrated, I have recourse to your Excellency, praying you to enforce the execution of my Decree of this date which will be notified by the Notary Peter Pedescloux [*sic*] to the end that neither Catherine Jolly nor Francis Hulin may alienate or dispose of any of the Slaves Sold at the Auction made by the Intendant Pro Tem— Don Juan Ventura Morales; that they may also be prevented from ill-treating them, as they pay their days work, and that the notaries be forbidden to make any Sale of the Same— until the cause be decided[.]

> May God Grant your Excellency a
> long Life.
> June 16th 1804
> (Signed) *The Marquis of Casa Calvo,*
> [*sic*]

I Certify the above to be a faithful
Translation
(Signed) *P. Derbigny*
Interpreter to the Government

---

1. It was this letter and its translation that Derbigny failed to bring to the attention of Claiborne. The unavoidable tardiness of the governor's response embarrassed him and nearly produced an international incident with Spain. Claiborne responded to Casa Calvo on September 5, 1804. For additional information, see Letter No. 185, To James Madison, [April 3,] 1805.

{107}
From Casa Calvo
TO HIS EXCELLENCY THE
GOVERNOR AND INTENDANT
GENERAL

Sir,

The Commissioner of his Catholic Majesty, who had reason to expect from your Excellency all the assistance of his Authority and faculties to Secure the Interest of the King his Master, observes with the greatest concern that without the least attention to the true informations which he had given in writing and verbally on the occasion of Don Pedro Villamil, all possible means are employed to Shackle the necessary measures, which he is taking in Business particularly relative to and peculiar of his nation. He Sees that credit is given to cabals and that attention is in preference paid to the ill-grounded pretensions of those who for private purposes are conspiring to defeat the just right of their Sovereign, and to usurp audaciously the property of his Subjects.

Placed in Such a predicament he is under the necessity of entering the most Solemn protest against the Decree issued by your Excellency's Court against Don Pedro Villamil a Spanish Subject, under frivolous pretexts and upon a false denunciation made by a certain Hulin. The undersigned has already assured your Excellency that the Sale of Villamils [*sic*] Slaves has been fraudulently made, with a view of causing the ruin of that Subject of His Majesty, after having unjustly deprived him of his Honor. He has also assured your Excellency that neither Villamil nor his Slaves Shall go out of the Province without your knowledge; and finally he has shewn to your Excellency that the Steps made by Hulin, those taken by Catherine Jolly Villamils [*sic*] wife and the machinations of their agents and favorers have no other object than to confound justice and obstruct my measures. Your Excellency will recollect that with your knowledge and assistance the undersigned is taking the necessary depositions in order to ground a rational decision on this matter, by making evident the right of His Catholic Majesty; he therefore had reason to expect from your Excellency all due attention, and that reflecting on the gravity of the Business, you would not let it be treated with the indifference he observes, but would at least do him the favor of believing what he Said, and waiting for the decision. If the apparent right of Hulin Should be hurt, he had Such recourse as the Law permits. He cannot therefore abstain from telling your Excellency that under the existing circumstances, and in a business directly connected with the Interest of the King his Master, your Excellency could not admit Mrs. Catherine Jolly to the oath of Allegiance, Since She could not herself renounce her fidelity towards her lawful Sovereign without the leave of Her Husband. Your Excellency therefore ought from the beginning to have deferred and refused to admit any petition on this Subject, much more So when the Undersigned, with due respect for the Territorial authority, assured your Excellency that you would be informed in time of whatever would occur. To pretend Sir to follow another line of conduct, is wounding the most Sacred rights of Nations. This cause has by no means any thing to do with your Excellency's Authority, nor with the Territorial priviliges [*sic*] of the United States. It would be unprecedented that his Catholic Majesty and his Subjects, by the cession of this Province to the French Republic, and the Sale made Subsequently of the Same to the United States Should be deprived of their rights of property, and even placed out of the Class of the Citizens of the Said States in the common course of Justice.

The undersigned therefore finds himself under the necessity of informing his Court and the President of the United States of these proceedings, Since he does not find in your Excellency that favorable disposition which natural rights entitle him to, which the rights of persons claim, and which he expected to obtain from the Harmony and good understanding that Subsist between both Nations, unless your Excellency be pleased to Stop and revoke the measure which you have taken, giving Such assistance as depends from your authority and leaving the undersigned at liberty to act with the prudent Liberty required by the Laws in order to secure the Interest of the King his Master and restore the property of one of his Subjects who has been violently dispossessed—

> May God grant your Excellency
> many years
> (Signed) *The Marquis of Casa Calvo*

Gov. Claiborne—
New Orleans 26th July 1804—
I certify the above translation.
P. Derbigny—

{108}
To Casa Calvo

> To His Excellency the Marquis of Casa
> Calvo
> New Orleans Sept 5th 1804[1]

Sir,

The Translator for the Government of Louisiana has this day returned to my Office translations of Your Excellencys [*sic*] Letters of the 16th June and 26th of July. The neglect of this Officer may in Some Degree be attributed to his indisposition and my own late illness. I however particularly regret the delay of the Translation of your Letter of the 16th June, because a speedy reply to it (which would have been made) might have prevented your extraordinary communication of the 26th of July the language of which I conceive highly exceptionable, and the Sentiments totally inadmissible.

The Affair of Villamil has taken a turn which I had not anticipated, and
your Excellency has exercised an Authority which I cannot approbate much
less can I enforce any Decree which you may take upon yourself to render on
this or any other occasion. I know of no Courts in Louisiana but those de-
riving their powers from the Government of the United States, nor can Judicial process issue from any other authorities. Having made these general
remarks I will proceed to give you a concise Statement of the affair of Villamil
as it falls within my knowledge, together with the part I have acted.— But
I wish it to be understood, that this Statement is offered not to Justify my
conduct to your Excellency, but Solely to place the Subject in its true point
of view. Shortly after the United States had taken possession of Louisiana and
previous to the time prescribed by treaty for the evacuation of the Province
by the Spanish forces. Don Juan Ventura Morales, late Contador of the armies and Intendant of Louisiana under the Government of Spain informed
me by Letter that "there are in the Public Deposit of this City a number of
Slaves Seized as the property of Don Pedro Villamil late Steward of the
Royal Hospital of this place in which employment the Superior Tribunal and
royal audience of accounts of Havana declared him indebted in the sum of 9734,
Dollars: for its reimbursement, as Villamil ~~as Villamil~~ not only has not furnished the Security which he had offered, but also has absented himself
from the Province and fled from its decision. His Honor the Auditor of War
has advised by his Decree of the 23rd Instant to which I have agreed, that
we should proceed to an evaluation of the Slaves by the Intelligent persons
named for that purpose;— that they Should be Sold at Public Auction and
the proceeds paid into the Treasury, giving notice in the Gazette that the public may be informed of it with a previous intimation from me, by an official
Letter as usual to your Excellency, for your cooperation as Territorial Judge.
In consequence I beg and intreat your Excellency will be pleased to give
your consent that Such notice may be given in the Moniteur, and the Sale
made at my dwelling House, that this business which concerns the revenue
may be finished with the expedition recommended to be by the Tribunal of
accounts with the further additions of damages and expences [sic] which
may accrue from the delay. I flatter myself your Excellency will have less difficulty in acceding to my request, inasmuch, as by So doing without injuring the rights of your Government, you will give an unequivocal proof of your
disposition to afford protection to the affairs, in which my Sovereign has
So great an Interest as what I have before mentioned[.]"

In my reply to the above Letter the Sale was assented to under an impression that the Statement of Mr. Morales was correct, that the decision of

the Superior Tribunal of Havanna was founded in Justice, and that the Sale
of the negroes would tend to promote the Interest of the King of Spain and
to draw to a close the operations of his Catholic Majestys [sic] Officers in
Louisiana, which were essential to a Speedy and complete evacuation of
the Province. The Sale I understood Shortly thereafter took place, and that a
Mr. Hulin a Citizen of Louisiana became the purchaser. I do not recollect
to have heard any thing further upon the Subject until the receipt of your Excellency's Letter of the 12th of May in which you remarked "I have received a Dispatch from the Royal Tribunal of accounts of Havana, to the end
of taking cognizance without the interference of Mr. John Ventura Morales
heretofore intendant of these Provinces, of the collection of the Kings revenue
whereof a Debtor Mr. Pedro Villamil receiver of the Royal Hospital of this
place, and it being necessary to make *Some researches* for the purpose of veri-
fying certain *Judicial proceedings* wherein the aforesaid Intendant has gone
beyond his faculties inasmuch as he has not obeyed the orders of the above
mentioned Superior Tribunal. I inform your Excellency of this circumstance with a view of obtaining the necessary assistance to enable me to terminate this business as Soon as possible, and the permission authorizing Peter
Pedesclaux formerly the Notary of the Government under the Spanish Dominion to act in this instance[.]"

To the above request I acceded from a conviction that the contemplated
researches was an investigation of the Official conduct of the late Intendant. I deemed it improper to withhold from your Excellency any of the Records of this Province which might throw light on that conduct, and
accordingly in my Letter of the 16th of May, you were advised that "I had
no objection to Mr. Peter Pedesclaux's assisting you in *the researches* you
were charged to make, and taking for your use, *extracts from or copies of
Such Judicial proceedings,* as may be on file in any of the Offices in Louisiana[.]"
From Subsequent conversations between us, I inferred that in addition to an
investigation of the Intendants [sic] conduct your *researches* in Villamils
[sic] affairs, were designed to enable you to aid Villamil in the prosecution of
a claim to the Negroes in question, before a competent Tribunal. But *I
never until this day supposed* that your Excellency would have thought yourself authorized to exercise Judicial Powers in Louisiana, and to make Decrees which were obligatory.—

Your Letter of the 16th June was delivered to me on the Same day by Mr.
Peter Pedesclaux, who through an Interpreter informed me that it related
to Villamils [sic] affair, and was of a nature to require my prompt interference, that you represented the Sale to Hulin as a fraudulent Transaction,

and that the Negroes were in fact Still the property of Villamil— Mr. Pedesclaux added, that Hulin was at that time endeavoring to make Sale of the
negroes, and that your Excellency Solicited me to notify the notaries public
in this City of the fraud Suggested, in order that no person might purchase
the Said Negroes without information of the exception which would be taken
to the Title.

Relying on the accuracy of Mr. Pedesclaux's Statement, desirous of preventing any Citizen of Louisiana from being benefitted by a fraudulent
transaction or imposing on others, and to manifest at the Same time a respectful attention to your Excellencys representations, I addressed to the Notary
Peter Pedesclaux a note of which the enclosed, *marked A²* is a copy intending
to apply particularly to your Letter as Soon as a Translation was furnished
by the translator for the Government Mr. Derbigny to whom, as is usual the
original was immediately transmitted[.]

I refer you to *that Letter* to the Notary, and on perusing it you will find
no part, that can be construed as Sanctioning any Decree of yours.— The
Notary is only informed "that the transaction has been represented to me as
fraudulent," and "to make known the Same to all persons, who may apply
for the Drawing or Registering Bills of Sale for the Slaves aforesaid with a
view that no person might purchase these Slaves or any of them without a
knowledge of the exceptions which might be taken to the Titles." *I know not*
to what your Excellency alludes when you Speak of a decree rendered by
my Court in this affair. No Judgment or Decree has been rendered by me, a
Suit commenced by Hulin against Villamil, but as it has not come to Trial
I remain uninformed of the merits of the case.

The charges contained in your Letter, that "credit is given to cabals, and
that attention, is in preference paid to the ill-grounded pretensions of those
who for private purposes are conspiring to defeat the just right of your Sovereign and to usurp audaciously the property of his Subjects" and further that
property the Subjects of His Catholic Majesty "are even placed out of the
class of Citizens of the United States in the common course of Justice" deserve
Sir, no other notice from me than a declaration that they are as illiberal as
they are groundless, and I must pray your Excellency in any future communications you may think proper to make to *the chief magistrate* of Louisiana,
to use a language less exceptionable and to manifest more respect for the integrity and Independence of his character. Hulin is in the peaceable possession
of certain Slaves, and of that possession he cannot be deprived, but by the Law
of the Land, and the agency of the constituted authorities of Louisiana. If Villamil has a claim to these Slaves, the Courts are open to him, and that Jus-

tice will be rendered which every Suitor receives in the Judiciary of the United States. If Villamil has in his possession Slaves which Hulin claims, he may likewise appeal to the Same Tribunals[.]

The moment a Subject of his Catholic Majesty or any other foreign power Sits his foot on the Territory of Louisiana, he is bound to respect our Laws, and for a breach of them is held responsible; he is also under the protection of the Same laws, and may appeal to them for a redress of any injury received. It was not necessary therefore to administer to Mrs[.] Jolly or to Hulin the oath of allegiance to the United States (nor has it been done to enable them to apply to the Courts of Louisiana for the maintenance of their rights[)]. Before I conclude this communication I must inform your Excellency that the menace in the last Sentence of your Letter will not in the least influence my conduct. To your boast Sir I owe no responsibility— I nevertheless Should be wanting in my duty, were I not *on all proper occasions* to manifest a readiness to Support the Interest of ~~the~~ an ally of the United States— With respect to your intended representation to the President of the United States, I can only observe, that it cannot fail to terminate Honorably to the officer who discharges the trust reposed in him with integrity and firmness.

> Accept assurances of my Respect and
> High Consideration
> (Signed) *William C. C. Claiborne*

His Excellency
The Marquis of
Casa Calvo—

1. Published as To the Marquis of Casa Calvo, September 5, 1804, CLB, 2: 320–5, with variations in punctuation and without the emphasis found here.
2. Not present.

{109}
FROM CASA CALVO
To His Excellency The Governor And
Intendant General &c &c

Sir,
The answer which you have been pleased to send me Dated the 5th Instant, opens a field to go into Polemical disputes of a disagreeable nature. I have examined over again my Official Letters of the 16th of June and 26th of July,

and I find nothing in them that can deserve the acrimony of expressions
which your Excellency in your last Letter used. I would not be Surprized to
See your Excellency defending with firmness his rights and priviliges, as
well those belonging to your office and authority as those which are relative
to the Citizens of the United States, but it has caused me much Sensation
that your Excellency Should have taken the trouble of advising me, nay in a
manner teaching me the respect which I owe to the Integrity and Independence of your character. Really I do not know that your Excellency has made
use of the Same consideration towards the person whom I have the Honor
to represent here, when upon Hulins Saying aided by his oath your Excellency
ordered Villamil to be arrested notwithstanding I had assured you in writing and *verbally* that Villamil neither *retained the Slaves* in question nor
would absent himself out of this City. My word was disregarded, Villamils
arrest was effected, and he only obtained his liberty on giving Security. I leave
it to your Excellency's consideration to appreciate my mortification, when
I was persuaded as I am Still, that my word without my oath is entitled to
more belief than Hulins Saying accompanied by a thousand formalities.
Time having Sufficiently proved the wantonness and falsity with which he
took his oath, considering *that,* why does your Excellency wonder when I
complain that the Subjects of His Catholic Majesty are in Some degree disregarded? To answer, article, by article to all the contents of your Excellency's Letter, would be too prolonging for this affair which in Spite of the
measures I had endeavored to take by writing, verbally and confidentially
with your Excellency is to my great sorrow troubling the perfect Harmony
which until now had Subsisted between our respective authorities and
Commissions[.]

    Your Excellency has taken for himself the expressions by which I Say "that
the Cabals and ill-grounded pretensions of those who for particular purposes endeavour to defeat the rights of my Sovereign." I am very far from
using them with Such intentions; but I will ~~mention~~ maintain that there is
intrigue on the part of *one* from whom I least Suspected it, for the purpose
of Supporting a conduct and caprice which has been disapproved by the
Supreme Court from which the authority was derived. In addition to my duty
and in fulfilment [*sic*] of my trust, I must endeavour to bring the truth to
light with impartiality, and to acquaint your Excellency with it So that you
may not be imposed upon. The affair of Villamil is now as clear as day light.
The Supreme Court of finances has disapproved what had been done by the
Contador Don Juan Ventura Morales. That Court declares that fraud has
been committed against the Law, in the Auction and Sale of Villamils [*sic*]

Slaves, and in consequence orders that the Business be examined into according to Justice, and that the property be replaced in its former State to Secure in a positive manner the Interest of the King. By the proceedings which have been carried on in this case it fully appears that Hulin has bought the Slaves at the Auction for Mrs Villamil, that She does not possess Sufficient property to make Such purchases, that in their depositions they both contradict one another he affirming that he left two female Slaves to Mrs Villamil to Serve her without compensation and She pretending that She used to pay him monthly their wages, it is proved that all the female Slaves paid the revenue of their daily wages into the hands of Mrs Villamil, it is also proved that after the auction, She, told herself to the Said Slaves, that although they had been Sold, She was the person who had bought them, and therefore Still was their mistress. It is fully made To appear that the Same Don Juan Ventura Morales was the very man who delivered in his own closet to the Treasurer of the Finances the Sum arising from the price of the Said Slaves, with a thousand other incidents which convince the mind, not only of those who are impartial, but even of the interested parties themselves, So as to force them to a confession of the above evident facts. I will now ask if there is any doubt or any motive of blame against my conduct, if in this case the Interests or prerogatives of the United States are at all concerned: if any individual enjoying the rights of Citizenship has any thing to do with it, for the only one who has meddled with it is no more than apparently interested as it is proved and will be formally Shewn in due time to your Excellency. Are not all my measures and provisions only applied to Subjects employed in the Service of His Catholic Majesty, who cannot have returned to this Country after its retrocession but have remained in it exercising the functions of their respective offices, for which they are answerable to their Sovereign and accordingly cannot be Subjected to the Territorial Government in this respect, but only to the Delegate of their King, to whom he has committed the necessary authority for the purpose of terminating not only the evacuation of the Province and demarkation [sic] of its limits, but also the other business therein pending, where his intervention may be requisite as in the present case which interests both the Royal Revenue, and the Justice ~~done~~ due to a faithful and honest Subject. I do not pretend to exercise all kinds of Jurisdiction in the Territory under the command of your Excellency; but by my commission and representation I may exercise the ruling economical justice towards the Subjects of His Catholic Majesty in cases which from their circumstances are totally unconnected with the Laws rights or priviliges of the Country, and which can in no manner cause any prejudice to the Territorial authority and prerogative.

That is the fact and the Situation of this case, Such has been my conduct which I will lay before my Superiors to be examined and when I tell your Excellency that I will take this Step, far from being a threat or an argument deserving your Excellency's reflection "That you owe no Responsibility to the Court of Spain" it is an act of frankness which your Excellency ought to have appreciated Since I wish that at the Same time this circumstance will be made known through my channel to the Court of Spain, the Same information may arrive to the president of the United States from your Excellency So that both Courts may resolve what they will think proper, the matter requiring an explanatory declaration unless as I told your Excellency before and now repeat you Should be disposed to consider the case, and would after being convinced of the truth of the facts which I have related give your assistance So that the course of Justice may not be embarrassed, and the interest of the King my master as well as our respective responsibilities be Served, without losing on either Side any of that decorum which is naturally due to them, for in Such a case the aforesaid information or report would become useless and be dropt.

I wish to preserve the Harmony which until now has Subsisted; I hope therefore, that your Excellency animated by the Same principle will in his correspondence adopt expressions which may not wound my character, being certain of all my consideration—

> May God grant
> your Excellency a Long life—
> (Signed) *The Marquis of Casa Calvo*

New Orleans
Sept. 12. [*sic*] 1804
His Excellency
Gov. Claiborne

I certify the above Translation
(Signed)— P. Derbigny Interpt &c

{110}
To the Mayor of New Orleans
New Orleans January 20th 1805
To the Mayor of New Orleans[1]

Sir,

I have received your Letter of the ——— Instant.[2] The Trespass committed by a Citizen on the Commons of the City, is a Subject which falls within the

Judicial Department, and it will be the duty of the Attorney General to take the necessary measures to obtain redress, I persuade myself that the Records and Papers of Mr. Ximines's Office have been delivered to the Members of the Municipality who were appointed to receive them. But lest this may not be the case I enclose you an order to Mr. Ximines to deliver to you Such papers relating to the property of the City as may be in his Possession.

> I am Sir very Respectfully
> Your obdt Hbe St—
> (Signed) *William C. C. Claiborne*

1. James Pitot. For a biographical sketch, see pp. 255–7.
2. Date left blank in the original.

{111}
TO NATHANIEL MACON
New Orleans January 21st 1805

Sir,

I have the Honour to enclose you a memorial[1] from the Legislative Council of this Territory, and to request that you would lay the Same before the House of Representatives of the United States.

> accept assurances of my great
> Respect and Sincere esteem
> (Signed) *William C. C. Claiborne*

The Honble
N. Macon
Speaker of
~~James Madison~~
~~Secty of State~~
the H. of Representatives

1. Not present.

{112}
TO JAMES MADISON
New Orleans January 21st 1805

Dear Sir,

On perusing the Copy of my Letter of the 19th Instant, I find that my feelings (when speaking of the difficulty of my Situation) led me to introduce a Military Similie [*sic*], which is inapplicable and improper— You will oblige me therefore, if you will correct that part of my Letter of the 19th instant where the Similie of the forlorne Hope appears,[1] in Such manner as to make it read "I considered myself as Sent on an undertaking Hazardous to my Political reputation, and placed in a station where every Arm raised against me was raised to advantage—["]

> I am Sir very Respectfully
> Your obt St
> (Signed) *William C. C. Claiborne*

The Secty of State

---

1. The passage may be found in Letter No. 102, To James Madison, January 19, 1805.

{113}
To Commissioner of Police
New Orleans January 22nd 1805

Sir,

In Conformity to your Letter of this morning, I have given the necessary orders for the immediate repair of the Chimneys of the Government House.

The precautionary measures taken by the Police with respect to Chimneys are wise and prudent, and as a Citizen and an officer, I cannot but approve your vigilance.

> I am Sir very Respectfully
> Your Obt Hbe St
> (Signed) *William C. C. Claiborne*

Mr. Rivere[1]
Commissary General
of Police—

---

1. Probably Pierre Achille Rivière, who is listed as commissioner of police in Mayor Etienne de Boré's administration. See "Biographies of the Mayors of New Orleans," comp. and ed. Works Project Administration (project 665-64-3-112; typescript; New Orleans, May 1939), 1, where his surname is spelled as "Rivery." It is most likely he is the same Rivière whose plantation home served as a polling place in the elections of 1805 and 1806. See the reference to A Similar Letter..., which follows To James Pitot, July 24, 1805, CLB, 3: 136, and Proclamation by Governor Claiborne, July 26, 1805, and Writ of Election, March 10, 1806, TP, 9: 479, 666, respectively.

{114}

To James Madison

New Orleans January 26th 1805[1]

Sir,

I enclose you the third Number of the Public accuser.[2] You will see the gall
of my enemies, and the zeal with which they embrace every occurrence to
annoy my feelings. I feel as if I was trespassing upon your important duties
in Soliciting your attention for one moment to News paper publications.— But
when you perceive the malignity of my opponents I trust you will excuse the
desire I manifest to keep the Executive advised of my answers to the
charges exhibited.

With respect to the Militia I need only observe that my conduct was Such
as duty prescribed and my Judgment approved.— The formation of the
Volunteer Corps was a Matter of expediency. In acknowledging the Battalion
of free people of colour[3] and presenting to them a Standard I acted in conformity to instructions from the Secretary of War, and the delay attending the organization of the Militia generally was the result of necessity. As to the
Guard Stationed at the Government House, it consists only of a Corporal and
three men who are designed to give Security to the Records of the Province
(delivered to the Commissioners) which are deposited in a Room on the
ground floor[.] I do not know that any person would feel a disposition to
disturb those Records, but as they are important and their present Situation
Somewhat insecure, it Seemed to me that (during the continuance of the
Troops in this City) there would a propriety in having a Centinel placed at
the Government House. As to the orderly guard alluded to, I was during
the Provisional Government, furnished every day with a Sergeant, who carried Messages, Letters &c from my office, and as I find Such a character
Still useful I continue to avail myself of the Politeness of the Commanding
Officer in this particular.

Upon the Subject of Lieutenant Doyles marriage my conduct has been cruelly misrepresented, and I Strongly Suspect that my Enemies have carried
their Malignity So far, as to have obtained (by artifice[)] from a young Creole,
who Speaks but a few words of English, a Statement upon oath, which does
not contain a Single fact. Mr. Doyles marriage was not with me an object of
any concern; I know the young Man only by name, his folly I regretted,
but the elopement being effected I thought it best to prevent the girl from
being dishonored to permit the Marriage— A License however was not
granted until the father Solicited it, and the part I acted was alone dictated

by the feelings of benevolence. The representation of Mr. Orso altho on oath, as to my agency in the Business is without the least foundation. Several Gentlemen having a knowledge of the facts attending the Marriage have furnished me with certificates upon the Subject which are herewith enclosed Marked Nos. 1.2 &c[.]

I do not know that I Shall again trouble you with any remarks on anonimous writers— I feel as if you would deem them unworthy of Serious attention— But really when Such a deposition as Mr. Orso's can be obtained I fear that neither integrity[,] prudence or any other virtue can Shield the reputation of a public officer from malignant calumniators.

> I am Sir very Respectfully
> Your obt St.
> (Signed) *William C. C. Claiborne*

The Honble
James Madison
Secretary of State

P.S. The Petition Published was I believe wrote [*sic*] by myself— The friend of Doyle (a Mr. Randall) besought a written application for a License, but being improper, I gave a form of a Petition, which form he preserved and by way of revenge because I would not make him an Auctioneer he has given it to the writer of the accuser.

W. C. C. C—

The Scty of State

1. Published as Governor Claiborne to the Secretary of State, January 26, 1805, TP, 9: 380–2 with variations in punctuation and text with only the Certificate (deposition) by John Watkins. The other certificates (depositions) referenced in ibid., 381 n. 31, plus one more by Lt. Joseph Taylor, follow the cover letter printed here.

2. Claiborne subsequently identified the "public accuser" as Edward Livingston. See Letter No. 142, To James Madison, February 21, 1805.

3. On the black militia in these years, see Roland C. McConnell, *Negro Troops of Antebellum Louisiana: A History of the Battalion of Free Men of Color* (Baton Rouge: Louisiana State University Press, 1968), particularly pp. 33–45.

{115}
CERTIFICATE [DEPOSITION] OF GEORGE KING
> Here follows the Certificates alluded to
> in the above Letter—
> New Orleans January 23rd 1805—[1]

I Certify that Lieutenant Doyle informed me, previous and Subsequent to his Marriage of the particulars of his elopement with Mnlle Orso, and I

never understood that the Governor had any other Agency in the Business
than giving a License. I further certify that when Mr. Doyle did elope he
came with the young Lady to my House, and was immediately followed by
Thomas Randall—This Gentleman was dispatched to the Governor for a
license and returned without it, Stating Some difficulty in the business, which
made Doyle very uneasy—Randall went a Second time to the Governor and
a Second time returned without A License, Saying that the Governor would
not grant it them unless at the request of the Parents of the Young Lady—
Mr. Doyle and the Lady walked to my House, and I never heard a Carriage
mentioned by either of them.

(Signed) George King

1. Referred to in Governor Claiborne to the Secretary of State, January 26, 1805, TP, 9:
381 n. 31, but not printed there.

{116}
Certificate [Deposition] of Lt. William Murry
New Orleans Jany 23rd 1805[1]

I do Certify that Lieutenant Doyle (in his lifetime, and previous to, and Subsequent to his Marriage[)], communicated to me the particulars of his elopement with Mademoiselle Orso—I was informed by Said Doyle of his
arrangement on the occasion, and I never understood that he had been assisted in the affair by the Governor in any other way than by his obtaining a
license, and even that was obtained with difficulty—

(Signed) William Murry
Lieutenant of the United States
Artillery

1. Referred to in Governor Claiborne to the Secretary of State, January 26, 1805, TP, 9:
381 n. 31, but not printed there.

{117}
Certificate [Deposition] of James W. Lanier[1]

I Certify that I was at the Principal on the night on which Lieutenant Doyle
failed in his attempt to elope with Miss Orso.—I was also present on the
night on which he Succeeded, and acted as the friend of Doyle—I further Certify that on neither of the nights did I See Governor Claiborne at the Principal, nor was his Carriage in waiting to my knowledge, the only Agency I ever

understood the Governor had in the Business was (after the elopement) to grant a License of Marriage, and then I was informed he would not do it, until the father of the Young Lady had consented.

(Signed) *James W. Lanier—*

January 23rd 1805

1. Referred to in Governor Claiborne to the Secretary of State, January 26, 1805, TP, 9: 381 n. 31, but not printed there.

{118}
CERTIFICATE [DEPOSITION] OF JOHN W. GURLEY[1]

Some time in the Month of April last I recollect being in the Office of Governor Claiborne, when Mr. Thomas Randall came in and Stated that a Lieutenant Doyle of the United States Army had that evening eloped with a young Lady whose name I do not remember, and that they were at the House of a Gentleman in this City. He Stated that they were very Solicitous to be married, and that he came from the place where they then were, at their request to Solicit the Governor for a License. The Governor I remember Stated to Mr. Randall that he could not grant a license without the consent of the Parents of the young Lady as that was essential. Mr. Randall I believe went to the House of the father of the young Girl, when Shortly after her Brother came in; Doctor Watkins was then present and I believe Mr. Randall had also returned. Doctor Watkins acted as Interpreter to what was Said— The Brother as I understood was very anxious that the Governor Should grant his license to the Marriage to Save the reputation of the family, and also requested him to call on their father. I think that Mr. Randall brought a paper which he presented as a Petition, and I am led to believe myself correct in this from the circumstance of the Governors Saying, which I perfectly recollect; that it was informal and improper, and from his writing a note and handing it to Mr. Randall Saying that Something in that form or manner would be more correct.

(Signed) *John Ward Gurley*

New Orleans
January 24th 1805

1. Referred to in Governor Claiborne to the Secretary of State, January 26, 1805, TP, 9: 381 n. 31, but not printed there.

{119}

CERTIFICATE [DEPOSITION] OF LT. JOSEPH TAYLOR[1]

On the night of ———[2] of April last I visited the Main Guard at the Principal early in the Evening with the Parole and Countersign where I remained until near tattoo, having been informed by Lieutenant Doyle that he was to elope with Miss Orso on that Evening—I do not recollect to have Seen Governor Claiborne on that Evening at or near the Principal, and to the best of my recollection, the Governor neither kept a Carriage or Carriage Horses at the period above alluded to.

(Signed) *Joseph Taylor Lieutenant*
of 2nd Regt of Infantry

New Orleans
25 Jany 1805

P.S. The Evening I allude to is that, previous to the Evening Lieut Doyle eloped with Miss Orso—
    J. T—

1. Referred to in Governor Claiborne to the Secretary of State, January 26, 1805, TP, 9: 381 n. 31, but not printed there.
2. Blank in the original.

{120}

CERTIFICATE [DEPOSITION] OF JOHN WATKINS[1]

With respect to the Marriage of Lieutenant Doyle and Miss Orso which has become a matter of News Paper Discussion, I give you the following particulars as coming within my knowledge.

On the Evening of the elopement I went to the Governors where I found him and Mr. Gurley conversing upon the Subject, which till then I had never heard of. The Governor Stated to me that he had just received information of the parties being together in a private house, and read to me a petition from them praying a License which he added would not be ~~granted~~ obtained without first obtaining the consent of the Parents of the young Lady. At this moment Mr. Thomas Randall came into the Room and was requested by the Governor (as he Spoke French and knew Mr. Orso's family) to wait upon the old Gentleman, and inform him that the Governor wished to See him upon the unfortunate Subject of his Daughters marriage. Mr. Randall Soon returned and Stated that Mr. Orso himself was ill & in bed, but that his Son had promised to come, who accordingly entered a few minutes after. Young Mr. Orso appeared greatly distressed, excused his fathers not complying with the Governors request and observed that a visit from his Excellency might Soothe the old Gentlemans mind, and would be gratefully acknowledged by the whole family.— The Governor consented to go under the impression that a reconciliation might be brought about, and asked me to accompany him. We found the family in the greatest distress. The old Gentleman was in bed and appeared to be deeply and Sincerely affected. The Governor regretted what had happened, told him that he had been Solicited to grant them a license; but that he would not do it without his consent and asked him what he wished to be done? The old Gentleman replyed [*sic*] that of two evils he would choose the least, and that although nothing Should ever induce him to be reconciled to them, yet he could wish that Since they were already together that the Marriage might take place immediately and prayed that his Excellency would See it accomplished— The Governor assured him that he would— The old man then took the Governor by the hand, and in Tears thanked him for Such marks of condescension and goodness— We retired and the ceremony was performed by Father Walsh between 10 and 11 oclock that night in the presence of the Governor and several reputable private Gentlemen.

I was fully persuaded at the time and do Still fully believe that the whole of the Governors conduct relative to this affair was governed by the purest motives of benevolence and the most conscientious regard for the reputation and happiness of the parties concerned[.] I view his agency in this affair not only as blameless, but as one of the most virtuous and praise-worthy acts ever performed by him or any other member of Society— I view in it the Salvation of innocence, and the laudable attempt to heal the wounds of an afflicted father.

(Signed) *John Watkins*

New Orleans 23rd Jany 1805—

1. Also published as Certificate of John Watkins, January 22, 1805, TP, 9: 382–3, but dated one day earlier than the document here and with variations in the text and punctuation.

{121}
To James Madison
New Orleans January 27th 1805

Sir,

The last northern Mail met with a misfortune. The Rider represented that about 12 Leagues from this City, he was thrown from his Horse in the night and when he overtook him the Portmanteau was missing. It was found a few days ago by an Inhabitant floating in the Mississippi near the Shore and was immediately forwarded by the Civil Commandant of the District to me. The Portmanteau had been forced open. The Letters and papers were very wet, but it did not appear that they had been examined. Many however are Supposed to have been lost. It is probable the Horse after flinging the Rider (who I supposed was Drunk) was met by Some person who opened the Portmanteau in Search of cloathing [*sic*] or money, and finding none threw it down near the Waters edge[.]

This misfortune delayed the departure of the mail from here to Washington for one Week. I have nothing of importance to communicate. The Council are Still in Session and their proceedings evince much prudence. The Members are of opinion, that their per Diem allowance should be paid out of the Treasury of the United States, and are desirous of receiving their compensation. If an appropriation for this object has been made, I will thank you to inform me thereof.

The intercourse between the white Citizens and the Indians West of the Mississippi is at present not Subject to much restraint. Since the first of october [*sic*] Several persons have carried on Trade with the Indians without License, and not having myself received instructions upon the Subject I feel a delicacy in interfering, and the more So, Since by the act for the Government of the Territory, the duties of Superintendant of Indian Affairs does not devolve upon the Governor.— I wish Sir you would mention this Subject to the President. if [*sic*] the intercourse with the Indians is not carefully guarded disputes will Soon arise— At present the most perfect good understanding exists, and until I receive your orders I shall give Such instructions from time to time to the Commandants of Frontier Posts as are best calculated to preserve the existing harmony.

> I have the Honor to be Sir
> very Respectfully your
> Most Obdt Hbe St
> (Signed) *William C. C. Claiborne*

The Honble
James Madison
Secty of State

{122}
TO EDWARD DEMARESQUE TURNER
New Orleans January 28th 1805

Sir,

Your Letter of the 22nd of December was duly received.— I persuade myself that the Masters of the Slaves you allude to, have consented to their liberation, and if So that in conformity to my last Letter to you they have been released from Prison. The Legislature are now engaged in framing a Law providing for the Speedy Trial and Punishment of Slaves who Shall commit offences. The Subject is an important one; and requires deliberation, but I expect the law will pass in Six or eight days[.]

In the case of the Person whom you have confined in consequence of an attempt to defraud the Creditors of his Testator, I cannot give you any instructions inasmuch as my Judicial Powers have ceased Since the first of October, and you know the danger (under our Government) of the Executive interposing with the Judicial Department. I however perceive in your Conduct on the occasion a disposition to be just, and in any further Steps you may take your own prudence and judgment will be your best guides. Altho my Judicial Powers have ceased, yet yours as Civil Commandant continue, and have lately been fully recognized by an act of the Territorial Legislature.

On any other Subject ~~but~~ than one of a Judicial nature I Shall not hesitate to give you my advice when desired; but your own reflections will Shew you the delicacy of my present Situation So far as relates to the Judiciary. Present me respectfully to your Lady, and believe me to be with esteem Sir,

Your most obdt Hble St

(Signed) *William C. C. Claiborne*

Capt Turner
Natchitoches

{123}
TO JAMES MADISON
New Orleans January 13th 1805

Sir,

The incipient Capital of the Louisiana Bank has been Subscribed and the following Gentlemen elected Directors to wit— Paul Lanuse, James Pitot, Julien Poydrass, Daniel Clark, Michael Fortier, John Soulie, Thomas L Harman, Thomas Urquhart, William Donaldson, John F Merieult, Francis

Duplisses, James Carrick, John McDonough, John B[.] Labuttut and Nicholas Girod—

The People have of late received an opinion that a Bank would be of great Public Utility, and notwithstanding they were advised of the doubt which existed as to the validity of the charter, they were determined to make the experiment. The Civil Government here will very Soon I trust be perfectly organized, and then unless our differences with Spain Should assume an unfriendly aspect, there will be no necessity for more than one Company of regular Troops in this City; the balance may be ordered to Plaquemine, and our Frontier Posts where they may be Serviceable;— The enclosed Letter which I have this moment received from the Commanding officer at Natchitoches will Shew you the great increase of the Spanish force in the Province of Taxus [Texas].

> I am sir very Respectfully
> Your Hble St
> (Signed) *William C. C. Claiborne*

The Honble
James Madison
Secretary of State

{124}
TO JAMES MADISON
New Orleans January 14th 1805[1]

Sir,

I have this moment received your Letter of the fifteenth of December enclosing my Commission[2] as Governor of the Territory of Orleans with the approval of the Senate and Sundry other Commissions for officers of the Territory of Orleans. I am greatly indebted to the Government for their renewed confidence, and I pray you to be assured that every effort will be used by me, to Support and advance the Interest of my Country. Your instructions concerning the Hero have in part been anticipated; all the French and most of the English have landed— Some of the Latter from considerations of humanity have been placed in the Marine Hospital as was Stated in a former Letter, and I learn the Vessel will depart in a few days. Your opinion and instructions relative to the introduction of Slaves into the Mississippi Shall regulate my conduct.—

> I have the Honor to be with
> Respect and Esteem Sir
> your most obt Sevt

(Signed) William C. C. Claiborne

The Honble
James Madison
Secty of State

1. Published as Governor Claiborne to the Secretary of State, January 14, 1805, TP, 9: 368–9.

2. See Commission of Governor Claiborne, December 12, 1804, ibid., 351.

{125}
To Ferdinand Leigh Claiborne[1]
New Orleans Jany 29th 1805[2]

Sir,

    I enclose you a Commission for Mr. Wooldridge[3] as Civil Commandant of the District of Concordia which I will thank you to deliver— You will be pleased also to deliver to Mr. Wooldridge all the Papers and Records belonging to that Post and take his receipt for the Same—

I am Sir very Respectfully
your Hbe St
(Signed) William C. C. Claiborne

Major Claiborne
Natchez

1. Brief biographical information on this older brother of the governor is in Letter No. 165, n.1.

2. Published as Governor Claiborne to Ferdinand L. Claiborne, January 29, 1805, TP, 9: 386–7.

3. L. Wooldridge probably was related to Dr. John Watkins through his mother, Elizabeth Watkins Wooldridge, later Moss. John Hale Stutesman, *Some Watkins Families of Virginia and Their Kin: Abbott, Anderson, Bass, Clay, Cox, Farrar, Hancock, Hundley, Montague, Moseley, Randolph, Walthall, Wooldridge* (Baltimore: Gateway Press, 1989), 248. Samuel Wooldridge, a kinsman of L. Wooldridge, served as U.S. marshal in Natchez in 1806. Ibid., 253.

{126}
To Washita (Ouachita) Commandant
New Orleans January 29th 1805[1]

Sir,

    I received a late Letter from you Stating Some difficulty with respect to the Indian Intercourse. Since the first of October my former powers relating to

Indians have ceased, and being without instructions upon the Subject from the Government, I feel a delicacy in prescribing any general rules for your Guide— I however am of opinion that you did right in Stopping the Trader who proposed to pass up the Washita, and for the present you will not permit the person alluded to, or any other one, except those who were licensed by me to trade with Indians unless Such person Shall be of good character, and in no instance will you permit any person to pass into the Indian Territory as a Trader unless he Shall give Bond payable to the Governor of the Territory and his Successors in Office with Security for four thousand Dollars, with a condition that he will traffic with the Indians for Peltry alone and that no other article Shall be taken in exchange for his goods.[2] This Condition I esteem necessary to prevent any person or persons under colour of a Trading Voyage from passing into the Spanish Country for the purpose of taking Horses or of encouraging the Indians to do So, a Species of Trespass which if not prevented might involve us in disputes with our Spanish neighbors[.]

> I am Sir very Respectfully
> your &c
> (Signed) *William C. C. Claiborne*

To The Commandant
at Washita—

1. Published as Governor Claiborne to Joseph Bowmar, January 29, 1805, TP, 9: 387. See pp. 578–9 herein for a short biographical sketch of Bowmar.
2. Governor Claiborne to Joseph Bowmar, January 29, 1805, TP, 9: 387 n. 43, points out that Governor Claiborne transmitted applications for trading licenses to the secretary of war, who acted on them after consulting with the president.

{127}
To James Pitot
New Orleans January 30th 1805

Sir,

The Legislature of this Territory having authorized the Governor thereof to borrow for the Public use a Sum of money not exceeding five thousand Dollars, I have the Honour thro you to address the Municipality on the Subject, and to ask whether any and what Sum, they could conveniently loan the Territory and upon what Terms.

The Law authorizing the Loan is enclosed, which I pray you to lay before the Municipality— Permit me to add that fifteen hundred or two thousand dollars would for the present answer the calls of the Government and I persuade myself that the Municipality will be enabled without injuring the City to Loan that amount for a few months.

I am Sir with great Respect
and Esteem your
most obdt st
(Signed) *William C. C. Claiborne*

The Honble
James Pitot
Mayor of
New Orleans

{128}
To Edward Demaresque Turner
New Orleans February 1st 1805

Sir,

Having understood by a Gentleman lately from your District that the Negroes who escaped to Nacogdoches Some time Since, and are now in confinement were dangerous persons of established bad fame, and that their liberation would give alarm to the good Citizens, I advise that they be detained in Safe Custody until liberated by due course of Law. The Suggestion made in a former Letter, that I had no objection to their liberation, provided their Masters wished it, I hope you have not acted upon.— But if they have been released from confinement, and their going at large Should give any uneasiness to your Society, I advise that they be immediately arrested.— Their further Support while in confinement may be at the public expense.

I am Sir very Respectfully
Your obdt St
(Signed) *William C. C. Claiborne*

Captain Turner
Natchitoches

{129}
To John Bishop Prevost
New Orleans February 2nd 1805[1]

Sir,

The Bearer Mr. Pailette it Seems having been appointed by the Civil Commandant of Natchitoches administrator of the estate of John Soburn[2] Deceased, has attended in this City to take charge of the Estate of the Said Deceased: But finding that another administrator has been appointed by the Superior Court, he knows not how to proceed. Under these circumstances I have taken the Liberty to request Mr. Pailette to State his case to the Judge— If there is any thing improper in this request I hope you will excuse me. The Citizens of this Territory are So accustomed to apply to the officers of Government for their advice, that we Shall for Some time be Subjected to frequent applications—

> I am Sir, your obdt St
> (Signed) *William C. C. Claiborne*

The Honble
Judge Prevost

    1. Also printed as Governor Claiborne to Judge Prevost, February 1, 1805, TP, 9: 389, with slight differences in spelling and punctuation. John B. Prevost was from the state of New York. He arrived in New Orleans to assume his duties as judge of the Superior Court on the evening of October 28, 1804. Letter No. 27, To James Madison, October 29, 1804. Originally, three judges were to have been appointed to assume the judicial duties in Orleans Territory, but others did not accept appointment for some months. As a consequence, Judge Prevost functioned alone under the increasingly heavy court load. Claiborne welcomed Prevost warmly, but in time their relationship cooled as Prevost became friends with Robert Livingston and others who opposed the policies of Claiborne and the Jefferson administration.

    2. This last name is spelled Sobuir in Governor Claiborne to Judge Prevost, February 2, 1805, TP, 9: 389.

{130}
To William Bayard Shields
New Orleans February 4th 1805[1]

Sir,

    I have the Honor to enclose you an abstract of all the Warrants or orders of Survey issued by the Spanish authorities in the District of Natchez. This Abstract is taken from the Records delivered to the American commissioners and was made out by a Gentleman of respectability Specially[2] employed for the purpose by the late Secretary Mr. Brown.[3]

    I will thank you to inform me your opinion as to the mode of compensating this Gentleman for his Services—and whether the Sum is to be fixed and paid by you or myself—[4]

> I am Sir with Respect
> and Esteem your Hbe St

(Signed) *William C. C. Claiborne*

William B. Shields Esqr
Natchez

1. Published as Governor Claiborne to William B. Shields, February 4, 1805, TP, 9: 389, with slight differences in text and punctuation.

2. Probably Carlos Ximines. See To James Brown, March 18, 1806, and Message to the Legislature, May 26, 1806, CLB, 3: 272, 311, respectively.

3. James Brown.

4. Shields apparently was acting as land agent for the United States. See Governor Claiborne to William B. Shields, February 4, 1805, TP, 9: 389 n. 48.

{131}

TO JAMES MADISON

New Orleans February 6th 1805[1]

Sir,

The Press in this City is indeed becoming licencious;— it even menaces the Tranquility of private life— But hitherto the executive of the Territory has been the principal object of abuse— I am happy however to add that the Louisianians have no concern in the abusive publications and very generally disapprove of them; the discontented party are composed principally of Natives of the United States, and I am enclined to think their number very inconsiderable. The Legislative Council do not proceed to Business with all the dispatch which Several influential Americans who are here desire; they are Solicitous that a Code of Laws, and Principles of Practice to which they have been accustomed Should be introduced, and are So impatient of delay that I fear ~~Some~~ former regulations will be too Suddenly innovated upon, and that the American System of Jurisprudence will be more generally adopted, than the present Situation of the Territory will justify.

Finding in this City Several Public Buildings unoccupied by Public officers, I permitted private Citizens to use the Same, upon their agreeing to pay Such Rent per month, as three disinterested men Should Say was just; in this Situation is the old Custom House, and a Building (formerly appropriated as a Stable) Which Mr. Bradford[2] a Printer at present occupies: it is not yet ascertained what Rent those Houses are to bring, but you Shall be advised thereof in due time, and the Same Shall be accounted for.

Colonel Freeman occupies a Public Building gratis, the Barracks not affording him comfortable accommodations, and House which was formerly possessed by Priests I have not interfered with— The House ~~formerly~~ occu-

pied by Colonel Freeman was formerly the Kings School house; it was very
Much out of repair, but it has been put in fine order by the Colonel, and is
now a comfortable Building; I hope it will be appropriated to the Same object for which it was originally intended, and that it may be presented by Congress to the City—

> I am Sir very Respectfully
> Your Most obdt Sevt
> (Signed) *William C. C. Claiborne*

The Honble
James Madison
Secty of State

    1. Published as Governor Claiborne to the Secretary of State, February 6, 1805, TP, 9:
390, with slight variations in text and punctuation and with emphasis not found here.
    2. James Morgan Bradford, a native of Kentucky, purchased and published the *Union*
newspaper after his arrival in New Orleans in October 1804. Soon after acquiring the newspaper, he was named to the lucrative post of public printer. On December 20, 1804, Bradford
changed the name of the *Union* to the *Orleans Gazette*. Clarence S. Brigham, *History and Bibliography of American Newspapers, 1690–1820*, vol. 1 (1947; Westport, Conn.: Greenwood
Press, 1976), 192.

{132}

To Casa Calvo

New Orleans February 7th 1805[1]

Sir,
    I have received your Excellency's Letter of yesterday informing me of the
arrival in this City of Colonel De Lassus formerly Lieutenant Governor of
Illinois, with thirty Privates of the Regiment of Louisiana on their way to Pensacola.
    I beg leave to inform your Excellency that the temporary continuance of
these Troops in this City, until they can conveniently proceed to their place
of destination will afford me no uneasiness. Since I am persuaded that their
officers will take Special care to prevent the Commission of any disorders,
and will on all occasions manifest a respect for the Laws of this Territory.

> Accept assurances of my Respect
> and high consideration
> (Signed) *William C. C. Claiborne*

His Excellency
The Marquis of
Casa Calvo

1. Published as one of two enclosures in Governor Claiborne to the Secretary of State, February 10, 1805, TP, 9: 392, with emphasis on the word *"temporary"* not found here. The second enclosure in ibid., 392, was the Marquis of Casa Calvo to Governor Claiborne, February 6, 1805, notifying Claiborne of the arrival from Illinois of Colonel Don Carlos Dehault de Lassus and thirty privates of the Regiment of Louisiana in New Orleans. All were to take lodgings in New Orleans until their departure for their final destination.

{133}

To the Postmaster General[1]

New Orleans February 8th 1805[2]

Sir,

I enclose you an account[3] which was rendered to me on this day by Robert Chew, for Beverly Chew who acted as a Post Master in this City for a few months by virtue of an appointment from me, during the late Provisional Government. By this account, it Seems that one Hundred and Sixty four Dollars remained in Mr. Chews hands, after deducting his Commissions, and paying to Mr. Seamans Post Master at Natchez the monies due that office. The above Sum I understand accrued upon the Postage of Letters between Natchez and this City while Mr. Chew acted as Post Master, and which being paid to me will be held Subject to your orders. You will remember that during the late Provisional Government and previous to the extension of the Post office Laws to Louisiana, I informed you that I had authorized a charge of the usual Postage on Letters passing by the Express Mail, between this City and Natchez and that I had named temporarily Mr. Chew the Post Master—

> I am Sir with great Respect and
> Esteem
> Your obdt &c
> (Signed) *William C. C. Claiborne*

~~The Secy~~
~~of State The~~
~~Treasury~~

1. The postmaster general was Gideon Granger.
2. Published as Governor Claiborne to the Postmaster General, February 8, 1805, TP, 9: 391, essentially as printed here, but with the correct title of the addressee at the bottom of the letter.
3. Not present.

{134}
To James Madison
New Orleans February 10th 1805[1]

Sir,

Colonel De Lassus formerly Lieutenant Governor of Upper Louisiana (with thirty Spanish Soldiers) is now in this City on his way to Pensacola. His arrival was announced to me by a Letter from the Marquis Casa Calvo, of which the enclosure No 1 is a translation,[2] and to which I returned the answer No 2.[3]

The delay attending the evacuation of the Ceded Territory has often been noticed by me, and the Marquis has been told that the continuance of Spanish officers in this District So long beyond the right and occasion for it, was not Seen with approbation— But it Seems the evacuation is not yet completed, and that Several Spanish Officers continue in this City; Some I learn have been permitted to retire on half pay, and others I believe feel a strong desire to resign their Commissions and Settle permanently in Louisiana, and of this number I am inclined to think the late Intendant Morales is one— But of this however I have no certain information[.]

I am Sir very Respectfully
Your Most obdt St
(Signed) *William C. C. Claiborne*

The Secretary of
State—

1. Also published as Governor Claiborne to the Secretary of State, February 10, 1805, TP, 9: 391–2, with slight variations in text and punctuation.

2. The enclosure was not present, but it is printed as Governor Claiborne to the Marquis of Casa Calvo, February 7, 1805, ibid., 392.

3. See Letter No. 132, To Casa Calvo, February 7, 1805.

{135}
From John Bishop Prevost
New Orleans Feby 15th 1805[1]

Sir,

I take the liberty to enclose the return of the Sheriff,[2] from which I think you will concur in the propriety of aiding him with a guard[.][3]

I have the Honor to be Sir
Your Hble St

(Signed) *J B Prevost—*

His Excellency
Gov. Claiborne

1. Also published as Judge Prevost to Governor Claiborne, February 15, 1805, TP, 9: 393, with slight differences in the punctuation and text.

2. The Report by the Sheriff, February 15, 1805, Letter No. 136, follows immediately.

3. Perspective on the need for guards to accompany the sheriff and/or his deputies in this particular incident may be found in the biographical sketch of Lewis Kerr, pp. 415–37.

{136}
REPORT BY THE SHERIFF[1]

Superior Court	15th February Sent Charles
	Bonville my Deputy to the
Pomerat	Defendants House to make a Seizure
vs	of certain segars [cigars] but was
L[.] Mazenge	prevented and Driven off by force
	by Mazenge the Son of the
	Defendant, and the wife of the
	Said Defendant—
	(Signed) Louis Kerr[2]
	Alguazil Mayor
	True Copy from the original on Record
	in the Clerks office—
	Jas [.] Johnston Acting Clerk

1. Also printed as Report by the Sheriff, February 15, 1805, TP, 9: 393, in a slightly different format.

2. See pp. 415–37 for biographical information on Lewis Kerr.

{137}
TO CONSTANT FREEMAN
New Orleans February 17th 1805[1]

Sir,
Upon the representation of the Honble Judge Prevost that the Alguazil Mayor[2] has been resisted by force in the exercise of his duty at the Plantation of one Mazenge near this City, and that the aid of Military force is necessary to Support the Civil authority,[3] I have to request of you to furnish the Alguazil Mayor with a Non-Commissioned officer and Six men for that purpose—

I am Sir very Respectfully
Your Hble Sevt

(Signed) *William C. C. Claiborne*

Lieutenant
Colonel Freeman
Commanding

1. Also printed as Governor Claiborne to Constant Freeman, February 17, 1805, TP, 9: 394, with slight variations in punctuation and text.
2. This refers to the sheriff, Lewis Kerr.
3. See Letter No. 129, To John Bishop Prevost, February 2, 1805, and Letter No. 135, From John Bishop Prevost, February 15, 1805.

{138}
To Casa Calvo
New Orleans February 20th 1805

Sir,

The American Government desirous of facilitating the intercourse between the United States and the Territory of Orleans, propose to establish a Post from the City of Washington for the conveyance of Letters in a direct Course ~~from~~ to Fort Stoddart on the Mobile, and from thence by the Mouth of Pearl River to New Orleans. This contemplated Post will pass about Seventy Miles through the Territory possessed by Spain, and as I persuade myself that the Spanish Government will not only assent thereto but will extend to the person or persons who may have charge of the Mail their friendly protections— Convinced of your Excellencys disposition to interpose usefully between our two Governments and to promote the harmony and good understanding which happily prevails between the two nations, I have addressed you this communication—

I renew to your Excellency
assurances
of my great Respect and Esteem
(Signed) *William C. C. Claiborne*

His Excellency
The Marquis
of
Casa Calvo

{139}
To William Terrell Lewis[1]
(Private)
New Orleans February 17th 1805

Honored Parents,

The feelings with which I now address you are not to be expressed. My residence in this Country has brought heavy afflictions on myself and my connexions;— On a former occasion I exhausted the language of Calamity in the doleful tale of our accumulating misfortunes. Another dreadful event has occured; to you perhaps my worthy Parents the cruellest of all. May Merciful God arm your Hearts with fortitude to hear with due resignation to the divine will, that it has pleased him our Creator to take from among us your Son Micajah by an untimely death on Tuesday last.[2] He had Supposed himself injured by a young Gentleman at the Bar here: The consequence was a Duel, and he died bravely and without a Pang on the field.[3]

I need not I hope tell you, that the whole affair was conducted without my knowledge; without even a Suspicion of it on my part. No my venerated friends my own bosom would have been cheerfully presented to the fatal Bullet, before that young mans life Should have been added to the Catalogue of losses which your family have Sustained in consequence of the ill-fated elevation of my Political reputation in this Country. I have only to add, and I trust in Heaven you will find Some Source of consolation in it, that all Ranks and descriptions of People here, view his conduct as excusable, and that he died as universally lamented as he had lived beloved. He was attended to his grave by a concourse of Citizens which for respectability, or numbers has been seldom equaled, and never exceeded in this City.

The occasion would Seem to demand a longer Letter, but even thus much is wrung by imperious duty from a Heart bleeding at once, as a Husband, a Father, a Brother and a Son.

May Heaven furnish you with motives of consolation, which our fate on Earth Seems to deny.—

> Adieu Honored Parents, and accept
> assurances of my filial affection
> and respect
> William C. C. Claiborne

Major Lewis
Nashville—

1. The father of Elizabeth, "Eliza," W. Lewis, Claiborne's deceased first wife. This William Terrell Lewis (d. 1813) was usually addressed as Major Lewis from his rank in the Tennessee militia. He has been characterized as a "wealthy land speculator and planter." Louis R. Harlan, "Public Career of William Berkeley Lewis," *Tennessee Historical Quarterly* 7, no. 1 (March 1948), 8.

2. The date of Micajah's death was February 14, 1805.

3. Details of Micajah Lewis's death are given in Letter No. 140, To Thomas Jefferson, February 17, 1805, which immediately follows this letter, and in Letter No. 170, To William Terrell Lewis, March 23, 1805, n. 2.

{140}
TO THOMAS JEFFERSON
New Orleans February 17th 1805[1]

My Dear Sir,

I have lately had but too much occasion to Solicit from your feelings a tribute of condolence for the private misfortunes which have marked my residence in this Country. Once more I have to resume the unfortunate recital by announcing to you the Death of my Brother in Law and Private Secretary Mr. Micajah G [*sic*] Lewis, who on Tuesday last was killed in a Duel near this City.

You have no doubt discovered that (like most men who fill exalted Stations), it has been my misfortune to have attracted the Envy, and excited the Malevolence and ill will of a portion of Society, and I presume you are apprized of the persecution I am Suffering here, thro the Vehicle of licensious Press. Every circumstance as well of a private nature as of my official conduct, that calumny could torture in to an accusation against me, has been brought into public view, and exhibited in every Shape that malignant Wit could devise. I early discovered that these ungenerous attacks excited greatly the Sensibility of Mr. Lewis, and with the most anxious Solicitude for his well-fare, I used every argument to induce him to view with calmness the Tempestuous Sea to which my Political elevation had exposed me.— On one occasion I *had* accommodated a Dispute in which his Sympathies had involved him, and I had persuaded myself that my advice, united to his mild and pacific disposition, would have ensured his future Safety. But unhappily for me, and unfortunately for my poor Brother, even my misfortunes became the Sport of party Spirit, and the ashes of his beloved Sister were not Suffered to repose in the grave. She was raised from the Tomb to give poignancy and distress to my feelings;— He sought and discovered the Author of the cruel production; a duel was the consequence, and my amiable young friend received a Bullet through his Heart at the Second fire.

I hope the assurance is to you unnecessary, that this melancholy affair was kept a Secret from me, and that the news of the fatal result was the first intimation I received of it. Gladly would I have made bear [*sic*] my own Bosom to the Stroke, before any friend of mine, and particularly one So dear to me as Mr. Lewis had fallen a victim *in this cause.*—

> I am Dear Sir with great Respect
> Your faithful friend
> (Signed) *William C. C. Claiborne*

Thomas Jefferson—
President of
the
United States

1. Also published as Governor Claiborne to the President, February 17, 1805, TP, 9: 393–4, without the emphases found on this copy.

{141}
TO JAMES PITOT
New Orleans February 20th 1805[1]

Sir,

The Enclosed Papers will present you with a Copy of "An Act to Incorporate the City of New Orleans,"[2] upon perusal thereof you will find certain duties devolving upon the Mayor and Municipality of this City which I persuade myself will be discharged with promptitude and cheerfulness.

In a few days I hope to be enabled to present you with an official Copy of the Law in the French Language.—

> Accept assurances of my great respect
> and High Consideration
> (Signed) *William C. C. Claiborne*

The Honble
James Pitot Esq.
Mayor of New Orleans

1. Also published as Governor Claiborne to James Pitot, February 20, 1805, TP, 9: 395.
2. Not present. The act cited was approved February 17, 1805. *Acts Passed at the First Session of the Legislative Council of the Territory of Orleans, Begun and Held at the Principal, in the City of New-Orleans, on Monday, the Third Day of December, in the Year of Our Lord,*

One Thousand Eight Hundred and Four, and of the Independence of the United States the Twenty-Ninth (New Orleans: James M. Bradford, 1805), 44–73.

{142}

To James Madison
New Orleans February 21st 1805[1]

Sir,

In my Letter of the 19th Instant I stated that about the last of July or first of August the Petition of Hulin was presented to me. I have Since found among my Papers the original Petition, which is without Date but one of the Documents refered to, bears Date on the eleventh of August ~~but~~ last. I had no recollection myself as to the particular period of presenting the Petition, but one of the young Gentlemen in my office (Mr. Kennedy) had Supposed it to have been about the last of July or first of August, and relying on the correctness of his memory I made the Statement. I however can now confidently inform you that the Petition of Hulin was not handed to me ~~before~~ previous to the first of September. I was taken ill of the fever on the 9th of August, and did not rise from my Bed until about the last of that month. A Document annexed to the Petition bears Date on 11th of August, and it cannot be presumed that those Papers would have been presented to me during my confinement. You will have observed Sir, that the writer who has So plausibly, but So unjustly attacked my official conduct States that the Petition of Hulin was laid before me early in July; If this had been true, I should feel as if I had been inattentive to my duties; but the fact being established, that the improper conduct of the Marquis of Casa Calvo remained unknown to me until September, I do believe the most malignant of my Enemies would agree that my Letter of the fifth of that month to the Marquis ought to exempt me from censure.

Mr. Livingston (who is the author of the piece Signed the Public accuser)[2] made Several applications to me for a view of Hulins Petition, but it was mislaid and could not be found, at length the Public accuser appeared which first acquainted me of Livingstons designs, and in that writing, this unprincipled Man (calculating no doubt upon the Loss of the original Petition) Suppresses the Document which bears date on the 11th of August, and roundly asserts, that the Petition was presented the 1st of July. I have experienced here a great Share of News-Paper abuse, but nothing like a Serious charge of improper conduct in office has been exhibited, except in the affair of Hulin and Villamil, I am therefore Solicitous that this transaction Should appear to you in its true colours. Perhaps it was unfortunate that I permitted my name to have been used by Morales as Sanctioning the Sale of the negroes: But I cannot think that in doing So I at the time acted improperly. It was very Soon after the transfer of Louisiana to the United States, and within the period allowed by Treaty for the evacuation of the Province by the Spanish forces, Morales represented Villamil as an officer of his Catholic Majesty, a Public defaulter and fugitive; He further Stated that a Judgment had been rendered at the Havana by a competent Tribunal, and that the Sale of the Negroes (who had been in Deposit for Some time) ["]would enable him to finish this affair (in which his King was interested) with the expedition recommended" [*sic*][3]

Under these circumstances, I was of opinion that my assent to the Sale could do injury to no one and would tend only ["]to draw to a close the operations of His Catholic Majesty's officers in Louisiana"[4] which were essential to a Speedy and complete evacuation of the Province—

> I am Sir with Respect and Esteem
> Your Hble Sevt
> (Signed) *William C. C. Claiborne*

The Honble
James Madison
Secty of State

1. Also published as Governor Claiborne to the Secretary of State, February 21, 1805, TP, 9: 395–6, with emphasis not found in this copy and variations in punctuation and text.

2. See Letter No. 114, To James Madison, January 26, 1805, which first mentions the "Public Accuser."

3. Claiborne appears to be paraphrasing and partially quoting from Casa Calvo to Claiborne, September 5, 1804, CLB, 2: 321. The missing quotation mark added here is taken from the copy of Governor Claiborne to the Secretary of State, February 21, 1805, TP, 9: 396.

4. The copy of this letter printed in TP, 9: 396, does not carry quotation marks for this portion of the letter. The missing quotation mark supplied here is from that portion of Claiborne to Casa Calvo, September 5, 1804, CLB, 2: 322.

{143}

TO JAMES PITOT

New Orleans February 27th 1805[1]
To The Mayor and Members of the
Municipality![2]

Gentlemen,

As the period is approaching which will put an end to your official functions, I cannot deny myself the pleasure of acknowledging how Sensible I am of your faithful public Services and of returning you my best thanks for the Support which you have uniformly given to the Government of the Territory.—

In your respective Stations Gentlemen you have manifested great vigilance and attachment to the general Interest— Under your auspices the Streets and levies of the City have been much improved, and the Police So directed as to ensure Safety to property, and the preservation of good order.

I pray you Sir to accept yourself and convey to the members of the Municipality this expression of my Confidence Esteem and Respect—

William C. C. Claiborne[3]

The Honble
Jas Pitot Esqr
Mayor of New Orleans

1. Printed as Claiborne to James Pitot, February 27, 1805, TP, 9: 404, without the paragraphing seen here and with slight variations in punctuation.
2. The paragraphing and "feel" of this document as it is read suggest that Claiborne delivered this as a brief speech to the members of the Municipality.
3. This letter did not carry the usual notation, "signed," to the left of the space bearing the governor's signature.

{144}
To James Madison
New Orleans February 27th 1805

Sir,

The Collector of the Revenue Mr. Brown has just informed me, that the Captain of the Revenue Cutter had lately proceeded up the Lake and finding a quantity of Coffee Stored in a House on the Shore of the Bay of St. Louis, which he Supposed had been illicitly introduced, the Captain had entered the House taken possession of the Coffee and was now at the Balize waiting for further orders. Mr. Brown added that the Captain had exceeded his instructions, by coasting further to the Eastward than he had authorized him— and that as the Seizure had taken place within the Territory claimed by the United States but possessed by Spain, he thought it best to direct the coffee to be conveyed to the place from whence it was taken and placed in the Same Situation in which it was found.— I approved of Mr. Browns [*sic*] determination under an impression, that pending the negociation with

Spain, the President would be desirous that things Should remain in their present Situation and that the officers of this Territory Should refrain from acts which were calculated to irritate the Spanish Authorities[.]

> I am Sir
> very Respectfully
> Your Hble St
> (Signed) *William C. C. Claiborne*

The Honble
James Madison
Secty of State

{145}
TO JAMES MADISON
New Orleans February 28th 1805[1]

Sir,

I have the Honor to enclose you a Copy of "an Act to Incorporate the City of New Orleans.["] The Provision which allows the Citizens to Elect Aldermen is very popular. It will be the first time the Louisianians ever enjoyed the right of Suffrage and I persuade myself they will on this occasion use it with discretion.

The news of the War between England and Spain and the opening of the Port of Havana to neutral Vessels have greatly benefitted the commerce of this City. The Leveé [*sic*] is crowded with flour, Salted Provisions, Red Wine and Dry Goods destined for exportation. We have in Port a number of vessels and it is probable all will readily acquire freight.—

> I am Sir, very Respectfully
> Your Hble Sevt
> (Signed) *William C. C. Claiborne*

The Honble
James Madison
Secty of State

1. Also printed in James Robertson, ed. and trans., *Louisiana Under the Rule of Spain, France and the United States, 1785–1807*, vol. 2 (1910–1911; Freeport, N.Y.: Books for Libraries Press, 1969), 281–2.

{146}

To James Pitot

New Orleans February 28th 1805[1]

Sir,

Desirous of availing the Public of your Services as Mayor of this City, I have the Honor to enclose you a Commission, and to Subscribe myself

> with Respect and Esteem
> Your Hble St
> (Signed) *William C. C. Claiborne*

The Honble
James Pitot Esquire
Mayor of New Orleans

1. Also printed as Governor Claiborne to James Pitot, February 28, 1805, TP, 9: 404.

{147}

To James Madison

New Orleans March 3rd 1805

Sir,

The Prize Brig Active and her Cargo are sources of great litigation.[1] It has [(]I understood) been made [to] appear that the Captors had Sold their Interest in the Prize to three different Persons, and on the investigation of the case in the District Court I learn a tremendous Scene of fraud was unfolded.

The French Consul having esteemed it his duty to make enquiries upon this Subject, I enclose for your perusal a Copy of his Letter[2] to me, and of my answer.[3]

> I am Sir very Respectfully
> Your obt St
> (Signed) *William C. C. Claiborne*

The Honble
James Madison
Secty of State—

1. The complex details on this captured ship may be traced in Decree, May 7, 1804; To James Madison, August 1, 1804; To Captain Davis Harbor Master, August 3, 1804; To Lewis Kerr Esqr., Sheriff of New Orleans and performing the duties of Marshall for the District of Orleans, August 4, 1804; To James Madison, August 4, 1804; and to James Madison, August

9, 1804; all in CLB, 2: 135–6, 285–6, 289, 290–1, and 300, respectively; To James Madison, May 22, 1806, ibid., 3: 306; and the biographical sketch of Evan Jones, pp. 374–88 herein.

2. The letter From Consul Martel, 10th Ventose Year 13 (March 1, 1805), Letter No. 148, follows immediately.

3. Letter No. 149, Claiborne's response To Consul Martel, March 3, 1805, follows.

{148}
FROM CONSUL MARTEL
New Orleans 10th Ventose Year 13[1]
March 1st 1805

Sir,

I learn from the discussions which have taken place these last days in the Courts of this Territory, concerning the English Prize the Active that both this Vessel and her Cargo, which were before under an attachment of the Government of the United States, have been restored to Messrs. Amory and Callender Merchants[2] of this City who are Said to be ~~owners~~ Agents of the English owners.

As long as the Prize remained in the hands of the Government of the United States, I thought it expedient to abstain from any interference on my part, and to wait until the decision of the Executive power was made known of which decision being still ignorant, and unacquainted also with the motives according to which those Merchants were put into possession of the Said Prize, it is incumbent with my duty in this circumstance, to Seek for the necessary information relative to this ~~Subject~~ affair, So as to regulate my conduct accordingly and to enable myself to adopt Such conservatory measures as the circumstances and the Interest of the French Government may require.

It is with this view I now address your Excellency, requesting that you will be pleased to communicate to me the decision rendered and the motives in consequence of which this Vessel was given over to the agents of the former owners thereof.

I remain with respect
Your Excellency's
Most Hble St
(Signed) *Martel*
French Consul in
New Orleans

His Excellency
Gov. Claiborne

1. This date reflects the dating system imposed in France after creation of the First French Republic. The March 1, 1805, date entered beneath the French Republic dating system may have been entered by the translator. The name of the translator is not provided. Pierre Derbigny had earlier served in this capacity, as had Louis Moreau Lislet.

2. Amory, Callender & Company, sometimes simply Amory & Callender, was one of the ten most influential merchant firms in early territorial New Orleans. John G. Clark, *New Orleans, 1718–1812: An Economic History* (Baton Rouge: Louisiana State University Press, 1970), 341–2. The firm is listed as one of the endorsers of Andrew Porter, Jr., for appointment as inspector and surveyor of the Port of New Orleans in the fall of 1804. See Recommendation of Andrew Porter, Jr., as Port Inspector, November 22, 1804, TP, 9: 337.

{149}
To Consul Martel
New Orleans March 3rd 1805

Sir,

In answer to your Letter of the 1st of March I have the Honor to inform you, that the disposition of the Prize Brig Active and her Cargo as well as of all other litigated property in this Territory belongs wholly and exclusively to the Judiciary Authority, of the decision in this particular case I am not advised; but on application to the Clerk of the District Court, you may obtain a transcript from the Record which will furnish you with the information desired.

> I pray you Sir to accept assurances
> of my respectful consideration—
> (Signed) *William C. C. Claiborne*

The Honble
Mr. Martel
French Consul
in New Orleans

{150}
To Albert Gallatin
New Orleans March 4th 1805

Sir,

I have the Honor to enclose you an account against the United States for two Hundred and fifteen dollars and twenty five cents, the Vouchers are enclosed which I request may be examined and the amount passed to my credit[.]

> I am Sir very Respectfully
> Your Hble St

(Signed) *William C. C. Claiborne*

The Honble
Albert Gallatin
Secty of the Treasury

{151}

TO JAMES MADISON
New Orleans March 4th 1805

Sir,

Messrs. P. Madan and Joseph McNeill two respectable Merchants of this
City were requested by Captain Davis and myself to examine the old Custom House and to give their opinion as to the Rent per month which Should
be paid the United States for the use thereof.

I now enclose you a Copy of the award, and of an agreement which I have
entered into with Captain Davis. The Rent from the first of August to the
first of February has been paid to me. Captain Davis had a claim against the
United States for public Services rendered by my order for 100 Dollars, and
the balance due from him to the United States to wit 350 Dollars has been
paid to me, and for which I am accountable, as also for all the monies which I
may receive on account of my late agreement with Captain Davis. I trust the
disposition I have made of this Public building will be approved. I thought
it better to Rent it by the month than that it should remain unoccupied.

I am Sir very Respectfully
Your Hble Sevt
(Signed) *William C. C. Claiborne*

The Honble
James Madison
Secty of the State [*sic*]

{152}

TO JAMES MADISON
New Orleans March 8th 1805

Sir,
The late Election for City Aldermen was conducted with great order, but the
apathy of the People on the occasion astonished me; but few voted and
none appeared interested as to the issues.

I have appointed Mr. James Pitot Mayor, and Doctor John Watkins Re-

corder of the City. The former is a French Gentleman of Talents and respectability who has resided here for many years. The character of the Latter
is known to you; I am Sorry to lose his Services in the Legislative Council,
but it was an object with me to confer the office of recorder on a native Citizen of the United States, and there was not one as well qualified as Doctor Watkins[.]

I am Sir very Respectfully
Your Hble st
(Signed) *William C. C. Claiborne*

The Honble
James Madison
Secty of State

{153}
To Abimael Youngs Nicoll
New Orleans March 9th 1805[1]

Sir,
I request that you would examine every Vessel coming from a Foreign Port,
and if you find any Slave or Slaves on Board, not composing a part of the Crew,
that you would detain Such Vessel, and not permit her to pass the Fort[2] until
you have reported the case to the Governor of the Territory and received
his instructions.

I regret the trouble which a compliance with this request will occasion
you— But I find that the examination and detention desired are necessary to
insure a due observance of our Laws[.]

I am Sir with Respect and Esteem
Your obdt Hble St
(Signed) *William C. C. Claiborne*

Captain
Nicoll
Plaquemine

1. Also printed as Governor Claiborne to Abimael Nicoll, March 9, 1805, TP, 9: 414–5,
with variations in paragraphing from that found here.

2. Fort St. Philip at Plaquemine Bend. See pp. 604–7 for a descriptive history of this early
fortification up to the War of 1812.

{154}

TO CHARLES XIMINES

New Orleans March 11th 1805

Sir,

Mr. Quinones[1] having been appointed a Keeper of Records you will be pleased to deliver to him the Public Papers, Documents Records Notarial Acts and proceedings now in your possession.[2]

> I am Sir very Respectfully
> Your obdt St
> (Signed) *William C. C. Claiborne*

Charles Ximines Esqr.

1. Estéban Quinones, a native of Spain, had lived for many years in Louisiana. As a reflection of his decision to remain in Louisiana, he anglicized his given first name to Stephen. List of Civil and Military Officers, April 21, 1809, Notaries Public, TP, 9: 837.

2. Carlos (Charles) Ximines was former notary of the Spanish government in Louisiana. Governor Claiborne to Richard Relf and [Blank], March 12, 1805; James Brown to the Secretary of the Treasury, December 11, 1805; The Secretary of State to Governor Claiborne, February 10, 1806; and James Brown to Governor Claiborne, March 19, 1806; in ibid., 416, 546, 580, and 614, respectively. The letter to Richard Relf and [Blank], March 12, 1805, appears in this letter book as Letter No. 155. Ximines worked with Pedro (sometimes Pierre, at other times Peter) Pedesclaux, who held title to the public records by virtue of his purchase of the offices of clerk and notary of the Spanish government of Louisiana, recorder of mortgages and clerk of the cabildo in 1788. Pedesclaux notified President Jefferson through Governor Claiborne that he had bought these offices for twenty-five thousand dollars as his personal property, transferable to his children by right of inheritance. Sales of office, Pedesclaux said, were "almost universally established" under Spanish practice. Petition of Peter Pedesclaux, April 1804 [*sic*], ibid., 236. Under the authority of an act approved on March 5, 1805, the records were placed in the custody of Stephen Quinones. In addition, by an act passed on March 7, 1805, Quinones also was made custodian of the records of the governor's court, which had been created shortly after establishment of the temporary territorial government. *Acts Passed at the First Session of the Legislative Council of the Territory of Orleans, Begun and Held at the Principal, in the City of New Orleans, On Monday the Third Day of December, in the Year of Our Lord, One Thousand Eight Hundred and Four, and of the Independence of the United States the Twenty-Ninth* (New Orleans: James M. Bradford, 1805), 80–3, 86–8; see also Governor Claiborne to Richard Relf and [Blank], March 12, 1805, TP, 9: 416, particularly n. 86.

{155}

TO RICHARD RELF AND *[Blank]*[1]

New Orleans March 12th 1805[2]

Gentlemen,

I have this day Commissioned Mr. Quinones a Keeper of Records and authorized him to receive possession of certain Records appertaining to the office of Charles Ximines late a Notary Public. The Law having required that a delivery of the Papers Should take place in the presence of two Commissioners, I have gentlemen nominated and appointed you with full authority to act in this particular, and I Solicit on the occasion your Services. Mr. Quinones will Shew you a Copy of the Law in which your duty as Commissioners is prescribed.

I am Gentlemen
very respectfully
Your Hble St
(Signed) *William C. C. Claiborne*

Richard Relf
and *[Blank] [Blank]*
Esqrs

1. Blank in the original.
2. Also printed as Governor Claiborne to Richard Relf and [Blank], March 12, 1805, TP, 9: 416, with slight variations from this copy.

{156}
To Pierre Bailly[1]
New Orleans March 14th 1805[2]

Sir,

Having understood that Francis Connell the Civil Commandant of your District[3] has withdrawn from this Territory and that the Archives of the District are exposed to loss and injury, I request that you would repair to the House of the Said Connell, and take possession of Said Archives and hold the Same in Safe Keeping until you Shall hear further from me on the Subject.

I am Sir with great Respect
Your Hble St
(Signed) *William C. C. Claiborne*

Monsieur
Bailey [*sic*]

1. For a biographical sketch of Bailly, see pp. 587–8.
2. Printed as Governor Claiborne to Monsieur Bailey, March 14, 1805, in TP, 9: 417–8, with slight variations in format.
3. The district was Iberville on the west bank of the Mississippi River a few miles below Baton Rouge. See Register of Civil Appointments in the Territory of Orleans, February 13, 1806, Judges, Enclosed in John Graham to the Secretary of State, TP, 9: 598.

{157}
To Pierre Bailly
New Orleans March 14th 1805[1]

Sir,

I have enclosed you a Commission as Civil Commandant of the District of
Iberville. The interest of your Fellow Citizens require that the office of
Commandant Should be to Some person better qualified and in whom greater
confidence can be placed than in Francis Connell. My choice has fallen
upon you and I persuade myself you will give to the people the benefit of your
Services—

> I am Sir with respect and
> Esteem your Hble St
> (Signed) *William C. C. Claiborne*

Monsieur
Bailey [*sic*]

P.S. The probability is your office of Commandant will not continue for
more than a few weeks; The Legislature are about establishing Courts in
the different Parishes, in which the present Powers of Commandants will be
vested—

W. C. C. C[.]

1. Printed as Governor Claiborne to Monsieur Bailey, March 14, 1805, TP, 9: 417, with
slight variations in text and punctuation.

{158}
To James Madison
New Orleans March 18th 1805[1]

Sir,

We have not received a Northern Mail for five Weeks of course I am without any late Letters from the Department of State or recent information
from the Seat of Government. Much anxiety exists here to learn the issue of
the Memorial to Congress, we have Seen the report of the Committee of
the House of Representatives, and as you may have conjectured the Plan of
Government proposed by the Committee, is a Subject of private discussion
and one on which the Society is divided. The Legislative Council are yet in
Session, and have passed many Laws of which copies Shall Soon be forwarded to you. It is probable, that the Council will adjourn in about two

Weeks. Late Letters from our frontiers represent every thing as tranquil, and the disposition of the Indian Tribes as very friendly to the United States. The Marquis of Casa Calvo remains in this City, and expects shortly to be employed in extending the line of Limits between the United States and the Mexican possessions— A dispute has arisen among the Members of the Catholic Church in this City. Mr. Walsh who claims to be the Vicar General of Louisiana took upon himself to dismiss a Priest who had the care of this Parish. The Priest appealed to his Parishioners who have ~~disaw~~ disavowed the authority of Mr. Walsh and Elected (amidst many Huzzas) the dismissed Priest their Pastor.

The Subject excites much Interest among the Catholics, but it is probable the affair will not eventuate in any unpleasant consequences—[2]

> I have the Honor to be Sir
> very Respectfully
> Your most obdt St
> (Signed) *William C. C. Claiborne*

The Honble
James Madison
Secty of State

1. Also printed as Governor Claiborne to the Secretary of State, March 18, 1805, TP, 9: 420–1, with slight variations in text and punctuation.

2. On this situation, see Stanley Faye, ed., "The Schism of 1805 in New Orleans," *Louisiana Historical Quarterly* 22, no. 1 (January 1939), 98–141, and Michael J. Curley, C.SS.R., *Church and State in the Spanish Floridas (1783–1822)* (Washington, D.C.: Catholic University Press of America, 1940), 282–309.

{159}
To ——— [NEVER SENT][1]
(Private)
New Orleans March 19th 1805

Sir,

Your Letter of the [blank] Ultimo has been duly received. The merits of the dispute between Mr. Laussat and yourself, I am not sufficiently informed of, to give an opinion thereon. In relation to your general conduct in Society I have understood, that it has been marked with propriety, and recommended you to the acquaintance and Esteem of many respectable Inhabitants of this City[.]

> I am Sir very Respectfully
> Your obdt St

(Signed) *William C. C. Claiborne*

This Letter never
forwarded

1. Blank in the original. Possibly intended for Casa Calvo, toward whom Laussat reacted
with polite coolness. In part, Laussat's conduct was a reflection of his anti-Spanish feelings as
well as an informed cautious distrust of Spanish opposition to the sale of Louisiana to the
United States. See Pierre Clément de Laussat, *Memoirs of My Life to My Son During the Years
1803 and After. . .*, trans. Sister Agnes-Josephine Pastwa, ed. Robe t D. Bush (Baton Rouge:
Louisiana State University Press, 1978), 5, 18, 19, 20, 28, 32, 75, 76, 83, 100, 102 (anti-Spanish feelings); 74, 76, 77–8, 79, 84–5 (Casa Calvo); and 125–6 n. 17 (Spanish opposition to
the transfer of Louisiana to the United States).

{160}
TO JOHN BOWYER[1]
New Orleans March 23rd 1805[2]
To Captain Boyer

Sir,

I have received one Letter from you Since your arrival in the Appelousas
District, and which I immediately answered.[3] The difficulty between yourself and the Commandant of Attakapas[4] I have Sincerely regretted, but as it
has arisen more immediately from causes of a military nature, a decision
cannot be made by me.

In your character as Civil Commandant I am persuaded you will dispense
justice with an impartial hand, and that your Deportment will be Such as
to Secure you the esteem of the Citizens, and conciliate their affections to the
United States.—

A Law will pass in a few days establishing inferior Courts in the Territory.
By this Law Appelousas will form a County, and I shall have to appoint
three Judges, a Clerk[,] Sheriff[,] Coroner and Several Justices of the Peace.[5]
I will thank you to give me the names of Such Honest men of your District,
as you may Suppose best calculated to fill the above offices—

I am Sir with great respect
Your Hble St
(Signed) *William C. C. Claiborne*

Captain
Bowyer
Commandant

1. The spelling of Captain John Bowyer's surname in this letter book and in TP, 9, is both with and without the *w*. This Virginia-born officer's name is spelled with the *w* by Francis B. Heitman in *Historical Register and Dictionary of the United States Army from Its Organization September 29, 1789, to March 2, 1903*, vol. 1 (1903; Urbana: University of Illinois Press, 1965), 138.

2. Also printed as Governor Claiborne to John Bowyer, March 23, 1805, TP, 9: 422, with variations in punctuation and content.

3. Not present.

4. The commandant at Attakapas was Lieutenant Henry Hopkins. The nature of Captain Bowyer's differences with Hopkins is unknown, but may have grown out of the fact that Hopkins formerly had been civil commandant of both the Attakapas and Opelousas districts before the arrival of Bowyer sometime in early 1805. James Robertson, ed. and trans., *Louisiana Under the Rule of Spain, France and the United States*, vol. 2 (1910–1911; Freeport, N.Y.: Books for Libraries Press, 1969), 267. About a month after Claiborne's letter to Bowyer, Hopkins was transferred to New Orleans. Governor Claiborne to Henry Hopkins, April 22, 1805, TP, 9: 440. Bowyer was described by General Wilkinson as superior to other officers available for command, but lacking in education, manners, and intelligence, and with a tendency to imbibe too much alcohol, a problem for many of the men facing the difficult and lonely military life in much of early U.S. history. James Wilkinson to the Secretary of War, January 3, 1803 [1805], TP, 9: 151.

Hopkins, a native of Maryland, became a resident of Louisiana after he left the U.S. Army in 1805. Claiborne's appointment of Hopkins as adjutant general of the territorial militia on November 11, 1805, reflected the governor's high regard for the lieutenant. In Governor Claiborne to the Secretary of State, December 4, 1805, TP, 9: 540, Claiborne said that Hopkins had performed his duties as civil commandant of Opelousas during the provisional government "in a manner very satisfactory to me; he preserved the most perfect good order, and acquired for himself, the esteem and confidence of the People." On Hopkins's appointments, see General Orders, November 11, 1805; Register of Appointments in the Militia of the Territory of Orleans, enclosed in Secretary Graham to the Secretary of State, May 8, 1806; and List of Civil and Military Officers, April 21, 1809, Militia Officers; in ibid., 591, 632, 838, respectively. The responsibilities that Claiborne delegated to Hopkins as adjutant general reinforced the trust that Claiborne placed in him. See To Col. Henry Hopkins, November 24, 1805, CLB, 3: 235–7.

5. The law referred to by Claiborne was approved on April 10, 1805. The same law also divided the territory into twelve counties. *Acts Passed at the First Session of the Legislative Council of the Territory of Orleans, Begun and Held at the Principal, in the City of New-Orleans, on Monday, the Third Day of December, in the Year of Our Lord, One Thousand Eight Hundred and Four, and of the Independence of the United States the Twenty-Ninth* (New Orleans: James M. Bradford, 1805), 144–88 and unnumbered p. 208. In all, fifty-two laws were passed in the first session of the legislative council creating various offices and duties of the territorial government: treasurer; attorney general; the judges and justices of the peace; the inferior courts and their jurisdictions; and the punishment of crimes and misdemeanors. Ibid., 24–5, 260–2, 388–98, 372–4, and 210–60, 358–72, 408–12, 416–54, respectively. In the second session of the Legislative Council, some of these laws were modified.

{161}

TO JOHN BISHOP PREVOST

New Orleans March 23rd 1805[1]

Sir,

Captain Carrick, the Civil Commandant of the District of St. Bernard, has acquainted me of the disorderly conduct of one of the Priests in his Parish.—[2] I have requested Captain Carrick to communicate the particulars to you, Since if there be cause for the interference of the Civil authority, the Judiciary can alone direct the proper measures.

> I am Sir
> very Respectfully
> your most obdt St
> (Signed) *William C. C. Claiborne*

The Honble
Judge Prevost

1. Also printed as Governor Claiborne to Judge Prevost, March 23, 1805, TP, 9: 423, with slight variations in punctuation and text.
2. Carrick's problems with the priests in St. Bernard are delineated in the biographical sketch of him on pp. 575–7.

{162}

TO JOSEPH BOWMAR[1]

New Orleans March 23rd 1805[2]

Sir,

In a Letter which you lately addressed to Colo. Freeman, it is Stated that a request made to you by Mr. Dinsmore to prevent the *Choctaw Indians* from Hunting in your District had excited much discontent among them, and you Solicited further instructions upon the Subject. Altho I am uninformed of the authority of Mr. Dinsmore to interfere with Indian affairs west of the Mississippi, I nevertheless will take upon myself to advise, that for the present, you refrain from a compliance with Mr. Dinsmore's request, and that your Deportment to the Indians generally be the most conciliatory. You will protect the well disposed peaceable Indians from injury, and you will prevent the vicious from acts of aggression on the Inhabitants.—

The enclosed extracts from acts of Congress "regulating Trade and Intercourse with Indian Tribes"[3] you will carefully peruse, and I advise that for the present, they Serve as your guide. I will thank you to give me the names of Such Citizens of your District whom you think best calculated to fill the offices of Justices of the peace.

> I am Sir
> with Respect and Esteem
> Your Hbe St
> (Signed) *William C. C. Claiborne*

Lieut
Bowmar
Civil Commandant Washita

1. Brief biographical information on Bowmar is given on pp. 578–9.
2. Also printed as Governor Claiborne to Joseph Bowmar, March 23, 1805, TP, 9: 421–2, without the emphasis shown here, and with variations in spelling and punctuation.
3. Not present.

{163}
To Joseph Bowmar
March 24th 1805— New Orleans

Sir,

By a late Law which ~~will~~ has passed the Legislature [several words blotted out and undecipherable here], the Ouachita Settlement is formed into a County, and an inferior Court is to be established therein. The Law makes it my duty to appoint for the County of Ouachita, three Judges of the Inferior Court, a Clerk[,] Sheriff[,] Coroner, Treasurer and Several Justices of the peace. You will oblige me therefore if you will give me the names of Such honest men of your District as you Suppose but calculated, to fill the Offices above enumerated.— Your powers as Civil Commandant will continue until the inferior Court is organized.

> I am Sir very Respectfully
> Your obdt St
> (Signed) *William C. C. Claiborne*

Mr. Bowmar
Commandant
Ouachita

{164}
To Edward Demaresque Turner
New Orleans March 24th 1805

Sir,

By a Law which will pass the Legislature in a few days, the Settlement of Natchitoches, or rather the Parish of St. Francis is to be formed into a County.

The Law makes it my duty to appoint for that County, three Judges of the Inferior Court, a Clerk[,] Sheriff, Coroner, Treasurer and Several Justices of the Peace, you will oblige me therefore by giving me the names of Such honest men of your District as you Suppose best calculated to fill the offices above enumerated.— Your Powers as Civil Commandant will continue until the inferior Court is orgain [organized]—

> I am Sir very Respectfully
> Your obdtSt [*sic*]
> (Signed) *William C. C. Claiborne*

Captn Turner
Natchitoches &c—

{165}
To Ferdinand Leigh Claiborne[1]
New Orleans March 24th 1805

Sir,

I will thank you to inform me what Sum of money you have collected on account of the Sales of Rifles previous to my departure from Natchez, and what amount yet remains due. I am Solicitous that this Business should be finally and Speedily adjusted;— you will oblige me also, if you would ascertain from Colo[.] West the number of arms which were in the arsenal at Fort Dearborn when he took possession of the Government of the Territory. I have mislaid the memorandum of the Number which I had taken.

A few days previous to my leaving Natchez, three old Horses[2] which had been received from the Chactaws were sold by my orders; one was purchased by you and the Sum ~~of~~ was thirty Dollars which you have not yet paid; After paying the expense of bringing those Horses in, of pasturage &c there was a balance due to the United States of between fifteen and twenty Dollars, and this account is not Settled. It is expected that you will remit me the thirty Dollars you owe as early as may be convenient.

> I am Sir very Respectfully
> Your obdt St

(Signed) *William C. C. Claiborne*

Major F. L[.] Claiborne

1. Ferdinand Leigh Claiborne (1771–1815), the older brother of the governor, lived in Natchez, Mississippi Territory. He had been an officer in the U.S. Army, but resigned his commission in 1802 and moved to Natchez, where he became a merchant. He served as a member of the Mississippi Territorial Assembly in 1804 and was successively appointed colonel and brigadier general of the territorial militia. The Postmaster General to Ferdinand L. Claiborne, April 4, 1804, TP, 5: 315 n. 25. More information is provided by Dunbar Rowland, ed., *Mississippi, Comprising Sketches of Towns, Events, Institutions, and Persons, Arranged in Cyclopedic Form*, vol. 1 (Atlanta: Southern Historical Publishing Association, 1907), 423–4. As this letter's easy openness indicates, William C. C. Claiborne enjoyed a close personal friendship with his brother.

After William C. C. Claiborne's duties took him to Louisiana, F. L. Claiborne bid on and received the contract to carry the express mail between New Orleans and Fort Adams, Mississippi Territory. Initially, the expense of this service was charged to the Orleans Territory governor's office. To Gideon Granger, June 17, 1804, CLB, 2: 213. When that contract was to expire, the cost of the service was to be paid for by the office of the postmaster general. Gideon Granger, the postmaster in the Jefferson administration, considered the arrangements made for this service by Governor Claiborne to be the "most extravigant [*sic*] I have ever received." The Postmaster General to Governor Claiborne, December 6, 1803, TP, 9: 134.

2. While trying to clear his Mississippi accounts with Secretary Henry Dearborn in the War Department in June 1805, the governor pointed out that the particulars of this transaction, along with other business mentioned in the letter, had been reported earlier in his official journal. To Henry Dearborn, June 3, 1805, CLB, 3: 69–70.

{166}
To L. Wooldridge
New Orleans March 24th 1805[1]

Sir,
By a Law of the Legislature which will pass in a few days, all that Tract of Country beginning at the Mouth of Red River, and ascending the Same to black [*sic*] River, thence along black river [*sic*] to the Tensa ~~Lake~~ River and along the Same to the Tensa Lake; thence by a right Line Easterly to the Mississippi and down the Same to the Beginning "is to compose a County & to be called Concordia [*sic*]."[2]

Provision is made by Law for the formation of a County Court for Concordia and I shall have to appoint three Judges a Clerk, Sheriff, Treasurer, Coroner and Several Justices of the Peace;— you will oblige me therefore, by giving me the names of Such Honest men residing within the limits afoursaid [*sic*], ~~and~~ as you may Suppose best calculated to fill the offices enumerated[.]

I am Sir very Respectfully
Your obdt St

(Signed) *William C. C. Claiborne*

Mr. Wooldridge
Civil Commandant
Concordia—

1. Also printed as Governor Claiborne to L. Wooldridge, March 24, 1805, TP, 9: 423, without the strikethroughs contained here and with slight variations in punctuation.

2. Claiborne appears to be quoting from the act of the territorial council, which created the counties and established their boundaries in its first session in early 1805. See *Acts Passed at the First Session of the Legislative Council of the Territory of Orleans, Begun and Held at the Principal, in the City of New Orleans, On Monday the Third Day of December, in the Year of Our Lord, One Thousand Eight Hundred and Four, and of the Independence of the United States the Twenty-Ninth* (New Orleans: James M. Bradford, 1805), 144–208.

{167}
To James Madison
New Orleans March 24th 1805[1]

Sir,

The disposition on the part of the Catholicks of this Territory (which I mentioned in my last Letter) to assume the prerogative of electing their own Priests is extending itself.—

On yesterday I was informed by the Civil Commandant of the District of St. Bernard, that a Priest who had been Superseded by the Vicar General, had assaulted his Successor at the door of the Church, and expressed a wish to Submit his case to the People.[2] The Commandant added that the dismissed Priest was exciting disorder in the District and he apprehended a Serious riot in the Church would ensue. In consequence of this information, I addressed a Letter to Judge Prevost of which the enclosed is a Copy—[3] I have Since heard that the Judge had issued a warrant against the Priest for a Breach of the Peace.

I have taken occasion to mention to the Mayor of the City, and to Several influential men, that in any religious contest that might arise the Government could not and would not interfere, unless the Public peace was disturbed; that the rights of conscience were Sacred and the people were at Liberty to worship almighty God in what manner they pleased; but that the *Law* which proclaimed good order, *would operate,* and the Civil Magistrate *must act* whenever the Public peace was disturbed.[4]

I am Sir very Respectfully
Your obdt St

(Signed) William C. C. Claiborne

The Honble
James Madison
Secty of State

1. Also printed in James Robertson, ed. and trans., *Louisiana Under the Rule of Spain, France and the United States,* vol. 2 (1910–1911; Freeport, N.Y.: Books for Libraries Press, 1969), 283–4, with different paragraphing and with emphasis not on this copy.

2. Roger Baudier, *The Catholic Church in Louisiana* (1939; Baton Rouge: Louisiana Library Association, 1972), 252–3, is silent on this incident, saying only that Father Domingo Joachin Solano had served as parish priest for a short time in 1802, but was transferred to Galveztown, leaving St. Bernard without a pastor until 1805, when Fr. Walsh, as acting vicar-general, appointed Father Jean Marie Rochanson, a French secular priest, to lead the St. Bernard Catholic Church. Presumably, it was Fr. Rochanson who was attacked at the door of the church, but by whom is not clear.

3. Not present, but probably Letter No. 161, To John B. Prevost, March 23, 1805.

4. For related letters dealing with this explosive situation, see Robertson, *Louisiana Under the Rule of Spain,* 2: 284 n. 142; and Governor Claiborne to the Secretary of State, April 16, 1805, TP, 9: 434 n. 26, and the references provided therein.

{168}

TO JAMES MADISON
(Private)
New Orleans March 16th 1805

Sir,

Your private Letter of the 14th of January (with its enclosures) was duly received. I have not yet attempted to Select any additional Members for the Council, inasmuch as few persons here would accept until the issue of the Memorial to Congress was ascertained. Eugene Dorciere, James Mather and George Pollock's Commissions bear date the 30th of August and William Floods the 12th of December— John Sibley has been offered an appointment, but no answer having been received the Commission is not yet filled up.

It is probable that Doctor Sibley will not accept in consequence of an Indian agency confered upon him by the President. Three of the Commissions which were ~~presented~~ first forwarded to me, were presented to Messrs. Dorcier, Mather and Pollock. The Gentlemen first named by the President having declined accepting, the blanks were filled with the names above mentioned. The Commissions were dated the 30th August.

The Council is now composed of Messrs. Julien Poydrass, Benjamin Morgan[,] William Wikoff, George Pollock, Eugene Dorciere, James Mather and

William Flood. The Seat of Doctor John Watkins has been vacated in consequence ~~of his appointment~~ of his appointment to the office of Recorder of
this City. When the Memorial to Congress is decided, there will be no difficulty in completing the Council, but I am unwilling at this time to offer ~~any~~
[*sic*] Commission to any Citizen lest my feelings Should be Subjected to the
Mortification of a refusal[.]

I am Sir yours very
Respectfully
(Signed) *William C. C. Claiborne*

The Honble
James Madison
Secty of State

{169}

To Thomas Jefferson

New Orleans March 25, 1805[1]

Sir,

    The late Indian Agency which has been confered [*sic*] on Doctor John Si-
bley has occasioned an investigation of his private Character; and I discover that it has received many injurious reproaches. Mr. Bradford the Editor
of the Orleans Gazette has addressed to me a Letter upon the Subject which
I deem it a duty to lay before you, more especially Since in Some of my former
Letters to you I may have Spoken respectfully of Doctor Sibbly [*sic*], and I recollect to have mentioned him as a proper person to fill a Seat in the Legislative
Council. I have myself no knowledge of the Doctors private character nor
did I ever learn until lately any serious exceptions to it. He passed a few weeks
in the Mississippi Territory in the year 1802 and was occasionally at my
House. I was pleased with him as an agreeable companion and a man of information; I have Since received many interesting Letters from the Doctor
which contained as I Supposed much valuable information. The reputation
of the Doctor in North Carolina can readily be acquired from Some of the
gentlemen of that State. Of his general conduct here I cannot give any Testimony, there are however other Citizens who Speak of him equally as disre-
spectfully as Mr. Bradford, and others again who represent him as a man of
integrity and profess a friendship for him. I persuade myself that when you
consider the motive which has induced me to address you this Letter, you will
excuse the liberty I have taken; I have always been careful in recommending

persons for office and whenever I should be So unfortunate as to have named in my Letters to you an unworthy character, you may be assured, it has arisen from my being myself deceived.— I Still hope Doctor Sibbly [*sic*] is not unworthy of your Patronage, the characters of the best of men have been misrepresented. Of the Doctors Private reputation, I have no formal knowledge, but as exceptions to it are Stated by Mr. Bradford, I esteemed it a duty to enclose you his Letter.[2]

The council are yet in Session. Among the good Laws which they will enact, I hope there will be one for the Support of Public Schools, and upon liberal principles. Many African Slaves are introduced into the Settlement of Baton Rouge by the way of Pensacola & Mobile, and from Baton Rouge they pass into Louisiana. These abuses are Seen and regretted but (under existing circumstances) cannot be prevented.

> I pray you to accept the best wishes
> of D Sir [*sic*] Your faithful friend
> (Signed) *William C. C. Claiborne*

Thomas Jefferson
President of
the United States

1. Also printed as Governor Claiborne to the President, March 26, 1805, TP, 9: 424–5.
2. Not present.

{170}
To William Terrell Lewis[1]
(Private)
New Orleans March 23rd 1805

Honored Parents,

The misfortunes in our family which my last letter communicated has made upon my mind a Sorrowful impression; But it is our duty to bear with fortitude and resignation the Decrees of almighty God & I trust your reflections have Suggested to you many considerations which cannot fail to communicate the Sweetest consolation. That God is omnipotent[,] wise[,] merciful and just, all the works of creation demonstrate. His decrees to us Short Sighted mortals are Sometimes mysterious; but their ultimate tendency is the promotion of human happiness. An affectionate Son[2] has left you, and exchanged a life of trouble for an abode of happiness. Let us then no longer grieve for him, our lamentations cannot be heard by those they are directed to;— we have lost more than we can express;— but our dear relative

has gained much. Our distress then is not for the departed, it is for ourselves;— he unquestionably has made a happy exchange[.]

You have indeed much to console you for your loss; your Son lived respected, died lamented, and has left behind him an untarnished reputation.
I think you ought to Suppress your Tears, and rejoice (with Humble joy) for
the great blessings which a kind providence has ~~guaranteed~~ continued to
you. The company of your younger daughters will Soothe your declining
years, and your adopted Sons will Honor and respect their aged Parents
and be the guardians and protectors of their amiable Sisters. My life has been
chequered with many misfortunes, but my fortitude enables me to bear up
against them all. Th[r]own upon the changeable Sea of Public Life and in tempestuous times, much has happened to wound my feelings, and many attempts have been made to injure my reputation. But a conscience void of
offence is my consolation and to the charges exhibited by my calumniators
I oppose a whole life of Integrity.

By Mr. Stumps Boat, I forwarded you a present of Some Sweet meats, and
a Box of assorted Cordial, receive them not for their value but as tokens
of my affectionate remembrance.

Mr. Stump has also in charge for you a Trunk. It contains many articles
which may serve as mementos of a virtuous female whom I tenderly loved
while living, and whose memory I respectfully cherish with gratitude to the
Parents who gave me So great a blessing, and ~~with~~ resignation to the will
of a benevolent being who has made her an angel in Heaven.

> Accept Honored Parents the best
> wishes of your affectionate
> and dutiful Son.
> (Signed) *William C. C. Claiborne*

Major Lewis
Nashville Tennessee

1. The father of Eliza W. Lewis, Claiborne's deceased first wife.
2. Micajah G. Lewis, the son of Major Terrell Lewis and younger brother of Eliza Lewis,
Claiborne's first wife. Micajah Lewis had been killed by Robert Sperry in a duel. Young Lewis
had issued the challenge because of an implied slight to Governor Claiborne in a poem by
Sperry published in one of the New Orleans newspapers. The manner in which the poem was
written suggested that the deceased Eliza disapproved of Claiborne's conduct during a social
outing prior to her death from yellow fever in September 1804. In the duel, Lewis's pistol misfired. Sperry's bullet pierced Lewis's heart, killing him instantly. A recent arrival in Louisiana,
Sperry became a zealot among those who were critical of Claiborne, perhaps in an attempt to

garner favor within the business community. See John S. Kendall, "According to the Code," *Louisiana Historical Quarterly* 23, no. 1 (January 1940), 156–60.

{171}
To Thomas Jefferson
(Private)
New Orleans March 26th 1805

DSir,

Mr. Robinson a Passenger on Board the Brig enterprize [*sic*] Bound for Baltimore has promised to convey to you a Barrel of excellent Brown Sugar manufactured by Mr. Fortier a respectable Planter of this Territory.

Mr. Fortier has requested me to forward to you this Sugar, and to pray your acceptance of it as a Sample of the productions of this fertile District.

> I am DSir
> with great respect
> your faithful friend
> (Signed) *William C. C. Claiborne*

Thomas Jefferson
President of the
United States—

{172}
To John Beckley
(Private)
New Orleans March 26th 1805

DSir

Mr. Robinson a Passenger on Board the Brig Enterprize Bound for Baltimore has promised to convey to you the Barrell of Brown Sugar, which I mentioned in my last letter and of which I pray your acceptance. This Sugar is of an Excellent quality and is manufactured in this Territory.

> Present me respectfully to your Lady
> I am DSir
> Your Sincere friend
> (Signed) *William C. C. Claiborne*

J. Beckley Esqr.
Speaker[1] of the
House of Representatives
United States—

1. Beckley was, of course, clerk of the House of Representatives. See Edmund Berkeley and Dorothy Smith Berkeley, *John Beckley, Zealous Partisan in a Nation Divided* (Philadelphia: American Philosophical Society, 1973), 260–5. The Speaker of the House of Representatives at this time was Nathaniel Macon of North Carolina. Dumas Malone, *Jefferson and His Time*, vol. 4, *Jefferson the President, First Term, 1801–1805* (Boston: Little, Brown, 1970), 90.

{173}

FROM JAMES MADISON
(Private)
Copy of a Letter from the Secretary of
State Dated
Department of State
Feby 25th 1805[1]

Sir,

Your Several Letters of 8th, 10th, 11th, 15th, 23rd & 31st of December and 1st, 5th, 6th, 13th, & 14th of January have been Successively received the most of them after having been long on the way. The Steps taken by the Spaniards as communicated in those of the latest dates, for Strengthening and advancing their Military Posts, justly claim attention. Whatever the motive ~~of them~~ may be, the tendency of them cannot be favorable to the tranquility and friendship between the two Nations, which it must be the Interest of Spain as much at least as of the United States to preserve. As long Since as the 26th of September last, Mr. Pinckney communicated to the Spanish Government a proposition and recommendation on the part of the President that no new positions or augmentations of military force Should take place on either Side within the Territories claimed by both Eastward of the Mississippi; and the manifest ~~im~~propriety of this mutual forbearance throughout the Territories in controversy whilst negociations [*sic*] were in train, ought to have been readily admitted and ought to have produced immediately Counter orders in relation to any Military dispositions which a jealousy or false policy in the Spanish Government might have previously Suggested. It is not impossible that Such Counter orders may have been issued, and that notwithstanding the lapse of time, they may not have reached the proper hands. Be this as it may the President has thought it expedient, that Some provisional arrangements for the case, which you will learn from the Department of War, should be made on our part; that this determination should be candidly imparted to the Marquis of Casa Calvo, if Still at New Orleans; and that with assurances that the arrangements are merely provisional, he Should be urged to take the most effectual measures in his power for restoring every thing to the Military footing which existed at the Cession of Louisiana to the United States. The relation which France has both to Spain and the United States on the Subject of Louisiana, makes it also proper in the judgment of the President that the views of this Government should be explained to the French Minister here, and an occasion thence given him for Superadding his Council and influence with the Spanish authorities. The weight of these explanations cannot fail to be the greater both with the French Minister, and the Marquis of Casa Calvo &c on account of the War which has commenced between Great Britain and Spain. The Manifesto of Spain is Dated on the 12th of December. The formal annunciation on the part of Great Britain has not yet appeared.

There can be no room for pretending that the Military Steps within the Territories in question, taken by the Spanish Officers, had, or can have refered [sic] to the danger of attacks from great Britain [sic]. The relations Subsisting between great Britain and the United States and the light in which any Such ~~instructions~~ intrusions of the former, would present itself to the Latter, are a Sufficient guarrantee that they will not be attempted.— I only add on this Subject, that the President relies on your vigilance in obtaining and communicating intelligence of every Spanish movement or project which it may be interesting to the Government to possess, and particularly that he wishes you to take immediate measures for ascertaining the nature and extent of the Spanish establishment made or contemplated at the Bay of St. Bernard[2] or its vicinity. Notwithstanding the approaching term of the Cession, Congress have come to no final decision with respect to the object of the Memorial from the Inhabitants of Louisiana. The papers enclosed contain the views entertained with respect to the future Government of The Territory, by the respective branches as far as these views have been developed.

I have the Honor to be Sir with
great Respect & Esteem
Your obdt Hble St—
(Signed) *James Madison*

Gov Claiborne

1. Also printed as The Secretary of State to Governor Claiborne, February 25, 1805, TP, 9: 397–8, with variations in the text and punctuation.

2. Today known as Galveston Bay. This report of Spanish preparations to erect forts and establish settlers at the mouth of the Trinity River, which flows into the bay, grew out of Casa Calvo's plans to populate the Gulf Coast of western Louisiana and east Texas with settlers loyal to Spain with a view to reclaiming all of Louisiana west of the Mississippi for Spain.

Saint Bernard Bay should not be confused with St. Bernard Parish, which was and is on the east bank of the Mississippi River below New Orleans. See James Pitot, *Observations on the Colony of Louisiana from 1796 to 1802*, trans. Henry C. Pitot (Baton Rouge: Louisiana State University Press, 1979), 97, 98; and To James Madison, June 6, 1805, and April 16, 1806, CLB, 3: 81–2, 289–90, respectively. On Casa Calvo's grand scheme, see his biographical sketch, pp. 484–94 herein.

{174}
To Casa Calvo
New Orleans March 28th 1805

Sir,

Desirous of Sending Some ~~necessary~~ Military Stores to the Garrison of Fort Stoddart on the Tombigbee River, and a few Goods to the United States Factory at Fort St. Stephens, I have freighted for that purpose the Sloop Castor[,] Captain Cooper.

This vessel is engaged Solely on account of the United States, and your Excellency will much oblige me, if you would take Such measures, as may insure to Said Vessel a free and unmolested passage by the Fort of Mobile in going and returning.[1]

Accept assurances of my great
respect &
Sincere Esteem—
(Signed) *William C. C. Claiborne*

His Excellency
The Marquis of
Casa Calvo—

1. For Casa Calvo's response, see Letter No. 177, From Casa Calvo, March 29, 1805.

{175}
To William Bayard Shields[1]
New Orleans March 28th 1805

DSir,

Your Letter of the 5th of March (with its enclosures) was duly received.— I am sorry to learn of your indisposition, and the more So Since it deprived me of the pleasure of Seeing you in this City. I hope however that your Health is by this time reinstated.

The contents of your Letter was communicated to Mr. Mandoz, the Gentleman who made the Extract from the Records, and a Letter from him to me upon the Subject is now enclosed for your perusal.[2] Mr. Mandoz wishes to receive from you more particular instructions and if you would furnish them, they Shall be executed with care and dispatch.

I am Sir with Esteem
Your very obdt Sevt.
(Signed) *William C. C. Claiborne*

William B[.] Shields Esq

1. For information on Shields and other correspondence on the land records in Louisiana, see Letter No. 83, To William Bayard Shields, December 19, 1804, n. 1.

2. Letter No. 176, From Ferdinand Mandoz, March 28, 1805, immediately follows this letter.

{176}
FROM FERDINAND MANDOZ
New Orleans March 28th 1805[1]

Sir,

In conformity with Mr. Wm B Shields [*sic*] request, I have the Honor to inform your Excellency that after a careful revival of the abstract I have made of all the orders of Survey belonging to the District of Natchez, having confronted it with the original Register of the warrants of Land issued by the Spanish Government in the Province of Louisiana, I have found it just as I expected, I mean as correct as possible.

If Mr. Shields finds fault with it, it must be owing to the great confusion said records are in. Previous to my beginning Said Abstract which by the by, I intended to make perfectly accurate, I applied to the former Surveyor-General Mr. Charles Laveau, to Don Andres Armesto late Secretary of the Spanish Government, and to Several other persons whom I might derive any information concerning this business. At last I was informed that the greatest number of the Books of Records had been destroyed by the conflagration we had in this town in 1788[2] that those that exist now were made Since that time by Guess, and consequently are So incorrect that in Some of them there is not only the District missed, but even the Date of the order. I must likewise observe to your Excellency that the district of Feliciana (which comprehends Thomsons Creek and Bayou Sara) being a part of West Florida, Still in the hands of the Spaniards, I did not think it necessary to mention in Said Abstract; any of the warrants belonging to it; altho they are considerable and Some of very late Date. I have Said Registers in my possession, and will keep them until you receive an answer from Mr. Shields, to whom you may mention likewise that there is in them many warrants of land recorded as late as the year 1799, for the District of Natchez as well as that of Feliciana[.]

I Shall not make any alteration in the abstract aforesaid until you hear from that Gentleman respecting the Subject in question, and I hope he will ~~follow~~ forward Such directions with respect to it, as may Spare me the trouble of doing things twice, and the mortification of not pleasing him.

> I am Sir with great respect your
> Excellencys most obdt & very Hble
> St
> (Signed) *Ferdinand Mandoz*

His Excellency
Gov. Claiborne

1. The date originally appears to have been March 27, but the 7 has been written over to read 8.

2. The extent of the damage of this great fire is described by Samuel Wilson, Jr., in *The Vieux Carré, New Orleans: Its Plan, Its Growth, Its Architecture* (New Orleans: Bureau of Governmental Research, 1968), 44–5.

{177}
FROM CASA CALVO
To His Excellency the Governor of the
Territory of Orleans

Sir,

The effects your Excellency wishes to Send to Fort Stoddart[1] by the Schooner Caster Captain Cooper are of Such a nature as cannot I think oppose in the least to those acts of Civility which ought to take place between contiguous powers; and although I am not certain whether the Colonel Don Vincent Folch Governor of West Florida, be directed by the Kings orders to receive a duty on the effects which may be either imported or exported by the Mobile, to and from the American Territory of Tombigbee and St. Stephens I have taken on myself to request his granting a free passage to the above mentioned Vessel, Sending advice thereof to the Court in order that Kings approbation may be obtained, requesting that in case it should Hereafter be found necessary, he would cause the amount of Such duties on importation to which the Said Schooner may be liable to be ascertained. Since the present is more a Suspension of the payment which is to be made in case his Majesty Shall not accede to the Liberty now granted[.]

> May God grant your Excellency
> many years
> (Signed) *The Marquis of Casa Calvo*
> The Marquis of Casa Calvo—

New Orleans
March 29th 1805

1. See Letter No. 174, To Casa Calvo, March 28, 1805, which requested the opening of this service.

{178}
TO JAMES MADISON
New Orleans March 30th 1805

Sir,

Mr. Chambers the United States Factor for the Chactaw Indians is now in this City— His Business here is to procure Some necessary Supplies for the Factory, and to engage a Vessel to transport thither a quantity of Peltry which he had collected. Colonel Freeman ~~was~~ is also Solicitous to Send to Fort Stoddart some Military Stores which the Garrison greatly needed, and the Contractor ~~was also~~ is desirous to forward to the Same place a Supply of Provisions; but each of these Gentlemen ~~were~~ are unwilling to Subject the articles under their care to inspection and the payment of duties at the Town of Mobile, to remedy which I addressed a Letter to the Marquis of which no. 1 is a copy[1] and received an answer of which no. 2 is a translation.[2] The Supplies to Forts Stoddart & St. Stephens will now be forwarded, and I trust the Marquis's interference will have the desired effect. I find no difficulty in transacting business with the Marquis, he possesses a great Share of Spanish pride and a warm irritable temper which sometimes betrays him into imprudences, but his disposition is generous and accommodating, and his general Deportment that of a Gentleman! Of Governor Folch I cannot speak as favorable, he has more temper than discretion, more genius than Judgment, and his general conduct ~~is~~ far from being ~~accommodating~~ conciliatory— at the moment of closing this Letter, I was visited by a Son of Governor Folchs immediately from Pensacola. He mentioned to me that the Garrison at that place were in want of Provisions and daily expected an attack from the British. I did not however learn the reasons which induced them to fear an attack[.]

> I am Sir very Respectfully
> Your Hble St
> (Signed) *William C. C. Claiborne*

The Honble
James Madison
Secretary of State

1. See Letter No. 174, To Casa Calvo, March 28, 1805.
2. See Letter No. 177, From Casa Calvo, March 29, 1805.

{179}
To Garrett Elliott Pendergrass [Pendergrast]
(Private)
New Orleans March 31st 1805

DSir,

I received by the last Mail your Letter of the 21st instant, and am Sorry it is not in my power to return a Satisfactory answer. The Hospital here is in Some measure under the controul of the City Corporation. During the late temporary Government the Municipality appointed a Committee to repair to the Hospital with instructions to examine the Same, and make report generally as to the Manner in which it was conducted. Between that Committee and the then Hospital Physician, a dispute arose, and it eventuated in a unanimous request on the part of the Municipality to me to obtain the Physicians Dismission, I accordingly made application to that effect to Madam Castillon; upon which the Physician resigned and a Doctor Blanket was immediately named his Successor. To this Gentlemans nomination I made exceptions, but he was a Frenchman and So great a favorite with Madam that my objections were overruled.[1]

I do not think the appointment of Physician to the Hospital as desirable as you Seem to think. The resources of the institution are limitted [*sic*], and but few persons partake of its benefits. I am inclined to think that in the pursuits of private practice in this City a greater field is opened for genius and Medical Skill. The diseases of the Climate are various and not well understood. Human life here is and has hitherto been particularly precarious, and the Physician who could tame the rage of mortality during the Summer Months could not fail to acquire esteem and confidence. Your Medical enquiries I learn have been extensive and your application considerable— A large City therefore presents the most flattering prospects. Whether or not New Orleans Should be prefered, you yourself can best determine.

> Accept my good wishes
> I am DSir [*sic*]
> very Respectfully
> Your obdt Sevt
> (Signed) *William C. C. Claiborne*

Doctor Pendergrass
Natchez

1. See Letter No. 10, To Jean Baptiste Victor Castillon, October 8, 1804.

{180}

TO JAMES MADISON

New Orleans March 31st 1805[1]

Sir,

I enclose you Mr. Walsh's Pastoral Letter.[2] The City Council having heard that this production was in the Press, requested and obtained from the Printer the Manuscript Copy.— After the perusal the Council being apprehensive that its publicity would divide and inflame the Public mind instructed the Mayor to use his best endeavours to have it Suppressed.— Efforts to that effect were made but the Printer (Mr. Bradford[3]) urged the freedom of the Press, and determined upon his own responsibility to publish the Letter.

> I am Sir very respectfully
> Your obdt Hble Sevt
> (Signed) *William C. C. Claiborne*

The Honble
James Madison
Secty of State

1. The original letter is in State Department Territorial Papers, Orleans Series, 1764–1813, roll 6, vol. 6, January 1, 1805–June 21, 1805, folio 93, National Archives Microfilm, microcopy T260 (City Archives, Louisiana Department, New Orleans Public Library).
2. Not present. Walsh's pastoral letter was dated March 27, 1805. A copy of it, in French from the *Télégraphe* newspaper, is ibid., folio 96. The letter also was printed in one of the

issues of the *Orleans Gazette*. Unfortunately, very few issues of this newspaper have survived, including the one that printed Walsh's letter.

3. James Morgan Bradford, editor/owner of the *Orleans Gazette*, which also published Walsh's pastoral letter.

{181}
To Edward Demaresque Turner
New Orleans March 31st 1805[1]

Sir,

Your Several letters of the 3rd, 6th & 16th of March have been duly received.[2] The explanation you have given upon the Subject of the Slaves recently released from confinement is Satisfactory, and your conduct in this affair Seems to have been ~~governed~~ directed by prudent and just considerations[.]

I have as yet received no application from those who wish the banishment of the Slaves, and if any is made, I shall know how to appreciate the motive. I am aware of the difficulty of organizing the County Courts.— The want of information among the body of the People, their former habits and existing prejudices present great impediments, but I will Select with care the officers of the Court, and if things Should not be conducted with propriety, I shall only be censured by *illiberal Men,* or *those who know not the difficulties in my way.* I hope the recent reports from Nacogdoches are incorrect.— I however will take an early opportunity to confer on the Subject with the Marquis of Casa Calvo, and ascertain the truth of the case. If the Spanish authorities in your vicinity Should encourage the elopement of Slaves from the Service of their Masters, and give protection to the fugitives, the consequences cannot fail to be unpleasant, and the Subject will demand the Serious attention of our Government.

I am Sir with Esteem
Your Hble Sert
(Signed) *William C. C. Claiborne*

Captain Turner
Natchitoches—

1. Also printed as Governor Claiborne to Edward D. Turner, TP, 9: 430–1, with differences in punctuation and without the emphases seen here.
2. Not present with this manuscript.

{182}

To Theodore Stark

New Orleans April 1st 1805[1]

DSir,

A Law dividing this Territory into Several Counties and providing for the establishment of Inferior Courts will pass the Legislature in a few days. The Settlements of Ouachita and Concordia, will each form a County, & if the Office of Clerk in either of these Counties would be worthy your acceptance, I Should be happy to confer it on you. Having heard that you were not at present engaged in business I have made you this communication[.]

> I am Sir, with great respect
> and Esteem your Sincere Friend
> (Signed) *William C. C. Claiborne*

Theodore Stack[2] Esqr
Natchez

1. Also printed as Governor Claiborne to Theodore Stark, TP, 9: 431–2, with variations in punctuation.

2. The correct name of the addressee is "Stark." Stark apparently was, or became, a lawyer. Whether he took the job in north Louisiana is not known, but he subsequently became a resident of New Orleans. It was Stark who took the deposition given by Daniel Carmick against Daniel Clark and James Sterrett. See the biographical sketch of Carmick, pp. 461–75.

{183}

To James Madison

New Orleans April 1st 1805[1]

Sir,

I enclose you an answer to Mr. Walsh's Pastoral Letter by Colonel Bellechasse.[2] Neither the Letter or answer are yet in circulation, but I learn both will be distributed in a few days[.] This religious contest occupies at present much of the public attention[.]

> I am Sir very Respectfully
> Your Hble St
> (Signed) *William C. C. Claiborne*

The Honble
James Madison
Secty of State—

P.S[.] The Post from the Northward continues irregular.— We were much disappointed in not receiving the Mail due on this Evening— I presume these failures may be attributed to the Severe Winter and to High Waters.

W C. C C [*sic*]

1. The original letter, William C. C. Claiborne to James Madison, April 1, 1805, is in State Department Territorial Papers, Orleans Series, 1764–1813, roll 6, vol. 6, January 1, 1805–June 21, 1805, folio 95, National Archives Microfilm, microcopy T260 (City Archives, Louisiana Department, New Orleans Public Library). Perspective on this personal quarrel may be found in the Bellechasse biographical sketch, pp. 266–81.

2. The Bellechasse answer to Walsh was not with this manuscript, but it is in ibid., folio 96.

{184}
To William Terrell Lewis
(Private)
New Orleans April 1st 1805

My Dear Sir,

I am honored with the receipt of your Letter of the 12th Ultimo, and am happy to find that you bear with ~~great~~ fortitude the great loss which it has pleased God to inflict us with. Your sons premature departure will never cease to be regreted [*sic*] by me, but generous men attach to his conduct no censure and a merciful God will excuse his last act. His Sympathy for my feelings and a desire to avenge the wrong offered to my character by unprincipled Scribblers urged him to the Combat which terminated in his loss to his relatives and to Society. The particulars which you desire, the friend of your Son, has promised to give me, and they Shall be forwarded probably by the next Mail. In the mean time be assured that the conduct of my unfortunate Brother through the whole affair manifested a high Sense of Honor and much personal firmness. He made no Will nor any request as to the disposition of his Property. His great objects seemed to be, to have the affair promptly adjusted, and to keep me uninformed of his intentions; So careful was he on ~~that~~ this point, that to Mr. Kennedy (my present private Secretary) with whom he Slept, and was in habits of the most friendly intimacy, and every individual of my Family remained ignorant of the affair until the fatal result was communicated. The challenge was given on the 12th of February about 10 oClock [*sic*] in the morning, and the Duel was fought about 1 oClock [*sic*] on the Same day. Your Son owed one Hundred Dollars to Mr. Kennedy, and to him he wrote a Letter enclosing a Note of Colonel Hays (to whom he had Sold a Horse) for one hundred and twenty Dollars; requesting that he would collect it, and after paying himself, that he would deliver the Balance

to the Governor. This Letter was delivered to Mr. Kennedy by the friend
of Mr. Lewis, the day after the duel. Your request with respect to the wearing
apparel, shall be attended to, and also as to the Tomb Stone, which shall
be procured from one of the northern States. I must again express a wish that
you Should meet as you ought a calamity that our Maker has inflicted and
for which we Should not repine. Our grief is not for the Dead, it is Selfish; it
is for ourselves. We indeed have lost much, but our dear relationsive haves [sic]
made a happy exchange. The calumnies which my political elevation have
Subjected me to, had had occasioned me very little inquietude. conscious
[sic] rectitude, a life devoted to honorable pursuits, and the approbation of
the President (manifested by my re-appointment) were the considerations
which led me to despise News-Paper abuse. Would to God my amiable young
friend had received like *impressions*— I had Endeavoured to inculcate *them*
in my conversations with him, and that occasioned him to conceal from me
the personal affair in which he engaged. I will only add what I know you
will believe, that the publication which occasioned the Duel was as cruel as
it was false.

In my character as Governor I gave a Dinner to Several foreign officers of
distinction and to many respectable Citizens. A Band of Music played Several airs during the repast, and nothing occured that justified a charge of inde-
corum against myself or any of my guests. I pray you Sir, to present me
most affectionately to my Mother, and all the family, and to believe me to be,
with great respect your sincere friend—

(Signed) William C. C. Claiborne

Major
Lewis
Nashville Tennessee

{185}
To James Madison
New Orleans 1805[1]

Sir,

I am honored with the receipt of your Letter of the 25th, Ultimo,[2] and
Shall be particularly attentive to its contents. The Marquis of Casa Calvo
is yet in this City, and I believe contemplates remaining for Some time;— there
at present exists between the Marquis and myself a friendly intercourse,

and I shall embrace an early opportunity to make to him the communication desired by the President.

The Spanish force at Pensacola and in West Florida amounts to about nine hundred effective men, two hundred are Stationed at Baton Rouge about 80 at the Town of Mobile and the Balance at Pensacola. I cannot State the number of Spanish Troops in the Province of Taxus [Texas], but if any credit can be given to reports they have of late been considerably augmented. At the Bay of St. Bernard the Spaniards have erected a Fort of the Strength of which I am not informed, but on the Coast they have Several garrisons, and I learn from a Source ~~not to be doubted~~ entitled to credit, that within 80 Leagues from the mouth of the Sabine River they have at this time about 2,000 troops;— I however will make further enquiries and communicate to you the result. The Schism among the Catholics of the Territory encreases. The vicar general (who claims precedence in the Church) is about publishing a Pastoral Letter, and proposes to give it general circulation: I very much regret this religious controversy, but I persuade myself it will not be productive of Serious consequences. Mr. Walsh is an Irishman, and his principal opponent Mr. Antoine is a Spanish Priest.— The Marquis of Casa Calvo is Said to take great interest in favor of the latter; but I have no evidence of the fact.—

I am Sir very Respectfully
Your most obdt Sevt

(Signed) *William C. C. Claiborne*

The Honble
James Madison
Secretary of State

P.S. As it is probable I may occasionally have confidential communications to make you, I should be happy to be furnished with a Cipher
W. C. C. C— [*sic*]

1. Although only the year is entered for the date on this letter, it most probably was written in early April 1805, perhaps April 3. This is deduced from its location among other letters written in early April 1805 and its occurrence between letters dated April 1 and April 4, 1805. In addition, reference to receipt of Secretary Madison's letter of the "25th Ultimo" fits within the four-to-six-week delivery pattern of letters received from Washington, D.C.

2. Probably Letter No. 173, From James Madison, February 25, 1805.

{186}

To Constant Freeman
New Orleans April 4th 1805[1]
To Colonel Freeman

Sir,

I have recognized a Company of Volunteer Militia in this City by the Title of the Orleans fusiliers [sic], and annexed it to the Battalion of Orleans Volunteers.[2]

This new Company have Solicited the loan of forty Stand of arms, and you will oblige me, if you will cause that number to be delivered to the order of Captain Davis upon his giving a receipt for the Same. The Volunteer Corps of Militia heretofore organized in this City were furnished with public arms, and the officers of the general government to whom the circumstance was communicated did not express their disapprobation[.]

> I am Sir very
> Respectfully
> Your obdt Sevt
> (Signed) *William C. C. Claiborne*

Sent on thus far
By the Mail of the
10th September 1805

1. Also printed as Governor Claiborne to Constant Freeman, April 4, 1805, TP, 9: 432, as one paragraph and without the note found at the bottom of this draft.

2. The Battalion of Orleans Volunteers was authorized by An Act Recognizing the Battalion of Orleans Volunteers and Providing for a Troop of Horse, which was passed by the Legislative Council on January 23, 1805. *Acts Passed at the First Session of the Legislative Council of the Territory of Orleans, Begun and Held at the Principal, in the City of New Orleans, On Monday the Third Day of December, in the Year of Our Lord, One Thousand Eight Hundred and Four, and of the Independence of the United States the Twenty-Ninth* (New Orleans: James M. Bradford, 1805), 26–8. Little more than two months later, the council authorized the governor to recognize as a volunteer company any group of thirty-five or more white male citizens who were willing to equip and uniform themselves. Such a company was not to exceed sixty privates and the governor was to commission its officers. An Act Concerning Volunteer Companies of Militia, March 29, 1805, ibid., 120. The Orleans Fusiliers was the first such company. It was organized by Samuel B. Davis, the friend and sometimes business partner of Daniel Clark.

{187}

To James Madison
New Orleans April 5th 1805[1]

Sir,

A late Letter from Captain Turner of Natchitoches contains the following Paragraph "I fear the return of the Negroes who had escaped to Nacogdoches will not remedy the evil.— The Commandant who restored them has been arrested for So doing, and his Successor has positive orders to carry the royal Decree concerning fugitive Slaves into effect. My informant is a gentleman immediately from Nacogdoches.["][2] I trust this information is not correct, it however was accredited at Natchitoches and has excited Some uneasiness.

Many of the Citizens West of the Mississippi are yet impressed with an opinion, that they are shortly to fall under the dominion of Spain, and the Spanish officers here and at Pensacola take frequent occasions to remark "that West and East Florida would be given in exchange for the Territory West of the Mississippi, but on no other conditions would a Cession be made.["]

> I am Sir very Respectfully
> Your obdt Sevt
> (Signed) *William C. C. Claiborne*

The Honble
The Secretary
of State—

1. Also printed as Governor Claiborne to the Secretary of State, April 5, 1805, TP, 9: 432–3, with variations in punctuation and with emphasis not found on this copy.

2. Turner's letter has not been found. His informant may have been the Irish-born Edward Murphy, syndic in Natchitoches, land speculator, tobacco planter, Indian trader, and merchant with extensive contacts in northwest Louisiana and Spanish Texas. On him, see David LaVere, "Edward Murphy: Irish Entrepreneur in Spanish Natchitoches," *Louisiana History* 32, no. 4 (fall 1991), 371–91. It is less likely the informant was Diego Morphy, businessman, sometime partner of Bellechasse, Spanish consul in Charleston, South Carolina, in 1800 and in New Orleans in the fall of 1810, and a resident of Natchitoches in 1804. For references to this shadowy operative for the Spanish, see David Hart White, *Vicente Folch, Governor in Spanish Florida, 1787–1811* (Washington, D.C.: University Press of America, 1981), 101. Morphy, by then acting as Spanish consul in New Orleans, reported to Vicente Folch, governor of West Florida, in the fall of 1810 that he had learned American rebels were planning to move against both Mobile and Pensacola. See also Stanley Faye, "Consuls of Spain in New Orleans, 1804–1821," *Louisiana Historical Quarterly* 21, no. 3 (July 1938), 679.

{188}

To James Madison
New Orleans April 8th 1805

Sir,

I enclose you a translation of an address[1] recently made to the Board of Aldermen. The Translation has done great injustice to the original. A perusal however of the paper[2] enclosed will give you Some information as to the present State of the City.

> I am Sir very Respectfully
> Your Hble St
> (Signed) *William C. C. Claiborne*

The Honble
James Madison
Secretary of State

1. Not present.
2. Not present.

{189}

To John Sibley
New Orleans April 8th 1805[1]

Sir,

Your Letter of the *[Blank]* Ultimo was delivered to me by Lieutenant Murry. The abuses in the Post Department I have long Seen and regretted, but a remedy Seems difficult. I however rely much on the vigilance, talents and attention of the Post Master general [*sic*], and trust that in a Short time, a due portion of care will be manifested at the various offices.

The Council are yet in Session, but an adjournment will probably take place in five or Six days. If a call of the Legislature during the Summer Should become necessary, you Shall be advised thereof.

I can assure you Sir, that I exercise no manner of controul over any newspaper printed in this City, and if you have read a regular file of the Orleans Gazette, you must have perceived that; that paper has given Currency to many Severe and illiberal Strictures, on my public conduct, private manners and general deportment in Life. Strictures which I confess were very disagreeable to me, but being unconscious of doing wrong to my Country or to Man, the calumnies which have appeared, occasion me no Serious inquietude. I do not know upon what authority the Editor of the Orleans Gazette made the attack on you which is refered to in your Letter, but I am persuaded that he would publish any piece in explanation which might be offered. I am thus impressed, because altho the various pieces which have appeared against me were as Hostile to my reputation as language could make them, I discovered that productions in my vindication were not refused a place in the Same Paper.

The Legislature have passed a Bill providing for the establishment of County Courts. Natchitoches is constituted a County, and an Inferior Court is to be organized therein to be called the County Court. I will carry this Law into Execution as soon as possible; but until the Court is organized, the Civil Commandant retains his present powers.

> I am Sir very respectfully
> Your Hble Sert
> (Signed) *William C. C. Claiborne*

Doctor Sibbly [*sic*]

1. Also printed as Governor Claiborne to John Sibley, TP, 9: 433–4, without the paragraphing in this copy and with variations in punctuation.

{190}
To the Master and Wardens, Port of New Orleans
> Circulair to the Master and Wardens of
> the Port of New Orleans[1]
> Dated 10th April 1805

Sir,

Desirous of availing the Public of your Services as a Warden of the Port of New Orleans, I have the Honour to enclose you a Commission and to Subscribe myself[2]

> Very Respectfully
> Your Hble Sert
> (Signed) *William C. C. Claiborne*

1. This is the undated circular referred to in Letter No. 211, Governor Claiborne to the Master and Wardens, Port of New Orleans, April 23, 1805.

2. The men commissioned as wardens of the Port of New Orleans on April 10, 1805, were Andrew Burke, Hugh Pollock, John B. Labatut, Michael Fortier, George Pollock, Thomas Urquhart, and Eugene Dorsière. Register of Civil Appointments in the Territory of Orleans, February 13, 1806, Wardens of the Port, TP, 9: 602.

{191}
To James Madison
New Orleans April 16th 1805[1]

Sir,

Since my last nothing has occured worthy communication. The Schism in the Church is not yet adjusted; the enclosed reply[2] to Colonel Bellechasse has greatly irritated him and his friends and will I fear eventuate in a personal combat. I have learned that the Marquis of Casa Calvo takes an Interest in the dispute between the Priests, and uses his influence on the occasion. I have it in contemplation to address a Letter to the Marquis on the Subject and to Suggest the indelicacy and impropriety of any interference on his part.

The Louisiana Bank is in operation and has acquired confidence. It has made considerable discounts and received large deposits. The Council will probably rise in a few days; they have by Law divided the Territory into twelve Counties, and directed the Establishment of an Inferior Court in each County. In order the better to organize these Courts, and to Select Suitable characters to fill the various offices, I propose visiting several of the Counties, but I shall take care not to be too distant from the City to permit of my prompt attention to any instructions which you may give me. I will thank you therefore to forward your communications (as usual) to New Orleans, and provision will be made to convey them immediately to me.

> I am Sir very Respectfully
> Your obdt Sert
> (Signed) *William C. C. Claiborne*

The Honble
James Madison
Secretary of State

1. Also printed as Governor Claiborne to the Secretary of State, April 16, 1805, TP, 9: 434–5.

2. Not present, but clearly a reference to a letter published as an extra of the *Orleans Gazette,* April 13, 1805, signed as "Un de vos Concitoyens" (One of your Citizens). The letter, in French, attacks Bellechasse for his polemical response to Fr. Patrick Walsh's pastoral letter of March 27, 1805. See also Governor Claiborne to the Secretary of State, April 16, 1805, TP, 9: 434 n. 26, and the references cited there.

{192}
To Manuel Andry

To M Manuel Andrey Commandant of
the Parish of St John the Babtist [*sic*]
New Orleans April 16th 1805[1]

Sir,

I have understood that the Levee in your District is in Several places in bad order, and that an early repair thereof, is essential to the Interest of the Farmers generally. I advise therefore that you immediately instruct the persons owning the Land where the Levee is bad, to repair the Same, and in case of their refusal or neglect So to do, that you call upon the Inhabitants of your District generally to make the necessary repairs, and the expense attending the Same, the owners of the Land will be bound to pay. If the Roads of your District should be out of repair, you will cause the Ancient regulations relative to roads to be observed, as these regulations are yet in force.

I am Sir very Respectfully
Your Hble Sert
(Signed) *William C. C. Claiborne*

1. Also printed as Governor Claiborne to Manuel Andry, April 16, 1805, TP, 9: 435 with variations in punctuation and text. Biographical information on this respected, French-speaking, sugar planter may be found in Governor Claiborne to the President, March 4, 1810, and Manuel Andry to Governor Claiborne, January 11, 1811, TP, 9: 870 and 915–6, respectively.

{193}
To Obadiah Crawford[1]

(Private) New Orleans April 16th 1805

DSir,

Your Letter by the last Post was duly received. The Model of your invention I gave in charge Several months ago to a Mr. Derbigny, who promised to convey it in Safety to the Seat of Government, and to lay it before the Secretary of State. I gave also to that Gentleman the fifty Dollar Bank Note which you enclosed me and requested him to pay the Fees attending a Patent.

Mr. Derbigny was one of the Louisiana agents to Congress; he has not informed me the result of your application, But I persuade myself he has been attentive to your Interest, and that a Patent has been obtained[.]

I am Sir very Respectfully
Your obdt Hble Sert
(Signed) *William C. C. Claiborne*

Mr. Crawford

1. Obadiah Crawford was a resident of the Mississippi Territory. Although Claiborne did not personally know Crawford, the governor apparently wrote Secretary Madison a letter of introduction on October 1, 1804, describing Crawford as a "Young Man of great Mechanical genius, and an industrious . . . member of society." The letter and the fifty dollars from Crawford to pay for registering the patent were carried by Pierre Derbigny with a box containing a model of Crawford's cotton machine to the secretary of state. The secretary of state's office at this time was responsible for registering patents. See also Dear Sir [*sic*], October 1, 1804, CLB, 2: 344.

{194}
TO JOHN BOWYER
New Orleans April 19th 1805[1]

Sir,

Having understood by Colonel Freeman that you were made a member of a Court Martial and ordered to this City, I have appointed Mr. Theophilus Collins[2] Commandant Pro tem of Opelousas and to whom you will be pleased to deliver the Records and Papers of the District now in your possession[.]

I pray you to accept my thanks for your faithful public Services[.]

> I am Sir very Respectfully
> Your Hble Sert
> (Signed) *William C. C. Claiborne*

Captain Boyer

1. Also printed as Governor Claiborne to John Bowyer, April 19, 1805, TP, 9: 437, with variations in punctuation and text.

2. Theophilus Collins (d. August 20, 1810) was described at the time of his death as "an old and respectable inhabitant" of the county of Opelousas. *Louisiana Gazette,* August 30, 1810, p. 3, c. 2. At the time he was under scrutiny as a potential appointee in the new American government, and was characterized as an American of "wealth, sense and respectability, long resident in" Louisiana. Persons recommended by Governor Claiborne for members of the Legislative Council of the Orleans Territory, enclosed in Joseph Briggs to the President, August 17, 1804, Opelousas, TP, 9: 277. List of Persons Born within the Limits of the United States Residing at New Orleans, August 31, 1803, enclosed in Benjamin Morgan to Chandler Price, August 11, 1803, ibid., 10, identifies Collins as living in New Orleans, but like many early Louisiana planters, Collins apparently also had a home in Opelousas. Claiborne recommended Collins to President Jefferson as a candidate for the territorial legislative council. Governor Claiborne to the President, August 30, 1804, ibid., 285, identified Theophilus Collins of Opelousas as a native American. Little more than a week later, April 29, 1805, Claiborne appointed Collins judge in Opelousas. Register of Civil Appointments in the Territory of Orleans, February 13, 1806, ibid., 598.

{195}
TO JAMES MADISON
New Orleans April 19th 1805[1]

Sir,

In conformity to your Letter of the 25th of February, I have taken occasion to communicate verbally to the Marquis of Casa Calvo the impressions of the Executive of the United States upon the Subject of the late encrease of the Spanish armament within and near the disputed Territories, and also the provisional arrangements which were in consequence contemplated.

I Said to him that "the *President* had been desirous that pending the negociation between our two Governments, the present State of things Should not be innovated on by either party, and particularly that no new positions or augmentations of Military force Should take place on either Side, within the Territories claimed by both, eastward of the Mississippi," "But ~~understanding that~~ Since Spain had not only augmented her forces within the Territory aforesaid, & its vicinity, but established new Military Posts *he* had thought proper to Strengthen the garrisons of the United States on the Mississippi.["] I added that "the President was nevertheless Sincerely desirous that the existing differences Should be amicably adjusted, and he entertained Strong hopes that Such would be the result." The Marquis replied "that the forces of His Catholic Majesty had not been augmented at Baton Rouge, Mobile, or Pensacola in any other manner, than by concentrating at these places the troops which had been withdrawn from the various parts of Louisiana now in possession of the United States;["] He further observed that "in consequence of certain impressions which the conduct of our Minister at Madrid (Mr. Pinckney) had made on the mind of his Catholic Majesty, and a recent act of Congress which was construed by his Court as giving authority to the President to take possession of a part of Florida, a Fleet had been ordered to be fitted out at Cadiz and Terrol, for the purpose of carrying four thousand regular Troops to Mexico, which were to occupy various Posts in the Province of Taxus [Texas], and to advance as far as the Western Bank of the Sabine River under the direction of a Mr. Gramara (a Man of Military Talents and a great engineer) who was named Captain General of Taxus.— But (said the Marquis) the Fleet has never Sailed, and I Suppose its departure is delayed by the Satisfactory explanation which the President gave of the Act of Congress;—["] [sic] I have also received Letters of a late Date from St. [sic] Antoine and I do not learn from them the arrival of the Captain General Gramara, or that the Military Posts in the Interior Provinces had been Strengthened." After Some other unimportant conversation, and re-ciprocating assurances of personal consideration and of great Solicitude for the preservation of a good understanding between our two Nations the conference terminated.

> I am Sir very Respectfully
> Your Hble Sert
> (Signed) *William C. C. Claiborne*

The Honble
James Madison
Secretary of State

P.S. The Marquis told me that of the contemplated departure of a Fleet from Cadiz and Terrol its object and destination he had (in conformity to his instructions) Some time Since informed the Minister near the United States Mr. D'Yrujo [*sic*].
  W. C. C. C[.]

  1. Also printed as Governor Claiborne to the Secretary of State, April 19, 1805, TP, 9: 435–7, with emphasis marks not found here and variations in punctuation and text.

{196}
To Theophilus Collins
New Orleans April 20th 1805[1]

Sir,
  Desirous of availing the Public of your Services as Commandant Pro tem of the District of Opelousas I have the Honor to enclose you a Commission and to request that you would apply to Captain Boyer for the Public Records and Papers.

  I do not expect that your Powers as Commandant will long continue; An Inferior Court will very Soon be organized in Opelousas and then your Authority as Commandant will cease, the organization is only delayed until the Law is printed.

  I hope to be able to visit Opelousas in the Course of a few weeks[.]

> Accept assurances of my High
> Consideration & Respect
>
> (Signed) *William C. C. Claiborne*

Theophilus Collins Esqr.
Opelousas

P[.]S. I Shall again Solicit your Services under the County Court Law[.][2]

1. See Letter No. 194, To John Bowyer, April 19, 1805, referencing this appointment when Bowyer was assigned to New Orleans for court martial duty.

2. Little more than a week later, April 29, 1805, Collins was appointed judge in Opelousas. Register of Civil Appointments in the Territory of Orleans, February 13, 1806, TP, 9: 598.

{197}

To James Madison
New Orleans April 21st 1805[1]

Sir,

I was this Morning visited by the Marquis of Casa Calvo. We conversed freely on various ~~topicks~~ Subjects. He lamented the part which Spain had been compelled to take in the War, but he complained much of the Conduct of the English in attacking the Spanish Frigates, the treachery and cruelty of which had excited throughout Spain a general Spirit of indignation and resentment. He Stated that there was not that disunion in the Spanish Cabinet which the news papers had represented. The Prince of Peace was high in the confidence of his King and had the management of the War; that Portugal would be compelled to declare against England, and a Spanish Army would take Post within her Dominions. I understood from the Marquis that he had received recent dispatches from his Court; he mentioned that Spain had in Commission Sixty Sail of the Line, and the French and Dutch Seventy, that the War would be conducted on the part of the allies with great energy. When Speaking of the pending Negociation between the United States and Spain, the Marquis expressed his Surprize at the desire of the American government to extend her limits; he introduced the old hackneyed argument that a Republican form of Government could not long exist over extensive Territories. He however Seemed to think that the issue of the Mission would be favorable to the wishes of the President. There is no doubt but the great object of the Spanish ~~Cabinet~~ Government will be to limit the possession of the United States Westwardly by the Mississippi and to attain which East and West Florida and other considerations would cheerfully be offered. I form this opinion from my various conversations with the Marquis, Governor Folch and other Spanish officers. Indeed many persons here yet believe that the Country West of the Mississippi will be receded to Spain; the Marquis in his private conversations encourages Such opinions, and until the issue of Mr. Monroe's Mission is known the Louisianians will not consider their Political destiny as fixed.[2]

I have always told you that the foreign agents here Saw with pleasure, and Secretly countenanced the discontents of the People, and I am persuaded, they have been mentioned to the Court of Spain as evidences of the favorable impressions which the former Masters of Louisiana had left behind them. Fearing that these discontents would tend to encourage Spain in her pretensions to West Florida, to lessen the Interest which France might otherwise take in effecting an accommodation and thus embarrass our administration, I Saw with regret and Surprize the unnatural part which three or four apostate Americans (of Talents) were acting here. But there are men Sir, whose Hearts are So organized, that no consideration not even the Interest of their Country could induce them to forego the pleasure of gratifying their personal resentments, and there are others in whose Breasts a Spirit of Avarice and Self aggrandizement has acquired Such an ascendency as to have stifled every honest emotion. But it is unnecessary to enlarge further on this Head. In every community there are degenerate characters, ~~and~~ but it affords me consolation to assure you that the great body of the Americans here are useful worthy members of Society and faithful to the Interests of their Country. I can add with like Sincerity that the Louisianians generally Speaking are a virtuous amiable people and will in a Short time become zealous Supporters of the American Union.

I am Sir very Respectfully
Your Obdt Sert
(Signed) *William C. C. Claiborne*

The Honble
The Secretary
of State

1. Governor Claiborne to the Secretary of State, April 21, 1805, TP, 9: 439 n. 38, refers to the letter printed here.

2. Claiborne reported to Madison the rumor and general belief among Louisianians that Spain was to regain Louisiana west of the Mississippi in Letter No. 78, December 11, 1804. This report on the conversation with Casa Calvo is the first intimation from a ranking Spanish official that Spain would be willing to swap the Floridas in order to establish the Mississippi River as the western boundary of the United States.

The extended, convoluted and ultimately unsuccessful diplomatic mission of James Monroe to Spain is succinctly and lucidly set forth in Dumas Malone, *Jefferson and His Time*, vol. 5, *Jefferson the President, Second Term, 1805–1809* (Boston: Little, Brown, 1974), 49–54. It is interesting to note that both Claiborne and Monroe were willing to rely on a direct, military solution for the border problems in the old Southwest.

{198}
FROM ALBERT GALLATIN

Copy of a Letter from the Secretary of
the Treasury
Dated Treasury Department February
25th 1805

Sir,

Agreeably to your request, I now enclose to you, copies of your two Letters of the 31st of December last and of the accounts accompanying them.[1]

I have the Honor to be very
respectfully
Sir your obdt Sert
(Signed) *Albert Gallatin*

Wm C. C. Claiborne Esqr
Governor of New Orleans
The accounts themselves not having
been examined, I cannot Say
whether all the Items will be thought
admissible
A. G.

1. See Letter No. 92, To Albert Gallatin, December 31, 1804. The second communication was Letter No. 200, W. C. C. Claiborne Disbursements during Temporary Government, Fourth Quarter 1804, December 31, 1804. There are slight differences in the text of the letter returned and the draft found here.

{199}
TO ALBERT GALLATIN

New Orleans December 31st 1804

Sir,

You will receive enclosed herewith an account, accompanied by the necessary receipts numbered from 1 to 12 inclusively, amounting to four Hundred and ten Dollars and forty five cents, for disbursements made by me during the Current quarter, on account of the incidental and contingent expenses of the Territory of Orleans[.]

I have the Honor to be very
Respectfully Sir your obdt Sert

(Signed) *William C. C. Claiborne*

The Honble
Albert Gallatin
Secty of the Treasury

{200}
W. C. C. Claiborne Disbursements
during Temporary Government,
Fourth Quarter 1804
The United States

To William C. C. Claiborne Governor of the
Territory of Orleans

To amount of Sundry Disbursements made on account of
the Incidental expenses of the Said Territory   Viz.

Nos. 1 & 2	For this Sum paid Messrs. Currell and Landall for white washing and painting the Interior of the Government House	cts Dls. $33.50
" 3 & 4	This Sum paid McNeil I[.] Montgomery and Pezerban for Stationary and Candles for the use of the office	" 52.75 "
5	This Sum paid James Workman for his Services as a Clerk, for the Month of October 1804	" 50 –"
6	This Sum paid Jos. Mammell for carrying Dispatches to Attackapas [sic]	" 30 –"
7 & 8	This Sum paid for repairing a Seal and making a Screw for Secretary's Office	" 31
9	This Sum for provisions &c furnished the Crew of the Brig Hero an English Cartel	" 41.20
10	This Sum paid Moreau Lisley for his Services as Interpreter for the Months of Nov. & Decr 1804	"120,–"
11	This Sum paid Benner and Horten for a Drip Stone for the use of the Govt House	" 12,–

12   This sum paid for 10 Cords of
            Wood for the Use of the Governors
            & Secretary's offices   " 40 -"

                                                       $410.45

New Orleans
Dec 31st 1804

{201}
To Albert Gallatin
New Orleans Dec 31st 1804

Sir,

You will receive herewith an account and Vouchers for Sundry Disbursements
of a Contingent nature, made by me during the Temporary Government of
Louisiana, amounting to three hundred and thirty four 34/100 Dollars [sic]—

In the Course of a few days, I shall prepare a general Statement of my
accounts and forward it to the Treasury. This Statement has hitherto been
delayed by insuperable difficulties.— Among others, the Death of one,[1] and
the Temporary absence of another Gentleman employed in my office, are
to be mentioned.

                              I have the Honor to be
                              very Respectfully
                              Your obdt Sert.
                              (Signed) *William C. C. Claiborne*

The Honble
Albert Gallatin
Secretary of the Treasury

1. Joseph Briggs, the son of Isaac Briggs, died of yellow fever on September 16, 1804. Governor Claiborne to the President, September 18, 1804, and Governor Claiborne to the Secretary of State, January 4, 1805, in TP, 9: 298 and 361, respectively. The notice of his death also
appeared in the *Union*, September 19, 1804, p. 1, c. 1.

{202}
W. C. C. Claiborne Disbursements
during Temporary Government, Third
Quarter 1804

The United States
            To William C. C. Claiborne Governor General and
            Intendant of the Province of Louisiana Dr. [sic] [Debit]

For Sundry Disbursements during the Temporary
Govert to Wit

Nos 1	This Sum paid P. Derbigny for his Services as Interpreter to the Government for the Months of July and August 1804 @ $60 p month	$120.00
2	This Sum paid Benjamin Morgan for the Hire of a Dispatch Boat	"20.0[0]
3	This Sum paid P. Derbigny Interpreter for the month of September — 1804	60–"
	Carried over	$200
	Brought over[1]	$200..0 [sic]
Nos 4	This Sum paid for Postage of Letters on public business from 1st of June to 30th of September 1804	"17.35
5	This Sum paid James Workman for his Services as a Clerk in my office for September 1804	50.00
6	This Sum paid John Watkins on account of Services performed as a Clerk in my office during the Temporary Govt	50."
		$334.35

1. Page 308 of the manuscript began with the entries on this line.

{203}
To James Madison
New Orleans April 21st 1805[1]

Sir,

I received by the last Mail your favours of the 10th & 11th Ultimo; The last ~~Evening~~ enclosing a copy of the Law for the Government of this Territory, the Inaugural address of the President and a Duplicate of your Letter of the 25th of February, the original of which I had previously received and acted upon. Having Some time Since been advised by the President himself of his intention to establish a Post Route from Washington by the Creek Nation, Fort Stoddart and the mouth of Pearl River to New Orleans, I immediately commenced a correspondence with the Marquis of Casa Calvo upon the

Subject, a copy of which I several weeks ago forwarded to the President. The Marquis had no objection to the contemplated Route, but to meet any exceptions which might be taken by Governor Folch, and at the Same time to pay him an attention with which he is pleased, I shall take an early opportunity to communicate with him also on the Same Subject, and will advise you the result.

My Letter of the [blank] Instant will inform you of the Substance of a conversation I had with the Marquis of Casa Calvo in relation to the late Military movements of the Spanish authorities in this quarter. The Marquis does not admit that the Military Posts in the Province of Taxus [Texas] have been Strengthened, but I cannot believe that the frequent Statements to the contrary made to me by Captain Turner of Natchitoches and from other respectable characters, are without foundation.

The expedition of Governor Folch to Baton Rouge was certainly unnecessary— Kempers insurrection as it is termed was in fact nothing more than a riot, in which a few uninformed ignorant men had taken a part, and the whole affair was at an end previous to Folchs departure from Pensacola: The Marching of Spanish Troops to Baton Rouge, the opening of a road to Pensacola[,] Governor Folchs Subsequent conduct at this place, United to the exertions which were made to keep alive among the Citizens here an attachment to Spain, all tend to confirm me in an opinion that about that time a rupture with the United States was deemed by the Spanish authorities a probable event. But of late their conduct has assumed a more pacific aspect.

The Law of Congress for the Government of this Territory will not give general Satisfaction. The people had been taught to expect greater priviliges, and many are disappointed— I believe however as much is given them as they can manage with discretion, or as they ought to be trusted with until the limits of the Ceded Territory are acknowledged, and the National attachments to our new Brothers less wavering, and the views and characters of Some influential men here better ascertained. I particularly allude to those persons who were formerly in the Spanish Service and are permitted by their Government to remain in Louisiana as pensioners, or in the enjoyment of their full pay. I am happy that my Letters of the 19th and 26th of January with their Several enclosures have reached you, and I indulge a hope, that their perusal have removed any impressions unfavorable to me which the intrigues and writings of a Small and unprincipled faction might otherwise have made upon your mind. I confess Sir, that the opposition, the cruel opposition I have experienced has harrowed up my feelings excissively [*sic*];—

but I found powerful consolation from an approving conscience, and a well founded hope that my Superiors to whom the difficulties I have combatted are known, would approbate a conduct which has throughout been directed by the purest motives of honest Patriotism[.]

I am Sir very Respectfully
Your most obdt Hbe Sevt
(Signed) *William C. C. Claiborne*

The Honble
James Madison
Secretary of State

1. Also printed as Governor Claiborne to the Secretary of State, April 21, 1805, TP, 9: 437–9, with emphasis not found here and with variations in punctuation and the text.

{204}
TO HENRY HOPKINS
New Orleans 22nd April 1805[1]

Sir,
Your Letter by Mr. Prevost has been received. I do not recollect to have omitted answering any of your Letters the contents of which Seemed to me to have been interesting to the Citizens of your District:— It is however very probable, that many of my communications to you may have miscarried.—

In the Dispute between Captain Boyer and yourself, I have not interfered;— the Subject was a delicate one, and I was not fully informed of the particulars. I however remember to have Said to you, in a Letter that altho I regretted the differences, my confidence in your integrity and Talents was undiminished, and gave you assurances of my esteem.— In a former Letter from you, I was advised of your determination not to pass any conveyances of Land Sold by Indians without instructions from me. I approved of that determination and thought it unnecessary to write upon the Subject. In relation to the persons confined for offences, I can only observe that I have long expected that provision would be made for the Speedy trial of minor offenders in the Counties where the offences were committed; But no provision of the kind is yet made, and I can only request that you would cause persons charged with breaches of the Law to be holden in Safe custody.

Having understood that you were ordered to this City[,] I will thank you to leave the records &c in the hands of Some Discreet Citizen and name him the Civil Commandant *Pro Tem;* One of the Cyndicks would be preferred.

> Accept assurances of my Sincere
> Esteem
> (Signed) *William C. C. Claiborne*

Lieutenant
Hopkins
Atakapas

1. Also printed as Governor Claiborne to Henry Hopkins, April 22, 1805, TP, 9: 440, with variations in the text and punctuation.

{205}
To James Madison
New Orleans April 22nd 1805

Sir,

Mr. Brown[1] the Collector, has just informed me of a Contest which the Revenue Cutter has recently had with two Privateers in the vicinity of the Balize.— The particulars are as follow. For Some time past two British Privateers from Providence[2] have been cruising off the Mouth of the Mississippi and were in the habit of Boarding every Vessel coming in and going out;— at length they captured an American Schooner (bound in) within view of the Block House, and not more than three miles distant from the Land.— The Captain of the Cutter thought it his duty to ~~arrest~~ rescue the Vessel which he did, after an engagement of one hour and convoyed her Safe into the River. During the engagement the Cutter Sustained little or no damage. The Schooner belonged to a Frenchman in this City; was from Campeachy and had on Board among other articles thirteen or fourteen thousand Dollars. If the war continues for any time I am fearful that the Gulph will be crowded with Privateers and that much Spoliation on our Commerce will be committed.

> I am Sir very respectfully
> Your Hble Sert
> (Signed) *William C. C. Claiborne*

The Honble
James Madison
Secty of State—

1. William J. Brown, who had been named collector of the Port of New Orleans following the death of the previous collector, Hore Browse Trist. Governor Claiborne to the President, August 29, 1804; Recommendation of William Brown as Collector [of the Port of New Orleans], enclosed in John M. Gelston to the President, September 1, 1804; the President to Governor Claiborne, October 28, 1804; and Governor Claiborne to the President, December 16, 1804; in TP, 9: 279–80, 289, 289–90, 316, and 355, respectively.

2. Providence, or New Providence, the Bahama island on which is located the town of Nassau, in the Bahamas Islands. The island was a traditional stronghold of pirates on the heavily traveled shipping routes from the Gulf of Mexico.

{206}
To Henry Hopkins

New Orleans April 22nd 1805
Private

My Dear Sir,

You are ordered to Detroit and transferred to the first Regiment. I regret your removal and wish it was in my power to change the place of your destination. If you Should feel inclined to leave the Service, I should be happy to confer on you Some civil appointment worthy your acceptance. But whether you continue in or retire from the army you may rely on the friendship of

(Signed) *William C. C. Claiborne*

Lieut Hopkins

{207}
To John Boyer [Bowyer]

New Orleans April 22nd 1805

Sir

Having understood that Mr. Collins was absent from Opelousas, I will thank you to leave the Records &c to the care of Mr. Peyten who will deliver the Same to Mr. Collins on his return. We have nothing new here; General Wilkinson is Governor of upper Louisiana.

I am Sir very Respectfully
Your obdt Sert
(Signed) *William C. C. Claiborne*

Captain Boyer [*sic*]

{208}

TO HENRY DEARBORN
New Orleans April 23rd 1805[1]

Sir,

To enable me to meet Some Small expenditures I have incurred in the Indian Department, to defray also the expenses of conveying by express to Pensacola a Letter to Governor Folch on public Business and other inconsiderable charges which accrued during the late temporary Government of Louisiana, and which remain unpaid I have drawn a Bill upon you on this day in favor of William Brown payable at five days Sight. I am not certain that yours is the proper Department to draw on But I was inclined to the opinion that until otherwise instructed it would be most regular. The accounts and vouchers Shall in due time be forwarded.

> I am Sir very Respectfully
> Your obdt Sevt
> (Signed) *William C. C. Claiborne*
>
> The Honble
> The Secty of War

1. Also printed as Governor Claiborne to the Secretary of War, April 23, 1805, TP, 9: 442.

{209}

TO CONSTANT FREEMAN
New Orleans April 23rd 1805[1]

Sir,

In order to execute a duty which devolves upon me as Governor of this Territory I find it necessary to visit the Several Districts on the Mississippi as far up as Concordia a Post opposite to Natchez. I propose to pass by Water and to Set out on the first day of next month[.]

If therefore the State of the Service will permit I shall be much obliged to you to furnish me with a non Commissioned Officer, Six privates and a comfortable Boat. On my Arrival at Concordia the Boat may immediately descend the river, and I do not believe that the soldiers whose Services I solicit will be more than three weeks absent from the City. You will oblige me by an early answer to this Letter.

> I am Sir very Respectfully
> Your Hble Sert
> (Signed) *William C. C. Claiborne*

Lieut Colonel Freeman

1. Also printed as Governor Claiborne to Constant Freeman, April 23, 1805, TP, 9: 442–3.

{210}
TO STEPHEN ZACHARY[1]
New Orleans April 23rd 1805

Sir

The Legislature of this Territory having authorized the Governor thereof to Borrow for the Public use a Sum of money not exceeding five thousand Dollars I have through you to address on the Subject the Directors of the Bank, and to Solicit the Loan of three thousand Dollars for Such period as they may prescribe, and on the usual Interest. A Copy of the Law authorizing the Loan is enclosed which I pray you to lay before the Directors.

Accept assurances of my great
respect & Sincere Esteem.
(Signed) *William C. C. Claiborne*

Stephen Zachary Esqr.
Cashier of the Louisiana
Bank

1. Stephen Zachary (sometimes the surname is spelled "Zacharie") is named on the list of persons submitted by Benjamin Morgan to Chandler Price in August 1803 as being born in another country, but speaking French and English. List of Persons Born Subjects of Great Britain or of this Colony Now Residing Here, enclosed in Benjamin Morgan to Chandler Price, August 11, 1803, TP, 9: 10. Zachary was a partner in "Holmes & Zackarie," merchants. See Memorial to Congress from Merchants of New Orleans, January 9, 1804, and Recommendation of William Brown as Collector, enclosed in John M. Gelston to the President, September 1, 1804, ibid., 158, 290, respectively.

{211}
TO MASTER[1] AND WARDENS,[2] PORT OF NEW ORLEANS
New Orleans April 23rd 1805[3]

Gentlemen,

Under the Act regulating the Port of New Orleans[4] it is made the duty of the Executive to appoint two or more Master Pilots. For the present I am of opinion that two Master Pilots are Sufficient for the Commerce of the Port, and I will thank you to recommend to me Suitable Characters. Captain Johnson[5] is now the only Acting Pilot; he is represented to me as an active, capable and honest man. A Mr. Bradish[6] has also been mentioned to me by a number of respectable Citizens as worthy of confidence; But as I would wish to make no appointments of Pilots without previously consulting the Board of Wardens, I have addressed you this Letter.

I am Gentlemen with great
Respect your obdt Sert
(Signed) *William C. C. Claiborne*

To the Master and
Wardens of the Port
of New Orleans

1. The Harbor Master of the Port of New Orleans was Samuel B. Davis, whom Claiborne appointed to office on April 10, 1805, and reappointed on April 21, 1809. Register of Civil Appointments in the Territory of Orleans, February 13, 1806, Wardens of the Port, and List of Civil and Military Officers, April 21, 1809, Harbor Master of New Orleans, TP, 9: 602, 836.

2. The port wardens appointed to office on April 10, 1805, were Andrew Burke, Hugh Pollock, and John B. Labatut. The dates of the appointments of Michael Fortier, George Pollock, Thomas Urquhart, and Eugene Dorsière are not listed, but probably were made the same date, or shortly thereafter. Register of Civil Appointments in the Territory of Orleans, February 13, 1806, Wardens of the Port, TP, 9: 602.

3. Also printed as Governor Claiborne to the Master and Wardens, Port of New Orleans, April 23, 1805, TP, 9: 443.

4. The act was approved March 31, 1805. *Acts Passed at the First Session of the Legislative Council of the Territory of Orleans, Begun and Held at the Principal, in the City of New Orleans, On Monday the Third Day of December, in the Year of Our Lord, One Thousand Eight Hundred and Four, and of the Independence of the United States the Twenty-Ninth* (New Orleans: James M. Bradford, 1805), 122–44.

5. William M. Johnson, who was appointed April 10, 1805. Register of Civil Appointments in the Territory of Orleans, February 13, 1806, Pilots, TP, 9: 602.

6. Captain George Bradish, who was appointed to office on April 27, 1805. Ibid.

{212}
FROM ANDREW BURK[1]

Wardens Office April 25th 1805
His Excellency Wm. C. C. Claiborne
Governor of the Territory of Orleans

Sir,

I have had the Honor to receive your Letter of the 23rd Instant addressed to the Master and Wardens of the Port of New Orleans requiring them to recommend to you two Suitable characters as Branch Pilots, and having Submitted the Same to the Wardens, I beg leave to in form your Excellency that

Captain Johnson and Captain Bradish are in their opinion as well as in mine fit and proper persons for that Office, and as Such we recommend them, being as far as we can learn Gentlemen of respectable professional ~~xxxxxx~~[2] ~~abilities~~ Talents and possessing considerable local knowledge and experience of the entrance of the Mississippi[.]

The Board of Wardens request your Excellency will accept of their respectful thanks for this mark of your confidence and attention them.

> I have the Honor to be Sir
> Your most obdt Sert
> (Signed) *Andrew Burk*

Master Warden

1. List of Persons Born Subjects of Great Britain or of this Colony Now Residing Here, enclosed in Benjamin Morgan to Chandler Price, August 11, 1803, TP, 9: 10, identified Burk as a native of Great Britain.

2. None of the letters in this word is decipherable.

{213}
TO VICENTE FOLCH Y JUAN
New Orleans April 26th 1805[1]

Sir,

For the convenience of the Officers, as well as the Citizens of this Territory, The President of the United States contemplates the establishment of a Post for the conveyance of Letters, from the City of Washington to Fort Stoddart on the Mobile and from thence by the Mouth of Pearl River to New Orleans[.]

As this contemplated Post will pass about ~~thirty~~ Seventy miles through the Territory possessed by Spain, I sometime Since advised the Marquis of Casa Calvo thereof, who promised to write to your Excellency on the Subject; But as I feel particularly solicitous that this Post which promises to be of Such public Utility Should meet no interruption, I cannot refrain myself ~~refrain~~ from addressing your Excellency upon the Same Subject, and to request that your friendly protection may be extended to the person or persons who may have the Mail in charge. Captain Carmick of the United States Army[2] will present your Excellency this Letter, and will convey to me your answer—

> Accept assurances of my great respect
> and High consideration

(Signed) *Wm. C. C. Claiborne [sic]*

His Excellency
Gov Folch
Pensacola—

1. Also printed as Governor Claiborne to the Governor of West Florida, April 26, 1805, TP, 9: 444–5.

2. Captain Daniel Carmick, commandant of the one hundred U.S. Marines assigned to New Orleans in May 1804. To Henry Dearborn, May 5, 1804, and To Edward D. Turner, May 6, 1804, CLB, 2: 129, 132, respectively. The identification of Carmick as a member of the United States Army is a mistake, but may reflect a simplified approach to the fact that command of all land forces in New Orleans formally rested with the U.S. Army, then commanded by Lieutenant Colonel Constant Freeman. Tommy Young, "The United States Army in the South, 1789–1835" (Ph.D. dissertation, Louisiana State University, 1973), 117.

{214}
PARDON OF WILLIAM COBB
Territory of Orleans

To all Persons to Whom these Presents Shall come &c
Whereas William Copp [*sic*] now in the Prison of the City of New Orleans in Said territory has been convicted before the Superior Court of Said Territory begun and Holden in the City of New Orleans of an assault on one Andrew Burk of the Said City, & one of the Justices of the peace thereof ~~for the Said City xxxx xxxxx xxxx~~[1] while aiding and assisting one of the Constables of the Said City in the exercise of his Office. Now therefore be it known that for divers good causes are thereunto moving I William C. C. Claiborne Governor of the Said Territory do by virtue of the Said powers in me vested grant full free and entire Pardon to the Said Cobb of and from the Said offence with which he Stands convict[ed] as aforesaid, and also all other offences with which he may Stand charged previous to the Date of these presents, and do hereby remit release and forever discharge him off and from all and Singular the pains penalties and forfeitures accruing by Law on account of the Same as aforesaid. Given under my hand and the Seal of the administration at the City of New Orleans this 28th day of April 1805 and in the 29th year of American Independence[.]

(Signed) *William C. C. Claiborne*

Seal

1. These words are obliterated with ink and undecipherable.

{215}
To James Madison
New Orleans 29th of April 1805[1]

Sir,

Since my last, I have addressed a letter to Governor Folch upon the Subject of the Road, and no private opportunity having offered, I have forwarded it by Captain Carmick of the Army,[2] who will also convey to me the Governors answer. Colonel Freeman was obliging enough, to grant me on this occasion the benefit of Captain Carmicks Services. Messrs[.] Sauvé[,] De[s]-trahan[,] and Derbigny reached their respective homes on the day before yesterday[.] On this morning Mr. Sauvé came to the City and paid me a visit. The Deputies are certainly dissatisfied, but I am inclined to think, that they will not attempt to enflame the public mind. The Council is yet in Session an adjournment, will take place in a day or two. I shall visit in a few days the Settlements on the Mississippi as high up as Point Coupeé [*sic*] but will return again to New Orleans in fourteen days; in the mean time Such dispatches for me as may arrive will be forwarded to me by my private Secretary who remains in the City.

> I am Sir very respectfully
> your obdt Sert
> *Wm[.] C. C. Claiborne*

The Honble
The Secty of State

1. Also printed as Governor Claiborne to the Secretary of State, April 29, 1805, TP, 9: 445–6, with variations in text and punctuation.
2. Daniel Carmick, commandant of the U.S. Marines stationed at New Orleans.

{216}
To the Legislative Council
New Orleans May 4th 1805[1]

Mr. President and Gentlemen of the Legislative Council!

A Committe[e] of your Honorable body having acquainted me that you had considered and exercised your Legislative Authority on the various Subjects which required immediate attention, and believing myself, that the Public Interest will Sustain no injury by a Short Recess, I come now to prorogue this assembly.—

Permit me to hope Gentlemen that the Acts which you have passed, will prove conducive to the object which we have all in view the general Welfare— Of the merit of Laws however experience is the only infallible Test. The result of our labors will as speedily as possible be laid before our fellow Citizens, and the public functionaries will proceed immediately to the execution of the Laws. Their defects will not escape the observation of the Judicious Citizen or enlightened magistrate; and it will devolve on the Legislature to provide the requisite amendments. To enable us to perform this duty with promptitude, I shall again at an early day, avail the Territory of your faithful public Services; I therefore declare that the Legislative Council is prorogued until the 20th day of June next.[2] Receive Gentlemen the assurances of my great respect and Esteem, accompanied with my best wishes for your prosperity and Happiness[.]

(Signed) William C. C. Claiborne

1. Also printed as Claiborne to the Legislative Council, May 4, 1805, TP, 9: 446, with emphasis not found here and variations in text and punctuation marks.

2. The legislative council did not resume its deliberations again until June 22, 1805, the first date that a quorum was present. To James Madison, June 26, 1805, CLB, 3: 105. In writing Secretary Madison in June 1805, nearly three weeks after he arrived to assume his duties, John Graham, then serving as territorial secretary, wrote that the "council formed a quorum the day before yesterday," which would have placed the first day of business on June 21, 1805. TP, 9: 457.

{217}

Circular to County Court Judges
(Circular)
To the different Judges of the County
Courts

Sir,

In conformity to a Law of this Territory, of which a copy is enclosed,[1] it becomes my duty to organize in the County of _____ [2] an Inferior Court of Law, and as it is of importance to Society, that the office of Judge Should be filled by a Citizen of Talents and Integrity, my choice has fallen upon you, and I persuade myself, that you will accept the Commission herewith forwarded.[3]

I am aware that your private concerns may render public employment inconvenien[t] to you— But we all are bound to contribute to the good of the Society with whom we live, and I do trust that on this occasion you will not withhold your Services. The Laws passed by the Legislature are now printing in the English and French languages, and as Soon as they are completed you shall be furnished with a copy. I will thank you to deliver the Commissions enclosed to the persons for whom they are intended, and to administer to each officer an oath to Support the Constitution of the United States, and also an oath faithfully and diligently to perform the duties of his Office[.]

> Accept assurances of my respectful consideration
> (Signed) *William C. C. Claiborne*

1. Not present. The law was titled An Act Dividing the Territory of Orleans into Counties and Establishing Courts of Inferior Jurisdiction Therein. See *Acts Passed at the First Session of the Legislative Council of the Territory of Orleans, Begun and Held at the Principal, in the City of New Orleans, On Monday the Third Day of December, in the Year of Our Lord, One Thousand Eight Hundred and Four, and of the Independence of the United States the Twenty-Ninth* (New Orleans: James M. Bradford, 1805), 144–208. Later the legislative council amended the law to stagger the sessions of the various county courts. See An Act to Amend an Act for Dividing the Territory of Orleans into Counties and Establishing Courts of Inferior Jurisdiction Therein, ibid., 372–4. Because of the confusion that could result from the shift of authority from the local commandants and syndics of the former Spanish government to the newly created county judges and justices of the peace under the U.S. government, the council belatedly adopted a statute stipulating that from the day the new judicial officials took their oaths of office the powers of the former authorities ceased. This law also defined the duties of the judges and justices of the peace. An Act Relative to the Judges of the County Courts, and Justices of the Peace in the Territory of Orleans, ibid., 388–98.

2. Clearly this was a form letter with the name of the county to be entered in the blank space provided. The form was used for each county except Concordia, whose appointed judge, James Williams, was a resident of Natchez. Compare with Letter No. 218, To James Williams, May 4, 1805.

3. The men initially appointed to the judgeships in the twelve counties and their locations were Theophiles [sic] Collins, Opelousas; John Alexander, Natchitoches; James Workman, Orleans; Edward C. Nicholas, Attakapas; Charles L. P. Danemours, Ouachita; James Williams, Concordia; William Miller, Rapides; Michael [sic] Cantrell, Acadia; James Mather, LaFourche; Pierre Bailley [sic], Iberville; Julien Poydras, Pointe Coupée; and Achilles Trouard, German Coast. Two of the men, John Alexander and William Miller, resigned their appointments by January 1806 and were replaced by Thomas Dawson (Rapides) and Edward Turner (Natchitoches). Register of Civil Appointments in the Territory of Orleans, February 13, 1806, Judges, TP, 9: 598; see also Marietta Marie LeBreton, *A History of the Territory of Orleans, 1803–1812* (Ann Arbor, Mich.: University Microfilms, 1973), 153.

{218}

To James Williams
New Orleans May 4th 1805[1]

Sir,

In conformity to a Law of This Territory of which a Copy is enclosed,[2] it becomes my duty to organize in the County of Concordia an inferior Court of Law, and as it is of importance to Society, that the office of Judge should be filled by a citizen of Talents and integrity, my choice has fallen upon you and I persuade myself that you will accept the Commission herewith forwarded.[3]

I am aware that your private concerns may render a removal to Concordia inconvenient. But it is not necessary that you Should pass all your time in your County, nor would your Official duties prevent your practicing in the Courts which may be held at Natchez or in its vicinity— I trust, ~~that~~ therefore that on this occasion you will give to the Territory of Orleans the benefit of your Services. The laws passed by the Legislature are now printing in the English and French Languages, and as Soon so they are completed, you Shall be furnished with a copy. I will thank you to deliver the Commissions enclosed, to the persons for whom they are intended, and to administer to each officer an oath to Support the Constitution of the United States, and also an oath faithfully and diligently to perform the duties of his office.

> Accept assurances of my respectful
> Consideration
> (Signed)
> *William C. C. Claiborne*

Mr. James Williams
Natchez

PS. I do not know the Christian name of Mr. Richardson, you will be pleased to insert it.
W. C. C. C[.]

1. Also printed as Governor Claiborne to James Williams, May 4, 1805, TP, 9: 447.

2. Not present.

3. This letter and the packet of other commissions sent with it were mailed by Claiborne to his brother, F. L. Claiborne, who, like Williams, also was a resident of Natchez, with the request that they be delivered to Williams. To Major Claiborne, May 4, 1805, CLB, 3: 36–7.

BIOGRAPHICAL SKETCHES

PREFACE TO THE
BIOGRAPHICAL SKETCHES

The occasion for writing these essays was the editing of the William C. C. Claiborne Letter Book, 1804–1805, on deposit in the Louisiana and Lower Mississippi Valley Collections of the Louisiana State University Libraries. The Claiborne letter book came to my attention during research for a paper dealing with Governor Claiborne's impact on the foreign policy of Jefferson and Madison toward Spain.[1] The lack of readily accessible information on the characters and personalities of the men—American, English, Spanish, and French—who people the pages of those letters prompted my efforts to identify them and the events in which they took part during the early years after the transfer of Louisiana to the United States.[2]

Not all of the individuals named in the letters are examined here. The men whose lives are traced were, or sought to be, important in the establishment of the United States government in lower Louisiana, the Orleans Territory that became the state of Louisiana. Some of these associates of Governor Claiborne might be thought of today as "middle managers." They were mayors of New Orleans, judges, sheriffs, members of the territorial legislature, and military officers, either in the armed services of the United

1. That research was published as a two-part essay, Jared W. Bradley, "W. C. C. Claiborne and Spain: Foreign Affairs Under Jefferson and Madison, 1801–1811," "Part I, The Early Negotiations, 1801–1806," *Louisiana History* 12, no. 4 (fall 1971), 297–314, and "Part II, A Successful Expansion, 1807–1811," ibid., 13, no. 1 (winter 1972), 5–26.

2. *A Dictionary of Louisiana Biography,* gen. ed. Glenn R. Conrad (Lafayette: University of Southwestern Louisiana, 1988), fills a gap in Louisiana historiography, but did not appear until approximately eighteen years after I had begun research on the men identified in these essays.

States or the Territory of Orleans. They served the governor as administrators and advisors in the years before the "Burr conspiracy" burst on Louisiana and the nation. They were either personal friends or political allies. Some of them started out as supporters of Claiborne, but later opposed him, both personally and politically. A few of the men identified in these sketches made no lasting contribution to the development of Louisiana. They briefly claimed the attention of the governor, and in turn ours today.

The chief problem in writing about any of the men named in the letter book is identifying and finding the limited amount of information available on them. Some factual information on their lives and activities has appeared in other studies, most often as an incidental part of the big picture of how Louisiana fits into the history of the United States. The history of Louisiana into the twentieth century has been developed chiefly from the national perspective through reliance on the writings of figures of national importance, particularly Thomas Jefferson and James Madison. Since publication of the six volumes of the *Official Letter Books of W. C. C. Claiborne, 1801–1806,* edited by Dunbar Rowland, early in the twentieth century, the perspective has shifted only slightly to include that "Jeffersonian Centurion."[3]

Previous histories dealt most often with the major events of the years through and beyond the conclusion of the War of 1812: the Louisiana Purchase itself; the Burr conspiracy; the victory of Andrew Jackson over the British at the Battle of New Orleans; the treachery of General James Wilkinson; the Barataria pirates, Jean Laffite and his brother Dominique You; the struggle of Daniel Clark's heir, Myra Clark Gaines, to obtain her inheritance; and the victory of the "ancient Louisianians" over the Americans in the sociopolitical tug-of-war that developed between the French and the Americans, who arrived in the years after the Louisiana Purchase.

Virtually all these histories covered their subjects in such a way as to gloss over the salient questions about Governor Claiborne and the men he chose to help him establish the government of the United States in Louisiana. This is particularly true of Dr. John Watkins, Lewis Kerr, Judge James Workman, Joseph Deville Degoutin Bellechasse, and Evan Jones. Partly, this has occurred because writers have chosen to "mine only the [romantic] surface levels" of Louisiana's rich veins of history.[4] In a few instances, this may

---

3. The reference is to the subtitle of the only biographical study of Governor Claiborne published to date: Joseph T. Hatfield, *William Claiborne: Jeffersonian Centurion in the American Southwest* (Lafayette: University of Southwestern Louisiana, 1976).

4. Joseph G. Tregle, Jr., "The Antebellum Period," in *A Guide to the History of Louisiana,* ed. Light Townsend Cummins and Glen Jeansonne (Westport, Conn.: Greenwood Press, 1982), 27.

be because the men surrounding Claiborne, like the governor himself, were not as colorful as some of their contemporaries.[5] A more compelling reason for the lack of studies of these men may well be the dearth and inaccessibility of research materials. In some instances, however, the problem for writers is not the lack of research materials, but the quantity of them that must be read, analyzed, and interpreted to stimulate interest, or to challenge and awaken new perspectives on long-held viewpoints.

An example is the definition of "ancient Louisianians." Governor Claiborne's use of the term suggested that he meant the French who had lived in the territory for a number of years; however, he never said how long, nor was he consistent in his application of the term.[6] Perhaps the clearest explanation of who the French in Louisiana were occurs not in any of the letters of Governor Claiborne, but in one of the despatches of the French consul in New Orleans in 1812. The consul divided the "'large number of Frenchmen'" living in his jurisdiction into four categories: (1) the planters and merchants who retained French citizenship after the Louisiana Purchase; (2) the French from the first direct emigration from Santo Domingo, which started in 1797; (3) the Santo Domingo refugees expelled by the Spanish from Cuba; and (4) the Frenchmen who came directly from France to Louisiana and were unable to return to their native country.[7] Some of the Santo Domingo refugees were in fact Frenchmen who had emigrated to New Orleans by way of Santo Domingo.[8] Strangely, this definition ignores the descendants of the earlier French settlers in Louisiana, many of whom, but not all, were Acadians. It was these earlier French settlers who John Watkins said were "already as good Americans as any in the U. States."[9]

A number of the men in these letters—Dr. John Watkins, Benjamin Mor-

---

5. R. Randall Couch, "William Charles Cole Claiborne: An Historiographical Review," *Louisiana History* 36, no. 4 (fall 1995), 453.

6. See, e.g., Letters No. 16, 18, and 25, To James Madison, October 16, 19, and 27, 1804.

7. Paul F. LaChance, "The 1809 Immigration of Saint-Domingue Refugees to New Orleans: Reception, Integration and Impact," *Louisiana History* 29, no. 2 (spring 1988), 110–2. The author points out (p. 110 n. 5) that several hundred refugees from Santo Domingo arrived in New Orleans before the Louisiana Purchase, and that as many as one thousand refugees from there arrived in 1803–1804. He further states (p. 109) that 10,000 French refugees arrived in 1809.

8. Ibid., 133.

9. John Watkins to Secretary Graham, September 6, 1805, enclosed in Secretary Graham to the Secretary of State, September 9, 1805, Clarence E. Carter, comp. and ed., *The Territorial Papers of the United States*, vol. 9, *The Territory of Orleans, 1803–1812* (Washington, D.C.: U.S. Government Printing Office, 1940), 504.

gan, James Workman, Lewis Kerr, Bellechasse—played significant roles in the history and development of Louisiana and the United States, but their contributions are largely unknown and unrecognized. This is surprising, considering that the addition of the Louisiana Purchase territory to the United States by President Jefferson doubled the size of the nation.

The objectives in writing these essays were to identify as many as possible of the important early territorial personalities; establish their known accomplishments; delineate their personalities; and cast some light on the interpersonal relationships in those years and thereby provide insights into the individual characters, all within the context of the place and time in which they lived. Hopefully, the readers of these essays will find them as interesting to read as they were to research and write.

Note: The sketches appear in the order in which the subjects became important in the letter book.

James Francis Pitot (November 25, 1761–November 4, 1831) by all accounts was a man of "unflattering disposition," but of "solid understanding."[1] The latter description provides insight as to why he was a prominent figure in the business and politics of early New Orleans.

Pitot was born in Villedieu-les-Poëles, Normandy, France. When he was about twenty-three years old, Pitot went to Cap-Français, Santo Domingo, where he settled into a business career. With the outbreak of the revolution in Santo Domingo in 1791, he returned to France. In the fall of 1793 he apparently set out to return to Cap-Français, but instead landed in Philadelphia. After becoming a naturalized citizen of the United States in June 1796, Pitot moved to New Orleans the following August, taking Jean Lanthois as a business partner. Lanthois also was a refugee from Santo Domingo and a naturalized citizen of the United States.[2]

In 1802–03, after reports began to circulate that Spain had ceded Louisiana back to France, Pitot visited France with both business and politics in mind. At least this seems to be the import of the unpublished manuscript

1. Characterization of New Orleans Residents, enclosed in James Wilkinson to the President, July 1, 1804, entry 52, and List of the most Recommendable persons for military offices, entry 100, in Clarence E. Carter, comp. and ed., *The Territorial Papers of the United States,* vol. 9, *The Territory of Orleans, 1803–1812* (Washington, D.C.: U.S. Government Printing Office, 1940), 252 and 256, respectively (hereinafter cited as TP, with volume and page range).

2. Henry C. Pitot, *James Pitot (1761–1831): A Documentary Study* (New Orleans: Bocage Books, 1968), 13–4, 20, 23, 33, 34, 39, 44. This brief biography by a descendant of James Pitot contains greater information than shall be given here, particularly on the personal life and two marriages of Pitot. A reproduction of his likeness faces the title page of that publication.

"Observations sur la Colonie la Louisiane de 1796 á 1802," which has been attributed to him.[3] This critique of Spanish rule in Louisiana certainly aids in understanding why Pitot was welcomed to public office after the United States acquired Louisiana.

Pitot apparently became involved in public affairs almost immediately after his return to New Orleans in 1803. He was one of the twelve men serving on the Municipal Council when Louisiana was transferred to the United States.[4] Following the resignation of Etienne de Boré as mayor of New Orleans (May 26, 1804), Claiborne appointed Pitot to that office (June 2, 1804) on the recommendation of the Municipality (city council).[5] Like his good friend Boré, Pitot was pro-French, but a businessman first. Before six months had elapsed, Pitot submitted his resignation to Claiborne twice (October 31 and November 30, 1804) because of the low salary that went with the office. However, Claiborne refused to accept the resignations and even persuaded Pitot to accept reappointment as mayor under the new territorial government (March 11, 1805). As a consequence, Pitot served as mayor of New Orleans for nearly fourteen months (until July 27, 1805).[6] Pitot also held appointment (May 13, 1805) as justice of the peace.[7] Later, he was appointed auctioneer (September 5, 1807), an office created separately from the office of notary public by ordinance of Governor Claiborne three days after the transfer of Louisiana to the United States.[8] After the New Orleans Library Society was chartered, Pitot served as one of its direc-

3. René J. LeGardeur, Jr., and Henry C. Pitot, "An Unpublished Memoire of Spanish Louisiana, 1796–1802," in John F. McDermott, ed., *Frenchmen and French Ways in the Mississippi Valley* (Urbana: University of Illinois Press, 1969), 73–86, evaluates the manuscript.

4. "Administrations of the Mayors of New Orleans, 1803–1936," comp. and ed. Works Project Administration (project 665-64-3-112, typescript; New Orleans, March 1940), 1.

5. Ibid., 5; Joseph Briggs to the President, August 17, 1804, enclosing, Persons recommended by Governor Claiborne for members of the Legislative Council of the Orleans Territory; Governor Claiborne to James Pitot, February 27 and 28, 1805, enclosed commission as Mayor of New Orleans; and Register of Civil Appointments in the Territory of Orleans, February 13, 1806; TP, 9: 277, 404, and 603, respectively; and Pitot, *James Pitot*, 55–6.

6. "Administrations of the Mayors," 9.

7. Register of Civil Appointments in the Territory of Orleans, February 13, 1806, Justices, TP, 9: 599.

8. Return of Civil Appointments, Pardons &c. from the 1st of July 1807, to the 31st Decr. 1807 inclusive—Orleans Territory, Auctioneer, *Official Letter Books of W. C. C. Claiborne, 1801–1816*, ed. Dunbar Rowland, vol. 4 (1917; New York: AMS Press, 1972), 147; and Louis Moreau Lislet, comp., *A General Digest of the Acts of the Legislature of Louisiana: Passed from the Year 1804, to 1827, Inclusive, and in Force at the Last Period with an Appendix and General Index*, vol. 1 (New Orleans: B. Levy, 1828), 37.

tors.[9] Following the organization of the state government in 1812, he was appointed (March 13) Orleans district (parish) judge. In this capacity Pitot served as president of the police jury, the governing body of Orleans Parish, for seventeen years (1813–30).[10]

Pitot complained of his low salary as mayor, but continued to be active in the business world of New Orleans. While mayor in 1804–05, he was elected (January 1805) to the board of directors of both the Bank of Louisiana, which Governor Claiborne chartered in 1804, and the Orleans Navigation Company, which the territorial council chartered in 1805. Pitot was a board member of the navigation company until 1812 and served as its president in 1808.[11] Pitot also was a member of the board of directors of the New Orleans Insurance Company (1807–10).[12] He was one of the regents of the University of Orleans when that body petitioned (1812) the national government for all or part of the land on which stood Government House, the structure built by the Spanish government for use as a public school, but converted into the territorial capitol and courthouse by the U.S. government.[13] Following the death of Daniel Clark in 1813, Pitot, with Joseph Deville Degoutin Bellechasse and Chevalier François Dusuau de la Croix, served as an executor of Clark's estate.[14]

9. Pitot, *James Pitot,* 88.

10. Ibid., 97–8.

11. Governor Claiborne to the Secretary of State, January 13, 1804 [1805]; New Orleans Navigation Company to the President, May [blank] 1808; TP, 9: 368 and 789, respectively; and John G. Clark, *New Orleans, 1718–1812: An Economic History* (Baton Rouge: Louisiana State University Press, 1970), 288, Table VI; 292 n. 9; and 293, Table VIII. See also *Louisiana Gazette and New Orleans Advertiser,* February 13, 1807, p. 3, c. 3.

12. Clark, *New Orleans,* Table XII, facing p. 342 (unnumbered page).

13. Memorial to Congress from the Regents of the University of Orleans, April 20, 1812, TP, 9: 1014–16.

14. Nolan B. Harmon, *The Famous Case of Myra Clark Gaines* (Baton Rouge: Louisiana State University Press, 1946), 272–3.

JAMES BROWN

James Brown (September 11, 1766–April 7, 1835) was the son of John Brown, a Presbyterian minister, and Margaret Preston of Virginia. His oldest brother, John, Jr., was U.S. senator from Kentucky.[1] James's younger brother Samuel, a doctor, came to New Orleans in 1806, but settled near Natchez and later moved to Alabama.[2]

James received his early education at Liberty Hall, the school established by his father in the Shenandoah Valley of Virginia. The school is known today as Washington and Lee University.[3] Later, James briefly attended the College of William and Mary before beginning a law career in Kentucky (1789), where his brother John was making a name for himself. James was doing well in Kentucky when he sought political appointment in Louisiana through both of Kentucky's U.S. senators: his brother John, who had studied law under Jefferson, and John Breckinridge, a distant kinsman who was Jefferson's closest political advisor on western affairs.[4] Unlike others who

1. On the oldest brother, see *Dictionary of American Biography*, s.v. "Brown, John."

2. See *Dictionary of American Biography*, s.v. "Brown, Samuel"; and James A. Padgett, ed., "The Letters of Doctor Samuel Brown to President Jefferson and James Brown," *Register of the Kentucky Historical Society* 35, no. 111 (April 1937), 100–1.

3. Freeman H. Hart, *The Valley of Virginia in the American Revolution, 1763–1789* (Chapel Hill: University of North Carolina Press, 1942), 31, 41, 74, 80, 165.

4. Reference to Brown's economic status may be found in several places. See, e.g., the President to Governor Claiborne, August 30, 1804; James Brown to John Breckinridge, January 15, 22, September 17, 1805, all in Clarence E. Carter, comp. and ed., *The Territorial Papers of the United States*, vol. 9, *The Territory of Orleans, 1803–1812* (Washington, D.C.: U.S. Government Printing Office, 1940), 282, 369, 378–80, 506, respectively (hereinafter cited as TP, with volume and page range). The kinship of the Browns and Breckinridge is mentioned

sought public office in Louisiana, Brown stated that he was willing to be a naval officer, customs collector, or attorney general.[5] Despite his apparent modesty, it soon became clear that Brown wanted a position better than secretary of state, his last public office in Kentucky,[6] as well as one that would challenge his ability and satisfy his ambition for greater reward and recognition.

Brown applied for a position in Louisiana in September 1803, but it was not until July 20, 1804, that Jefferson advised Brown that he had been appointed Orleans Territory secretary effective that fall (October 1, 1804).[7] Brown and his wife had left Lexington, Kentucky, about June 1, so they received the news of his appointment en route to Louisiana.[8] Although he left Kentucky in the spring, Brown did not assume his duties as territorial secretary until the end of November 1804, presumably because of the prevalence of yellow fever in New Orleans.[9] In the meantime, Jefferson, without Brown's knowledge, appointed the Kentuckian judge on the Orleans Territory Superior (Supreme) Court because of his knowledge of the French and Spanish languages.[10] Brown could not have been at work much more than

in *Dictionary of American Biography,* s.v. "Brown, John." On the contacts between John Brown and Jefferson, and Breckinridge and Jefferson, see Dumas Malone, *Jefferson and His Time,* vol. 4, *Jefferson the President, First Term, 1801–1805* (Boston: Little, Brown, 1970), 241–3; and vol. 5, *Jefferson the President, Second Term, 1805–1809* (Boston: Little, Brown, 1974), 37, 252–3.

There is no biography of James Brown. Lawrence K. Fox, "The Political Career of James Brown" (master's thesis, Louisiana State University, 1946), provides most of the personal data about Brown's life, but does not fully come to grips with his subject and often must be cross-checked. The best departure point for a study of Brown's life is *Dictionary of American Biography,* s.v. "Brown, James." A likeness of Brown is reproduced in Padgett, "Letters of Doctor Samuel Brown," between pages 120 and 121.

5. Arthur P. Whitaker, *The Mississippi Question, 1795–1803: A Study in Trade, Politics, and Diplomacy* (1934; Gloucester, Mass.: Peter Smith, 1962), 240; and Recommendation of James Brown as Collector [for the Port of New Orleans], December 28, 1803, TP, 9: 145–6.

6. "Kentucky State Papers. Excerpts from Executive Journal No. 1, Governor Isaac Shelby," *Register of the Kentucky Historical Society* 27, no. 81 (September 1929), 587.

7. The President to James Brown, July 20, 1804, TP, 9: 269.

8. Padgett, "Letters of Doctor Samuel Brown," 123–4.

9. See Letter No. 4, To James Brown, October 4, 1804, and Letter No. 65, To James Madison, November 26, 1804. The *Louisiana Gazette,* November 30, 1804, p. 3, c. 1, reported that "On Monday last [November 23] . . . , the Honorable James Brown of Kentucky, Secretary for the Territory of Orleans," arrived in this city "with his Lady and Suite, all in good health."

10. On Brown's knowledge of French and Spanish, and his appointment as Superior Court judge, see James Brown to John Breckinridge, January 15, 1805; the President to James Brown,

five weeks when he resigned as territorial secretary and declined the territorial judgeship (January 8, 1805), both on the same grounds, the low salaries.[11] Jefferson wanted Brown to take the judgeship until May or June
1805. Brown performed the territorial secretary's duties for two weeks
longer (until January 22, 1805), even though Jefferson had declared the office vacant on December 1, 1804, nearly two weeks before Brown's appointment as judge was confirmed.[12]

Two months after relinquishing the territorial secretary's duties, Brown
accepted the first of three appointments that he was to hold through most
of Jefferson's second term as president. Brown accepted appointment from
the U.S. attorney general (March 22, 1805, and March 31, 1808) as district
attorney of Orleans Territory, the post Jefferson had promised John Brown
he would give to James.[13] Later in the year James accepted appointment
(July 8, 1805) as U.S. agent for the eastern district of Orleans Territory and
New Orleans to investigate land claims.[14] Prior to any of these appointments, Brown was named as one of the seventeen founding regents of the
elaborate, but unfinanced, educational system known as the University of
Orleans, created by the legislative council and approved by the governor on
April 19, 1805.[15]

December 1, 1804; the President to Governor Claiborne, January 7, 1805; and James Brown
to the President, January 8, 1805; in TP, 9: 282, 341–2, 363, and 365, respectively.

11. James Brown to the President, January 8, 1805, and James Brown to John Breckinridge, January 15, 1805, in TP, 9: 365–6 and 369, respectively. Marietta M. LeBreton, *A History of the Territory of Orleans, 1803–1812* (Ann Arbor, Mich.: University Microfilms, 1973),
181, points out that Brown resigned the office of territorial secretary sixteen days after arriving
in New Orleans to accept the post of Superior Court judge.

12. The President to Governor Claiborne, January 7, 1805; Secretary Graham to the Secretary of State, October 23, 1805; and James Brown to the Secretary of State, January 7, 1806;
in TP, 9: 363, 516, and 559, respectively.

13. The President to Governor Claiborne, January 7 and March 14, 1805; James Brown
to the Secretary of State, May 7, 1805; and James Brown to the Secretary of State, December
23, 1807; in ibid., 363, 417, 448–9, 770–1, respectively.

14. Secretary of the Treasury to the President, June 26, 1805; Secretary of the Treasury to
Allan B. Magruder, James Brown, and Felix Gundy, July 8, 1805; James Brown to the Secretary
of the Treasury, August 21 and September 3, 1805; James Brown to Governor Claiborne,
March 19, 1806; and Governor Claiborne to the Secretary of the Treasury, December 14,
1808; all in ibid., 457, 468–9, 495, 496–7, 613–5, and 812, respectively.

15. *Acts Passed at the First Session of the Legislative Council of the Territory of Orleans,
Begun and Held at the Principal, in the City of New Orleans, On Monday the Third Day
of December, in the Year of Our Lord, One Thousand Eight Hundred and Four, and of the
Independence of the United States the Twenty-Ninth* (New Orleans: James M. Bradford,
1805), 306.

On November 27, 1805, Brown was appointed second lieutenant in the territorial militia. The following spring he was appointed (May 6, 1806) justice of the peace.[16] The same spring (June 7), he and Louis Moreau Lislet were authorized by the territorial legislature to prepare a guide to the laws in force in Louisiana at the time the United States received the colony from France.[17] The work was published two years later under the title *Digest of the Civil Laws Now in Force in the Territory of Orleans, with Alterations and Amendments to Its Present System of Government. By Authority* (New Orleans [Bradford and Anderson], 1808). Governor Claiborne's criticism of the English language portion of the digest for its many inaccuracies and his belief that the French language portion would have to be declared the legal text calls into question Brown's reputed command of French and Spanish.[18]

Claiborne's criticism of Brown's portion of the 1808 digest reflects the open disagreement that had developed between the two by 1806, and raises the question of the origins of their differences. Initially, Claiborne welcomed Brown into the territorial government, but was defensive about what he felt was his most vulnerable point, his inability to speak French. In responding to Jefferson on Brown's appointment, Claiborne noted Brown's knowledge of French, saying it would be useful. The governor also added that he hoped his current study of French would give him a tolerable knowledge of the language in a few months.[19]

After he arrived in the territory, Brown privately criticized Claiborne because he did not speak or read either French or Spanish.[20] The criticism may reflect not only Brown's personal pride, but also his desire to be territorial governor. A basis for this view is seen in Brown's political maneuvering to gain appointments as territorial secretary and district attorney. Also,

16. Register of Appointments in the Militia of the Territory of Orleans, enclosed in Secretary Graham to the Secretary of State, May 8, 1806, Tenth Regiment; and Register of Civil Appointments January 1–June 30, 1806, enclosed in Richard Claiborne to [the Secretary of State], Justices of the Peace, June 30, 1806; TP, 9: 639 and 662.

17. *Acts Passed at the First Session of the First Legislature of the Territory of Orleans Begun and Held in the City of New-Orleans, on the 25th Day of January, in the Year of Our Lord One Thousand Eight Hundred and Six, and of the Independence of the United States of America the Thirtieth* (New Orleans: Bradford and Anderson, 1807), 214–9.

18. On the criticisms, see George Dargo, *Jefferson's Louisiana: Politics and the Clash of Legal Traditions* (Cambridge, Mass: Harvard University Press, 1975), 156–7; and Governor Claiborne to the Secretary of State, October 7, 1808, TP, 9: 802–3.

19. Governor Claiborne to the President, October 5, 1804, ibid., 307, 309.

20. James Brown to John Breckinridge, January 22 and September 17, 1805, ibid., 379, 508.

Brown's irritable reaction to notification by Claiborne that he had been appointed territorial secretary suggests more than the surviving correspondence of either man indicates.[21] Finally, the attempt made in Washington in the fall and winter of 1804 to replace Claiborne as governor of Orleans Territory reinforces the belief that Brown wished to be territorial governor.[22] How Brown felt about Claiborne became known to both Madison and Jefferson through one of Brown's letters to John Fowler, one of the men who recommended Brown for appointment as collector of the port of New Orleans.[23] Referring to the letter, Madison reported that "Brown without indicating any personal ill will agst the Govr appears to concur fully in denouncing his want of talents and weight of Character."[24]

James Brown's desire to be territorial governor may have affected his attitude toward Claiborne, but there were other factors that placed a strain on the relationship of the two men. After arriving in New Orleans, Brown became a friend of Edward Livingston, the disgraced former district attorney of New York who sought to restore his reputation through acquisition of wealth in New Orleans. Their friendship led to difficulties for Brown. Claiborne immediately became suspicious of the association. Livingston was persona non grata to Jefferson and was far from friendly to the Jefferson administration.[25] There is little doubt of the closeness of Brown and Livingston. Within a matter of weeks after assuming his duties as territorial secretary, Brown joined the unsuccessful movement to have Livingston named as his assistant to draft a much-needed legal code for the territory.[26] After appointment as district attorney, Brown was retained (1806) by Liv-

21. See Secretary Brown to the Secretary of State, October 26, 1804, and the President to Governor Claiborne, January 7, 1805, ibid., 313–4 and 363, respectively. The Claiborne missive is Letter No. 4, To James Brown, October 4, 1804. Henry Johnson to J. F. H. Claiborne, May 4, 1806, stated that Brown wished to supersede W. C. C. Claiborne as governor. John Francis Hamtramck Claiborne Papers, 1797–1884, Southern Historical Collection, Wilson Library, University of North Carolina, Chapel Hill.

22. On attempts to replace Claiborne late in 1804, see Everett S. Brown, ed., *William Plummer's Memorandum of Proceedings in the United States Senate, 1803–1807* (New York: Macmillan, 1923), 220–1 (entry for December 12, 1804).

23. See Recommendation of James Brown as Collector, December 28, 1803, TP, 9: 145.

24. Governor Claiborne to the Secretary of State, January 19, 1805, ibid., 375 n. 26.

25. William B. Hatcher, *Edward Livingston: Jeffersonian Republican and Jacksonian Democrat* (University: Louisiana State University Press, 1940), 99, 106–8, 118–22, 135–6, 143–51, 197 n. 34. See also Dargo, *Jefferson's Louisiana,* 75.

26. Dargo, *Jefferson's Louisiana,* 113–5.

ingston to represent him in the celebrated batture case. Since Brown's capacity as district attorney made him counsel for the government, his service to Livingston raises the dual questions of conflict of interest and moral turpitude.[27] Brown's conduct in this instance alienated Jefferson, who had taken a personal interest in the case. Claiborne and John W. Grymes, newly appointed district attorney in 1808, sought to have Brown replaced as U.S. agent for land claims with Grymes in that year, but were unsuccessful.[28] Ultimately, the relations between Brown and Claiborne were so strained that Brown once referred to Claiborne as leaving a wake of filth behind wherever he went.[29]

During the Burr conspiracy, General James Wilkinson suspected James and Samuel Brown of being intimates of Aaron Burr. Wilkinson's suspicions may well have sprung from James Brown's opposition to Wilkinson's suspension of the writ of habeas corpus.[30] Since Burr's father had been president of the College of New Jersey (Princeton) when John Brown, Sr., attended the college, and Burr and John Brown, Jr., had been colleagues in the U.S. Senate for several years, it is quite likely that Burr visited James in New Orleans as he had visited John in Frankfort, Kentucky, on the way south. However, no evidence has been found to indicate that the contacts between Aaron Burr and the Browns were anything more than social courtesies.[31]

Nothing in James Brown's conduct or personality suggests that he had any part in the expansionist schemes afloat in territorial New Orleans. By nature, he found mixing with people distasteful.[32] A contemporary who knew him in Kentucky described Brown as a "towering & majestic person,

27. See Hatcher, *Edward Livingston,* 147.

28. Prior to departing from Virginia for the Territory of Orleans to establish his residence, Grymes sought any position the president might believe him "capacitated to discharge" (TP, 9: 772); subsequently, he sought a better-paying position, pointing out that the office and salary he anticipated were withheld from him by James Brown, whom Grymes described as being openly opposed to the Madison administration. Philip Grymes to [the President], August 27, 1808 (ibid., 802–3). Grymes subsequently was supported by Claiborne for the post of register of the land office (Governor Claiborne to the Secretary of the Treasury, December 14, 1808, ibid., 812–3).

29. James A. Padgett, ed., "Some Letters of James Brown to Presidents of the United States," *Louisiana Historical Quarterly* 20, no. 1 (January 1937), 87.

30. Dargo, *Jefferson's Louisiana,* 201 n. 34.

31. Fox, "Political Career of James Brown," 35–9.

32. On Brown's disdain for mixing with the people, see his reference to "moboratory" quoted in Whitaker, *Mississippi Question,* 242.

very proud, austere & haughty[,] in fact repulsive in manner, and . . . exceedingly unpopular."[33] The only time Brown was elected to public office by the people was in 1811, when he, with Alexandre Labranche and Jean N. Destréhan, was chosen to represent the German Coast, the district above New Orleans in which he owned a plantation with his nephew, John Humphreys.[34] Brown's election to the constitutional convention was a tribute to his legal knowledge and extensive law practice. When the convention assembled, Brown was appointed to the committee to compose a draft constitution. On the last day of the convention, he was called to preside during the presentation of a gift to the permanent president, Julien Poydras.[35]

After Louisiana was admitted to the Union, Brown was twice chosen by the state legislature (1812–17, 1819–23) to represent the state in the U.S. Senate. His election in 1812 came after Jean N. Destréhan declined the office and Governor Claiborne's interim appointee, Thomas Posey, was rejected by the state legislature.[36] Brown was defeated for reelection in 1817 by Claiborne.[37] Before his second term in the Senate ended, Brown resigned (December 10, 1823) to accept appointment by President James Monroe as U.S. minister to France.[38] Like Albert Gallatin, who preceded him in the Paris mission, Brown found it frustrating. Having agreed to a treaty of commerce in the spring of 1822, the French were not yet ready to discuss the claims of Americans that grew out of the undeclared naval war with France during the Napoleonic War. As a consequence, Brown regarded his arrangements for the visit of Marie Joseph Paul Yves Roch Gilbert du Motier, the Marquis de Lafayette, to the United States in 1824–25 as the highlight of his service in France.[39] James's part in arranging for Lafayette's visit may have been given additional poignancy because the marquis had been John Brown, Jr.'s, commanding officer in Virginia during the American Revolu-

33. "Memoirs of Micah Taul," *Register of the Kentucky Historical Society* 27, no. 79 (January 1929), 356.

34. Fox, "Political Career of James Brown," 40, 67, 69, 70; and *Journal de la Convention D'Orléans de 1811–12* (Jackson, La.: Jerome Bayon, August 3, 1844), 3.

35. *Journal de la Convention D'Orléans*, 4, 19.

36. To General Posey, January 25, 1812, in *Official Letter Books of W. C. C. Claiborne, 1801–1816*, ed. Dunbar Rowland, vol. 6 (1917; New York: AMS Press, 1972), 209–11; and *Journal of the Senate during the Second Session of the First Legislature of the State of Louisiana* (New Orleans: Peter K. Wagner, 1813), 11.

37. *Dictionary of American Biography*, s.v. "Brown, James."

38. Ibid.

39. Fox, "Political Career of James Brown," 63.

tion.[40] Before the results of the 1828 presidential election were known, James Brown asked to be relieved of the diplomatic post in Paris. He returned to the United States in August 1829 and shortly thereafter retired from public life. In the fall of the year (November 6, 1829) Brown was given a farewell banquet in New York, which was attended by many men prominent in national political and social circles, among them Daniel Webster.[41]

James Brown's wife was Anna, better known as "Nancy" Hart, the daughter of Thomas Hart of Kentucky. Her youngest sister, Lucretia, married Henry Clay. Thus, during the mission to France, Brown's immediate superior was his brother-in-law, Henry Clay, who was secretary of state under President John Quincy Adams. Both James and Nancy Brown died in Philadelphia, where they established residence after returning to the United States. They had no children.[42]

40. See *Dictionary of American Biography,* s.v. "Brown, John."
41. Fox, "Political Career of James Brown," 64–5.
42. Ibid., 14–5, 67.

BELLECHASSE

Joseph Deville Degoutin Bellechasse (June 21, 1761–1837?) was born in New Orleans, one of three sons of Joseph Deville Degoutin and Marie Jeanne Caron.[1] An older brother named Charles was born in 1757 and a younger brother named François Marie was born in 1765.[2] No evidence has been found to indicate that a distinction was ever made between Joseph Deville Degoutin the father *(ainé, père)* and the son *(fils, jeune)* of the same name. It is known that the senior Degoutin died before his daughter Maria Francisca was married in 1786.[3] Like many of the eighteenth-century French settlers in lower Louisiana, Degoutin *père* was born in Acadia, Nova Scotia, where his father, Mathieu Desgouttins, had been *greffier* (recorder, or clerk of court) and lieutenant general in the colonial militia.[4]

The name of Joseph Deville Degoutin, *jeune,* is variously spelled among the Spanish and American documents. Until the early 1790s, the junior Degoutin's name appears as Deville, Deville Degoutin, Desgoutens, and de

1. Baptism of Joseph Deville Degoutin, July 1761 [*sic*], St. Louis Cathedral, Orleans Parish, Louisiana, Baptismal Register, vol. 4, 78. In his deposition given in support of Myra Clark Whitney Gaines's attempts to win her inheritance, Bellechasse said that he was born in 1760. See the *New Orleans Weekly Delta,* January 28, 1850, p. 3, c. 2.

2. Baptism of Charles Deville Degoutin, October 17, 1757, St. Louis Cathedral, Orleans Parish, Louisiana, Baptismal Register, vol. 3, 85; and Baptism of Marie Deville Degoutin, June 16, 1765, ibid., 5: 95, respectively.

3. Elizabeth Becker Gianelloni, *The Notarial Acts of Estevan de Quinones, 1785–1786,* vol. 2 ([Baton Rouge:] n. p., 1966), 68–9.

4. Bona Arsenault, *Histoire et Généalogie des Acadiens,* vol. 1 (Quebec: Conseil de la Vie Française en Amérique, 1965), 382.

Grontin. In one record, which granted Degoutin *jeune* permission to spend eight months in Principé, Santo Domingo, to arrange family matters in 1788, his name is given as "Josef Deville de Butein."[5] Unfortunately, Degoutin's application for the Principé visit is missing and only the index to the letter has survived.[6] Perhaps the most outrageous spelling of Bellechasse's name occurs in Governor Claiborne's correspondence. There it appears as "Bellchap Assilla Degantico."[7] Bellechasse apparently most often signed his name in later years, as he affixed it to the Louisiana Constitution of 1812, "J. D. Degoutin Bellechasse."[8]

The title Bellechasse, by which the younger Degoutin is best known in Louisiana history, is a commemorative and honorary French appellation associated with land, meaning fine hunting, or chase.[9] The title first was linked with the younger Degoutin late in April 1793 and appears to have grown out of one or more events in his life. In Deville Degoutin's military life the Bellechasse title could have stemmed from a demonstration of the same kind of physical prowess that his older brother Charles exhibited in 1796 when, after a ten-league (circa 30 miles) foot race, he captured near Pensacola a number of deserters from the Spanish Army.[10] References to "DeVille"— that is, Bellechasse—as the bearer of correspondence between Don Estéban Miró, governor of Louisiana, and Alexander McGillivray, leader of the

5. *Archivo General de Indias. Sección V, Gobierno. Audiencia de Santo Domingo Sobre la Época Española de Luisiana, legajo* 2545, folio 42, microfilm reel 111, Special Collections, Library, Loyola University, New Orleans, Louisiana (hereinafter cited as *AGI, Audiencia de Santo Domingo,* with *legajo* and folio numbers). Before 1793, Bellechasse's signature usually appeared as "Joseph Deville Degoutin."

6. See José de la Peña y Camara, Ernest J. Burrus, S.J., Charles E. O'Neill, S.J., and Maria T. G. Fernandez, *Catalogo de Documentos del Archivo General de Indias, Sección V, Gobierno. Audiencia de Santo Domingo Sobre la Epoca Española de Luisiana,* vol. 1 (Madrid: Dirección General de Archivos y Bibliotecas and New Orleans: Loyola University of New Orleans, 1969), 24, entry 227, 1) a).

7. A List of the Councellors [*sic*], undated, may be found in *Official Letter Books of W. C. C. Claiborne,* ed. Dunbar Rowland, vol. 2 (1917; New York: AMS Press, 1972), 375 (hereinafter cited as CLB, with volume and page numbers).

8. See Cecil Morgan, comp., *The First Constitution of the State of Louisiana* (Baton Rouge: Louisiana State University Press, 1975), "Facsimiles," 30, 29, and end pages, "Authentic Signatures."

9. Jack A. Reynolds, "Louisiana Place-Names of Romance Origin" (Ph.D. diss., Louisiana State University, 1942), xxxiii, 42–3.

10. Jack D. L. Holmes, *Honor and Fidelity: The Louisiana Infantry Regiment and the Louisiana Militia Companies, 1766–1821* (Birmingham, Ala.: [Jack D. L. Holmes,] 1965), 110–1.

Creek Indians, may be found in the surviving correspondence between these men.[11]

It also is possible the Bellechasse title grew out of ridicule. When Colonel Francisco Bouligny, a New Orleanian known for his sharp tongue and pen, applied the title to the thirty-two-year old Degoutin in the spring of 1793, it may have been because "Bellechasse" had just gotten engaged to Francisca Emilia Olivier. She was the daughter of cabildo member Carlos Honorato Olivier and had been one of the parties in a civil suit involving the question of marriage six years earlier.[12] Bellechasse applied for permission to marry Francisca in June 1793, but for reasons unknown they were never married.[13]

If events in the military and personal life of Degoutin *jeune* were insufficient to evoke use of the complimentary Bellechasse title, his numerous business transactions could have done it, although this seems less likely. Bellechasse's business life centered chiefly on the development and sale of land, ventures that may have begun about the time of his assignment as commandant at New Feliciana. In January 1801, Degoutin *jeune*, Pedro Olivier, and Louis de Clouet granted Santiago Jarreau of Pointe Coupée their power of attorney to sell land in New Feliciana.[14] Bellechasse's occasional references to his involvement with land development in Louisiana suggests that he was proud of his association with this business and that his connection with it was well known.[15]

Interest in the sale and/or development of land in frontier Louisiana was not new to the Degoutin family. When Degoutin *père* settled in Louisiana, he acquired property in New Orleans six miles below the town on the west bank of the Mississippi River, as well as in the Attakapas country. Indeed, Degoutin *père* was one of the early Acadian applicants for a land grant from the French government in the Attakapas.[16] It is quite likely that the family

11. See John W. Caughey, *McGillivray of the Creeks* (1938; Norman: University of Oklahoma Press, 1959), 234, 235.

12. Jack D. L. Holmes, "Three Early Memphis Commandants: Beauregard, Deville Degoutin, and Folch," *West Tennessee Historical Society Papers,* 18 (1964), 32 n. 162.

13. The application may be seen in *AGI, Audiencia de Santo Domingo, legajo* 2562, folio 345, microfilm reel 129.

14. Act of January 26, 1801, Notarial Acts of Pierre Pedesclaux, Notarial Archives, New Orleans.

15. See, for example, the reference in his March 30, 1808, letter printed in *Louisiana Gazette,* April 8, 1808, p. 2, c. 3.

16. Bellechasse's father was one of the earliest Acadian settlers from Nova Scotia to receive a land grant in Louisiana after the expulsion/migration of these people from Canada. He received a grant of 2,115.70 acres along Bayou Teche in south central Louisiana on June 13, 1764. See the map by Gertrude C. Taylor, *Land Grants Along the Teche, Part I, Port Barre to*

matters Joseph Deville Degoutin *jeune* arranged in Santo Domingo in 1788 involved land owned by his father and grandfather.

By 1806, Bellechasse was living below New Orleans, apparently on some of the riverfront property acquired by his father.[17] When he left Louisiana in 1814, his complimentary Bellechasse title was so strongly associated with this property that it was retained as the name of the place when Theodore Packwood and Judah P. Benjamin acquired it in the 1840s. The Bellechasse name for this locale continues to this day.[18] Prior to 1806, Bellechasse divided his time between residence in New Orleans and a plantation on the Côte des Allemandes, the first "German Coast" above the city.[19] In short, there is little reason to believe that anyone in New Orleans in the spring of 1793 other than Joseph Deville Degoutin was called Bellechasse.[20]

The young Joseph Deville Degoutin entered the military service of Spain as a distinguished soldier (June 1, 1777), a category that was open to him because his father served in the militia. By application and bravery, he rose through the ranks to cadet (June 1, 1780), sublieutenant (August 23, 1781), lieutenant (November 22, 1786), and captain (1797). During the American Revolution, in which Spain's chief objective was to regain colonial possessions, Degoutin participated in the captures of Fort Bute and Baton Rouge (1779), Mobile (1780), and Pensacola (1781). From 1786 into 1792, he was stationed in West Florida with various duties at Pensacola, Mobile, and Fort St. Stephens. Vicente Folch, commandant at Mobile, 1787–1792, credited young Lieutenant Joseph Deville Degoutin with the actual construction of Fort Estéban, later known as Fort St. Stephen, in the spring of 1789.[21] One

St. Martinville (1979). The senior Degoutin land concession was in the northwestern present-day St. Martin Parish near the town of Arnaudville. Mrs. Taylor states the acreage and boundaries depicted are approximate, but that the map is a copy of southwestern Louisiana surveys dating from 1810 to 1856 and is based on research in the *American State Papers* and the *Louisiana Register of State Land Claims*.

17. B[arthélémy]. Lafon, *Calendrier de Commerce de la Nouvelle-Orléans, pour l'Année 1807* (New Orleans: Jean Renard, 1806 [*sic*]), 63.

18. Robert D. Meade, *Judah P. Benjamin: Confederate Statesman* (New York: Macmillan, 1943), 57.

19. Governor Claiborne to the President, November 13, 1805, Clarence E. Carter, comp. and ed., *The Territorial Papers of the United States*, vol. 9, *The Territory of Orleans, 1803–1812* (Washington, D.C.: U.S. Government Printing Office, 1940), 526 (hereinafter cited as TP, with volume and page range); and *Louisiana Gazette*, August 14, 1804, p. 1, c. 2.

20. For a contrary view, see Holmes, "Three Early Memphis Commandants," 27.

21. The fort was named for Estéban Miró, ranking officer under Galvéz, the governor-general of Louisiana (1776–1782) and uncle of Vicente Folch. David Hart White, *Vicente*

of his frontier duties during this time (February 1789) was participation in the capture of fourteen escaped slaves camped on the Tensaw River in south Alabama.[22]

Bellechasse was well liked by governors Miró, Carondelet, and Gayoso, each of whom employed the robust young officer with one walleye,[23] as courier to deliver messages to secret agents in the western United States.[24] Carondelet described Bellechasse late in November 1796 as a "firm officer of talent" who could be depended on to exercise energy and courage in military and business matters.[25] By this date Bellechasse had been effectively in command of the newly built Fort San Fernando de las Barrancas (present-day Memphis, Tennessee) for almost six months, having replaced his recent commander at Mobile, Lieutenant Colonel Vicente Folch.[26] Perhaps to alleviate the shortage of food brought about by the severe flooding in St. Louis and St. Genevieve in 1797, Bellechasse provided St. Louis and the Illinois Country with their first shipment of sheep.[27] Bellechasse remained at Las Barrancas for its dismantling and evacuation by Lieutenant Colonel Carlos Howard in March 1797, working closely with Howard and receiving his praise when their work was completed. After brief stays in Campo de la Esperanza (Hopewell, Missouri) and St. Louis, Bellechasse was brought back to New Orleans by Gayoso near the end of September 1797.[28]

Folch, Governor in Spanish Florida, 1787–1811 (Washington, D.C.: University Press of America, 1981), 10–1.

22. *Archivo General de Simancas. Sección de Guerra Moderna. Hojas de Servicias Militares de América, 1787–1799, legajo 7291, cuaderno 1, Regimiento de Infantería de Luisiana, Diciembre 1787*, [p.] 52. See also Holmes, "Three Early Memphis Commandants," 28, 33; and Holmes, *Honor and Fidelity*, 111.

23. See the portrait of Bellechasse reproduced in Louisiana Historical Society, "Celebration of the Louisiana Centennial," *Publications of the Louisiana Historical Society* 6 (1912), facing p. 69.

24. Caughey, *McGillivray*, 234, 235.

25. Louis Houck, ed. and trans., *The Spanish Regime in Missouri; A Collection of Papers and Documents Relating to Upper Louisiana Principally within the Present Limits of Missouri during the Dominion of Spain . . . ,* vol. 2 (1909; New York: Arno Press, 1971), 130. The letter is dated 1795, but internal evidence clearly establishes that it should be 1796.

26. Abraham P. Nasatir, *Spanish War Vessels on the Mississippi, 1792–1796* (New Haven: Yale University Press, 1968), 117 n. 59, and 134.

27. Nicolas de Finiels, *An Account of Upper Louisiana*, eds. Carl J. Ekberg and William E. Foley; trans. Carl J. Ekberg (Columbia: University of Missouri Press, 1989), 64.

28. Ernest R. Liljegren, "Lieutenant-Colonel Carlos Howard and the International Rivalry for the Mississippi Valley, 1796–1798" (master's thesis, University of Southern California, 1939), 28 n. 30; 32 n. 5; 44–5; 46, nn.5, 6; 47–50; 53; 129; 140; 142. Copy owned by the author.

It was while in New Orleans in the fall of 1797 that Bellechasse married Adelaida Maria Josefa Lalande Dalcour. The two declared her dowry before the royal notary on March 11, 1796, and Bellechasse applied for the marriage license the following month.[29] Royal approval of the match was given September 19, 1796, but the wedding was delayed until after Bellechasse returned from the Las Barrancas assignment.[30] It seems likely, too, that while in New Orleans in the fall of 1797 Bellechasse was recommended for promotion to captain, the rank that appeared beside his name for the first time in the records of his next assignment, Pensacola.[31]

Bellechasse had not been assigned to Pensacola very many months when Gayoso selected him to command New Feliciana, the post being established on Thompson's Creek above Baton Rouge.[32] The New Feliciana assignment, which Bellechasse assumed early in 1798, was much like that at Fort San Fernando de las Barrancas in that it, too, was an observation post. However, New Feliciana was situated almost two hundred miles south of Las Barrancas, halfway between Baton Rouge and the disputed border with the United States. New Feliciana almost literally overlooked New Valentia, the settlement proposed for Bayou Sara by the U.S. senator from Ohio, John Smith.[33] However, there were significant differences between the assignments at Las Barrancas and New Feliciana. Barrancas was already operational, though in poor condition, when Bellechasse assumed command of it, whereas New Feliciana had to be built and organized. At Barrancas, Bellechasse was a bachelor, comparatively free of personal responsibilities. At New Feliciana, he was a married man. Most important, the superior officers with whom Bellechasse had established rapport during previous assignments were soon to depart the Louisiana scene.

The extant records do not reveal whether Bellechasse's quick temper and poor education were hindrances in the demanding assignment at New Feliciana, but personal problems manifested themselves. The effects of the

29. Act of March 11, 1796, Notarial Acts of Carlos Ximines, Notarial Archives, New Orleans.

30. Marriage of Joseph Deville Degoutin and Adelaida Maria Josefa Lalande Dalcour, October 4, 1797, St. Louis Cathedral, Orleans Parish, Louisiana, Marriage Register, vol. 2, 116, Act 425. The marriage was recorded in 1798, but the register does not further specify the date. Two fellow officers of Bellechasse, Joseph Crozat and Carlos Reggio, witnessed the ceremony.

31. Holmes, "Three Early Memphis Commandants," 33.

32. Ibid.

33. Thomas P. Abernethy, *The South in the New Nation, 1789–1819* (Baton Rouge: Louisiana State University Press, 1961), 333–4.

added financial responsibility, which a married man and post commander must assume, made themselves known first. On August 4, 1798, Bellechasse applied for reestablishment of his license for unlimited trade.[34] The following year the strain that Las Barrancas and New Feliciana made on Bellechasse's health made itself known. By May 1799, he had served nearly twenty-two years with the Spanish military. Citing his poor health, Bellechasse applied for retirement, but asked to be allowed to return to duty if his health improved. Bellechasse's desire to retire was so great that he offered to contribute five dollars a month to the war effort if the king would grant him retirement at half pay.[35]

Bellechasse apparently expected the two applications to be acted on favorably, but no decision on either had been made when Governor Gayoso unexpectedly died in July 1799. Eleven months after the death of Gayoso, Bellechasse still had heard nothing from either application, so he renewed both through the Marqués de Casa Calvo, interim military governor-general of Louisiana. Finally, in November 1801, the Marqués de Someruelos, newly appointed captain-general in Havana, granted Bellechasse the retirement as requested. However, the license for unlimited trade was denied. The captain-general advised Bellechasse through Casa Calvo that he knew nothing of such licenses for Bellechasse or anyone else.[36]

The immediate reaction to Someruelos's decision is not known, but the thirty-nine-year-old Bellechasse must have been shocked and angry. For the present, he apparently kept busy as executor of his mother-in-law's estate (she died in 1799) and job hunting. It may have been at this time that Bellechasse became associated with the plantation in the Côte des Allemandes and with Daniel Clark. As New Feliciana post commander, Bellechasse would have known that Clark wished to develop his extensive landholdings in Feliciana and Cabanocey.[37]

In August 1803, additional information on the seemingly abrupt end to Bellechasse's military career was provided by Pierre Clément Laussat. The

34. Salvadore Muro y Salazar, Marqués de Someruelos, to Antonio Cornel, November 8, 1800, refers to the date of Bellechasse's application. *AGI, Audiencia de Santo Domingo, legajo* 2568, folio 50, microfilm reel 135.

35. Holmes, "Three Early Memphis Commandants," 33.

36. Someruelos to Cornel, November 8, 1800, *AGI, Audiencia de Santo Domingo, legajo* 2568, folio 50.

37. Abernethy, *South in the New Nation*, 262–3, 335–6; and Sidney A. Marchand, *The Flight of a Century (1800–1900) in Ascension Parish, Louisiana* (Donaldsonville, La.: S. A. Marchand, 1936), 23 n. 5, 29, 37.

French colonial prefect for the transfer of Louisiana from Spain to France reported that he had obtained the services of Bellechasse as commander of the colonial militia. Laussat noted the Creole had twenty-four years of military experience and was "not personally well-disposed towards the Marquis de Casa-Calvo" because the Spaniard had "dismissed [him] from active service on unfavorable terms."[38]

More than a decade after Laussat's remarks, Louis de Clouet wrote that Casa Calvo released Bellechasse from service because he aided Daniel Clark in gathering information to document the perfidy of General Wilkinson. It seems that Bellechasse allowed Clark access to the secret communications from Governor Carondelet to Wilkinson. This was tantamount to treason to Casa Calvo, who regarded Clark as an American spy.[39] Although de Clouet's statement eventually may prove to be correct, it was not until the request from John Watkins in 1804 that Clark first sought evidence to prove Wilkinson had been in the pay of the Spanish. Equally important, it was not until after events centering about the "Burr conspiracy" that Clark began his own search for such evidence. Chronologically, therefore, de Clouet's statement is not supported by these events in the relations between Casa Calvo and Bellechasse. Until supporting evidence is brought to light, it must be concluded that Casa Calvo's treatment of Bellechasse was a reflection of the decision by Someruelos, the captain-general in Havana, and Casa Calvo's imperious personality.

Bellechasse regarded de Clouet as a friend, and they were associates in the development of Pointe Coupée. De Clouet, nonetheless, later characterized Bellechasse as a fool; but neither he nor Casa Calvo understood their former fellow officer, nor do they seem to have grasped the circumstances in which the altered balance in international power had left Spain and, as

38. Baron Marc de Villiers du Terrage, *Les Dernières Années de la Louisiane Française. Le Chevalier de Kerlérec, D'Abbadie—Aubry, Laussat* (Paris: E. Guilmoto, 1904), 418. Laussat pointed out in July 1803 that Casa Calvo required "all the military officers," which included virtually everyone of any note, to meet him, at which time they were required to sign an order saying yes or no, "whether they would remain in the service of the king of Spain." Laussat pointed out that the "pensions and the fortune of an infinite number of them depended upon their yes answer. Some of the mulattoe militiamen were held in prison for twenty-four hours to force them to say yes." James A. Robertson, ed. and trans., *Louisiana Under the Rule of Spain, France, and the United States, 1785–1807*, vol. 2 (1910–1911; Freeport, N.Y.: Books for Libraries Press, 1969), 44.

39. Stanley Faye, ed., "Louis de Clouet's Memorial to the Spanish Government, December 7, 1814 (Conditions in Louisiana and Proposed Plan for Spanish Reconquest)," *Louisiana Historical Quarterly* 22, no. 3 (July 1939), 810–1.

it were, them. Bellechasse may not have understood the realities of world power either, since he at first rejected Laussat's offer to head the militia, but on the advice of Clark decided to accept the appointment.[40] What Clark may have said to cause Bellechasse to change his mind can only be surmised, but it surely must have touched on the business arrangements between them as well as Clark's personal political ambitions. Clark also may have played on Bellechasse's resentment of Casa Calvo. Bellechasse disliked Casa Calvo because of his roles in the executions of French settlers in Louisiana under Governor O'Reilly and in the murders of hundreds of Frenchmen in Santo Domingo during the bloody Toussaint l'Ouverture rebellion. He also disliked Casa Calvo because he was part Irish.[41] The economic and emotional scars left on Bellechasse by the Casa Calvo-Someruelos decision in 1801 now began to work against Spanish interests.

Bellechasse advised Claiborne that he was declining the appointment to the territorial legislative council for fear that service on the council would attract the resentment of his creditors, foremost of whom was Daniel Clark.[42] A late-nineteenth–early-twentieth-century historian has said Bellechasse declined the appointment to the territorial council because he had been "active in calling public meetings to protest against the division" of Louisiana.[43] Although this is partly true, the real reason that Bellechasse declined the appointment may have been his dislike of Claiborne. Bellechasse's opinion of Claiborne was not publicly known until his testimony in behalf of Myra Clark Gaines was revealed in 1850. In the deposition he gave for that case, Bellechasse described Claiborne as "weak-minded" and his policies as "not wise or conciliatory."[44] After the transfer of Louisiana to the

40. Nolan B. Harmon, *The Famous Case of Myra Clark Gaines* (Baton Rouge: Louisiana State University Press, 1946), 53, 270–1. Isaac J. Cox, in *The West Florida Controversy, 1798–1813: A Study in American Diplomacy* (1918; Gloucester, Mass.: Peter Smith, 1967), 194, described Louis de Clouet as a confidant of General Wilkinson. Therefore, Bellechasse's situation was considerably more complicated than it appears.

41. On Bellechasse's anti-Irish sentiment, see George Dargo, *Jefferson's Louisiana: Politics and the Clash of Legal Traditions* (Cambridge: Harvard University Press, 1975), 45.

42. Claiborne to Madison, November 5, 1804, James Madison Papers, Series I, General Correspondence and Related Items, 1723–1859, *Presidential Papers Microfilm No. 2974*, reel 8, Troy H. Middleton Library, Louisiana State University Libraries.

43. Alcée Fortier, *Louisiana, Comprising Sketches of Parishes, Towns, Events, Institutions, and Persons, Arranged in Cyclopedic Form*, vol. 1 ([Madison, Wis.:] Century Historical Association, 1914), 82.

44. *New Orleans Weekly Delta*, January 28, 1850, p. 3, c. 2. Perry Scott Rader, "The Romance of American Courts: Gaines vs New Orleans," *Louisiana Historical Quarterly* 27, no. 1 (January 1944), 72–3 does not print all of Bellechasse's deposition.

United States, Bellechasse tried to relinquish command of the militia organized by Daniel Clark and other Americans for reasons of poor health, "insufficiency of means," and poor command of the English language, but was persuaded to remain.[45] Claiborne apparently kept Bellechasse as head of the militia to draw on his military experience, knowledge of Louisiana, and popularity with the Louisiana populace.[46]

Partly in response to Bellechasse's discouragements and partly because he did not completely trust the native Louisianian because of his ties to Clark, Claiborne tried to reduce his reliance on Bellechasse as the breach developed with Clark early in 1804. At the end of March, Claiborne called on the second in command of the volunteer militia, Major Eugene Dorsière, to organize the militia of the Territory of Orleans.[47] Perhaps because Dorsière, too, was obligated to Clark and subordinate to Bellechasse, nothing came of this early attempt to organize the territorial militia.[48]

It was not until after the territorial council provided for the creation of the militia in the spring of 1805 that organization of the military arm of the territorial government began. Claiborne credited Bellechasse with ultimate completion of the task,[49] but wavered when it came to recommending the native Louisianian for promotion to brigadier general in command of the militia. After first recommending Bellechasse for the rank, Claiborne advised Secretary of War Henry Dearborn that the colonel was honest, but lacked the independence, strength, and energy necessary for the post. The general officer promotion would have to go to an American, whom Claiborne said he would name in the summer of 1806.[50]

Two factors may have influenced Claiborne to delay naming the militia commander. First, and most important, was Bellechasse's attempt to resign (May 1806) from the territorial legislature over the attempt to reinstate Spanish legal practices. Bellechasse had accepted appointment to the council

45. To Col. Bellechasse, March 17 and March 22, 1804, CLB, 2: 49–50 and 53, respectively; and Register of Appointments in the Militia of the Territory of Orleans, enclosed in Secretary Graham to the Secretary of State, May 8, 1806, TP, 9: 632.

46. To Col. Bellechasse, March 17, 1804, CLB, 2: 49; and Governor Claiborne to the Secretary of State, December 4, 1805, TP, 9: 541.

47. To Maj. Dorsier [sic], March 30, 1804, CLB, 2: 71.

48. To James Madison, June 28, 1804, and July 5, 1804, ibid., 231 and 236–7, respectively.

49. Militia General Orders, September 20, 1804, CLB, 2: 337; and To James Madison, October 16, 1804, ibid., 354; Governor Claiborne to the Secretary of War, December 13, 1807, TP, 9: 768.

50. To Henry Dearborne [sic], May 31, 1806, CLB, 3: 320.

in the fall of 1805. His attempt to resign followed the resignations of Jean Destréhan and Pierre Sauvé. Destréhan and Sauvé quit the territorial legislature shortly before Claiborne vetoed the legislation that would have reinstituted Spanish civil law and blocked the further introduction of common law into Orleans Territory.[51] Second, Claiborne may have suspected Bellechasse would never take up arms against Spain or France. However, it is unlikely the governor knew such a report had been made to the Spanish government as recently as May 12, 1806, by Bellechasse's friend Ignacio Fernandez de Velasco, or that the report contained the added statement that Bellechasse accepted a colonelcy in the Orleans Territory Militia only because of popular pressure and politics.[52]

The timing of Velasco's report on Bellechasse's loyalty should be noted. The report was not made until after Bellechasse had asked John Watkins about rumors of invasion plans being made by prominent members of the territorial militia who also were known to be members of the recently organized Mexican Association.[53] Equally noteworthy is the fact that Velasco's report was made less than three months before the Spanish incursion near Natchitoches; less than six months before revelation of the Burr conspiracy; and about seven months before Casa Calvo joined the pro-French faction in the Spanish government. It also should be noted that during the 1805–06 war scare with Spain, while Claiborne was at Natchitoches, Bellechasse was left with responsibility for protecting New Orleans from attack.[54] Before the frontier crisis had passed, Claiborne praised both Bellechasse and John B. Macarty, another Louisiana native who was colonel of the Fourth Regiment of the territorial militia, for their efforts to rally Louisianians to support the territorial government.[55]

Less than three months later, perhaps as a result of General Wilkinson's sweeping accusations about the involvement of businessmen and public officials in New Orleans in the Burr conspiracy and Bellechasse's close association with Daniel Clark, Claiborne developed doubts about the trust he had placed in Bellechasse. Writing Bellechasse on January 7, 1807, the governor demanded to know the names of the men who had invited him to join with them in plans for "an unauthorised expedition to Mexico" and "to seize the present Governor of the Territory of Orleans and send him away

51. To James Madison, May 26, 1806, ibid., 313; To Henry Dearborn, October 10, 1806; ibid., 4, 28; and Dargo, *Jefferson's Louisiana,* 136.

52. Holmes, "Three Early Memphis Commandants," 34.

53. See James Workman, *The Trials of the Honb. James Workman, and Col. Lewis Kerr, Before the United States Court* . . . (New Orleans: Bradford & Anderson, 1807), 43.

54. To R. Claiborne, August 17, 1806, CLB, 3: 379.

55. To Henry Dearborn, October 19, 1806, ibid., 4: 31.

by force." Linking his request to Bellechasse's appointment as commander of the First Brigade in the territorial militia and his position in the territorial council, thereby implying a threat of dismissal from both positions, Claiborne demanded an answer.[56] Bellechasse denied the charge and proved by his conduct throughout the crisis that there was no foundation to the imputation to his name. He gave an affidavit to that effect on March 20, 1807.[57] Whatever de Clouet thought of Bellechasse, it is clear that the Creole colonel had not lost contact with reality. Bellechasse had no intention of jeopardizing his retirement and commission with the Spanish government, or his economic and social position in the Orleans Territory, in a vain attempt to restore Spanish rule in Louisiana.

Eighteen months after Claiborne advised against the promotion of Bellechasse to brigadier general, the governor recommended appointment of either Bellechasse or John B. Macarty to the rank. The change in Claiborne's opinion regarding Bellechasse came about as a result of the dramatic reversal in local political alignments during the "reign of terror" conducted by General Wilkinson as he played out the Burr conspiracy. Wilkinson's actions immobilized and/or banished Claiborne's supporters and critics in the English-speaking community, and won for the governor a following in the French-speaking community.[58] Ironically, it was Bellechasse, the self-proclaimed friend of Spain and France, and Daniel Clark's cohort in undermining Wilkinson's reputation, who confirmed the evidence given by James Workman that was used by Wilkinson to expose and destroy the Mexican Association and bring down Claiborne's political allies and friends.[59]

As previously indicated, Bellechasse declined to serve in the territorial council in 1804. He apparently wished to serve in the territorial house of representatives and announced his candidacy for that body in September the following year. When he was not elected to the house, Bellechasse was nominated by the house and accepted a five-year appointment (November 1805)

---

56. To Col. Bellechasse, January 7, 1807, ibid., 85.

57. Daniel Clark, *Proofs of the Corruption of Gen. James Wilkinson, and of His Connexion with Aaron Burr, with a Full Refutation of His Slanderous Allegations in Relation to the Principal Witness Against Him* (1809; New York: Arno Press, 1971), n. 68, Affidavit of Colonel Bellechasse, 145.

58. Dargo, *Jefferson's Louisiana*, 57–63; and Governor Claiborne to the Secretary of War, December 13, 1807, TP, 9: 768. Claiborne's new circle of advisers became Julien Poydras, James Mather, Bellechasse, Jean Baptiste Macarty, and Pierre Foucher. Governor Claiborne to the Secretary of State, March 27, 1807, TP, 9: 723.

59. See To Col. Bellechasse, January 7, 1807, and To James Brown, January 17, 1807, CLB, 4: 85, 98–9, respectively. On Workman's role in this major political shift, see his biographical sketch.

to the territorial council by the Jefferson administration.[60] During his last year on the council, Bellechasse served it as president.[61] Earlier, he had been elected to the New Orleans City Council, representing the third district (1804–05) under Mayor James Pitot and the sixth district (March 1805–November 1812) under Mayors Pitot, John Watkins, and James J. Mather.[62] Bellechasse also held appointments as recorder (February 27, 1805–May 6, 1807) of the New Orleans City Council and justice of the peace (May 13, 1805) in the Faubourg Ste. Marie.[63] On taking office as recorder, Bellechasse announced to the members of the council that he so "deeply . . . felt the honor" of presiding at the council that "he would accept no emoluments attached" to the office, but would instead use this income to pay the construction costs of those "persons known to be unable to pay" for the construction of their banquettes (raised wooden sidewalks). The council members "heartily applauded" his generosity and decided to announce it in the newspapers of the city.[64] Just as many other French and some Spanish businessmen in New Orleans in these early years, Bellechasse also became a Freemason, serving as a member of Perfect Union Lodge from 1808 onward.[65]

Near the end of the territorial period, Bellechasse was appointed (June

60. The President to Governor Claiborne, August 30, 1804; the President to the Secretary of War, September 6, 1804; Governor Claiborne to the Secretary of State, October 29, 1804; Governor Claiborne to the President, November 19, 1804; Members Originally Named for the Council . . . [and] Recently Named . . . . [Followed by list of] Members Now Attending in the Legislative Council, enclosed in Governor Claiborne to the President, December 2, 1804; and Governor Claiborne to the Secretary of State, February 20, 1806; all in TP, 9: 283, 291, 317, 334, 346, and 604, respectively.

61. Memorial to Congress by the Legislature [March 12, 1810], ibid., 877; and B[arthél-émy] Lafon, *Annuaire Louisianais pour L'Année 1809* (New Orleans: By the Author, 1808), 162.

62. "Administrations of the Mayors of New Orleans, 1803–1936," comp. and ed. Works Project Administration (project 665-64-3-112, typescript; New Orleans, March 1940), 5, 14.

63. New Orleans Conseil de Ville: Official Proceedings, no. 1, book 2 (April 4, 1805– February 12, 1806), 75, City Archives, Louisiana Division, New Orleans Public Library; Register of Civil Appointments in the Territory of Orleans, enclosed in John Graham to Secretary of State, February 13, 1806, TP, 9: 599, 601; and Lafon, *Calendrier de Commerce,* 63. Bellechasse was succeeded in office by Charles (also known as Carlos and/or Laveau) Trudeau, a relative of Zenon Trudeau. See "Administrations of the Mayors of New Orleans, 1803–1936," 9, and Register of Civil Appointments, January 1–June 30, 1806, enclosed in Richard Claiborne to [the Secretary of State], June 30, 1806, TP, 9: 663.

64. New Orleans Conseil de Ville: Official Proceedings, no. 1, book 1 (November 20, 1803–July 6, 1807), 75-6.

65. Powell A. Casey, "Masonic Lodges in New Orleans," *New Orleans Genesis* 20, no. 77 (January 1981), 1.

1, 1811) to the administrative council of the new Charity Hospital created by the territorial legislature in April 1811.[66] When the constitutional convention opened in New Orleans in November 1811, Bellechasse was present as one of the twelve delegates elected to represent New Orleans.[67] The following spring, he sought election to the state senate, but was defeated by Thomas Urquhart.[68] In the fall of 1812, Bellechasse was one of six men who stood for election as mayor of New Orleans. In this political contest he came in a poor third behind Nicholas Girod and James Pitot.[69] After this election Bellechasse apparently held no other public office in Louisiana and does not appear to have sought any other public office. His last recorded service to the city while on the city council was as a committee member (September 1812) with Paul Jean Blanque and the architect William Brand, who were authorized to receive bids for reconstruction of the city market, which had been destroyed by the hurricane that hit the city August 19–20, 1812.[70]

Just as many other Catholics in New Orleans in 1805–06, Bellechasse opposed the claims of Father Patrick Walsh to be vicar-general of the church in Louisiana. However, Bellechasse came in for particular censure from Fr. Walsh when he publicly opposed Walsh's claims and used the occasion to isolate Walsh as an Irish, not a Spanish or French, priest. Bellechasse accomplished this by publicly reminding New Orleanians that it was "an Irishman, one of [Walsh's] compatriots, [who] brought mourning and desolation" to Louisiana families in 1769.[71] This reference to the harsh res-

66. Members of the Council of Administration of the Charity Hospital of New-Orleans for 12 Months, Return of Civil Appointments from 1st June 1811 [to] Dec. 31 of same year, in the Orleans Territory, enclosed in Thomas B. Robertson to Secretary of State James Monroe, January 18, 1812, TP, 9: 987, and *Louisiana Gazette,* May 16, 1811, p. 3, c. 1.

67. Philip D. Uzée, "The First Louisiana State Constitution: A Study of Its Origins" (master's thesis, Louisiana State University, 1938), appendix 1, 36.

68. *Louisiana Gazette,* June 8, 1812, p. 2, c. 3. Ibid., July 2, 1812, p. 2, c. 3, reported that Urquhart received 528 votes and Bellechasse 350.

69. New Orleans Conseil de Ville: Official Proceedings, vol. 2, book 3 (January 12, 1811 to November 17, 1812), 240, 245.

70. Ibid., 229.

71. Bellechasse's attack on Fr. Walsh is undated, but was written before April 1, 1805. Walsh's *Lettre Pastorale* was published in the March 27, 1805, issue of the *Orleans Gazette.* William C. C. Claiborne to James Madison, April 1, 1805, which enclosed Bellechasse's answer to Patrick Walsh's pastoral letter as published in the *Télégraphe.* Both are contained in State Department Territorial Papers, Orleans Series, 1764–1813, reel 6, vol. 6, January 1, 1805–June 21, 1805, folios 95 and 96, respectively. National Archives Microfilm, microcopy T260, New Orleans Public Library, City Archives, Louisiana Department. Later, Bellechasse's letter was separately published as *Bellechasse Aux Habitants De La Nouvelle-Orléans* (New Orleans: de L'Imprimerie du *Télégraphe,* no date). Florence Jumonville, *Bibliography of New*

toration of Spanish rule by Governor O'Reilly clearly was intended to isolate Walsh. It was a piece of pure demagoguery that Bellechasse knew would
win public sympathy, if not strong support, among the growing numbers of
émigrés from Santo Domingo in New Orleans.[72] To lend additional weight to
his opposition to Walsh, Bellechasse used his full name, Joseph Deville Degoutin Bellechasse, and his official titles in the published piece, "Colonel Commandant des Milices et Membre du Conseil de la Commune," commandant
of the militia and member of the territorial council.[73] The slur on Irishmen
also may have been aimed at the Marqués de Casa Calvo, who has been described as the "grand counsellor" (sic) of the Catholic Church in Louisiana
at this time.[74] Although Claiborne feared the exchanges between Fr. Walsh
and Bellechasse might lead to personal combat, this did not happen, and the
whole issue became dormant with the death of Walsh on August 22, 1806.[75]

Bellechasse's anti-Irish sentiment does not appear to have influenced his
close business relationship with Irish-born Daniel Clark. In a letter published in one of the New Orleans newspapers early in 1808, Bellechasse defended Clark, describing him as "esteemed and . . . incorruptible," and as
uniting "talents to his other good qualities."[76] Although the warm friendship between Bellechasse and Clark appears to have cooled after 1808, the
change in their relationship apparently stemmed from Clark's altered outlook on life. There is no indication that Clark's criticism of the organization
of the territorial militia was in any way intended for Bellechasse.[77] More-

Orleans Imprints, 1764–1864, 1st ed. (New Orleans: Historic New Orleans Collection, 1989),
34, entry 107.

72. Paul F. LaChance, "The 1809 Immigration of Saint-Domingue Refugees to New Orleans: Reception, Integration and Impact," *Louisiana History* 29, no. 2 (spring 1988), 110 n.
5, points out that several hundred refugees from Santo Domingo arrived in New Orleans before the Louisiana Purchase, and that as many as one thousand refugees arrived from there in
1803–1804. More arrived before the end of the decade.

73. Letter No. 183, To James Madison, April 1, 1805, enclosed Bellechasse's answer to
Walsh, but the copy was not in the Claiborne letter book on deposit with the Louisiana and
Lower Mississippi Valley Collections, Louisiana State University. However, it may be seen in
William C. C. Claiborne to James Madison, April 1, 1805, State Department Territorial Papers,
folios 95–6.

74. Roger Baudier, *The Catholic Church in Louisiana* (1939; Baton Rouge: Louisiana Library Association, 1972), 258.

75. Governor Claiborne to the Secretary of State, April 16, 1805, TP, 9: 434. Notice of
Walsh's death on August 22, 1806, appeared in the *Télégraphe,* August 23, 1806, p. 3, c. 1.

76. *Louisiana Gazette,* April 8, 1808, p. 2, cc. 3, 4, and p. 3, cc. 1, 2.

77. For Clark's criticisms, see Governor Claiborne to Daniel Clark, May 23, 1807, TP, 9:
738 and n. 95 the same page. Clark's remarks clearly were intended for Claiborne and led to
Claiborne's demand for "satisfaction" on the dueling field.

over, it was nearly two years after Clark's criticism that Bellechasse resigned his commission (December 17, 1808) in that body.[78]

It has been suggested that Bellechasse resigned his commission in the militia as a protest against the treatment of Clark by the territorial government.[79] In light of Bellechasse's independent conduct in the past, it is much more likely that personal factors were of greater importance in determining this action than events in the public life of Daniel Clark. As a result of the strenuous duty at Las Barrancas, Bellechasse's health appears to have been weakened. There is no record of a specific complaint, but he apparently felt to a greater degree the seasonal fevers that were the general complaint of most Louisianians until well into the nineteenth century. Most important, since the opportunity for leading Louisiana back into the Spanish fold had passed, it is possible, in view of subsequent developments, that Bellechasse was planning to reclaim his pension by returning to active service in the Spanish army in Cuba.

Bellechasse's failure to be elected to public office in 1812 and the death of Daniel Clark in August 1813 undoubtedly influenced the fifty-two-year-old Creole to move to Cuba. His function as one of three executors of Clark's will apparently was Bellechasse's last public responsibility in Louisiana.[80] Sometime in 1814, he left the United States for Havana. There he re-entered the military service of Spain and became a sugar planter in Matanzas Province. It was here that he was visited in 1833 by Daniel Clark's daughter, Myra Clark Whitney, on her quest for information about her father and her inheritance in Louisiana. Subsequently, the aging Bellechasse, now a retired lieutenant colonel, gave evidence in behalf of Myra's suits to claim her inheritance.[81] He died, date unknown, in Cuba after having served France, Spain, and the United States with honor, while preserving his integrity at a time when the pressures and temptations to do otherwise were great.[82]

78. To Colonel Bellechasse, December 17, 1808, CLB, 4: 272.

79. Harmon, *Myra Clark Gaines,* 116.

80. Ibid., 272–3.

81. Bellechasse apparently gave two depositions in support of Myra's quest to claim her inheritance, once in December 1834 and again in 1837. See ibid., 175–81, and Rader, "Romance of American Courts," 72–4.

82. Bellechasse was still living in 1837 when he gave the second deposition in support of Myra's claims. Rader, "Romance of American Courts," 74.

BENJAMIN MORGAN

Benjamin Morgan (?–November 10, 1826)[1] did not want a career in politics, nor did he initially seek it. Writing to a friend in Philadelphia in the summer of 1803, Morgan said that although he expected to continue to live in "this young country," he did not want an office in the American government that was soon to be established in New Orleans.[2] Nonetheless, he, like Dr. John Watkins, became very important to the establishment of American government in lower Louisiana, that portion of the Louisiana Purchase that

1. No birth date for Benjamin Morgan has been found. The statements of Benjamin's contemporaries and others later that Benjamin was from Philadelphia suggest that he, like his older brother Jacob, was born there. Because no record of Benjamin Morgan's birth and baptism has been found, it is possible poor health as an infant and plans to baptize him later were forced aside by the beginning of the American Revolution. The records of the first Protestant Episcopal Church in Reading, Pennsylvania, where Morgan's ancestor settled, ended in 1784, but there is no record of Benjamin Morgan's baptism. The second Protestant Episcopal Church in Reading began in 1826. It is possible that St. Thomas Episcopal Church, Whitemarsh, Montgomery County, a suburb of Philadelphia, is where a birth and baptismal record should have been. The records there extend from 1786–1864, but are not continuous. Notice of Benjamin Morgan's death was printed in the English language section of the *Courier de la Louisiane,* November 10, 1826, p. 1, c. 3, and in the French language portion of the same paper on p. 2, c. 3.

2. Benjamin Morgan to Chandler Price, August 18, 1803, in Clarence E. Carter, comp. and ed., *The Territorial Papers of the United States,* vol. 9, *The Territory of Orleans, 1803–1812* (Washington, D.C.: U.S. Government Printing Office, 1940), 9 (hereinafter cited as TP, with volume and page range). Chandler Price may have been an in-law of Rebecca Morgan, Benjamin's sister, through her marriage to John Price. Abstracts of Wills and Administrations, Berks County, Pennsylvania, Will Book B, Jacob Morgan Will, May 28, 1792, B-290 [497–98], reveals that Rebecca was the wife of John Price.

became the Orleans Territory. Ultimately, Morgan, like Watkins, served in both chambers of the territorial legislature and the New Orleans City Council. Unlike Watkins, however, Morgan was one of the very few men of financial means in New Orleans not engaged in land speculation, which was an additional reason for Claiborne to seek Morgan's involvement in the establishment of U.S. government in the former French and Spanish colony.[3] Benjamin Morgan's lack of interest in gaining wealth from land may have stemmed from his knowledge of the confusion in land titles in Louisiana, a confusion compounded by the land dealings of the Spanish intendant, Juan Ventura Morales, after the Louisiana Purchase. Morgan also may have been influenced by the fact that his father, Jacob, received rights to extensive acreage through his service as an officer in the Pennsylvania militia during the American Revolution, as sales of this land would benefit the Morgan siblings.[4]

Claiborne described Morgan to Jefferson on May 29, 1804, as a "man of business and great integrity."[5] The characterization certainly is accurate, but for many years this tribute, in combination with the difficulty in identifying even the most basic factual information on Morgan's life before he settled in New Orleans, has discouraged and halted examination of the significant role he played in establishing the U.S. government in lower Louisiana.

The initial importance of Morgan derives from his accurate and dispassionate insights on specific personalities on the New Orleans scene before and after the United States assumed control over the lands of the Louisiana Purchase. The foundation of that importance was, as Claiborne noted, Morgan's integrity, but it also was founded in his powers of discernment and ability to characterize succinctly. Claiborne's reliance on Morgan was both

---

3. Governor Claiborne to the President, August 30, 1804, TP, 9: 285, narrowed this point specifically to West Florida lands, but no indication has been found that Benjamin Morgan sought financial gain from any land speculation. There is evidence he acted as realtor in 1808 for the sale of land within the Faubourg St. Marie (Mary), which was bounded by Magazine, Camp, and Gravier Streets, the growing American portion of New Orleans in which his home and business were located. See Morgan's advertisement in the *Moniteur de la Louisiane*, September 21, 1808, p. 4, c. 4 (hereinafter cited as *Moniteur*).

4. Abstracts of Wills and Administrations, Berks County, Pennsylvania, Will Book B, Jacob Morgan Will, May 28, 1792, B-290 [497–8], mentions land claims he received as a result of his militia service in the American Revolution.

5. To Thomas Jefferson, May 29, 1804, in *Official Letter Books of W. C. C. Claiborne, 1801–1816*, ed. Dunbar Rowland, vol. 2 (1917; New York: AMS Press, 1972), 176 (hereinafter cited as CLB with volume and page numbers).

political and personal. Describing Morgan as "my friend," the governor entrusted management of some of his personal business to Morgan.[6]

The governor also steered business opportunities to Morgan on occasion. Shortly after the American government was established in New Orleans, Morgan was licensed to trade with the Indians in Louisiana. He requested and received the license for himself and Jacob Bright on September 28, 1805.[7] How much this license reflected Morgan's belief there was money to be made in the Indian trade and how much it may have reflected Claiborne's continuing interest in curbing, if not stopping, Spanish influence among all the Indians of the old Southwest is not known.[8] More significant attempts to help Morgan came some years later, in February 1812 and September 1813.[9] In both these instances, it is much more likely Claiborne acted out of concern for Morgan and his family. By these years, Morgan no longer held an appointive office and had been defeated in his bid to be elected mayor of New Orleans in 1811. Most important for Morgan, these were years in which he and many other Louisianians, along with most of the nation outside of New England, were suffering from the embargoes instituted by the Jefferson and Madison administrations leading into the War of 1812.

Jefferson also demonstrated great confidence in Morgan. After learning from newspaper reports that Claiborne was dangerously, if not mortally, wounded as a result of his duel with Daniel Clark in June 1807, the president asked Morgan to "undertake the office of [territorial] Secretary" until someone could be appointed to fill the post. In asking Morgan to take the office for "a short time," Jefferson said he was concerned the territory might be "without any executive head" because the office of territorial secretary was then vacant.[10] Although two New Orleans newspapers, the *Louisiana*

6. See, for example, To Col. F. L. [Ferdinand Leigh] Claiborne, October 14, 1808, CLB, 4: 228.

7. The bond required for this trade was four thousand dollars and had to be posted before the licensee could enter into the trade. Governor Claiborne to Joseph Bowmar, January 29, 1805, TP, 9: 387.

8. Marietta Marie LeBreton, "A History of the Factory System Serving the Louisiana Indians, 1805–1825" (masters thesis, Louisiana State University, 1961). On Claiborne's earlier interest in the Indian trade, see Jared W. Bradley, "William C. C. Claiborne, the Old Southwest and the Development of American Indian Policy," *Tennessee Historical Quarterly* 33, no. 3 (fall 1974), 265–78.

9. To Benjamin Morgan, February 7, 1812, and [To] Benjamin Morgan, Esqr., September 8, 1813, CLB, 6: 50 and 266, respectively.

10. Jefferson to Benjamin Morgan, July 18, 1807, in Thomas Jefferson, *The Writings of Thomas Jefferson*, vol. 11, ed. Andrew A. Lipscomb and Albert Ellery Bergh (Washington, D.C.: Thomas Jefferson Memorial Association, 1905–07), 288.

Gazette and the *Moniteur de la Louisiane,* reported in September that Morgan was to be appointed territorial secretary, Morgan already had declined the nomination. Morgan notified Jefferson in August that he should have by then received "Communications from Governor Claiborne" making it "unnecessary" for Morgan to take the office.[11]

Not all of Morgan's associates in New Orleans shared a high opinion of him. In July 1804, General James Wilkinson tersely described Morgan as "not deficient in understanding."[12] The characterization, written for President Jefferson, displayed a circumspection unlike descriptions of other New Orleanians supplied by the general. Its brevity suggests that Wilkinson certainly was wary of Morgan and may have disliked him. Perhaps the general feared that if he praised Morgan, the former Pennsylvania businessman would gain ascendancy over him through political preference.

Claiborne advised Jefferson in May 1804 that Benjamin Morgan was "formerly of Philadelphia."[13] Benjamin had been in business with his father in Philadelphia from sometime after the American Revolution into the year 1800 under the name of Jacob & Benjamin Morgan & Company.[14] Presumably their business was that of commission merchant, which was the kind of business Morgan operated when he settled in New Orleans.[15] The initial home of this Morgan family in Pennsylvania was not Philadelphia, but Mor-

11. The *Louisiana Gazette,* September 1, 1807, p. 3, c. 2, and the *Moniteur,* September 2, 1807, p. 2, c. 2, carried the story of Morgan's appointment. Benjamin Morgan to the President, August 27, 1807, TP, 9: 762, is Morgan's refusal of the appointment. See also Governor Claiborne to the President, September 4, 1807, TP, 9: 764, which speaks of Morgan's declining the appointment.

12. Characterization of New Orleans Residents, July 1, 1804, entry number 40, enclosed in James Wilkinson to the President, July 1, 1804, TP, 9: 251.

13. To Thomas Jefferson, May 29, 1804, CLB, 2: 176.

14. The Caernarvon Township, Berks County, Pennsylvania, Tax Records for 1794 and 1795 contain the name of Benjamin Morgan's business. Ms. Susan S. Koelble to the author, December 17, 1996.

Benjamin Morgan's father is identified as Jacob Morgan and his mother as Rachel Pensol in Charles R. Maduell, Jr., *New Orleans Marriage Contracts, 1804–1820. Abstracted from the Notarial Archives of New Orleans* (New Orleans: Polyanthos Press, 1977), 38 (entry 145). However, Pennsylvania records reveal that Benjamin Morgan's mother's maiden name was Piersol, not Pensol. John W. Jordan, ed. *Colonial and Revolutionary Families of Pennsylvania. Genealogical and Personal Memoirs,* vol. 3 (1911; Baltimore: Genealogical Publishing, 1978), 1022–3.

15. Numerous advertisements by Benjamin Morgan appear in the several newspapers published in early nineteenth-century New Orleans. A representative example of them may be seen in the *Moniteur,* September 21, 1808, p. 4, c. 4.

gantown, a village about fifty miles west of Philadelphia and thirteen miles south of present-day Reading, Pennsylvania. Jacob Morgan's father, Thomas, settled on the land surveyed for him in Caernarvon Township in the southernmost tip of Berks County about the time Jacob was born. Thomas Morgan (d. 1740) is believed to have been a native of Wales.[16] It was Jacob (1716–November 11, 1792) who laid out Morgantown in 1779 on the land claimed by his father in Caernarvon Township.[17]

Some of the respect accorded Benjamin Morgan flowed from the distinguished record of his father. Colonel Jacob Morgan became known early in his life for service to his community, first as an Indian fighter, then as sheriff in Berks County, and as an officer in the Pennsylvania militia during the French and Indian War (1754–63) and, later, in the American Revolution (1776–84).[18] Colonel Morgan lived most of his life in Morgantown except for the years of the American Revolution, when he is described as living "principally in the city of Reading," Pennsylvania.[19] After the American Revolution, Jacob apparently settled permanently in Philadelphia. Benjamin appears to have been the younger of two sons born to Colonel Morgan and his wife, Rachel. It is possible Rachel was the second wife of Jacob Morgan, Sr., and that Benjamin was an unexpected dividend in the family. An older son, Jacob Morgan, Jr., was born in 1742 and died in 1812.[20]

Scattered evidence reveals that, after Colonel Morgan's death in the fall of 1792, young Morgan continued the company that he and his father had founded.[21] Little more than a year after his father's death, Benjamin married

16. Jordan, *Colonial and Revolutionary Families*, 2: 1022–3. Much of the information given on these pages also may be found in ibid., 2: 658–60. However, the information on pp. 658–60 is not as lucidly or coherently presented.

17. Ibid., 2: 1022–3.

18. Jacob was elected sheriff in Berks County with Benjamin Lightfoot in 1752, 1753, and 1754. See Kenneth Scott and Janet R. Clarke, *Abstracts from the Pennsylvania Gazette, 1748–1755* (Baltimore: Genealogical Publishing, 1977), 197, 253, 309. Jacob Morgan's service in the Pennsylvania militia is set forth in Jordan, *Colonial and Revolutionary Families*, 2: 1022–3. Jacob Morgan's Revolutionary War service in the important post of superintendent of the Pennsylvania County Commissioners of Purchases is identified in the *Papers of Robert Morris, 1781–1784*, vol. 3, ed. E. James Ferguson (Pittsburgh: University of Pittsburgh Press, 1973–1995), 32; other references to Jacob's service in this capacity may be found in the indexes to these volumes. Jacob Morgan is sometimes confused with his son, Jacob Morgan, Jr., who also served in the Pennsylvania militia during the American Revolution.

19. Jordan, *Colonial and Revolutionary Families*, 2: 1023.

20. Ibid.

21. Jacob Morgan appears to have prepared his will less than six months before his death. Abstracts of Wills and Administrations, Berks County, Pennsylvania, Will Book B, Jacob Mor-

Harriet Ashton, in Christ Church, Philadelphia.[22] In the fall of the same year, 1793, Benjamin was described as a "merchant of the city" when he and Harriet sold some of the property in Caernarvon Township left to him by his father.[23]

The date of Benjamin Morgan's arrival in New Orleans is unknown, but it appears to have been in the spring or early summer of 1800, although other records indicate that Benjamin was still living and working in Philadelphia that spring. On April 17 that year, Morgan sold to Chandler Price the 263 acres of land in Caernarvon Township. The general tenor of this document and the reference to Morgan as "merchant" in the transaction, suggest that by this date he and Price may have been business partners.[24] Because there is no mention of Morgan's wife in the sale, it is possible she had died by this date, perhaps in the yellow fever epidemic that struck Philadelphia that year. The death of Harriet may have precipitated Benjamin's decision to move to New Orleans. Close examination of Morgan's correspondence with Chandler Price, particularly Morgan's letter of August 18, 1803, suggests, on the basis of what is known about his other actions, that he then had been in New Orleans for some time, perhaps as much as three years.[25]

The death of Harriet Ashton Morgan may have triggered Benjamin's decision to relocate, but the move to New Orleans clearly was intended to take advantage of the widespread belief at the end of the eighteenth century that the dusty and humid river town was destined to become one of the world's leading trade centers. Like the Irish-born George Pollock, who made New Orleans his home about this same time, Benjamin Morgan also intended to capitalize on the opportunities to be found in the growing port.

Morgan relied on his contacts in Philadelphia, New York, and elsewhere to develop business after settling in New Orleans.[26] Initially, his contact in

---

gan Will, May 28, 1792, B-290 [497–8]; and Jordan, *Colonial and Revolutionary Families*, 2: 1023.

22. *Record of Pennsylvania Marriages, Prior to 1810*, vol. 1 (Baltimore: Genealogical Publishing, 1987), 182, citing the "Marriage Record of Christ Church, Philadelphia, 1709–1806." Benjamin Morgan and Harriet Ashton were married on June 27, 1793.

23. Philadelphia Land Records, *Deed Book* 14, p. 492. Photocopy in the possession of the author.

24. Philadelphia Land Records, *Deed Book* 18, p. 376.

25. See n. 2 above.

26. Morgan's trade with Philadelphia and New York is discussed by John G. Clark in *New Orleans, 1718–1812: An Economic History* (Baton Rouge: Louisiana State University Press, 1970), 204.

Philadelphia appears to have been Chandler Price. Later, he also relied on Daniel W. Coxe, a Philadelphia merchant identified as the friend of Daniel Clark. Perspective on Benjamin Morgan's business contacts with both Daniel Coxe and Daniel Clark may be glimpsed in the June 2, 1808, deposition of Coxe. Included in the deposition is Clark's February 1806 letter telling Coxe that he and Benjamin Morgan, along with a third party yet to be named, were to use the schooner *Patty* consigned to Morgan to ship cargo amounting to forty thousand dollars on a Spanish certificate granted by the Marqués de Casa Calvo. The *Patty* belonged to John Craig of Philadelphia.[27] It was Morgan's business dealings with Clark that provided the basis for his acerbic description of Clark in August 1803 as "deficient in dignity of character & sterling veracity."[28] Despite this harsh appraisal, Morgan continued to regard Clark as a friend.[29]

Morgan was one of the large number of men, particularly Americans, who supported Daniel Clark in the organization of the volunteer militia in the weeks before December 20, 1803, the date on which the United States assumed control of Louisiana. The volunteer militia came into existence because of the great local concern that Spanish rancor over the loss of their colony would result in open hostilities during the brief period of French control of Louisiana under Pierre Clément de Laussat.[30] Earlier, Morgan had declined appointment by Laussat to the reorganized city council of New Orleans. Morgan refused the office, saying he was not qualified for the appointment because he did not speak either French or Spanish.[31]

Morgan consistently supported Claiborne after he assumed the reins of

27. Daniel Clark to Daniel W. Coxe, 6th February 1806, in Daniel Clark, *Proofs of the Corruption of Gen. James Wilkinson, and of His Connexion with Aaron Burr, with a Full Refutation of His Slanderous Allegations in Relation to the Principal Witness Against Him* (1809; New York: Arno Press, 1971), Notes, pp. 126–7.

28. Benjamin Morgan to Chandler Price, August 18, 1803, TP, 9: 9.

29. Ibid.

30. John Monette, *History of the Discovery and Settlement of the Valley of the Mississippi, By the Three Great Powers, Spain, France, and Great Britain, and Subsequent Occupation, Settlement and Extension of Civil Government by the United States, Until the Year 1846*, vol. 1 (1846; New York: Arno Press, 1971), 561. For additional information on the volunteer militia assembled by Clark with the assistance of Samuel B. Davis at Clark's ropewalk, see "Military Association," pp. 591–5 herein.

31. Pierre Clément de Laussat, *Memoirs of My Life to My Son during the Years 1803 and After . . .*, trans. Sister Agnes-Josephine Pastwa, ed. Robert D. Bush (Baton Rouge: Louisiana State University Press, 1978), 126 n. 18. Despite Morgan's stated reason for declining the appointment, it is possible he refused the office because of the difficulties many had in dealing with Laussat and to protect his business.

government of the Orleans Territory even though the businessman believed, on the basis of what he knew of the young Mississippi governor, that Claiborne was "unsuitable" for the office. Morgan believed, like many others, that the man needed for Louisiana should be a strong leader from the United States. Whoever was appointed, Morgan said, should "know their rights" and exercise them.[32]

Benjamin Morgan was among the first four men Claiborne recommended to Jefferson for appointment to the legislative council, despite Morgan's desire to stay out of politics.[33] Along with two of the other men named, John Watkins and Gaspard DeBuys, Morgan was among the first to accept appointment to the territorial council in 1804–05 because most of Claiborne's initial appointees declined to serve.[34] Jefferson regarded Morgan as part of the "American contingent" on the council.[35] In January 1806, Morgan was elected to the territorial house of representatives to replace Robert Avart, who had resigned from the office.[36] Morgan also served on the city council from July 1807 through July 1811.[37] His election to the city council clearly points to Morgan's continued willingness to help Claiborne establish American government in Louisiana after John Watkins was dismissed from the office of mayor by Claiborne. It is possible that Morgan also agreed to stand for election to the city council because the responsibilities of that office would directly affect his livelihood as a merchant in New Orleans. Following his terms on the city council, Morgan stood for election as mayor of New Orleans in September 1812, but lost to Nicholas Girod.[38]

32. Benjamin Morgan to Chandler Price, August 18, 1803, TP, 9: 9.

33. To Thomas Jefferson, May 29, 1804, CLB, 2: 175–6.

34. To James Madison, October 22, 1804; A List of the Councellors [sic], undated; and To James Madison (DUPLICATED) [sic], November 18, 1804; in ibid., 372, 375, and 393, respectively.

35. The President to Governor Claiborne, April 17, 1804, TP, 9: 225; and George Dargo, *Jefferson's Louisiana: Politics and the Clash of Legal Traditions* (Cambridge, Mass.: Harvard University Press, 1975), 33.

36. Sir [The Honble. James Madison], January 23, 1806, CLB, 3: 247; and H. Molier to Governor Claiborne, January 21, 1806, TP, 9: 574.

37. New Orleans Conseil de Ville: Official Proceedings, no. 1, book 3 (February 15, 1806–July 1, 1807); no. 2, book 1 (July 6, 1807–December 28, 1808); book 2 (January 14, 1809–December 26, 1810), and book 3 (January 12, 1811–November 7, 1812). See also "Administrations of the Mayors of New Orleans, 1805–1936," comp. and ed. Works Project Administration (project 665–64–32–12, typescript; New Orleans, 1940), 14.

38. New Orleans Conseil de Ville: Official Proceedings, book 3 (January 12, 1811–November 7, 1812), 240. Other mayoral candidates at the time were James Pitot, Joseph Deville Degoutin Bellechasse, Charles Trudeau, and Andrew Villamil.

The respect that Morgan commanded among his business peers is suggested by the number and variety of business boards to which he was elected, either as a director or president. Among them were the Louisiana Bank (March 1804), the first bank authorized in the Orleans Territory;[39] the New Orleans Navigation Company (*Compagnie de Navigation;* 1806–09);[40] the New Orleans Insurance Company (*Compagnie d'Assurance Maritime;* 1808 and 1809);[41] the branch Bank of the United States, 1808–1811, over which he presided in 1811 during its liquidation;[42] the Bank of Orleans, which he helped found and organize in 1811;[43] and the New Orleans branch of the Second Bank of the United States when it was established in 1816.[44]

A story that appeared in the *Louisiana Gazette* in March 1811 indicates that Morgan was elected president of the branch Bank of the United States by one vote. His narrow victory apparently precipitated some strong criticism of him in the newspapers of, in the words of the editor of the *Louisiana Gazette,* the "*French Editors.*" The editor of the *Gazette* responded to the criticisms, saying "We know Mr. Morgan well, we have known him many years, and can draw a true picture of his *virtues* and *vices*—We have wished to heal the wounds that our society received under martial law, in 1806 and '7—but much as we are disposed to peace, we are ready for war." Alluding to the political preferment the French faction enjoyed under Claiborne, the editor of the *Gazette* went on to say in defense of Morgan: "We are willing to let those exclusive patriots enjoy the *loaves* and *fishes,* and let them bask in the sun-shine of executive patronage; but they should not abuse and traduce characters, who are equal if not superior to them, in all the qualities that adorn society."[45]

39. Ordinance Providing for the Establishment of a Bank, March 12, 1804, CLB, 2: 30.

40. *Louisiana Gazette,* February 9, 1808, p. 3, c. 4, and February 7, 1809, p. 3, c. 2; and B[arthélémy] Lafon, *Annuaire Louisianais pour L'Année 1809* (New Orleans: de L'Imprimerie de L'Auteur, 1808), 203. See also Clark, *New Orleans,* 290.

41. *Louisiana Gazette,* April 26, 1808, p. 3, c. 1, and April 28, 1809, p. 2, c. 4; and Lafon, *Annuaire Louisianais,* 202.

42. *Louisiana Gazette,* April 1, 1808, p. 2, c. 4, and Lafon, *Annuaire Louisianais,* 201. The election of directors for 1810 may have been held in Philadelphia. See the *Louisiana Gazette,* March 13, 1810, p. 3, c. 1.

43. *Louisiana Gazette,* May 25, 1811, p. 3, c. 3. Morgan was elected president of this bank at its organizational meeting. Ibid., June 18, 1811, p. 2. c. 3.

44. Clark, *New Orleans,* 290.

45. *Louisiana Gazette,* March 22, 1811, p. 2, c. 4. Emphasis in the original. One of the owners, or perhaps the owner, of the *Gazette* at this time may have been Dr. John Watkins.

Benjamin Morgan's involvement with establishing American government in the Orleans Territory clearly indicates his strong support of the United States. Similarly, his participation in nonremunerative community activities further strengthens his image as a good citizen. In April 1806, Morgan joined with George Pollock, Julien Poydras, and nine other New Orleans businessmen who subscribed fifty dollars each to establish the Alarm Fire Company and to purchase a fire engine from Philadelphia.[46] Morgan also was a founder of two other organizations in New Orleans. In July 1805 he was one of the seventeen founders of Christ Church, the first Protestant Episcopal Church established in the Orleans Territory.[47] After Christ Church was chartered by the territorial council on July 3, 1805, Morgan served it as vestryman and warden (1805–06 and 1810–11, respectively).[48] In June 1805 he was one of the founders of the New Orleans Library Society chartered by the territorial council, but there is no indication he served as one of the trustees in the actual establishment of a public library.[49]

Morgan escaped the wrath of Wilkinson during the Burr conspiracy because he was well known as a supporter of Claiborne and the government,

See the biographical sketch of John Watkins, n. 284. Clark, *New Orleans,* 348, sees Morgan's election in 1811 as a "victory for the 'French faction.'"

46. New Orleans Municipal Papers, box 1, 1770–1806, folder 13, Special Collections, Howard-Tilton Memorial Library, Tulane University.

47. *Acts Passed at the Second Session of the Legislative Council of the Territory of Orleans, Begun and Held at the Principal, in the City of New Orleans, on Thursday the Twentieth Day of June, in the Year of Our Lord, One Thousand Eight Hundred and Five, and of the Independence of the United States the Twenty-Ninth* (New Orleans: James M. Bradford, 1805), 88.
Although there were men who were not Episcopalians who helped to establish this church, there is evidence to suggest that Morgan was Episcopalian. As pointed out in note 22, his first marriage was in Christ Episcopal Church, Philadelphia. Of greater significance, perhaps, is the fact that his parents were buried in the cemetery of St. Thomas Protestant Episcopal Church in Reading, Pennsylvania. Jordan, *Colonial and Revolutionary Families,* 2: 1023.

48. Georgia F. Taylor, "The Early History of the Episcopal Church in New Orleans, 1805–1840," *Louisiana Historical Quarterly* 22, no. 2 (April 1939), 439. See also Philander Chase, *Bishop Chase's Reminiscences: An Autobiography,* 2nd ed., vol. 1 (Boston: James B. Dow, 1848), 57.

49. *Acts Passed at the First Session of the Legislative Council of the Territory of Orleans, Begun and Held at the Principal, in the City of New Orleans, On Monday the Third Day of December, in the Year of Our Lord, One Thousand Eight Hundred and Four, and of the Independence of the United States the Twenty-Ninth* (New Orleans: James M. Bradford, 1805), 322. The trustees are identified in Roger P. McCutcheon, "Libraries in New Orleans, 1771–1833," *Louisiana Historical Quarterly* 20, no. 1 (January 1937), 152–3.

thereby leaving no opening for General Wilkinson to attack him. Because of his strong support for Claiborne, Wilkinson categorized Morgan as one of the "ancient Louisianians," those who became the base of Claiborne's political support in the aftermath of the Burr conspiracy.[50] Later events revealed that Morgan was not accepted by the members of this group because he was not French. He was, of course, vitally important to Governor Claiborne and continued to play a significant, but barely visible role in the establishment and maintenance of U.S. government in Louisiana.

The invaluable support that Morgan gave Claiborne may be glimpsed during the events of the Burr conspiracy and the development of plans to defend New Orleans in the War of 1812. During the Burr conspiracy, when the New Orleans business community did not support the request by Wilkinson and Claiborne for men and money to refurbish and man the two decrepit navy gunboats in port, Claiborne privately appealed to Morgan and Paul Lanusse, another New Orleans businessman, for assistance. On December 16, 1806, the governor wrote the two men asking them to help recruit the "necessary number of Seamen" to man the two useable naval vessels remaining in New Orleans. When the ships were ready and could be manned, they were stationed on the Mississippi River, one above and one below New Orleans, as protection against the anticipated assault of Aaron Burr and his accomplices.[51] Claiborne expressed his appreciation of Morgan's sustained support late in the summer of 1808. Writing Secretary Madison on September 7, Claiborne said that Benjamin Morgan, Joseph Saul, and Dr. William Flood were among those "who have been more uniform in support of the Administration, of the Laws and good order" than any other Americans.[52] One year later, after it became known that William Brown, the collector of the Port of New Orleans, had absconded with public money, Claiborne asked Benjamin Morgan to take the post. The governor said he wanted the position filled by a "Citizen of high standing . . . whose Integrity and Love of Country, have been well attested." For reasons unknown, Morgan would not take the post.[53]

Several years later, when the British invasion of Louisiana seemed imminent and native Louisianians had not turned out in response to the gover-

---

50. Dargo, *Jefferson's Louisiana,* 62.
51. [To] Paul Lanusse and Benjamin Morgan, December 16, 1806, CLB, 4: 62.
52. To James Madison, September 7, 1808, ibid., 211–2.
53. Governor Claiborne to the President, November 19, 1809, TP, 9: 858.

nor's call for militia to defend New Orleans, Claiborne relied on Benjamin Morgan to draw up the outline of plans to defend the city by water and land. It was during this time that Morgan penned his first known criticism of the governor. After watching Claiborne's inept attempts to prepare New Orleans against British invasion, Morgan wrote his friend Chandler Price, to say: "Our poor nervous, indecisive Governor although honest and warmly attached to his country, has been the ~~cause~~ principal cause of all the party rage that is now afflicting our State and which if we have no army to combat [it] may end in civil Strife and bloodshed."[54] The frustration and disgust that elicited these opinions from Morgan at this time were reminiscent of the opinions expressed privately by former mayor and former speaker of the territorial house of representatives, John Watkins, and territorial Secretary John Graham in 1805.[55] More important, Morgan's opinions expressed in February 1814 were almost identical to those expressed publicly by Watkins in 1807 during his break with Claiborne over the Burr conspiracy.[56]

Benjamin Morgan's sense of civic responsibility also revealed itself in other ways. Sometime in 1806 he followed the lead of Mr. V. Rillieux, who had used "pebble stones," or what would be called gravel today, to cover the heavily used passages, or alleys, between his warehouses on Tchoupitoulas and Poydras Streets. Morgan improved on Rillieux's idea by placing gravel on Gravier Street, between Tchoupitoulas and Magazine Streets, near his business. He subsequently enlarged the project, using ballast from the holds of ships docking in New Orleans.[57] Morgan's efforts were noteworthy for their success and led, by the early 1820s, to a municipal policy of paving all the streets of New Orleans using ballast.[58] Initially, Morgan's project ap-

54. Benjamin Morgan to Chandler Price, February 27, 1814, in Uselima Clarks Smith Collection, William Jones Papers, Historical Society of Pennsylvania. Strikeover in the original. This letter is identified as a copy of the original. Photocopy owned by the author.

55. On the views that Watkins and Graham privately shared with Claiborne and Secretary of State Madison in 1805, see the biographical sketch of John Watkins.

56. See *Debate in the House of Representatives of the Territory of Orleans, on a Memorial to Congress, Respecting the Illegal Conduct of General Wilkinson* (New Orleans: Bradford & Anderson Printers, 1807), 17–8, 37–8.

57. John Adems Paxton, *The New Orleans Directory and Register; Containing the Names, Professions & Residences, of All the Heads of Families and Persons in Business, of the City Suburbs; Notes on New-Orleans; with Other Useful Information* (New Orleans: Printed for the author, 1822), 20–1.

58. Ibid., 21.

pears to have been ridiculed because the public believed the ballast rocks would sink out of sight in the mud flats on which New Orleans was built.[59]

Unlike many of the men surrounding Claiborne, Benjamin Morgan held no military appointment on the governor's staff. Morgan declined appointment as inspector of the Port of New Orleans, a position calling for the rank of naval officer, in the summer of 1804 and later.[60] However, the disastrous effects of the embargo policies of Jefferson and Madison on business apparently forced Morgan to accept a similar appointment in 1809.[61] The closest Morgan appears to have come to service in the military occurred during the War of 1812. When New Orleans was threatened with British invasion, he was elected to the Committee of Public Defense on September 16, 1814, at a meeting of a "great number of the citizens of New-Orleans . . . held at the Exchange Coffee-house." Edward Livingston was chosen to serve as president of the committee, the purpose of which was to make known the "patriotic sentiments" of the people of Louisiana, whose loyalty had been questioned in the past.[62]

At the request of Claiborne, Morgan and Colonel Bartholomew Shaumberg subsequently descended the Mississippi River in October 1814 to examine how best to defend the river approach to New Orleans and its inhabitants. Their report formed the basis for Claiborne's recommendation that Fort St. Philip and points below New Orleans be manned and readied for the defense of the city. These actions, the governor told General Andrew Jackson, were "absolutely essential to the security of this City against all approaches by way of the Mississippi."[63] This recommendation represented a complete reversal of policy by Claiborne. On February 27, 1814, Morgan wrote Chandler Price that Claiborne then was so heavily courting public popularity, which was strongly influenced by the anti-American sentiment of Frenchmen who had recently arrived in New Orleans from Europe and

59. Roger Baudier, "Sanitation in New Orleans," *Southern Plumber* 9, no. 5 (December 1930), 11.

60. The Secretary of the Treasury to Hore Browse Trist, February 27, 1804; Hore Browse Trist to the Secretary of the Treasury, April 1, 1804; and Hatch Dent to James H. McCulloch, July 14, 1804; TP, 9: 193, 218, 267, respectively, anticipate and confirm Morgan's refusal.

61. Lafon, *Annuaire Louisianais,* 159, lists Morgan as one of seven "Commis aux Inspections," that is, port inspectors.

62. Pierre Foucher, Dussuan de la Croix, George M. Ogden, Dominique Bouligny, Jean Noël Destréhan, Jean Blanque, Augustin Macarty, and Richard Relf also were elected to the committee. Paxton, *New Orleans Directory and Register,* 49. See also *Louisiana Gazette,* September 20, 1814, p. 3, c. 1, and September 24, 1814, p. 2, c. 3.

63. To Andrew Jackson, November 4, 1814, CLB, 6: 307.

Santo Domingo, that he had taken several highly questionable actions. Among these, Morgan reported, were Claiborne's decisions to abandon his call for the militia to defend the state and the advice to abandon Balize, the small military station at the mouth of the Mississippi River at which pilots boarded vessels destined upriver for New Orleans. This advice, Morgan said, came "after Wilkinson had nearly completed a log battery that would have kept off or sunk any vessel that could come over the [sand] Bar" at the mouth of the Mississippi River.[64]

The reversal in Claiborne's stand clearly may be attributed to Morgan. Morgan, through his friend Chandler Price, brought to the attention of the national government Claiborne's vacillation and capitulation to the influence of a misguided segment of public opinion. On February 27, Morgan asked Price to "use every exertion in your power with the general government to have 2 or 3,000 regulars troops [sic] placed in our neighborhood."[65] Price received Morgan's February 27 letter on April 5 and immediately forwarded it to William Jones, who was secretary of the navy and acting secretary of the treasury in President Madison's cabinet. In forwarding the letter, Price asked Jones to "hand it to the Secretary of War or the President or such authority as you may think proper."[66]

The advice Benjamin Morgan gave to the government through Chandler Price ultimately became the policy of the United States government. However, the pieces of the puzzle that could be seen clearly and understood from New Orleans did not fall into place until after Andrew Jackson arrived in New Orleans in the fall of 1814 to take command of all U.S. military forces. By then a more obvious picture of the precarious situation facing the United States in New Orleans had begun to emerge. Nonetheless, the need for a properly equipped army to defend Louisiana was not realized until after General Jackson was on the spot in command in New Orleans.[67] Later, after

64. Benjamin Morgan to Chandler Price, February 27, 1814, in William Jones Papers.

65. Ibid.

66. Ibid. A native of Philadelphia, Jones served as secretary of the navy from January 12, 1813–December 2, 1814 and as acting secretary of the treasury from May 1813 into February 1814 during President Madison's second term. During President Jefferson's first term, Jones served in the U.S. House of Representatives (1801–03) as a Republican from Pennsylvania. After the War of 1812, Jones served (July 1816–January 1819) as first president of the Second Bank of the United States (*Dictionary of American Biography*, s.v. "Jones, William.")

67. Claiborne's letter of August 24, 1814, to Jackson, and James Monroe's letter of October 10, 1814, to Jackson, the newly appointed military commander along the Gulf Coast, provided him with the necessary information. The Claiborne letter described conditions in New Orleans. Monroe's letter advised Jackson that the British expedition for seizing New Orleans had sailed from Ireland in September. Robert V. Remini, *Andrew Jackson and the Course of*

the successful defense of New Orleans, Morgan, like many other Louisianians, was present for the farewell dinner given General Andrew Jackson in
the spring of 1815.[68]

Benjamin Morgan suffered considerable financial losses during and after
the War of 1812, just as many other businessmen in Louisiana and elsewhere in the United States. He may have been hurt again by the Panic of
1819.[69] Morgan's close ties to the banking community in New Orleans and
Philadelphia suggest that even though Louisiana was not badly hurt in the
Panic of 1819, he may have been financially hurt. The business downturn
of 1822 in combination with the flooding of many planters by the Mississippi River in 1823 may have been too much for Morgan to recover from.[70]

There is evidence that Claiborne's close association with Morgan continued up to the time of the governor's death. Claiborne wrote his sister-in-
law Magdalene (Mrs. Ferdinand L. Claiborne) early in the second week of
October 1817, about six weeks before his death from the effects of yellow
fever, that Benjamin Morgan had advised him on October 6 not to come to
or enter New Orleans before the twentieth of the month because of a yellow
fever epidemic then raging in the city. Morgan also advised Claiborne that
the ship *Ohio* would be leaving New Orleans for Philadelphia near the end
of the month or the beginning of November 1817, suggesting that good accommodations were still available.[71] Normally, cooler weather settles into
south Louisiana by this time, killing or driving away mosquitos bearing yellow fever.

American Empire, 1767–1821, 1st ed. (New York: Harper & Row, 1977), 237, 239, 245, 247,
251. Major A. Lacarrière Latour served as the chief engineer in the construction of defenses
of New Orleans for Jackson. His perspective on the battle of New Orleans is in his book, A.
Lacarrière Latour, *Historical Memoir of the War in West Florida and Louisiana in 1814–1815*
(Gainesville: University of Florida Press, 1964).

68. *Louisiana Gazette,* April 4, 1815, p. 2, c. 1.

69. On the reasons for and the general effects of the Panic of 1819, see George Dangerfield, *The Era of Good Feelings* (1952; New York: Harbinger Books, 1963), 175–89. Louisiana
came through the economic crisis of 1819 relatively unscathed, as pointed out by Larry
Schweikart, *Banking in the American South from the Age of Jackson to Reconstruction* (Baton
Rouge: Louisiana State University Press, 1987), 57.

70. There were numerous crevasses on the Mississippi River in 1823, most of them below
the mouth of the Red River. D. O. Elliot, *The Improvement of the Lower Mississippi River
for Flood Control and Navigation,* vol. 1 (Vicksburg, Miss.: U. S. Waterways Experiment Station, 1932), 107.

71. William C. C. Claiborne to Magdalene [Mrs. Ferdinand L.] Claiborne, October 10,
1817, Magdalene H. Claiborne Papers, 1815–1836, Southern Historical Collection, Wilson
Library, University of North Carolina, Chapel Hill.

At the time of Morgan's death in 1826, his business was known as Benjamin Morgan and Son.[72] The "son" was his sole surviving and youngest son, Benjamin, who died at the age of thirty-one on September 8, 1849.[73] Earlier, during the years 1818–1822, Morgan had been in partnership in New Orleans with Samuel Dorsey. Their business was known as Morgan, Dorsey & Company. In addition to serving as commission merchants, the firm also served as a forwarding and collection agency, accepting products from the Mississippi and Ohio valleys, and shipping products to ports on the east coast of the United States and to England.[74] At the time of his death, Morgan apparently was broke. His will, filed November 13, 1826, opens: "having surrendered all my property to my creditors for the payment of my own debts and for the commitments I am under for others and being thus without any property in possession to bequeath. . . ." Morgan named his sons Samuel P. Morgan and William H. Morgan, who were identified as being "at Cambridge in Massachusetts," as executors. The will instructed his sons "to hold [any] surplus in trust" for his wife Mary and six other children: Harriet, Mary, Rachel, Sarah, Elizabeth, and Benjamin.[75]

Settlement of Benjamin Morgan's estate is attributed to his youngest surviving son, Benjamin, because Samuel and William both died before the estate could be settled. Benjamin was a minor, approximately eight years old at the time of his father's death. For this reason it seems likely that family members and/or friends handled the settlement. Papers filed with the court in Philadelphia reveal that the value of Morgan's estate in that city did not exceed one thousand dollars. Settlement of the estate there was handled by William M. Stretch at the request of young Benjamin. Others signing the final administration included Morgan's longtime friend, Chandler Price, who was listed as "merchant," and Thomas A. Morgan, also identified as a merchant representing the city of Philadelphia.[76]

72. See *Courier de la Louisiane,* November 10, 1826, p. 1, c. 4.

73. *Daily Picayune,* October 24, 1849, p. 2, c. 7.

74. Morgan[,] Dorsey & Company Account Book, 1818–1822, Special Collections, Howard-Tilton Memorial Library, Tulane University.

75. Benjamin Morgan Will, Orleans Parish, Louisiana. Court of Probate, Record of Wills, Will Book, 1824–1833, vol. 4, 118. Benjamin Morgan's second marriage took place in 1804 in New Orleans. Maduell, *New Orleans Marriage Contracts,* 38 (entry 145), identifies Morgan's second wife as Mary "Walsh." However, a transcript of a Plaquemine Parish Courthouse record titled "An Exchange Sale Between Benjamin Morgan and James Wilkinson," May 18, 1819, spells Morgan's second wife's maiden name "Welsh." James Wilkinson Papers, box 1, folder 4, Special Collections, Howard-Tilton Memorial Library, Tulane University.

76. Philadelphia Register of Wills, Administration Book N (1826), Administration #372, p. 131. Photocopy owned by the author.

Four of Benjamin Morgan's five daughters—Harriet, Rachel, Sarah, and Elizabeth—died forty-one years later in a train wreck at Lockland, Ohio, on November 21, 1867, without issue. The fifth daughter, Mary Eve, died on September 26, 1905, in New Orleans, also without issue.[77] Benjamin Morgan's second wife, Mary Welsh, died at age sixty-seven on October 18, 1848.[78]

77. Leonard Huber and Guy F. Bernard, *To Glorious Immortality: The Rise and Fall of the Girod Street Cemetery, New Orleans' First Protestant Cemetery, 1822–1957* (New Orleans: Alblen Books, 1961), 34.

78. *Daily Picayune*, October 20, 1848, p. 2, c. 7.

JOHN WATKINS

The rise of Dr. John Watkins to prominence in the politics of early territorial Louisiana was so unexpected and swift that even in an age of telecommunications it seems magical.[1] Several factors, most of them beyond Watkins's control, combined to give him what must be considered a spectacular political career.

John Watkins was unknown in politics and a relative newcomer to lower Louisiana. He had lived in Spanish Upper Louisiana from sometime in the latter half of 1795 to the opening year of the nineteenth century, when he formally made New Orleans his home. Nothing in Watkins's life prior to 1803 suggested that he sought or wanted a career in politics. Eventually, his honest and nonpartisan patriotism brought an end to his political pursuits. The brevity of his political career, which began in April 1803 and entered its rapid decline when William C. C. Claiborne removed him as mayor of New Orleans in early March 1807, accentuates its brightness. Claiborne opposed Watkins's unsuccessful bid to be territorial delegate to Congress in 1809, but Watkins did return to the political arena to play a significant role

1. John Watkins and John Watson sometimes are confused. Writing in the 1930s, one of the Works Project Administration writers, aware of John Watkins's importance and rapid rise to prominence, wrote that Watkins arrived in New Orleans from Philadelphia on May 26, 1804, and was appointed to office by Claiborne. That writer appears to have confused John Watkins with John Watson. See "Administrations of the Mayors of New Orleans, 1803–1936," comp. and ed. Works Project Administration (project 665-64-3-112, typescript; New Orleans, March 1940), 11. John Watson apparently did arrive in New Orleans in May 1804. Georgia Fairbanks Taylor, "The Early History of the Episcopal Church in New Orleans, 1805–1840," *Louisiana Historical Quarterly* 22, no. 2 (April 1939), 428 n. 7, and 435.

as a member of the 1812 constitutional convention, which wrote the state's
first constitution. Death from yellow fever at the age of forty-one late in the
summer of the same year lends poignancy to his shortened life.[2]

John Watkins's life was much like that of the restless, mobile Americans
Alexis de Tocqueville wrote about in his study of the United States and its
people between 1835 and 1840. De Tocqueville characterized Americans as
being in "incessant" motion and "continuous" movement.[3] Elsewhere in his
study de Tocqueville described Americans as "'constantly changing . . .
[their] domicile and . . . continually forming new enterprises.'"[4] Although
devoted to the practice of medicine, Watkins seemed to be constantly on the
move and to have engaged in more than one major project at a time. As a
consequence, information on his activities, particularly before 1803, is
sparse and scattered from Virginia through Kentucky to Philadelphia, to
Missouri, and down the Mississippi River to New Orleans. It also is found
in archival depositories in Scotland and Spain. The effect of this scattered
information, along with the absence of any personal papers, has been to discourage an examination of Watkins's life.

John Watkins most probably was born in 1771, near Midlothian, Chesterfield County, Virginia, south of the James River and southwest of Richmond.[5] He identified his parents at the time of his second marriage in 1804.[6]

2. Watkins died on August 30, 1812, and was buried about six o'clock that evening. His
will was filed the following day, August 31, 1812. John Watkins Will, Orleans Parish, Louisiana, Court of Probate, Record of Wills, 1805–1837, Will Book, 1805–1817, vol. 1, 1805–
1817, 510–11; and "Administrations of the Mayors," 13.

3. Alexis de Tocqueville, *Democracy in America,* ed. Phillips Bradley, vol. 1 (New York:
Alfred A. Knopf, 1948), 292–3.

4. James T. Schleifer, *The Making of Tocqueville's Democracy in America* (Chapel Hill:
University of North Carolina Press, 1980), 42.

5. On one of his proselyting missions into Spanish Missouri, the Reverend John D. Shane
noted that he met Dr. John Watkins from Woodford County, Kentucky, in the vicinity of St.
Louis. Shane also recorded that Watkins told him he was "originally from" Chesterfield
County, Virginia. State Historical Society of Wisconsin, Draper Manuscript Collection, Kentucky MSS, Draper MSS 15CC7 (entry 16), microfilm 3074, reel 86 (hereinafter referred to as
Draper MSS Collection). Comparison of events referred to in this entry by the Reverend Shane
and other sources suggest that Shane met Watkins sometime between September 1800 and September 19, 1801, most probably not long after Watkins had returned from his failed mission
to Spain. Michael F. Doran, *Atlas of County Boundary Changes in Virginia, 1634–1895* (Athens, Ga.: Iberian, 1987), 23–4, shows the boundaries of Chesterfield County and establishes
that it was formed in 1749 from that portion of Henrico County below the James River.

6. See Charles R. Maduell, Jr., *New Orleans Marriage Contracts, 1804–1820. Abstracted
from the Notarial Archives of New Orleans* (New Orleans: Polyanthos Press, 1977), 38 (entry
143), citing the Notarial Files of Narcise Broutin.

John Watkins, junior, was born on land his father, John (1742–1807), in-
herited from his father, also named John Watkins (1710–1765), but known
as the "Planter." The progenitors of this Watkins family in America were
Henry Watkins (1638–1715) and his son Edward Watkins (1676–1717).[7]
The father of Dr. John Watkins was a veteran of the American Revolution.[8]
He moved his family, household goods, and slaves to Kentucky in 1785.
There were approximately seventy members in the Watkins wagon train
when it left Virginia in the fall of 1785. They included his wife, Mary, and
their five children, along with the husband of his eldest daughter. The senior
Watkins made his home in the heart of what became known as the Blue
Grass region of Kentucky, arriving about the time of the first snowfall.[9]

   The senior John Watkins became a part of the landed gentry in Kentucky,
much as he and his forebears had been in Virginia. He was one of the founders of the town of Versailles, the Woodford County seat, and served as a
member of the Kentucky constitutional convention of 1792. When the new
constitution was approved, the senior John Watkins was elected to the
house of representatives of the first Kentucky legislature, and was chosen
elector for Woodford County.[10] Late in June of that year, he was nominated

   7. John Hale Stutesman, *Some Watkins Families of Virginia and Their Kin: Abbott, Anderson, Bass, Clay, Cox, Farrar, Hancock, Hundley, Montague, Moseley, Randolph, Walthall,
Wooldridge* (Baltimore, Md.: Gateway Press, 1989), 205.

   8. John Watkins, Sr., is referred to as "Captain" in Daniel Trabue, *Westward into Kentucky: The Narrative of Daniel Trabue*, ed. Chester Raymond Young (Lexington: University
Press of Kentucky, 1981), 135–6. John H. Gwathmey, *Historical Register of Virginians in the
Revolution. Soldiers, Sailors, Marines, 1775–1783* (1938; Baltimore: Genealogical Publishing,
1987), 809, lists eight men named John Watkins from Virginia, but does not provide information showing which might be the father of Dr. John Watkins.

   9. *Westward into Kentucky*, ed. Young, 134–6. The children of John and Mary (Hudson)
Watkins, in approximate birth order, were Elizabeth ("Betsey"), John, Mary ("Polly"), Samuel,
Sarah, Martha ("Patsey"), and Phebe (Phoebe) Watkins. The married daughter was Elizabeth.
Her husband was James Lockett of Virginia. Two minor boys, Hudson and Erasmus Watkins,
were named in the 1807 will of John Watkins, Sr., but no further identification of them was
provided. The will of the senior John Watkins stipulated that Erasmus was to be sent to live
with Dr. John Watkins in Louisiana. Stutesman, *Some Watkins Families*, 201–11. See also John
Stutesman, "From Virginia to Kentucky—The Pioneer Family of John and Mary Watkins,"
Kentucky Ancestors 20, no. 2 (autumn 1984), 91–3.

   10. Richard H. Collins, *History of Kentucky*, rev. ed., vol. 1 (Covington, Ky.: Collins,
1878), 355, 357. On the senior John Watkins's role in the establishment of Versailles, Kentucky, see also Zachary F. Smith, *The Clay Family*, Part First, *The Mother of Henry Clay* (Louisville, Ky.: John P. Morton, 1899), 22; and Dabney Garrett Munson and Margaret Ware
Parrish, eds., *Woodford County, Kentucky: The First Two Hundred Years, 1789–1989* (Lexington, Ky.: By the Editors, 1989), 57–8.

by Governor Isaac Shelby of Kentucky to be a Shelby County justice of the peace, then a position of greater importance in the structure of American society.[11]

The growing affluence of John Watkins, senior, made it possible for his eldest son, John Watkins, junior, to pursue his interest in the study of medicine with Dr. Benjamin Rush in the Medical School of the College of Philadelphia. While in private study with Rush, Watkins became a good friend of two other Virginians also studying with Rush, William Henry Harrison, future governor of the Indiana Territory and president of the United States, and Samuel Brown. Harrison left medicine to pursue a career in the army, but Watkins and Brown continued their medical studies.[12]

Watkins came under the influence of Benjamin Smith Barton, professor of *materia medica,* while at medical school in Philadelphia. Barton was internationally recognized as the leading naturalist and botanist in the United States. Barton helped Watkins discover a lifelong interest in natural history.[13] Watkins maintained contact with Barton after leaving Philadelphia and for several years supplied him with information on the natural history of the Mississippi Valley. One of Watkins's letters to Barton was published in the *Transactions of the American Philosophical Society* as "Notices of the Natural History of the Northerly Parts of Louisiana; in a Letter from Dr. John Watkins to Dr. Barton."[14] The proceedings of the society also reflect that Watkins sent information to the society on rock salt found on the earth's surface in Missouri. At a later date, September 16, 1803, he sent

11. "Kentucky State Papers. Excerpts from Executive Journal No. 1, Governor Isaac Shelby," *Register of the Kentucky Historical Society* 27, no. 81 (September 1929), 591.

12. Jerah Johnson, "Dr. John Watkins, New Orleans' Lost Mayor," *Louisiana History* 36, no. 2 (spring 1995), 189. On Harrison's medical studies and departure for the army, see Freeman Cleaves, *Old Tippecanoe, William Henry Harrison and His Time* (New York: Charles Scribner's Sons, 1939), 7–8.

13. Johnson, "New Orleans' Lost Mayor," 189.

14. *Transactions of the American Philosophical Society* 6, Part 14 (1809), 68–72. The letter is dated St. Louis, October 20, 1802, with the notation that it was read for Watkins at a meeting of society members on January 1, 1803. However, the *Proceedings of the American Philosophical Society* 22, no. 119 [July 1885], Part 3, 330, indicate that Watkins's letter was read on January 21, 1803. Before the letter was published, the publications committee, John Vaughan and Benjamin Latrobe, asked Watkins to "furnish the Linnaean Nomenclature" of the plants and animals "as far as can be done." The use of the scientific names in the published paper indicates that Watkins, or someone, complied with the request. "Report of the Committee on the Papers of John Watkins, Philadelphia, March 4, 1803," American Philosophical Society. Photocopy of the original owned by the author.

information on the "Discovery of a Cantharides," a kind of beetle commonly known as the "Spanish fly." As a powdered preparation, it formerly was used internally as a diuretic and genitourinary stimulant, and externally as a skin irritant.[15]

Young Watkins left the medical school of the College of Philadelphia, later known as the University of Pennsylvania, for the University of Edinburgh Medical School, Scotland, where he studied for two years, 1792–94. In his first year Watkins attended clinical lectures and classes in anatomy and surgery, chemistry, and the "practice of physik." During his second year he studied midwifery and the theory and practice of medicine.[16] Watkins apparently went to Edinburgh to study on the recommendation of Dr. Benjamin Rush. Shortly after arriving in Edinburgh, Watkins wrote Rush to thank him for "the attention and favors, which I received from you during my stay in Philadelphia." Watkins also expressed his gratitude to Rush for the "politeness and attention" extended to him by Doctor Duncan in Edinburgh because of Rush's "generous friendship." Betraying perhaps a touch of homesickness, Watkins also told Rush that the "advantages of study" in Edinburgh "at least equaled" those in Philadelphia. He closed his letter to Rush saying that the "Good will" he felt toward the University of Philadelphia and his "respect for its professors" would make him "defer taking a degree until I return to America."[17]

Watkins did not follow through on his plan to receive his degree, despite his stated intention. Why he did not is unknown. Perhaps, like the vast majority of medical students then, he felt the additional two years of expense were not justifiable, or necessary. Although he did not receive his medical diploma, Watkins was devoted to the practice of medicine. Some New Orleans residents ranked Watkins "among our best Physicians."[18] Regardless of his political career, most of his associates thought of him as Doctor Wat-

15. *Proceedings of the American Philosophical Society* 22, no. 119, 328 and 341, respectively.

16. The unpublished Matriculation Albums, Edinburgh University Library, Edinburgh, Scotland. Mrs. Jo Currie, Assistant Librarian, Special Collections, Edinburgh University Library, to Jared W. Bradley, May 12, 1995.

17. John Watkins to Dr. Benjamin Rush, July 20, 1792, *Benjamin Rush Papers,* vol. 19 (Philadelphia: Library Company of Philadelphia), 40. Photocopy of the transcription owned by the author.

18. James Sterrett to Nathaniel Evans, December 2, 1809. Nathaniel Evans and Family Papers, Louisiana and Lower Mississippi Valley Collections, Louisiana State University Libraries.

kins, although the family may have called him "Watkins" as his first cousin John Clay did in 1804.[19]

When he returned to Kentucky, Watkins began to practice medicine in Lexington in association with Basil Duke, an older man with an established practice. They subsequently welcomed Frederick Ridgely, another recently arrived young doctor, to the practice.[20] Within a year of returning home, Watkins married Salley Clay, his first cousin. Salley was the sister of John and Henry Clay, the latter being the political figure who dominated much of Kentucky and United States history in the years between 1812 and 1850. Two months after Watkins and Salley were married, she died.[21] Apparently heartbroken and disillusioned after her death, Watkins closed his practice in Lexington and left Kentucky. Thereafter, nothing is known of his activities for nearly two years.

Watkins is heard of again from his location in Spanish Upper Louisiana in what today is known as Missouri, but then was called the Illinois Country. There, Watkins was identified in 1797 as "an American speculator," claiming 7,057 arpents, a square league, of land near the mouth of the Meramec River.[22] The records indicate he then was living in St.

19. John Clay to Henry Clay, New Orleans, July 6, 1804, *The Papers of Henry Clay*, ed. James F. Hopkins, vol. 1, *The Rising Statesman, 1797–1814* (Lexington: University of Kentucky Press, 1959), 140.

20. Johnson, "New Orleans' Lost Mayor," 189. *Papers of Henry Clay,* 1: 141 n. 7, refers to the Watkins practice in Lexington, but provides no details.

21. Salley (Sarah) Clay was the daughter of Elizabeth Hudson and John Clay. Elizabeth Hudson Clay was the sister of Mary Hudson Watkins, the mother of John Watkins. Stutesman, *Some Watkins Families*, 205–6. See also Winston de Ville, "Old Letter in Virginia Archives Reveals Data on Early Louisiana Families: Trudeau and Duralde," *New Orleans Genesis* 19, no. 73 (January 1980), 19. Watkins gave the date of Salley's death as June 12, 1795, at the time of his second marriage in New Orleans in 1804. However, the marriage bond of John Watkins and Salley Clay is dated June 12, 1795. Photocopy of Marriage Bond Number 242, Woodford County, Kentucky, owned by the author. Johnson states that Salley died of yellow fever on August 12, 1795 ("New Orleans' Lost Mayor," 189). On the relationship of the Hudson girls and further evidence of Mary Hudson's marriage to John Watkins, senior, see George H. S. King, "Will of George Hudson of Hanover County, Virginia," *Virginia Magazine of History and Biography* 66, no. 1 (January 1958), 85–7.

22. Louis Houck, *A History of Missouri from the Earliest Explorations and Settlements Until the Admission of the State into the Union,* vol. 1 (Chicago: R. R. Donnelley & Sons, 1908), 75 n. 154 (continued from 74). This claim, dated February 6, 1797, ultimately was not allowed by the Missouri Land Commission, despite the sworn testimony of Antoine Soulard, surveyor for the Spanish and later the United States, that he "had seen among the official pa-

Louis.[23] Of course, Watkins's plans for the settlement and development of the land in Missouri depended on Spanish policy. For this reason, it is believed that he did not immediately settle in Upper Louisiana when he left Lexington, but began to indulge his interest in the natural history of the Illinois Country. With nature as his balm, Watkins gradually returned to society and the practice of medicine. On his journey back from disillusionment and grief, Watkins became a fur trapper, trader, and occasional interpreter to the Indians, and he began to move into the business of land developer.

Indications of Watkins's activities in the Illinois Country are drawn from several sources: his 1799 St. Louis will; references to his occasional work as interpreter to the Indians;[24] and his association with the Chouteaus (Pierre, Sr., and Auguste) and Manuel Lisa.[25] In his 1799 will, Watkins spec-

---

pers of Zenon Trudeau, an order from the Baron de Carondelet to grant . . . a league square" to Watkins. *American State Papers: Public Lands,* vol. 2 (Washington, D.C.: Gales & Seaton, 1834), 444.

Houck states that Watkins also bought the Jean Marie Cardinal place known as "Fontaine à Cardinal" a few miles north of St. Louis sometime after 1780 (*History of Missouri,* 2: 38 n. 87). It may have been this plantation that Watkins described in his 1799 will as being "in the Grand Prairie near to this Village [St. Louis]" (John Watkins Will, December 16, 1799, Instrument No. 2267, *St. Louis Archives,* Missouri Historical Society. Photocopy in the possession of the author). A deposition with this will states that it was found unopened among the French and Spanish archives in the office of the clerk of the St. Louis County Court, on October 14, 1847.

23. Houck, *History of Missouri,* 2: 75 n. 154 (continued from p. 74), and 100 n. 44. Watkins may have chosen not to live on the land near the Meramec for two reasons. First, he was frequently on the move. Second, the Osage Indians in that vicinity were more troublesome than in other localities and as late as 1793 repeatedly drove the settlers away. In addition, vagabond Indians of other tribes from the southeastern United States, some from as far away as the Gulf of Mexico, made the area even more unsafe. The Indians used the tributaries of the Meramec River as meeting places from which they made their predatory excursions. Ibid., 75–6.

24. The Reverend John D. Shane identified Watkins as "interpreter to the Indians." Draper MSS Collection. The contents of Watkins's letter published in *Transactions of the American Philosophical Society* in January 1803 support his wide-ranging acquaintance with the land and Indians of the Great Plains as far west as the Rocky Mountains, as far north as the Dakotas and Minnesota, and as far south as present-day Oklahoma and Arkansas.

25. Evidence of Watkins's business dealings with the Chouteaus and Manuel Lisa is in the Auguste Chouteau Papers and the Manuel Lisa Papers, in the *Chouteau Family Papers* on deposit with the Missouri Historical Society. Dennis Northcott, assistant archivist, Missouri Historical Society, to the author, July 26, 1995. Watkins is not mentioned by Louis Houck as being among the numerous persons identified in the fur trade in early Missouri in Louis Houck,

ified that his "lawful debts be paid . . . with Peltries and that the balance" of his estate be converted into silver. With this silver, the debt he owed John Neighbour (sometimes spelled Neybour), who was then living on "my [Watkins's] plantation at the Marameq [*sic*]," was to be paid.[26] Quite possibly, Watkins was attracted to the Spanish colony by the wise and discreet settlement policies of Zenon Trudeau, the lieutenant governor of Upper Louisiana, who appears to have been a shaping influence on the life and career of Watkins after he settled in Louisiana.[27]

Other contemporary evidence also points to Watkins's association with the settlers and the Indian tribes living near the confluence of the Missouri and Ohio Rivers with the Mississippi River. In the fall of 1798, in a chance meeting at St. Genevieve, Missouri, Watkins assisted Moses Austin as translator of French in a dispute Austin was having with his partners over the lead mining business he was under contract with the Spanish to develop.[28] It may have been at this time that Watkins collected the information on rock salt in Missouri that he sent to the American Philosophical Society.[29]

Watkins wrote his 1799 will in anticipation of a dangerous journey. The document begins: "I, John Watkins Junior, native of Virginia, now living in the Town of St. Louis, Illinois, intend a long and dangerous voyage." What kind of voyage and to where is not specified, but the will stipulates that, in the event of Watkins's death while on this long journey, "a certain tract of

---

ed. and trans., *The Spanish Regime in Missouri: A Collection of Papers and Documents Relating to Upper Louisiana Principally with the Present Limits of Missouri . . . ,* (New York: Arno Press, 1909). For this reason, it is believed that Watkins's involvement with the fur trade and work as interpreter to the Indians grew out of his interest in natural history, that they were occasional, and that they were used chiefly to keep him in "currency" to advance his acquisition of land. Richard Edward Oglesby, *Manuel Lisa and the Opening of the Missouri Fur Trade* (Norman: University of Oklahoma Press, 1963), 20, points out that the "only currency of value" at the end of the eighteenth and beginning of the nineteenth centuries in the Illinois Country "was peltry."

26. John Watkins Will, December 16, 1799.

27. A brief biographical sketch of Trudeau may be seen on pp. 372–3.

28. In this meeting, Austin referred to Watkins as "Dr. John Watkins of St. Louis," suggesting that Watkins continued to practice medicine. David B. Gracy II, *Moses Austin: His Life* (San Antonio, Tex.: Trinity University Press, 1987), 76. Antoine Soulard, the surveyor general for Upper Louisiana, wrote on June 30, 1806, that "Austin speaks and understand[s] French, . . . can also read it." Clarence E. Carter, comp. and ed., *The Territorial Papers of the United States,* vol. 13, *The Territory of Louisiana-Missouri, 1803–1806* (Washington, D.C.: Government Printing Office, 1948), 524 (hereinafter cited as TP, with volume and page range).

29. Reference to this unpublished contribution is noted in the *Proceedings of the American Philosophical Society* 22, no. 119, 328. See also n. 14 to this biographical sketch.

land lying upon the little rock River," which he had purchased earlier, was to "be conveyed to Philip Nolan or his heirs." Watkins's Missouri property, or the proceeds from its sale, were to go to his younger brother, Samuel Watkins, who had settled in Missouri after John moved there.[30]

Despite its commonplace practicality as a frontier estate planning tool, Watkins's 1799 will raises a number of questions because of the inclusion of Philip Nolan. Watkins and Nolan had known one another as youths in Lexington, where Nolan lived as foster son of General James Wilkinson and his family from about 1785 to 1791. Nolan, like Watkins, was born in 1771. It is quite likely that the two youngsters received their secondary education in the Latin school of William Steele in Kentucky.[31] The Nolan and Wilkinson families apparently had known one another in Maryland. After the deaths of his parents, young Nolan followed the Wilkinsons to Kentucky and lived with them in Lexington until 1791, when Nolan became the general's agent in New Orleans.[32] Watkins and Nolan most probably renewed their friendship in 1796–97, when Nolan was in Missouri making a map for Carondelet.[33] The naming of Nolan by Watkins in his will clearly implies a strong friendship between the two young men.

30. John Watkins Will, December 16, 1799. Eighteenth- and early-nineteenth-century wills similar to Watkins's 1799 will were not unusual and were written because of the dangers inherent in living on the frontier. Ella Chalfant, *A Goodly Heritage: Earliest Wills on an American Frontier* (Pittsburgh: University of Pittsburgh Press, 1955), 3–4, 81–3, and *passim*.

31. Johnson, "New Orleans' Lost Mayor," 188.

32. Maurine T. Wilson and Jack Jackson, *Philip Nolan and Texas: Expeditions to the Unknown Land, 1791–1801* (Waco, Tex.: Texian Press, 1987), 2, 5–8, tell of Nolan's early ties to Wilkinson and are the best source for information on his tragic life. Jack Jackson, in *Los Mesteños: Spanish Ranching in Texas, 1721–1821* (College Station: Texas A&M University Press, 1986), 452–64, places Nolan at the forefront of the "mustanger" trade with Texas.

33. James Ripley Jacobs, *Tarnished Warrior: Major-General James Wilkinson* (New York: Macmillan, 1938), 184, points out Nolan's mapmaking ability and journey to the Illinois country in 1796–97. Nolan probably was in Missouri to map the location of the secret Spanish Fort Carondelet, which was built in 1794–95 on the upper Osage River. See also Wilson and Jackson, *Philip Nolan*, 79–80, particularly n. 15 (p. 138). The fort, described as a glorified trading post, was used to manage the Osage Indians, the tribe least amenable to Spanish control. The Osage were the most important tribe living in the western part of Spanish Illinois during the years of Spanish rule. Carl H. Chapman, "The Indomitable Osage in Spanish Illinois (Upper) Louisiana 1763–1804," in John Francis McDermott, ed., *The Spanish in the Mississippi Valley, 1762–1804* (Urbana: University of Illinois Press, 1974), 287–8, 300–7. Nolan also intended to make a map of Natchez in the spring of 1797, but advised Wilkinson that he could not make it without antagonizing Gayoso. Nolan to Wilkinson, April 24, 1797, Register of Letters Received by the Secretary of War, Unregistered Series, 1789–1860, Record Group 107, microcopy 222, reel 1, 1789–1804.

Long after Nolan's disappearance in Texas, Watkins, like many others, probably wondered what had happened to his friend and, as time passed without any news, he undoubtedly harbored a growing suspicion and resentment of the Spanish. These feelings most likely were reinforced by the anti-American attitudes and activities of the Spanish in the Lower Mississippi Valley following the transfer of Louisiana to the United States. Such feelings would account, in part, for Watkins's friendship with James Workman, who was known for his anti-Spanish views, and for Watkins's membership in and support of the Mexican Association in New Orleans a few years later in 1805–07. It is in this sense that the lives of Watkins, Nolan, and Mexico are linked with Louisiana and early U.S. history.

The linking of Watkins, Nolan, and Mexico raises additional pertinent questions: What prompted Watkins to reach out to his friend through his will in 1799? The chief conclusion is that Watkins knew of the financial embarrassment Nolan was suffering at the time and of his great love for and desire to marry the socially prominent Frances Lintot of Natchez. This conclusion leads to another question: from whom did Watkins learn of Nolan's love for Fanny Lintot? Obviously, Watkins must have gained this information from Nolan himself. Watkins's decision to leave Nolan real property appears to have been altruistic, but was it known to Nolan? The answer to this question may never be known. Finally, does Watkins's will in any way suggest that he may have considered joining Nolan on his next, and final, expedition into Texas? Or did the long and dangerous journey Watkins referred to in his will mean some other, possibly less hazardous journey?[34]

34. It has been suggested that on his last venture into Texas in 1801 Nolan, unlike Aaron Burr and others who most certainly were intended victims of Wilkinson in 1807, may have been the unwitting victim of the man who had befriended and partly reared him, General James Wilkinson. Nolan's mission may have been "to go into central Texas and establish a fortified point from which Nolan's men could threaten the entire" Texas colony, while "General Wilkinson was to lead a column of men down from Kentucky." The project is similar to the proposal advanced by President John Adams a few years earlier. According to that plan, Alexander Hamilton was to lead an American army from Fort Washington (Cincinnati) into Missouri and on to Mexico. Noel M. Loomis and Abraham P. Nasatir, *Pedro Vial and the Roads to Santa Fe* (Norman: University of Oklahoma Press, 1967), 233. See also "The Real Philip Nolan," *Publications of the Mississippi Historical Society* 4 (1902), 286, 284; and Noel M. Loomis, "Philip Nolan's Entry into Texas in 1800," in McDermott, *The Spanish in the Mississippi Valley*, 130–2. This scenario seems doubtful for two reasons. First, as protection for himself and Wilkinson, Nolan usually kept knowledge of all his plans from the general. See Nolan to Wilkinson, Frankfort, Kentucky, June 10, 1796, in General James Wilkinson, *Memoirs of My Own Times*, vol. 2 (1816; New York: AMS Press, 1973), Appendix II. Second, it is doubtful because of Wilkinson's espionage work for and financial dependence on the Spanish.

If Watkins impulsively had thought of joining Nolan's final expedition to Texas, he may have decided not to participate in the scheme when he learned of the extent of Spanish opposition to Nolan's return to the "unknown land."[35] Nonetheless, Watkins's 1799 will suggests, superficially at least, that his first involvement with plans for seizing and occupying Texas and Mexico may have been 1799, rather than 1805–07. However, unless or until collateral evidence is discovered, the will stands chiefly as an example of frontier estate planning and a reflection of friendship between two young men struggling to make their ways in the world. Corroborating evidence for this version of the story is in documents dated 1800 from the Spanish Archives of the Indies and in depositions given in 1806 by knowledgeable contemporaries of Watkins. These papers clearly indicate that Watkins's 1799 will was prepared in anticipation of his journey to Spain to make a personal appeal to the Spanish court for a large land grant in the Illinois Country. The project coincided with Watkins's move to New Orleans.

John Watkins began to call New Orleans his home early in 1800, suggesting that he initiated the move to lower Louisiana from the Illinois Country soon after Zenon Trudeau left office as lieutenant governor of Upper Louisiana in July 1799.[36] Watkins is known to have been in New Orleans on March 4, 1800, the date he offered a proposal to the Spanish governor of Louisiana for the settlement and further development of Upper Louisiana by himself and unnamed partners.[37] The cover letter that accompanied this two-part proposal was addressed to the Marqués de Casa Calvo, who was

35. Nolan to Wilkinson, New Orleans, January 6, 1796 (Wilkinson, *Memoirs of My Own Times,* 2: 117) referred to Texas as the "unknown land," by which he meant the present day politico-geographic entities of Texas, New Mexico, and Mexico. Watkins could have been advised by Zenon Trudeau, if he did not already know, of the strong opposition of the Spanish officials in Louisiana and Texas to intrusions into the "unknown land" by any foreigners, especially Americans.

36. Late in October 1804, Claiborne wrote Secretary Madison that the "Physician of the Port [Dr. Watkins] . . . has resided in the Territory for four years" To James Madison, October 27, 1804, in *Official Letter Books of W. C. C. Claiborne, 1801–1816,* ed. Dunbar Rowland, vol. 2 (1917; New York: AMS Press, 1972), 377 (hereinafter cited as CLB, with volume and page range). Presumably, the governor obtained this information from the French prefect Laussat and Watkins.

37. John Watkins to Señor Marqués de Casa Calvo, March 4, 1800, *Archivo General de Indias, Papeles de Cuba, legajo* 2366, folios 235–44. Watkins refers to his unnamed company and partners on folios 241 and 243 (hereinafter cited as AGI, *Papeles de Cuba, legajo* 2366 with folio numbers).

appointed interim governor of Louisiana following the death of Governor-General Manuel Gayoso de Lemos on July 18, 1799. The salutation "Señor Marqués" at the top of the first part of the proposal also could have been intended for the Marqués de Someruelos, captain-general in Havana.[38] The contents of this document indicate Watkins had knowledge of Upper Louisiana that would have come from living in and traversing that part of the Mississippi Valley for a number of years, and also from having access to statistical data collected by a governmental agency.[39]

Watkins played the chief role in presenting the application for the large land grant, but the evidence reflects that the project also may have originated, in part, with Kentucky Circuit Court Judge Benjamin Sebastian, associate justice of the Kentucky Court of Appeals, who became a key figure in Spain's efforts to separate Kentucky from the Union in the 1780s and 1790s.[40] Others named in the original articles of incorporation were John A. Seitz of Lexington; A. Steele of Shelbyville, Kentucky; Dr. Frederick Ridgely, the doctor who had joined the medical practice of Drs. Duke and Watkins in Lexington; and a Mr. Grayson of Bardstown, Kentucky. Watkins was one of the stockholders, but his chief role was that of agent for the group, perhaps because of his command of the French and Spanish languages, and his rapport with the lieutenant governor of Spanish Upper Louisiana, Zenon Trudeau. The name of the corporation, whether given at its inception or later, was "The Kentucky Spanish Association." The stated purpose of the company was to encourage Americans, particularly Kentuckians, to settle on the land grant they were to receive in Upper Louisiana.[41] Presumably, the death of Gayoso in July 1799 and the appointment of the Marqués de Casa Calvo as acting governor of Louisiana contributed to the decision of the association members to try to present their case to the court

38. Ibid., folio 241.

39. See ibid., folios 235–7, in which Watkins cites detailed information on population growth, agricultural development, the mining of lead by Moses Austin and others, and the actual increase in the cost of flour, corn, and cooking lard for the years from 1795 through 1799.

40. Sebastian's role as a paid agent of the Spanish was revealed in the Federalist *Frankfort (Ky.) Western World* newspaper in 1806 and proved beyond any doubt, at which point he resigned from office. Thomas P. Abernethy, *The Burr Conspiracy* (New York: Oxford University Press, 1954), 88–9, 94–5.

41. *Western World,* August [23,] 1806, p. 4, cc. 1–2. The corporation members are named in the deposition of Richard Steele published in ibid., December 13, 1806, p. 4, c. 2, and in the Lexington *Kentucky Gazette and General Advertiser,* December 11, 1806, p. 2, c. 4 (hereinafter cited as *Kentucky Gazette*).

of Spain, where it might receive a more favorable hearing. Watkins obviously was selected to act as agent for the group because of his travel experience and his ability to speak both French and Spanish.[42]

Watkins set out on his journey in June 1800 with a planned stop in Philadelphia to visit Dr. Benjamin Rush. When Watkins reached Philadelphia, however, the yellow fever quarantine then in effect in the city prevented the visit with Rush so that he was forced to go on to New York City. Watkins wanted to call on Rush to ask him for a "letter of introduction to Mr. Humphreys the American Minister at the Court of Madrid," or to other friends of Rush in Lisbon or Pennsylvania who might be helpful to his mission.[43] Unfortunately, whatever letters Rush subsequently provided Watkins were stolen from him after he arrived in Spain. According to newspaper reports in 1806, Watkins was "ensnared by a band of robbers" in Spain who took not only his money, but also the papers "necessary for his introduction" at court in Madrid.[44] As a consequence, Watkins returned to New Orleans and submitted the Kentucky Spanish Association proposal to Casa Calvo, with whom the backers must have felt the chances of success were not as great.

The opening sentence of the long cover letter that accompanied the reworked proposal confirms other reports that after Watkins left Kentucky he lived in Missouri. In the letter, Watkins refers to himself as a resident of Illinois in the province of Upper Louisiana and asks the Spanish government for a grant of up to one million acres of land "between the most eastern branch or arm of the river Saint Francis and the Arkansas River."[45] It apparently was this grant that Henry Clay some years later laughingly described

42. Johnson, "New Orleans' Lost Mayor," 196, mentions the books written in Spanish and French that were listed in the inventory of Watkins's papers after his death. The books may have been used by Watkins to teach himself those languages and to keep informed regarding medical practices of those countries.

43. John Watkins to Benjamin Rush, June 24, 1800, in *Benjamin Rush Papers,* vol. 19, p. 40, Library Company of Philadelphia.

44. The *Western World* described Watkins as an inexperienced traveler in Spain and unflatteringly compared him to Gil Blas, the literary figure in the early-eighteenth-century novels *Gil Blas de Santillane* by Alain-René Lesage. Blas, the hero of the novels, is taken from the innocence of a respectable middle-class background by rogues and robbers into corruption, but returns to respectability with the triumph of virtue through wisdom learned along the way (*Western World,* August [23,] 1806, p. 4, c. 2).

45. Specifically, the document begins: "Dn Juan Watkins Vecino del Districto de Ilinoa en la Provincia de la Luisiana," John Watkins to Señor Marqués de Casa Calvo, March 4, 1800, AGI, *Papeles de Cuba, legajo* 2366, folio 235. Ibid., folio 243 (numbered paragraph 1), contains the request for the land grant. The original plan apparently requested three million acres. See the *Western World,* August [23,] 1806, unnumbered p. 4, c. 2.

as "big enough to form a respectable state."[46] The proposal stipulated that one-third of the four hundred families who were to be permitted to settle on the land requested were to be Germans.[47] All the settlers were to be "farm-workers, artisans, and other members useful to society who will bring with them cattle, tools and all kinds of useful articles."[48] A comparison of the hand that wrote this document with the three signatures of Watkins within it and his 1799 holographic will suggests that the final transcription of this proposal was by a public scribe, but that the document itself most probably was the product of several minds. This conclusion is drawn from a comparison of the three signatures of Watkins on folios within the proposal with the hand of the scribe employed to copy the documents for submission to the Spanish authorities.[49] It also is drawn from analysis of the original articles of incorporation printed in the Kentucky newspapers.[50] At least one of the authors appears to have been Carondelet, who authorized the grant to Watkins.[51]

Despite the thought and preparation that went into the proposal submit-

46. Stutesman, *Some Watkins Families*, 206, citing an 1853 letter of Edmund Wooldridge to F. N. Watkins in the George Brown Goode Papers, the Virginia State Library.

47. John Watkins to Señor Marqués de Casa Calvo, March 4, 1800, AGI, *Papeles de Cuba, legajo* 2366 folios 243–4 (numbered paragraph 6). The guidance of Zenon Trudeau, or someone of comparable or higher rank in the Spanish colonial administration, seems implicit at this point in the document more than in any other place. The bid to attract German settlers clearly was an attempt to build on the example of the settlers of the "German Coast" along the banks of the Mississippi River above New Orleans and the 1785 suggestion of Martin Navarro, the *contador* and later intendant of Louisiana, that one thousand German families, especially from German Lorraine, be settled in Louisiana. James A. Robertson, ed. and trans., *Louisiana Under the Rule of Spain, France, and the United States, 1785–1807*, vol. 1 (1910–1911; Freeport, N.Y.: Books for Libraries Press, 1969), 248–49. A similar suggestion was made by Governor Manuel Gayoso de Lemos on July 5, 1792 (ibid., 288). Although Watkins may not have known about the earlier policy suggestions, Zenon Trudeau, as lieutenant governor of Spanish Upper Louisiana, certainly would have. Most important, the references to German settlers clearly were intended to conform to the Spanish government's new settlement policy issued in 1798. Under the new immigration policy, Americans were banned and the "God-fearing Flemings and Germans" greatly desired by the Spanish Crown were to be attracted to Louisiana if at all possible. Arthur P. Whitaker, *The Mississippi Question, 1795–1803* (1934; Gloucester, Mass.: Peter Smith, 1962), 156–7.

48. John Watkins to Señor Marqués de Casa Calvo, March 4, 1800, AGI, *Papeles de Cuba, legajo* 2366, folios 243–4 (numbered paragraph 6).

49. Watkins's signature may be seen in ibid., folios 240, 241, and 245.

50. See the *Western World*, August [23,] 1806, unnumbered p. 4, cc. 1–2, and the Lexington *Kentucky Gazette*, December 11, 1806, unnumbered p. 2, c. 4.

51. See *American State Papers: Public Lands*, 2: 444.

ted to the colonial administration of Spanish Louisiana, the project was turned down. Watkins learned this within a year, or less, after submitting the plan. He revealed this fact to the Reverend John D. Shane in Missouri sometime after September 1800 when they met near St. Louis. At least that seems to be the meaning of an entry in Shane's journal that said, "Watkins told me the Spanish had ceased to make grants."[52]

Equally suggestive of the support and covert guidance of an older, experienced administrator like Zenon Trudeau in the land development scheme is the fact that Watkins continued to pursue its implementation after the arrival in New Orleans of Pierre Clément de Laussat, the French prefect who was to govern Louisiana following its return to France. Watkins's continued pursuit of the proposal was revealed by Daniel Clark. In his capacity as U.S. consul in New Orleans, Clark reported to Secretary of State Madison on April 27, 1803, that "Doctor Watkins whom I have already mentioned to you as a Land Speculator is proposing Plans to the French government for colonizing a part of the upper Country, the Tract included between the River St. Francis and Arkansas."[53]

Despite his high hopes of becoming a wealthy land developer in Upper Louisiana, Watkins's dream was dashed again, this time by the sale of Louisiana to the United States by Napoleon. As Watkins's hoped-for avenue to wealth faded, he, along with many others in New Orleans, began to give his attention to speculative land ventures in the Orleans Territory and West Florida. This is revealed in the notarial archives in New Orleans and in a letter written by General Wilkinson to Secretary of War Henry Dearborn on January 3, 1804. The notarial acts of John Lynd reveal that Watkins bought 500 acres of land—part of the tract formerly granted to the Baron de Bastrop—from John W. Gurley in Ouachita County in September 1805 for $500.00.[54] In his letter to Dearborn, Wilkinson reported: "Doct. Watkins last evening assured me" that Laussat had informed him that prior to his departure from France Laussat had "'expressly requested Instructions, to justify his taking possession of West Florida, but . . . instead . . . was informed that Spain had positively refused it,'" despite "'repeated applications of the French Consul.'" Wilkinson went on to say that "Almost the whole of the Americans, English & Irish here, with many Frenchmen &

52. Draper MSS Collection, 15 CC7 (entry 16).

53. [Arthur P. Whitaker, ed.,] "Despatches from the United States Consulate in New Orleans, 1801–1803, II," *American Historical Review* 33, no. 2 (January 1928), 339.

54. Act of September 16, 1805, Notarial Acts of John Lynd, Notarial Archives, New Orleans.

Spaniards are engaged on the speculation[,] and every valuable spot" between the Mississippi River and Mobile "will be granted away." Without
mentioning Clark by name, the general said that even "our ex Consul stands
at the Head of the list."[55] In time, the momentum for land speculation in
West Florida grew until by early August 1805, Claiborne reported that Juan
Ventura Morales, the Spanish intendant still resident in New Orleans, was
to open an office in the city for the sole purpose of disposing "of all the
Vacant Lands in West Florida."[56]

Watkins's interest in land development seems never to have slackened.
Late in August 1804, Claiborne reported to Jefferson that Watkins was
"said to be in a small degree interested in the Florida purchases."[57] Nearly
two years later, on June 12, 1806, Claiborne, apparently at the request of
Watkins, recommended the doctor to Jefferson for a position on the "Board
of Land Commissioners for the New Orleans district," if such a vacancy
occurred.[58]

The association of Watkins with the highly respected and well-connected
Zenon Trudeau in combination with his pursuit of land development in
Upper Louisiana brought the doctor to the attention of Laussat. However,
it most probably was a combination of Watkins's association with Zenon
Trudeau, his activities as a land developer, his training as a doctor, and,
most importantly, his command of French, Spanish, and English that focused Laussat's attention on him. Laussat saw in Watkins someone who
could help smooth the way for his plans to reorganize the cabildo, the administrative body that governed the city of New Orleans. When that reorganization was complete, Laussat appointed Watkins to the *conseil de ville*
(city council), the new name of the reorganized cabildo, in April 1803.[59]

55. James Wilkinson to the Secretary of War, January 3, 1803 [1804], TP, 9: 151.

56. To James Madison, August 3, 1805, and From Casa Calvo [August 8, 1805], both in
CLB, 3: 145–6, and 159–60, respectively. The Casa Calvo letter incorporates verbatim Mo-
rales's long-winded response to Casa Calvo's inquiry confirming Claiborne's concern. See also
To Casa Calvo, August 21, 1805, ibid., 179.

57. Also named in Claiborne's letter with Watkins were William Kenner and William Donaldson. Governor Claiborne to the President, August 30, 1804, TP, 9: 284, misspells Donaldson's name as "Donelson."

58. To Thomas Jefferson, June 12, 1806, CLB, 3: 326.

59. Pierre Clément de Laussat tells in his memoirs of appointing Watkins to the city coun-
cil. *Memoirs of My Life to My Son During the Years 1803 and After, Which I Spent in Public
Service in Louisiana as Commissioner of the French Government for the Retrocession to
France of that Colony and for Its Transfer to the United States*, trans. Sister Agnes-Josephine
Pastwa, ed. Robert D. Bush (Baton Rouge: Louisiana State University Press, 1978), 76. Wat-
kins served on the city council until he took office as mayor on February 27, 1805.

At the time of Watkins's appointment to the *conseil de ville,* Laussat also assigned Watkins and a Mr. Allard, another member of the city council, responsibility for inspecting the Charity Hospital of Saint Charles and all bakeries in the city.[60] Perhaps as a result of this responsibility, Watkins applied for, and shortly was granted, a medical license to practice in New Orleans on July 22, 1803.[61] In essence, this responsibility made Watkins and Allard the de facto board of health for New Orleans. At the same time, the city council passed an ordinance requiring all garbage, refuse, and sewage to be thrown into the Mississippi River. Anyone who violated the ordinance would be fined and all such proceeds were to be used to support the Charity Hospital.[62]

The importance of their political positions in the governments of Louisiana and New Orleans after the Louisiana Purchase presented numerous occasions for Watkins and Claiborne to have met, but Watkins said in March 1807 that he "had been upon terms of intimacy and friendship with both" Claiborne and Wilkinson "all my life."[63] Clearly, Watkins had known Clai-

60. "Allard" most probably was Jean Pierre Allard, not Louis Allard, who was appointed captain in the territorial militia on March 1, 1806. Jean Pierre's appointment to the city council is mentioned in Laussat, *Memoirs of My Life,* 76. He is cursorily identified in Characterization of New Orleans Residents, entry 19, July 1, 1804, enclosed in James Wilkinson to the President, July 1, 1804, TP, 9: 250. Louis Allard may be the Allard whose military evaluation is in *Archivo General de Simancas. Sección de Guerra Moderna. Hojas de Servicias Militares de América, 1787–1799, legajo 7292, cuaderno 5, Compañías de Carabineros Distinguidos de Luisiana, Diciembre 1796,* folio 3. The appointment of Louis as captain in the militia is listed in Register of Appointments in the Militia of the Territory of Orleans, May 8, 1806, enclosed in Secretary Graham to the Secretary of State, May 8, 1806, TP, 9: 633.

61. Johnson, "New Orleans' Lost Mayor," 191. It may have been at this time that Laussat also appointed Watkins physician to the port of New Orleans.

62. John Duffy, ed., *The Rudolph Matas History of Medicine in Louisiana,* vol. 1 (Baton Rouge: Louisiana State University Press, 1958), 231–2, 420–1. About this date, May 29, 1804, Watkins, in his capacity as physician of the port of New Orleans, wrote Claiborne urging the removal of filth-laden barges at the city docks for the general good of public health. Marietta Marie LeBreton, *A History of the Territory of Orleans, 1803–1812* (Ann Arbor, Mich.: University Microfilms, 1973), 196–7.

63. *Debate in the House of Representatives of the Territory of Orleans, on a Memorial to Congress, Respecting the Illegal Conduct of General Wilkinson* (New Orleans: Bradford & Anderson Printers, 1807), 38 (hereinafter cited as *Debate on a Memorial to Congress*). A kinsman of John Watkins, also named John Watkins, of King William County, Virginia, married Betty Claiborne (born April 20, 1751) on April 22, 1772. It may have been through this family connection that Dr. Watkins and Governor Claiborne had known one another as children. Betty Claiborne was the daughter of Philip Whitehead Claiborne of "Liberty Hall," King William County, Virginia. *Genealogies of Virginia Families from the Virginia Magazine of History*

borne before circumstances brought them together in New Orleans. Once in office in New Orleans, several factors fostered friendship between the two. Both were natives of Virginia with strong ties, respectively, to Kentucky and Tennessee, the first trans-Appalachian territories to become states. A significant factor in their association was Watkins's command of the French and Spanish languages. Claiborne did not speak either language and for this reason often felt inadequate for his duties as civil official in the transfer of Louisiana to the United States. For a few years the feelings of friendship between the two men grew as Claiborne increasingly relied on Watkins to assist him in establishing the U.S. government in the Orleans Territory.[64]

Following the transfer of Louisiana to the United States on December 20, 1803, Watkins, like most of Laussat's appointees to government, was continued in office by Claiborne.[65] However, the minutes of the city council indicate that Watkins did not begin to attend council meetings until mid-March 1804, after his mission as personal representative of the governor to the river parishes above New Orleans.[66] By the late winter of 1804, Claiborne already had found Watkins to be indispensable as an intermediary in learning about the needs of and dealing with the foreign language-speaking peoples of Louisiana. In a very real sense, Watkins became Claiborne's interpreter, advisor, and confidant. By February 1804, Watkins had become Claiborne's eyes, ears, and spokesman.

One of the early tasks Claiborne gave Watkins was to check on the rumor circulating in New Orleans early in 1804 that General Wilkinson had been "corruptly" paid ten thousand dollars by the Spanish government while serving as the U.S. military commissioner to take possession of Louisiana.[67]

---

and Biography, vol. 2, Claiborne-Fitzhugh (Baltimore: Genealogical Publishing, 1981), 9 (entry 50) and 8 (entry 24), respectively.

64. Governor Claiborne to the President, October 5, 1804; and James Brown to John Breckinridge, September 17, 1805, in TP, 9: 307, 309, and 508, respectively.

65. LeBreton, in *History of the Territory of Orleans,* 43–4, points out that the mayor and all but two of the twelve city council members appointed by Laussat continued in office under Claiborne. The two council members who resigned were Evan Jones and Pierre Sauvé.

66. Watkins attended the council meetings of March 17, 28, and 31, 1804. He did not begin to attend meetings regularly until his appointment as recorder of the city council on March 11, 1805. New Orleans, Conseil de Ville: Official Proceedings, no. 1, book 1 (November 20, 1803–March 19, 1805), 55, 68, 69, City Archives, Louisiana Division, New Orleans Public Library.

67. Affidavit of James M. Bradford, March 17, 1809, *American State Papers: Miscellaneous Series,* vol. 2 (Washington, D.C.: Gales and Seaton, 1834), 95.

At Watkins's request, Daniel Clark made inquiries and even checked the Spanish treasury records, but reported back to Watkins that the money "had not been paid."[68] Because nothing damaging to Wilkinson was found, Clark asked Evan Jones, a good friend of Wilkinson, to tell the general the circumstances and result of his investigation.[69]

Just as the year 1803 marked the opening of a new phase of Watkins's career, 1804 marked the beginning of changes in his personal life. On January 11, 1804, he married Eulalie Trudeau, the nineteen-year-old daughter of Zenon Trudeau.[70] Apparently, Watkins's interest in Eulalie also had been a factor in his decision to make New Orleans his home. With income from his medical practice, and appointments as physician to the port of New Orleans and to a seat on the New Orleans City Council, Watkins's life had taken a more positive turn and he felt ready once more to assume the responsibilities of a married man.[71]

In February 1804, Claiborne sought Watkins's help in a vital assignment. The governor appointed Watkins to serve as his confidential representative to the parishes on both the east and west banks of the Mississippi as far upriver as Baton Rouge. The overall objective of Watkins's mission was to impress Louisianians favorably with the "change of Government." However, Watkins also carried specific instructions "to make Suitable appointments of Commandants"; to assure the people that "their liberty, property and religion" would be protected, and that Louisiana would "never revert to France, or be detached from the United States."[72] In reporting Watkins's appointment to perform this important task, Claiborne told Secretary Madison he could not leave New Orleans because of the demands on him there, but said the mission was necessary to check discontent and curb the few

---

68. It may have been this records search that Louis de Clouet said angered the Marqués de Casa Calvo. See Stanley Faye, ed., "Louis de Clouet's Memorial to the Spanish Government, December 7, 1814 (Conditions in Louisiana and Proposed Plan for Spanish Reconquest)," *Louisiana Historical Quarterly* 22, no. 3 (July 1939), 810–1, and the Bellechasse biographical sketch, particularly n. 39.

69. Deposition of Daniel Clark to the U.S. House of Representatives, January 11, 1808, in *American State Papers: Miscellaneous Series*, 2: 112.

70. Maduell, *New Orleans Marriage Contracts*, 38 (entry 143).

71. Watkins's office at this time may have been located at 43 Levee Street. *New Orleans in 1805: A Directory and a Census, Together with Resolutions Authorizing Same, Now Printed for the First Time from the Original Manuscript*. Facsimile. (New Orleans: Pelican Gallery, 1936), 30.

72. To John Watkins, February 9, 1804, CLB, 1: 367–9. Claiborne's letter appointing Watkins also is printed in Robertson, *Louisiana*, 2: 309–10.

disturbances he had heard about in the rural parishes.[73] Watkins, Claiborne said, was "pleased to undertake" the assignment, adding that "he is a perfect Master of the French and Spanish languages, possesses good general information, and supports the character of a very honest man."[74] In the governor's words, the appointment was "high proof" of his confidence in the "discretion and judgment" of Watkins.[75] This appears to have been the initial appointment of Watkins as clerk in the governor's office, a position he held into April 1804.[76]

Watkins delivered eight commissions and administered the oaths of office to four returning commandants and four new commandants while on this assignment.[77] In combination with the five commandant appointments made by Claiborne, all the local political offices of the temporary government were then filled.[78] Aside from the positive impact that Watkins had on the people with whom he came into contact while reestablishing local government for the United States, perhaps the greatest benefit Claiborne derived from Watkins's mission was the valuable information he brought back about conditions in the rural areas of the territory.

Claiborne learned from Watkins that the local governments, as the re-

73. In the spring of 1804, Claiborne wrote Madison: "I find myself overwhelmed with business, communications from the different Commandants pour in upon me, and may require immediate answers; the Citizens present themselves daily for redress of grievances, and my Court which has hitherto been held once a week is crowded with suits, and which together with the necessary attention to the Militia and to the ordinary business of my department render my official labours incessant." To James Madison, April 11, 1804, CLB, 2: 91.

74. To James Madison, March 1, 1804, ibid., 14.

75. To John Watkins, February 9, 1804, ibid., 1: 368.

76. See Governor Claiborne to the President, April 15, 1804, TP, 9: 222, and Letter No. 202, entry 5, W. C. C. Claiborne Disbursements during Temporary Government, Third Quarter, 1804, where Watkins is paid for "Services performed as a Clerk in my office during the Temporary Govt."

77. Dr. Watkins' Report, February 2, 1804, CLB, 2: 3–8, and Robertson, *Louisiana*, 2: 311–6. The report date, February 2, 1804, obviously is an error. It most probably should be dated March 2, 1804. The date of Watkins's appointment for the mission was February 9, 1804. Ibid., 309, 311, and To John Watkins, February 9, 1804, CLB, 1: 367.

78. On these, see To Julien Poidras [*sic*], January 14, 1804, and February 25, 1804; CLB, 1: 333–4 and 384–5; To James Madison, January 24, 1804; ibid., 347 (Henry Hopkins); To Edward D. Turner, October 17, 1804, ibid., 2: 385–6; To Edward Menillon, ibid., 2: 87; To Lieutenant Bowmar, May 14, 1804, and May 15, 1804, ibid., 2: 147–8 and 149, respectively; and Joseph Bowmar to Governor Claiborne, April 15, 1804, TP, 9: 223–4. Amos Stoddard was appointed civil commandant in Upper Louisiana. To Armos [Amos] Stoddard, January 24, 1804, CLB, 1: 350.

organized and reconstituted cabildo in New Orleans had been, were disorganized and corrupt. More important, Watkins reported that a "large majority of the most respectable people of the Country" wanted law and order restored, and were impatient for the establishment of the U.S. government. They suggested to Watkins that the best way to do this was to continue the commandant system of local government established by the Spanish until the American political and judicial systems were introduced. With this objective in mind, Watkins suggested that the governor instruct the commandants to revive and enforce laws neglected by the Spanish authorities, such as those pertaining to the building and repairing of levees, roads, and bridges; the subordination of slaves; and the licensing of taverns.[79]

Watkins closed his report to Claiborne on the mission with the inclusion of some complaints of the commandants concerning their circumstances and conditions. The complaints centered on expenses and the funding of the local governments. The costs of maintaining "public Buildings, Court houses, [and] prisons," they said, were greater than the revenue fees to which they were entitled by law. The commandants also complained of the "difficulty . . . almost impossibility of finding persons to act as constables." The "inhabitants," Watkins reported, were "unwilling to leave their farms and neglect their crops for a service so disagreeable in its nature, and productive of so little profit." To meet this need, the commandants suggested that a "Hundred Dollars a year for each . . . [constable] would be a Sufficient gratification." Watkins believed this salary was unrealistic, but he nonetheless passed it along to the governor, advising him the commandants "pretend" it would be sufficient.[80] With the information brought back by Watkins, Claiborne gained solid, firsthand knowledge of lower Louisiana and was able to move forward with plans to provide for the peace and safety of the territory until a permanent system of government could be adopted and implemented.[81]

79. Dr. Watkins' Report, February [March] 9, 1804, ibid., 2: 8–10.

80. Ibid., 10–12.

81. LeBreton, *History of the Territory of Orleans,* 57, points out that the commandant system functioned as the local government until April 10, 1805, when the legislative council adopted "An Act Dividing the Territory of Orleans into Counties, and Establishing Courts of the Inferior Jurisdiction Therein" (*Acts Passed at the First Session of the Legislative Council of the Territory of Orleans, Begun and Held at the Principal, in the City of New Orleans, On Monday the Third Day of December, in the Year of Our Lord, One Thousand Eight Hundred and Four, and of the Independence of the United States the Twenty-Ninth* [New Orleans: James M. Bradford, 1805], 144–208).

Watkins's report also touched on two subjects that were beyond Claiborne's authority to remedy. These were requests for the continued importation of slaves from Africa and a member of Congress to represent "the true interests and situation" of Louisianians.[82] Both issues soon demanded Claiborne's attention and, by a curious turn of events, Watkins returned from his mission to the river parishes in time to temporarily defuse both.

Louisianians had been following newspaper reports of the debates in Congress about the form of government being drafted for them. The most important parts of the legislation being considered pertained to the legislature, the judiciary, and slavery. As the people of Louisiana read about the debates through January and February, they began to openly grumble about and oppose some of the laws passed on their behalf. Just as public opinion was forming on the actions of Congress, there arrived in New Orleans from France in the last week of February 1804 a Bostonian named Benjamin Tupper. He moved to take advantage of the agitated state of the public mind, probably with the encouragement of Etienne de Boré, mayor of New Orleans, and his friend, Jean Noël Destréhan, both of whom were Francophiles. Arrogating to himself responsibility as tutor in the operation of democracy, Tupper issued invitations to a March 12 public meeting at which the persons present were to "State their grievances to Congress and to elect an agent" to carry the memorial to Congress.[83]

The meeting was held as scheduled at the "House of a private Gentleman" presided over by Boré.[84] Claiborne tried to discourage the "respectable Citizens" from attending, but the meeting was more heavily attended than he expected. Most of those present were New Orleans merchants and planters living near the city. Few Americans attended.[85] The governor received a report on the meeting from "a Gentleman who attended the assembly" at his request.[86] Whether Watkins was the gentleman Claiborne asked to attend is not known, but he was present. Most important, as a result of his prudent comments, the anger and frustration of those who attended

82. Dr. Watkins' Report, February [March] 9, 1804, CLB, 2: 10–11.

83. Ibid.

84. Boré was described by General Wilkinson as "principally distinguished by his vanity & a blind attachment to the French Nation." Characterization of New Orleans Residents, July 1, 1804, entry 1, enclosed in James Wilkinson to the President, July 1, 1804, TP, 9: 248.

85. To James Madison, March 10, 1804, and March 16, 1804, CLB, 2: 25 and 42, respectively.

86. To James Madison, March 16, 1804, ibid., 43.

were kept from creating immediate problems for the governor. The most outspoken Louisianian present was Destréhan, a man known for his strong opinions.[87] Destréhan called on those assembled to authorize the district commandants to hold meetings in their commandancies to elect delegates to a future convention to be held in New Orleans at which two delegates would be chosen to go to Congress to present the views of Louisianians.[88] Tupper also spoke at the meeting, but was regarded by those present as an interloper.[89] It was the comments of Destréhan, generally thought to be the richest planter in Louisiana and a good friend of Mayor Boré, that seemed to sway the assembled crowd.

Watkins sought to counter the effects of both Tupper's and Destréhan's remarks. Initially speaking in English, Watkins conducted a short civics class on the functioning of the U.S. government for those present, explaining its principles, showing the necessity for deliberation in the framing of laws, and the good that might flow from measures founded in "sound reason and mature reflection." On the slave trade and the demand for representation in Congress, Watkins said the wishes of the people of Louisiana "had already been conveyed to the Seat of Government, in the official communications of Governor Claiborne."[90]

Mayor Boré reminded those present, when Watkins finished his remarks, that "'this was a French Assembly'" and that he trusted the doctor's "'example would not be followed.'" On hearing this comment, Watkins expressed "nearly the same Sentiments" in French. In translating his ideas into French, Watkins also put them in the form of a motion, which was adopted unanimously. Under the terms of the motion, those present appointed a committee of three men to "draft a memorial to Congress, to be reported" at the next meeting of the participants.[91] Watkins was one of the three men

87. A little more than two years later, Claiborne described Destréhan as a man of "strong prejudices, and altho they may be founded in error, it is not in the power of Man to remove them." To Jefferson, July 10, 1806, ibid., 3: 364. Destréhan's last name is often misspelled as "Detrion" in the correspondence at this time. See To James Madison, March 16, 1804, ibid., 2: 43 and *passim*, as well as Governor Claiborne to the Secretary of State, July 13, 1804, TP, 9: 261.

88. On Destréhan's partisan French attitude, see TP, 9: 261.

89. To James Madison, March 16, 1804, CLB, 2: 44.

90. Ibid., 45. Claiborne endorsed the request of Louisianians for a delegate in Congress, saying they should have the same privileges extended to other territorial governments. To James Madison, March 1, 1804, ibid., 14.

91. To James Madison, March 16, 1804, ibid., 45.

appointed to the committee, but no date was set for a future meeting.[92] Watkins's astute conduct deflected both issues briefly, but they emerged with greater ferocity in June in the Orleans Memorial written by Edward Livingston, Daniel Clark, and Evan Jones after the provisions of the act creating the Territory of Orleans became known.[93]

Claiborne was so elated at the outcome of the March 12 meeting that he acknowledged Watkins's role in it with praise greater than he had given to any one. Writing to President Jefferson on April 15, 1804, Claiborne described Watkins as one of the men "whose Conduct I highly appreciate, and who must eventually hold high Rank in the estimation of good Men." The governor, who was about four years younger than Watkins, went on to say of the doctor that he "unites to great integrity of character, a well informed mind, a correct Judg'ment, and a benevolent, friendly disposition." In addition, Claiborne said Watkins has "by his merit . . . acquired great influence among the People." The governor succinctly summarized it all when he wrote that the doctor was of "great assistance"to him. About this time, Claiborne also persuaded Watkins to join his staff and recommended the doctor to Jefferson for the position of territorial secretary, if it had not already been filled.[94]

Watkins was not appointed territorial secretary, but Claiborne kept the doctor's name before Jefferson for the next five months, almost as if to remind the president that this good and faithful servant was awaiting appointment to office. Near the end of May 1804, Claiborne asked Jefferson to appoint Watkins to another post, the Territorial Legislative Council, saying

92. The other two men named to the committee were Jean François Merieult (Meriult, Merriult), a businessman and slave trader in New Orleans, and James Pitot, the businessman who succeeded Boré as mayor of New Orleans. Ibid., 46.

93. To James Madison, July 1, 1804, ibid., 233–4, and Governor Claiborne to the President, July 1, 1804, TP, 9: 246–7 both point out the roles of Livingston, Clark, and Jones in drafting the new memorial to Congress. LeBreton, *History of the Territory of Orleans,* 120 n. 61, points out that this June memorial was different from the one that was to have been drafted by Watkins, Merieult, and Pitot in March.

94. Governor Claiborne to the President, April 15, 1804, TP, 9: 222. The salaries of Watkins and other clerks employed by Claiborne may be seen in For Sundry Disbursements During the Temporary Government, June 10, 1805, CLB, 3: 90. Although he is listed as clerk in Claiborne's official expenses, Watkins also may have been used as interpreter. Claiborne said he "found it necessary to employ" an interpreter early in 1804. Claiborne to James Madison, January 10, 1804, CLB, 1: 331. The man retained by Claiborne with the designation of interpreter at this time was Pierre Derbigny, who delivered the governor's address in French on October 2, 1804, the date Claiborne was sworn into office by Mayor James Pitot. *Louisiana Gazette,* October 5, 1804, p. 3, c. 2.

this time he was confident the doctor was one man who would "discharge with fidelity any confidence" he might be given.[95] Perhaps because the president had not responded to any of his suggestions regarding Watkins, Claiborne mentioned Watkins again in a late June letter to Jefferson, saying that both Joseph Briggs, his private secretary, and Watkins were very unwell from the raging epidemic of yellow fever.[96] In August 1804, Claiborne again mentioned Watkins in one of his letters to Jefferson, pointing out that Watkins was "decidedly attached to Republican principles."[97] Clearly, Watkins's work to establish the U.S. government in lower Louisiana had earned him the great respect and admiration of Claiborne, who very much wanted the doctor to play a greater role in territorial government.

John Watkins continued his leadership role in public health matters on the city council while Claiborne sought the doctor's appointment to a higher post in territorial government. In June Claiborne agreed with the city council's request to establish a municipal board of health to deal with matters affecting the health and well-being of the city's residents. Although it was to change its configuration again in a few months, this action enlarged the health committee created during Laussat's brief tenure into the board of health, the modern name by which it came to be known. After this reorganization, the board included two doctors, John Watkins and Robert Dow, and three lay members selected by the city council.[98] The creation of the board of health appears to have been in response to the discovery of two major diseases in New Orleans in June, smallpox and yellow fever.[99] In the same month, Watkins drafted the city ordinance prescribing the procedure by which newly arrived physicians were to be licensed to practice in the city.[100]

---

95. To Thomas Jefferson, May 29, 1804, CLB, 2: 175–6.

96. To Thomas Jefferson, June 28, 1804, ibid., 231.

97. Governor Claiborne to the President, August 30, 1804, TP, 9: 284.

98. The lay members of the board of health were Gaspard Debuys, Francis Duplessis, and Felix Arnaud. LeBreton, *History of the Territory of Orleans,* 197.

99. To James Pitot, June 16, 1804, CLB, 2: 208–9, tells of the presence of smallpox. Duffy, *History of Medicine,* 372–3, points out that because Watkins had notified the governor first, he and all the doctors were admonished "'never to neglect to inform the municipal body of the existence of this scourge.'" Captain Daniel Carmick, commanding officer of the contingent of U.S. Marines that had arrived in New Orleans in May 1804, reported that twenty-two of his men were bedridden with yellow fever in June 1804. Ultimately, at least twelve hundred people died in this epidemic, "chiefly Strangers, one hundred" of them from the army. See George W. Morgan to David Rees, October 23, 1804, David Rees Papers, Special Collections, Howard-Tilton Memorial Library, Tulane University.

100. Duffy, *History of Medicine,* 1: 326–7.

Early in July 1804, Watkins had sufficiently recovered from his bout with yellow fever that he could deliver a speech at the Fourth of July celebration conducted in the city. His cousin John Clay, who had recently arrived in New Orleans, described the events of that day in a letter to his brother, Henry, in Kentucky, as a positive display of American power. The remarks of Watkins and Pierre Derbigny, Clay said, "displayed much ingenuity" and were "listened to with much attention." The speeches and the parade of about two thousand volunteer militia and U.S. military forces, Clay reported, were "conducted with a pleasing regularity" and "eclat."[101] Watkins gave his address at the Principal, as did Pierre Derbigny, who made his speech in French for the benefit of the French-speaking residents of New Orleans. Another observer of the New Orleans scene at this time believed the speeches of both Watkins and Derbigny would "tend to quiet the discontent which has begun lately to manifest itself."[102]

Finally, on September 27, 1804, Claiborne received notification from Secretary Madison that President Jefferson had recommended John Watkins for appointment to the territorial legislative council.[103] Jefferson later said that he had waited "almost to the 12th hour to get all the information" he could "respecting characters at N. Orleans" before sending the commissions to Claiborne.[104] Eight days after he received them, the governor officially advised Watkins of his nomination. Three days later Watkins notified Claiborne that he would accept the appointment as long as there was no conflict with his position as port physician. If there was a conflict, Watkins advised the governor, "I wish it to be understood that I cannot consent to become a member of the legislative Council."[105] Claiborne saw no conflict, nor apparently did Madison or Jefferson. Claiborne sent Watkins's letter of acceptance to Madison when he notified the secretary that Watkins had accepted the appointment.[106]

Watkins's tenure on the territorial council was for only three months,

---

101. From John Clay, July 6, 1804, *Papers of Henry Clay,* 1: 140.

102. Hatch Dent to James H. McCulloch, July 14, 1804, TP, 9: 266.

103. Madison to Claiborne, August 30, 1804, James Madison, *Letters and Other Writings of James Madison, Fourth President of the United States,* vol. 2 (Philadelphia: J. B. Lippincott, 1865), 204. For the date on which Claiborne received the letter, see Governor Claiborne to the Secretary of State, September 27, 1804, TP, 9: 299.

104. The President to the Secretary of War, September 6, 1804, ibid., 291.

105. To James Madison, October 8, 1804, and From John Watkins, October 8, 1804, CLB, 2: 349 and 351, respectively.

106. To James Madison, October 8, 1804, ibid., 349.

but it was a busy period. Among the bills he was identified as being involved with the passage of were An Act to Incorporate the City of New Orleans; An Act Providing for the Removal and Safekeeping of Certain Papers, Records and Documents, now in the Possession of Peter Pedesclaux and Charles Ximenes; and An Act Making Provision for the Attorney-General of the Territory of Orleans. All three of these bills appear to have been adopted by the council on February 28, the day after Watkins's appointment as recorder of the city council[107] Although Watkins resigned from the legislative council on the twenty-seventh of the month, he apparently continued to work closely with the council to attain passage of these important acts until he began to function as recorder of the city council.

An indication of how busy Watkins may have been in these months is suggested by the newspaper notice offering a reward of $180 for papers "Lost or stolen" from his house "some time in the course of last month." The missing items were described as a note in the French language for $300, another in the amount of $150 payable to Zenon Trudeau, and a third note in the amount of $30, along with a "memorial from Edward C. Nicholls, Esq. Secretary to the Governor's court, under the late temporary government, to the Legislative Council." Watkins asked that the notes be returned to him with no questions asked. He made his appeal to the publisher of the *Louisiana Gazette* because part of the Nicholls Memorial had been unexpectedly published in that newspaper a few days earlier.[108] It may have been about this same time that Watkins established his residence on Bayou St. John. The change of residence appears to have occurred before he sought passage of an act for opening the Metairie Road from Bayou St. John to the settlement of Cannes Brulees about fifteen miles above New Orleans.[109]

Claiborne continued to advance Watkins within the city government of New Orleans while seeking a variety of positions for Watkins within the territorial government. On March 11, 1805, the date that James Pitot assumed his duties as mayor of New Orleans, John Watkins began to exercise his responsibilities as recorder for the city council, using the title "president" when he presided at council meetings.[110] In appointing Watkins to the

---

107. *Louisiana Gazette*, March 15, 1805, p. 1, c. 3.

108. *Louisiana Gazette*, February 8, 1805, p. 3, cc. 3, 4.

109. Passage of this act was reported in ibid., March 8, 1805, p. 2, c. 4.

110. *Conseil de Ville: Official Proceedings*, no. 1, book 1 (November 20, 1803–March 19, 1805), 254. The official title "recorder" appeared in the minutes, but the title "president" followed Watkins's name, who was the first to use the title "president of the council." The actual minute clerk, or *greffier*, was "M. Bourgeois."

post of recorder, Claiborne advised Secretary Madison on March 8, 1805, that his objective was to "confer the office . . . on a native Citizen of the United States, and there was not one as well qualified as Doctor Watkins."[111] When Claiborne appointed Watkins recorder, the doctor relinquished his position on the territorial council, having served only three months on that body. Watkins's resignation from the territorial council was effective on February 27, 1805, the same date of his appointment as recorder of the city.[112]

As Watkins's responsibilities in the administration of the rapidly growing city of New Orleans increased and his availability to the governor decreased, Claiborne moved to keep near him the one man in whom he placed great trust. On April 17, 1805, little more than six weeks after Watkins resigned from the territorial council, Claiborne appointed him aide-de-camp with the rank of major.[113] Less than a month later, May 13, 1805, Watkins was appointed justice of the peace.[114]

After Pitot's resignation as mayor of New Orleans in July, Watkins immediately was appointed to succeed him and began to perform mayoral duties before officially taking possession of the office.[115] On July 26, Watkins notified Claiborne that he had found various proclamations approved by the council and signed by Pitot among the papers of the former mayor. These decrees reflected the plans of the Pitot administration to improve the health and beauty of the city by cleaning and draining the streets and ditches; removing the "ancient Custom house"; razing the dilapidated fortifications and batteries surrounding the city that had been transferred to the

111. Robertson, *Louisiana,* 2: 282–3. Watkins's appointment to this position suggests that Claiborne intended for the doctor to become mayor once Pitot determined to return to the business world. Watkins was succeeded as recorder of the city by Joseph Deville Degoutin Bellechasse. See "Administrations of the Mayors," 9.

112. *Conseil de Ville: Official Proceedings,* no. 1, book 2 (November 20, 1803–March 19, 1805), 253–5; and Register of Civil Appointments in the Territory of Orleans, February 13, 1806, enclosed in John Graham to the Secretary of State, February 13, 1806, Recorders, TP, 9: 601.

113. Appointed to the same rank at the same time were Michael Fortier, junior, Joseph Faurie, and William Nott. General Orders, April 17, 1805, TP, 9: 583.

114. Register of Civil Appointments, February 13, 1806, Justices, ibid., 599.

115. Claiborne accepted Pitot's resignation on July 24, 1805, and appointed Watkins on the same date. See To James Pitot, July 24, 1805, CLB, 3: 136. However, the official date for the change in officers was made July 27. The date of Pitot's resignation is given in Register of Civil Appointments, February 13, 1806, Mayors of New Orleans, TP, 9: 603. The date that Watkins officially assumed his duties as mayor of New Orleans was July 27, 1805. *Conseil de Ville: Official Proceedings,* no. 1, book 2 (April 4, 1805–February 12, 1806), 75.

United States by the Spanish and French officials; and, on the "Petition of the officers of the town Guard," removing the riotous guards from the first floor of the *Hôtel de Ville* (city hall) to a separate barracks where they were to be placed under the close control of their officers.[116]

Claiborne responded to Watkins's inquiries about the proclamations by subject. Regarding the old customhouse and the fortifications, the governor reminded the mayor that these were the property of the United States government. Claiborne said he expected federal commissioners to arrive in a "few Months . . . to investigate, and determine the validity of claims to Land" on which the decaying customhouse stood. Until a ruling was made by the commissioners, the governor said it was not within his power to accede to the wishes of the council. For the same reasons, he could do nothing about the dilapidated fortifications. However, these were so full of accumulated stagnant water that Claiborne "cheerfully consented to the Levelling of them all, except forts St. Charles and St. Louis." They were garrisoned by troops of the U.S. Army and could not be evacuated without orders from the president.[117]

Claiborne initially demurred to Watkins's request that the detachment of regular U.S. Army troops at city hall be replaced with a "City Guard." The governor was concerned that the cost of this new city service would be large. As a consequence, he suggested that it might be advisable, on the "Ground of economy, and expediency," to continue relying on the troops of the U.S. Army.[118] Known as the *Maréchaussée,* or gendarmerie, the city guard was actually a paid company of the First Regiment of the territorial militia commanded by Colonel Bellechasse. However, the immediate supervision and command of the city guard was the responsibility of the mayor and city council under the authority granted them by the act that incorporated the city of New Orleans and allowed it to maintain the internal security of the city.[119] On March 14, 1806, Watkins notified the president and council that

116. John Watkins to Governor Claiborne, July 26, 1805, TP, 9: 481–3.

117. To John Watkins, August 2, 1805, CLB, 3: 144.

118. Ibid., 144–5.

119. James Brown to John Breckinridge, September 17, 1805, TP, 9: 510, identifies the city guard members by their French names. Claiborne, or his secretary, brutalizes the spelling of the word *gendarmes* in An Ordinance, July 21, 1804, CLB, 2: 259, and To James Pitot, July 1, 1805, ibid., 3: 107. To John Watkins, October 31, 1805, ibid., 219–20, and LeBreton, *History of the Territory of Orleans,* 210–11, tell of the lines of command over the city guard. Pitot's original proposal stipulated that the mayor was to have "sole authority to name all the officers and agents . . . and . . . to administer the regulations of the service." See New Orleans Conseil de Ville, Messages from the Mayor, 1805–1836 (translations), no. 15, May 6, 1805,

the "City Guard began yesterday its regular work." The guard then consisted of "25 *watchmen,* two assistant chiefs and the Commandant."[120] Unfortunately, the city guard failed to perform their police duties, spending most of their time carousing in the streets and cabarets with free blacks or slaves whom they were supposed to be regulating.[121] James Brown, the former territorial secretary, said the guard was staffed, particularly the officers, by renegade French soldiers from Santo Domingo.[122]

Despite Claiborne's reluctance to end reliance on the U.S. Army for police duty, two weeks later, on August 18, before he set out on his planned tour of the interior counties of Orleans Territory, Claiborne accepted Watkins's proposal that New Orleans have its own city guard, or police force. Before implementing this significant change on the local scene, the governor did modify it with the stipulation that the city guard should be quartered at the city hall only at night. During the daylight hours, the U.S. troops were to be in place there as usual. On the same date, Claiborne also asked Lieutenant Colonel Freeman to move from city hall to the quarters for the army in the barracks and notified Watkins of his action.[123] Even the governor's trip to the interior counties north of Pointe Coupée, his first since assuming his official duties in the territory, owed much to Watkins.[124] Claiborne advised both Watkins and Secretary Madison that he felt he could leave New Orleans because "the City Authorities are now completely organized, and there is every reason to Hope that safety and good order will continue."[125]

Shortly after assuming his duties as mayor, Watkins also asked that the building dedicated by the Spanish for use as a public school be returned to the city.[126] Claiborne had granted Lieutenant Colonel Freeman authority to

---

p. 25, City Archives, Louisiana Department, New Orleans Public Library. An overview of the attempts to organize and finance the police in these years is provided by Dennis Charles Rousey in *The New Orleans Police, 1805–1889: A Social History* (Ann Arbor: University Microfilms, 1984), 26–33.

120. New Orleans Conseil de Ville, Messages from the Mayor, 1805–1836, vol. 2 (January 4, 1806–December 30, 1807), no. 30. Emphasis in the original.

121. James Brown to John Breckinridge, September 17, 1805, TP, 9: 510; and LeBreton, *History of the Territory of Orleans,* 211.

122. James Brown to John Breckinridge, September 17, 1805, TP, 9: 510.

123. To Colonel Freeman, August 18, 1805, CLB, 3: 176–7; and To John Watkins, Mayor, August 18, 1805, ibid., 177–8.

124. To Casa Calvo, August 21, 1805, ibid., 179, indicates the governor finally got away on that date on his proposed trip to Concordia.

125. To John Watkins, Mayor, August 18, 1805, ibid., 178 and To James Madison, August 20, 1805, ibid., 179.

126. John Watkins to Governor Claiborne, August 2, 1805, TP, 9: 487–8.

use the building as headquarters for the American troops in New Orleans. Because he occupied the second floor, the colonel refused to move from the building unless ordered by the secretary of war.[127] Plaintively, Watkins wrote Claiborne asking, "What has Minerva done in this part of the American dominions, that she should be compeled [sic] to cede her place to Mars?" Reflecting his earlier efforts to establish a public library in Lexington, Kentucky, Watkins wanted the former school building to house the public library, which was to be part of the educational system for the territory.[128]

Watkins's request for the use of the building was not the first one received by Claiborne. The issue had arisen in May when Judge Dominick Hall asked the governor for the old school to use as quarters for the United States district court. When Claiborne received Watkins's request for use of the building, he forwarded it to Secretary Madison with another of his own, asking again that the whole issue be laid before the president for a decision.[129] Freeman did finally vacate the building sometime in late October or early November, but not for the use proposed by Watkins. The building became the home of the district court. Claiborne did say, however, that eventually the old brick school building was to be returned to the educational purposes for which it had been built.[130]

Watkins was elected to serve in the newly created twenty-five member house of representatives while Claiborne was on his tour of the interior counties. James Brown believed Watkins's election to this post was because of his marriage to Eulalie Trudeau, whose "numerous connections amongst

127. To John Watkins, August 3, 1805, CLB, 3: 147.

128. John Watkins to Governor Claiborne, August 2, 1805, TP, 9: 488. Johnson, "New Orleans' Lost Mayor," 189, tells of Watkins's efforts to establish a public library in Lexington, Kentucky.

129. To Gov. Claiborne from Judge Dominick A. Hall, May 13, 1805; Copy of a Letter from the Honble. Judge Hall to Governor Claiborne Dated June 1, 1805; Copy of a Letter from Gov. Claiborne to Colonel Freeman Dated June 1, 1805; Copy of Letter from Colonel Freeman to Gov. Claiborne Dated June 2, 1805; Copy of a Letter from Gov. Claiborne to Colonel Freeman Dated June 3, 1805; To Colonel Freeman, June 5, 1805; To Judge Hall, June 6, 1805; To Governor Claiborne from Judge Hall, June 6, 1805; To James Madison, June 6, 1805; Claiborne to James Madison, August 3, 1805; all in CLB, 3: 55–6, 60–1, 61–2, 62–3, 63–6, 72–3, 74–5, 75–6, 76–7, and 148–9, respectively. Secretary of War Henry Dearborn informed Freeman on June 14, 1805, that Claiborne had authority over the building in question if it was attached to the civil government. John Watkins to Governor Claiborne, August 2, 1805, TP, 9: 488 n. 36.

130. A List of Buildings in the City of New Orleans belonging to the United States, enclosed in Claiborne to Thomas Jefferson, October 23, 1805, CLB, 3: 211.

the old settlers" brought him their vote and support.[131] In the election Watkins was considered part of the "American ticket," which was elected to office on September 11, 1805.[132]

Less than a week before the election, Watkins was informed of a plot to foment an insurrection among free men of color and slaves in New Orleans. He immediately investigated the story and, in the absence of the governor, made a formal report to John Graham, the newly appointed territorial secretary. The report is one of the few documents that provides insight into the personality and thinking of John Watkins. It reveals an intelligent, multitalented man concerned about providing for the safety and security of all the Orleans Territory in the face of what appeared to be a genuine threat, not so much from a slave insurrection as from public uncertainty and the lack of U.S. protection from domestic and foreign intrigue.

The leader of the insurrection being planned was a Frenchman who called himself "Le Grand." According to the plot, the white residents of New Orleans were to be massacred and the insurrectionists were to become masters of the city, or destroy it by "pillage or fire." Evidence belonging to Le Grand suggested that he had begun making comprehensive plans to revolutionize the whole territory by contacting those slaves and free blacks who could be quietly drawn into his scheme without attracting notice. Watkins learned of Le Grand's activities from a "mulatto Slave named Celestin," who brought the initial report to him in mid-August "accompanied by two Gentlemen."[133]

The potential danger in Le Grand's plot caused Watkins to seek the assis-

131. Secretary Graham to Governor Claiborne, September 16, 1805; and James Brown to John Breckinridge, September 17, 1805, in TP, 9: 506 and 511 n. 73, respectively.

132. Other candidates in this New Orleans grouping were the merchant James Carrick, Bellechasse, James Brown, Thomas Harman, Jean (John) Baptiste Macarty (McCarty), and John McDonogh (McDonnaugh), Jr. Secretary Graham to Governor Claiborne, September 16, 1805, postscript, ibid., 506.

133. John Watkins to Secretary Graham, September 6, 1805, ibid, 500–4. The quotation is from p. 500. Fears of a slave revolt surfaced during yellow fever outbreaks, partly because blacks seemed to be less affected than whites by the disease and because in the total population, blacks, whether slave or free, outnumbered whites. In New Orleans the disparity was greater by more than four thousand. Jo Ann Carrigan, *The Saffron Scourge: A History of Yellow Fever in Louisiana, 1796–1905* (Lafayette: Center for Louisiana Studies, University of Southwestern Louisiana, 1994), 33, 39, 67–8; and Petition of the Inhabitants & Colonists of Louisiana, September 17, 1804; Governor Claiborne to the President, September 18, 1804; and the Secretary of State to the President, February 4, 1811, enclosing A General Return of the Census of the Territory of Orleans taken for the Year 1806, December 31, 1806, all in TP, 9: 297, 298, and 923, respectively.

tance of Colonel Bellechasse and Major Eugene Dorsière, the two ranking officers in the territorial militia. With their support Watkins made plans to entrap Le Grand during one of his late-night ventures into the suburbs, where he had scheduled another meeting with a group of free mulattos and slaves. At the clandestine meeting, Le Grand and a trunk full of his papers were seized along with a few would-be insurrectionists. The papers revealed that his real name was Grand Jean, a pardoned deserter from the French army, who had entered the United States at Baltimore after fleeing Santo Domingo. Le Grand said that he had been in New Orleans six weeks, but papers in his trunk indicated he had been there nearly four months, after brief stays in Baltimore and in Lexington, Kentucky. The trunk also contained two passports, one recently issued by Casa Calvo for travel to Havana and another issued by William Brown, the collector of the Port of New Orleans. The U.S. passport falsely identified Jean as a native-born Louisianian.[134] Subsequently, Le Grand was tried for attempting to incite insurrection of slaves and found guilty on December 23, 1805.[135]

Le Grand's insurrectionist plotting alarmed many of the residents of New Orleans, but led nowhere because of the vigilance of Celestin and his owners, and the quick action of Mayor Watkins.[136] Nonetheless, the potential in the plot disturbed Watkins. As a consequence, in his report on the incident the mayor urged several important truths on Secretary Graham and Governor Claiborne about United States ownership and control of Orleans Territory. Bluntly, the mayor said the United States government must increase the number of troops in the territory and place them in strategic locations for its safety and security. Watkins must have known this recommendation was in direct opposition to Claiborne's views. On July 27 the governor had advised Secretary Madison that he "no longer" saw the "necessity for stationing of regular Troops in the Interior" of the territory and that "one Company might be usefully employed, as a guard for the Public Property" in New Orleans. A "greater number," Claiborne said, appeared to be "unnecessary."[137]

134. John Watkins to Secretary Graham, September 6, 1805, enclosed in Secretary Graham to the Secretary of State, September 9, 1805, TP, 9: 501–02.

135. *Government* v. *Le Grand Jean,* Superior Court case no. 50, November 22, 1805.

136. One week after Territorial Secretary Graham's letter to Secretary of State Madison, Graham advised Claiborne that the "alarm occasioned by the contemplated Insurrection of Le Grand or Grand-Jean seems in a great measure to have died away." Secretary Graham to Governor Claiborne, September 16, 1805, TP, 9: 505.

137. To James Madison, July 27, 1805, CLB, 3: 137.

Watkins also said in his report on the plot that the United States government should do everything it could to increase the American population in Orleans Territory, so that it would be made to "overballance [*sic*] that of every other description of persons." In addition, he recommended that Louisiana must rid itself of all the "agents and influence of foreign Governments." Speaking "in confidence to the Government of my Country," Watkins wrote: "It is high time that the people of this country and more particularly the Strangers who reside among us should be convinced . . . beyond a possibility of doubt that the Sovereignity [*sic*] of Louisiana is irrevocably fixed in the hands of the United States." Finally, the mayor said, "Many of the old Inhabitants . . . are already as good Americans as any in the U. States," but that the "character, the manners, the language of the country must become American if we wish the Government to be such."[138]

John Graham believed Watkins's report on Le Grand was potentially so incendiary that he would not put it in the mail to the governor, presumably because of his concern that it might be stolen and then revealed. Instead, Graham alluded to the receipt of disturbing news when he wrote Claiborne and urged the governor to return quickly to New Orleans. Claiborne received Graham's letter in Concordia, where a fever had so incapacitated him that he was kept from arriving in New Orleans until October 4. How Claiborne reacted to Watkins's strongly urged recommendations is not known. However, after he returned to the city and surveyed the situation himself, Claiborne acted on only one of Watkins's suggestions, that calling for strengthening the military in the territory. Specifically, Claiborne urged the Jefferson administration to refurbish the military installations in and around New Orleans, particularly forts St. John, at the mouth of Bayou St. John on Lake Pontchartrain, and St. Philip, on the Mississippi River below New Orleans; and the stationing of a "few Gun Boats" on the "Mississippi and the Lakes." Although his suggestions implied increasing the number of military men stationed in the Orleans Territory, Claiborne never specifically requested this.[139] Perhaps because he was aware of Jefferson's penchant for economy and knew of the president's actions to strengthen the defenses of the lower Mississippi Valley, Claiborne may have been reluctant to speak too boldly on this point.[140]

138. John Watkins to Secretary Graham, September 6, 1805, enclosed in Secretary Graham to the Secretary of State, September 9, 1805, TP, 9: 503–4.

139. To James Madison, October 24, 1805, CLB, 3: 212–3.

140. On the measures taken by the Jefferson administration, see Secretary of War to Governor Claiborne, April 26, 1806, TP, 9: 627–8.

Territorial Secretary John Graham did not share that reluctance. Writing to Madison on January 2, 1806, Graham said: "If we could get clear of every Spaniard in the Country I should rejoice for we should then be free from our most dangerous enemies . . . from the returns made to the Mayor there are about two hundred & thirty of these people . . . who would be ready to seize–[sic] any moment of disturbance to commit the vilest depredations . . . whether in Peace or War they are a nuisance to the country[.]"[141]

Clearly, the opinions shared by Watkins and Graham could not have pleased Claiborne, but what his personal reaction to them may have been is not discernible from his correspondence.

Watkins played a key role in most of the actions taken by the newly elected members of the territorial house of representatives when it gathered in New Orleans for its initial meeting on November 4, 1805. After being sworn into office, the house received Claiborne's request for the names of ten nominees from whom President Jefferson would choose five to be members of the territorial council, the newly created upper house of the legislature.[142] With this task out of the way, the house then began to consider legislation for governing the territory. One of the first acts passed by the house authorized the translation and publication of several documents that the representatives felt were important to the citizens of Louisiana: the Constitution of the United States; the Northwest Ordinance of 1787, on which the laws of the Orleans Territory were based; and all the laws passed by Congress relating to the Orleans Territory. Watkins supported the motion, but successfully amended it with a provision requiring a committee report on the results when both branches of the territorial legislature were to meet the following year.[143] His objective apparently was to assure that what was done would be acceptable.

Watkins also presented and read the final draft of the address to President Jefferson from the new territorial house of representatives.[144] In addition, he was appointed to the committee ordered to draft the provisional

141. Secretary Graham to the Secretary of State, January 2, 1805 [1806], ibid., 553.

142. Address to the House of Representatives, November 4, 1805, CLB, 3: 223–4. The names of the nominees to the council and the number of votes they received on November 8, 1805, may be found in Extract from the Journal of the House of Representatives of the Territory of Orleans, November 8, 1805, enclosed in Jean Noël Destréhan to the President, November 11, 1805, TP, 9: 524.

143. Proceedings of the Territorial House of Representatives, November 11, 1805, TP, 9: 521.

144. Ibid.

rules that were to govern the conduct of business in the newly created body.[145] Finally, acting for the committee responsible for drafting a planned memorial to Congress, Watkins both presented and read the English language version of the document that was accepted on the last day of the session and subsequently translated into French.[146]

The house adjourned at five o'clock on the evening of November 14, believing, as did Governor Claiborne, that both houses of the new territorial legislature would be convened in the latter part of February 1806.[147] However, it was not until February that Claiborne learned President Jefferson's choices for the territorial council, and it was not until March 25, 1806, that the legislature convened. When the session did begin, Watkins almost immediately was chosen Speaker of the House when Destréhan resigned to take the seat to which he had been elected in the territorial council.[148]

Watkins now was at the pinnacle of his power and influence as a doctor, mayor of New Orleans, Speaker of the House of Representatives, and aide-de-camp to the governor. As Speaker, his first task was to prepare the response of the house members to Claiborne's March 25, 1806, address to the joint session of the territorial legislature. Watkins's reply echoed much of what Claiborne already had said, and in this sense it seems almost to have

145. Ibid., 522.

146. Ibid.

147. To James Madison, November 20, 1805, CLB, 3: 234; and Proceedings of the Territorial House of Representatives, November 14, 1805, five o'clock, P.M., TP, 9: 522. On February 5, 1806, Watkins resigned his position as major and aide-de-camp to Claiborne. He was replaced by John W. Gurley. Ibid., 597. The timing may be coincidental, but the resignation may reflect growing differences between Watkins and Claiborne, particularly over the lack of military preparedness and inadequate defenses in the Orleans Territory.

148. LeBreton, *History of the Territory of Orleans,* 160 n. 42, points out that the March 24, 1806, date given for Claiborne's Address to the Legislature of the Territory of Orleans in CLB, 3: 274, is an error. The actual meeting date was March 25, 1806. See also the *Louisiana Gazette,* March 28, 1806, p. 2, c. 1. The meeting on the twenty-fifth was a joint session of both branches of the legislature at which Claiborne touched on the chief pieces of legislation he felt were needed. Among the items he mentioned were legislation for internal improvements (rivers, roads, and levees); revision of the judicial system; establishment of a prison; development of codes of law to deal with criminals and slaves, respectively; the need to provide financing for the system of education adopted by the first legislative council; and legislation to provide for the continuance of the Charity Hospital. In a separate message, apparently delivered at the same time, Claiborne dealt with the need to finish the reorganization of the militia. See Fellow-Citizens of the Legislative Council, and of the House of Representatives, CLB, 3: 279–81, which immediately follows the Address. Together the two pieces extend from page 274 into page 281.

been designed to reassure the governor and, similarly, the members of the house, that they understood what their duties were. In comparison to the smooth flow of Destréhan's brief response for the council, Watkins's reply to the governor is sincere, but pedagogical in its stiff and studied phraseology. The issues of particular interest to Watkins must be winnowed from the longer listing lifted from the governor's address. These were calls for placing the "charity Hospital upon such a footing as to make it more generally beneficial"; taxes to pay for the educational system; and a census of the numbers of people living in the territory, which Watkins had requested earlier.[149]

Among the acts adopted on the first day of the session was one providing for the privileges of the members of the legislature.[150] Presumably, this act, the second to be passed in the session, was the product of the rules committee to which Watkins had been added in November 1805. The act providing for the establishment of public free schools in the counties of the territory was adopted on May 2, but no provision for funding them was made.[151] The law providing for taking a census of the inhabitants of the territory was approved on May 20.[152] Adopted the same date was the act fixing compensation for the members and officers of the two houses of the legislature.[153] The house of representatives also provided for financing the government by levying a tax on all real property in the territory except that owned by the U.S. government.[154] In addition, the legislature authorized the governor to borrow up to $16,000 for twelve months "to answer the expences [*sic*] of the government."[155] The Code Noir (Black Code), which prescribed the rules and conduct to be observed between blacks, whether slave or free, and

149. Compare Destréhan's reply with that made by Watkins. See Jean Noël Destréhan to Governor Claiborne, March 29, 1806, in TP, 9: 618–9, and John Watkins to Governor Claiborne, ibid., 620–2.

150. *Acts Passed at the First Session of the First Legislature of the Territory of Orleans, Begun and Held in the City of New Orleans, on the 25th Day of January, in the Year of Our Lord One Thousand Eight Hundred and Six, and of the Independence of the United States of America the Thirtieth* (New Orleans: Bradford & Anderson, 1806), 4.

151. Ibid., 8.

152. Ibid., 20.

153. Ibid., 26.

154. Ibid., 132, 134.

155. Ibid., 62, 64. Claiborne made application with the bank to borrow the money on May 26, 1806. Claiborne to Cashier Louisiana Bank, May 26, 1806; and Obligation to Louisiana Bank, June 9, 1806, both in CLB, 3: 316–7 and 324–5, respectively.

whites, was virtually the last act adopted. It was signed into law by the governor on June 7, the date the session adjourned.[156] In all, thirty-three laws were enacted by the legislature. Watkins played a significant role in getting all of them adopted.

One noteworthy development of the first session of the first territorial legislature was the friction that developed between the legislative and executive branches of government. As the legislators came to understand their acquired political power, they began to dispense with the politeness that initially characterized their relations with the governor. By April the legislators were asserting their independence and were at such cross purposes with Claiborne that on May 26 the council passed a resolution calling for the immediate dissolution of the legislature.[157] Most of the friction that developed was in the council, where the membership chiefly was made up of "ancient Louisianians." What precipitated the resolution was Claiborne's veto of the council's act that committed the territory to the old customs and civil laws that had been in effect in Louisiana when it was ruled by France and Spain.[158] As the governor wrote Julien Poydras on the date he vetoed the act, the legislation dictated the "Treatises and Writers on the Civil Law which should be practised in our Courts of Justice." Regarding this provision of the legislation, Claiborne told Poydras, "I think with you that our present Judicial system is defective; it neither suits the Interest or habits of the People."[159]

When Claiborne reported these developments to Secretary Madison, he said the resolution to dissolve the legislative session was attributed to Pierre Derbigny, whom he described as having acquired a "decided ascendency" over the council through his capacity as secretary to that body.[160] When the

156. *Acts Passed at the First Session of the First Territorial Legislature,* 150.

157. To James Madison, May 26, 1806, CLB, 3: 309.

158. The views of the council members were printed in the *Telegraphe,* June 3, 1806. See [Translation] *Le Télégraphe.*—New Orleans.—Tuesday, June 3, 1806.—Excerpt [*sic*] from the Session of the Legislative Council of May 26, 1806, TP, 9: 650–7.

159. To Julien Poidras [*sic*], May 26, 1806, CLB, 3: 315.

160. To James Madison, May 26, 1806, ibid., 309. Derbigny was characterized at this time as "much attached to his native Country," France, and "a devoted Friend of Laussat & Boreé [*sic*]." Characterization of New Orleans Residents, July 1, 1804, enclosed in James Wilkinson to the President, July 1, 1804, entry 28, TP, 9: 251. See also entry 70, ibid., 254, which is considerably less flattering, and entry 115, ibid., 257, which confirms the initial assessment and Claiborne's estimate of Derbigny. Claiborne told Jefferson that he considered Derbigny an honest man, but doubted "whether, at this time, he is altogether an American in sentiment or attachment." Governor Claiborne to the President, November 13, 1805, ibid., 525.

house voted on the resolution for dissolution on May 27, the day after it was received, only ten of its twenty-five members supported the act. Watkins was one of the fifteen members who voted it down.[161] As a consequence, the Destréhan/Derbigny attempt to reject Americanization of the territory failed. In reviewing the events a day after the house vote, Claiborne wrote Madison that, "As far as I can learn the public sentiment, the proceeding [the resolution] is not approved."[162]

In mid-May, before the resolution to dissolve the legislature, the house began to consider selection of the territorial delegate to Congress. Watkins was one of three nominees for the post. The other two candidates were Daniel Clark and Evan Jones. Claiborne advised Jefferson that Watkins was supported in the legislature "by native Citizens of the United States." Support for Clark and Jones was divided among the "ancient Louisianians." Claiborne thought Jones would be elected, but when the vote was taken on May 19, Clark was the winner.[163]

Early in the second week of April, before Clark's election, when the differences between the legislative and executive branches were beginning to emerge, Claiborne advised Jefferson that the "ancient Louisianians" were "greatly jealous of the few Native Americans" in the house of representatives.[164] No names were mentioned, but John Watkins obviously was one of the targets of criticism then and later because of his close association with the territorial government of Claiborne. One of the men who undoubtedly was critical of Watkins was Daniel Clark. Less than a month after his election, Clark revealed that his hostility toward Claiborne included anyone associated with the governor. After the session ended on June 16, 1806, Clark announced a comprehensive and personal vendetta. Writing to General Wilkinson, Clark said that "in order to oppose Governor Claibornes Creatures and Schemes with success," he had "found it necessary to accept" appointment as Orleans Territory delegate to Congress. Further into the letter,

161. See *Le Télégraphe.*—New Orleans, Tuesday, June 3, 1806.—Excerpt from the Session of the Legislative Council of May 26, 1806, in TP, 9: 650. About this time, Destréhan stepped down as president of the legislative council and was replaced by Pierre Sauvé. Destréhan's name last appeared as president on a bill adopted on May 22. Sauvé's name appeared on the next act adopted, May 26, 1806. *Acts Passed at the First Session of the First Territorial Legislature*, 62.

162. To James Madison, May 28, 1806, CLB, 3: 319.

163. To James Madison, May 14, 1806, ibid., 298 (belief that Jones would be elected); To Thomas Jefferson, May 21, 1806, ibid., 303–4.

164. To Thomas Jefferson, April 10, 1806, ibid., 288.

Clark bragged that his election was "a severe shock to W C. C. C [*sic*] and his Gang." They were, he said, "much chop-fallen." Clark went on to add that "all the first character[s] & best men here" had "united against" Claiborne and the men surrounding him.[165]

Initially, Watkins showed no concern about any criticisms intended for him. After the close of the legislative session, however, something caused him to feel uneasy about his relationship with the governor. In the latter part of June, or in July, Watkins wrote Claiborne, touching on a number of matters that concerned both of them. The doctor's letter has not been found, but it is obvious from Claiborne's July 29 response that Watkins wrote about some of the events in the recent legislative session and apparently asked about his very visible roles in some of those events as Speaker of the house and mayor of New Orleans. In his reply, Claiborne reassured Watkins that he had "abundant reason to be satisfied" with Watkins's "public Duties." The governor added that even though some men, "constitutionally enclined [*sic*] to find fault, may complain, I pray you to believe, that your fidelity in office, will always be acknowledged by the good and the discerning."[166]

The overall tone of Claiborne's response to Watkins's letter certainly was affable, but it is clear the governor did not himself endorse Watkins's private conduct. In light of the tensions that developed between the two men in the fall and winter of 1806–07, Claiborne's reference to "public Duties" raises questions about what he meant. Use of the phrase suggests knowledge of some other activity by Watkins that may not have pleased the governor. If that is true, what was the activity? Was it rumors of his role in the 1799–1800 Kentucky Spanish Association land development scheme soon to be reported in the August 23, 1806, issue of the Frankfort *Western World* newspaper? Did Watkins discuss the project and his role in it in his letter to the governor? Reports of the story to be carried in the *Western World* were known and talked about in New Orleans, but with General Wilkinson, not Watkins, as the target.[167] Perhaps there was something else not discernible in the extant Claiborne correspondence or some other source.

Claiborne's July letter to Watkins also touched on other subjects, both

165. Daniel Clark to James Wilkinson, June 16, 1806, TP, 9: 660–1.

166. To John Watkins, July 29, 1806, CLB, 3: 371.

167. James Sterrett talked quite knowledgeably about the *Western World* story approximately eight days before its publication. James Sterrett to Nathaniel Evans, August 15, 1806, Nathaniel Evans and Family Papers.

personal and public. Apparently Watkins was recovering from a fever, either malaria or a mild case of yellow fever, when he wrote the governor. Claiborne noted that he, too, had been "much enfeebled" from days of incessant fever, but "exercise and a Change of Climate" had been of great benefit.[168] Generally, New Orleans was free of yellow fever in the summer of 1806. Referring to this good fortune, Claiborne said he hoped it would last and that Watkins's recovery would "continue uninterrupted thro'out the season."[169]

In the same letter, Claiborne also demonstrated a supervisory stance toward Watkins that he had not exhibited before. The tone is subtle, but nonetheless suggests a change in the governor's attitude toward Watkins. The change is seen in Claiborne's remarks about a recent fire in New Orleans that Watkins had mentioned in his letter. Claiborne said he "learned with regret" that public assistance in putting out the fire was not effective.[170] He suggested the city council should pass an ordinance comparable to one in effect in Philadelphia that called on every citizen to act with "celerity and order" in putting out a fire. Enforcement of the ordinance in Philadelphia rested with the police of that city. Claiborne also suggested that Watkins begin planting trees in New Orleans. The streets were too narrow to permit extensive plantings, but the governor believed they easily could be "introduced on the Levee, and in the Square fronting the Principal." The "good

168. To John Watkins, July 29, 1806, CLB, 3: 373.

169. Ibid., 372.

170. The fire destroyed the ropewalk owned by Daniel Clark and threatened the entire city of New Orleans on June 4, 1806. The ropewalk extended perpendicularly from near the low-lying levee along the Mississippi River toward Lake Pontchartrain. Lying just beyond the original upriver boundary of New Orleans, the ropewalk blocked access via Chartres, Royal, and Bourbon Streets to Faubourg St. Mary, the developing American suburb. In short, the ropewalk blocked the growth of the American sector of New Orleans and continued to do so after the ropewalk burned because Clark would not relocate it when he had it rebuilt. The city filed suit in Superior Court on February 2, 1805, to obtain the land in front of Chartres, Royal, and Bourbon Streets, but was unsuccessful because the land belonged to Daniel Clark. The jury impaneled to determine what legal action might be necessary met in December 1805. The suit was discontinued on April 15, 1807, after Watkins no longer was mayor or a member of the city council. New Orleans, Messages from the Mayor, vol. 1, no. 58 (July 10, 1805); vol. 2, no. 65 (June 11, 1806); no. 74 (June 22, 1806); and no. 94 (August 13, 1806). Page 67 of the June 11, 1806, message refers to "a crowd" of men who refused to "help extinguish the fire." Their conduct may have been a reflection of their resentment of Clark as well as the circumstances in which they were caught. The lawsuit brought by the city was Mayor of New Orleans v. Samuel B. Davis, Superior Court case no. 1093, February 2, 1805.

effects," he said, "would soon be perceived." Alluding to "improvements to the Streets" launched by Watkins in the spring, Claiborne said he thought this "contributed much" to the cleanliness and health of the city.[171]

The clean streets that Claiborne referred to were the result of the *arrète* (ordinance) Watkins had been instrumental in getting through the city council. The ordinance required property owners to repair the *banquettes* (sidewalks) and street gutters fronting their property or pay the city for having it done. The ordinance covered all property, public and private. These improvements were begun while the legislature was in session and were the cause of additional friction between Watkins and Claiborne on the one hand and Lieutenant Colonel Freeman on the other. When the United States government did not improve the sidewalks adjoining the military barracks, the city did the work and presented the bill, $642, to the governor for collection.[172] Claiborne, in turn, asked Freeman to authorize payment of the bill, but he refused. Ultimately, the bill was paid, but not until after Claiborne brought it to the attention of Secretary Madison as a project essential to the health of the residents of New Orleans.[173] While waiting for an answer to his request from Madison, Claiborne advised Watkins "to suspend all further improvements to Lots claimed by the United States."[174]

The summer of 1806 provided a respite between the noisy, upsetting first session of the first legislature and the Burr conspiracy. The events leading into the Burr conspiracy began with the movement of Spanish troops to Bayou Funda, seven miles from Natchitoches, in late July.[175] Claiborne officially informed Watkins of the incursion at Natchitoches from Natchez on September 17. The governor's letter to the mayor was prompted out of concern that Spanish forces from Mobile and Pensacola would attack New Orleans from the east.[176] To provide for the defense of the city, Claiborne

171. To John Watkins, July 29, 1806, CLB, 3: 371–3.

172. To Col. Freeman, June 12 and 13 (two letters this last date), 1805, ibid., 91–2, 93, and 94. A similar ordinance adopted on March 17, 1804, also required property owners to fence their property. See the *Louisiana Gazette,* January 18, 1805, p. 4, c. 2.

173. LeBreton, *History of the Territory of Orleans,* 209.

174. To James Madison, June 27, 1806, CLB, 3: 137.

175. From Edw. D. Turner, August 8, 1806, ibid., 382. Subsequently, the Spanish force, numbering fewer than seven hundred men, fell back to Bayou Pierre, which Claiborne described as about fifty-five or sixty miles from Natchitoches. To Henry Dearborn, August 28, 1806, ibid., 388.

176. Fearing an attack on West Florida by the Americans, the Spanish governor of that province, Vicente Folch, had begun to map defense strategy with a *junta de guerra* (war committee), which he assembled in Pensacola in January 1806. A part of the committee's strategy included construction of gunboats at Mobile. David Hart White, *Vicente Folch, Governor in*

instructed Watkins to keep in contact with Cowles Mead, the acting governor of the Mississippi Territory, and "if necessary to communicate . . . by Express." Watkins was instructed to keep Mead informed of "every occurrence of an Interesting nature." Claiborne said the Mississippi governor would, if it became necessary, "detach to New Orleans, such number of his Militia, as may be in his power" to help defend the city.[177]

In New Orleans the report of the Spanish incursion near Natchitoches was carried in the *Orleans Gazette*. The editor of this newspaper, James Morgan Bradford, assumed in his report that fighting on the frontier was already underway.[178] Bradford, a native of Kentucky, was known for his strongly held anti-Spanish and proexpansionist sentiments, which frequently were expressed in his newspaper. Often his opinions mirrored those of a significant segment of the businessmen in New Orleans, most of whom, by all accounts, were members of the Mexican Association. It undoubtedly was this mind-set throughout the West that Aaron Burr sought to capitalize on in his bid to return to popularity and public office.[179]

In the next issue of the *Orleans Gazette,* September 23, Bradford announced the time had come to "give the wretched subjects of despotic Spain" the blessings of American republicanism. The story voiced the opinion undoubtedly held by many Americans in the trans-Appalachian West when it said that "we may sincerely rely that our President, who had so large a share in accomplishing the independence of the United States, will

---

Spanish Florida, 1787–1811 (Washington, D.C.: University Press of America, 1981), 84. However, about this same time, Folch also had begun to map strategy for taking New Orleans and Natchez, and for fomenting sedition in Kentucky and Tennessee as the "preliminary step in acquiring the western bank of the Mississippi." Isaac J. Cox, *The West Florida Controversy, 1798–1813: A Study in American Diplomacy* (1918; Gloucester, Mass.: Peter Smith, 1967), 176.

177. [To] Doctor John Watkins, August 17, 1806, CLB, 3: 378.

178. *Orleans Gazette,* September 22, 1806, as reported in Milton Lomask, *Aaron Burr: The Conspiracy and Years of Exile, 1805–1836* (New York: Farrar, Straus, Giroux, 1982), 156. It was well known in the West that Secretary Dearborn had given a standing order to General Wilkinson in June to repulse any Spanish soldiers who sought to occupy any position east of the Sabine River.

179. Burr said the Creole committee from Orleans Territory carrying the petition to Congress "offered to elect him Congressional delegate from the new territory." Royal Ornan Shreve, *The Finished Scoundrel: General James Wilkinson, Sometime Commander-in-Chief of the Army of the United States, Who Made Intrigue a Trade and Treason a Profession* (Indianapolis: Bobbs-Merrill, 1933), 145. Abernethy, *Burr Conspiracy,* 89, points out that the "people in general, thinking that Burr's object was merely to lead an expedition against the hated Dons, were enthusiastic supporters."

seize with eagerness and exultation an honorable occasion that may offer for conferring on our oppressed Spanish brethren in Mexico those inestimable blessings of freedom enjoyed in the United States."[180]

Unfortunately, neither Bradford nor most Americans, especially western settlers, grasped the tortured complexity of Jefferson's approach to managing the unruly nation he had wrested from Federalist control in 1801. Most important, no one could have anticipated the unusual twists and turns that General Wilkinson would give to events.

Wilkinson's machinations ultimately ensnared Watkins and Claiborne in a confrontation that ended their association, politically and personally, and radically altered the political alignments in Orleans Territory. For this reason, the general's conduct must be evaluated as it affected the life of Watkins. Wilkinson's actions in the unfolding events of the so-called Burr conspiracy were all ad hoc and reveal that he had several objectives: The first and most important was to continue to conceal his longstanding role as a paid agent of the Spanish government and, if possible, to wring more money from them; second, he sought to conceal his role in encouraging Aaron Burr to believe that he could use the disgruntled interests of the Orleans Territory, or one of the other territories or states in the trans-Appalachian West, to return him to a place of importance in American politics; third, he sought to embarrass and drive Claiborne from office as governor of Orleans Territory, if the Jefferson administration did not replace him; and finally, he sought to destroy the power and influence of John Watkins in the administration of the Orleans Territory and the city of New Orleans for his attempts in 1804 to reveal the general's role as a paid agent for the Spanish in the old Southwest.

The opening act of the Burr conspiracy began with the two letters Wilkinson wrote to President Jefferson from Natchitoches on October 20 and 21, 1806. Both letters were carried by the general's trusted aide, Lieutenant (subsequently Lieutenant Colonel) Thomas A. Smith, to Washington, where he took them from his shoe to hand to Jefferson on the night of November 25, 1806.[181] The letters advised Jefferson that "a powerful association" was about to "rendezvous eight or ten thousand men in New Orleans" for an

180. Lomask, *Aaron Burr*, 161–2, quoting from the *Orleans Gazette*, September 23, 1806. Lomask (p. 162) believes the words "could have been uttered by Aaron Burr." However, they sound much more like Bradford or Judge James Workman than Aaron Burr. Bradford, like Watkins, was from Kentucky. His father, Daniel Bradford, was editor of the *Kentucky Gazette* in Lexington. Few issues of the *Orleans Gazette* have survived.

181. Abernethy, *Burr Conspiracy*, 150–2; Lomask, *Aaron Burr*, 162, 179.

expedition against Veracruz, Mexico. A part of this action, Wilkinson said, included a general insurrection during which the American government was to be subverted; the western states and territories were to be severed from the United States to establish an empire based in Mexico; and the bank in New Orleans was to be seized and its money used to conquer Mexico with the aid of the British navy. The general concluded the melodramatic presentation of his messages with the lie that he was completely perplexed as to the identity of the person or persons responsible for these developments.[182]

The impact of Wilkinson's statements in his first letter so distracts the reader that it is often overlooked the letter also revealed the true reason for his incredible report. Early in this letter, Wilkinson lashed out against charges made against him in the July 7, 1806, issue of the Frankfort, Kentucky, *Western World* newspaper. In this, its first issue, the Federalist newspaper reopened the nearly forgotten "Spanish Conspiracy" of the 1790s in Kentucky by linking it to the current intrigues of Burr and Wilkinson.[183] To save himself from disgrace and the loss of his job, Wilkinson had to come up with a story that would depict him in a positive light and distract the Jefferson administration. The two weeks that it took Wilkinson to travel from Natchez to Natchitoches in September/October 1806 apparently was when he devised parts of the scheme that enabled him to do just that. The plan was based on Wilkinson's knowledge of people and events in the West, Jefferson's fears and foibles, and Claiborne's naïveté. According to the plan, set in motion with his October letters, Wilkinson could pose as the great savior of the United States. The lynchpin in the scheme was Jefferson. The two keystones in the plan were Jefferson's dislike and distrust of Burr, and his great fear that the union of states might disintegrate during his presidency. Wilkinson's inability to maneuver Claiborne into displacement as governor of the Orleans Territory was the only unsuccessful portion of his diabolical scheme. Failure to achieve this objective nearly exposed the whole plan several times as Wilkinson and Claiborne both were buffeted by developments in the fall and winter of 1806–07.

Wilkinson arrived in New Orleans on the evening of November 25, the same date Lieutenant Smith handed the general's letters to Jefferson, and five days after the president's proclamation ordering the seizure of Burr reached the city. Using nightfall as his pretext, immediately after he debarked Wilkinson retired from all public access, despite the excitement his

182. Lomask, *Aaron Burr,* 179; Abernethy, *Burr Conspiracy,* 150–2.
183. Abernethy, *Burr Conspiracy,* 92–3, 150.

arrival created in the city.[184] No one, not even territorial Governor Claiborne, got to speak with Wilkinson until the following day.[185] Watkins subsequently managed to visit with the general for a few minutes during what appears to have been a purely social occasion at the home of James Carrick, an English-born businessman in New Orleans and the civil commandant of St. Bernard.

According to Wilkinson's memorandum of their brief meeting, Watkins spoke of the "rumors in circulation" and observed that it was "nonsense to attempt to fortify the city, for if the people expected from above, should come down, the general could not resist them with his regular force, and that he would not find a man to assist him" in New Orleans. According to Wilkinson's memorandum, Watkins also said that "we might talk of discontents on the Mississippi, but they were to be found on the Atlantic also."[186] Watkins's statements were predicated on his well-known beliefs that the five hundred regular American troops stationed in the Orleans Territory and the six thousand poorly armed, poorly trained, sickly, and scattered territorial militia would be inadequate to maintain American ownership and control of the Territory in the face of any real military threat to its security.[187] Wat-

184. Claiborne advised Madison that "Wilkinson has this moment arrived in New Orleans." To James Madison, November 25, 1806, CLB, 4: 37–8. The *Louisiana Gazette,* November 28, 1806, p. 3, c. 1, noted that "Wilkinson and suite" arrived in the evening. The same story reported that on the morning following his arrival, it was "announced by a federal salute." On October 23, 1806, before leaving Natchitoches, Wilkinson had ordered Lt. Col. Freeman to secure the French artillery and ammunition left in New Orleans from the transfer of Louisiana from France to the United States, and to put forts St. Charles and St. Louis in New Orleans "in the best state of defence" possible. Freeman was ordered to make these preparations without arousing suspicion or revealing who ordered them. Wilkinson, *Memoirs of My Own Times,* 2: Appendix CI. Needless to say, the work on these tasks did not go unnoticed by New Orleans residents.

185. To James Madison, November 25, 1806, CLB, 4: 37–8.

186. James Wilkinson, *Burr's Conspiracy Exposed; and General Wilkinson Vindicated against the Slanders of His Enemies on That Important Occasion* ([Washington City: Printed for the Author] 1811), 125, Appendix No. 114. The date of Watkins's conversation with Wilkinson is not known, but it apparently came after Claiborne saw the general, which means it took place sometime between November 26 and December 4 or 5, the date Claiborne briefed Watkins. The most probable date of Watkins's conversation with Wilkinson was November 27, 1806.

187. During the territorial house debate on March 16, 1807, Watkins said, "we never have had at any time, (if my information be correct,) for two or three years past, more than from 150 to 300 troops fit for actual service in this city or its vicinity." *Debate on a Memorial to Congress,* 17.

kins's comments were the observations of an educated, intelligent, informed public official familiar with public opinion in Philadelphia and elsewhere along the Atlantic seaboard as well as the Mississippi and Ohio valleys of the United States. Yet, in Wilkinson's deposition, they became the basis for depicting the mayor as an untrustworthy and disloyal citizen.

Wilkinson did not provide Governor Claiborne with any details of what he knew about the Burr conspiracy until December 3, nine days after he arrived in New Orleans, in spite of the apparent urgency of the situation facing the nation in the Orleans Territory. Even then, Claiborne was not brought into the general's confidence. Wilkinson briefed Claiborne along with Captain John Shaw, the U.S. naval commander of the New Orleans Station.[188] To all outward appearances, the general was taking the correct actions. He had briefed the two most important civil and military officials in the territory and was coordinating possible defense strategy with them. Wilkinson's treatment of Claiborne certainly was at best coldly polite. The treatment accorded John Watkins, the mayor of the most important city in the West, by both the general and the governor was worse. When Claiborne called a meeting of New Orleans businessmen for Wilkinson to address them six days later, Watkins again was not present. From his subsequent reference to this meeting, Watkins appears to have been aware that he was deliberately excluded from both meetings.[189]

Claiborne briefed Watkins either on December 4 or 5. On hearing what Wilkinson had said, the mayor immediately urged the governor to notify by courier the various governors of the western states and territories. Because Wilkinson had neglected this responsibility, Watkins offered to "set out the next day, if necessary, to Kentucky." The mayor thought there might yet be time to alert the people of the "upper country," those living in Kentucky, Indiana, Ohio, and Tennessee, to the danger they faced.[190] During their meeting Claiborne also told Watkins that General Wilkinson had asked him

188. Important Statement [by Governor Claiborne and Captain Shaw], December 3, 1806, CLB, 4: 38–40.

189. *Debate on a Memorial to Congress*, 29. The *Louisiana Gazette*, December 9, 1806, p. 3, c. 1, carried a report on the meeting that took place that day. See also Walter F. McCaleb, *The Aaron Burr Conspiracy and A New Light on Aaron Burr* (1936; New York: Argosy-Antiquarian Ltd., 1966), addendum, 48. (The second part of this book, *A New Light on Aaron Burr*, is separately paginated. Therefore, hereinafter references to this separate section will be cited as McCaleb, *Burr Conspiracy*, addendum, with page numbers.)

190. *Debate on a Memorial to Congress*, 25. The governor of Indiana Territory was a fellow Virginian and College of Philadelphia Medical School classmate of Watkins, William Henry Harrison. Cleaves, *Old Tippecanoe*, 32–3.

to declare martial law and to suspend the writ of habeas corpus. Watkins advised against both these actions, saying he "considered such measures unnecessary, illegal & calculated to excite alarm." They would, the mayor said, "destroy all confidence in the civil authority, & throw the whole government into the hands of the military chief."[191] Finally, the governor also asked the mayor about the "best measures that could be adopted for the safety of the country." In response to this question, Watkins urged Claiborne to take "a strong ground; calling out and putting into actual service several hundred of his militia, . . . retaining" command of them himself.[192]

The manner in which Claiborne handled his meeting with Watkins suggests that it encompassed more than briefing the mayor on what Wilkinson had said about Burr's possible schemes. This inference is drawn not only from what the governor said and did during the meeting, but also from his conduct afterwards. During the meeting Claiborne employed Wilkinson's stratagem of sworn secrecy, asking Watkins "under the most solemn injunction of secrecy," for "all the particulars of Burr's projects." The phraseology that Watkins used when quoting Claiborne's question suggests that Wilkinson already had successfully shaken the governor's trust in Watkins. The mayor later said Claiborne "asked me whether I had any knowledge" of Burr's plans, and "intreated [sic] me if I had[,] to communicate it to him with that candor and love of my country which he did me the honor to say he knew I possessed."[193] More important, Watkins responded that he "never had heard" of such a scheme by Burr as that reiterated by Claiborne, and that he "firmly believed there was not a man in the territory (the agents and officers of foreign governments excepted) who would not risk his life" in defense of the country.[194]

The fact that Claiborne distrusted Watkins by the time of their meeting is most clearly seen in the governor's reaction to some of the advice solicited from Watkins. For example, Claiborne did not accept Watkins's offer to ride to the "upper country" to alert the officials there, nor is there evidence he took any action to implement the suggestion. The governor did write a circular letter to the governors of Tennessee, Kentucky, Ohio, and Indiana on December 5, 1806, but he apparently never sent it.[195] Both these actions

191. *Debate on a Memorial to Congress,* 25.
192. Ibid.
193. Ibid., 24.
194. Ibid.
195. McCaleb, *Burr Conspiracy,* 172, citing the *Orleans Gazette,* April 7, 1807, regarding Watkins's suggestion. However, McCaleb believes the circular letter "never left" Claiborne's

are clear signals that Claiborne's attitude toward Watkins and others on whom he had formerly relied was changing, or had already changed. The change clearly is attributable to General Wilkinson, who has left evidence of the seeds of doubt he planted in Claiborne's mind and the intense pressure he brought to bear on the deceived and credulous young governor.

Insight about how Wilkinson played on Claiborne's credulity may be glimpsed in two sources, Watkins's remarks from the floor of the house of representatives during the debate on the memorial to Congress on March 16 and 17, 1807, and Wilkinson's correspondence. In the course of the house debate, Watkins described Claiborne's state of mind after his conference with Wilkinson as "confounded with fear & *astonishment*."[196] Clearly, Wilkinson had frightened Claiborne into believing that "Burr had many powerful friends in this city" who were to be feared.[197] Watkins's few descriptive remarks about Claiborne during their meeting leave the picture of a man genuinely shaken and afraid, not only for his country, but for his very life. This picture is confirmed in a deposition Claiborne gave later in which he stated that he, like Wilkinson, feared he would be assassinated.[198]

In the deposition Claiborne also revealed the extent to which he had turned against John Watkins. Claiborne said he "concealed" his intentions from his former friends with the "double view of preserving my person from assassination, and to keep open the channels of communication by which I received information" about the "secret designs and movements" of the traitors to the United States.[199] The general obviously employed his insider's knowledge of the men in Kentucky involved with the Spanish conspiracy in the 1790s to turn Claiborne against Watkins. Specifically, Wilkinson undoubtedly used his knowledge of Watkins's role as agent in the land development project of the Kentucky Spanish Association, which involved the

---

office because "no trace of it elsewhere has been found." The circular letter may be seen in To Governors [of Tennessee, Kentucky, Ohio and Indiana], December 5, 1806, CLB, 4: 42.

196. Emphasis in the original. *Debate on a Memorial to Congress*, 24. In responding to Claiborne's January 12 opening address to the General Assembly of the territorial legislature, Julien Poydras also referred to "your [Claiborne's] astonishment," thereby suggesting that both Watkins and Poydras closely paraphrased Claiborne's remarks when describing the governor's reaction to Wilkinson's story. See From Julien Poydras, January 22, 1807, CLB, 4: 110.

197. *Debate on a Memorial to Congress*, 24.

198. Claiborne's deposition appeared in an affidavit submitted by Wilkinson. Nathan Schachner, *Aaron Burr, A Biography* (New York: Frederick A. Stokes, 1937), 367.

199. Ibid.

disgraced Kentucky judge Benjamin Sebastian, in Spanish Upper Louisiana in 1799–1800 to turn Claiborne against the mayor.

The specifics of Wilkinson's comments to Claiborne probably will never be known, but enough clues are in Watkins's account of his meeting with Claiborne to provide perspective on what was said to the mayor. In the December meeting Claiborne apparently spoke of the doubtful patriotism of Kentuckians. This blanket indictment of the loyalty of Kentuckians caused Watkins to declare then and later that he "had confidence in the patriotism and integrity of the upper country," by which he chiefly meant Kentucky. Watkins obviously regarded Claiborne's remark as a slur on his father and others who had helped to establish the state of Kentucky and, by implication, himself. Watkins's reaction to the meeting with Claiborne in December suggests the governor may have accused the mayor then of being a traitor. Whether intended for Kentuckians or the mayor, and whether it was made in December 1806 or in February 1807 after Claiborne learned of Watkins's membership in the Mexican Association, the accusation angered Watkins and it rankled. His angry reaction to it was revealed in his remarks during the territorial house debate on the memorial to Congress.

Insight on how Wilkinson isolated Claiborne from Watkins and his other friends also is in the general's correspondence with Claiborne during the tense and tumultuous months in New Orleans from late November 1806 into March 1807. On December 7, 1806, Wilkinson again asked Claiborne for a declaration of martial law. In this second written request, Wilkinson began to display the psychological pressures he employed against Claiborne when he said, "I believe I have been betrayed, and therefore shall abandon the idea of temporizing or concealment, the moment I have secured two persons now in this city."[200] However, it was not until the following month that Wilkinson divulged who he felt had betrayed him.

Wilkinson again tried to get Claiborne to declare martial law on January 3, 1807. The letter containing the request this time was elaborate and openly coercive. The name of the person who Wilkinson believed had betrayed him was revealed in the postscript highlighted with the forceful initialism, "NB," nota bene, meaning "note well" or "take notice." There, Wilkinson accused Claiborne of being his betrayer. The general told the governor that the district attorney, James Brown, had assured him "Dr. Watkins had communicated to his Brother, information which I had revealed to you and Mr. J. Brown only." Wilkinson also accused Claiborne

200. McCaleb, *Burr Conspiracy*, 174. [To] General Wilkinson December 17, 1806, CLB, 4: 63–5, is the governor's written refusal of this request.

of having failed in three years time to get the territorial militia organized.[201] The accusations were made as Wilkinson pressured Claiborne for an oath of secrecy about the plans he had enumerated in the body of his letter. The plans called for daily checks on people entering or leaving the city and other steps for "galvanizing" New Orleans against attack by Burr and his followers. At the same time, Wilkinson also demanded that Claiborne "Proclaim Law Martial" over New Orleans, "or agree that I may exercise it." If this was not done, Wilkinson said, "the world must condemn you as the author of the ruin . . . and everlasting loss of a country."[202]

Claiborne continued to refuse either to issue the declaration of martial law or to suspend the writ of habeas corpus in spite of Wilkinson's outrageous accusation. It is possible that Watkins's earlier advice on these two points helped reinforce Claiborne's decision to take no actions "which my Superiors have not sanctioned."[203] The suspicion that the general might have succeeded in pressuring Claiborne into these two actions is suggested by the fact that five weeks later the governor himself sought the suspension of habeas corpus. There seems little doubt, therefore, that by January 1807, Wilkinson had successfully isolated Claiborne from all his former advisors and destroyed Watkins's influence with the governor. Up to this point, Watkins had been Claiborne's chief advisor and was the one man possibly strong enough to have checked Wilkinson's roughshod ride over the constitutional rights and privileges of citizens in the Orleans Territory.

The meeting of the territorial legislature for its regular session on January 12 offered the prospect of a change in the tense atmosphere that had permeated New Orleans since the early fall of 1806. However, the chain of events set in motion by Wilkinson in October had yet to run its course. Claiborne's address to the joint session on January 13 touched on a number of matters

201. The brother referred to here was Dr. Samuel Brown, sibling of John and James Brown. Samuel Brown (1769–1830) and John Watkins had studied medicine together in Philadelphia and at the University of Edinburgh Medical School, Scotland. Samuel Brown lived in New Orleans from sometime in 1806 to 1808, when he married Catherine Percy of Natchez and settled there. Johnson, "New Orleans' Lost Mayor," 194. It is possible that John Watkins shared with Samuel Brown some of the things Claiborne said to him, but according to James Brown on September 17, 1805, his brother Samuel was "too much engaged in the *Natural* to spend a thought on the *political* world" (emphasis in the original). James Brown to John Breckinridge, September 17, 1805, TP, 9: 506.

202. "NB" occurring at the end of James Wilkinson to Governor Claiborne, January 3, 1807. James Wilkinson Papers, Special Collections, Howard-Tilton Memorial Library, Tulane University, New Orleans, Louisiana.

203. To Cowles Mead, September 5, 1806, CLB, 4: 1.

important to the territory, but only alluded to an "unauthorized expedition to Mexico."[204] There was no direct reference to the Burr conspiracy, nor were there any references to the half-dozen attention-grabbing arrests made by Wilkinson. As a consequence, it was left to the territorial legislature to speak of the circumstances in which they met. The council and house individually passed resolutions pledging their support to the national government and the president, and condemning any actions to subvert the Constitution. Yet, neither legislative chamber was quick to respond to Claiborne's January 13 address. Julien Poydras, president of the council, replied on January 22. John Watkins, in his capacity as Speaker, replied for the house on January 26.[205] Poydras's response to Claiborne's address was more restrained and circumspect than was Watkins's response.[206]

Addressing the issues Claiborne had ignored, Watkins said that although the governor had "not thought proper to reveal" to the house the reasons that led to the "extraordinary measures for some time past in this Territory," the members considered it a "sacred duty which they owe to themselves and their fellow citizens, fully to investigate those measures and the motives which have induced them, and to represent the same to the Congress of the U.S."[207]

The house then convened itself into a committee of the whole to take up the matter of a memorial "To the Honorable Senate and House of Representatives of the United States in Congress Assembled." The memorial was to describe the illegal conduct of General Wilkinson and Claiborne's support of it.

The "propriety of such a measure" had been suggested by John Watkins and was unanimously approved by the house.[208] The objective of the memorial was not to punish Wilkinson and Claiborne for dereliction of duty, but to place before Congress a record of their conduct so that the Senate, the confirming authority for both appointments, could "punish the officers who shall be found to have disregarded their duty."[209] The original committee

204. [Governor Claiborne's] Speech to the two Houses of the Assembly, January 13, 1807, ibid., 88–9.

205. From the House of Representatives, January 26, 1807, ibid., 112–4.

206. From Julien Poydras, January 22, 1807, ibid., 110–2.

207. From the House of Representatives, John Watkins, Speaker, January 26, 1807, ibid., 113.

208. *Debate on a Memorial to Congress,* 15. Strangely, the few writers who have examined the memorial have not credited John Watkins as its originator. See, e.g., McCaleb, *Burr Conspiracy,* 198–9.

209. *Debate on a Memorial to Congress,* 9.

members selected by the two chambers of the territorial legislature were John W. Gurley, William Donaldson, and Benjamin Morgan.[210]

The memorial began by pointing out there were no extenuating circumstances that "might excuse some" of the "violent measures" used by Wilkinson and permitted by Claiborne. There was, it said, "no foreign enemy or open domestic foe," nor had one "yet been proved to have been within any perilous distance of this city," nor had it been proven that "treason lurked within our walls."[211] It went on to state that the "acts of the high-handed military power to which we have been exposed . . . [are] . . . too notorious to be denied, too illegal to be justified, too wanton to be excused."[212]

In short, the memorial to Congress placed the blame for the "reign of terror" in New Orleans squarely on Wilkinson with the indulgent support of Claiborne.

Wilkinson and Claiborne, of course, opposed adoption of the memorial. If successfully reported to Congress, the memorial could result in their disgrace and the loss of their jobs. Under pressure from the governor and the general, the house began to react with uncertainty. As a consequence, the memorial began its journey through the house with detours through several committees, each of which unsuccessfully sought to refine its points for acceptability to all the members. Claiborne became so frightened that Watkins and his supporters outside the legislature would win passage of the memorial to Congress that he discreetly joined Wilkinson in soliciting the help of Vicente Folch y Juan, governor of Spanish West Florida, to pressure members of the territorial legislature to defeat the memorial and to pass a resolution praising Wilkinson for his successful defense of the territory and nation. In the words of Wilkinson, Folch's assistance was sought because Wilkinson knew that "those who control the legislative council are all friends of yours."[213]

Sometime early in 1807, Claiborne wrote Folch, who was still in Baton

210. *Moniteur de la Louisiane*, January 28, 1807, p. 2, c. 1 (hereinafter cited as *Moniteur*).

211. *Debate on a Memorial to Congress*, 8.

212. Ibid., 9.

213. [Arthur P. Whitaker, ed. and trans.,] "Documents. 5. An Interview of Governor Folch with General Wilkinson, 1807," Folch to Someruelos, June 25, 1807, *American Historical Review* 10, no. 4 (July 1905), 839. See also Abernethy, *Burr Conspiracy*, 213–4, and Wilkinson to Folch, n.d., AGI, *Papeles de Cuba, legajo* 2375, folios 95, 96. The members of the legislative council at this time were Julien Poydras, James Mather, Sr., Joseph Deville Degoutin Bellechasse, Jean Baptiste Macarty, and Pierre Foucher. Governor Claiborne to the Secretary of State, March 27, 1807, TP, 9: 723.

Rouge, urging the West Florida governor to return to Pensacola through New Orleans.[214] When Folch did not respond to the written entreaties of Claiborne and Wilkinson, a delegation of "persons of position and distinction" was sent from New Orleans to intercept the Spanish governor on his return to Pensacola. The delegation found Folch's schooner at the "mouth of the Lower Manchac," where "contrary wind prevented" its entry into Lake Pontchartrain. The purpose of the delegation from Wilkinson and Claiborne was "to induce" Folch to come to New Orleans. Both Wilkinson and Claiborne were so eager for his support to oppose the memorial, Folch remarked, "that if the President himself had come to New Orleans they could not have given him a better reception than the one I experienced." Bellechasse, longtime military associate and one-time assistant commander under Folch, was to have been a member of the delegation sent to Folch, but because he was ill the Hispanophile Louis Brognier de Clouet took his place.[215] Watkins and his friends in the legislature also had outside support, in their case from a group of New Orleans lawyers, among them Edward Livingston. The "association of lawyers" promoting adoption of the memorial particularly frightened Wilkinson.[216] Claiborne attributed the authorship of the memorial to Edward Livingston.[217]

While the memorial was being shunted from committee to committee in the house, Claiborne suddenly sent a special secret message to the legislature on February 10, asking that the writ of habeas corpus be suspended.[218] The

214. Whitaker, "Interview of Governor Folch," 837, points out that the specific Claiborne letter Folch referred to has not been found, but that Claiborne's April 24, 1807, letter to Folch could be the one meant. See Governor Claiborne to the Secretary of State, April 24, 1807, TP, 9: 727–8.

215. Whitaker, "Interview of Governor Folch," 838. De Clouet's given names were Louis Brugny, or Brognier. His middle name was given in the *Moniteur,* December 9, 1807, p. 3, c. 1. His surname is spelled variously as *Decluet, de Cluet,* and *Declouits.* The most common spellings of his last name are *de Clouet* and *Declouet.* The spelling used here is from the List of Civil and Military Officers of the Territory of Orleans, shewing [*sic*] their several places of Nativity, April 21, 1809, TP, 9: 837–8.

216. Whitaker, "Interview of Governor Folch," 839.

217. A notation in the hand of Governor Claiborne at the bottom of the first page of the copy of the memorial he sent to Secretary Madison reads: "This Memorial was written by Mr Ed: Livingston;— at least am so informed by a gentleman, who [is an assistant ?] of Mr. Livingston[.] W. C. C. Claiborne." See the Library of Congress copy of *Debate on a Memorial to Congress,* 1. At some point, either before or after this copy of the memorial was bound, part of the original notation was cut off so that its precise wording cannot be determined.

218. Message [of Governor Claiborne to Legislative Council & of the House of Representatives], February 10, 1807, CLB, 4: 118–9. From the House of Representatives, February 18,

date of Claiborne's message is significant. February 10 was the same date that he wrote Robert Williams, governor of the Mississippi Territory, saying that John Watkins was one of the "most respectable" of several men in New Orleans implicated in the "Mexican association whose proceedings were secret, & the members bound by an Oath." In the letter to Williams, who had recently resumed his gubernatorial duties, Claiborne went on to say, "I have heretofore esteemed the Doctor an amiable & useful Citizen; But unless he can rescue his character from the reproach to which it is now subjected, painful as it may be to me, my confidence in him shall be withdrawn forever."[219]

Claiborne's sudden action apparently was triggered when he learned of Watkins's membership in the Mexican Association. He became aware of Watkins's affiliation with the group from testimony given by the mayor in defense of Lewis Kerr in his misdemeanor trial.[220] Claiborne's actions indicate that he now intended to deal summarily with Watkins much as Wilkinson had dealt with others for their supposed roles in the Burr conspiracy. The governor's move to suspend the writ of habeas corpus also may have been triggered by the news received on the same date that a mistrial had been declared by the judge hearing the case against Lewis Kerr. Motivated by panic and anger, Claiborne for the moment seems to have opted for Wilkinson's heavy-handed approach to rid himself of his former friends, whom he now believed to be untrustworthy, if not traitors.

Whatever plans Claiborne may have contemplated, he was forced to alter them exactly one week after his letter to Governor Williams. On February 17, in his capacity as Speaker of the house of representatives, Watkins notified Claiborne the house had "Examined with attention the Constitution of the United States, and the ordinance of Congress" by which the territory was "Governed, and they are of [the] opinion that they cannot, without violating the Constitution, suspend under any restriction whatever the writ of

---

1807, ibid., 122, reveals that Claiborne's February 10, 1807, message to the legislature was secret.

219. Governor Claiborne to ? [, March 2, 1807], fragment of letter following Claiborne's letter To Robert Williams, February 10, 1807, ibid., 120. Internal evidence in this letter fragment suggests that it was written on March 2, 1807, the opening date of the second trial of Lewis Kerr and James Workman.

220. James Workman, *The Trials of the Honb. James Workman, and Col. Lewis Kerr, Before the United States Court, for the Orleans District on a Charge of High Misdemeanor, in Planning and Setting on Foot, Within the United States, an Expedition for the Conquest and Emancipation of Mexico* (New Orleans: Bradford & Anderson, 1807), 74. See also the biographical sketches of Lewis Kerr and James Workman.

Habeas Corpus."[221] Watkins's report to the governor was based on the February 13 decision rendered by three judges—Hall, George Matthews, Jr., William Sprigg—and the district attorney, James Brown, after they had read the laws creating the Orleans Territory.[222] It apparently was during the week of February 10–17, 1807, that the relations between Claiborne and Watkins experienced a complete rupture. Watkins's report so upset Claiborne that on February 20 he wrote Secretary Madison suggesting the "necessity" of an amendment to the "Ordinance for our Government" which would "give the right of suspension" of the writ of habeas corpus to "*all,* or some *one* of the branches of the Territorial Legislature" so that "persons against whom just causes of suspicion may arise" could be arrested or confined.[223] It seems clear that Claiborne had intended to arrest and jail Watkins, but was stopped by the decision of the judges consulted by Watkins and the legislature.

The failure of Claiborne's apparent intention to suspend the writ of habeas corpus in order to arrest Watkins was the latest in a series of setbacks that left the governor and General Wilkinson reeling from the reaction against them in the territorial legislature. It was during this time that Claiborne began to meet with "five members of the legislative Council"—Julien Poydras, James Mather, Sr., Joseph Deville Degoutin Bellechasse, Jean Baptiste Macarty, and Pierre Foucher. Claiborne said these were "men in whom the Government and myself could confide."[224] Less than four weeks after his February 10 letter to Governor Williams, Claiborne replaced Watkins as mayor of New Orleans with James Mather, Sr.[225]

Claiborne's February 10 letter to Governor Williams suggests that Watkins was dismissed from office because of his involvement with the secret Mexican Association. However, an examination of all the evidence relating to Watkins's dismissal suggests that his membership in that group was the pretext for his dismissal. The real reason Claiborne dismissed Watkins as mayor was his successful and independent leadership of the territorial legis-

221. February 17, 1807, Resolved That the House of Representatives . . . . [signed by] John Watkins, Speaker of the House of Representatives, CLB, 4: 123.

222. "Faithful Picture of the Political Situation of New Orleans at the Close of the Last and the Beginning of the Present Year, 1807," ed. James E. Winston, *Louisiana Historical Quarterly* 11, no. 3 (July 1928), 421 n. w-53.

223. To Madison, February 20, 1807, CLB, 4: 121 (emphasis in the original).

224. Governor Claiborne to the Secretary of State, March 27, 1807, TP, 9: 723. Foucher's name is variously spelled as Fouché, Fouchet, and Fourchet.

225. Ibid., 723–4.

lature, particularly the house of representatives, and the New Orleans City Council. As governor of the territory, Claiborne could not afford to have someone who was opposed to him and the policies of the Jefferson administration occupy such important governmental posts. Specifically, Claiborne dismissed Watkins as mayor of New Orleans because he feared Watkins would obtain passage of the damaging Memorial to Congress.

John Watkins did not leave office without offering strong opposition privately and publicly to the lies and distortions of General Wilkinson that were overwhelming the governor and the nation.

Evidence of Watkins's personal debate with Claiborne is suggested by the governor's belated attempts to determine the truthfulness of the rumor that Wilkinson received money from Casa Calvo in 1804. When this rumor was first bruited, Wilkinson tried to cloud the question with the response that the money was to be used to make a large purchase from the sugar planter John McDonough. Claiborne's reaction to this statement was that "all was not right." To allay his own suspicions, as well as to satisfy the Jefferson administration, the governor asked Wilkinson about the rumor. Claiborne also subsequently made inquiry with Governor Folch in January 1807 about any payments by the Spanish government to Wilkinson. Claiborne could find no support for the rumor that Wilkinson received money from any Spanish source. As a consequence, he was left with no recourse but to accept the general's statement that the money he received was reimbursement by the U.S. Army "for extra services in running [boundary] lines" between U.S. and Spanish territory.[226] This development in the chain of events appears to have put a seal of finality to Claiborne's impending break with Watkins.

The governor relieved Watkins of his duties as mayor of New Orleans on March 7. Four days later, March 11, Claiborne confessed to Secretary Madison that he believed Watkins "meditated nothing against the American Government—and that he sincerely loves his country." The governor added, however, he was of the opinion that Watkins's "zeal for the liberation of Mexico led him into some imprudences."[227]

Watkins wrote a brief letter to the members of the city council on his last day as mayor that was notable for its simplicity and touch of poignancy.

226. Daniel Clark, *Proofs of the Corruption of Gen. James Wilkinson, and of His Connexion with Aaron Burr, with a Full Refutation of His Slanderous Allegations in Relation to the Principal Witness Against Him* (1809; New York: Arno Press, 1971), 52–3 n. 25, Deposition of James M. Bradford.

227. McCaleb, *Burr Conspiracy,* 33, citing Claiborne's letter in Letters in Relation to Burr's Conspiracy MSS, U.S. State Department of Archives, Washington, D.C.

Regarding his more than four years of service, first as city council member and then mayor of New Orleans, Watkins said he was happy to "have served the public usefully." Much of what he had done, he said, was "mostly due to the assistance" given him by council members and "to the wisdom of the measures" they adopted. He closed his letter with the "offer of my gratitude" and the assurance that "if there is anything which can add to the satisfaction furnished by a pure conscience, in my retirement, it will be found in the hope that you will honor me with your esteem."[228]

The quickness with which Claiborne supplied Secretary Madison with an explanation of his dismissal of Watkins seems to suggest the governor felt guilty about his treatment of the man who had served him and his country well and faithfully since February 1804. Ten weeks later, on May 19, Claiborne wrote Jefferson lamenting the loss of Watkins, saying: "I am much afflicted at the course which Doctor Watkins has taken; I had long entertained the best opinion of his Talents and intentions and given him a great share of my confidence and patronage; but the intrigues of designing men have, I fear made him abandon those principles which he once professed and practiced."[229]

Claiborne's anger with Watkins ended not only the doctor's involvement with the administration of the city, but also his lucrative post as port physician, because both positions were at the pleasure of the territorial governor.[230] However, Watkins's difficulties with Claiborne did not end his elected responsibilities in the territorial house of representatives, which the doctor continued to serve as Speaker to the end of his term in June.

Debate on the Memorial to Congress was scheduled for March 16 in anticipation of the end of the legislative session. On that date, the house assembled as a committee of the whole with Doctor Ebenezer Cooley, the representative from Pointe Coupée, occupying the Speaker's chair. Watkins apparently removed himself as Speaker so that he could fully participate in the debate. This record of these sometimes heated discussions supplies some knowledge of what Watkins knew and thought about the Burr conspiracy, as well as the conduct of Wilkinson and Claiborne during those momentous events. The record of that debate also provides a glimpse of the local politi-

228. Watkins to the President and members of the City Council, March 7, 1807, in *New Orleans Messages from the Mayor*, vol. 2, 131 (March 11, 1807). The letter is quoted in "Administrations of the Mayors," 9, 13.

229. Governor Claiborne to the President, May 19, 1807, TP, 9: 734.

230. Letter No. 25, To James Madison, October 27, 1804, described the port physician's post as "lucrative."

cal turmoil created by and in the wake of the Burr conspiracy in New Orleans.

Final debate on the Memorial to Congress began with the motion of Colonel Alexander Fulton from Rapides County to reject it.[231] William Donaldson seconded Fulton's motion because, he said, reading of the memorial was
"fulsome to the ears of many in the house." When Fulton's motion failed,
Donaldson moved to recommit the memorial to committee on the grounds
that it "was not confined to facts, and was vindictive." This motion, too,
was defeated.[232] There then followed two days of discussion in which the
most vocal advocates for adoption of the memorial were Joseph O. Parrot,
of Opelousas County, John Hughes of Ouachita, and John Watkins. Those
house members known to have actively opposed its adoption were Alexander Fulton, William Donaldson, John W. Gurley, and John Collins, the
other representative from Opelousas.

In his remarks, Watkins characterized his situation during the first day of
debate. Caught between Claiborne and Wilkinson, the former mayor said,
"suspicion alone was sufficient" to stigmatize one as a friend of Burr. "If
you dared to assert from your knowledge of the patriotism of the Western
states, that Burr would not succeed . . . you were accused of wishing to lull
the people into a state of dangerous security" and attempting "to stifle the
vigilance of government" and "were therefore denounced as a friend of
Burr." On the other hand, Watkins said, if you "gave implicit confidence to
all the general's information . . . you were equally his friend, and a traitor
to your country."[233] Speaking of himself, Watkins said, "I have from my
infancy adored the principles upon which the American constitution is
founded." The "possibility of a case in which any officer of the government" could "be justified in a departure from the written laws" of the country never occurred to him, Watkins said.[234] Taking aim at the heart of his
predicament, Watkins added, "such is my love of truth, and respect for the
honor and dignity . . . of the legislature," and "for freedom in general,"
that what he "most ardently" desired to see was less subservience "to party
spirit."[235]

Watkins's description of the situation in New Orleans in 1806–07 re-

231. *Debate on a Memorial to Congress*, 3. At the time the memorial was being considered, Orleans Territory's political subdivisions were identified officially as counties.

232. Ibid., 3, 9, 10.

233. Ibid., 26.

234. Ibid.

235. Ibid., 38.

veals a city and territory under siege from the commanding general of the United States Army supported by the territorial governor. The situation was so bad, Watkins said, that it was "dangerous for a private citizen to express any sentiment in opposition to the measures of the day."[236] Watkins accused Claiborne "of having abandoned his duty" by "consenting to and approving the military arrests and the transportation" of citizens by General Wilkinson.[237]

Representative John Hughes reminded those present that "no member" of the territorial legislature "had courage enough to condemn the conduct of General Wilkinson," except when the legislature was in session and its doors were closed.[238] Even then, Hughes said, house members were not safe because Wilkinson had stationed a guard in the house, "which insulted" members "and violated its privileges."[239] Representative Joseph Parrot reminded the house members that "It was the unanimous voice" of the house ten weeks earlier that a memorial should be forwarded to the government, "containing [the] facts of which we complained." Equally to the point, Parrot said he did "not believe" the opposition measures being sought stemmed from "upright motives."[240]

Watkins revealed in his remarks on the second day of debate, March 17, that developments outside the legislature directly affected the debate on the memorial and determined whether it would pass. Before the debate began, he said, "before the subject had been investigated, or even submitted to this committee," several of the house members had "actually pledged themselves to vote against it." Without naming anyone, Watkins said these members had "pledged themselves . . . in the Coffee-House, or upon the banking table to reject" the memorial.[241] The reference to discussions around the banking table could have been intended for Donaldson, who was then engaged in developing Donaldson Town, the future Donaldsonville.[242] Regardless of whom Watkins had in mind when he made the remark, his barb on this

236. Ibid., 15.
237. Ibid., 41.
238. Ibid., 15.
239. Ibid., 11.
240. Ibid., 9–10.
241. Ibid., 37.

242. Advertisements for land sales in the new town began to appear in several of the New Orleans newspapers at this time. See, e.g., *Louisiana Gazette*, June 27, 1806, p. 3, c. 4. See also the sales notice in the *Moniteur*, October 25, 1806, p. 4. c. 4. Property sales apparently began in June 1806.

point was quite sharp. Posing a rhetorical question, he asked "how many persons are there in this busy city of ours, who do not stand now and then in need of assistance from the banks?"[243]

During the second day of the debate, Gurley came closest to providing a balanced perspective on the situation facing the house when he characterized the memorial as an attempt to make the legislature "a mad partizan in the quarrels and contests of individuals," a clear reference to the ongoing, bitter quarrel between Claiborne and Wilkinson and their critics, which now included Watkins.[244] The seeming objectivity in Gurley's statement must be balanced with the knowledge that he was heavily obligated to Claiborne and the Jefferson administration through his appointments as register of lands for the eastern district of Orleans Territory, territorial attorney, and aide-de-camp to the governor.[245] Ironically, Gurley had been appointed aide-de-camp by Claiborne to fill the position vacated by Watkins on February 5, 1806.[246]

Despite Watkins's statement that he was aware the situation in New Orleans was fraught with politics, he initially does not appear to have perceived his own altered political base. The sudden strength of the opposition to the memorial surprised and angered Watkins, who had not anticipated the subtle shift in favor of Claiborne and Wilkinson among house members brought about by the passage of time and the influence of Vicente Folch.[247] Warming to his subject, Watkins told house members they owed their "salvation not to general Wilkinson or governor [*sic*] Claiborne, but to the patriotism and integrity of the people of Kentucky." It was they who upheld the principles of liberty and independence the citizens of Orleans Territory enjoyed, he said.[248] Here Watkins's anger at Claiborne suggests how Wilkinson's knowledge of Watkins's role as agent for Judge Benjamin Sebastian and other Kentuckians in 1800 to obtain a large grant of land in the Illinois Country from the Spanish government may have been used with telling effect against the mayor. The initial reports of the plans, first revealed in December 1806, cast doubt on Watkins's loyalty. The report was doubly

243. *Debate on a Memorial to Congress*, 37.

244. Ibid., 31.

245. John W. Gurley to the Secretary of the Treasury, June 3, 1805, and Register of Civil Appointments in the Territory of Orleans, February 13, 1806, Attornies [*sic*], TP, 9: 453 and 602, respectively.

246. General Orders, February 5, 1805, ibid., 597, 632.

247. See *Debate on a Memorial to Congress*, 15.

248. Ibid., 27.

damaging to Watkins because Judge Sebastian tried to conceal his part in the scheme by using the fictitious name "Andrew Watkins."[249]

Watkins went on to remind his fellow legislators that Wilkinson's assault on the body politic was so severe that at one time they were all afraid to express their true opinions outside the closed doors of the legislative chamber.[250] The memorial, he said, recorded that the "citizens of this territory" were "not only stopped" as they passed quietly through their neighborhood, "but [were] fired upon, by order of General Wilkinson." In another instance, Watkins said a member of the house of representatives "was imprisoned until he had suffered an illegal examination of his private papers."[251] The Speaker did not identify either the citizens fired on or the imprisoned house member.

Ultimately, the memorial was rejected on March 17 by a vote of fourteen to seven on the motion offered by Gurley.[252] Gurley's motion rejected the memorial "in toto" because he "was perfectly convinced" there was "not the slightest ground" for alterations that would meet the approval of a majority of the house. John Collins, representative from Opelousas, seconded Gurley's motion. He believed the memorial contained statements that were

249. *Western World,* December 13, 1806, p. 4, c. 2. For information on Sebastian, see Thomas Robson Hay, *The Admirable Trumpeter: A Biography of General James Wilkinson* (Garden City, N.Y.: Doubleday, Doran, 1941), 267–8; and Shreve, *Finished Scoundrel,* 168–70. The standard on the "Spanish conspiracy" in Kentucky is still Thomas Marshall Green, *The Spanish Conspiracy: A Review of Early Spanish Movements in the South-West....* (1891; Gloucester, Mass.: Peter Smith, 1967), iii–iv, vi, 86–7, 120–38, and *passim.*

250. *Debate on a Memorial to Congress,* 15.

251. Ibid., 8. The memorial, which was not passed by the territorial House, may be read in the *Debate on a Memorial to Congress,* 3–9. The privately printed copy of the memorial sent by Claiborne to Secretary Madison is no longer among the territorial papers of the State Department. Governor Claiborne to the Secretary of State, March 23, 1807, TP, 9: 722 n. 70. The annotated copy that Claiborne sent to Madison subsequently was made a part of the Rare Book and Special Collections Division, the Library of Congress, where it was bound as part of that Library's *Political Pamphlets,* vol. 105. See Whitaker, "Interview of Governor Folch," 839 n. 1, and George Dargo, *Jefferson's Louisiana: Politics and the Clash of Legal Traditions* (Cambridge, Mass.: Harvard University Press, 1975), 202 n. 39. Dargo points out (ibid., 202 n. 38), that the five-page draft of the memorial, with documents appended, may be seen in the Joseph Dubreuil de Villars Papers, Duke University.

252. Those voting to reject the memorial were Manuel Andry; Felix Bernard; J. Etienne de Boré; John Collins; William Conway; Dr. Ebenezer Cooley; William Donaldson; Alexander Fulton; John W. Gurley; A. Hébert; J. Hébert; Monchoufee; David B. Morgan; and Henry S. Thibodaux. Those voting against rejection of the memorial were Joseph Arnauld; John Hughes; Chevalier de LaCroix; Hazure de Lorme; Joseph Parrot; Joseph Sorrel; and Watkins. *Debate on a Memorial to Congress,* 42.

"not true, and ought not to come before this house."[253] Unfortunately, Claiborne's annotations to the copy of the memorial that he sent to Madison do not address any of these points. In essence, Claiborne's notations are non sequiturs—that is, they have nothing to do with the accusations made about incidents that occurred during the "reign of terror." Neither are his annotations defenses of his or Wilkinson's conduct. The annotations simply brush aside all the charges made against him and Wilkinson. After characterizing the memorial as emanating from Edward Livingston, Claiborne said that the actions and statements attributed to Wilkinson and himself were "not fair Representations of the General's Communications,"[254] and that the accusations were "false,"[255] but he offered no rebuttal to the specific allegations. With regard to Claiborne's request that the legislature suspend the writ of habeas corpus, the governor lamely indicated "a copy of the Messages here alluded to was sent to the Department of State."[256] On the last page of the pamphlet, the governor scrawled: "Note. To correct the various Errors in this pamphlet, & to expose the falsehoods it demands, it would be necessary [to] Write a Book."[257] The rest of this annotation, the longest at seven and a half lines, is undecipherable because of the governor's writing, the manner in which the pamphlet was bound, and damage to the page over time. Perhaps the most important annotation is on page seven, where Claiborne asserts that if he had opposed General Wilkinson at the time of Erick Bollman's second arrest, it "would have . . . raised the standard of Civil War."[258] Because a portion of this annotation appears to have been cut off, the meaning in the reference to "Traitors wish [?]. . . ." cannot be determined.[259]

Before the final vote for or against passage of the memorial was taken, Watkins acknowledged the "impossibility of ever bringing forward . . . a memorial" that "would accord with the ideas of all the members" of the house. In support of this view, he pointed out the "very grievances that we complain of in the memorial have been made meritorious acts" by virtue of the address approving "measures adopted by gen. [*sic*] Wilkinson in this city." The address, Watkins said, "has been signed and presented to him,"

253. Ibid., 10, 29.
254. Annotation made at the bottom of page, ibid., 3.
255. Annotations made at the bottom of page, ibid., 3 and 6.
256. Annotation made across the bottom of page, ibid., 9.
257. Annotation across the bottom of page, ibid., 42.
258. Annotation across the bottom of page, ibid., 7.
259. Ibid.

with the "names of some of the members of the house . . . subscribed to it."[260] One of the signers was William Donaldson, who had renewed his motion to recommit the memorial on March 17.

It now is known that passage of the address Watkins spoke of was considerably aided by the support of Spanish West Florida Governor Vicente Folch and his friends in the Orleans Territory, particularly those in the legislature. Regarding his role in the passage of this resolution, Folch said, "I thought that I ought to lend myself to it in order to show them that Spain could be useful to them even in their own country."[261] Following the dismissal of Watkins from office as mayor and adoption of the addresses endorsing Wilkinson and Claiborne, the New Orleans scene became quiet. As one local observer characterized the situation, "Our war is all over. Nothing but the greatest harmony & Confussion [sic] prevails. . . . the Troops are all to be parcelled out to the different Stations, and are almost all affronted."[262]

Watkins's last official act as Speaker of the house may have been to inform President Jefferson on May 10, 1807, of the names of the men nominated by the house to fill the vacancy in the legislative council created when James Mather, Sr., was appointed mayor.[263] The fact that Watkins notified Jefferson, rather than Claiborne, suggests the continued strain in the relations between the former mayor and the governor, as well as the determination of Watkins to fulfill his responsibilities as Speaker.

The loss of income as mayor of New Orleans and the end of his elected term in the territorial house of representatives, along with the cessation of Claiborne's patronage at nearly the same time, appear to have adversely affected Watkins's financial situation almost immediately. At least, this seems to be the implication in the doctor's offer to sell "Archer," his twenty-five-year-old "valet de chambre," in May. In the newspaper sales notice Watkins described the slave as an intelligent, excellent domestic who spoke French, English, and passable Spanish. The sale price for the slave was set at five hundred *piastres,* the common medium of exchange in much of the Mississippi Valley and Gulf Coast in the first half of the nineteenth century.[264] The

260. Ibid., 29.

261. Whitaker, "Interview of Governor Folch," 839–40.

262. James Sterrett to Nathaniel Evans, March 20, 1807, Nathaniel Evans and Family Papers.

263. John Watkins to the President, May 10, 1807, TP, 9: 732–3.

264. *Moniteur,* May 27, 1807, p. 4, c. 2. The original date of the sales notice apparently was May 12, 1807. Five hundred piastres then would have been the approximate equivalent of eight hundred to one thousand dollars. The piastre was the Spanish dollar, the medium of

one positive development in his life at this time was election to the board of directors of the Orleans Navigation Company, which occurred on February 9, 1807, two days after he was replaced by Claiborne as mayor of New Orleans.[265]

Feelings still ran high among those who opposed Wilkinson and Claiborne, but most of their opposition was blocked or silenced by the end of the legislative session in April 1807. As a result, when the territorial elections were held in September, they "terminated very much to . . . [the] satisfaction" of Claiborne. As the governor wrote Madison, "Doctor Watkins & those of his Party, were but partially supported." Most of the men elected to the legislature were generally "ancient Louisianians, of honest reputations and Supporters of the Government," Claiborne said.[266] Watkins himself apparently did not seek public office. His position on the city council was filled, in a real sense, by two men, James Mather, the newly appointed mayor, and Benjamin Morgan, who was elected in July 1807.[267] Thomas Urquhart, the only man of English lineage elected to the territorial house of representatives from New Orleans in 1807, was chosen Speaker over three other candidates, Eugene Dorsière, Chevalier La Croix, and Joseph Villars, in January 1808.[268]

Watkins's name was not advanced for public office again until 1809, when he was nominated for election by the territorial legislature as delegate to Congress for the "ensuing two years." Revealing a still active animus toward the former mayor, Claiborne wrote Madison on February 13, 1809, that Watkins "received all the support" that Daniel Clark "could give him."

---

exchange in the colonial possessions of Spain and other nations rimming the Gulf of Mexico and beyond in the eighteenth and into the nineteenth centuries. It can be equated with the peso of Mexico and other South American countries as well as with the American dollar. It was divided into five livres or eight "bits," or "rials" (*reales*). In 1936 the equivalent value of the peso was approximately $1.7151. J. Villasana Haggard, *Handbook for Translators of Spanish Historical Documents* (Austin: Archives Collection, University of Texas, 1941), 106.

265. *Louisiana Gazette*, February 10, 1807, p. 3, c. 1. Named to the board at the same time were Benjamin Morgan, Stephen Zacharie, James Pitot, and William Kenner.

266. Governor Claiborne to the Secretary of State, October 5, 1807, TP, 9: 766.

267. Morgan served on the city council until the city elections of 1812. New Orleans Conseil de Ville: Official Proceedings, no. 1, book 3 (February 15, 1806–July 1, 1807); no. 2, book 1 (July 6, 1807–December 28, 1808); book 2 (January 14, 1809–December 26, 1810); book 3 (January 12, 1811–November 7, 1812).

268. In addition to Urquhart, the men elected to the territorial House in the fall of 1807 were Chevalier de La Croix, John (Jean) Blanque, Dominque Bouligny, Joseph Villar, and Magloire Guichard. All except Villar were elected to office for the first time. *Moniteur,* January 13, 1808, p. 2, c. 3.

Nonetheless, Watkins's opponent, Julien Poydras, was elected by a vote of 20 to 5.[269]

In the years that followed, Watkins apparently kept busy with his medical practice, various business interests, and some civic responsibilities. He continued to live on Bayou St. John, approximately two miles from the city, where he had established his residence early in 1805.[270] Six years later, sometime during the first five months of 1811, Watkins apparently changed residences on Bayou St. John. On May 22 that year, he purchased number 10 St. John Road, in the St. John Faubourg, from Daniel Clark, taking on a mortgage in the amount of $1,420.00.[271] In the same year his office was at 7 St. Louis Street.[272]

Following the loss of the election as territorial delegate in 1809, nothing is heard of Watkins until after the news reached New Orleans that Congress had authorized the Territory of Orleans in February 1811 to draft a constitution as the initial step toward being granted admittance to the union of states. Watkins's desire to see the Orleans Territory become a state was well known. While serving in the territorial house, he formally proposed statehood and the drafting of a constitution. He also served on the committee to write the judicial section of that document.[273]

Late in June 1811, after official word reached Louisiana that it could become a state, Watkins's name appeared on the first of several lists as one of a number of men who would be "well supported for the Constitutional Convention."[274] Three days later, on June 28, Dr. Galipot wrote the editor of the *Louisiana Gazette* saying, "I cannot for the soul of me, see why one

269. (Private) Secy of State, February 13, 1809, CLB, 4: 316–17.

270. B[arthélémy]. Lafon, *Annuaire Louisianais pour L'Année 1809* (New Orleans: By the Author, 1808), 215, lists Watkins's residence on Bayou St. John.

271. Act of June 13, 1812, Notarial Acts of John Lynd, Notarial Archives, New Orleans.

272. Thomas H. Whitney, *Whitney's New-Orleans Directory, and Louisiana & Mississippi Almanac for the Year 1811* (New Orleans: Printed for the Author, 1810), 55.

273. Cecil Morgan, comp., *The First Constitution of the State of Louisiana* (Baton Rouge: Louisiana State University Press, 1975), 26, and the sources cited there.

274. Claiborne was not officially notified that President Madison had signed the enabling act into law on February 20, 1811, until May 9, 1811. Notification was not received in New Orleans until after the middle of June 1811. Philip Uzée, "The First Louisiana State Constitution: A Study of Its Origins" (master's thesis, Louisiana State University, 1938), 8. The first list carrying Watkins's name was published in the *Louisiana Gazette,* June 25, 1811, p. 2, c. 3. Subsequently, his name appeared on lists published in the same newspaper on June 28, p. 2, c. 3; July 16, p. 2, c. 3; July 27, p. 2, c. 3; August 3, p. 2, c. 3; August 22, p. 2, c. 3; and September 11, 1811, p. 2, c. 2.

Doctor should have the preference (in the political world) over another" and suggested the names of twelve other doctors, including Watkins, who would "most probably form a *Sound healthy Constitution,* and should it prove sickly, would administer medicine for its recovery *Gratis.*"[275] When the votes for the Constitutional delegates were tallied and reported on September 20, Watkins was one of the twelve men elected to represent New Orleans, proving that he still had many friends in the community.[276]

The constitutional convention delegates first met informally on November 4 "in a large room of Mr. Tremolet's [*sic*] Coffee House . . . fitted for their accommodation."[277] Their initial action was to choose Francis Joseph Le Breton Dorgenois as president pro tempore and Morel as secretary.[278] Because New Orleans was not yet free of an outbreak of yellow fever that fall, concern for the health of the "country members" was expressed at the meeting. Fully cognizant of the dangers to the delegates and aware that a number of them were not present because of the yellow fever danger, John Watkins moved for adjournment until the third Monday of the month, November 18. Thomas Urquhart seconded the motion. In the brief discussion that followed, Jean Blanque, the strongly pro-French Bonapartist delegate from Orleans County, countered that the convention "could not legally adjourn for any considerable length of time" because Congress might regard their actions as "contemptuous and illegal."[279] In a move that exposed the

275. Emphasis in the original. In addition to Galipot, who apparently wrote the letter, and Watkins, the other doctors named were Louis Fortin; William Rogers; Oliver H. Spencer; Robert Dow; Joseph Montigue (Montague); Nicholas Robelot; William Flood; William Barnwell; James D. Russel; Cyprien (?) Grosse; and (?) Davies. *Louisiana Gazette,* June 28, 1811, p. 2, c. 3.

276. Ibid., September 20, 1811, p. 2, c. 3.

277. Ibid., November 5, 1811, p. 2, c. 3.

278. The pro tempore secretary named here most probably was the French-born P. L. (Pierre Louis) Morel, who frequently was employed as a translator because of his command of French, Spanish, and English. At one time he was employed in this capacity by Grandpré. Later Morel entered the legal profession and in this capacity defended Louis Louaillier in his dispute with Andrew Jackson over continuation of martial law in New Orleans in March 1815. James A. Padgett, ed., "The Difficulties of Andrew Jackson in New Orleans Including His Later Dispute with Fulwar Skipwith, as Shown by the Documents," *Louisiana Historical Quarterly* 21, no. 2 (April 1938), 369. Additional information on Morel may be found in Jane Lucas DeGrummond, *The Baratarians and the Battle of New Orleans: With Biographical Sketches of the Veterans of the Battalion of Orleans, 1814–1815,* by Ronald R. Morazan (Baton Rouge: Legacy, 1979), 166–7.

279. Blanque is characterized as a Bonapartist by Louis de Clouet. See Stanley Faye, ed., "Louis de Clouet's Memorial to the Spanish Government, December 7, 1814 (Conditions in Louisiana and Proposed Plan for Spanish Reconquest)," *Louisiana Historical Quarterly* 22,

uneasy new political alignments in the territory, Urquhart suddenly supported Blanque. Watkins, backed by Jean Destréhan, Alexander Porter, and
Daniel J. Sutton, said that "it was the duty of Governor Claiborne to furnish
the Convention with a list of the members elected for each county," but that
he had not yet done so. As a consequence, Watkins pointed out, they were
meeting "without any other authority than" that collected from newspaper
stories. Although Blanque, known for his "animated style," strongly objected, Watkins's motion was carried.[280]

The minor political skirmish over the election of the convention's temporary officers points out that the new supporters of Claiborne were struggling
to gain their political wings and still insecure in their recently awarded positions of power and importance. This observation seems to be confirmed by
the subsequent attack made on both Watkins and Destréhan by J. B. S.
Thierry, editor of the *Courier* newspaper. Both men, particularly Watkins,
were "highly censured" by Thierry, whose newspaper had displaced the *Orleans Gazette* in 1808 as the official public printer.[281]

After Thierry's attack was published, a writer calling himself "Truth"
wrote the *Louisiana Gazette* pointing out there was "neither room for censure or praise in the whole business." Watkins's remarks, "Truth" said, "did
not cast the least shade of censure" on Claiborne. The anonymous writer
went on to say that "on the contrary," Watkins had included in his remarks
the assumption that *sickness or some other cause* had prevented the returns from being made" by the governor's office. "Truth" then went on to
say Thierry would agree with him if he had been present at the meeting. The
unknown writer then accused Thierry of being the "*legitimate guardian* of
Mr. Claiborne's honour." "Truth" closed his review of the matter with the

---

no. 3 (July 1939), 811. Blanque, characterized as a thirty-five-year-old merchant at the time
of the first constitutional convention, was a native of Nay, France. As did many of the men in
early New Orleans, Blanque belonged to one of the several Masonic lodges then active in the
city. Powell A. Casey, "Masonic Lodges in New Orleans," *New Orleans Genesis* 20, no. 77
(January 1981), 7.

280. Jean Paul Blanque's demeanor is characterized in the *Louisiana Gazette,* November
23, 1811, p. 2, c. 3, and is supported by insight provided in Laussat, *Memoirs of My Life,* 47.
Blanque had come to Louisiana in 1803 with Laussat, who described him as "my faithful
friend" (ibid., 127 n. 20). Elsewhere Blanque is described as Laussat's cousin. Governor Claiborne to the Secretary of State, March 24, 1804, TP, 9: 201 (in this letter, Blanque is erroneously identified as "Blanche"). When Claiborne notified Madison of the reason for the
adjournment, he referred to the "Apprehensions, that the City was not yet free from Yellow
Fever," but he did not mention Watkins's role in the decision. To James Monroe, November
14, 1811, CLB, 5: 380.

281. Dargo, *Jefferson's Louisiana,* 40, 71, 208 (n. 116).

suggestion that if Thierry was the "man of honour and probity" that he professed to be, he would correct his error; publicly acknowledge that he had been "wrong[ly] informed; and apologize to Mr. Watkins" for his "rude attack."[282]

The conduct of Claiborne's supporters continued to betray their insecurity and apparent fear of Watkins's political acumen when the convention delegates assembled on November 18. Instead of calling Dorgenois and Morel to the chair to fulfill their service as temporary officers of the convention, the quorum present called Julien Poydras to preside as president pro tempore and proceeded with the election of permanent officers. The two nominees for president of the convention were Poydras and John Watkins. In the balloting that followed, Poydras received 24 votes and Watkins 10. Eligius Fromentin was nominated and elected secretary without opposition.[283] Thereafter, the delegates met each day at ten o'clock through November twenty-third.

The convention delegates received official certification of the election results from Claiborne when they assembled in Tremoulet's on the morning of November 19. They then began to consider whether they wished to organize a state government under the terms offered by Congress. John Watkins gave direction to this discussion when he offered a resolution calling on the convention members to accept the terms and conditions of the February 17, 1811, act of Congress enabling the territory to become a state.[284] Discussion of Watkins's resolution favoring statehood was postponed until the November 20 session.

282. Emphasis in the original. *Louisiana Gazette*, November 11, 1811, p. 2, c. 3.

283. Ibid., November 19, p. 2, c. 3.

284. Ibid., November 21, 1811, p. 2, c. 3, and *Journal de la Convention D'Orléans de 1811–12* (Jackson, La.: Jerome Bayon, August 3, 1844), 3, 4. Because the journal of the 1811–12 convention was not published until 1844, it must be used in conjunction with contemporary newspaper reports published following the sessions of the convention in 1811–12. Often the names of individual delegates are misspelled and even incorrect. For example, John Watkins most often is referred to as "Jones" Watkins. Occasionally he is called "Tom" Watkins. At other times, his correct given name, John Watkins, is used. Ibid., 4, 14, 17.

The convention apparently did not employ a stenographer. Regarding this great need, the editor of the *Louisiana Gazette*, November 21, 1811, p. 2, c. 3, said, "We fondly hope the Convention will employ a *Stenographer*. The debates yesterday were so very interesting, that every member must be impressed with the advantage it would be to the public to have them fairly taken" (emphasis in the original). See also ibid., p. 2, c. 4.

The most complete study of the proceedings of the 1811–12 constitutional convention with perspective on the political climate of the territory and city of New Orleans from 1803 to 1812 is Uzée, "First Louisiana State Constitution." See also Morgan, *First Constitution*.

When the delegates assembled on November 20, Magloire Guichard, Jean Blanque, and Bernard Marigny supported Watkins's resolution, but Destréhan, and Alexander Porter, a young Irishman who had settled in southwest Louisiana on the recommendation of Andrew Jackson, spoke against it.[285] The following day, November 21, Destréhan and Porter were joined by five other delegates. Those who objected to the enabling act did not oppose statehood for the territory, but rather those provisions of the act that would, in time, diminish the distinctive French character of the territory and assure its Americanization. They also objected to the boundaries that were to be established by Congress; the reversion of all vacant lands, then heavily used by Louisiana residents, to the U.S. government; and publication of the legislative and judicial proceedings of the state-to-be in English.[286] Nonetheless, following a "short impressive speech" by Watkins and comments from others, all of whom endorsed the resolution for statehood, the delegates voted 35 to 7 at three o'clock on the afternoon of November 21 to form a state constitution.[287] The seven negative votes were cast by Destréhan, Bela Hubbard, Henry S. Thibodaux, Andrew Goforth, James Dunlap, David B. Morgan, and Alexander Porter.[288]

After voting for statehood on November 21, the delegates then unanimously agreed to all the provisions of the Constitution of the United States, which was a requirement of the enabling act. They then appointed a seven-man committee to draft a constitution for the state.[289] Perhaps because he was not a lawyer and had long been identified with land development, Watkins was named to the committee charged with the responsibility to com-

285. *Louisiana Gazette,* November 21, 1811, p. 2, c. 3, and *Journal de la Convention D'Orléans,* 4. On Porter, see Wendell Holmes Stephenson, *Alexander Porter: Whig Planter of Old Louisiana* (Baton Rouge: Louisiana State University Press, 1934), 13–5.

286. According to the *Journal de la Convention D'Orléans,* 4, these objections were not made until the meeting on November 23, 1811, but they are recorded in various issues of the *Louisiana Gazette,* November 19, 21, and 22, 1811, p. 2, c. 3. As indicated, the reports on the convention appeared on the same pages and columns of the newspaper. See also LeBreton, *History of the Territory of Orleans,* 487–8.

287. *Louisiana Gazette,* November 22, 1811, p. 2, c. 3, and *Journal de la Convention D'Orléans,* 4.

288. *Journal de la Convention D'Orléans,* 4. *Louisiana Gazette,* November 20, p. 2, c. 3; November 21, p. 2, c. 3; November 22, p. 2, c. 3, 1811; LeBreton, *History of the Territory of Orleans,* 487–8.

289. The members of this committee were James Brown; Allan B. Magruder; Jean Blanque; Henri Bry; Jean N. Destréhan; Henry Johnston; and Michel Cantrelle. *Louisiana Gazette,* November 23, 1811, p. 2, c. 3; and *Journal de la Convention D'Orléans,* 4.

pose a resolution to Congress "praying for an extension" of the boundaries of the new state to "embrace West Florida to the river Perdido," which then was the southeastern boundary of the Orleans Territory. Although Watkins was named to this committee, he is not mentioned as one of the speakers who sought the inclusion of West Florida in the new state. The two named were Jean N. Destréhan and James Brown.[290] After these actions, the convention adjourned until November 29, when the committee charged with providing a draft constitution was to return with a document ready for consideration.[291]

The first constitution of the state of Louisiana essentially was taken from the second constitution of the state of Kentucky, which was written in 1799. This circumstance may be attributed to the number of influential members in the convention who were from Kentucky, or who had lived there before settling in the Orleans Territory. In addition to John Watkins, whose ties to Kentucky were well known, two of the five committee members appointed to draft the Louisiana constitution—James Brown and Allan Bowie Magruder—also were from Kentucky. Magruder was a native of Kentucky who had been admitted to the Kentucky bar at the age of twenty in 1795. Although a native of Virginia, Brown had practiced law in Kentucky and served there as secretary of state before settling in Louisiana.[292]

Watkins was not a member of the committee charged with the responsibility to provide the convention with a draft constitution, but he did play key roles in other actions that shaped the final document. During the December 9 session, Watkins's motion to take up the constitution as reported on November 23 by the committee, section by section and article by article, was passed.[293] Also adopted in this session was Watkins's motion to confine the preamble of the constitution to the very words of the act of Congress in which the name "Louisiana" was used.[294] In this sense, although most of the members of the convention preferred "Louisiana" as the name of the state, he played a major role in assuring that this name would be chosen.[295] During the session of December 10, Watkins presided as convention chair.

290. *Journal de la Convention D'Orléans,* 4; and *Louisiana Gazette,* November 23, 1811, p. 2, c. 3.

291. *Louisiana Gazette,* November 23, 1811, p. 2, c. 3; and *Journal de la Convention D'Orléans,* 4.

292. Morgan, *First Constitution,* 9–10, 17, 20–1. On Brown, see his biographical sketch.

293. *Louisiana Gazette,* December 10, 1811, p. 2, c. 3.

294. Ibid.

295. Ibid.

Also in this session, the delegates changed the day of elections for the new state of Louisiana from the third Monday in October to the third Monday in November.[296]

During the session on January 7, 1812, ten of the twelve members comprising the Orleans County delegation protested when denied their demand that New Orleans be granted three seats in the senate chamber rather than the two all other counties were given. The two delegates who did not join the walk-out led by Jean Blanque are identified only as Americans. Whether John Watkins was one of the two is not known.[297] He is identified as one of the New Orleans delegation who supported more senatorial representation for New Orleans.[298] There seems little doubt that when the convention members voted unanimously on January 22, 1812, to accept the constitution for the state of Louisiana, John Watkins must have felt pride in the notable role he had played in bringing the task to fruition.[299]

The last known public political act of Watkins was to sign the April 12, 1812, memorial to Congress requesting all or part of that "lott [sic] of ground on which the Government House is situated" be made the location of the University of Orleans. Watkins signed the memorial as one of the original trustees of the university. This simple act was a hard-won milestone in his longstanding efforts to provide Louisiana with even a modicum of public education. By 1811 the college had 70 students and expected to see the "rapid and great augmentation of the number" in the future. The request was endorsed by Claiborne in his capacity as chancellor of the University of Orleans. Among the other signers were Moreau Lislet, Francis X. Martin, and James Mather.[300]

One business that Watkins engaged in after his career in politics was newspaper ownership. It is not known when he acquired the *Orleans Gazette,* but it is a matter of record that he sold it in the spring of 1812. The mortgage/sale of the newspaper to Peter K. Wagner and Joseph B. Baird was recorded on May 25, 1812. Wagner had arrived in New Orleans that spring. The sale included not only the printing office, the paper, and other stock in

296. Ibid., December 11, 1811, p. 2, c. 3.

297. Ibid., January 8, 1812, p. 2, c. 3, tells of the walk-out protest.

298. Uzée, "First Louisiana State Constitution," 18.

299. *Louisiana Gazette,* January 23, 1812, p. 2, c. 3, reported the Constitution for the State of Louisiana had been passed "yesterday, by an unanimous vote."

300. Memorial to Congress from the Regents of the University of Orleans, April 20, 1812, TP, 9: 1014–6.

trade, but also the "outstanding debts due" to the paper, along with the "monies in hand."[301]

Why a notice of the death of John Watkins was not published is not known. If one appeared in the *Orleans Gazette,* the issue carrying the story is among the many of that newspaper that have been lost. John Watkins was survived by his wife, Eulalie, and their only child, Jean Zenon Watkins, who was born on August 6, 1805.[302] Like his father, Jean Zenon also became active in politics. Known in his adult life as "John," the younger John Watkins was elected to represent St. James Parish in the state house of representatives. Taking his seat on January 4, 1831, this younger Watkins was returned to office for nearly twenty years.[303] He fell out of favor with the Democrats when he voted for Pierre Soulé rather than John Slidell for the U.S. Senate in January 1848. Because of this vote, young John Watkins was denounced as "'another Whig traitor.'"[304] Jean (John) Zenon Watkins died February 10, 1863. He was survived by his wife, née Lucie Elise (or Elsie) Ducros, and his mother.[305] Mrs. John Watkins, née Eulalie Trudeau, died September 21, 1867, at the age of 82.[306]

301. Act of May 25, 1812, Notarial Acts of John Lynd, Notarial Archives, New Orleans. Watkins may have become a silent partner about the time of Thomas Anderson's death, August 18, 1811, if he was not already a partner. There is no reference to Watkins as an owner in Clarence S. Brigham, *History and Bibliography of American Newspapers, 1690–1820,* vol. 2 (Westport, Conn.: Greenwood Press, 1961), 190. There also are no references to him as an owner in the surviving issues of the newspaper.

302. *Sacramental Records of the Roman Catholic Church of the Archidiocese of New Orleans,* vol. 8, *1804–1806,* ed. Charles E. Nolan, trans. J. Edgar Bruns (New Orleans: Archdiocese of New Orleans, 1993), 326 (entry for Jean Zenon Watkins).

303. *Journal of the House of Representatives of the State of Louisiana, Tenth Legislature, First Session* (New Orleans: John Gibson, 1831), 7.

304. Arthur Freeman, "The Early Career of Pierre Soulé," *Louisiana Historical Quarterly* 25, no. 4 (October 1942), 1100.

305. There was no reference to children in the death notice that appeared in the *New Orleans Bee,* February 11, 1863, p. 1, c. 7.

306. *New Orleans Bee,* September 22, 1867, p. 1, c. 7.

ZENON TRUDEAU

Zenon Trudeau and his family would be considered among the "ancient Louisianians" sometimes referred to by Governor Claiborne. Trudeau was born in New Orleans on November 28, 1748, the son of *Sieur* Jean-Baptiste Trudeau, a lieutenant in the French army, and Marie de Carrière. One of his siblings was Charles Laveau Trudeau, the surveyor-general of Louisiana. Well educated, Zenon, like his father, made the army his career, joining the Regiment of Louisiana as a cadet in 1769. During the American Revolution he participated in the battles of Baton Rouge in September 1779 and Pensacola in 1781 with Gálvez.[1] He married Eulalie de Lassize, daughter of Nicolas de Lassize, a captain in the royal army and commandant at Pointe Coupée, in 1781.[2] Appointed governor of Upper Louisiana in 1792, Trudeau served at the post until succeeded by Carlos Dehault Delassus de Luzières in the summer of 1799. Trudeau was given the opportunity to retire on a pension in 1797, but refused because he thought he was needed while Spain was at war with England. In 1800 he commanded the infantry troops sent from Mexico and Louisiana, some of whom were mulattos, to capture William Augustus Bowles in East Florida.[3] Trudeau was well liked as an administrator, possessed a friendly disposition, a pleasing personality, and a

1. *Archivo General de Simancas. Sección de Guerra Moderna. Hojas de Servicias Militares de América, 1787–1799, legajo 7291, cuaderno 9*, Regimiento de Infanteria de Luisiana, June 1794, folio 12.

2. Derek N. Kerr, "Trudeau, Zenon," in *A Dictionary of Louisiana Biography*, Glenn Conrad, gen. ed., vol. 2 (Lafayette: University of Southwestern Louisiana, 1988), 799.

3. David Hart White, *Vicente Folch, Governor in Spanish Florida, 1787–1811* (Washington, D.C.: University Press of America, 1981), 54.

very mild temper. Following the transfer of Louisiana from Spain to France, he requested the pension previously offered and asked to remain in the former Spanish colony rather than serve outside of Louisiana.[4]

It is doubtful that Trudeau's request to remain in Louisiana was granted, or, if granted, it was revoked. He and his brother, Felix, were named on July 30, 1805, by Casa Calvo, along with three other officers of the Louisiana Regiment, as "Having not yet . . . joined their corps."[5] Some, or all five, may have lost their commissions and pensions at the hands of Casa Calvo, who was inflexible in his demands for obedience to him and allegiance to the Spanish crown. Trudeau died in St. Charles Parish, Louisiana, on September 12, 1813.[6] Unfortunately, there is no study of Trudeau and his contributions to the establishment of European civilization in the Mississippi Valley.

4. Abraham Nasatir, *Spanish War Vessels on the Mississippi, 1792–1796* (New Haven: Yale University Press, 1968), 59 n. 2; and 135 n. 8.

5. A list of the officers, in his C. M.'s service, who are to depart immediately after having terminated their business, July 30, 1805, enclosed in the Marquis of Casa Calvo to Governor Claiborne, August 2, 1805, in Clarence E. Carter, comp. and ed., *The Territorial Papers of the United States,* vol. 9, *The Territory of Orleans, 1803–1812* (Washington, D.C.: U.S. Government Printing Office, 1940), 486.

6. Abraham Nasatir and Ernest R. Liljegren, "Materials Relating to the History of the Mississippi Valley from the Minutes of the Spanish Supreme Council of State, 1787–1797," *Louisiana Historical Quarterly* 21, no. 1 (January 1938), 67 n. 143.

Evan Jones (August 17, 1739–May 11, 1813) was born and reared in New York.[1] His association with the lower Mississippi Valley had its origins in the trade that flourished briefly between the English colonies and Spanish Louisiana after the close of the Seven Years War in 1763. The earliest record of Jones's participation in this trade is 1765, when he arrived in New Orleans from Mobile, which then was the great outlet on the Gulf of Mexico for the British involved in the Indian fur trade. On this visit to New Orleans, Jones entered into a contract with the merchants Petit and Durand. He sold not only his cargo, but also his ship.[2]

The sale of his ship did not end Jones's participation in the profitable coasting trade. In July 1766, George Johnstone, governor of British West Florida and one of the benefactors of Evan and his brother James, described a Mr. Jones as "the most reputable man among us to make my compliments" to the new governor of Spanish Louisiana, Antonio de Ulloa. It is quite likely the Jones referred to was Evan, for in the same letter, Johnstone stated that he gave Jones bills of exchange to be negotiated at New Orleans.[3]

Evan Jones's acquaintance with Governor Johnstone probably stemmed

1. [Arthur P. Whitaker, ed.,] "Despatches from the United States Consulate in New Orleans, 1801–1803, I," *American Historical Review* 32, no. 4 (July 1927), 805 (hereinafter cited as Whitaker, "Despatches, I"); and St. Louis Cemetery Card File, Louisiana State Museum Library, New Orleans. Efforts by the author to further document the family and birthplaces of Evan Jones and his younger brother, James, were unsuccessful.

2. Mrs. Fred O. James (Thelma Coignard), "Index to French & Spanish Translations of Original Documents," *New Orleans Genesis* 3, no. 11 (June 1964), 202.

3. The complete letter is printed in Clinton N. Howard, *The British Development of West Florida, 1763–1769* (Berkeley: University of California Press, 1934), 127.

from the anticipated and real contributions of Jones to the settlement and trade of West Florida. Among the latter was the good working relationship that Evan and James had with such trading companies as William Walton & Co. of New York City.[4] The anticipated contributions initially may have hinged on adoption of Governor Johnstone's plans to encourage settlement of the colony by paying ship captains from a schedule of proposed fees for transporting able-bodied persons from England, Europe, North America, and Jamaica. Particularly sought were Englishmen trained as carpenters, blacksmiths, bricklayers, shipwrights, millwrights, and indigo makers.[5] Nothing is known of the numbers of persons Jones may have brought to live in West Florida, but either in the fall of 1765 or in the spring of 1766 the New Yorker joined the growing list of landholders in the newest British colony. There is a Jones listed among the recipients of fifteen grants approved by Governor Johnstone sometime before November 2, 1765.[6] If that was not Evan Jones, there is no doubt that he acquired patents to a commercial lot fronting on Pensacola harbor and four hundred acres bordering East Lagoon near the governor's house in April and May 1766.[7] Fifteen months later, Evan, with his brother James, received title (September 29, 1767) to some islands in Middle River and fifty acres of land on the mainland at Pensacola.[8] Whether this association of Evan and James was a continuation or an initiation of their partnership is not known, but the arrangement was clearly mutually advantageous. James was a member of the West Florida Council, the governing body of the colony headquartered in Pensacola.[9] In December 1767, Evan and James joined with Jacob Blackwell, who was collector of customs at Mobile, a member of the West Florida Council, and a leader in the British attempts to settle the new colony, to acquire title to five hundred acres of land on East River above Pensacola.[10]

4. On the Jones brothers' reliance on William Walton and James Beekman of the William Walton Company, see James Jones to General Haldimand, March 14, 1770, in the *Sir Frederick Haldimand Papers, 1769–1772*, Library of Congress microfilm 2964, Louisiana and Lower Mississippi Valley Collections, Louisiana State University Libraries.

5. George Johnstone to John Pownall, Secretary to the Board of Trade, July 27, 1766, Great Britain, Public Record Office, *Colonial Office Papers*, Series 5, vol. 574: 2, microfilm 1753, Louisiana and Lower Mississippi Valley Collections, Louisiana State University Libraries.

6. Howard, *British Development of West Florida*, 66.

7. Ibid., 73, 74.

8. Ibid., 84.

9. James is known to have served on the council from sometime in 1769 into June 1771. See *Colonial Office Papers*, 5/586: 309, and ibid., 5/588: 288.

10. Howard, *British Development of West Florida*, 92.

By 1770 the Jones brothers were regarded as important to the settlement and economic development of West Florida. Through his contacts in New Orleans, Evan not only obtained the assistance of Governor Alexander O'Reilly in collecting debts owed to the Jones brothers and other English merchants trading with that Spanish port, but also, like Oliver Pollock about this same time, persuaded the Spanish governor to permit the Jones brothers to continue in the trade, which was important to both the English and Spanish colonies.[11] Perhaps it was for this reason that Evan was recommended by Lieutenant Governor Elias Durnford for a seat on the council in January 1770.[12] About this same time, through his friendship with General Frederick Haldimand, James's attention was directed toward using the Florida Keys in the program for settling and developing West Florida.[13]

Less than two weeks after Evan was recommended for appointment to the council, his life came perilously close to an end. On February 4 or 5, Evan was involved in a duel on Gage Hill outside of Pensacola with former lieutenant governor Montfort Browne.[14] The immediate cause of the duel is not known, but it appears to have originated in the dismissal of James Jones and David Hodge from the council in August 1769 by Browne amidst charges that Browne had misused his office. Browne accused the two councilors of having "labour'd by the most insidious means to obstruct every sort of Harmony and Order" within the colony.[15] The two council members and one or two others apparently angered Browne when they questioned an account he presented as though it had been certified as examined in council,

---

11. See Lawrence Kinnaird, ed., *Spain in the Mississippi Valley, 1765–1794*, Part 1, *The Revolutionary Period, 1765–81*. American Historical Association *Annual Report, 1945* (Washington, D.C.: U.S. Government Printing Office, 1946), 179; James, "Index to French & Spanish Translations," 205; and Mrs. Fred O. James (Thelma Coignard), "Index to French and Spanish Translations of Original Documents," *New Orleans Genesis* 3, no. 12 (September 1964), 330.

12. Durnford to Earl of Hillsborough, January 27, 1770, *Colonial Office Papers* 5/587: 88.

13. James Jones to General Haldimand, March 14, 1770, *Haldimand Papers*.

14. Cecil Johnson provides an overview of this incident in *British West Florida, 1763–1783* ([New Haven: Yale University Press, 1943], 70–3). The most probable date of the duel was February 5, 1770. See the correspondence between Browne and Durnford, and Durnford and Edmond R. Wegg, attorney general of West Florida, in *Colonial Office Papers, 5/587*: 173, 175, 177, 179, 181. See also the Council Minutes of February 7, 1770, in *Colonial Office Papers, 5/587*: 215.

15. Browne to Earl of Hillsborough, August 20, 1769, in *Colonial Office Papers, 5/586*: 309.

when in truth it had not.[16] Since Browne was suspected of fraud, the reason for the meeting with Evan Jones may well have involved the question of Browne's integrity or that of the Jones brothers. In the duel, Evan's pistol misfired. Browne then shot Jones, wounding him in the abdomen. Although Evan's survival was in doubt for days, he recovered because the wound was a clean one in which the bullet passed completely through his body without damaging any vital organs.[17]

About two years after the duel with Montfort Browne, Evan and James Jones were backers of the largest speculative land venture advanced for West Florida. The scheme called for the location of settlers from New York on a 25,000-acre township that was to be established overlooking the Mississippi River. This project in community planning also was backed by two New Englanders, Israel and Rufus Putnam, and others.[18] Nothing ever came of the township project because of the political and economic difficulties that began to affect the English colonies and the lucrative Gulf Coast trade in the early 1770s. The nature of those problems can be glimpsed from Evan Jones's complaint to the Privy Council in 1772.

The minutes of the council for July 28, 1772, reveal that Alexander McPherson, judge and register, and James Ferguson, marshal, of the Vice Admiralty Court for East and West Florida, would not give Jones clear title to a brig that had been condemned by the court and bought by him at public auction. Jones's petition for redress of this grievance demonstrates the unanimity of outlook and spirit that corrupt use of the British admiralty courts then was producing in pre-Revolutionary British North America. Jones said that the court, as managed by its present officers, had "become more pernicious in its consequences than a Roman Catholic Inquisition; and the abuses

16. Durnford to Earl of Hillsborough, January 27, 1770, in ibid., 5/587: 85. Perspective on the problems caused by Lt. Governor Browne's inflated travel expenses and attempts to have the government pay for his travels to see lands as far west of Pensacola as the Mississippi River may be glimpsed in Julius Groner and Robert R. Rea, "John Ellis, King's Agent, and West Florida," *Florida Historical Quarterly* 66, no. 4 (April 1988), 394. The issue between Evan Jones and Browne may have involved expenses for gifts to the Indians on behalf of Elias Durnford and Browne, as well as expenses Browne tried to transfer out of his account in favor of a friend, deputy superintendent for Indian Affairs, Leonard B. Westrupp.

17. Statement of Dr. John Lorrimer, Surgeon General, West Florida Council minutes, February 18, 1770, in *Colonial Office Papers*, 5/587: 216–7.

18. Albert C. Bates, ed., *The Two Putnams: Israel and Rufus in the Havana Expedition 1762 and in the Mississippi River Expedition 1772–73 with Some Account of the Company of Military Adventurers* (Hartford: Connecticut Historical Society, 1931), 130, 258, and *passim*; Johnson, *British West Florida*, 140; and James A. James, *Oliver Pollock: The Life and Times of an Unknown Patriot* (New York: D. Appleton-Century, 1937), 41–4.

daily practiced in it, to the prejudice of the subjects, call loudly for redress."[19]

The British government closely began to regulate the trade and westward movement of its North American colonists about the time that the traditional Spanish policy of excluding foreigners from trade with Spanish colonies was resumed in Louisiana.[20] The resulting slump in trade along the Gulf Coast was aggravated by a simultaneous decline in trade with the interior. As a consequence, the English merchants along the Gulf Coast began to focus their attention on the Mississippi River and the commerce there. The actions of the Jones brothers reflect these circumstances. In the spring and summer of 1772, Evan and James received patent rights to 2,600 acres of land east of present-day Baton Rouge.[21] Thereafter, Evan, like Oliver Pollock, appears to have focused his attention on developing business prospects in Spanish territory.

In 1775, Evan received grants from the Spanish government of two parcels of land in the Acadia District on the Mississippi River above New Orleans and one of 1,713 arpents of land in the Lafourche District.[22] By his own admission, Evan regarded 1775 as the year in which he entered on the more settled life of a planter,[23] but the land acquisitions and other enterprises he and his brother James were individually and jointly involved in suggest that they both were entrepreneurs. Certainly they sought to take advantage of the competitive British and Spanish policies that were designed to use the English-speaking settlers to develop the lower Mississippi Valley. This is demonstrable particularly with regard to land. In 1776, Evan and James sold land six leagues above Baton Rouge to John Nash.[24] The following year they were in business on the Amite River, apparently on some of the land acquired in 1772. Subsequently, they appear to have used land acquired from Joseph Richard and Santiago McCollock on the right bank of Bayou Manchac in present-day Iberville Parish as the base for their business operations.[25]

19. Johnson, *British West Florida*, 230.

20. James, *Oliver Pollock*, 49–56, and the references cited therein.

21. *American State Papers: Public Lands*, vol. 3 (Washington: Gales & Seaton, 1834), 46.

22. Ibid., 2: 270; and *Lafourche Parish Surveys, 1790–1803*, Louisiana and Lower Mississippi Valley Collections, Louisiana State University Libraries.

23. Whitaker, "Despatches, I," 805.

24. *Archives of the Spanish Government of West Florida*, vol. 9 (Baton Rouge: Survey of Federal Archives in Louisiana, 1937–40), 205.

25. On the Bayou Manchac property, see *American State Papers: Public Lands*, 2: 275. Albert Casey lists, illustrates, and references all of the early land transactions in *Amite County, Mississippi, 1699–[1890]*, vol. 4, *Environs, Land Plats, Florida Parishes of Louisiana; and Set-

During the American Revolution, Evan was a member of the Spanish Company of Distinguished Carabineers Militia, having joined that cavalry unit (October 24, 1779) after the capture of Baton Rouge. It was at this time, apparently, that he became a Spanish subject.[26] Subsequently, Evan served with the Iberville Militia and the German Coast Disciplined Militia. More than seven years later he was promoted to the rank of sublieutenant (January 17, 1787). Almost exactly five years after that, he was promoted to captain (February 12, 1792). On the urging of Governor Gayoso, Evan became commandant pro tempore (September 13, 1797–September 27, 1798) of the Acadian Coast of Lafourche de Chitimachas. There is no record that Evan ever fought in any of the American Revolutionary War battles in the old Southwest, or any other Spanish campaign, during his more than twenty-one years of militia service in Spanish Louisiana. Nonetheless, he was credited with valor and note made of his "good" application, capacity, and conduct.[27]

As the British military presence in West Florida declined and was terminated, the business of Evan and James Jones prospered under the Spanish. In 1780, Evan bought 797 arpents of land with a dwelling house and picket fence adjacent to the grant of 1775 in the Lafourche District for twelve hundred dollars. The following year (February 26, 1781) he married Marie Verret, daughter of Nicholas Verret and Marie Cantrelle, whose family was prominent in the Lafourche de Chitimachas District and New Orleans. Later, Evan's son-in-law, Henry McCall, named the combined Lafourche properties Evan Hall Plantation.[28] By 1784 the Evan and James Jones Company, trading in flour, indigo, fur, and hides, was established in New Orleans. Among the companies they served as agents in New Orleans were Nicholas Low of New York and William and James Walton & Company of Philadelphia.[29]

---

tlers, *Louisiana-Mississippi-Missouri Maps* (Birmingham, Ala.: Amite County Historical Fund, 1969), 8, 9, 21, 86, 99, 266, 289, 291, 293, 401.

26. Whitaker, "Despatches, I," 805.

27. *Archivo General de Simancas. Sección de Guerra Moderna. Hojas de Servicias Militares de América, 1787–1799, legajo 7291, cuaderno 2, Regimiento de Milicias Provinciales Disciplinadas de Alemanes. Floridas,* folio 10, microfilm 3124, Louisiana and Lower Mississippi Valley Collections, Louisiana State University Libraries. See also Jack D. L. Holmes, *Honor and Fidelity: The Louisiana Infantry Regiment and the Louisiana Militia Companies, 1766–1821* (Birmingham, Ala.: [Jack D. L. Holmes] 1965), 193–4.

28. Sidney A. Marchand, *An Attempt to Re-Assemble the Old Settlers in Family Groups* (Baton Rouge: Claitor's Book Store, 1965), 52–3 (entry 368), citing Ascension Catholic Church Register No. 1, 140.

29. John G. Clark, *New Orleans, 1718–1812: An Economic History* (Baton Rouge: Louisiana State University Press, 1970), 162–5, 265, 272.

Shortly after relinquishing his position as commandant of the Lafourche de Chitimachas in 1798, Evan visited the United States for several months. His age, fifty-nine, and the deaths of his eldest and youngest sons, John and Thomas, as well as business matters, may have precipitated the long visit to New York and Philadelphia.[30] When he returned to New Orleans in the second week of August 1799, Evan learned that his friend Governor Gayoso had died about three weeks earlier. Since he held appointment as U.S. consul (recess appointment May 11, 1799, confirmed December 5, 1799), Jones presented his credentials to Colonel Francisco Bouligny, the officer temporarily responsible for governing Louisiana. Bouligny advised Jones that the matter would have to be passed on by the Marqués de Someruelos, captain-general in Havana. In the meantime, Bouligny assumed that William E. Hulings of Philadelphia would continue to act as consul in accordance with Jones's wishes. About a week later, in response to a communication from Bouligny, Jones resigned his commission in the Spanish militia.[31]

After the Marqués de Casa Calvo arrived in mid-September to assume the duties of interim governor-general of Louisiana, Jones inquired of him whether the captain-general had given orders for his recognition as consul. The marqués advised Jones that as long as he was a subject and militia officer of Spain he could not be U.S. consul. Casa Calvo did not tell Jones that Someruelos also had ordered Jones's arrest and deportation to Havana. The intercession of Casa Calvo prevented this portion of the captain-general's orders from being carried into effect. The marqués pointed out to Someruelos that Jones was a man of "independent fortune, married, with grown-up children and large family connection [sic], and enjoying the esteem of the principal men" in Louisiana. If Jones were arrested, it might precipitate "commotions and murmurings," and cause the United States to deport Don José Vidal, the Spanish consul recently sent to Natchez. As a result, Jones was not arrested, but he was ordered to cease his activities as consul.[32]

30. On the sons, see Evan Jones Will, Orleans Parish, Louisiana. Court of Probate, Record of Wills, 1805–1837. Will Book 1805–1817, vol. 1, 36 (hereinafter cited as Evan Jones Will with page numbers).

31. Whitaker, "Despatches, I," 806.

32. Ibid., 806. Casa Calvo's reference to Jones as a man of "independent fortune" probably reflects recognition of the fact that the marqués could not control Jones through any threat to reduce or stop pension payments Jones may have been receiving from the Spanish government. Casa Calvo did take this action against Bellechasse and appears to have used it, or threatened to use it, against other Spanish citizens. See the biographical sketches of Bellechasse and Casa Calvo.

Despite the prohibition order of the Marqués de Someruelos, Jones continued to function as acting consul without pay for more than a year and a half. As a consequence, Casa Calvo advised Jones on April 30, 1801, to stop his activities.[33] When he did not, Intendant Don Ramon de López y Angulo initiated proceedings in the *audiencia* (court) at Santo Domingo to have Evan Jones's national trading privileges revoked.[34] Although the revocation of the trade license was still pending a year later, the issue was dead.[35] Spain had ceded Louisiana to France in October 1800 and Daniel Clark had been appointed U.S. consul in New Orleans on July 16, 1801. For these reasons, as well as the ones Casa Calvo pointed out to Someruelos, no formal action against Evan Jones ever was taken by the Spanish government.

After the retrocession of Louisiana to France in 1803, Jones served as a member of the *conseil de ville,* the new city council created by Laussat to replace the cabildo, from its creation (November 30, 1803) until December 20, 1803, when he and Pierre Sauvé submitted their resignations.[36] Thereafter, Jones apparently held no other local or territorial office, although he actively opposed Governor Claiborne in the early years of the territorial government.

Contact between Evan Jones and Claiborne was initiated by Jones in March 1802, a few months after Claiborne had assumed his duties as governor of the Mississippi Territory. Jones wrote the governor that he had "received *three Hogsheads & three Boxes,* containing Hoes & Axes & marked 'U.S. Chictaw [*sic*] Indians.'" The boxes had been shipped in February or March of 1801 from Philadelphia on the brig *Thomas* and consigned, without his knowledge, to Evan Jones, apparently because he had been appointed U.S. consul at New Orleans. While en route to New Orleans, the *Thomas* was captured and taken into Providence, The Bahamas, and condemned as a prize. All her cargo, except the hogsheads and boxes of axes

33. Whitaker, "Despatches, I," 807.

34. López y Angulo to Soler, July 13, 1801, *Archivo General de Indias, Audiencia de Santo Domingo, legajo* 2617, folio 1, microfilm reel 172, Library, Special Collections, Loyola University, New Orleans. (Hereinafter the *Archivo General de Indias* shall be cited as AGI.)

35. López y Angulo to Soler, July 2, 1802, AGI, *Audiencia de Santo Domingo, legajo* 2531, folios 624–32, microfilm reel 102.

36. New Orleans Conseil de Ville: Official Proceedings, no. 1, book 1, November 30, 1803–March 29, 1804, City Archives, Louisiana Department, New Orleans Public Library, 2, 4, 50; and "Administrations of the Mayors of New Orleans, 1803–1936," comp. and ed. Works Project Administration (project 665-64-3-112, typescript; New Orleans, March 1940), 1. The reorganized city council occasionally was referred to in its early years as the "Municipal," the "Municipality," or the *conseil de ville.*

and hoes, was sold. These were shipped to Jones by his representatives in the Bahamas.[37] Claiborne agreed to accept the farming utensils in order to send them on to the Choctaw Indians and to reduce the storage costs to the United States government.[38] In his capacity as superintendent of Indian Affairs for the Southern Department, Claiborne authorized payment of the eighty or ninety dollars in charges that accrued against the United States government. In his request for reimbursement for this cargo, Jones also presented "a small demand of Twenty one Dollars" against the government of the United States for goods still in his hands.[39] In responding to Jones on this point, Claiborne advised him that it was "not in my power to act," and that Jones would have to submit his claim to the Treasury Department for payment.[40]

Although this exchange was businesslike and devoid of any apparent personal feelings of animus, the relations of the two men gradually worsened. The differences between them became significant. They were too strong to have been based only on Jones's objections to the Jefferson administration's refusal to give Louisianians immediate representative government. There is about them the suggestion of a personal antagonism. The wellsprings of Jones's opposition are known chiefly through the correspondence of Claiborne and for this reason may be only partially correct. Claiborne believed that Jones was opposed to the U.S. government on principle. Claiborne also thought that Jones disliked him personally for ordering the seizure (May 1804) of the brigantine *Active*.[41] This British ship, formerly known as the *Hector* out of Jamaica, was suspected of being taken on the high seas and brought into New Orleans for sale under other pretenses.[42]

---

37. From Evan Jones, March 17, 1802, in *Official Letter Books of W. C. C. Claiborne, 1801–1816*, ed. Dunbar Rowland, vol. 1 (1917; New York: AMS Press, 1972), 74–5 (hereinafter cited as CLB, with volume and page range).

38. To Henry Dearborn, April 8, 1802, ibid., 71–2.

39. From Evan Jones, March 17, 1802, ibid., 75.

40. To Evan Jones, April 7, 1802, ibid., 76.

41. To James Madison, May 22, 1806, ibid., 3: 306.

42. Decree (Auction), May 7, 1804; To James Madison, August 1, 1804; To Captain Davis[,] Harbor Master, August 3, 1804 (examine cargo to determine discharge); To Lewis Kerr, Sheriff of New Orleans and performing the duties of marshal for the district of Orleans, August 4, 1804 (Discharge of Cargo, the Prize Brig Active); To James Madison, August 4, 1804; and To James Madison, August 9, 1804, in CLB, 2: 135, 285–6, 289, 290, and 300, respectively. Additional details on this complicated story may be found in *Evan Jones v. Shaw et al.*, Superior Court Case No. 24, December 10, 1804, in the City Archives, Louisiana Department, New Orleans Public Library.

The origins of Claiborne's antipathy are clear. After receiving Jones's October 8, 1804, letter declining to serve on the territorial council, the governor expressed his concern to Secretary Madison that "a few designing men" intended to "acquire a mischievous influence in Louisiana."[43] His fears were accurate and Evan Jones was the man who confirmed them. Two days after Jones declined serving on the council, his letter of declination was printed in the New Orleans *Telegraphe*.[44]

There is little doubt but that Claiborne shared the view expressed by "Fair Play" five days later in the New Orleans newspaper *Union* that Jones was agitating to create an opposition party while at the same time deprecating party spirit. Claiborne also may have agreed with the rest of "Fair Play's" assertion that Jones wished to place himself at the head of the party he sought to create.[45] How accurate "Fair Play's" assessment of the situation may have been is conjectural. Jones, like Daniel Clark, may have thought his donated service as U.S. consul entitled him to greater recognition from the national government. However, it seems more likely that Jones inherently identified with the mercantile and financial interests courted by Alexander Hamilton. Therefore, it would follow that Jones was motivated by the same feelings that controlled many Federalists in their attitudes toward the farmer-oriented Jeffersonian Republicans. If this is true, and the scattered evidence strongly suggests that it is, Jones's feelings undoubtedly were reinforced by his successful suit in the *Active* case and by his successful suit against several prominent Jeffersonian Republicans in Mississippi.

The second law suit Jones won was brought in April 1809 against Isaac Briggs, John Ellis, William Dunbar, and Ferdinand L. Claiborne, the governor's brother, for the failure of these men to pay the note contracted earlier by Isaac Briggs and his sons Samuel and Joseph as part of an agreement to build some kind of steam engine in Natchez, Mississippi Territory, for Jones.[46] Isaac Briggs, Ellis, Dunbar, and F. L. Claiborne cosigned the note on November 15, 1806. Under the terms of the agreement, the three Briggs men were to pay Jones $505.56 on or before July 1, 1807. If they defaulted

43. To James Madison, October 8, 1804, CLB, 2: 349.

44. The October 10, 1804, issue of the *Télégraphe*, which carried Jones's letter of refusal, has not survived, but Jones's letter was reprinted in the *Union*, October 15, 1804, p. 1, cc. 3–4.

45. The *Union*, October 15, 1804, p. 1, cc. 1–2.

46. The steam engine in question may be the one for which a patent was issued on October 9, 1802, to Samuel Briggs, Jr. The engine was for use in "all kinds of mills—saw mills, sugar mills, cotton gins, grits mills[,] etc." *Télégraphe*, January 25, 1804, p. 3, c. 2.

on the payment, Jones was to be paid almost ten times that amount, or $5,096. Jones initiated legal proceedings in April 1809 to collect the principal due, plus interest and court costs. By late September 1810, he had received $2,024 from Chew and Relf, who were Dunbar's agents in New Orleans.[47]

Jones's association with politically ambitious Daniel Clark and anti-Jeffersonian Edward Livingston suggests that they did seek to establish an opposition party in New Orleans. Jones certainly did not make this move without thought, for he was not the kind of personality who would allow his name to be used lightly. His decisions to participate in preparing the memorial to Congress in 1804, to decline service on the territorial council, and to publish his letter of declination all appear to reflect a point of view and pattern of thought. From one perspective, Jones's actions suggest the concern that businessmen like James Pitot and Daniel Clark exhibited for the governance of New Orleans when they learned of the retrocession of Louisiana to France. From another perspective, Evan's actions suggest his long-established connections from early residence along the Gulf Coast and in Louisiana. For example, his association with Edward Livingston undoubtedly harked back to Evan's association with Philip Livingston, Jr., Edward's oldest brother, nearly a generation earlier in Pensacola. Philip had served as secretary to British West Florida governor Peter Chester and, as had virtually all the early settlers in that province, had been involved with land development.[48]

Much as Evan Jones had a basis for rapport with Edward Livingston, he also had connections with men who had personal reasons to oppose Claiborne. Often these associations had their roots in the mercantile and Federalist-oriented opposition to Claiborne in Mississippi Territory. Noteworthy here was the close cooperation of Jones with John Sargent, the Mississippi territorial governor whom Claiborne severely criticized from the floor of the U.S. House of Representatives, and John Steele, the former secretary of Mississippi Territory who served as acting governor of that territory in the eight months before Claiborne assumed those duties in November 1801.

Steele has been described as Claiborne's "patron & friend in early life." When Claiborne arrived in Natchez, Secretary Steele opened his home to

47. *Evan Jones* v. *Shaw et al.*, Superior Court Case No. 24, December 10, 1804, and *Evan Jones* v. *Isaac Briggs, John Ellis, William Dunbar, and F. L. Claiborne*, Superior Court Case No. 2139, April 17, 1809.

48. Johnson, *British West Florida*, 22, 130, 140.

him, befriending the young man again, until the governor found his own accommodations in the Mississippi Territory. However, relations between the two men gradually deteriorated, reportedly because Steele "occasionally associated with [former] governor Sargent and other gentlemen of federal politics." Claiborne apparently never told Steele that he disapproved of his association with Sargent. Friends of Steele and the territorial secretary himself were led by Claiborne to believe the governor wanted Steele to remain in the secretary's post for another four years. Steele learned this was not true from a friend whom he had written in the U.S. Senate. How Claiborne really felt was revealed to the senator by Madison when he called on the secretary of state to say he was "very happy" to hear that Col. Steele and Governor Claiborne were such good friends that the colonel had accepted appointment again as territorial secretary. Madison expressed surprise at this news, saying to the senator, "'There must be some mistake; we have letters exactly contrary to the colonel's.'"[49] After learning of Claiborne's duplicity, Steele turned against the governor. Before he completed his duties as territorial secretary in May 1802, Steele openly functioned from his office as the leader of opposition to Claiborne in the Mississippi Territory.[50] The irregular correspondence of Jones with Sargent and Steele, before and after Steele's break with Claiborne, reflects their interest in business and political affairs that touched each of them.[51] One other factor that undoubtedly influenced the outlooks of both Jones and Claiborne was the difference in their ages. In 1804, Jones was sixty-five and Claiborne was twenty-nine.

One person who associated with Jones as a friend was General James Wilkinson.[52] Initially, the men probably identified with one another because of their mutual pursuit of business. In time, their relationship appears to have been reinforced by their dislike of Claiborne as well as their feelings of being slighted by the Jefferson administration after being passed over for appointment to preferential office in the acquisition of Louisiana. At one point in 1804, Daniel Clark relied on Evan Jones to convey the message to Wilkinson that he, Clark, had inquired and then "satisfied myself, by an

49. *Louisiana Gazette*, January 25, 1812, p. 2, cc. 3–4.

50. Joseph T. Hatfield, *William Claiborne: Jeffersonian Centurion in the American Southwest* (Lafayette: University of Southwestern Louisiana, 1976), 50.

51. For example, see Jones to Sargent, September 27, 1799, Evan Jones Letter, Miscellaneous Collections, Special Collections, Howard-Tilton Memorial Library, Tulane University.

52. Jones is identified as a "friend of the general" in the Deposition by Daniel Clark to the U.S. House of Representatives, January 11, 1808, in *American State Papers: Miscellaneous*, vol. 2 (Washington: Gales & Seaton, 1834), 112.

inspection of the treasury book for 1804," that, contrary to rumors then circulating in New Orleans, Wilkinson had not been paid ten thousand dollars by the Spanish.[53] Clark's inquiry had been initiated in response to a request from Claiborne made by John Watkins.[54]

Despite the legitimacy of his interests, the opposition of Jones was misguided. The Clark-Livingston-Jones combination, which produced the memorial to Congress in 1804, failed to enlist significant public support.[55] Jones subsequently moved closer to the American community, but the turn events had taken isolated him from Governor Claiborne, thereby precluding any opportunity to build on the insights he had provided Secretary Madison about government in Louisiana.[56] Claiborne continued the commandant-magistrate system of local government employed by the Spanish and, as Jones suggested to Madison, strengthened it by stationing U.S. troops throughout the territorial districts, where they could be called on to enforce the local, oral, civil rulings *(procés verbal)* rendered by the commandant-magistrate.[57] However, in taking these actions Claiborne most likely was adhering to advice given to him by Dr. John Watkins. After Jones published his letter declining to serve on the territorial council, Claiborne would have nothing to do with Jones. Claiborne's reaction to Jones's public refusal to serve in the new territorial government suggests the governor's surprise. The extent of that surprise and the depth of Claiborne's resentment is suggested by the attacks on Jones that followed the publication of Jones's letter.[58] The mixture of politics and personalities did not end there. Early the following year, Claiborne exercised his influence with Jefferson to keep Jones out of the council.[59]

Although Evan Jones held no political office after December 1803, he continued to be active on the social scene and in the business world of New Orleans. His trade in the sale of slaves, sugar, and construction materials ex-

53. Ibid.

54. Ibid.

55. George Dargo, *Jefferson's Louisiana: Politics and the Clash of Legal Traditions* (Cambridge, Mass.: Harvard University Press, 1975), 35–8.

56. On these, see Hints of Evan Jones: Administration of Justice, enclosed in Daniel Clark to the Secretary of State, October 21, 1803, Clarence E. Carter, comp. and ed., *The Territorial Papers of the United States*, vol. 9, *The Territory of Orleans, 1803–1812* (Washington, D.C.: U.S. Government Printing Office, 1940), 83–4 (hereinafter cited as TP, 9:).

57. Insight on Jones's ideas may be seen in ibid.

58. See not only the letter of "Fair Play," but also the communication from "A Louisianian" in the *Union*, October 15, 1804, p. 1, cc. 1–2 and cc. 2–3, respectively, and also "To Mr. Evan Jones Esqr." by "Flagellus" dated October 15, 1804, in ibid., October 20, 1804, p. 1, cc. 1–4, and p. 2, c. 1.

59. Governor Claiborne to the President, November 13, 1805, TP, 9: 525, 526.

panded.[60] The building materials were supplied to, among others, the federal government, which used them to rebuild Fort St. Philip at Plaquemine Turn.[61] In 1804, Evan was one of the incorporators of the Bank of Louisiana and was to have been its president, but declined the position when Claiborne withdrew his support from the project after Jefferson advised the governor that the bank was illegal and a "nullity."[62] A few months later, Claiborne reported that Jones was one of the men trying to revive the bank.[63]

In 1805, Jones was one of the incorporators of Christ Church, the first Protestant Episcopal Church in Louisiana chartered by the territorial council, and a trustee of the University of Orleans.[64] The following year he was nominated for election as territorial delegate to the U.S. House of Representatives. Claiborne believed that Jones would be elected, but Daniel Clark won the seat. Later, Claiborne reported that Jones was quite unhappy about the defeat.[65] By 1807, Jones had established his business on Magazine Street in the Faubourg St. Mary, the developing business section favored by Americans upriver from the old city.[66]

Evan Jones's role in the Burr conspiracy has been nearly lost from view, but an excerpt from Wilkinson's published defense of his actions provides

60. Clark, *New Orleans,* 318; and Sidney A. Marchand, *The Flight of a Century (1800–1900) in Ascension Parish Louisiana* (Donaldsonville, La.: S. A. Marchand, 1936), 23.

61. See the two letters of Abraham D. Abrahams to Secretary of War, dated April 18, 1808, in *Letters Received by the Secretary of War, Registers of Letters Received, 1800–1860,* vol. 4, April 10, 1808–December 31, 1809, entry nos. 29, 30, document F 26, reel 4, record group 107.

62. Ordinance Providing for the Establishment of a Bank, March 12, 1804, CLB, 2: 30, for the bank incorporators; and The President to Governor Claiborne, April 17, 1804; Governor Claiborne to the Secretary of State, April 25, 1804; Governor Claiborne to the President, August 30, 1804; and Governor Claiborne to the Secretary of State, January 1, 1805; TP, 9: 225–6, 232–3, 285, and 361, respectively, on the legality and establishment of the bank.

63. Governor Claiborne to the Secretary of State, January 4, 1805, TP, 9: 362.

64. *Acts Passed at the First Session of the Legislative Council of the Territory of Orleans, Begun and Held at the Principal, in the City of New Orleans, on Monday the Third Day of December, in the Year of Our Lord, One Thousand Eight Hundred and Four, and of the Independence of the United States the Twenty-Ninth* (New Orleans: James M. Bradford, 1805), 307; *Acts Passed at the Second Session of the Legislative Council of the Territory of Orleans, Begun and Held at the Principal, in the City of New Orleans, on Thursday the Twentieth Day of June, in the Year of Our Lord, One Thousand Eight Hundred and Five, and of the Independence of the United States the Twenty-Ninth* (New Orleans: James M. Bradford, 1805), 88; also TP, 9: 1014.

65. To James Madison, May 14, 1806, and To Julien Poidras [*sic*], May 26, 1806, CLB, 3: 298, 314.

66. B[arthélémy] Lafon, *Calendrier de Commerce de la Nouvelle-Orléans, pour l'Année 1807* (New Orleans: Jean Renard, 1806 [*sic*]), unnumbered page.

a revealing glimpse of the depth of Jones's dislike of Claiborne, even with allowances for Wilkinson's exaggeration. Jones is quoted by the general as urging "with all his force and eloquence, to join Burr and aid him in 'pulling down the detestable government under which we live, to make way for a better.'"[67] Wilkinson deliberately left undefined the government about which Jones may have been speaking. However, it seems clear on the basis of Jones's refusal to serve in any capacity in the territorial government that he found the Orleans Territory government established by the Jefferson administration and headed by Claiborne distasteful. Later, in the wake of the revelations surrounding the Burr conspiracy, Jones served as foreman of the grand jury that indicted Judge James Workman and Lewis Kerr for their alleged roles in the Mexican Association's purported invasion of adjacent Spanish territory.[68] After the Bank of the United States opened a branch in New Orleans, Evan served on the board of directors for two years, 1810–1811.[69]

Evan Jones died May 11, 1813, and was buried in the "Protestant burying ground of New Orleans."[70] He was survived by his wife, Marie Verret; one son, Evan; and three daughters, Matilde, Lise, and Celeste. A fourth daughter, Marie Anne, who married Bernard Philippe de Marigny de Mandeville, died in 1808, leaving two sons, Prospere and Gustave.[71] The son named Evan (born November 12, 1785) died on July 3, 1813, less than two months after his father.[72] Matilde was made coexecutrix of her father's estate because of the "especial confidence" that he placed in her "prudence and good sense."[73] Henry McCall married Celeste and Lise in that order, but left no issue from these marriages.[74] Evan's wife died in 1821.[75]

67. James Wilkinson, *Burr's Conspiracy Exposed; and General Wilkinson Vindicated Against the Slanders of His Enemies on That Important Occasion* ([Washington City]: Printed for the Author, 1811), 92 n.

68. Presentments to the Grand Jury Against James Workman and Lewis Kerr, enclosed in Claiborne to Madison, April 21, 1808, CLB, 4: 170–3.

69. Clark, *New Orleans,* 165 n. 3, Table VI following p. 287.

70. Evan Jones Will, 36.

71. Ibid.

72. Hewitt L. Forsyth and various contributors, "Tombstone Inscriptions from New Orleans Cemeteries," *New Orleans Genesis* 1, [no. 2] (March 1962), 188.

73. Evan Jones Will, 36, 39. Evan's brother James died before Evan made out his will in 1810, leaving thirty thousand dollars in money, land, and other property to Evan, along with the guardianship of a slave boy named Jim. Ibid., 37.

74. *Henry McCall Speech, 1899,* Louisiana and Lower Mississippi Valley Collections, Louisiana State University Libraries.

75. Marie Verret, Widow of Evan Jones, Will, Orleans Parish, Louisiana. Court of Probate. Records of Wills, 1805–1837, Will Book, 1817–1824, vol. 3, 210.

JAMES WORKMAN

James Workman (177?–August 1832) has been described as "a man of energy and ideas, [who was] significantly involved in the affairs of his time and place."[1] The element of truth in this characterization is more a description of Workman's aspirations than his accomplishments, because the impact of his career had results other than those he intended. More nearly accurate is the description of Workman by one of his peers as a "man of ability and courage, but lacking in self-restraint."[2] Another contemporary said of Workman, "I am sure that I never beheld a face upon which the signs of inward benevolence and integrity were more impressively stamped."[3] All these personality traits were manifested in Workman's life and his last will.

Before settling in the Orleans Territory, Workman served in the British army and then studied law in England, after which he pursued a career in political journalism in both England and the United States.[4] Because he was born in Ireland, Workman was prohibited by English law from becoming a

1. Charles S. Watson, "A Denunciation on the Stage of Spanish Rule: James Workman's 'Liberty in Louisiana' (1804)," *Louisiana History* 11, no. 3 (summer 1970), 252.

2. "Faithful Picture of the Political Situation of New Orleans at the Close of the Last and the Beginning of the Present Year 1807," ed. James E. Winston, *Louisiana Historical Quarterly* 11, no. 3 (July 1928), 395 n. w-32.

3. Henry S. Foote, *The Bench and Bar of the South and Southwest* (St. Louis: Soule, Thomas & Wentworth, 1876), 195.

4. Workman publicly said he had served in the British army and felt capable of commanding a regiment. See James Workman, *The Trials of the Honb. James Workman, and Col. Lewis Kerr, Before the United States Court, for the Orleans District on a Charge of High Misdemeanor, in Planning and Setting on Foot, Within the United States, An Expedition for the Conquest and Emancipation of Mexico* (New Orleans: Bradford & Anderson, 1807), 30.

solicitor. As a consequence, he did what many other well-educated Irishmen before him had done. He entered the world of commerce. There, he became well trained in the law merchant, that international body of practices and customs rooted in Roman law and continental trading experience.[5]

In territorial Louisiana, his legal training, like that of Lewis Kerr, whom he met after coming to New Orleans, played a key role in the development of Louisiana's legal system. Unfortunately, Workman is not remembered for his positive contributions to Louisiana and American history, but only as an advocate of common law and for championing, at least in their early association, Governor William C. C. Claiborne, who used but apparently never genuinely liked the doughty Irishman.

Most information on the life of James Workman remains shrouded by the unrecorded past. It is known that he was born in Cavan, Ireland, the only son of John Workman. It also is known that when James entered the Middle Temple, London, in June 1789 to study law, his father was deceased.[6] Following his admission to the Middle Temple, nothing more is known of Workman until the spring of 1795. Near the end of May that year, the young man called attention to himself with a privately printed letter in which he supported the argument against England's continuing war with Napoleonic France.[7] It is possible that Workman hoped to further his career with this attention-getting device, because the privately printed letter was one of the techniques used by young men in later eighteenth-century England to get ahead in a profession. Subsequently, someone who read Workman's letter wrote the *Monthly Review* appraising his views and describing him as above party and of "superior abilities."[8]

The views that Workman advocated in his letter were similar to those of the Duke of Portland, the privy councilor in charge of Irish affairs. There

---

5. On Workman's education in law, see H. A. C. Sturgess, comp., *Register of Admissions to the Honourable Society of the Middle Temple from the Fifteenth Century to the Year 1944,* vol. 2 (London: Butterworth, 1949), 405; vol. 3, 158.

Workman's admittance to the Middle Temple suggests that he may have been Protestant. Catholics were not permitted to practice law in England until after Parliament passed the Catholic Relief Act of 1792. See Sidney A. Low and F. S. Pulling, eds., *The Dictionary of English History,* rev. ed. (London: Cassell, 1904), 237.

6. Sturgess, *Register of Admissions,* 3: 158.

7. The letter is reprinted in James Workman, *Political Essays Relative to the War of the French Revolution . . .* (Alexandria, Va.: Cottom & Stewart, 1801), 5–65.

8. *Monthly Review,* 18 (November 1795), 330. Workman's reviewer did not reveal his name. Because Workman often wrote for publication and was the source of most of the information that we know about him, it is possible he was the unknown reviewer.

is no evidence that Workman's letter brought him the support he may have hoped to receive from the duke. On the other hand, the praise Workman received in the pages of the *Monthly Review* may have encouraged him to write a second letter to the duke. Published in January 1797, this letter was an answer to the two public letters of Edmund Burke, the great conservative political journalist, who opposed peace with the French Republic.[9] No reaction to this letter has been found, but it appears to have led to Workman's employment by the *Monthly Review* in 1797–1798. Subsequently, the prospects for Workman apparently dimmed. Sometime in the early spring of 1799 the aspiring political journalist sailed for the United States.[10]

Workman's decision to leave England clearly was related to the political situation between Ireland and Great Britain at that time. Frustrated in their desire for independence by intransigent Englishmen and selfish Irishmen, the nationalist United Irishmen entered into an agreement with France to wrest their freedom from England, precisely the situation Workman had warned Englishmen about in his letter to the Duke of Portland.[11]

The hopes of the United Irishmen died in their crushing defeat by the British at Vinegar Hill, Ireland, in 1798.[12] Thereafter, it was virtually impossible to adhere to a middle position on the Irish question. Because he had opposed the war with France, Workman may have been suspected of being an Irish sympathizer. At the least, his Irish background and public stand on the Irish question cast a shadow on his future in Great Britain. Undoubtedly, it was for these reasons that Workman decided to leave England for the United States sometime early in 1799. Significantly, Workman chose to live in several cities in the recently established United States where the British merchant class influence was still strong and where the Federalists were strongest: Norfolk, Virginia; New York; and Charleston, South Carolina.[13]

9. See Workman, *Political Essays*, 69–141.

10. Workman became a citizen of the United States on May 21, 1804. Marion R. Hemperley, comp., "Federal Naturalization Oaths, Charleston, South Carolina, 1790–1860," *South Carolina Historical Magazine* 66, no. 1 (January 1965), 227. United States immigration laws then required a five-year residence before naturalization, suggesting that Workman most probably arrived in the country in April or May 1799.

11. See Workman, *Political Essays*, 150, 152, 174.

12. J. H. Plumb, *England in the Eighteenth Century (1714–1815)* (Middlesex, England: Penguin Books, 1950), 184–5.

13. On British merchant influence in the very early history of the newly independent United States, particularly South Carolina, see Lisle A. Rose, *Prologue to Democracy: The Federalists in the South, 1789–1800* (Lexington: University of Kentucky Press, 1968), 51, 105–12, 120, 129, 270, 246–7.

Debarking at Norfolk, the young man appears to have used his legal training and writing skill to earn his way along the Atlantic coast from Richmond to Philadelphia and then on to New York before returning to settle briefly in Alexandria, Virginia. In Alexandria the booksellers and stationers Cottom & Stewart printed Workman's first known publication in the United States, his *Political Essays,* which contains his letters of 1795 and 1797.

Political Essays also contains a provocative piece that Workman began writing in the summer of 1799. This essay, titled "A Memorial Proposing a Plan, for the Conquest of Spanish America, by Means which Would Promote the Tranquility of Ireland," has escaped the attention of most writers dealing with early U.S. and Louisiana history, but it is crucial to understanding the circumstances that ensnared Workman and his friend Lewis Kerr in the wake of the Burr conspiracy. Workman's essay unquestionably derived from and was a source of the rumor that had been prevalent for several years in parts of the United States, Great Britain, and Europe that England was considering seizure of Spanish territory in North America.

Workman submitted his elaborately conceived proposal to the British minister of war, Henry Dundas, Viscount Melville, one of the leading advocates of a Spanish American policy for England.[14] Workman's essay was one of a number of similar proposals considered by the British cabinet at the time. Many of them called for military attacks on the southeast (Argentine) and southwest (Chilean) coasts of South America and the West Indies.[15] However, Workman called for the seizure of Spanish territory to begin in North America with the conquest of Louisiana and the Floridas, and for their occupation and settlement by Irish Catholics.[16] This last feature of the plan supposedly would aid the expedition in Spanish America, where only the Catholic Church was legally permissible. New Orleans and Pensacola were to serve as the "Place d'Armes" for the British-backed conquerors, who were to move into South America via the Caribbean possessions of Spain.[17]

There were several objectives inherent in Workman's scheme. First, he

---

14. The essay was submitted to Dundas in the summer of 1800 after Workman arrived in the United States, which suggests he had not completely given up hope of attaining a better position for himself in England. See Workman, *Political Essays,* 147.

15. See John Lynch, "British Policy and Spanish America, 1783–1808," *Journal of Latin American Studies* 1 (1969), 11–3.

16. Workman, *Political Essays,* 157–9.

17. Ibid., 156, 163, 174.

sought to "completely cure" Great Britain's "only dangerous wound," Ireland, by drawing away the nearly 100,000 disgruntled and professionally trained Irish soldiers involved in the insurrection there in the 1790s. Second, he wanted to place Britain's "wealth and power on a foundation which no combination of enemies could shake, and which time itself could hardly destroy." Third, he wished to replace other cultural traditions with Anglo-Saxon ones. Specifically, Workman wanted British common law introduced wherever conquests were made.[18] Workman submitted his proposal to Dundas in the summer of 1800, but by then the British cabinet had determined that the Mediterranean was, for the present, of greater importance to British interests than Spanish colonial possessions in the Western Hemisphere.[19]

The British government's rejection of any adventures in colonial Spanish America apparently ended any hope Workman may have harbored for career advancement in Great Britain. However, this did not end the itinerant career of the *Political Essays*. In 1801 Workman sent a copy of his *Political Essays* to President Jefferson with a cover letter urging the president to take Louisiana and the Floridas from Spain before France seized them.[20] Although he was misguided in this approach to Jefferson, Workman's decision to send his essays to the president also may have been influenced by the expansionist sentiment prevalent in the South, particularly among Federalists in western Georgia, the Carolinas, and the trans-Appalachian West.[21] The cool reception that Jefferson gave Workman's proposal is suggested by the lack of any evidence that the president ever acknowledged receipt of the *Political Essays*.

Ironically, after being rejected by the British and shunned by Jefferson,

18. Ibid., 156.

19. Lynch, "British Policy and Spanish America, 1783–1808," 14.

20. Workman's submission of his scheme to Jefferson is noted in Watson, "Denunciation," 249.

21. Thomas P. Abernethy, *From Frontier to Plantation in Tennessee: A Study in Frontier Democracy* (Chapel Hill: University of North Carolina Press, 1932), 89, 113–4, 142–3, 164–7, points out the Federalist strength in frontier Tennessee centered on the need to defend the settlers from Indian attacks sponsored by the Spanish in Florida and Louisiana. Lisle A. Rose, *Prologue to Democracy: The Federalists in the South, 1789–1800* (Ann Arbor, Mich.: University Microfilms, 1972), 13–4, says this also was true of the frontiers of western Georgia and both Carolinas. In the published version of his dissertation, which incorporates additional material, Rose emphasizes that by 1800 the elitist Federalists in Virginia and the Carolinas had begun to give way to Republican doctrines of equality and democracy. Rose states that by 1800 they had "abandoned their political positions and either joined with the Republicans or withdrew from public life." Rose, *Prologue to Democracy,* 288.

Workman's "Memorial" became the source of the Marqués de Casa Calvo's schemes to colonize Texas lands claimed by the United States as part of the Louisiana Purchase.[22] Perhaps the greatest irony of the plan advanced in the "Memorial" is that its ideas appear to have become, without ever being named, the basis for General Wilkinson's indictment of Workman and Kerr for conspiracy in the train of the Burr conspiracy.

The influence of Southern Federalist views on Workman may have been greater than is apparent. About the time *Political Essays* was published, Workman moved to Charleston, South Carolina, the seedbed of a number of plans in the 1790s to seize Louisiana and the Floridas.[23] He was friendly with Stephen C. Carpenter, another Irish expatriate, who arrived in Charleston shortly after Workman. A journalist by trade, Carpenter intended to establish a newspaper, but gave up the idea when Loring Andrews, a transplanted New Englander, established the pro-Federalist Charleston *Courier* in January 1803.[24] Although his name was not listed in the *Courier*, Carpenter apparently was employed by Andrews in an editorial capacity before he became one of the newspaper's owners in early September 1805.[25]

22. Casa Calvo's scheme to colonize lands claimed by the United States in the Louisiana Purchase territory was little more than a copy of the colonization plan set forth by Workman in his "Memorial." See Casa Calvo to Miguel Cayetno Soler, March 20, 1805, *Archivo General de Indias, Papeles de Cuba, legajo* 179-B (hereinafter *Archivo General de Indias* will be referred to as AGI). See also the Casa Calvo biographical sketch, particularly n. 13. It is quite likely the marqués obtained a copy of the *Political Essays* in New Orleans, perhaps from Workman. A complete copy of the 1801 publication was advertised for sale for seventy-five cents in the *Moniteur de la Louisiane*, April 11, 1807, p. 1, cc. 3–4.

23. On these, see Francis S. Philbrick, *The Rise of the West, 1754–1830* (New York: Harper & Row, 1966), particularly pp. 184–205. Rumors of a possible attempt by Americans from the Carolinas and Georgia to seize New Orleans in 1792 caused the then governor of Louisiana, the Baron de Carondelet, to surround the town of New Orleans with a ditch and a palisade connecting it to the Mississippi, from which he could divert water. The dirt from the ditch was used to form a parapet around the town. In addition, Carondelet built five bastions from which the curtain walls erected behind the parapets could be defended. Samuel Wilson, Jr., *The Vieux Carré, New Orleans: Its Plan, Its Growth, Its Architecture* (New Orleans: Bureau of Governmental Research, December 1968), 45–6.

24. On Carpenter, see *Dictionary of American Biography*, s.v. "Carpenter, Stephen Cullen, d. 1820"; and A. S. Salley, Jr., comp. and ed., *Marriage Notices in [the] Charleston Courier, 1803–1808* (Columbia: State Company for the Historical Commission of South Carolina, 1919), 5.

25. On Carpenter's affiliation with the *Charleston Courier*, see Clarence S. Brigham, *History and Bibliography of American Newspapers, 1690–1820*, vol. 2 (1961; Westport, Conn.: Greenwood Press, 1976), 1029. See also Charles S. Watson, "Stephen Cullen Carpenter, First

Through his contacts with Carpenter and his reputation as a writer, Workman may have supplemented his income as a writer for the *Courier*.[26]

While living in Charleston, Workman moved closer to attaining the influence in government that he had sought earlier. In the spring of 1804 his stage play *Liberty in Louisiana* opened in Charleston. Later in the year it was performed in New York and Philadelphia.[27] The play apparently grew out of an essay on political conditions in Louisiana that Workman had been writing, but abandoned for the more dramatic play form when it became known that the United States had bought Louisiana from France. Rich in metaphor and reminiscent of Richard B. Sheridan's style of comedy, Workman's play depicted Liberty as a young maiden who suffered from injustices inflicted on her through Spanish colonial rule, specifically the corrupt administration of justice. She was saved from further wrongs by the timely arrival of U.S. law, which accompanied the acquisition of Louisiana.[28] Reflecting his own political tendencies, the influence of the Southern Federalist circles in which he moved, and possibly the effects of the rebuff from Jefferson in 1801, Workman dedicated his play to John Marshall, the high Federalist chief justice of the U.S. Supreme Court.[29]

The previously published *Memorial* and Workman's play defined him, in the eyes of the few who then and later evaluated his life and career, as an Anglophile and champion of common law over civil law. Sometime after his play closed in Charleston, Workman moved to New Orleans, perhaps as a result of friendship with Dr. John Watkins, a native of Virginia who was rising to prominence in the territorial government of the Orleans Territory.[30]

Drama Critic of the Charleston *Courier*," *South Carolina Historical Magazine* 69, no. 4 (October 1968), 243–52.

26. Watson, "Denunciation," 247.

27. Ibid.

28. Ibid., 252–7, 258.

29. Ibid., 257 n. 40. See also Watson, "Stephen Cullen Carpenter," 249, in which that author says the "Federalist viewpoint pervades the comedy." On Marshall's Federalist views, see Robert Kenneth Faulkner, *The Jurisprudence of John Marshall* (Princeton, N.J.: Princeton University Press, 1968), 8–9, 18–22, 166–9, 173–85; and Leonard Baker, *John Marshall: A Life in Law* (New York: Macmillan, 1974), 13, 46, 94, 107–8, 109, 119, 127–36, 160–2, 166–9, 186–9, 195–6, 588–604, 626, 648, 689–90. A succinct and useful overview of the life and career of Marshall is in the *Encyclopedia of Southern Culture*, s.v. "Marshall, John."

30. Watkins served as clerk in Governor Claiborne's office "during the temporary govt." See Letter No. 202, W. C. C. Claiborne Disbursements During Temporary Government, Third Quarter 1804, undated, entry 6, and the John Watkins biographical sketch, n. 66.

Workman arrived in New Orleans sometime in the spring of 1804.[31] Whether he had been practicing law before settling in Louisiana is not known, but in New Orleans Workman soon became a force in shaping Louisiana's legal system because of both his knowledge of law and his writing ability. In September and October 1804, he was employed as a clerk, that is, secretary, in Governor Claiborne's office.[32] In December of the same year, he was appointed secretary to the territorial legislative council on the recommendation of John Watkins.[33] It was in the latter capacity, Workman said, that the council asked him to draft the two acts that brought criminal law in the Orleans Territory into conformance with the laws of the United States. Despite numerous subsequent attempts to rewrite Louisiana's criminal code, Workman's 1805 draft of the law with Louis Casimir Elisabeth Moreau Lislet remained the state's basic criminal code until 1942.[34]

During the fall of 1804 Workman defended Claiborne against the attacks made on him by Pierre Derbigny in the *Esquisse de la Situation Politique;* in doing so he also elucidated his views on civil law in general and Spanish law in particular.[35] Although Workman dealt with all the subjects touched on in the *Esquisse,* when he addressed the subject of the Spanish laws in

31. In a letter dated March 28, 1807, Workman stated that he then had been in New Orleans for almost three years. See James Workman, *Essays and Letters on Various Political Subjects,* 2nd American ed. (New York: I. Riley, 1809), 112.

32. See Letter No. 202, entry 5, W. C. C. Claiborne Disbursements During Temporary Government, Third Quarter 1804, undated; and Letter No. 200, entry 5, W. C. C. Claiborne Disbursements During Temporary Government, Fourth Quarter, undated, respectively.

33. Workman, *Essays and Letters,* 115–6.

34. In an 1835 letter to Adrien-Emmanuel Rouquette, who was then in Paris and considering a career in law, Edward Livingston advised the young man, "the ground work," meaning the origins of Louisiana law, which Rouquette was seeking, began with "a law passed in 1805." In the next sentence, without mentioning Workman by name, but to make his meaning absolutely clear, Livingston went on to say, "The first and most important of these laws (1805) enumerates the offences and annexes the penalties. But for the definitions and modes of proceeding, refer to the common law of England." Rouquette became famous later in Louisiana history for his work among the Choctaw Indians as *Père* Rouquette. Dagmar R. LeBreton and Mitchell Franklin, "Bench and Bar: A Late Letter by Edward Livingston on the Criminal Code of Louisiana," *Tulane Law Review* 17, no. 2 (November 1942), 286.

35. [Pierre Derbigny], *Esquisse de la Situaton Politique et Civile de la Louisianae, depuis le 30 novembre, 1803, jusqu'au 1er octobre 1804. Par un Louisianais* (New Orleans: de l'Imprimerie du Telegraphe, 1804). Derbigny also had been employed as interpreter in Governor Claiborne's office during the months of July, August, and September 1804. See Letter No. 202, W. C. C. Claiborne Disbursements During Temporary Government, Third Quarter 1804, undated, entry nos. 1 and 3.

force in Louisiana, he said they were "generally excellent in themselves; for they are founded on the Roman Code, one of the most perfect and elegant systems of jurisprudence ever promulgated to the world." The precepts of the Roman Code, he said, were the maxims of the law of nature applied to civil society. Only the manner in which the Spanish enforced the law, Workman said, was objectionable. This had been the message of Workman's play *Liberty in Louisiana.* Unfortunately, Workman chose to say these things in the *Mississippi Messenger,* a Natchez, Mississippi, newspaper, under the fictitious name of "Laelius."[36] Most later writers have not been aware of the balanced scope of Workman's understanding of both civil and common law because the early writers of Louisiana history have portrayed the political events of the early years of the state as a Gallic victory over Anglo-Saxon culture. From the vantage point of the late twentieth century it is clear Workman's 1805 work melding common and civil law was a bridgehead to future law in Louisiana.[37] The importance of Workman's 1805 law became apparent in the spring of 1806 when Claiborne vetoed an attempt by the wealthy planter element in the territorial legislature to create and force on the Orleans Territory a system of sixth-century Roman law and Spanish law from the Middle Ages.[38]

While serving as secretary to the legislative council in the fall of 1804 Workman also was called on to draft the laws that provided for establishment of libraries and the University of Orleans, the ambitious title given to the system of education created in the Orleans Territory. Subsequently, he was appointed one of the regents of the University of Orleans and a trustee

36. Isaac Briggs identified Workman as "Laelius" in his February 9, 1805, letter to Jefferson. George Dargo, *Jefferson's Louisiana: Politics and the Clash of Legal Traditions* (Cambridge, Mass.: Harvard University Press, 1975), 123–4, particularly nn. 74 and 75. Dargo provides great insight onto Workman's thought and his position in the development of law in Louisiana.

37. Respected Louisiana Judge Douglas Gonzales of the Baton Rouge First Circuit Court of Appeal said in 1994, " 'Generally, [the laws of] Louisiana and other states are moving together,' " so much that the original distinction between civil law and common law is disappearing. Judge Gonzales went on to say in this interview that most of the states of the United States are moving toward codification of all their laws. See *Directory '94, Special Edition, The (Baton Rouge) Advocate,* September 6, 1994, p. 26.

38. Mitchell Franklin explores the antirevolutionary French and anti-American origins of the proffered legislation, which Claiborne vetoed on May 26, 1806, in his essay, "The Eighteenth *Brumaire* in Louisiana: Talleyrand and the Spanish Medieval Legal System of 1806," *Tulane Law Review* 16, no. 4 (June 1942), 514–61. An overview of the 1805 law is provided in Dargo, *Jefferson's Louisiana,* 136–7. Dargo's study has done much to establish a more balanced view of all the legal and political issues of territorial Louisiana.

of the New Orleans Library Society.[39] In addition, Workman rewrote the two bills that had been drafted by Edward Livingston for the improvement of inland navigation in the territory. Under Workman's pen, the two pieces of legislation became one. This was done, he said, at the request and on the instructions of another council member, George Pollock.[40] During this same period, Workman's Protestant background again was suggested. In June 1805, he was named to a committee charged with the responsibility for establishing the Episcopal church in New Orleans.[41]

Workman not only worked for Claiborne, but he also was close to the governor politically. Isaac Briggs, surveyor-general for the Mississippi Territory, wrote Jefferson early in 1805 that Workman defended Claiborne under the pen names of "Projector" and "Laelius."[42] Shortly after Claiborne and Workman became alienated, a writer known only as "Libertas" described Claiborne as Workman's benefactor.[43] Claiborne certainly recognized and used Workman's valuable legal training and writing skills when he appointed the Irishman as secretary in his office in the fall of 1804 and as judge in Orleans County (the geographical entity that was New Orleans and later became Orleans Parish) in May 1805.[44] In the latter position, Workman also served as judge of the court of probate for the territory.[45] What held these two men in brief lawyerly alliance was the shared belief that Latin Louisiana, with its civil law base, could be joined to the United States and its Anglo-Saxon heritage through uniformity of law. To both

39. *Acts Passed at the First Session of the Legislative Council of the Territory of Orleans, Begun and Held at the Principal, in the City of New Orleans, On Monday the Third Day of December, in the Year of Our Lord, One Thousand Eight Hundred and Four, and of the Independence of the United States the Twenty-Ninth* (New Orleans: James M. Bradford, 1805), 306; and Roger P. McCutcheon, "Libraries in New Orleans, 1771–1833," *Louisiana Historical Quarterly* 20, no. 1 (January 1937), 153.

40. Workman, *Essays and Letters,* 115–6.

41. *New Orleans Louisiana Gazette,* June 4, 1805, p. 2, c. 4.

42. Clarence E. Carter, comp. and ed., *The Territorial Papers of the United States,* vol. 5, *The Territory of Mississippi, 1798–1817* (Washington, D.C.: U.S. Government Printing Office, 1937), Isaac Briggs to the President, February 2, 1805, 382.

43. *New Orleans Louisiana Gazette,* April 14, 1807, p. 3, c. 3.

44. For Workman's appointment as judge, see Register of Civil Appointments in the Territory of Orleans, February 13, 1806, Judges, Clarence E. Carter, comp. and ed., *The Territorial Papers of the United States,* vol. 9, *The Territory of Orleans, 1803–1812* (Washington, D.C.: U.S. Government Printing Office, 1940), 598 (hereinafter cited as TP, 9 with page range).

45. Workman, *Essays and Letters,* 122.

men, this initially meant a change in the substance and procedure of the law in Louisiana.[46]

Despite the prestigious positions Workman held with the executive, legislative, and judicial branches of the territorial government, there are indications that his course was not always easy. In the spring of 1806 he brought suit against George W. Morgan, treasurer of Orleans Territory, for five hundred dollars, the amount Workman claimed was owed him for service as secretary to the legislative council from December 4, 1804, to November 5, 1805. Workman supported his claim with a certificate from Julien Poydras, president of the first legislative council, and the January 26, 1805, territorial law that confirmed his appointment. However, Morgan declined to pay the claim on the grounds that Congress stipulated the date of dissolution of the legislative council was four months earlier, on July 4, 1805.[47] The difficulty Workman encountered with Treasurer Morgan was an omen of greater troubles to come.

The revelation by General James Wilkinson of Aaron Burr's vaguely defined intentions in the fall of 1806 was followed by the rumor that the former vice president of the United States had enlisted the support of a locally organized paramilitary group in his project.[48] Although not widely known, the members and purposes of this group, known as the Mexican Association, were generally public knowledge. They were, or had been, depending on whose statements are accepted, preparing for the war expected throughout much of the old Southwest in 1805 and 1806 between the United States

46. Dargo, *Jefferson's Louisiana*, 124, 168–9.

47. *James Workman v. G. W. Morgan*, Superior Court Case No. 1228, May 5 [, 1806 ?]. The council had authorized payment of four hundred dollars to Workman on May 4, 1805, "as compensation for his extra services." See *Acts Passed at the Second Session of the Legislative Council of the Territory of Orleans, Begun and Held at the Principal, in the City of New Orleans, on Thursday the Twentieth Day of June, in the Year of Our Lord, One Thousand Eight Hundred and Five, and of the Independence of the United States the Twenty-Ninth* (New Orleans: James M. Bradford, 1805), 410.

48. See the decoded letter to Wilkinson, which the general claimed triggered all his actions, in Henry Adams, *History of the United States of America During the Second Administration of Thomas Jefferson*, vol. 1 (New York: Charles Scribner's Sons, 1890), 252–4; and To James Madison, November 25, December 5, and December 9, 1806; Important Statement, Private, December 1, 1806; and To Governors, December 5, 1806; all in *Official Letter Books of W. C. C. Claiborne, 1801–1816*, ed. Dunbar Rowland, vol. 4 (1917; New York: AMS Press, 1972), 37–8, 42–4, and 52; 38; and 42, respectively (hereinafter cited as CLB with volume and page range).

and Spain. During the anticipated war the members of the association were to liberate the Spanish colonies bordering the United States and along the Gulf of Mexico, including the Floridas, Texas, and Mexico. Hence, the name Mexican Association.[49] The origin of the group, some of its members later declared, lay in the bellicose message that President Jefferson delivered to Congress early in December 1805; the unstable political and military atmosphere that had permeated New Orleans since the acquisition of Louisiana in the fall of 1803; and the lack of military preparedness of the United States in general and territorial Louisiana in particular.

Jefferson's early December 1805 message was the most warlike that he had sent to Congress. Without specifying whether his concern was for infringement of U.S. rights by Great Britain, France, or Spain, the president called for the strengthening of harbor defenses, reorganization of the militia, and augmentation of the navy.[50] In New Orleans about a dozen of the territory's leading citizens, among them James Workman and Lewis Kerr, reacted as Daniel Clark and others had in November 1803 before the transfer of Louisiana to the United States. They organized the volunteer Mexican Association. Ultimately, the association numbered as many as three hundred members and, much like the earlier "Volunteer association," began to function extralegally and in a semisecret fashion.[51] This tactic paralleled the local action in November 1803 when the "Volunteer association . . . of the most respectable people" was organized out of fear that Spanish unwillingness to surrender Louisiana to the French might erupt in public disorder. In November and December 1803, before American troops arrived, members

49. Secretary Graham to the Secretary of State, January 2, 1805 [1806], TP, 9: 554–5; and To James Madison December 5 and 9, 1806, CLB, 4: 42–4 and 51–2, respectively.

50. Dumas Malone, *Jefferson and His Time*, vol. 5, *Jefferson the President, Second Term, 1805–1809* (Boston: Little, Brown, 1974), 69–70.

51. Secretary Graham to the Secretary of State, January 2, 1805 [1806], TP, 9: 554, alluded to "about three hundred and fifty men other than French, Spanish or natives" on whom the territory could rely to defend itself. In his February 1807 testimony, John Watkins spoke of three hundred members in the Mexican Association. See Workman, *Trials,* 74. Workman and Kerr are identified as leaders in organizing the Mexican Association in 1805–06 by Thomas P. Abernethy, *The Burr Conspiracy* (New York: Oxford University Press, 1954), 25. See also Samuel H. Wandell and Meade Minnigerode, *Aaron Burr, A Biography Written, in Large Part, from Original and Hitherto Unused Material,* vol. 2 (New York: G. P. Putnam's Sons, 1925), 124–7. A company of men at this time consisted of approximately one hundred enlisted men and officers. Additional perspective on this question can be found in Winston, "Faithful Picture," 359–433. See also the "Mexican Association/Associates" essay in this appendix.

of the "Volunteer association" actually patrolled the streets for approximately three weeks.[52] The 1803 volunteers became the nucleus of the militia provided for in 1805 by the Orleans territorial council.[53]

Official provision for the territorial militia ended the need for expedient arrangements, but the failure to get the official militia organized and ready to defend the territory provided the vacuum in which the Mexican Association continued its shadowy existence. Perhaps the greatest reason for the continued life of the Mexican Association, a number of whose members were officers in the official militia, was the conduct of Joseph Deville Degoutin Bellechasse. A former commander of the volunteer militia and the highest ranking officer in the organization, Bellechasse was known to be obligated to Daniel Clark, who was becoming increasingly estranged from Governor Claiborne. In addition, Bellechasse was reputed to have said he would never take up arms against Spain or France.[54] Given the unstable political situation in New Orleans for several years after acquisition of the Louisiana Purchase, the inadequate defenses of the Orleans Territory, and Workman's well-known opinions, it is not surprising that he continued to support Daniel Clark and other public officials and businessmen in the formation of the Mexican Association, if only for protective covering. It also is possible that Workman and Kerr, with the governor's tacit approval, sought to keep a check on Clark on behalf of Claiborne.

52. [Arthur P. Whitaker, ed.,] "Another Dispatch from the United States Consulate in New Orleans," *American Historical Review* 38, no. 2 (January 1933), 291–2, prints Daniel Clark's December 3, 1803, letter to Madison in which he tells of the public tension in New Orleans and of the 180 American men and their friends who spontaneously decided to organize the "Volunteer association" in November 1803. For additional perspective on the issue see [Arthur P. Whitaker, ed.,] "Despatches from the United States Consulate in New Orleans, 1801–1803, II," ibid., 33, no. 2 (January 1928), 355–6, particularly n. 43 on the latter page. See also John W. Monette, *History of the Discovery and Settlement of the Valley of the Mississippi, by the Three Great Powers, Spain, France, and Great Britain, and Subsequent Occupation, Settlement and Extension of Civil Government by the United States, Until the Year 1846*, vol. 1 (1846; New York: Arno Press, 1971), 561. Claiborne to Madison, October 16, 1804, CLB, 2: 353–4, tells of the organization of "several Companies" of the "Volunteer Corps" by "the Citizens of the United States, residing" in New Orleans prior to his arrival and his acceptance of their offer to be of service during the transition of governments.

53. To James Madison, December 27, 1803, CLB, 1: 313–4, 339, and October 16, 1804, ibid., 2: 354.

54. Jack D. L. Holmes, "Three Early Memphis Commandants: Beauregard, Deville Degoutin, and Folch," *West Tennessee Historical Society Papers*, 18 (1964), 34, cites evidence that such assurances were given to the Spanish government for Bellechasse on May 12, 1806. One year earlier, Claiborne had described Bellechasse to Secretary of War Dearborn as lacking independence. (Private) To Henry Dearborne [sic], CLB, 3: 320.

The affable relationship between Claiborne and Workman collapsed in the "reign of terror"—military arrests, illegal abductions, and defiance of court orders—conducted by General Wilkinson for about a month beginning in mid-December 1806 after revelation of the Burr conspiracy.[55] Workman, like other vocal members of the Mexican Association, advocated upholding U.S. law and protection of citizen's rights in opposition to the actions of General Wilkinson. Workman went so far as to appeal publicly to Claiborne on January 5, 1807, to act on the words he often had uttered in private conversations about safeguarding individual rights.[56] However, the governor would not take any decisive action. He refused to issue the proclamation of martial law requested by Wilkinson in December 1806 and January 1807, or to support those men who were directly and adversely affected by Wilkinson's actions.[57] Although Workman regarded the impasse as a complete collapse of law, he apparently hoped that Claiborne might yet be pressured into action. As a consequence, he notified the governor on January 12, 1807, that he was closing his court.[58] Workman also revealed that his next step would be to appeal to the territorial legislature, which convened on the same date.

The threat to rally overt opposition to Wilkinson undoubtedly led to Judge Workman's arrest two days later.[59] On orders issued by Wilkinson, both Workman and Lewis Kerr were seized by a detachment of U.S. Army dragoons and marched through the streets of New Orleans to spend the night in jail. The charge against both men was the high misdemeanor of conspiracy, independent of whatever plans Burr may have had. Sounding very much as though he had been apprized of Workman's Memorial for the

55. Events manipulated by Wilkinson in October and November 1806, while at Natchitoches and before he arrived in New Orleans, are clearly traced by Milton Lomask in his study *Aaron Burr: The Conspiracy and Years of Exile, 1805–1836*, vol. 2 (New York: Farrar, Straus, Giroux, 1982), 163–74. Wilkinson's actions in New Orleans are set forth on pp. 182–5 of this study.

56. Workman, *Essays and Letters*, 120–2.

57. Wilkinson's requests for martial law are in From James Wilkinson, December 6, 1806; From James Wilkinson, December 7, 1806; and From James Wilkinson, December 15, 1806; all in CLB, 4: 46, 49, and 58. Claiborne's responses are in To James Wilkinson, December 8, 1806, and [To] Genl. Wilkinson, December 17, 1806, both in ibid., 4: 49–50 and 63–5.

58. Workman, *Essays and Letters*, 119–20.

59. See Wilkinson to Secretary of War, January 10, 1807, *Letters Received by the Secretary of War, Unregistered Series, 1789–1860. Records of the Office of the Secretary of War*, document F-25, microcopy 222, reel N-2, 1805–1807; and From James Wilkinson, January 14, 1807, CLB, 4: 95.

conquest and emancipation of Spanish America, Wilkinson arrested Workman and Kerr for planning to seize Mobile, Pensacola, and Mexico, and for planning to revolutionize the Territory of Orleans. This was the charge returned by the grand jury convened earlier on the request of Wilkinson.[60]

Without revealing his own role in any of the events, Wilkinson obtained the information he used to arrest Workman from Lieutenant Colonel Constant Freeman, commander of all U.S. military forces in New Orleans and second in command under General Wilkinson. Freeman's revelations came from two interviews of Judge Workman in December 1806. The judge freely shared his views on the innocent character of the Mexican Association during a visit with Freeman "on a court martial matter" of interest to the two men. On the request of Freeman, Workman allowed him to communicate the substance of his remarks to Wilkinson.[61] It also appears that the arrests of Workman and Kerr owed much to Abner L. Duncan, whom General Wilkinson retained as his counsel prior to the "reign of terror." Duncan "urged the General, repeatedly," to seize all suspects and to declare "martial law" in the city.[62]

In spite of the excessive show of force used to arrest him and the humiliation to which he was subjected, Workman continued to oppose the courses pursued by Wilkinson and Claiborne. Four days after his arrest, the judge indicated his rejection of the authority of both Wilkinson and Claiborne by notifying the territorial legislature that he was closing his court.[63] On February 11, while his trial was in progress, Workman publicly rebuked Claiborne, saying that the governor was to blame for the unlawful arrests in the territory.[64] Before his retrial on the misdemeanor charge, Workman relinquished his judicial duties in disgust.[65]

---

60. Workman, *Essays and Letters,* 125–6. See also Marietta Marie LeBreton, *History of the Territory of Orleans, 1803–1812* (Ann Arbor, Mich.: University Microfilms, 1973), 427 n. 60.

61. Wandell and Minnigerode, *Aaron Burr,* 2: 124–5.

62. "Affidavit of A. L. Duncan esq.," in James Wilkinson, *Memoirs of My Own Times,* vol. 3 (1816; New York: AMS Press, 1973), 332–3.

63. Workman, *Essays and Letters,* 142.

64. Workman's January and February letters to Claiborne were all printed in the *Louisiana Gazette* and read into the record of the lower chamber of the territorial legislature. They also were published in pamphlet form. See James Workman, *A Letter to the Respectable Citizens, Inhabitants of the County of Orleans, Together with Several Letters to His Excellency Governor Claiborne, and Other Documents Relative to the Extraordinary Measures Lately Pursued in this Territory* (New Orleans: Bradford & Anderson, 1807).

65. Workman, *Essays and Letters,* 148.

Workman had strong support in the territorial house of representatives among American delegates, particularly from John Watkins, who was then Speaker of the house and mayor of New Orleans. However, it is doubtful that anything Watkins or Workman might have done would have moved Claiborne to support opposition to Wilkinson. The governor and the general were not personally close, and Claiborne continued to have doubts about the general's loyalty,[66] but the linchpin in Wilkinson's support was not Claiborne. It was President Jefferson. The president placed no restraints on Wilkinson because of his concern that whatever Burr was doing was illegal.[67] Toward Workman, Jefferson had little sympathy and quickly perceived political motives in the judge's actions. The important facts to Jefferson were that Workman was "known to be one of the Mexican league" and had used his office as judge "to liberate his accomplices." In short, Workman had acted from political motives and was irresponsible.[68] Claiborne also was held in check by the knowledge that Secretary of War Dearborn was a strong supporter of General Wilkinson.[69] A contemporary of Workman later characterized the judge as one of Burr's "most trusted associates."[70] Because Workman's opinions of the Spanish and their administration of justice was well known, it is quite likely this characterization of the judge says more about the desperate and opportunistic Burr than it does about Workman.

Workman's defense against the charge of conspiracy paralleled that of Lewis Kerr. Workman admitted having thought about leading an expedition against the Spanish in the Floridas and Mexico, but stated that he had not

66. On Workman's support in the territorial legislature, see Dargo, *Jefferson's Louisiana,* 58, 59. On Claiborne's continuing distrust of Wilkinson, see Vicente Folch y Juan's February 17, 1808, negative response to Claiborne's inquiries about Wilkinson's secret connection with Spanish officials from the time of the governorship of Estevan Miró in AGI, *Papeles de Cuba, legajo* 144.

67. See Jefferson's November 27, 1806, proclamation in James D. Richardson, ed., *A Compilation of the Messages and Papers of the Presidents, 1789–1897,* vol. 1 (Washington, D.C.: Government Printing Office, 1896), 404–5.

68. Dargo, *Jefferson's Louisiana,* 202–3 n. 41, quoting Jefferson to Joseph C. Cabell, March 18, 1807, Jefferson Papers, University of Virginia Collection. Workman, on application from Lewis Kerr, ordered the release of Peter Ogden and Samuel Swartout, who had been arrested at Fort Adams, Mississippi Territory, on orders from General Wilkinson.

69. See Andrew Jackson to Henry Dearborn, March 17, 1807, in John Spencer Bassett, ed., *The Correspondence of Andrew Jackson,* vol. 1 (Washington, D.C.: Carnegie Institution of Washington, 1927), 173.

70. Foote, *Bench and Bar,* 195.

violated any laws because he made no attempt to prepare an expedition against the neighboring Spanish provinces. The idea occurred to him, he said, in the weeks following President Jefferson's belligerent message to Congress in early December 1805. As Kerr had done, Workman also argued that politics was not tantamount to treason and that political societies were not illegal. In comparison to Kerr's defense, however, Workman's was rambling and argumentative, raising more questions than it resolved. Where Kerr persuasively depicted himself as one of the victims caught in the events manipulated by General Wilkinson with the indulgence of Governor Claiborne, Workman pugnaciously depicted himself as the foremost victim.[71] Neither Workman nor Kerr was acquitted on the merits of these defenses, but rather on the testimony of Joseph Thomas, a prominent New Orleans merchant and acquaintance of Kerr. Called as a witness during the retrial, Thomas testified that Lieutenant Francis W. Small, whose secret testimony had led to the arrests and trials of Workman and Kerr, had been arrested and confined by General Wilkinson until Small revealed the names of the men who had discussed with him vague schemes to invade the nearby Spanish colonies.[72]

Workman was acquitted of the charge of conspiracy, but his career continued to suffer, partly because he had fallen from favor with the Claiborne administration and partly because of his fighter's spirit. The former judge's presence in New Orleans appears to have made Claiborne nervous, particularly when the governor learned that Workman was one of the founders of a new weekly newspaper, *La Lanterne Magique* (the *Magic Lantern*). In mid-March 1808, Claiborne wrote Secretary Madison that Workman was among the "Society of 'Choice Spirits'" who were to publish the paper, even though the newspaper carried the names of Johnson and Ravenscraft as publishers.[73] Claiborne also named Lewis Kerr as one of the backers, saying that all of them were "distinguished for [their] friendly dispositions toward the 'would be Emperor,'" Aaron Burr. The purpose in founding the newspaper, Claiborne believed, was to deprecate "every friend of Government" in the territory, particularly the governor.[74]

A number of issues of the *Magic Lantern* did appear in the spring and

71. Workman, *Trials*, 161–4.

72. Ibid., 12–5, 101, 106, 126–7. A brief story about the verdict, reprinted from the *Orleans Gazette*, was carried in the *Louisiana Gazette*, March 10, 1807, p. 3, c. 2.

73. To James Madison, March 17, 1808, CLB, 4: 167; and Brigham, *History and Bibliography of American Newspapers*, 1: 186.

74. To James Madison, March 17, 1808, CLB, 4: 167–8.

fall of 1808, and a few more appeared early in 1809 before the newspaper ceased publication. An editorial in one of the 1808 issues reported that the paper halted publication because of the "dearth of amusing matter. . . . Scarcely had three of our numbers made their appearance, when the legislature, as if to spite us, adjourned *sine die.*"[75] Workman's involvement with a floundering weekly newspaper probably did not trouble Claiborne and the Jefferson administration as much as the possibility that the former judge might somehow obtain a position of political importance in the territory. Such an opportunity presented itself to Workman in the summer of 1808.

Through circumstances beyond the control of Workman, he was offered temporary appointment to the vacant post of territorial attorney general. The office became vacant when the appointee, William Thomson, declined the position and his deputy, Abner Duncan, was kept from performing the duties by illness. At this point, Judge Louis Moreau Lislet, one of Workman's former associates on the bench, tried to appoint Workman attorney general pro tempore.[76] As a territorial judge, Moreau Lislet had no authority to make the appointment. That he tried to do so was acknowledgment of Workman's training in law as well as his balanced judgment regarding civil law and common law. In the eyes of both men, the question of what law was to govern Louisiana must have been regarded as resolvable through a marriage of civil and common law to the advantage of all Louisianians. Lewis Kerr and Moreau Lislet had already demonstrated that in their work on the *Exposition of Criminal Laws of the Territory of Orleans* in 1806, as had James Workman with his work on the criminal laws in 1805.

Judge Moreau Lislet's endorsement of Workman should have caused later writers, if not Workman's contemporaries, to reevaluate his role in the development of Louisiana law. Moreau Lislet's great reputation as a codifier of Louisiana's complex legal system lay nearly twenty years in the future, although he already was highly regarded as an expert in civil law. It seems clear that in September 1808 Moreau Lislet wanted Workman not only to shoulder some of the legal workload facing the territorial bench and bar, but also to be on hand to assist in the integration of common law with civil law in the development of a coherent legal system for the business-oriented port of New Orleans and Orleans Territory.[77] Workman must have been

75. Brigham, *History and Bibliography of American Newspapers,* 1: 186.

76. Moreau Lislet tried to appoint Workman to the office on September 18, 1808. See To William Thomson, November 5, 1808, CLB, 4: 239–40.

77. See Robert A. Pascal, "A Recent Discovery: A Copy of the 'Digest of the Civil Laws' of 1808 with Marginal Source References in Moreau Lislet's Hand," *Louisiana Law Review* 26, no. 1 (December 1965), 25–7.

sorely tempted by Moreau Lislet's offer, but he knew that the right to appoint the attorney general lay with the executive rather than with the judicial branch of the government and declined the office.[78]

Moreau Lislet's desire to retain Workman's expertise was well intentioned, but the effect of his action may have been to contribute to the worsening situation facing the former judge in the Orleans community. The situation came to a head in the fall of 1808. In November, Philip Grymes, Jefferson's newly appointed district attorney in the Orleans district, accused Workman of having a deep *"rooted enmity to the government."*[79] Grymes made the accusation during a superior court hearing on the batture case in which he represented the municipal government of New Orleans and Workman represented Edward Livingston.

How much of Grymes's outburst was a reflection of his inexperience and frustration with the difficult case that placed him in opposition to the more experienced Workman can only be estimated. Workman responded to Grymes's offensive remark, branding it a "falsehood," whereupon Grymes hurled a pewter inkwell at Workman's head.[80] The inkwell missed Workman, but splattered other lawyers and onlookers with ink. Grymes was taken into custody, but both men were placed under a five hundred dollar bond and ordered to appear in court the following day, at which time they were both fined twenty-five dollars and imprisoned for eight hours.[81] The incident might have ended here except for Workman's lack of restraint and the involvement of Judge Joshua Lewis, a Jefferson appointee and the presiding judge in the batture case.

Immediately following their sentencing, Workman challenged Grymes to a duel. After Grymes repeatedly and positively declined to meet him in personal combat, Workman had handbills in French and English posted in several public places calling Grymes a coward.[82] Grymes replied with handbills of his own, offering an apology to the public along with a copy of Workman's indictment and acquittal of the high misdemeanor charge in 1807.[83]

---

78. To William Thomson, November 5, 1808, CLB, 4: 240.

79. *The Case of Mr. Workman on a Rule for an Alleged Contempt of the Superior Court of the Territory of Orleans* (Philadelphia: William Fry [, 1809]), 6. Emphasis in the original.

80. Ibid.

81. Ibid., 6–9.

82. Ibid., 9–10. The differences between Grymes and Workman may also be found in H. H. C. [Heloise H. Crozat], "When Knighthood Was in Flower," *Louisiana Historical Quarterly* 1, no. 4 (April 1918), 367–71.

83. H. H. C. [Crozat], "When Knighthood Was in Flower," 367–8, prints the handbills by Workman calling Phillip Grymes a coward. Also printed is Grymes's response, saying Workman owed the public an apology, along with the indictment returned by the grand jury for

On December 3, 1808, the date that Grymes's handbill attack on Workman appeared, the *Orleans Gazette* carried a story of the courtroom incident between Grymes and Workman.[84] The following day, Judge Lewis
ordered Workman to show cause why he "should not be excluded from the
bar of . . . [the superior] court" for "perversion of the observations made
by the court" in the sentencing of Grymes.[85] Specifically, Judge Lewis objected to that portion of the newspaper story in which he was represented
as having said that Grymes's behavior was not only unbecoming a gentleman, but would be "disgraceful even in a tavern."[86] All the harsh statements
attributed to him, the judge said, were erroneous and tantamount to contempt of court.[87]

Workman's narrative of the reprimand of Grymes was based on the
firsthand report of another lawyer and former court reporter, Auguste Davezac, the brother-in-law of Edward Livingston.[88] Workman had not been
in the court when Judge Lewis made his comments to Grymes about his conduct because the judge had taken the precaution of reprimanding and sentencing the lawyers separately. For his part in writing the newspaper story,
Davezac also was punished. Initially, he, too, was barred from practicing in
the superior court, but this sentence was reduced when the judge reluctantly
agreed that a reprimand would be sufficient.[89]

Faced with the possibility of losing his means of earning a living, Workman retained Lewis Kerr as his attorney. Kerr responded to Judge Lewis's
objections to Workman's newspaper story by pointing out the story was
"derived from others" who had been present and could be corroborated by
still others who had been present. However, Judge Lewis, supported by the
territorial attorney general, Abner Duncan, would not allow any witnesses
to be presented.[90] Workman also gathered numerous signed statements upholding Davezac's report of what the judge had said in court, and he solicited testimonials from both his friends and enemies in his attempts to
persuade Lewis to omit the suspension from the bar.[91]

Workman's trial. The indictment carried the signature of Evan Jones, who served as foreman
of the jury. See also *Case of Mr. Workman,* 10–1.

84. *Case of Mr. Workman,* 11.
85. Ibid., 11–2, 13.
86. Ibid., 9, 11–2, 33.
87. Ibid., 12.
88. Ibid., 32.
89. Ibid., 12–3, 32.
90. Ibid., 12, 13.
91. Ibid., 11, 31, 33–43.

Judge Lewis's ruling against Workman, however, was absolute. In the judge's opinion, it was Workman's responsibility to be "perfectly certain of the correctness of the statement before he ventured to publish it."[92] The only way this could have been done, Workman believed, was to have the judge review the story before it was printed, but this would have been an infringement of the freedom of the press guaranteed by the Constitution.[93]

In his subsequent evaluation of the difficulties with Grymes, Workman believed Grymes's attack "to have been premeditated . . . from the commencement" of his arguments in court on November 25, 1808.[94] Judge Lewis's motives for ruling as he did were characterized by Workman as "some of the least excusable ones which can actuate the human mind."[95] On the one hand, Judge Lewis sought to cripple Edward Livingston's case against the city of New Orleans over the batture. On the other, the judge sought to protect Grymes, who had made a number of serious mistakes in handling the case since assuming his duties as district attorney in September.[96] The hint of a vendetta against him and all those considered hostile to the Jefferson appointees in Orleans Territory became stronger when Workman stated that an attempt to disbar Edward Livingston was made in February 1809, but was rejected when it was placed before a grand jury.[97] The whole incident with Grymes, Workman believed, was manipulated as "a convenient mode of getting rid of their competitors."[98] No names other than the principals in the cases were mentioned, but it seems clear that Workman blamed the territorial administration of Governor Claiborne for his disbarment.

92. Ibid., 13.

93. Ibid., 27–30.

94. Ibid., 7. Workman may have been correct, but the problem may have been more a reflection Jefferson's reaction to political attacks on his administration, particularly after the Burr conspiracy. Patriotism was the camouflage used by all those who wished to establish themselves in Jefferson's understanding as opposed to any perceived threat to the unity of the United States, or to the idea that the Louisiana Purchase was a threat to the security of the new nation. Grymes's verbal assault on Workman in court during the batture case was a continuation of the patriotism he stressed in his request for appointment. See Philip Grymes to the President, January 15, 1808, TP, 9: 772. Benjamin Morgan's recommendation of Grymes to head the office of Register of Land also emphasized Grymes's devotion to the United States. See Benjamin Morgan to the President, December 12, 1808, ibid., 810.

95. *Case of Mr. Workman,* 21.

96. Ibid., 20–1. Grymes said he arrived in New Orleans on August 18, 1808, and immediately assumed his duties. Philip Grymes to [the President], August 27, 1808, TP, 9: 801.

97. *Case of Mr. Workman,* 26.

98. Ibid.

Workman left New Orleans sometime in March or early April 1809, with his means of earning a livelihood seriously impaired. By that time, he was fully aware of the lengths to which the territorial government under Claiborne would go to be rid of him. He apparently went to Philadelphia, where he had his explanation of the latest events in New Orleans published by William Fry. While in Philadelphia, Workman undoubtedly called on his old friend Stephen C. Carpenter, who had moved there in 1807 after a brief stay in New York in 1806.

Following the visit to Philadelphia, it is unclear where Workman settled. The slight evidence thus far uncovered does not point to any one place. This is probably intentional, considering the treatment Workman received at the hands of the Claiborne administration in New Orleans. Given the fact that he named Anne Carpenter, the eldest daughter of his friend Philip C. Carpenter, a recipient of one of the legacies in his will, it is most probable that Workman stayed in Philadelphia. However, he just as easily may have settled in Charleston, South Carolina, or New York City, or any of the ports along the eastern seaboard. Charleston, of course, was the site of Workman's personal successes before moving to New Orleans in 1804. New York was a bustling port city roughly comparable to New Orleans in its growing importance, but it also was the base of operations for the family of Edward Livingston, with whom Workman had become friendly before the break with Governor Claiborne. In addition, New York was the residence of Workman's aunt, Sarah M. Workman, who served as governess in the family of the British consul in New York.[99]

Wherever Workman settled, he apparently kept informed about developments in New Orleans and appears to have planned to return when he thought it was feasible. In any event, sometime in November 1817, about the time of Claiborne's death, Workman returned to New Orleans.[100] Before long, he had established a profitable law practice and involved himself once more in the social and business life of the city.

99. James Workman Olographic Will, Dated April 24, 1831, filed October 18, 1832. *Orleans Parish, Louisiana. Court of Probate, Record of Wills,* Will Book, *1824–1833,* vol. 4., 384. No evidence has been located that would place Workman in New York City or Charleston.

100. Claiborne died on November 23, 1817, as a result of the effects of yellow fever. The date of his death may be found in the memorial offered by Governor Jacques Villere in the state legislature on January 6, 1818. *Journal of the House of Representatives of the State of Louisiana, Second Session, Third Legislature* (New Orleans: J. C. de St. Romes, 1818), 6, microfilm L-222, reel 1, Louisiana Department, State Library of Louisiana, Baton Rouge, La.

Among his clients after returning to New Orleans was the Orleans Navigation Company, which he successfully defended before the state supreme court in 1822, upholding the validity of the company charter and the company's right to recompense for its improvements to navigation of Bayou St. John and the Carondelet Canal. As was his custom, Workman took this occasion to advertise his success with publication of *The Defence of the Orleans Navigation Company*.[101] Two other cases that Workman successfully defended after he returned to New Orleans were for the Caricaburu, Arieta & Company, merchants of Havana. He was so proud of his success in these cases that he published the brief of them in 1820.[102]

In 1822, Workman's excellent legal training was acknowledged by his peers once again. He was one of eight nominees considered by a joint meeting of the Louisiana House of Representatives and Senate on March 14 to revise the civil code and the code of procedure and to prepare a commercial code of law for Louisiana. The work entailed harmonizing and unifying all details of the existing law with particular reference to the introduction of the common law of England. Although Workman was not one of the three jurisconsults selected, he received twenty-three votes, two less than Pierre Derbigny and Edward Livingston. Moreau Lislet received the most votes, forty-three.[103]

As might be expected, Workman continued his friendship with Moreau Lislet, Edward Livingston, Auguste Davezac, and others with whom he had been friendly before his departure from New Orleans in the spring of 1809. Indeed, a New Orleans newspaper described Workman in December 1828 as one of the men working untiringly for the success of the public dinner honoring Livingston and promoting his candidacy for the U.S. Senate. Others who were involved in advancing Livingston's candidacy were Denis Prieur, then the mayor of New Orleans, and John Slidell.[104] As he had in the territorial period, Workman continued his efforts to develop libraries in

101. James Workman, *Defence of the Orleans Navigation Company, Before the Supreme Court; in the Suit Instituted Against Them by Scire Facias, Pursuant to a Resolution of the Legislature of the State of Louisiana* (New Orleans: Benjamin Levy, 1822).

102. James Workman, *Brief of the Case of Caricaburu, Arieta & Company, Merchants of the Havana, Appellants in the Following Suits: First the Josefa Segunda, Her Tackle, Cagro* [sic] *&c versus the United States. Second . . . Caricaburu, Arieta & Company versus the Josefa Segunda, Her Tackle, Cargo, and 152 Negroe Slaves. Now Pending in the Supreme Court of the United States for the Louisiana District* (New Orleans: Benjamin Hanna, 1820).

103. William B. Hatcher, *Edward Livingston: Jeffersonian Republican and Jacksonian Democrat* (University: Louisiana State University Press, 1940), 242.

104. Ibid., 329.

New Orleans. He was chosen as one of the commissioners of the Law Library Society, which was incorporated in 1828.[105]

As nullification and disunion sentiment rose with the tariff question in the South in the 1820s and early 1830s, Workman publicly opposed them. He joined with Governor André B. Roman; Alexander Porter, Jr.; Francis X. Martin; Charles Gayarré; Denis Prieur; J. C. de St. Romes, editor of the *Louisiana Courier;* John Slidell; and Charles M. Conrad on June 27, 1832, in leading opposition to the spirit of nullification and disunion before the Tariff of 1832 was adopted.[106] Perhaps as a result of being drawn back into politics, Workman ran for election to one of the Orleans Parish seats in the Louisiana House of Representatives in 1830 and won. William C. C. Claiborne, Jr., the eldest son of the former governor, also won a seat in the house in this election, as did John (Jean Z.) Watkins, the son of John Watkins, the man who had been instrumental in bringing Workman to Louisiana in 1804.[107]

When the first session of the tenth legislature convened in the fall of 1831, Workman was called to the chair to serve as Speaker pro tempore until the house elected Alexander Mouton as Speaker.[108] As the new legislature organized, Workman was appointed to several committees: Public Education; Judiciary; the Consolidated Association of the Planters of Louisiana; and a Committee to Investigate the State of the Charity Hospital in New Orleans.[109] Workman also was present for the special session of the legislature that convened on November 14, 1831, and the regular session that convened in January 1832.[110] Like most of the members of the legislature,

105. McCutcheon, "Libraries in New Orleans," 158.

106. Joseph G. Tregle, Jr., "Louisiana and the Tariff of 1816–1846," *Louisiana Historical Quarterly* 25, no. 1 (January 1942), 91.

107. *Journal of the House of Representatives of the State of Louisiana, Tenth Legislature, First Session* (New Orleans: John Gibson, 1831), 1, 7. This William C. C. Claiborne was the first son of the governor and his second wife, Clarisse Duralde. Most of his youth was spent in Kentucky with John Clay and his wife, who was a sister of his mother. Legal tutorial responsibility was assigned to them by Governor Claiborne on his deathbed. See Jane Lucas DeGrummond, "Cayetana Susana Bosque y Fanqui, 'A Notable Woman,'" *Louisiana History* 23, no. 3 (summer 1982), 286.

108. *Journal of the House of Representatives of the State of Louisiana, Tenth Legislature, First Session,* 1, 4.

109. Ibid., 9, 16, 20, 21.

110. *Journal of the House of Representatives, Extra Session, Tenth Legislature* (New Orleans: John Gibson, 1831), 1; and *Journal of the House of Representatives, Second Session, Tenth Legislature* (New Orleans: John Gibson, 1832), 1.

Workman opposed the relocation of the state government to Donaldson-ville, even though he seems to have favored moving the government out of New Orleans. What he and most of the members of the legislature objected to were the totally inadequate facilities made available for use in Donaldson-ville by the townspeople and Antoine Peytavin.[111]

Sometime in the late summer or early fall of 1832, Workman, along with the two black men on a sailboat with him, was drowned in the Mississippi Sound while returning from a visit to Bay St. Louis.[112] His olographic will was filed on October 18, 1832.[113] At the time he wrote his will, April 24, 1831, Workman apparently was suffering from the effects of yellow fever. Early in the document he alludes to being in "feeble health." As Workman said in his will, he had "no wife & no relation in either the ascending or the descending line." He left $2,500 to Anne Carpenter of Philadelphia, the eldest daughter of his friend Stephen C. Carpenter; $2,500 to his aunt, Sarah M. Workman, governess in the family of the British consul in New York; $1,000 to John G. Greeves, iron monger of New Orleans; $1,000 to James Workman Greeves, the son of John G. Greeves; $1,000 to the Society for the Relief of Orphan Boys; $150 to John R. Grymes, payment for "pro-fessional services which he refused to accept any fee," and several other be-quests to friends and daughters of friends in New Orleans.[114] One large bequest of $10,000 was left to the American Colonization Society and the Auxiliary Society of Maryland for use "as they think it right to do."[115]

Reflecting his longstanding interest in books and libraries, Workman di-vided his large collection among several of his friends in the legal profession, as well as "Louisiana College at Jackson" and the Commercial Library, which was "established or about to be established" in New Orleans. Inter-estingly, he left to the wife of George W. Morgan, then sheriff of Orleans Parish, "Plutarch's lives, the History of the Jews, He[r]bert['s] india [sic], and the History of Roman Literature." The "French translation of the body of the Roman Civil Code," Workman left to Christopher de Armas, coun-

---

111. *Journal of the House of Representatives of the State of Louisiana, Tenth Legislature, First Session,* 6, 7, 13. For additional information on Peytavin, see his biographical sketch in this appendix.

112. *Louisiana Advertiser,* October 18, 1832, p. 2, c. 3. The names of the two black men were not given in the story, nor were they identified in other sources consulted.

113. Orleans Parish, Louisiana. Court of Probate, Record of Wills, Will Book, 1824–1833, vol. 4., 384–5.

114. Ibid.

115. Ibid., 385.

selor-at-law and son of Felix de Armas, the notary public in New Orleans. Workman's law books were left to Samuel Porter, judge of the Louisiana Superior Court and resident of Donaldsonville, and John MacReady, a lawyer in New Orleans.[116]

After Workman's death, the *Louisiana Advertiser* reported that the Hibernian Society of New Orleans was made the "universal legatee" of the "residue of his ample fortune" to be used for the "relief and maintenance of destitute and indigent emigrants from Ireland and Scotland." The newspaper reported that Workman was "always a very prominent member and President of their deliberations."[117] No provisions of this nature were recorded in the will registered in Orleans Parish. A few days later, the same newspaper reported that Workman was memorialized by the New Orleans Bar Association. The resolution for the memorial was drafted by John R. Grymes, John Slidell, and others of the New Orleans bar. The motion for adoption of the resolution was offered by Pierre Soulé. Presiding at the meeting was Workman's longtime friend, Louis Moreau Lislet.[118]

116. Ibid. These are not all the provisions of Workman's will, which was quite specific in detail about bequests.

117. *Louisiana Advertiser,* October 19, 1832, p. 2, c. 3.

118. Ibid., October 22, 1832, p. 2, c. 3.

LEWIS KERR

Lewis Kerr (August 11, 1772–October 7, 1834) was described not long after his death as a man who "possessed great suavity of manners and . . . a most facetious and private conversation."[1] The same contemporary also described Kerr as "an accomplished scholar[;] an eloquent and graceful orator; and an ingenious writer."[2] In short, Lewis Kerr was an eighteenth-century gentleman of ability with a keen wit. Surprisingly, this is not the image of him that has survived. If Kerr is remembered in U.S. history, it is as one of the Aaron Burr conspirators. This recollection is unfair since he was tried and acquitted of the conspiracy charge. Yet the effects of his trials and subsequent establishment of his residence in the West Indies have only encouraged a general belief in his complicity in the Burr episode, and discouraged investigation of his life and career. As a consequence, Kerr's contributions to the development of Louisiana law and the maturation of U.S. politics, and his service as a public official in the Orleans Territory and the West Indies have gone virtually unnoticed.

Lewis Kerr was the second son of an Anglican minister and school teacher also named Lewis Kerr, who established his reputation as founder and headmaster of one of the most popular public schools in Dublin, Ireland.[3] Young Kerr's mother was Elizabeth Lyndon of Dub-

1. *Nassau Royal Gazette and Bahama Advertiser* (New Providence, The Bahamas Islands), October 18, 1834, p. 3, c. 1.

2. Ibid.

3. The senior Lewis Kerr served as master of Cavan School, Cavan County, Ireland, 1764–68. George D. Butchaell and Thomas U. Sadleir eds., *Alumni Dublinenses: A Register of the Students, Graduates, Professors, and Provosts of Trinity College in the University of Dublin*

lin.[4] Like his father and older brother, Richard, young Lewis attended Trinity College of Dublin University, graduating with the B.A. degree in the summer of 1793.[5] Before graduation Kerr decided on a career in law and, in accordance with the legal requirements then imposed on Irish residents, sought admission simultaneously to the Inns of Court in London and the Kings Inns, Dublin. Although he was admitted to the Inner Temple, London, on June 18, 1791, as with most Irish barristers in this period of British history, Kerr neither matriculated with the Inner Temple nor practiced law in England.[6] He was admitted to practice at the Dublin bar either at the Michaelmas (September) term of 1794, soon after filing his petition for admission, or early in 1795.[7]

From approximately 1795 until sometime in 1797, young Kerr appears

---

(1593–1860) (new ed. with suppl.; Dublin: Alexander Thom, 1935), xvii, 465, and Appendix B, Addenda and Corrigenda, 140. Young Lewis Kerr gave the names of his parents in his "Memorial of Lewis Kerr to be Admitted to the Degree of Barrister, Addressed to the Benchers of the Honourable Society of the Kings Inns, Dublin, 3rd November 1794," Kings Inns Library, Dublin (photocopy owned by the author).

4. "Memorial of Lewis Kerr"; and marriage license of the Rev. Lewis Kerr and Elizabeth Lyndon, in Dublin Consistorial Office Marriage License Books, 1635–1825, vol. 2, E–M, inclusive, p.124, Irish Records in the LDS Family History Library, Salt Lake City, Utah.

5. The Rev. Lewis Kerr received the B.A. (1741), M.A. (1744), and M.B. (1759) degrees from Trinity. His son Richard received the B.A. degree from Trinity in 1788. Butchaell and Sadleir, *Alumni Dublinenses,* 465.

6. R. L. Lloyd, ed., *Admissions to the Inner Temple, 1505–1850,* vol. 4 (typescript; London: n.p., 1950–1960), 137. Information provided by Robert D. Mills, assistant librarian, Kings Inns Library, Dublin, to the author, February 1, 1977.

Although inns were established in Ireland for the benefit of law as far back as the reign of Edward I (1272–1307), no Irish lawyer was permitted to practice at the bar from 1542 to May 1885 without simultaneously registering at one of the English Inns of Court. The only compulsory training required by the inns in London during these centuries was the eating of a certain number of dinners in the common hall of one of the English Inns of Court and of the King's Inns, Dublin. Neither attendance at lectures nor qualifying examinations was required. Beginning in May 1885, Irish law students were no longer required to pay periodic visits to London for the purpose of consuming the dinners believed necessary to complete their legal education. The Inns of Court clearly were considered more than law schools. They were "'graduate schools of gentlemanly culture.'" Ronald Ray Swick, *Harman Blennerhassett: An Irish Aristocrat on the American Frontier* (Ann Arbor, Mich.: University Microfilms International, 1995), 13–4, particularly n. 27 on the latter page.

7. Butchaell and Sadleir, *Alumni Dublinenses,* 465, indicates that Lewis Kerr was admitted to the Dublin bar in 1795, but the "Judges and Barristers at Law with the Dates of Their Admissions" indicates that Kerr was admitted to the Dublin bar in the Michaelmas term, 1794. *Treble Almanac,* Part III, *The Dublin Directory for the Year 1798* (Dublin: William Wilson, 1798), 121.

to have supported himself on the small income he received as one of several coroners of Dublin, while at the same time trying to build a law practice.[8] Unfortunately for Kerr, he launched his career amidst deteriorating economic and political conditions in his homeland. Ireland at the end of the eighteenth century was seriously divided. Political moderates, who wanted what would be known today as commonwealth status within the British Empire, were frustrated by those in Ireland who wanted independence and by those in England who wanted tighter economic and political control over Ireland. As hope faded for even a slight measure of independence, many Irishmen turned to revolutionary France for succor. Thereafter, events moved inexorably to confrontation in 1798 at the Battle of Vinegar Hill, in which opposition in Ireland to British policy suffered a crushing defeat.[9] Young Kerr does not appear to have played any part in the Irish rebellion. Sometime in 1797, he sought his fortune in India, the foundation stone of the second British Empire and the route to professional and financial success for aspiring, unconnected young Englishmen into the twentieth century.

Kerr obtained a barrister's position in Calcutta about the time that Richard Colley, the Marquess of Wellesley and the elder brother of the Duke of Wellington, was appointed governor-general of India. It is unlikely that Kerr owed his appointment to Wellesley. It is more likely that Kerr obtained the barrister's post through the intercession of his kinsman, General Lord Hely-Hutchinson, with Henry Dundas, Viscount Melville.[10] Dundas was an influential member of the ministry of the young William Pitt. It was through Dundas that Pitt usually conducted his military operations. In the case of India, Dundas combined his military responsibilities with the placement of well-trained young men, usually Scots, in government service.[11] Late in Jan-

8. *The City and Country Calendar; or The Irish Court Registry for the Year . . . 1795* (Dublin: s. n., 1795), 147; *The City and Country Calendar; or The Irish Court Registry for the Year . . . 1796* (Dublin: s. n., 1796), 180; and *The Irish Court Register, and the City and Country Calendar for the Year . . . 1797* (Dublin: n.p., 1797), 145.

9. J. H. Plumb, *England in the Eighteenth Century (1714–1815)* (Baltimore: Penguin Books, 1959), 184–5, 198–200.

10. The kinship of Lewis Kerr and General Lord Hely-Hutchinson is revealed in James Workman, *The Trials of the Honb. James Workman, and Col. Lewis Kerr, Before the United States Court, for the Orleans District on a Charge of High Misdemeanor, in Planning and Setting on Foot, Within the United States, An Expedition for the Conquest and Emancipation of Mexico* (New Orleans: Bradford & Anderson, 1807), 13. On Hely-Hutchinson, see *Dictionary of National Biography*, (1921–22, reprint), s.v. "Hely-Hutchinson, John, Baron Hutchinson."

11. George M. Trevelyan, *History of England*, vol. 3, *From Utrecht to Modern Times: The Industrial Revolution and the Transition to Democracy* (Garden City, N.Y.: Doubleday Anchor Books, 1952), 102, 126.

uary 1798, not long after his arrival in India, Kerr was praised as a "very impressive and relevant" speaker before the colonial Supreme Court in Calcutta for his part in the prosecution of a perjury case.[12] Toward the end of the year 1798, Kerr was employed in editing *The Rules and Orders of the Supreme Court of Judicature at Fort William in Bengal* and in drafting some additional rules for the court.[13] For reasons unknown, Kerr left India within a year. Why he left the promising niche he appeared to be making for himself is not known.[14] If he returned to Ireland, it must have been only for a brief visit, since the next record of location places him in the United States.

Lewis Kerr arrived in the United States in 1799 or early in 1800 and apparently set out for the trans-Appalachian West, stopping first in the Ohio Territory.[15] There he may have visited Harman Blennerhassett or Joseph Kerr, both of whom had settled in Ohio in 1796. Kerr would have known of the large and prominent Blennerhassett family of Ireland and may have been acquainted with Harman from their both having attended Trinity College, or through their duties as lawyers and coroners in Ireland. Blennerhassett was admitted to the Irish bar in 1790 and held appointment as coroner of Tralee, Kerry County, Ireland, from 1795 into 1797.[16] Whether Lewis Kerr was related to Joseph Kerr is not known. Joseph moved to Ohio from Kerrsville, Pennsylvania (later named Chambersburg), and was one of Ohio's early United States senators. Many years later, after economic reversals, he settled and eventually died in northeast Louisiana.[17]

12. The "Supreme Court" notices of the *Calcutta Monthly Journal*, February 1798. Extract courtesy of Mrs. Henry Z. Pain, July 28, 1976.

13. See the authorship identified with pages 122–95 of this larger work listed in the British Museum, *General Catalogue of Printed Books*, photolithographic ed. (London: Trustees of the British Museum, 1965), 14: 1039, and 122: 478.

14. Thomas P. Abernethy quotes an unspecified source as saying that Kerr "'fled from Bengal for his virtuous deeds.'" *The Burr Conspiracy* (New York: Oxford University Press, 1954), 25.

15. Claiborne described Kerr as "from the State of Ohio, & lately of Natchez." Governor Claiborne to the President, August 30, 1804, in Clarence E. Carter, comp. and ed., *The Territorial Papers of the United States*, vol. 9, *The Territory of Orleans, 1803–1812* (Washington, D.C.: U.S. Government Printing Office, 1940), 286 (hereinafter cited as TP, with volume and page range).

16. *Dictionary of American Biography*, s.v. "Blennerhassett, Harman"; and Mrs. Henry Z. Pain to the author, October 17, 1976, citing unspecified pages from *The City and Country Calendar; or The Irish Court Registry for the Year . . . 1795; The City and Country Calendar; or The Irish Court Registry for the Year . . . 1796; and The Irish Court Register, and the City and Country Calendar for the Year . . . 1797.*

17. William E. Gilmore, "General Joseph Kerr," *Ohio Archaeological and Historical Publications* 12, (1903), 164–6; and *Biographical Directory of the American Congress, 1774–1971. The Continental Congress, September 5, 1774, to October 21, 1788. The Congress of*

Lewis Kerr next visited Tennessee, which is probably where he met Andrew Jackson. Meeting Jackson set Kerr on the path that earned him a footnote in history. It was on the recommendation of Jackson that Kerr settled in Natchez, Mississippi Territory, in March 1801 and began to practice law.[18] After William C. C. Claiborne assumed his gubernatorial duties in the territory in November 1801, the occasional references to Kerr in the governor's correspondence suggest that a friendship developed between the two men, partly as a result of their mutual friend Andrew Jackson.[19] However, it was not until after the Louisiana Purchase that events provided perspective on Kerr's relationship with Claiborne.

Claiborne once described Kerr as possessing "great talents & address," and his reliance on Kerr for selected duties supports this opinion.[20] Indeed, Kerr generally was known to be "a great favorite" of Claiborne's until well into the period of the Burr conspiracy.[21] It was Kerr who brought Claiborne what may be considered his first report on the "perfectly useless" defense works at New Orleans and the inadequate number of regular Spanish troops on garrison duty there. With this oral eyewitness report, Kerr also delivered to Claiborne a despatch from Daniel Clark in New Orleans.[22] Following Claiborne's appointment as civil official to receive Louisiana from the French in the fall of 1803, Kerr joined the governor's entourage, serving as U.S. marshal during the temporary civil government that functioned before the creation of the Orleans Territory.[23] Subsequently, Claiborne ap-

the United States from the First through the Ninety-First Congress, March 4, 1789, to January 3, 1971, Inclusive (Washington, D.C.: Government Printing Office, 1971), 1228–9. It most probably was Joseph Kerr who visited Blennerhassett in Richmond during the Burr trial. See William Safford, *The Blennerhassett Papers, Embodying the Private Journal of Harman Blennerhassett, and the Hitherto Unpublished Correspondence of Burr, Alston, Comfort Tyler, Devereaux, Dayton, Adair, Miro, Emmett, Theodosia Burr Alston, Mrs. Blennerhassett, and Others . . .* (Cincinnati: Moore, Wilstach, Keys, 1861), 366, 392.

18. On Jackson's role in Kerr's decision to settle in the Mississippi Territory, see George Cockran to Andrew Jackson, March 26, 1801, Andrew Jackson Papers, Series I, General Correspondence and Related Items, 1775–1860, Presidential Papers microfilm no. 2725, reel 2, Troy H. Middleton Library, Louisiana State University Libraries.

19. See, for example, Claiborne to Seth Lewis, October 19, 1802, in *Official Letter Books of W. C. C. Claiborne, 1801–1816*, ed. Dunbar Rowland, vol. 1 (1917; New York: AMS Press, 1972), 204–5 (hereinafter cited as CLB with volume and page range).

20. Claiborne to Madison, March 17, 1808, ibid., 4: 167.

21. *Louisiana Gazette and New Orleans Daily Advertiser*, January 16, 1812, p. 2, c. 3.

22. Compare Claiborne to Daniel Clark, Natchez, November 18, 1803, CLB, 1: 287–90, with Claiborne to Madison, November 18, 1803, ibid., 286.

23. Governor Claiborne to the Marshal and Sheriffs of New Orleans, July 30, 1804, TP, 9: 270. See also To Henry Dearborn, June 9, 1804, CLB, 2: 200, in which Claiborne says that Kerr "came to this City [New Orleans] a member of my family," meaning a member of his

pointed Kerr to serve as *alguazil major* (sheriff) of New Orleans from at
least January 4, 1804, to late February or early March 1805.[24]

Kerr's duties as sheriff were sometimes not only unpleasant, but also
dangerous. He played a key role in quieting a mob of two hundred angry
men who gathered in front of the Marqués de Casa Calvo's residence on
the evening of November 16, 1804. The cause of this incident was the arrest
of Manuel García y Muñiz, captain of the small fleet of Spanish war vessels
on Lake Pontchartrain being used to transport Spanish troops to West Florida.[25] García and nearly three hundred Spanish soldiers and sailors from the
West Florida command of Vicente Folch were in New Orleans on their way
back to Pensacola, having recently quashed the Kemper brothers' attempts
to seize Baton Rouge.[26] García was arrested on the warrant sworn to by an
American, David Bannister Morgan, and issued by Judge John B. Prevost of
the territorial superior court. Morgan had been seized by the Spanish while
working on an authorized surveying job above the north shore of Lake
Pontchartrain. He filed his complaint after a dramatic escape from the
schooner under García's command as it stood about a mile off the mouth
of Bayou St. John.[27] To assist Kerr in maintaining public order, Claiborne
requested Colonel Thomas Butler to strengthen the guard.[28] The following

---

official family for the transfer of Louisiana to the United States; and Letter No. 65, To James
Madison, November 26, 1804.

24. The *Union,* January 9, 1804, p. 3, c. 3, indicates that Kerr was appointed *alguazil
major* and sheriff on January 4, 1804. The *Louisiana Gazette,* March 5, 1805, p. 2, c. 4, states
that Kerr resigned as sheriff and George Ross was appointed to the position. Kerr also simultaneously served as marshal for the district of New Orleans. See To Lewis Kerr Esqr., Sheriff of
New Orleans and performing the duties of Marshall for the District of Orleans, August 4,
1804, CLB, 2: 289, and Letter No. 65, To James Madison, November 26, 1804. Kerr may
have held the post of marshal until the appointment of Francis Joseph LeBreton Dorgenois in
October 1804. Governor Claiborne to the President, October 22, 1804, TP, 9: 311, tells of
Dorgenois's appointment as U.S. marshal.

25. See Abraham P. Nasatir, *Spanish War Vessels on the Mississippi, 1792–1796* (New
Haven: Yale University Press, 1968), 103 n. 29; and Jack D. L. Holmes, "*Dramatis Personae*
in Spanish Louisiana," *Louisiana Studies* 6, no. 2 (summer 1967), 169–75, for information on
Manuel García y Muñiz.

26. David Hart White, *Vicente Folch, Governor in Spanish Florida, 1787–1811* (Washington, D.C.: University Press of America, 1981), 77–8.

27. To James Madison, November 23, 1804, CLB, 3: 13–6; Governor Claiborne to the
President, November 19, 1804, TP, 9: 334; and George W. Morgan to David Rees, October
23, 1804; George W. Morgan to David Rees, December 6, 1804; and David B. Morgan to
David Rees, December 6, 1804; all in the David Rees Papers, Special Collections, Howard-
Tilton Memorial Library, Tulane University.

28. To James Madison, November 23, 1804, CLB, 3: 16.

winter, on February 15, 1805, Judge Prevost requested an armed guard from the U.S. Army to assist Kerr in the performance of his duties as sheriff in a difficult case.[29] On this occasion, one of Kerr's deputies, Charles Bonville, was forcefully prevented from seizing a shipment of cigars from L. Mayenge by Mayenge's son, son-in-law, and wife.[30] In response to Prevost's request, Claiborne asked Colonel Freeman to furnish Kerr with a noncommissioned officer and six enlisted men to assist him in carrying out his duties.[31]

Kerr held other appointments to public office, as did most of the men with ability and a legal background in early territorial Louisiana. He was appointed in June 1804, with Michel Fortier, to command the battalion of free people of color.[32] After the company of Orleans Fusiliers was organized by Samuel B. Davis in March 1805, Kerr became a member, rank unknown, but withdrew from the company in late November of the same year.[33] Perhaps because of his support of the Orleans Fusiliers, the first independent militia company recognized by Claiborne, Kerr was appointed brigade major on the governor's staff on August 11, 1805.[34] On January 27, 1806,

29. Judge Prevost to Governor Claiborne, February 15, 1805, TP, 9: 393.

30. Characterization of New Orleans Residents, July 1, 1804, entry 3, enclosed in James Wilkinson to the President, July 1, 1804, TP, 9: 249, carries an unflattering description, probably written by Daniel Clark, of the volatile Mayenge. In Letter No. 65, To James Madison, November 26, 1804, the surname is spelled "Mazenge."

31. Letter No. 137, To Constant Freeman, February 17, 1805. It may have been for expenses growing out of this kind of duty, associated with the Superior Court, that the legislative council voted to reimburse Kerr the "sum of two hundred and six dollars, for articles furnished by him to the superior court" on May 4, 1805. See *Acts Passed at the Second Session of the Legislative Council of the Territory of Orleans, Begun and Held at the Principal, in the City of New Orleans, On Thursday the Twentieth Day of June, in the Year of Our Lord, One Thousand Eight Hundred and Five, and of the Independence of the United States the Twenty-Ninth* (New Orleans: James M. Bradford, 1805), 410.

32. To Henry Dearborn, June 9, 1804, and December 22, 1804, CLB, 2: 199–200, 217–8, respectively.

33. The company, and others like it, was authorized by the territorial council on March 29, 1805. "An Act Concerning Volunteer Companies of Militia," *Acts Passed at the First Session of the Legislative Council of the Territory of Orleans, Begun and Held at the Principal, in the City of New Orleans, On Monday the Third Day of December, in the Year of Our Lord, One Thousand Eight Hundred and Four, and of the Independence of the United States the Twenty-Ninth* (New Orleans: James M. Bradford, 1805), 306. Samuel B. Davis initially served as company commander. On Davis's role and Kerr's limited service in the company, see Governor Claiborne to the Secretary of State, April 5, 1805; and Letter [to] Captain S. B. Davis from William Nott, a.d.c. [aide-de-camp], November 23, 1805; both in TP, 9: 432, 593, respectively.

34. Register of Appointments in the Militia of the Territory of Orleans, May 8, 1806, enclosed in Secretary Graham to the Secretary of State, May 8, 1806, TP, 9: 632.

Kerr received appointment as justice of the peace.[35] When the legislative council created the University of Orleans in April 1805, Kerr was named as one of the founding regents.[36] Finally, Kerr, with Pierre Derbigny, was retained by the city of New Orleans in 1806 to search for legal documents that would support the city's claim to as much common land as possible along the Mississippi River in the dispute with Daniel Clark and Samuel Davis.[37] Since the suit was brought against Davis on February 2, 1805, the placing of Kerr on retainer appears to reflect the territorial government's search for collateral support in its case against Edward Livingston in the batture controversy.[38]

Shortly after resigning his post as sheriff of New Orleans in the late winter of 1805, Kerr was retained by Governor Claiborne on the authorization of the territorial council to write the criminal code and procedures for the courts of the Orleans Territory and produce both English and French versions.[39] In turning to Kerr, Claiborne said that he needed a "Gentleman Learned in the Law," someone in whom he had "great confidence" because of his "professional talents and Industry." Claiborne said he wanted the work to be "concise, . . . the Style . . . plain . . . , and ready for the Press as speedily as possible." Claiborne also turned to Kerr because "your time is not wholly engaged" as a result of "the present suspension of Business in our Courts."[40] The task was reminiscent of the one Kerr had done for the Supreme Court in Bengal, India. When the Louisiana procedures were completed, they were published in two separate printings, one by Bradford and Anderson, the printers to the territorial government, and the other by John Mowry, in 1806. The Bradford and Anderson printing was the bilingual

35. Register of Civil Appointments, January 1–June 30, 1806, Justices of the Peace, enclosed in Richard Claiborne to [the Secretary of State], June 30, 1806, TP, 9: 662; and Barthélémy Lafon, *Calendrier de Commerce de la Nouvelle-Orleans, pour l'Année 1807* (New Orleans: Jean Renard, 1806 [*sic*]), 63.

36. Lafon, *Calendrier de Commerce,* 73; and *Acts Passed at the First Session of the Legislative Council . . . ,* 306.

37. Derbigny and Kerr to the Mayor, October 6, 1806, Governor's Office: American Documents, 1804–1814, City Archives, Louisiana Department, New Orleans Public Library.

38. *The Mayor of New Orleans* v. *Samuel B. Davis,* Superior Court case no. 1093, February 2, 1805. The city attempted to obtain at a reasonable price the land between the city and its adjacent upriver suburb, St. Mary. The land in question lay beyond the ends of Chartres, Royal, and Bourbon Streets and was claimed by Daniel Clark. The suit against Davis, who was regarded as Clark's agent, was discontinued on April 15, 1807.

39. To Lewis Kerr, August 14, 1805, CLB, 3: 166.

40. Ibid.

(French and English) edition. The Mowry printing was the English language portion of the publication issued separately.[41] Translator for the French language portion of the finished publication was Louis Moreau Lislet, a former resident of Santo Domingo who also was considered an expert in civil law.

The *Exposition of Criminal Laws* presaged the course that law in Louisiana ultimately would take. Its authors drew on civil law for content and common law for administrative procedures. Unfortunately, after publication of the code, a political quarrel developed between those who favored civil law and those who favored common law as the basis of statute law. Those who wished to negate the influence of Jefferson's republican policies, along with his gubernatorial appointee, William C. C. Claiborne, and the Americanization of Louisiana's Romanist legal heritage were attracted to this means of defense. They made it a struggle between the onslaught of Anglo-Saxon society and their traditional French society. It is likely that Kerr anticipated the ugly fight among the several factions vying for political control in territorial Louisiana and wanted no part of it. As a world traveler, Kerr probably was quite aware that the developing quarrel between arriving French émigrés and some native Louisianians, on one side, and arriving Americans on the other was much broader in scope than the local issues. The quarrel attained political structure when the native Louisianians were empowered by Governor Claiborne, who began to rely on them for political support during the Burr conspiracy.

In legal circles outside of Louisiana, the attack on common law derived its respectability from the longstanding discussion of whether common law should be replaced with a rival system or a completely new system of laws. This debate had begun in the colonial period of American history and was given impetus by the defeat of the British in the American Revolution. It was never fully resolved, but after the French Revolution the Napoleonic

---

41. The title of the publication was *An Exposition of the Criminal Laws of the Territory of Orleans: The Practice of the Courts of Criminal Jurisdiction, the Duties of Their Officers, with a Collection of Forms for the Use of Magistrates and Others. Published in Pursuance of An Act of the Legislature of the Territory, Entitled "An Act for the Punishment of Crimes and Misdemeanors," Passed May 4, 1805* (New Orleans: Bradford & Anderson, 1806). An added title page in French indicates that Louis Moreau Lislet translated the French edition, which was published by Jean Renard as part of the same volume. The pagination for the two-part work is continuous. See Florence Jumonville, *Bibliography of New Orleans Imprints, 1764–1864*, 1st ed. (New Orleans: Historic New Orleans Collection, 1989), 38 (entries 127 and 128). Warren M. Billings, "A Neglected Treatise: Lewis Kerr's Exposition and the Making of Criminal Law in Louisiana," *Louisiana History* 38, no. 3 (summer 1997), 261–86, examines this publication and points out that it is to be reprinted.

Code was regarded in some American legal circles as a model of clarity and order.[42] In comparison, common law seemed to be feudal and barbaric. Law in early Louisiana was a bewildering mixture of French and Spanish practice derived from "a mélange of codes, customs, and doctrines of various ages."[43]

Claiborne and Kerr were good friends until the Burr conspiracy burst on the public in late 1806. In August 1804, Claiborne described Kerr to Jefferson as one of the three known republicans among the thirty lawyers in New Orleans. Equally important, Claiborne said that he appointed Kerr sheriff because he "enjoyed my confidence, & was himself possessed of legal information."[44] Isaac Briggs, the surveyor-general for the Mississippi Territory and one of Jefferson's chief informants in the Southwest, wrote the president early in 1805 that Kerr defended Claiborne under the pen name of "Curtius."[45] In the spring of 1806 Claiborne engaged Kerr to defend the sale of a tract of land by a tribe of friendly Indians in the territory to a native Louisianian. The sale had occurred under the Spanish government. Kerr sought one hundred dollars as his fee, which he said was the lowest figure offered in New Orleans in a cause of importance. Claiborne offered fifty dollars as just compensation. Both men agreed to submit the question of the fee to the secretary of war for resolution.[46]

During the bitter and divisive quarrel between the Catholic priests Patrick Walsh and Antonio Sedella, both of whom claimed the title vicar-general of the Catholic Church in Louisiana, Kerr sided with the Irish-born Walsh. Their friendship apparently was based on more than political convenience. When Walsh died, it was Kerr who notified Bishop Carroll, head of the Catholic Church in the United States, of the priest's death late in August

42. Not everyone rushed to embrace the Napoleonic Code. Among the wealthy commercial and landed classes in the United States, the Napoleonic Code was regarded as provocative and disruptive. In this sense Jefferson was regarded as the representative of the French Revolution and the agent of change within the American Revolution, which placed Claiborne in a very awkward position for laying the foundations of government in territorial Louisiana. See Mitchell Franklin, "The Eighteenth *Brumaire* in Louisiana: Talleyrand and the Spanish Medieval Legal System of 1806," *Tulane Law Review* 16, no. 4 (June 1942), 514–61.

43. Lawrence M. Friedman, *A History of American Law* (New York: Simon and Schuster, 1973), 151.

44. Governor Claiborne to the President, August 30, 1804, TP, 9: 286.

45. Isaac Briggs to the President, 9th of the 2nd mo. 1805 [*sic*], in Clarence E. Carter, comp. and ed., *The Territorial Papers of the United States*, vol. 5, *The Territory of Mississippi, 1798–1817* (Washington, D.C.: U.S. Government Printing Office, 1937), 382.

46. To Henry Dearborn, June 26, 1806, CLB, 3: 348–9.

1806. In his letter to Bishop Carroll, Kerr described Walsh as "my respected friend."[47]

Following the revelation of the Burr conspiracy, Claiborne learned of a connection between Burr and the Mexican Association from the cipher letters between Jonathan Dayton and Burr. The letters were shown to Claiborne by General James Wilkinson after he arrived in New Orleans from Natchitoches.[48] Although the Mexican Association was not mentioned by name, the references to "associate" and "association" alarmed Claiborne. The semisecret Mexican Association had been known to exist in New Orleans since sometime in 1805.[49] It had been organized by about a dozen of the territory's leading citizens, among them Judge James Workman, Kerr, John Watkins, and Daniel Clark. Kerr and Workman were credited with taking a leading role in organizing the association.[50] Workman provided most of what is known about the objectives of the group in his December 30, 1806, statement to Lieutenant Colonel Constant Freeman.[51] It is possible Kerr joined in the organization of the association with the idea of checking on its activities, with the knowledge and approval of Claiborne. As an officer in the territorial militia and on the governor's staff, Kerr had an immediate need to know what was being done by the business interests of the community to protect itself. Although not widely known, the existence of the organization and its purposes were public knowledge. At its inception,

47. Peter Guilday, *The Life and Times of John Carroll, Archbishop of Baltimore, 1735–1815* (1922; Westminster, Md.: Newman Press, 1954), 706 n. 17. Apparently, Walsh died on August 22, 1806. *Télégraphe*, August 23, 1806, p. 3, c. 1.

48. To James Madison (Private), December 4 and December 5, 1806, CLB, 4: 40 and 42–3.

49. Writing about what he knew of it, Vicente Folch y Juan, governor of Spanish West Florida, told the Marqués de Someruelos, captain-general, on February 10, 1807, that the Mexican Association had been established "About two years ago" and that it was "dependent on the one in New York." Folch called it a *"Comisio Revolucionario,"* meaning a revolutionary commission. Walter F. McCaleb, *The Aaron Burr Conspiracy and A New Light on Aaron Burr* (1936; New York: Argosy-Antiquarian, 1966), 90, 91. (The second part of this book, *A New Light on Aaron Burr,* is separately paginated. Therefore, references to this separate section will be cited as McCaleb, *Burr Conspiracy,* addendum, with page numbers). This background information may have been provided to Folch by Marqués de Yrujo.

50. Abernethy, *Burr Conspiracy,* 25, cites from the testimony of Lt. W. A. Murray in 1807 from the Burr Conspiracy MSS in the Library of Congress on Workman's and Kerr's involvement in the organization of the Mexican Association.

51. Samuel H. Wandell and Meade Minnigerode, *Aaron Burr, A Biography Written, in Large Part, from Original and Hitherto Unused Material,* vol. 2 (New York: G. P. Putnam's Sons, 1925), 124–7.

the group was known to be preparing for the war expected between the United States and Spain late in 1805 and early in 1806. During the expected war, the associates were to take Baton Rouge and Mobile, and "then march into the Spanish provinces west of the Mississippi."[52]

The organization of the military association sought by Graham and Watkins paralleled and continued the local action taken in New Orleans in November 1803 when a volunteer militia of Americans was organized by Daniel Clark out of fear that the Spanish officers and their friends might try to stop the transfer of Louisiana to France and its sale to the United States.[53] There is no evidence that Claiborne approved or allowed the military association to be organized. When Burr visited New Orleans in June 1805, he contacted some of the men who had been active in the Mexican Association and apparently received assurances of unspecified support for his future project from a few of them.[54] Claiborne was aware of the connection between the association and Burr by early December 1806, if not before.[55]

52. Ibid., 124–5. Charles Gayarré, *History of Louisiana,* 4th ed., vol. 4 (1903; New Orleans: Pelican, 1965), 124, speaks only of the military association described by John Graham in Secretary Graham to the Secretary of State, January 2, 1805[6], TP, 9: 555. George Dargo, *Jefferson's Louisiana: Politics and the Clash of Legal Traditions* (Cambridge, Mass.: Harvard University Press, 1975), 55, 199 n. 14, regards the two groups as one and the same, but this does not appear to be completely true. See the "Military Associates/Association" and "Mexican Associates/Association" essays in this appendix.

53. See [Arthur P. Whitaker, ed.,] "Another Dispatch from the United States Consulate in New Orleans," *American Historical Review* 38, no. 2 (January 1933), 291–2, which prints Daniel Clark's December 3, 1803, letter to Madison telling of the public tension in New Orleans, and of the 180 American men and their friends who spontaneously decided to organize the "Volunteer association" in November 1803; and [Whitaker, ed.,] "Despatches from the United States Consulate in New Orleans, 1801–1803, II," ibid., 33, no. 2 (January 1928), 355–6, particularly n. 43, on the latter page, provides additional perspective on the issue. To James Madison, October 16, 1804, CLB, 2: 353–4, says the "Volunteer Corps" was organized by "the Citizens of the United States, residing in the City." The governor added that "several Companies were form'd, and . . . some of the ancient Militia were enroll'd in the new Corps." See also John W. Monette, *History of the Discovery and Settlement of the Valley of the Mississippi . . . Until the Year 1846,* vol. 1 (reprint; New York: Arno Press, 1971), 561; and Marietta Marie LeBreton, *A History of the Territory of Orleans, 1803–1812* (Ann Arbor, Mich.: University Microfilms, 1973), 68.

54. Henry Adams, *History of the United States of America During the Second Administration of Thomas Jefferson,* vol. 1 (New York: C. Scribner's Sons, 1890), 223–4; and Abernethy, *Burr Conspiracy,* 25, 26, 30, 269–70.

55. It is possible that Claiborne had no knowledge of the rumored intent to use the Mexican Association to seize Spanish colonial possessions nearby, but it seems unlikely. See the

Thus, at the outset Burrism was linked to well-known local figures. Some of them, including Kerr; John Watkins, mayor of New Orleans and speaker of the territorial House of Representatives; Sheriff George T. Ross; and Workman were close to Claiborne either as friends or public officials. Kerr and Judge Workman shortly became outspoken leaders of opposition to the measures taken by General Wilkinson to halt what he said were the plans of Burr.

Two weeks after revealing what he had learned about Burr's schemes, Wilkinson launched what has been described as a "reign of terror" against Burr's associates and men in New Orleans who were known by him to be members of the Mexican Association. The delay, Wilkinson said, was a stratagem to trap the conspirators, many of whom believed the general was part of whatever Burr's scheme may have been. In mid-November, before leaving Fort Adams for New Orleans, Wilkinson sent Claiborne a message designed to frighten the unsuspecting governor and turn him from his friends. Wilkinson wrote Claiborne, "You have spies on your every movement and disposition" and advised him not to share any information with even "the most intimate friend of your Bosom."[56] Similar private messages, tailored to persuade whomever he was addressing, either in writing or in person, of the accuracy of his information were made to Jefferson and John Watkins.[57] Once in New Orleans, Wilkinson took command of the situation by force of his position as supreme commander of U.S. military forces in the West, his closely held command of the facts, and his strong personality. Soon afterwards he launched a series of actions consisting of military arrests, illegal abductions, defiance of court writs, and the threatened use of force against anyone who opposed him.[58]

Kerr, like most members of the Mexican Association, opposed Wilkinson's high-handed actions as an abridgment of individual rights and liberties guaranteed under the Constitution. However, Kerr acted on his beliefs. After two of Burr's associates, Samuel Swartwout and Peter Ogden of New York, were arrested at Fort Adams, Mississippi Territory, in mid-December 1806, Kerr applied to Judge Workman for their release. Swartwout, like another Burr associate, Dr. Erick Bollman, was sent to Baltimore by Wilkinson before

---

"Mexican Associates/Association" and "Military Associates/Association" essays in this appendix.

56. From James Wilkinson, November 12, 1806, CLB, 4: 55.

57. Dargo, *Jefferson's Louisiana,* 56 and 200 n. 18.

58. Ibid., 56–7.

his freedom could be effected. Young Ogden was rearrested on December 19, two days after being given his freedom. Because he actively opposed General Wilkinson and was a known associate of Wilkinson's most vocal critic, Judge James Workman, Kerr fell under the general's suspicion. Three weeks later, on the evening of January 14, 1807, both Kerr and Workman were arrested while at dinner by a detachment of U.S. Army dragoons. The two men were charged by the grand jury, summoned at Wilkinson's request, with the high misdemeanor of setting on foot military expeditions against the Spanish provinces of Florida and Mexico with weapons and ammunition that were to have been taken from the U.S. arsenal at Fort Adams.[59] However, the real reason for Kerr's arrest may have been Wilkinson's fear that Kerr would arrest him. A week before his arrest, Kerr, a colonel in the militia, was given the responsibility of arming the regular militia of the city. In that week, he had received "nearly a thousand stand of arms."[60] More important, Kerr was known to have suggested to Governor Claiborne that he "authorize him," Kerr, to arrest General Wilkinson "*on his own responsibility,* and ship him" to Washington.[61] After spending twelve to fifteen hours in jail, Kerr was paroled in the custody of Governor Claiborne.[62] What Claiborne and Kerr may have said to one another on Kerr's release is not known. In the course of his trial, Kerr alluded to his friendship with Claiborne only once.

To refute the charges lodged against him by General Wilkinson, Kerr retained Edward Livingston, Philip L. Jones, and William A. Duer as counsel. However, Livingston and Jones were ill throughout much of the trial so that

59. From James Wilkinson, January 14, 1807, and Presentments against James Workman and Lewis Kerr at a Grand Jury of the Superior Court in the County of Orleans in the Territory of Orleans, January 12, 1807, enclosed in To James Madison, April 21, 1808, CLB, 4: 94–5 and 170–1 respectively; Workman, *Trials,* 5–7, 102; and James Workman, *Essays and Letters on Various Political Subjects,* 2nd American ed. (New York: I. Riley, 1809), 147.

60. "Faithful Picture of the Political Situation of New Orleans at the Close of the Last and the Beginning of the Present Year, 1807," ed. James E. Winston, *Louisiana Historical Quarterly* 11, no. 3 (July 1928), 409–10 (original publication pp. 31–2). A few years later, someone identifying himself only as "Cato" said that Colonel Henry Hopkins received one thousand stand of arms, and that Kerr and Colonel Jacques Villeré each received three hundred stand of arms, but "not one hundred stand of them have ever been returned into the arsenal" *(Louisiana Gazette,* January 16, 1812, p. 2, c. 3).

61. Emphasis in the original. Winston, "Faithful Picture," 409–10.

62. Ibid., 410, and Workman, *Essays and Letters,* 147, both tell of the closeness of Claiborne and Kerr. This fact appears to have been common knowledge. Five years later, when the "reign of terror" was becoming a memory, someone identifying himself only as "Cato" described Kerr as "a great favorite" of Claiborne in 1806 and early 1807 *(Louisiana Gazette,* January 16, 1812, p. 2, c. 3).

Kerr, assisted by Workman, was allowed to plead his own case. Early in the trial U.S. Army Lieutenant Francis W. Small quoted Kerr as saying he would appeal to his relative, General Lord Hely-Hutchinson, for money and ships from the British government, thereby assuring the success of the proposed expedition against Spanish territory. In his defense Kerr pointed out that anything he said must be considered in the context of the widely held belief in 1805 and early 1806 that the United States and Spain would soon be at war. He further pointed out that no preparations for any expedition had ever been made by him or anyone else. Kerr went on to declare that all statements made to the jury should be balanced against the knowledge that the Mexican Association had been dissolved in the spring of 1806 when it seemed clear there would be no war between the United States and Spain.[63]

The surviving record of Kerr's remarks in his trial provides excellent insight into his powers of discernment and his personality. There is a flash of brilliance when he develops the concept of the Mexican Association as nothing more than "loyal opposition." The association, he suggested, was simply a private political organization without sinister or subversive motives. This was a departure from the usual meaning of *political* in early nineteenth-century U.S. history. It was not until after the Jacksonian era that *political* meant anything other than divisiveness in American history.[64] In Louisiana at this time *political* usually was applied to those who favored the retrocession of all or part of Louisiana to Spain or France. Arguing that "Vulgar minds" were "too easily led to believe that all political projects, in a mere citizen, are nearly allied to treason," Kerr attempted to show that "politics" was not treason and political societies had a role in society.[65]

In dealing with the reasons for his arrest, Kerr claimed that his incarceration was the result of his opposition to the illegal and unconstitutional actions of General Wilkinson. His arrest and confinement, Kerr said, were based on testimony forced from Lt. Small during his close confinement on the orders of Wilkinson.[66] Unfortunately, Kerr produced no witness to corroborate this point. Regarding Small's testimony, Kerr said, "I do not accuse the witness of one single misstatement. I admit the whole with pleasure."[67] Gently alluding to the gullible naïveté demonstrated by the youthful Lt. Small, Kerr acknowledged that he had lodged himself in his present difficult

63. Workman, *Trials*, 102–13, 120–2.
64. Ibid., 125–30. See also Dargo, *Jefferson's Louisiana*, 201 n. 36.
65. Workman, *Trials*, 174.
66. Ibid., 174–6.
67. Ibid., 127–8.

position by his unguarded wit. The whole incident, Kerr said, amounted to a "whimsical farrago of light and frivolous conversation set forth as matter of solemn fact and sober speculation."[68]

Despite the disarming nature of Kerr's testimony, in the absence of any witnesses to support his statements the jury could not agree on a verdict after three days of deliberation, and on February 15, 1807, was discharged.[69] However, this did not conclude the case. The attorneys for the prosecution, James Brown, John W. Gurley, and Abner L. Duncan, argued that a new jury should be impaneled. The presiding judge, Dominic A. Hall, agreed with them and on his instruction the date for the new trial was set to begin in two weeks, March 2, 1807.[70]

In the second trial, Kerr served from the outset as his own counsel and was acquitted in a matter of minutes after the trial began. He was acquitted on the testimony of a new witness for the defense, Joseph Thomas, a prominent merchant and acquaintance of Kerr through the Battalion of Orleans Volunteers. Thomas testified that he had seen and conversed with Lt. Small in the headquarters of the Orleans Volunteers a few days after Small had been arrested and confined by Wilkinson. During the conversation, Small stated that he was being held because he "would not give up the names of some gentlemen who had spoken to him about an expedition to Mexico." Thomas went on to testify that Small said he "never . . . thought" the expedition was illegal, nor did he think there was "anything criminal in the expedition."[71] Thomas said he urged Small to reveal the names of the men, saying that by withholding them he was doing them an injustice as well as himself, but Small would not.

On the introduction of this testimony, several members of the jury requested permission to consult on the verdict of the case, stating that after hearing the testimony of Thomas their opinions could not be altered by the debates from the bar. Under the circumstances the attorneys and the court agreed to submit the case to the jury without further comment. The jury retired and within a few minutes brought in the not-guilty verdict.[72]

---

68. Ibid., 127.

69. Ibid., 95, 173–4. A fragment of a letter following To Robert Williams, February 10, 1807, CLB, 4: 119–20, indicates that Kerr was tried first and says the jury was discharged on February 10, 1807. Internal evidence in the letter fragment suggests that it most probably was written on March 2, 1807, the opening date of the second trial of Kerr and Workman.

70. Workman, *Trials*, 176.

71. Ibid., 177.

72. Ibid., 178. The verdict was reported in the *Orleans Gazette*, Thursday, March 5, 1807, p. 3, c. 2, and carried the following day in the *Louisiana Gazette*, Friday, March 6, 1807, p. 2, c. 3.

Before revelation of the Burr conspiracy and his alleged association with it, Kerr's career flourished. During the trial, Lt. Small quoted Kerr as having said that he was "comfortably enough situated; that he wanted nothing."[73] After revelation of the conspiracy and his trial, Kerr found that he no longer was a member of that Anglo-American quadrumvirate of Kerr, Workman, Watkins, and Ross that had surrounded Claiborne.[74] Indeed, Kerr not only was excluded from the governor's presence, but during his trial wondered aloud, "which day of my life most to regret, that on which I made Wilkinson an enemy, or that on which Claiborne became my friend."[75] Although it was not immediately apparent, Kerr's career suffered and he soon was forced to borrow money. One person to whom he obligated himself in the months after his trial was the wealthy merchant George Pollock. Because of business reverses, Pollock, too, soon found himself in straitened financial circumstances. Less than two weeks after Kerr borrowed one hundred dollars from Pollock, the Irish-born merchant filed for bankruptcy. Subsequently, he sold Kerr's note to the merchants Hart, Bartlett & Cox, who brought suit to collect from Kerr. Ultimately, on November 21, 1808, the plaintiffs were awarded judgment for principal, interest, damages, and costs.[76] Either from a desire to correct the gross injustice suffered at the hands of Wilkinson, or from a genuine need of income, Kerr brought suit in the territorial Superior Court against the army officer, Captain E. Bradish, who arrested him and marched him off to jail. The report of the suit said Kerr sought twenty thousand dollars in damages for assault and false imprisonment.[77]

The continued presence of Kerr in New Orleans appears to have made Claiborne nervous. On March 17, 1808, approximately eight months before the court decision in favor of Hart, Bartlett & Cox, Claiborne wrote Madi-

73. Workman, *Trials,* 13.

74. Dargo, *Jefferson's Louisiana,* 57–8, 60, and passim touches on political alignments in Orleans Territory, particularly after the Burr conspiracy.

75. Workman, *Trials,* 131.

76. *Thos. Hart, Jr., John S. Bartlett, and Nathaniel Cox* v. *Lewis Kerr,* Superior Court case no. 1643, May 27, 1808, and Superior Court case no. 1748, August 1, 1808. A second record of the latter case is dated only August 1808, but contains essentially the same information. The proceedings in George Pollock's bankruptcy are set forth in *George Pollock* v. *His Creditors,* Superior Court case no. 1503, March 5, 1808. The records reflect that it was Pollock who initiated the proceedings.

77. *Kentucky Gazette,* February 16, 1808, p. 3, c. 2, citing the original report carried in the *Orleans Gazette.* No record of the case has been found, so that its final disposition is unknown.

son that Kerr had applied for his passport to visit England.[78] The following month, the governor privately advised Secretary of War Dearborn that Kerr supposedly was to return to Ireland.[79] The city directory for this year lists his address at 23 "royale sud" (south Royal Street).[80] There are indications that as long as he was in New Orleans, Kerr not only was involved in litigation, but also continued to practice law.[81]

One case in which he served as counsel was the contempt of court charge brought against James Workman in December 1808 by Judge Joshua Lewis. The case grew out of the exchanges in the court between Philip Grymes, attorney for the city, and Workman, attorney for Edward Livingston, during the batture case. Despite the preponderance of evidence assembled on behalf of Workman, Judge Lewis barred him from practicing law in the Superior Court of the Orleans Territory.[82]

There also are indications that Kerr actively continued to fight the wrongs he saw taking place at the instigation of Wilkinson and the inaction of Claiborne. With James Workman, Kerr was identified by Claiborne as one of the backers of the short-lived newspaper *La Lanterne Magique* (the *Magic Lantern*).[83] Other evidence indicates Kerr attacked Wilkinson in the *Philadelphia Gazette* under a pseudonym, "Curtius," associated with his name in the past. In the anonymous piece, "Curtius" said the general's conduct in New Orleans was to disguise his character and role in everything that had transpired.[84]

78. To James Madison (Private), March 17, 1808, CLB, 4: 167.

79. Governor Claiborne to the Secretary of War, April 21, 1808, TP, 9: 784.

80. B[arthélémy]. Lafon, *Annuaire Louisianais pour L'Année 1809* (New Orleans: L'Imprimerie de L'Auteur, 1808), 214.

81. See To James Madison, April 21, 1808, CLB, 4: 170. One of the cases with which Kerr was involved was that of Peter Pedesclaux, former recorder of mortgages in New Orleans, in May 1807. Claiborne had removed Pedesclaux from office, but Pedesclaux maintained that he had bought the office from the government of Spain and would not relinquish the office or its papers. As a consequence, Governor Claiborne brought suit. Subsequently, Claiborne reported that Kerr, Workman, Livingston, and James Alexander had volunteered their services as counselors for Pedesclaux. Governor Claiborne to the President, May 19, 1807, TP, 9: 735.

82. [James Workman,] *Case of Mr. Workman on a Rule for An Alleged Contempt of the Superior Court of the Territory of Orleans* (Philadelphia: William Fry, [1809]), 15.

83. To James Madison, March 17, 1808, CLB, 4: 167.

84. Winston, "Faithful Picture," 386 n. w-25 (original publication p. 16). The correct date on which the *Philadelphia Gazette* story was carried in the *Louisiana Gazette* was September 2, 1808, p. 2, c. 4, and p. 3, cc. 2–3, not September 8, 1808. Although "Curtius" may have been the nom de plume used by Kerr, the story from the *Philadelphia Gazette* sounds more as though it were written by Workman. McCaleb, *Burr Conspiracy*, addendum, 56–7,

If Kerr had not already decided to leave New Orleans, the decision against Workman in the contempt case and how it arbitrarily was made by Judge Lewis and Abner L. Duncan, the Orleans Territory attorney general, revealed the extent to which the territorial administration under Claiborne was willing to go to destroy any opposition. As a consequence, Kerr decided to move on. He apparently left New Orleans sometime in the first quarter of 1809, perhaps March, to settle in the Bahama Islands.[85] Kerr's last official act before leaving New Orleans suggests that his financial circumstances may have further deteriorated. In mid-February 1809, Kerr transferred ownership of Maria, a thirteen-year-old slave girl, to James C. Williamson to satisfy the six hundred dollar mortgage he owed Williamson.[86]

Except for a few years, from approximately 1828 to 1830, when depressed economic conditions in the Bahamas caused him to move to Kingston, Jamaica, Kerr lived the rest of his life in Nassau. In the Bahamas he became a well-known and respected lawyer. One of his peers there regarded Kerr as the "most eloquent lawyer that ever addressed judge or jury in Nassau."[87] Whenever it was known he was to appear before the court, the hall reportedly would be "crowded to suffocation."[88] Although this praise of Kerr may be exaggerated, there is little reason to doubt that he was an accomplished speaker with a keen intellect.

The combination of Kerr's speaking ability, training in law, and prior public experience pointed toward a career in public service. That career began in the Bahamas on November 23, 1810, when he took his seat in the house of assembly. For the next twenty-four years, Kerr served the people of the Bahamas as assemblyman (1810–32), council member (1832–34), solicitor general (1833–34), and attorney general (1833–34).[89]

After the War of 1812, Eligius Fromentin, a state senator from Louisiana, wrote to a "friend in Baltimore" that Lewis Kerr was believed to have

---

cites evidence that Wilkinson maintained contact with the Spanish throughout the Burr episode.

85. Workman, *Case of Mr. Workman,* 26, says Kerr "quitted the territory shortly" after the contempt trial.

86. Act of February 18, 1809, Notarial Acts of John Lynd, Notarial Archives, New Orleans, Louisiana.

87. *Nassau Royal Gazette and Bahama Advertiser,* October 18, 1834, p. 3, c. 1.

88. Ibid.

89. David E. Wood, archives assistant, Public Records Office, Nassau, The Bahamas, citing unspecified pages of the "Miscellaneous and Indexes Journal of the House of Assembly" and the *Blue Book, 1834.* Enclosed in D. Gail Saunders, archivist, Public Records Office, Nassau, Bahamas, to the author, November 10, 1976.

been with the British forces in the attack on New Orleans. The report was carried in *Niles' Weekly Register,* but no evidence has been found to substantiate the story.[90]

During his years of public service in the Bahamas, Kerr came to be regarded as a distinguished leader of the opposition to gubernatorial authority and to the attempts of the government in England to force the colony to adopt laws that would improve the condition of the slaves brought to the Bahamas.[91] Although Kerr generally supported the islanders' views in the matter of slavery, he firmly believed the slaves should be treated humanely, or Parliament would adopt laws for the islands regulating the conduct of slave and master. This appears to have been the basis of Kerr's actions toward his fellow assemblyman James Wildgoose in 1831.

Wildgoose precipitated a crisis in the Bahamas by having one of his female slaves flogged.[92] This was a violation of the laws regulating slavery in the islands, but it created an uproar when the incident was critically noted in the house of assembly. The debate that followed developed along the lines of the continuing struggle for power between the governor and the assembly, but it was one of the avenues by which Kerr moved from the assembly to the council and then on to be attorney general. In the debate Kerr took the position taken later by Viscount Goderich, secretary of war for the colonies, that "in the case of slaves, as of freemen, the Common Law must, in the absence of positive Statute, afford the rule of decision."[93] What punishment, if any, may have been given Wildgoose over this infraction of the law is not known, but the extended debate precipitated by the incident must

90. *Niles' Weekly Register* (Baltimore), February 14, 1815, 360, c. 2. Attempts to corroborate this published story have been unsuccessful. The military records in the British Public Record Office are not indexed. John Wood, Reader Services Department, Public Record Office, Kew, Richmond, Surrey, U.K., to author, June 29, 1995.

91. See Kerr's obituary in the *Nassau Royal Gazette and Bahama Advertiser,* October 18, 1834, p. 3, c. 1. Wilbur H. Siebert, *The Legacy of the American Revolution to the British West Indies and Bahamas* (Columbus: Ohio State University, 1913), 30–4; Michael Craton, *A History of the Bahamas* (London: Collin, 1962), 187–204. A Captain Kerr, commander of the Brown Rangers, a company of black infantrymen that participated in the April 23, 1824, parade celebrating King George IV's birthday, is referred to in Michael Craton and D. Gail Saunders, *Islanders in the Stream: A History of the Bahamian People,* vol. 1, *From Aboriginal Times to the End of Slavery* (Athens: University of Georgia Press, 1992), 252. See also ibid., 245, which mentions the Kerrs attending a social function without further identification of them.

92. Craton and Saunders, *Islanders in the Stream,* 201.

93. Lewis Kerr to J. Carmichael-Smyth, January 31, 1832, Public Records Office, London, Colonial Office 23/86, photocopy owned by the author.

have been embarrassing and frustrating to him. Wildgoose had begun his law career as a clerk in Kerr's law office.[94]

Whether it was a lingering bitterness toward Kerr over this incident, or simply that Wildgoose and his friends were unwitting victims of Kerr's compulsion for tall tales, is not known, but later Wildgoose told a story containing the mixture of fact and misinformation that was characteristic of Kerr's brand of facetiousness—the kind of whimsy that helped to bring on the trial for high misdemeanor in New Orleans. The tale harked back to Kerr's years in Louisiana and the Burr conspiracy. According to Wildgoose, in the "early part of 1807, a gentleman calling himself Louis [sic] Kerr arrived at Nassau" and began practicing law. Nothing was known of the man's past, but his knowledge of law, his eloquence, and his success at the Nassau bar soon won him appointment as attorney general. Shortly thereafter the barrister married "Miss M'Pherson, a daughter of Major M'Pherson, then in command of the West India Regiment stationed at New Providence."[95] Subsequently, near the end of the year 1809, Wildgoose went on to report, an American schooner arrived in Nassau from some port in South America. On board was a beautiful lady who began inquiring for Mr. Blennerhassett. As James Stark recounts the matter:

> no one knew of any such person being in any of the Bahama Islands. Accident, however, revealed to her that the Attorney General of the Colony, Louis Kerr, was no other than Blennerhasset. *The lady was his wife.* Blennerhasset sought an interview with her and prevailed on her, after giving her a large sum of money, which was afterwards turned into an annuity, to leave the island, pointing out to her that if the secret was divulged it would be his ruin. . . . But one person at that time, James Wildgoose, Blennerhasset's confidential clerk, and afterwards himself a lawyer, knew these facts; he religiously kept the secret until years after Blennerhasset's death.[96]

It is possible that new and unshakable evidence could appear to confirm Wildgoose's story as repeated by Stark, but from what is presently known there is no basis in fact for the statements made about Kerr. As has been

94. James H. Stark, *Stark's History and Guide to the Bahama Islands* (Boston: Stark, 1891), 184.

95. Ibid.

96. Stark, *History and Guide,* 184–5. Emphasis in the original.

pointed out, Kerr was involved in lawsuits as defendant and counsel in New
Orleans in 1807 and 1808. Although he applied for his passport in March
1808, it is apparent that he did not leave the Orleans Territory until nearly
a year later. Equally important, Kerr's rise to political importance in the Bahamas was not as meteoric as Stark's narrative leads the reader to believe.
Kerr served twenty-two years in the Bahamas Assembly before his appointments as council member, solicitor general, and attorney general, all of
which coincided with his defense of some aspect of slavery. For example,
Kerr used his talents as a writer to provide arguments for the opposition to
Lord Goderich's unsuccessful attempt in 1832 to abolish slavery in the British Empire.[97] A pamphlet by Kerr dealing with this topic was regarded by
some in England and the Bahamas as the "best written on the subject, of
any that emanated, [sic] from the Colonies."[98] Of course, slavery was an
issue of paramount importance to the planters of the Bahamas and elsewhere in the West Indies, where badly worn soil offered little hope of much
more than a minimum standard of living between the ebb and flow of a
continually decreasing port traffic.

It seems likely, too, that Wildgoose's statement that Kerr paid Mrs.
Blennerhassett an annuity to prevent revelation of his supposed bigamy
is without foundation. Kerr married Isabel McPherson, daughter of a Dr.
McPherson of Nassau, on March 9, 1811.[99] There is no known record of a
prior marriage by Kerr under any name. It is possible he could have paid
an annuity to Mrs. Blennerhassett, but not for the reasons given by Wildgoose. Kerr may have supported Margaret Agnew Blennerhassett and her
children out of his own generosity as long as he could, since the financial
hardship that she and her children faced after the death of Harman Blennerhassett was well known.[100] It is more likely that Kerr may have served as
legal counsel in the distribution of any inheritance due Blennerhassett, his
wife, and children. If Kerr gave Blennerhassett's wife financial assistance

---

97. On Goderich's failure, see Wilbur D. Jones, *"Prosperity" Robinson: The Life of Viscount Goderich, 1782–1859* (New York: St. Martin's Press, 1967), 222–7, 235. Although the
legislatures of the West Indian colonies are spoken of generally, there are no references to Lewis
Kerr and the Bahamas.

98. *Nassau Royal Gazette,* October 18, 1834.

99. Register of Marriages, 1805–1828, Christ Church, Nassau, The Bahamas Islands.

100. Mrs. Blennerhassett's circumstances are touched on in *Dictionary of American Biography,* s.v. "Blennerhassett, Harman," and Safford, *Blennerhassett Papers,* 585ff. Blennerhassett actually died in 1831, so that even here the pieces of Wildgoose's story as related by Stark
are not logical.

from his own resources, it could not have been great, or for very long. Cyclical economic conditions in the Bahamas periodically forced Kerr to live in straitened circumstances. During one of these periods near the end of the 1820s, Kerr moved to Kingston, Jamaica. The relocation clearly was intended to improve his financial standing, but apparently did not. In his will, written during the residence in Kingston, Kerr described his circumstances there as "unsatisfactory and unsettled." He was then receiving "little income . . . to enjoy" from his law practice.[101]

The illness from which Kerr suffered at the time he wrote his will in 1829 and at the time of his death in 1834 may have been the same, but its nature is unknown. He died in Philadelphia, Pennsylvania, where he had gone with the permission of the governor of the Bahamas to seek medical aid.[102] With Kerr at the time of his death was his sister-in-law, Mary McPherson Macdonald, who accompanied him in the capacity of a nurse and close family friend.[103] Kerr's wife Isabel apparently remained in Nassau.

There were eight children born to Lewis and Isabel Kerr: Lewis Lyndon (born September 15, 1812), Eliza (born August 24, 1814), Mary Isabel, Richard Hulton (born July 1, 1820), Ann, Claudius (born February 17, 1826), and Octavia (born February 21, 1828).[104] Sometime after the death of Lewis Kerr, his wife moved to New Orleans, where she died at the age of sixty-seven in March 1856. The notice of her death stated that Mrs. Kerr was survived by her sons L. L. Kerr and R. H. Kerr.[105]

101. Will of Lewis Kerr, March 26, 1829. Register of Wills, Book C 4, pp. 68–9, Nassau, The Bahamas Islands. Photocopy owned by the author.

102. Excerpt from the dispatch of the governor of the Bahamas, October 16, 1834.

103. See the September 16, 1834, codicil to the will of Lewis Kerr written in Philadelphia. Photocopy owned by the author.

104. The Kerr children are named by Kerr in his will. The known birth dates are from the *Register of Baptisms,* Christ Church, Nassau.

105. *New Orleans Daily Picayune,* March 27, 1856, p. 4, c. 3.

GEORGE POLLOCK

George Pollock (1755–August 23, 1820) was known to his contemporaries as a "gentleman of fortune and great respectability," and "one of the best educated, best informed and most polished citizens of New Orleans."[1] Yet the researcher who seeks information on Pollock's life is left almost with an enigma because of the absence of solid facts. For example, Benjamin Morgan, a contemporary and friend in New Orleans, wrote that Pollock was born in Great Britain.[2] Many years later, a scion of the Biddle family of Philadelphia who claimed to be a distant kinsman of George Pollock seemed to imply that George was born in colonial North America. Biddle described Pollock as the son of Thomas Pollock, who settled in New Bern, North Carolina, about 1740, and Eunice Edwards, granddaughter of Jonathan Edwards, the great New England divine. Thus, through his mother, George Pollock was reputed to be a first cousin of Aaron Burr, whose mother was Esther Edwards, an older sister of Eunice.[3] Biddle also described Burr and

1. This description of George Pollock may be found in several places, but the quotation used here is from William Safford, *The Blennerhassett Papers* . . . (Cincinnati: Moore, Wilstach, Keys, 1861), 513.

2. List of Persons born subjects of great Britain [*sic*] or residing here, August 31, 1803, enclosed in Benjamin Morgan to Chandler Price, August 11, 1803, in Clarence E. Carter, comp. and ed., *The Territorial Papers of the United States,* vol. 9, *The Territory of Orleans, 1803–1812* (Washington, D.C.: U.S. Government Printing Office, 1940), 10 (hereinafter cited as TP, with volume and page numbers).

3. See Charles Biddle, *Autobiography of Charles Biddle, Vice-President of the Supreme Executive Council of Pennsylvania, 1745–1821* (Philadelphia: E. Claxton, 1883), 323; and Safford, *Blennerhassett Papers,* 367, 486–7, 489, 513. Years later this incorrect information was incorporated in Horace E. Hayden, *Pollock Genealogy: A Biographical Sketch of Oliver Pol-*

George Pollock as close friends, and contemporary reports on contacts between the two men support this description. More recently, a monographic
study of early New Orleans refers to George Pollock as the brother of Oliver
Pollock, the financier of the American Revolution in the West.[4]

The truth apparently is that George Pollock was born in Dublin, Ireland,
the son of John Pollock and Elizabeth Carlile. George is believed to have
come to the United States between 1780 and 1786 with two of his brothers,
Hugh and Carlile. The three lived in New York City, where they established
businesses, sometimes together, and became naturalized U.S. citizens. Soon
after settling in New York, George married. He and his first wife, name unknown, had one child, a daughter named Ann. At the age of ten, after the
death of her mother, Ann was sent to live with a Mrs. Hartigan, her aunt
in Dublin. George took as his second wife Catherine Yates of New York
City in 1787. His country home, named Monte Alta, was located on the
banks of the Hudson River, the present site of General Ulysses S. Grant's
tomb.[5]

Much of the mystery about George Pollock stems from the several
changes of residence he made in his lifetime—Dublin, New York, Philadelphia, New Orleans—and confusion with his distant cousin, Oliver Pollock.
At least one writer assumed that George settled in New Orleans in the 1780s
as an employee of Oliver.[6] However, a careful examination of the available
evidence indicates that George Pollock did not make New Orleans his domicile until nearly twenty years later, after having lived in New York and Philadelphia. This information is derived from several sources. The first is

lock, Esq., of Carlisle, Pennsylvania, United States Commercial Agent at New Orleans and
Havana, 1776–1784. With Genealogical Notes of His Descendants (1883; Harrisburg, Pa.:
Lane S. Hart, 1976), 47–8. This book was reprinted in its entirety in New Orleans Genesis
15, no. 57 (January 1976), 1ff.

4. See John G. Clark, New Orleans, 1718–1812: An Economic History (Baton Rouge:
Louisiana State University Press, 1970), 351. James A. James, Oliver Pollock: The Life and
Times of an Unknown Patriot (New York: D. Appleton-Century, 1937), does not name the
two brothers who he said accompanied Oliver, his father, and a nephew to North America
about 1740.

5. Years later, Pollock's daughter Ann returned to the United States and became the wife
of Commodore Daniel Todd Patterson of the United States Navy. Melva Mae Guerin Fournier
and Jess Bergeron, "The Pollock and McDonnell Family," Terrebonne Life Lines 6, no. 2 (summer 1987), 60. This daughter was identified by George Pollock in his will as Catherine Carlisle.
George Pollock Will, September 7, 1819, Orleans Parish, Louisiana. Court of Probate, Record
of Wills, Will Book, 1817–1824, vol. 3, 161–2. City Archives, Louisiana Department, New
Orleans Public Library (hereinafter cited as George Pollock Will).

6. John G. Clark, New Orleans, 351.

Labigarre, a brief resident of New Orleans and a contemporary of George Pollock, who, with Evan Jones, compiled a list of characterizations of New Orleans residents that General James Wilkinson forwarded to President Jefferson in July 1804. In the Labigarre portion of the list Pollock is described as a native of Ireland, but "long [a resident] in New York."[7]

When and why George Pollock left New York is not known, but from about 1800 to near the end of 1807, Pollock maintained a residence at 172 Chestnut Street, Philadelphia.[8] Although Labigarre does not say when Pollock moved to New Orleans, he speaks of Pollock's presence in the city in such a way as to suggest that his arrival was comparatively recent. In addition, Labigarre's statement that Pollock's "family and fortune are rooted" in New Orleans seems intended to remove any doubt about where George Pollock officially resided.[9] The further description of Pollock as an active supporter of Governor Claiborne appears to be accurate on the basis of the appointments to public office received from or with the support of Claiborne.[10]

Aside from the statements of Benjamin Morgan and Labigarre about George Pollock, the earliest official record of his presence in New Orleans is from 1804. Late in the spring of that year, apparently after Claiborne appointed James Pitot mayor of New Orleans, Pollock was appointed to the New Orleans City Council, a post he held until early in the second week of March 1807.[11] Pollock's career as a public official had begun in December 1804 and seemed to blossom soon thereafter. In that month he was appointed, with Eugene Dorsière, to the territorial legislative council after others refused Claiborne's offer of the appointment.[12] Also in December 1804,

7. Characterization of New Orleans Residents, July 1, 1804, no. 102, enclosed in Governor Claiborne to the President, July 1, 1804, TP, 9: 256. The progenitor of this Pollock line was John Pollock, the great-grandfather of George. How Oliver Pollock may have been related to George is not known. See Fournier and Bergeron, "Pollock and McDonnell Family," 60.

8. Safford, *Blennerhassett Papers,* 513, indicates that George Pollock was living in his Chestnut Street home as late as November 17, 1807. See also Hayden, *Pollock Genealogy,* 47–8.

9. Characterization of New Orleans Residents, no. 102, TP, 9: 256. Hayden, *Pollock Genealogy,* 48, states that George Pollock moved to New Orleans in 1803.

10. As early as 1804, Pollock was identified as "active in the support of Governor Claiborne." Characterization of New Orleans Residents, no. 102, TP, 9: 256.

11. "Administrations of the Mayors of New Orleans, 1803–1936," comp. and ed. Works Project Administration (project 665-64-3-112, typescript; New Orleans, March 1940), 6, 9.

12. The President to Governor Claiborne, August 30, 1804; The President to the Secretary of War, September 6, 1804; Governor Claiborne to the President, December 2, 1804; and Gov-

Pollock, Benjamin Morgan, and Dr. John Watkins were appointed a committee of three to draw up a code of civil law and a code of superior court practice, a task they apparently arranged for Lewis Kerr to complete, but that eventually was completed by James Workman and Louis Moreau Lislet.[13] Then, on the last day of December 1804, the *Orleans Gazette* reported in an extra edition that Pollock had introduced in the territorial legislature a resolution denouncing the conduct of the Spanish guards posted near the Marqués de Casa Calvo's house as derogatory to the United States and an infringement of its sovereignty.[14] In the spring of the following year, Pollock was appointed to a number of important public offices. On April 10, 1805, he was appointed port warden; he was reappointed to the office on April 21, 1809.[15] Late in the month of April 1805, Pollock also was appointed justice of the peace.[16] His reappointment to this position of public trust two years later on June 30, 1807, suggests that, like the port warden office, Pollock may have held it throughout the territorial period.[17]

George Pollock's sense of public responsibility manifested itself in other ways, too. With Benjamin Morgan and Dr. William Flood, Pollock founded the New Orleans Library Society in June 1805.[18] In April 1806 he joined with Benjamin Morgan, Julien Poydras, and eight other businessmen or

---

ernor Claiborne to the President, December 21, 1804, in TP, 9: 283, 291, 344–5, and 358, respectively.

13. George Dargo, *Jefferson's Louisiana: Politics and the Clash of Legal Traditions* (Cambridge, Mass.: Harvard University Press, 1975), 114. Kerr apparently preferred to work on the *Exposition of Criminal Laws,* an accomplishment that has been ignored while his failure (or refusal) to codify the civil law has been overemphasized.

14. Resolution of the Legislative Council, December 31, 1804, TP, 9: 360–1. Ibid, 360 n. 1, states that the resolution was printed "In the form of a small printed handbill," apparently for distribution in New Orleans and elsewhere. The text of the bill also is printed in James A. Robertson, ed. and trans., *Louisiana Under the Rule of Spain, France and the United States, 1785–1807,* vol. 2 (1910–1911; Freeport, NY: Books for Libraries Press, 1969), 246 n. 122.

15. Register of Civil Appointments in the Territory of Orleans, Wardens of the Port, enclosed in John Graham's February 13, 1806, letter; and List of Civil and Military Officers, April 21, 1809, Wardens [of the Port], in TP, 9: 602 and 836, respectively.

16. Register of Civil Appointments in the Territory of Orleans, Justices [of the Peace], enclosed in John Graham's February 13, 1806 letter, ibid., 599.

17. A Register of Civil Appointments, June 30, 1807, Justices of the Peace, ibid., 750.

18. *Acts Passed at the First Session of the Legislative Council, of the Territory of Orleans, Begun and Held at the Principal, in the City of New Orleans, On Monday the Third Day of December, in the Year of Our Lord, One Thousand Eight Hundred and Four, and of the Independence of the United States the Twenty-Ninth* (New Orleans: James M. Bradford, 1805), 322.

businesses in New Orleans, to subscribe fifty dollars each for the purchase and maintenance of a fire engine from Philadelphia. It was around this engine that the Alarm Fire Company was organized.[19] The following year, on May 11, 1807, Pollock agreed to serve with Dominick Hall, Pierre Derbigny, John Watkins, Alexander Bonamy, George W. Morgan, and F. Fromentin as one of the trustees of the New Orleans Library, which had been established two years before.[20] In the same year, Pollock was elected president of the New Orleans Chamber of Commerce[21] and served as a director of the lottery established in 1805 to finance the University of Orleans, the newly created territorial system of education.[22] Perhaps the most important mark of George Pollock's reputation as a respected businessman and citizen was his appointment as a director of the branch Bank of the United States, which opened in New Orleans early in 1805. He was appointed to this position in 1806.[23] Pollock also served as one of the directors of the *Compagnie de Navigation* in 1808–09.[24]

As did most of the able-bodied and responsible men in territorial Louisiana, George Pollock also served in the militia. He was appointed captain in the Orleans Volunteers on May 30, 1806, apparently serving in the company of carabineers.[25] The appointment appears to have been a continuation of his service in the volunteer militia organized in December 1803 when the French again briefly ruled Louisiana and it was feared the Spanish would oppose American ownership of the colony. It was in this capacity that Pollock served with Eugene Dorsière, John Lynd, and others in the court martial of Samuel B. Davis in October 1805.[26] During the War of 1812, Pollock

19. New Orleans Municipal Papers, box 1, 1770–1806, folder 13, Special Collections Department, Howard-Tilton Memorial Library, Tulane University.

20. See the minutes of the May 11, 1807, meeting reported in the *Louisiana Gazette,* May 22, 1807, p. 4, c. 2, and B[arthélémy]. Lafon, *Calendrier de Commerce de la Nouvelle-Orléans, pour l'Année 1807* (New Orleans: Jean Renard, 1806 [*sic*]), 72.

21. "Premier 'Directory' de la Nouvelle-Orleans, 1807," in *La Diamant* 1, no. 14 (May 1, 1887), p. 45, c. 2.

22. Lafon, *Calendrier de Commerce,* 73.

23. Ibid., 71; and the *Louisiana Gazette,* April 1, 1808, p. 2, c. 4.

24. B[arthélémy]. Lafon, *Annuaire Louisianais pour L'Année 1809* (New Orleans: By the Author, 1808), 202–3.

25. Lafon, *Calendrier de Commerce,* 99; and Register of Appointments in the Militia of the Territory of Orleans, enclosed in Secretary Graham to the Secretary of State, May 8, 1806, Orleans Volunteers, TP, 9: 639.

26. General Court Martial, October 19, 1805, and General Orders, Captain Davis, October 26, 1805, TP, 9: 587 and 588–9, respectively.

again saw military service as a rifleman in Captain Thomas Beale's Company of Orleans Riflemen (December 1814–March 1815).[27] The limited service and low rank undoubtedly reflect the emergency defense needs of New Orleans as well as Pollock's age and health.

George Pollock's relocation to New Orleans in 1803 clearly was intended to take advantage of the general belief that the frontier river town was destined to be one of the world's leading trading centers.[28] The development did not take place as rapidly as anticipated in the early nineteenth century, and Pollock, like many of the merchants in New Orleans and elsewhere in the strife-filled Napoleonic era, soon faced such serious business reverses that he was forced to seek relief in court. On March 5, 1808, Pollock petitioned the Orleans Territory Superior Court to grant him relief from his obligations as provided for by the law for insolvent debtors. In petitioning the court, Pollock said he had become unable to pay his just debts "by various unforeseen accidents and misfortunes in business."[29] The petition made it clear that what he sought was not escape from any payment of his obligations, but an assembly of his creditors at which an assignment of his estate could be made under the provisions of the applicable statute. Attached to the petition was an itemized list of creditors in New Orleans, Philadelphia, New York, London, and Belfast, Ireland. The total amount owed exceeded $60,000. Following acceptance of the agreement among his creditors, the court granted Pollock bankruptcy status on July 1, 1808.[30]

Pollock's financial problems may have been hastened by his support of Aaron Burr. The evidence that Pollock was closely involved with Burr is significant and raises more questions than the known evidence answers. By how many years did Pollock's involvement with Burr antedate Burr's trial for treason? Was it Pollock who initially stimulated Burr's interest in the old Southwest? In the wake of the revelation of the Burr conspiracy by General Wilkinson, Pollock was accused by Judge James Workman of having used

27. Powell A. Casey, *Louisiana in the War of 1812* (Baton Rouge: [by the author], 1963), "Rosters of Louisiana Troops in the War of 1812," "Separate Companies and Troops," p. lxx. For perspective on the men who comprised this company, see Jane L. DeGrummond, *The Baratarians and the Battle of New Orleans* (Baton Rouge: Louisiana State University Press, 1961), 80.

28. In the fall of 1806, Pollock's business place was at 28 Chartres Street, New Orleans. *Louisiana Gazette*, November 7, p. 4, c. 3.

29. *George Pollock v. His Creditors*, Superior Court case no. 1503, March 5, 1808.

30. Ibid.

his position as justice of the peace to certify that depositions were sworn in the "reign of terror" by General Wilkinson when, in truth, they had not been.[31] In August 1807, before the end of Burr's trial for treason, the former vice president obtained a large personal loan from Pollock.[32] Harman Blennerhassett, the chief source of information on the relationship of the two men, suggested that Burr used the loan from Pollock for personal expenses, since Luther Martin, William Langburn, Thomas Taylor, John G. Gamble, and Burr himself were named as Burr's bondsmen in May 1807.[33]

Knowledge of Pollock's support of Burr came with the revelations of General Wilkinson, but the extent of their association suggests friendship rooted in past associations in more placid times. On one level, Burr apparently was somehow involved with the education of George Pollock, perhaps when they both lived in New York.[34] Of greater significance, Pollock seems to have been well acquainted with Burr's plans for financing the Spanish American venture. Indeed, Pollock may have used some of his business contacts in the United States and Europe in an effort to advance the Burr scheme.[35] When Burr's trial was over and he left Richmond on November 3, 1807, he went directly to Philadelphia as the houseguest of George Pollock.[36] Although Burr was supposed to be living incognito, with Pollock as his host, the former vice president "opened an audience-chamber" from which he continued to pursue his plans for Spanish America.[37] His residence with Pollock was so well known that it was there Burr was arrested by the sheriff of Philadelphia on the complaint of the Pittsburgh merchant William Wilkins. Wilkins accused Burr of failing to comply with the contract between them on some aspect of the scheme revealed by General Wilkinson.[38]

31. "Faithful Picture of the Political Situation of New Orleans at the Close of the Last and the Beginning of the Present Year, 1807," ed. James E. Winston, *Louisiana Historical Quarterly* 11, no. 3 (July 1928), 403 (original page number 27).

32. Safford, *Blennerhassett Papers,* 367.

33. J. J. Coombs, *The Trial of Aaron Burr for High Treason, in the Circuit Court of the United States for the District of Virginia, Summer Term, 1807 . . .* (Washington, D.C.: W. H. & O. H. Morrison, 1864), 36–7.

34. Safford, *Blennerhassett Papers,* 482.

35. Ibid., 487, 489.

36. Ibid., 483, 485, 513.

37. Ibid., 486–7, 489, and *passim.*

38. Biddle, *Autobiography,* 323. Only perusal of Wilkins's suit would reveal the issues between Wilkins and Burr. Unfortunately, those documents were not available to the author. They may be available in Philadelphia. Thomas P. Abernethy, *The Burr Conspiracy* (New York: Oxford University Press, 1954), 62, 76, 101, has slightly more information on William

Perhaps because his earlier gamble on Burr had failed badly, or because he belatedly realized that some of his looming business difficulties may have stemmed from his ties to Burr,[39] Pollock did not immediately offer to serve as Burr's bondsman. Instead, Pollock accompanied Burr and one of the sheriff's deputies to the home of a neighbor, Charles Biddle, who was asked to endorse Burr's note. Biddle was then regarded as "one of his [Burr's] most attached friends,"[40] but he, too, declined to endorse the note. Biddle did assist in getting his neighbor, a lawyer named Hollowell, to vouch for Burr's appearance in court the next morning, when Pollock was accepted as bondsman in this matter. Later, Pollock was discharged from the obligation because of "some mistake of the plaintiff's attorney."[41]

Perhaps because he was fundamentally a businessman and did not oppose either General Wilkinson or Governor Claiborne during the "reign of terror" in New Orleans, George Pollock was not attacked either privately or publicly as were James Workman and Lewis Kerr. As a consequence, after the tumult in New Orleans and the trial in Richmond, Pollock could devote his energies to rebuilding his fortune. This task was made somewhat easier because he did not lose all his appointments at the hands of Claiborne. Pollock continued to serve as port warden and notary public and kept those positions not dependent on the administration of Governor Claiborne. In this manner, Pollock apparently preserved his business contracts with agencies of the national and territorial governments. One of these contracts, with the army in New Orleans, was signed on December 3, 1807. Under this agreement with Colonel Freeman, Pollock agreed to supply the United States with 10,000 pieces of pitch pine to be delivered to Carondelet Canal. The agreement stipulated that part of the timbers were to be twelve feet long and nine inches in diameter, the other part (five thousand of the timbers) nine feet long and five to six inches in diameter.[42] One wonders

---

Wilkins and his brother John Wilkins in the Burr affair. Milton Lomask, *Aaron Burr: The Conspiracy and Years of Exile, 1805–1836* (New York: Farrar, Straus & Giroux, 1982), does not mention Wilkins or the suit he brought against Burr.

39. Blennerhassett believed that Pollock was "unaware" of how Burr was using him. Safford, *Blennershassett Papers,* 487.

40. Ibid., 501.

41. Biddle, *Autobiography,* 323.

42. Colonel Constant Freeman to Secretary of War Henry Dearborn, December 3, 1807, in Register of Letters Received by the Secretary of War, Unregistered Series, 1789–1860, record group 107, microcopy no. M222, reel 2.

whether the timbers came from the forty thousand acres of land Pollock claimed on the east bank of the Amite River.[43]

George Pollock died on August 23, 1820, in Madisonville, Louisiana, near where the Tchefuncte River disgorges into the north shore of Lake Pontchartrain.[44] His will, made on September 7, 1819, named his five children. Carlile, his son, was born in New York City in 1790. His daughters Catherine Carlile, born in 1791; Lorenza, born in 1795; and Charlotte, born in 1799, also were born in New York City. One daughter, Maralla, then "about a year and half old," was "born of Maria Herrera[,] an unmarried woman." He expressed the desire that his youngest child by Maria Herrera be brought up "in a decent manner."[45] Pollock named as executors of his will his son Carlile; son-in-law, Captain Daniel Todd Patterson; and nephew, Captain Thomas Pollock.[46] With reference to the children born of his two marriages, Pollock said they were "heirs of all I may be possessed of at the time of my decease." However, he did note that his daughter Ann had married well and was independent, and that his son Carlile had "a good office" and also was independent.[47]

43. Winston De Ville, "Some Louisiana Land Claims," *Louisiana Genealogical and Historical Register* 16, no. 2 (June 1969), 127.

44. Fournier and Bergeron, "Pollock and McDonnell Family," 61.

45. George Pollock Will, pp. 161–2. The dates and places of birth of the children from Pollock's two marriages are given in Fournier and Bergeron, "Pollock and McDonnell Family," 61.

46. George Pollock Will, p. 162. The January 13, 1820, marriage of Thomas Pollock to Ana Sarpy of New Orleans in St. Louis Cathedral reflects that he was the son of Santiago (James) Pollock and Jenny St. Claire of Ireland. Alice D. Forsyth, "St. Louis Cathedral Archives, Marriages, 1806–1821. Names of Persons of Irish Birth and/or Scottish Extraction," *Louisiana Genealogical and Historical Register* 21, no. 4 (December 1974), 317.

47. George Pollock Will, p. 162.

GEORGE T. ROSS

George Thompson Ross (1773–June 5, 1816) was the son of Colonel James Ross and Mary Sabina Kuhn of Lancaster County, Pennsylvania. Sabina was the daughter of Adam Simon Kuhn, a prominent physician and land speculator in Lancaster. James was the son of George Ross, a lawyer and land speculator in Lancaster, and one of the signers of the Declaration of Independence.[1] James is remembered in American history for organizing the volunteer company of riflemen from Lancaster County that reputedly was the first formed and ready for action after the Continental Congress called on the colonies for troops.[2] His brother-in-law and military superior in the Revolution was General William Thompson, commander of Thompson's Pennsylvania Rifle Battalion. The Irish-born Thompson, from Carlisle,

1. On the earlier George Ross, see *Dictionary of American Biography,* s.v. "Ross, George."

2. Undated memorandum among the Ross Family Papers, Lancaster County Historical Society, Lancaster, Pennsylvania. James Ross also was associated with Louisiana. He was appointed clerk of the Third Superior Court District and judge of Concordia Parish on January 1, 1807, and June 4, 1808, respectively. He was succeeded in these offices in September and October 1808 by William Haughey and David Latimore, respectively. See Register of Civil Appointments, Clerks, June 30, 1807, and Return of Proclamations, Pardons, and Appointments, June 30, 1808, in Clarence E. Carter, comp. and ed., *The Territorial Papers of the United States,* vol. 9, *The Territory of Orleans, 1803–1812* (Washington, D.C.: U. S. Government Printing Office, 1940), 749 and 796 (hereinafter cited as TP, with volume and page numbers). It apparently was James's wife who Claiborne reported left New Orleans for New York in March 1809. See To Judge Claiborne, March 27, 1809, in *Official Letter Books of W. C. C. Claiborne, 1801–1816,* ed. Dunbar Rowland, vol. 4 (1917; New York: AMS Press, 1972), 337–8 (hereinafter cited as CLB, with volume and page numbers).

Pennsylvania, married Catherine, one of James Ross's sisters.[3] It was for his grandfather, George, and his uncle General William Thompson that George Thompson Ross was named.

The military service of his father and uncle influenced the development of George T. Ross's career. He first entered the army in Pennsylvania as a lieutenant in the first Corps of Artillerists and Engineers at the age of twenty-three (December 19, 1796). Possibly because of President Jefferson's economy moves, Ross left the army after four years and five months service (May 20, 1801). He reentered the army less than a year later (May 3, 1802) with appointment as a second lieutenant in the Second Infantry Regiment.[4] Following this enlistment Ross was stationed at Fort Adams, Mississippi Territory. He came to Louisiana in the contingent of U.S. troops that accompanied Governor Claiborne to New Orleans to receive the Louisiana Purchase Territory from France in December 1803.[5]

After coming to Louisiana, Ross's lackluster career began to brighten and move in new directions. Nearly three months after the historic ceremonies in the Place d'Armes, Ross was appointed adjutant (February 29, 1804) of his regiment. Subsequently, he also served as judge advocate.[6] Early in July 1804, Ross married Henrietta Cowperthwaite, daughter of Jacob Cowperthwaite of Philadelphia and Charlotte O'Brien of South (?) Carolina.[7] Approximately three months later (October 6, 1804), Ross resigned his commission and returned to civilian life.[8]

For the next two and a half years, Ross appeared to have found his métier in a combination of private business, public service, and political appoint-

3. John Ward Willson Loose, secretary, Lancaster County (Pa.) Bicentennial Commission, to the author, December 24, 1975; George O. Seilhamer, "'Old Mother Cumberland,'" *Pennsylvania Magazine of History and Biography* 24 (1900), 37; and "Queries," ibid., 50, no. 1 (1926), 94.

4. Francis B. Heitman, *Historical Register and Dictionary of the United States Army from Its Organization September 29, 1789, to March 2, 1903*, vol. 1 (1903; Urbana: University of Illinois Press, 1965), 846.

5. General James Wilkinson's Order Book, December 31, 1796–March 8, 1808, Records of the U.S. Adjutant General's Office, record group 94, microcopy M-654, reel 3, 406, 436.

6. Ibid., 460; and postscript by George T. Ross in Henriette Ross to Mrs. James Ross, August 10, 1804. Transcription of original in Ross Family Papers. Photocopy owned by the author.

7. Henriette Ross To Mrs. James Ross, August 10, 1804, in Ross Family Papers. Baptism of Henriette Ross, Ursuline Convent Chapel, Baptismal Book I (1805–1838), Act 189; and marriage of Jacob Cowperthwaite to Carlota O'Brin [sic], April 10, 1787, Saint Louis Cathedral, Orleans Parish, Louisiana, Marriage Book 2 (1784–1806), Act 181, 52.

8. Heitman, *Historical Register,* 1: 846.

ment. Immediately after leaving the army, he established himself as a merchant in New Orleans.[9] The following spring (May 2, 1805), Governor Claiborne appointed Ross sheriff of New Orleans.[10] The Pennsylvanian may have assumed the duties of this office early in March, because the former sheriff, Lewis Kerr, resigned in late February and notice of Ross's appointment appeared in a New Orleans newspaper early the following month.[11] Ross also was appointed (May 30, 1805) captain in the Battalion of Orleans Volunteers, a branch of the territorial militia.[12] Finally, Ross was one of the seventeen founders of Christ Church, the Protestant Episcopal Church chartered by the territorial council on July 3, 1805.[13]

The high point in the cordial relations between Claiborne and Ross occurred in dealings with the Marqués de Casa Calvo. On the evening of December 5, 1804, Ross formally reported to Claiborne the gist of a heated exchange with a Spanish officer who was part of the guard at Casa Calvo's home. Apparently, the officer in charge of the guard objected to the conversation Ross and Dr. John Lynd carried on at a "distance of a Square from Casa Calvo's residence." The Spanish officer hailed them "from the opposite corner," advising them to be quiet, and even placed his hand on his sword as though he meant to draw it on Ross after he had followed the officer, "reproaching him for his insolence."[14]

Little more than thirteen months later, January 10, 1806, Claiborne ordered Ross and a detachment of the Orleans Rangers to northwest Louisiana to find and expulse Casa Calvo from U.S. territory. Ross was given authority to use force to carry out his orders. Unfortunately, the sheriff/mili-

9. Recommendation of Andrew Porter, Jr., as port inspector, November 22, 1804, TP, 9: 337.

10. Register of Civil Appointments in the Territory of Orleans, enclosed in Secretary Graham to the Secretary of State, February 13, 1806, Sheriffs, ibid., 600.

11. See the *Louisiana Gazette,* March 5, 1805, p. 2, c. 4.

12. Register of Appointments in the Militia of the Territory of Orleans, enclosed in Secretary Graham to the Secretary of State, May 8, 1806, Orleans Volunteers, TP, 9: 639.

13. *Acts Passed at the Second Session of the Legislative Council of the Territory of Orleans, Begun and Held at the Principal, in the City of New Orleans, on Thursday the Twentieth Day of June, in the Year of Our Lord, One Thousand Eight Hundred and Five, and of the Independence of the United States the Twenty-Ninth* (New Orleans: James M. Bradford, 1805), 88; and Georgia F. Taylor, "The Early History of the Episcopal Church in New Orleans, 1805–1840," *Louisiana Historical Quarterly* 22, no. 2 (April 1939), 434, 435, 439.

14. See Letter No. 75, From George T. Ross, December 6, 1804. In his letter, Ross described the incident and its circumstances, saying he was "convinced" of Claiborne's "disposition to preserve the dignity of our characters."

tia captain could not locate the troublesome Spaniard. Ross looked for the marqués on the road from Natchitoches, but Casa Calvo returned to New Orleans via the Red River. Yet the long horseback ride to the Louisiana-Texas border was not without results. Ross's report on the activities of the Spanish official confirmed Claiborne's belief that Casa Calvo was the source of the continuing rumor that most of Louisiana was to be returned to Spain.[15]

One year later, Claiborne and Ross were in such disagreement that the governor refused to reappoint him sheriff. The difficulties between Claiborne and Ross grew out of the revelations surrounding the Burr conspiracy. Like many of the prominent business and political leaders in New Orleans, Ross had joined the Mexican Association, a group advocating the conquest of Spanish territory. Claiborne reported to President Jefferson that he declined to reappoint Ross because of his "oath of secrecy, relative to the invasion of Mexico" and because of "some improper Conduct in the settlement of his public Accounts."[16]

The nature of Ross's "improper Conduct" in the matter of his "public Accounts" may never be known unless some of Ross's papers are located, and anyone who attempts to sort out the sheriff's problems on the basis of presently known information is left to ponder several questions: Did the disagreement between Claiborne and Ross involve the Orleans Rangers? What parts did Richard Claiborne, the governor's private secretary and kinsman, and Catherine Ross, George's sister, have in the events leading up to Ross's dismissal? And, lastly, what was Daniel Clark's role, if any, in the disagreement? Unfortunately, only partial answers to these questions have thus far been established. Whatever the problem, or problems, Ross certainly had the support of local merchants, who advertised their objection to his being terminated in April 1807.[17]

Ross's resignation from the Orleans Rangers at about the same time Claiborne refused to reappoint him sheriff suggests a connection between his membership in the Rangers and his dismissal from office. When Catherine

15. George T. Ross to Governor Claiborne, February 11, 1806, TP, 9: 581–2.

16. Governor Claiborne to the President, May 3, 1807, ibid., 731. See also George Dargo, *Jefferson's Louisiana: Politics and the Clash of Legal Traditions* (Cambridge, Mass.: Harvard University Press, 1975), 60.

17. Among those who signed the protest were George Pollock, Bellechasse, Samuel B. Davis, J. Touro, A. R. Ellery, James Workman, John W. Gurley, Pierre Derbigny, Edward Livingston, James Brown, Abner L. Duncan, and Lewis Kerr. See the *Louisiana Gazette*, April 21, 1807, p. 2, c. 4.

Ross came to Louisiana is unknown, but on March 5, 1807, she and Richard Claiborne were married.[18] Six weeks later it was reported that George Ross was not to be reappointed sheriff.[19] Whether it was at this time, or in 1808, when Richard Claiborne was judge of Rapides Parish and accused of misappropriation of funds, that George and Catherine became estranged is not known. There is no doubt, however, that the break between the two was permanent, or that the resentment was mutual. George recognized numerous other family members in his last will and testament, but never mentioned Catherine.[20] There also appears to have been trouble between George and his father, because when Catherine applied for a pension in 1845, she presented sworn testimony, including her own, that she was her father's only heir at the time of his death in 1809.[21]

It is clear from the extant evidence that at the bottom of Claiborne's disagreement with Ross lay the sheriff's membership in the Mexican Association. For this reason, it is pertinent to note here other facts germane to the troubles that befell Ross.

The similarity between the founding of the Mexican Association and the establishment of the Orleans Volunteers by Daniel Clark and others in November 1803 may be more apparent than real. Nonetheless, it is striking. There is no indication Clark's critical interest in the militia extended to the establishment of the Orleans Rangers. However, Clark's influence on men inside and outside of the territorial government in 1807 was at its peak, and the figure of the imperious Irishman cast a long shadow across the events centering on the Burr conspiracy.[22] It is not surprising, therefore, that later observers of these events might wonder if the Orleans Rangers and the Mexican Association comprised many of the same men. Only a comparison of

18. "Newspaper Notices, Louisiana Gazette (New Orleans)," *Louisiana Genealogical Register* 5, no. 6 (December 1958), 42.

19. *Louisiana Gazette*, April 21, 1807, p. 3, c. 1.

20. George Ross Will, May 28, 1816, Lancaster County Court House, Lancaster, Pennsylvania, Register of Wills Office, Orphans' Court Book, M-1-72. Transcription of original in Ross Family Papers. Photocopy owned by the author.

21. John Ward Willson Loose to the author, December 24, 1975. Another son named James drowned at sea in February 1805. *Louisiana Gazette*, April 2, 1805, p. 3, c. 3. Siblings Rebecca and Mary Ann (Maria Sabina) married Dr. James Barefoot and John Brindley, respectively. A third son, William, married Jane Whitaker. Florence I. Gallagher to the author, May 6, 1975 [1976]. Miss Gallagher identified herself as the great-great-granddaughter of Mary Ann Ross and John Brindley.

22. See Thomas P. Abernethy, *The Burr Conspiracy* (New York: Oxford University Press, 1954), 171-2.

the membership lists of both groups would resolve this question. Unfortunately, no membership list of the Mexican Association has been found.

There is reason to believe that Ross, too, became a political scapegoat since it is known that Claiborne used the Burr conspiracy to banish or immobilize his political enemies, even at the expense of hurting his friends.[23] Whether or not this is true, the idea is fostered and reinforced by events before and after Ross was turned out of the sheriff's office. The Orleans Rangers were organized in the spring of 1805, when Ross received his commission in the militia.[24] In 1804–05, Claiborne was vitally interested in organizing and strengthening the territorial militia, and would have been receptive to the service of a newly organized militia unit commanded by an experienced and trustworthy officer.

Early in 1807, after it became known that Ross was not to be reappointed sheriff, a dozen prominent New Orleanians publicly protested his removal as sheriff and his departure as commander of the Orleans Rangers. Their objections were capped by a testimonial dinner less than three weeks later on the evening of May 9 at Madam Fourage's, a popular restaurant. In the course of the evening's festivities, Ross's service and departure from the Orleans Rangers was memorialized with expressions of appreciation and thanks for his "nobleness and firmness of mind," which the memorialists said "ought always to be the innate principle of a soldier." The memorial and evening closed with best wishes for the future prosperity and happiness of Ross.[25] Some of the protesters, like Edward Livingston, Pierre Derbigny, and James Brown, were avowed opponents of Claiborne. Others, such as W. W. Montgomery, Joseph Deville Degoutin Bellechasse, and John W. Gurley, were not. Montgomery was a businessman from Philadelphia, Bellechasse was head of the territorial militia, and Gurley was territorial attorney general.

The remaining nine years of George Ross's life were much like the earlier

---

23. On this point, see Dargo, *Jefferson's Louisiana*, 57–8.

24. On the organization of the Orleans Rangers, see the *Louisiana Gazette*, April 2, 1805, p. 3, c. 1, and June 14, 1805, p. 3, c. 3. Provision for a cavalry unit of the Orleans Volunteers had been made by the territorial council and signed into law by Claiborne on January 23, 1805. *Acts Passed at the First Session of the Legislative Council, of the Territory of Orleans, Begun and Held at the Principal, in the City of New Orleans, On Monday the Third Day of December, in the Year of Our Lord, One Thousand Eight Hundred and Four, and of the Independence of the United States the Twenty-Ninth* (New Orleans: James M. Bradford, 1805), 23.

25. *Louisiana Gazette*, May 12, 1807, p. 2, c. 3, and p. 3, c. 2.

ones, with one exception. Sandwiched among the years devoted to business, political appointment, and military service, Ross began to practice law. He had been admitted to the Lancaster bar in 1797, but apparently did not begin to practice law until the latter part of 1810 when he was admitted to the Louisiana bar.[26] Ross's turn to law appears to have grown out of his appointment in August 1810 as official notary for the city of New Orleans after the death of the previous notary, Eliphelet Fitch.[27] Immediately after his departure from the sheriff's office, Ross entered the auction business. In the newspaper advertisements for this venture, he billed himself as "Late Sheriff."[28] Toward the end of the month of August 1810, Ross also entered into partnership with Daniel Murgtroyd as shipping commission merchant. The partnership was potentially a lucrative one because of Murgtroyd's Philadelphia background and his capacity in New Orleans as agent for the Kentucky Bank of Frankfort. The business does not appear to have fared well, probably because of Jefferson's embargo and the British blockade of Europe. The business was done irreparable damage when Murgtroyd died in April 1811.[29] During this time, Ross also appears to have intermittently operated a liquor store on the corner of Conti and Chartres Streets. His involvement with this business began in mid-May 1807, about the time he was replaced as sheriff, and was resumed in May 1812, a month before hostilities between the United States and Great Britain formally commenced.[30] Less than three months after reentering the liquor business in 1812, Ross abandoned it to resume his military career.

Ross's renewed interest in a military career began in the spring of 1811 when he assumed command of the Columbian Infantry, a private militia company badly in need of reorganization. One year later the company was a revitalized and fully uniformed military unit.[31] After Congress declared war on Great Britain, this company of forty-four men was the first militia unit from Louisiana to volunteer for active duty in defense of the country

26. John Ward Willson Loose to the author, December 24, 1975; and *Louisiana Gazette,* November 7, 1810, p. 3, c. 3.

27. *Louisiana Gazette,* August 10, 1810, p. 3, cc. 1, 3.

28. See, e.g., ibid., April 19, 1808, p. 1, c. 4.

29. Ibid., August 29, 1810, p. 3, c. 3, and Daniel Murgtroyd Will, April 1, 1811, Orleans Parish, Louisiana, Court of Probate, Record of Wills, Will Book, 1805–1817, vol. 1, 376.

30. *Louisiana Gazette,* May 12, 1807, p. 3, c. 2, carries such an advertisement dated May 8, 1807.

31. "Louisiana Military Data. Louisiana Militia, 1811–1814," ed. P. L. Dupas (Works Project Administration, typescript; Jackson Barracks, La., 1941), 23, 25, 29, 32, 54, 64.

(July 12, 1812). Ross's action harked back to his father's conduct in the Revolutionary War, for the Columbian Infantry became the nucleus of the First Battalion of Louisiana Volunteers created in November 1812 in response to concern that the British were going to attack New Orleans.[32]

By the fall of 1812, Ross held the rank of major. Subsequently, he was promoted to lieutenant colonel (April 30, 1813) and made commander of the First Battalion of Louisiana Volunteers the following day.[33] His promotion came on the orders of Governor Claiborne's brother, General Ferdinand L. Claiborne, who commanded the regiment of volunteers from Mississippi Territory assembled at Baton Rouge in November 1812 to protect the lower Mississippi Valley from attack by the British via the lakes, Pontchartrain and Maurepas, and Bayou Manchac.[34]

The fear of a British attack on Louisiana in 1812 proved to be a false alarm, but the threat of Indian assaults on settlements in the Mississippi Territory was very real. As a consequence, the Louisiana and Mississippi militiamen assembled at Baton Rouge were designated the Brigade of Louisiana and Mississippi Territory Volunteers, and ordered late in June 1813 into eastern Mississippi Territory to protect the settlers there from raids by the Creek Indians. Ross was one of a number of Louisianians who accepted duty with General Claiborne's brigade to fight the Indians.[35] Unusually rainy weather in the summer of 1813 and a shortage of supplies delayed General Claiborne's departure from Baton Rouge until early July. Ross commanded the rear of Claiborne's brigade and was still at Buhler's Plain, twenty-one miles from Baton Rouge, on the ninth.[36] By the end of the month, however, both Claiborne and Ross were at Mt. Vernon, the fortified settlement immediately west of the Tombigbee River above its confluence

32. Powell A. Casey, *Louisiana in the War of 1812* (Baton Rouge: [by the author], 1963), 5. Meetings to discuss the call to active duty were held in the days prior to the event. See the *Louisiana Gazette,* July 9, 1812, p. 3, c. 3, and July 11, 1812, p. 3, c. 3.

33. The date given for Ross's promotion to commander of the First Battalion is April 31, 1813, but clearly should have been May 1, 1813. See Casey, *Louisiana in the War of 1812,* 5, 6. Ross's promotion to colonel in the U.S. Army may be found in the *Journal of the Executive Proceedings of the Senate of the United States,* 14th Cong., 2nd sess. (Washington, D.C.: Duff Green, 1828), 417, 435.

34. Casey, *Louisiana in the War of 1812,* 6; and J. F. H. Claiborne, *Mississippi, as a Province, Territory, and State, with Biographical Notices of Eminent Citizens,* 2nd ed. (Baton Rouge: Louisiana State University Press, 1964), 318–9.

35. Casey, *Louisiana in the War of 1812,* 6.

36. "Louisiana Military Data," 117.

with the Mobile River.[37] Ross apparently remained in the vicinity of Mt. Vernon through the winter of 1813, returning to Baton Rouge with other Louisiana volunteers in March 1814.[38]

Ross was appointed (August 1, 1813) commander of the 44th U.S. Infantry Regiment while on duty in the Mississippi Territory. This regular army unit was created to replace army units, particularly the 3rd U.S. Infantry, that had been moved to other parts of the United States.[39] He received the appointment over Governor Claiborne's nominees for the command, Alexander Laneuville, then adjutant general of Louisiana, and Charles Tessier of Baton Rouge.[40] After release from duty with General Claiborne's brigade, Ross began to recruit men for his command. Many of the officers who joined the 44th had served with Ross in the First Battalion of Louisiana Volunteers and were Creoles. Very few of the enlisted men were native Louisianians.[41] On August 15, Ross advised General Andrew Jackson that the regiment consisted of three hundred men, excluding officers, and he expected the number to increase to five hundred by November.[42]

As commander of the 44th Infantry Regiment, Ross took part in the planning for and destruction of the pirate lair maintained by the Laffite brothers on Grand Terre Island in Barataria Bay northwest of the mouth of the Mississippi River.[43] Ross was second in command to Master Commander Daniel T. Patterson, the U.S. Navy commander at New Orleans.

37. Albert J. Pickett, *History of Alabama and Incidentally of Georgia and Mississippi, from the Earliest Period* (1850; New York: Arno Press, 1971), 526.

38. Claiborne, *Mississippi*, 320, 334; John Reid and John H. Eaton, *The Life of Andrew Jackson*, ed. Frank L. Owsley, Jr. (University: University of Alabama Press, 1974), 117; and Casey, *Louisiana in the War of 1812*, 6.

39. Casey, *Louisiana in the War of 1812*, 7, 42; and Heitman, *Historical Register*, 1: 846.

40. Casey, *Louisiana in the War of 1812*, 42.

41. Ibid., 6, 42. Ross to Andrew Jackson, August 15, 1814, in John Spencer Bassett, ed., *Correspondence of Andrew Jackson*, vol. 2 (Washington, D.C.: Carnegie Institution of Washington, 1927), 26–7, provides perspective on the enlistment problems.

42. Bassett, *Correspondence of Andrew Jackson*, 2: 26. Casey, *Louisiana in the War of 1812*, lxxvii (appendix), lists forty officers in the 44th Regiment, and states (p. 42) that there were 400 men in the unit on December 23, 1814.

43. Insight on the planning phases of this politico-military operation may be gained from Jane Lucas De Grummond, *The Baratarians and the Battle of New Orleans* (1961; Baton Rouge: Legacy Press, 1979), 43; Wilbur S. Brown, *The Amphibious Campaign for West Florida and Louisiana, 1814–1815* (University: University of Alabama Press, 1969), 39–42; and "Louisiana Military Data," 143–6. The last named source prints Patterson's October 10, 1814, letter to Secretary of the Navy William Jones, but erroneously dates it as 1813.

Patterson and Ross left New Orleans on September 11, 1814, with seventy men from the 44th Regiment on board the USS *Sea Horse,* a one-gun schooner acquired by the navy in New Orleans in 1812 for use as a tender.[44] They were joined at Fort St. Philip on the following day by the USS *Carolina,* a fourteen-gun schooner ordered to New Orleans expressly to reinforce the military operation against the Baratarians. From there Patterson and Ross moved on to Balize, the lighthouse and river pilot station located near the Northeast Pass of the Mississippi River. Here they were joined on the thirteenth by U.S. gunboats number 5, 23, 156, and 163. The flotilla sailed out of the Southwest Pass of the Mississippi on the evening of September 15 and arrived off Grand Terre at 8:00 A.M. on the sixteenth.[45]

The Baratarians were aware that the United States was sending a military expedition against their stronghold, but they were surprised when it appeared off Grand Terre. They instead had expected the British, who had threatened on September 3, 1814, to destroy their base on Grand Terre unless the Baratarians helped them to invade the United States.[46] Presumably, it was the British threat that caused Jean Laffite to remove most of the papers, maps, specie, and slaves, and some of the merchandise, arms, and ammunition from Grand Terre to Isle Dernière sometime before the arrival of the U.S. military force. Despite this precaution, Patterson and Ross seized merchandise, flour, and salt valued at more than five hundred thousand dollars, along with some weapons and ammunition, and a small amount of gold and silver. In addition, twenty-six vessels of brigantine, schooner, and launch size were taken. Ross and the men of the 44th Regiment took eighty prisoners among the forty palmetto-thatched huts on Grand Terre, but more than four hundred Baratarians escaped across the shallow bay into the surrounding bayous and swamp. Their decision to flee most likely had been reinforced by Jean Laffite's admonition not to oppose the U.S. expedition since it would cause them to lose the amnesty he sought from Governor Claiborne for all Baratarians. Pierre Laffite, fresh from two months of imprisonment in New Orleans and ailing, had already left Grand Terre by pirogue for a plantation on Bayou Lafourche.[47]

44. On the USS *Sea Horse,* see Howard I. Chapelle, *The History of the American Sailing Navy: The Ships and Their Development* (New York: Bonanza Books, 1949), 246, 533.

45. "Louisiana Military Data," 143–4.

46. DeGrummond, *Baratarians and the Battle of New Orleans,* 37–41.

47. Ibid., 46. Jean Laffite tells of these incidents in his journal. See Jean Laffite, *The Journal of Jean Laffite: The Privateer-Patriot's Own Story,* trans. John A. Laffite (New York: Vantage Press, 1958), 52–4, 72.

Patterson praised Ross for his part in the expedition against the Baratarians. Writing to Secretary of the Navy Jones, Patterson said: "It affords me great satisfaction to inform you . . . [of] . . . the most cordial co-operation of Colonel Ross, and the detachment of his regiment—in [sic] every measure adopted or duty performed, the utmost harmony existing between the two Corps during the whole expedition, himself, officers, and men sharing in every enterprise or arduous duty where their services could be useful."[48]

Fifty of the seventy men from Ross's regiment were left to guard the booty captured at Grand Terre.[49]

News of the success of the expedition against the Baratarians reached New Orleans before Patterson and Ross left Grand Terre on September 20, but the public was not given a glimpse of the action at Barataria until four days later, when part of Ross's September 19 letter to Major Michael Reynolds was published in one of the New Orleans newspapers.[50] Following the return of Patterson and Ross to New Orleans on October 10, reports of the treasure taken at Grand Terre appeared in newspapers in New Orleans and Baltimore.[51] On October 17, 1814, Patterson, Ross, and the men who participated in the expedition filed suit claiming one fourth of the proceeds from the sale of the ships and cargoes seized at Grand Terre.[52]

The lawsuit filed by Patterson and Ross of necessity languished in the courts while they and other public officials devoted their thoughts and energies to strengthening the defenses of New Orleans against the impending British attack. As a ranking regular U.S. Army field officer in New Orleans and

48. "Louisiana Military Data," 146.

49. *Journal of Jean Laffite*, 54.

50. *Louisiana Gazette*, September 24, 1814, p. 3, c. 2. Michael Reynolds of Virginia was Ross's brother-in-law. Reynolds married Catherine Cowperthwaite on July 28, 1808, in Ursuline Convent Chapel. One of the witnesses was James Sterrett. Alice D. Forsyth, archivist, St. Louis Cathedral, to the author, February 9, 1976. Reynolds was then on the staff of Louis de Clouet's Regiment of Louisiana Drafted Militia. Casey, *Louisiana in the War of 1812*, vi (appendix). Reynolds had served in the U.S. Marine Corps from May 1, 1799, until 1807 or 1808, following his assignment to New Orleans in 1807. His prior service in 1805–06 included duty as adjutant to the corps commandant, Lieutenant Colonel Francis Wharton. Office of Naval Records and Library, Navy Department, *Register of Officer Personnel United States Navy and Marine Corps and Ships' Data, 1801–1807* (Washington, D.C.: U.S. Government Printing Office, 1945), 66.

51. See *Louisiana Gazette*, October 11, 1814, p. 2, c. 4, and p. 3, c. 1; and *Niles' Weekly Register* (Baltimore) 6, October 22, 1814, p. 92, c. 2, and p. 93, c. 1.

52. Stanley C. Arthur, *Jean Laffite, Gentleman Rover* (New Orleans: Harmonson, 1952), 90–1, prints the suit filed by Patterson, Ross, and others. See also *Journal of Jean Laffite*, 65–6, 71–2, 75.

commander of the 44th Regiment, Ross's role was important. The conduct of his men set the standard for the inadequately trained and sometimes unruly militia, particularly the men of Louis de Clouet's Louisiana Drafted Militia Regiment. Because of insufficient volunteers, the men in de Clouet's regiment were drawn from various militia units scattered over the state. This fact, and de Clouet's conduct, which to some extent masked his strong pro-Spanish feelings, are doubtless two reasons why discontent appeared among the men of his regiment about a month after muster at Baton Rouge in September 1814. In mid-November the discontent had grown to disobedience. By this time the regiment was stationed eighteen miles below New Orleans at English Turn and assigned the task of building a parapet from the Mississippi River to the swamp. Their unruliness required the presence of Governor Claiborne, who took Colonel Ross and some of the men of Ross's 44th Regiment with him to the camp. After a number of arrests and courts-martial, the attitude of the Drafted Militia men improved and progress was made on the parapet. Nonetheless, men from the 44th Infantry Regiment also were assigned to English Turn before Claiborne and Ross left the camp, partly because of the problems with the men in the Drafted Militia and partly because of the belief that the British invasion force was then off the Louisiana coast.[53]

During the battle of New Orleans, Ross exercised the authority of a brigadier general. He commanded the right side of the nineteen-hundred-yard "Line Jackson," which extended from the Mississippi River along the Rodriguez Canal into the swamp south of the Gentilly Plain. His command of 1,327 men included the 7th and 44th U.S. Army Infantry regulars, the U.S. Marines stationed in New Orleans, and the Louisiana militia units, all of which manned the line for nearly six hundred yards beginning at the river.[54] In the surprise attack ordered by Jackson on the evening of December 23, before the siege line was stabilized, Ross's men held the left flank and even took thirty prisoners in the savage hand-to-hand fighting which took place when the British counterattacked. Although the militia men clamored for it, Ross would not permit a bayonet charge. His decision undoubtedly was correct; the British troops being rushed to the front during the battle were veterans thoroughly experienced in the use of that weapon. There is no indication that General Jackson questioned Ross's decision. Indeed, about

53. Casey, *Louisiana in the War of 1812,* 17.

54. Reid and Eaton, *Life of Andrew Jackson,* 292–3; Powell A. Casey, *Louisiana at the Battle of New Orleans* (New Orleans: Louisiana Landmarks Society, 1965), 17; and *Niles' Weekly Register* (Baltimore) 26, February 25, 1815, p. 404, c. 1.

an hour after the success of Ross's men, Jackson withdrew from the attack because of the heavy fog that settled over the battlefield about 8:00 P.M. and because his scattered forces were out of effective control.[55]

Between the defeat of the British on January 8, 1815, and his death in Lancaster on June 6, 1816, Ross spent some time in Washington, D.C. He apparently was discharged from the army (June 15, 1815) while in Washington.[56] The exact date of Ross's departure from New Orleans is unknown, but it appears to have been after January 13, 1815, the birth date of his youngest son.[57] In the codicil to his last will and testament, Ross refers to this child as having been "born since I left home" and expresses the wish that he be named George Thompson Ross, Jr.[58] While in Washington, Ross lobbied Congress for the right to the proceeds from the sale of the vessels and cargoes taken by the officers and men on the expedition against the Baratarians. He was assisted in this task by a friend, William P. Zantzinger, who lived in Washington.[59] Ultimately, their efforts were successful. On February 22, 1817, President Madison signed into law the amended bill approved by Congress that directed the secretary of the treasury to pay Ross and Patterson $50,000 from the proceeds of the booty taken at Barataria.[60]

55. Brown, *Amphibious Campaign*, 101–2, 103–4.

56. Heitman, *Historical Register*, 1: 846.

57. Baptism of Jorge Rosse [George Ross], "Saint Louis Cathedral Baptism Register," vol. 9 (1818–1822), Act 158, in a letter from Alice D. Forsyth, archivist, St. Louis Cathedral, to the author, February 9, 1976.

58. George Ross Will, May 28, 1816. Ross's memory of events may have been clouded. The marriage certificate of Ross's sister-in-law, Marguerite Cowperthwaite, and Daniel Carmick, dated March 4, 1815, bears the names of Marguerite's sister, Henriette, and her husband George Ross. Estrait des Archives de l'Eglise de Ste. Marie, New Orleans, November 16, 1855, Daniel Carmick pension record, Navy and Old Army Branch, Military Archives Division, National Archives and Records Service.

59. George Ross Will, May 28, 1816.

60. The bill for the relief of Ross and Patterson was read for the first time in April 1816. Its progress may be traced in the *Annals of Congress: The Debates and Proceedings in the Congress of the United States, 1789–1824* (Washington, D.C.: Gales and Seaton, 1826), 14th Cong., 1st sess., 1401, 1412, 1432; ibid. (1854), 14th Cong., 2nd sess., 870, 873, 951, 1279; and *Journal of the House of Representatives of the United States* (Washington, D.C.: William A. Davis, 1816), 14th Cong., 2nd sess., 345, 350, 394, 423, 459.

The ships seized at Barataria were purchased by front men for the Laffites when the government offered them at public auction, according to John S. Kendall, "The Huntsmen of Black Ivory," *Louisiana Historical Quarterly* 24, no. 1 (January 1941), 24. The *Journal of Jean Laffite*, 54, states the fifty men of Ross's 44th Regiment left to guard Grand Terre were taken prisoner by the men of three of his later arriving ships. Laffite is not clear, but the infantrymen apparently were released before the British attacked New Orleans.

In his will Ross charged his friend John Dick in New Orleans with the responsibility for seeing that the sum granted him by the surviving officers and men of the Barataria expedition was paid to his wife and children.[61] What Ross's share of the proceeds was and whether it was paid to his wife and children is not known.

Ross went to Lancaster in the fall of 1815 to recover his health, which had been adversely affected by the strenuous military duty in Mississippi and Louisiana, and to recover his and his mother's claim to land in nearby Dauphin County.[62] In Lancaster he was nursed by his Aunt Susana (Mrs. John) Kuhn and her two daughters, Sarah and Maria. Undoubtedly, it was his lobby work in Washington and efforts to recover the Dauphin County land that did irreparable damage to his health. At least this seems to be part of the meaning of the statement by the rector of St. James Episcopal Church in Lancaster, who said that Ross "might have recovered but was imprudent."[63] In reporting his death, the local Lancaster newspaper described Ross as a man who was "all *heart* and *soul*."[64]

Ross was survived by his wife and daughter, both named Henrietta, and two sons, Alonso and George, Jr. In his will Ross directed his friend and physician, Dr. Eberly, to prepare his body for shipment to New Orleans in a "Hogshead of Strong Rye Brandy" via the merchants Boyle and Hand of Baltimore.[65] Since there is no official burial site for him in the family plot at the St. James Episcopal Church graveyard in Lancaster, Pennsylvania, Ross's body apparently was shipped, as he specified, by William P. Zantzinger to New Orleans for burial. His will further directed that the portraits of himself as a lieutenant in the artillery and of his father as a young man be sent from their places of safekeeping with friends and relatives in Pennsylvania to his sons Alonso and George in New Orleans. Although William P. Zantzinger and John Dick were charged with certain responsibilities, Ross named his wife as sole executrix of his estate.[66]

61. George Ross Will, May 28, 1816. Robert C. Vogel, in "The Patterson and Ross Raid on Barataria, September 1814" (*Louisiana History* 33, no. 2 [spring 1992], 158), establishes that Ross was disappointed in the results of the confiscated booty.

62. George Ross Will, May 28, 1816; *Lancaster Journal,* June 7, 1816; and photocopy of death notice owned by the author.

63. George Ross Will, May 28, 1816; and Rector's Record Book, St. James Episcopal Church, Lancaster Pennsylvania, entry dated June 7, 1816, without a page number.

64. *Lancaster Journal,* June 7, 1816. Emphasis in the original.

65. George Ross Will, May 28, 1816.

66. Ibid.

DANIEL CARMICK

Major Daniel Carmick (April 4, 1773–November 5, 1816) was the second highest ranking officer in the United States Marine Corps before he received a fatal head wound while defending New Orleans in the War of 1812.[1] Because the marine barracks at New Orleans carried three hundred or more men on its roster, Carmick was authorized by Congress to use the title "Commandant of a Separate Post."[2] Previously, only the ranking officer in command of all the Corps was allowed to use the title "commandant." Carmick's tour of duty in New Orleans during the War of 1812 was his third. He had served there previously in 1804–05 and 1807.

William Ward Burrows, first commandant of the Marine Corps after it was organized as a separate branch of the U.S. Navy, once described Daniel

---

1. Carmick's date of birth is given in Lewis D. Cook, "Carmick of Salem, N.J., and of Philadelphia." Typescript on deposit in the Historical Society of Pennsylvania (Philadelphia, 1949), 5. Cook cites the Stephen Carmick family Bible and Christ Episcopal Church records, Philadelphia. Carmick died in the U.S. Naval Hospital in New Orleans. The date of his death is given in the *Louisiana Gazette,* November 6, 1816, p. 2, c. 2, and the November 6, 1816, letter of his friend, James Sterrett, enclosed in the letter of Lt. Francis B. de Bellevue to Colonel Franklin Wharton, Commandant, U.S.M.C., November 7, 1816, Card Register of Communications Sent and Received, 1798–1918, Entry 40, Daniel Carmick, USMC, Officer. Records of the United States Marine Corps, Historical Division. Record Group 127. Carmick's wife, the former Marguerite Cowperthwaite, declared that Daniel died on or about November 6, 1816, thus confirming the date given by the newspaper and James Sterret. *War of 1812, Bounty Land Warrant Applications, Records of the Veterans Administration, Record Group 15,* Daniel Carmick, BLWT-49626-160-55, Deposition of Marguerite Cowperthwaite Carmick, November 23, 1855, New Orleans. Photocopy in possession of the author.

2. *American State Papers: Naval Affairs,* vol. 1 (Washington: Gales & Seaton, 1834), 264.

Carmick as a "Man of Spirit," a fact demonstrated in his conduct as a marine.[3] For example, in Marine Corps history, Carmick traditionally is credited with helping to establish the sobriquet "leatherneck" for the marines. The leather stock, or neckpiece, which was part of the original Marine Corps uniform, was worn for nine years by Carmick, who "only laid it aside because it was out of fashion."[4] Despite the questionable hygienics of this practice, Carmick was known for his good grooming habits, which he tried to instill in those who served under him.[5] Carmick also was known for his loyalty to the Marine Corps, which he demonstrated by coolly winning over to his point of view those early critics of the newly organized Corps, regardless of their rank or station in life.[6] Carmick also was known within the

3. Lt. Col. Burrows to Lt. Henry Caldwell, September 22, 1800, in *Naval Documents Related to the Quasi-War Between the United States and France. Naval Operations from June 1800 to November 1800* (Washington, D.C.: Government Printing Office, 1938), 374 (the unnumbered volumes in this set shall hereinafter be cited as *Naval Documents Related to the Quasi-War,* followed by the inclusive dates covered by each volume).

4. Robert D. Heinl, Jr., *Soldiers of the Sea: The United States Marine Corps, 1775–1962* (Annapolis, Md.: United States Naval Institute, 1962), 29.

5. See Carmick to Burrows, August 24, 1799, in *Naval Documents Related to the Quasi-War Between the United States and France. Naval Operations from August 1799 to December 1799* (Washington, D.C.: United States Government Printing Office, 1936), 123, in which Carmick tells of his continuing struggle to keep his men in clean uniforms (hereinafter cited as *Naval Documents Related to the Quasi-War, August 1799 to December 1799*). A copy of this letter, dated May 21, 1799, with slightly different spelling of a few words, is printed in *Naval Documents Related to the Quasi-War Between the United States and France. Naval Operations from April 1799 to July 1799* (Washington, D.C.: United States Government Printing Office, 1936), 227. Because no other records indicate that Carmick had sea duty in May 1799 and other evidence places him on duty in Pennsylvania and New York, the August 24, 1799, date is assumed to be the correct one.

Eventually, Carmick resorted to issuing a sailor suit of clothes to the men under him in an effort to keep the marine uniforms clean, but even this did not work. *Naval Documents Related to the Quasi-War, August 1799 to December 1799,* 91. This may have been the beginning of the similarity in daily uniforms used by U.S. marines and sailors.

6. One of the most outspoken critics of the marines was Commodore Thomas Truxton, who considered the Marine Corps unimportant, "especially in time of peace." (see Heinl, *Soldiers of the Sea,* 616). In anticipation of serving under Truxton on the USS *Chesapeake* in early 1801, Carmick called on him and had a very long conversation on the "duty of a Marine." Afterward, Carmick concluded that if the commodore adhered to what he said, the marines on the *Chesapeake* would be "better treated than on board any of our ships." (*Naval Documents Related to the United States Wars with the Barbary Powers,* vol. 2, *Naval Operations Including Diplomatic Background from January 1802 through August 1803* [Washington, D.C.: United States Government Printing Office, 1940] 58 (hereinafter cited as *Naval Documents, Barbary Powers,* vol. 2, *January 1802 through August 1803*). Later, while in service on

Corps to be a steadfast friend to younger officers in need of guidance and counseling.[7] In building his reputation as a staunch defender of the Marine Corps, Carmick worked closely early in his career with Commandant Burrows, taking advice from the older man and providing him with observations on shipboard conditions and treatment of marines assigned to other ships in the navy as well as his own.[8]

It is no exaggeration to say that Daniel Carmick's service in the United States Marines lifted him from obscurity to fame as a national hero. Prior to the spring of 1798, when he was commissioned lieutenant in the marines, almost nothing is known about his life.[9] Scattered evidence suggests that he, like his grandfather Peter Carmick (d. 1759), his father Stephen (1718/19–1774), and his older brother, also named Peter (1759–1786), was employed in Philadelphia in some aspect of the import business when the undeclared naval war with France in 1798–1800 changed the course of his life.[10] A con-

---

the USS *Constitution*, Carmick reported that "Officers of the ship do not interfere with my men" (*Naval Documents Related to the Quasi-War, August 1799 to December 1799*, 91).

7. See *Naval Documents Related to the Quasi-War, June 1800 to November 1800*, 374, 444, for the favorable outcome of a very difficult situation for Lieutenant Henry Caldwell because of the intercession of Carmick.

8. See Carmick's report to Commandant Burrows on the terrible conditions on the *Constitution* before Captain Talbot assumed command and the changes that came about afterward in *Naval Documents Related to the Quasi-War, April 1799 to July 1799*, 480–1, and ibid., *August 1799 to December 1799*, 91, as well as Commandant Burrows to Secretary of Navy Benjamin Stoddert, January 26, 1800, in which the commandant referred to the "Tyranny spoke of to me by Capt Carmick" on board the USS *Herald* in *Naval Documents Related to the Quasi-War Between the United States and France. Naval Operations From January 1800 to May 1800* (Washington, D.C.: United States Government Printing Office, 1937), 136 (hereinafter cited as *Naval Documents Related to the Quasi-War, January 1800 to May 1800*).

9. Carmick's commission is printed in *Naval Documents Related to the Quasi-War Between the United States and France. Naval Operations from February 1797 to October 1798* (Washington, D.C.: United States Government Printing Office, 1935), 66–7 (hereinafter cited as *Naval Documents Related to the Quasi-War, February 1797 to October 1798*).

10. Peter Carmick, Daniel's grandfather, was said to have come to America from Scotland "in the train of William Penn," but he was not a Quaker (William Sawitzky, "The American Work of Benjamin West," *Pennsylvania Magazine of History and Biography* 62, no. 4 [October 1938], 452). See also A. Van Doren Honeyman, ed., *Documents Relating to the Colonial History of the State of New Jersey,* First Series, vol. 32, *Calendar of New Jersey Wills, Administrations, etc.,* vol. 3, *1751–1760* (Somerville, N.J.: Unionist-Gazette Association of Printers, 1924), 53; and William Nelson, ed., *Documents Relating to the Colonial History of the State of New Jersey,* vol. 23, *Calendar of New Jersey Wills,* vol. 1, *1670–1730* (Paterson, N.J.: Press Printing and Publishing, 1901), 54–5.

nection between his previous work and new military duties is suggested by
Daniel's first military assignment and his rapport with Commandant Bur-
rows. Burrows, a lawyer and Revolutionary War veteran from Charleston,
South Carolina, had become a resident of Philadelphia after the Revolution.
He was appointed commandant of the U.S. Marine Corps by President John
Adams on July 12, 1798, the day after the Corps was established by law.[11]
Three weeks after establishment of the Marine Corps as a distinct body
within the Navy Department, young Carmick was promoted to captain.
With this promotion, he became the third-ranking officer in the newly organized Corps.[12] It is most likely Carmick and Burrows became acquainted
through business contacts in Philadelphia, perhaps through work that was
done for the Philadelphia merchants Willing and Francis, who sold the
newly built USS *Ganges* to the U.S. government for use in the quasi-war
with France.[13] The *Ganges* was Carmick's first sea duty assignment.[14] The
Carmick and Willing families appear to have been close; Thomas Willing
was one of the executors of the will of Stephen Carmick, Daniel's father.[15]

During the quasi-war with France, Carmick's second sea duty assignment was to the USS *Constitution*. He initially refused to serve on the ship
because at this point in its history, it had the reputation of being "miserably
managed."[16] Under a new captain, the Revolutionary War hero Silas Talbot,

11. Heinl, *Soldiers of the Sea*, 10. Ibid., 12–3, deals briefly with Burrows as a role model
for marines. In a very real sense, the relationship between Burrows and Carmick was much
like that between father and son. There is little reason to believe Carmick had any personal
recollection of his father. When Stephen Carmick died in June 1774, Daniel was fourteen
months old. Cook, "Carmick of Salem," 2.

12. Henry E. Williams, "Biographical Sketch of Daniel Carmick, Major, USMC," typescript, rev. and ed. Ralph W. Donnelly; History and Museums Division, Department of the
Navy (1972; Washington, 1973), 7. This typescript is useful in developing the military career
of Carmick, but cites no sources.

13. See the purchase agreement in *Naval Documents Related to the Quasi-War, February
1797 to October 1798*, 63–4. The ship apparently was intended for use in the East India trade.
Originally, there were three owners: Thomas Willing; his son, Thomas Mayne Willing; and his
nephew, Thomas Willing Francis. As business partner with Robert Morris, Thomas Willing
had helped to finance the new American nation. Willing later served as president of the Bank
of North America and its successor, the Bank of the United States. Burton A. Konkle, *Thomas
Willing and the First American Financial System* (Philadelphia: University of Pennsylvania
Press, 1937), 116, 118, 136.

14. *Naval Documents Related to the Quasi-War, February 1797 to October 1798*, 66.

15. Cook, "Carmick of Salem," 3, who cites *Philadelphia Will Book Q*, 28.

16. Carmick to Burrows, June 28, 1799, *Naval Documents Related to the Quasi-War,
April 1799 to July 1799*, 349–50.

and a new crew, the *Constitution* began to build the reputation that made it famous in American history. Carmick and his detachment of marines played a significant role in making the new image.

One of the several prizes taken by the *Constitution* under its new captain and crew was the British ship *Sandwich*. The capture of this copper-bottomed packet, believed to be one of the fastest ships then afloat, was widely heralded when it was reported in the United States in 1800. The venture also involved the first landing on foreign soil by the U.S. Marine Corps. The expedition generally is regarded as one of the best planned and executed missions that involved the early navy and marines.[17] Carmick and the other marines and sailors who participated in the action were praised by Captain Talbot for the "handsome manner and great address with which they performed this dashing adventure." Regardless of how well the venture played with the participants and the American public when it was reported in the newspapers of Philadelphia and elsewhere, the incident had taken place within the Spanish territorial waters of Santo Domingo and was a violation of Spanish neutrality. To avoid the serious complications of an international incident, the *Sandwich* had to be returned on the orders of the president of the United States.[18]

Following his duty on the *Constitution*, Carmick returned home to take a long furlough, at the end of which he was assigned for about a year to the marine barracks at Philadelphia.[19] During this time his younger brother, Edward, the twin of younger sister Elizabeth, died.[20] When Captain Carmick returned to duty, he was assigned to the USS *Chesapeake,* which was ordered to the Mediterranean Sea to protect American shipping against the Barbary pirates of North Africa.[21]

Following his tour of duty in the Mediterranean, Carmick received the first of his three assignments to Louisiana. Sometime in April 1804, Car-

17. *Naval Documents Related to the Quasi-War, January 1800 to May 1800*, 503–4; and Heinl, *Soldiers of the Sea*, 13.

18. *Naval Documents Related to the Quasi-War, January 1800 to May 1800*, 503–4. Under U.S. law at that time, the members of a capturing party were permitted to receive a portion of any prize money from any vessels seized. See *Naval Documents Related to the Quasi-War, August 1799 to December 1799*, 195, in which the prize money from the *Amelia* was denied to the men of the *Constitution* because the ship's owners and its origin were in a neutral country, Germany.

19. Williams, "Daniel Carmick," 4.

20. Cook, "Carmick of Salem," 5, and Christ Church, Philadelphia, *Burial Record*, p. 3587, January 1, 1801.

21. *Naval Documents, Barbary Powers*, vol. 2, *January 1802 through August 1803*, 58.

mick sailed under orders on the USS *Superior* from Norfolk, Virginia, for New Orleans in the newly acquired Louisiana Purchase territory. Under his command were three lieutenants, one surgeon, and a company of enlisted men.[22] On May 5, 1804, the morning after the *Superior* docked in New Orleans, Carmick marched his men through the streets of the city to their barracks.[23] The parade of the company of one hundred marines in their red, white, and blue uniforms with gold buttons and gold trim must have made quite an impression on the Spanish and French citizens of the town, as Carmick no doubt intended.[24] About a week later, Captain James Sterrett, paymaster for the U.S. Army in New Orleans, described the newly arrived marine officers as "fine young men."[25] Before the end of June nearly one-fourth of Carmick's command was ill, causing him to report that New Orleans certainly had a "very unhealthy climate."[26] Most of the men on the sick roster were ill with yellow fever, that scourge of the seaports of the world into the twentieth century.[27]

Soon after Carmick assumed his duties in New Orleans, Governor Claiborne called on him to represent the United States in negotiations with Vicente Folch y Juan, the governor of West Florida, to establish a postal route through that Spanish colony. Claiborne seems to have chosen Carmick to handle this duty for two reasons: first, Carmick appears to have been acquainted with George T. Ross, a fellow Pennsylvanian, who had been in the military contingent that accompanied Governor Claiborne in taking posses-

22. James Sterrett to Nathaniel Evans, May 5, 1804, identifies the men who landed as "One Captain three Subalterns one Surgeon and about 110 Men of the Marine Corps," Nathaniel Evans and Family Papers, Louisiana and Lower Mississippi Valley Collections, Louisiana State University Libraries. To Edward D. Turner, May 6, 1804, in *Official Letter Books of W. C. C. Claiborne, 1801–1816*, ed. Dunbar Rowland, vol. 2 (1917; New York: AMS Press, 1972), 132 (hereinafter cited as CLB, with volume and page numbers) also mentions Carmick's arrival and the number of men under his command.

23. To Henry Dearborn, May 5, 1804, CLB, 2: 129, gives the date Carmick and his men arrived in New Orleans.

24. The uniform of the early Marines is described in Charles L. Lewis, *Famous American Marines: An Account of the Corps: The Exploits of Officers and Men on Land, by Air and Sea from the Decks of the "Bonhomme Richard" to the Summit of Mount Suribachi* (Boston: L.C. Page, 1950), 23–4.

25. James Sterrett to Nathaniel Evans, May 12, 1804, Nathaniel Evans and Family Papers.

26. Williams, "Daniel Carmick," 6.

27. Jo Ann Carrigan, *The Saffron Scourge: A History of Yellow Fever in Louisiana, 1796–1905* (Lafayette: Center for Louisiana Studies, University of Southwestern Louisiana, 1994), 32–5, provides a broader perspective on the yellow fever epidemic in New Orleans in 1804 and the problems the disease caused into the twentieth century.

sion of Louisiana in 1803 and soon was to become sheriff of New Orleans.[28] Second, and perhaps most important, Claiborne may have chosen Carmick for this duty because of the young captain's publicized participation in the capture of the *Sandwich* in Santo Domingo. The fact that he had an impressive physical appearance and military manner were factors the governor undoubtedly also was relying on to impress the difficult Spanish governor.[29]

Carmick had to travel to Pensacola to meet with Folch. The negotiations were successful, but throughout the mission it must have seemed to Carmick that his efforts were doomed to failure. The first ship on which he booked passage in late April 1805 was shipwrecked "on the lake."[30] Carmick booked passage on a second vessel, which was "pursued and driven back by a British Privateer."[31] Because of the delays, it was not until June 5 that he reached Pensacola. Two days later, Carmick met with Governor Folch. Either on that date, June 7, or soon thereafter, the two men agreed on the

28. For information on George T. Ross, see his biographical sketch.

29. The earliest known likeness of Carmick, a profile physiognotrace by Charles Balthazar Julien Févret Saint-Mémin, shows a young man with a well-shaped head covered with short cut, slightly wavy and curly hair. Above the leather stock and high coat collar then worn by U.S. Marines, Saint-Mémin depicts a firm, nearly square jaw line sporting a tapered sideburn that extends down almost to Carmick's chin. The large, open eyes, straight nose, and almost sensuous mouth, together with the smooth brow, convey an expression of youthful anticipation and determination. Although the likeness is in the characteristic black on white that became the hallmark of Saint-Mémin and his partner Thomas Bluget de Valdenuit, the viewer senses the blond hair and gold in the epaulet on the right shoulder, and the blue in the long coat with its red lapels, white facings, and gold buttons. The total image is that of an intelligent, well-groomed, and efficient young man, exactly the kind Commandant Burrows sought for the Marine Corps and that Claiborne wanted to use to impress Governor Folch. This likeness of Carmick is in *Naval Documents Related to the Quasi-War, August to December 1799,* facing p. 122. It most likely was made soon after Carmick entered the Marine Corps in 1798, which was the year after Saint-Mémin settled in Philadelphia. This physiognotrace is different from those in Heinl, *Soldiers of the Sea,* following p. 30, and Richard S. Collum, *History of the United States Marine Corps* (Philadelphia: L.R. Hamersly, 1890), facing p. 58, both of which appear to be of a later date. The later likenesses show Carmick wearing a queue.

30. To James Madison, May 5, 1805, CLB, 3: 40, tells of the misfortune on the lake, presumably Pontchartrain. Carmick apparently set out on this journey in late April, but was back in New Orleans before May 4, 1805. Governor Claiborne to the Secretary of State, April 29, 1805, suggests that Carmick began his odyssey in April and erroneously refers to him as an army officer (Clarence E. Carter, comp. and ed., *The Territorial Papers of the United States,* vol. 9, *The Territory of Orleans, 1803–1812* [Washington, D.C.: U.S. Government Printing Office, 1940]; hereinafter cited as TP, with volume and page range). The army officer in New Orleans sometimes confused with Carmick was George Washington Carmichal.

31. To the Post Master General, June 7, 1805, CLB, 3: 83.

arrangements for the overland U.S. postal route through West Florida.[32] However, after the negotiations were completed, Governor Folch would not allow Carmick to leave Pensacola.[33]

Uncertain of the implications of Folch's unfriendly action and knowing that he had accomplished his mission, Carmick determined to return to New Orleans by land regardless of Folch's attitude.[34] Sometime in late June, Carmick reached Pass Christian on the Mississippi Gulf coast. There, he met a vessel bound for Mobile. Because the ship ultimately was bound for New Orleans, Carmick took passage on it. While the ship was docked in Mobile, Carmick suffered the second setback of the mission: the dispatches from Governor Folch intended for Governor Claiborne were stolen from Carmick's baggage on the wharf. Carmick arrived back in New Orleans about July 4, 1805, without the dispatches.[35] Eventually, the purloined documents were replaced with copies from Governor Folch's file, but Carmick could not have been proud of his diplomatic venture.[36] Eight days after his return to New Orleans, Carmick received orders recalling him to Washington. In late August, Carmick was given orders stationing him in Philadelphia, where he remained until early May 1806, when he was ordered to duty in Washington.[37]

The assignment to headquarters in Washington appeared to be good for Carmick. In reality, it spelled trouble because of the latent hostility between him and the new commandant of the Marine Corps, Lieutenant Colonel Franklin Wharton. Carmick's attitude toward Wharton is vividly set forth in a June 27, 1804, letter on the occasion of Wharton's promotion. Carmick wrote Wharton that he was happy to hear of the promotion to lieutenant-colonel and command of the Marine Corps. However, by his next statement

32. William C. C. Claiborne to Vicente Folch, April 26, 1805, State Department Territorial Papers, Orleans Series, 1764–1813, reel 6, vol. 6, January 1, 1805–June 21, 1805. National Archives microcopy T260, City Archives, Louisiana Department, New Orleans Public Library, folio 119, contains a copy of the letter Carmick hand-delivered to Folch requesting establishment of the postal route through Spanish West Florida.

33. Carmick reported to Claiborne that Folch kept him from leaving Pensacola while a brig from New Orleans was outfitted as a privateer. Daniel Carmick to Gov. Claiborne, July 4, 1805, CLB, 3: 113–4.

34. The unfriendly and antagonistic attitudes of Folch and Casa Calvo toward one another and the United States are clearly discernible in To Gov. Claiborne from the Marquis of Casa Calvo, July 16, 1805, CLB, 3: 130.

35. Daniel Carmick to Gov. Claiborne, July 4, 1805, ibid., 114.

36. To James Madison, August 9, 1805, ibid., 156.

37. Williams, "Daniel Carmick," 6.

Carmick negated all appearance of friendly feelings. Carmick told Wharton that his promotion was unprecedented and little expected, and then closed by saying he had "no doubt the next session of Congress will revoke it."[38] Clearly, Carmick had hoped to become commandant of the Marine Corps and resented Wharton for his sudden and unexpected promotions.

Carmick's outspokenness certainly established that he did not have a high opinion of his new superior. Hostility and resentment between the two men grew until Wharton advised Secretary of the Navy Robert Smith of the situation. In his letter, Wharton severely criticized Carmick for an "opposition to orders which amounts not to a disobedience of them," but which exhibits a "concealed hostility" that avoids violation of the articles of war just enough to prevent his arrest.[39] Wharton's letter to Smith was followed immediately by an order from the secretary suspending Carmick from his command for "contumacious conduct."[40] Wharton followed Secretary Smith's action with notice to Carmick that he was calling a "Court of Inquiry" to investigate the complaints he had lodged against Carmick. The complaints included disobedience of orders, disrespect to commanding officers, remaining away from headquarters without permission, and disregarding regulations pertaining to uniform.[41] Carmick responded eight days later, requesting that he be tried by court martial so that his guilt or innocence could be determined.[42] The court martial apparently met in early August to investigate Wharton's charge of disrespect. After the investigation, the court acquitted Carmick and ordered that he be restored to his command. The verdict was approved by Commandant Wharton, but it is doubtful he was happy with it.[43]

Carmick's court martial did not end the differences between the two highest ranking officers in the corps. About a year after Carmick's court martial, Commandant Wharton forwarded to Secretary Smith allegations made by Lieutenant Samuel Baldwin against Carmick and a Lieutenant Creuse involving Wharton. Baldwin and Creuse both were serving under Carmick, who by this time was completing his second tour of duty in New Orleans. Baldwin's allegations were filed from New Orleans. Whatever the complaints were, Wharton wrote Navy Secretary Smith he was "unwilling

38. Card Register of Communications.
39. Williams, "Daniel Carmick," 6–7.
40. Ibid., 7.
41. Wharton to Carmick, July 11, 1806, Card Register of Communications.
42. Carmick to Wharton, July 19, 1806, ibid.
43. Wharton to Carmick, August 23, 1806, ibid., and Williams, "Daniel Carmick," 7.

to act" on them because they "embrace personal [opinions] which I should prefer to notice only with silent contempt."[44]

Carmick's court martial did not resolve the differences with Wharton, but it was the occasion in which the question of uniform regulation was resolved. Commandant Wharton had objected to Carmick's wearing the leather stock, but the regulations regarding this part of the marine uniform apparently were not clear. As a consequence, the charge was dismissed. Nonetheless, Wharton's complaints had the result he wished. Carmick laid the leather stock aside because, as he said, it was "out of fashion." Ironically, the lasting effect of this charge against Carmick is that he is credited with establishment of the tradition of the marines being called "Leathernecks."[45]

Baldwin's allegations against Carmick and Creuse were filed by Commandant Wharton with Secretary Smith about the time Carmick returned from his second tour of duty in New Orleans. Carmick's tour had begun with his arrival in the territorial capital late in January 1807, about the time the "reign of terror" created by General Wilkinson in the Burr conspiracy was near its peak. The assignment reflected the continuing concern of the national government with security for the important Mississippi estuary and outlet for American trade beyond the Appalachian Mountains. As with the first tour in New Orleans, Carmick arrived aboard a U.S. naval vessel, in this instance the brigantine USS *Franklin*. He had with him a detachment of two lieutenants, four sergeants, four corporals, two musicians, and sixty-four privates. Except for the gossipy report by Baldwin, the second tour of duty in the Crescent City apparently was uneventful, despite the excitement generated by the tumultuous events of the Burr conspiracy. By August 8, 1807, the crisis in New Orleans had passed and Carmick was ordered back to headquarters, where he assumed command of the marines at the Washington barracks.

During the year he was commander of the Washington barracks, Carmick again became involved with recruiting, something he did well and had done since he had joined the Corps.[46] He had been in command at Washington about a month when he advised Commandant Wharton that eighteen

44. Wharton to Robert Smith, August 14, 1807, Card Register of Communications.
45. Heinl, *Soldiers of the Sea*, 29.
46. *Naval Documents Related to the Quasi-War, February 1797 to October 1798*, 66–7. According to the recruitment regulations then in effect, for every man brought into the corps, the recruiting officer was to receive a "reimbursement fee" of one dollar. See ibid., 34.

new recruits had been brought into service.[47] Carmick also sought to make certain the new young officers in the Corps knew the drill commands necessary to train enlisted men how to march. Shortly after he assumed command, Carmick issued an order that the new officers were to familiarize themselves with the commands for "marchings, wheelings, forming and reducings of divisions and such simple maneuvers."[48]

The Washington assignment was followed early in 1808 by another tour of duty at Norfolk, Virginia, where Carmick remained for nearly eighteen months.[49] During this assignment he was promoted, on March 7, 1809, to major. The rank had not been used in the Marine Corps since Carmick's mentor, William Ward Burrows, had been promoted from it on April 22, 1800.[50] Congress brought the rank back into use only three days before Carmick was appointed to it, so that the newly revived rank appears to have been intended for him alone. The promotion came in conjunction with President James Madison's desire to station three hundred marines at New Orleans and the need for an officer of greater rank than captain to command such a large contingent of troops.[51] Carmick assumed command of the marine post at New Orleans on July 5, 1809.[52]

Nearly three months after taking command in New Orleans, Carmick was pulled into the swirl of actions generated by General James Wilkinson in his efforts to defend himself against charges that he was a paid espionage agent for the Spanish and, as such, had played a leading role in the Burr conspiracy. In response to the demand of his superior, General Wilkinson, Carmick provided a deposition on September 25, 1809, that was damaging to both Daniel Clark and James Sterrett.[53] No details are known about how

47. Carmick to Wharton, September 14, 1807, Card Register of Communications.

48. Williams, "Daniel Carmick," 7.

49. Ibid.

50. Ibid.

51. *American State Papers: Naval Affairs*, 1: 264; Heinl, *Soldiers of the Sea*, 616 n. 19.

52. Williams, "Daniel Carmick," 7. On the same page it is pointed out that the Marine Corps dropped the rank of major from use again, effective March 3, 1817, four months after Carmick's death.

53. James Wilkinson, *Burr's Conspiracy Exposed; and General Wilkinson Vindicated Against the Slanders of His Enemies on That Important Occasion* ([Washington City,] 1811), 94. Sterrett had arrived in New Orleans as part of the American military contingent from Fort Adams, Mississippi Territory, for the transfer of Louisiana to the United States. James Wilkinson to Secretary of War, January 24, 1803 [1804], and General Orders, October 21, 1805, TP 9: 169, 587, respectively. Sterrett was commissioned a lieutenant in the army in Pennsylvania in June 1794 and resigned on September 20, 1805, to make New Orleans his home. Francis B. Heitman, *Historical Register and Dictionary of the United States Army from Its Organization*

Carmick came to give the deposition, but it is unlikely he willingly gave this sworn statement against his future brother-in-law. Wilkinson's wrath in this instance was directed more at Sterrett than Clark. Sterrett, like several other young army officers stationed in New Orleans, had left the army in 1805 because of Wilkinson.[54] Wilkinson described Sterrett as "notoriously hostile to the government" and "a miserable dependent" of Clark. There is no truth to the first part of this statement, and the latter part is true only to the extent that Sterrett, like many businessmen in New Orleans at this time, was suffering from the loss of business as a result of the embargo adopted by the Jefferson administration and needed work to provide for his family.[55] Sterrett was doubly hurt by the embargo and the obligations left to him to pay when his former business partner, John Clay, returned to Kentucky, leaving the debts owed by their partnership, Clay & Sterrett.[56] Among the jobs he took in an effort to meet his obligations and provide for his family was that as editor of the New Orleans *Louisiana Gazette* newspaper, which is how he was identified in the deposition taken by James Tharp.[57]

During this third tour of duty in New Orleans, Carmick lived in the marine barracks with the men under his command, as he apparently did in his

---

September 29, 1789, to March 2, 1903, vol. 1 (1903; Urbana: University of Illinois Press, 1965), 921.

54. James Sterrett to Nathaniel Evans, October 15, 1804, identifies several young officers who were forced out of the army by Wilkinson. James Sterrett to Nathaniel Evans, April 22, 1805, alludes to Sterrett's difficulties with Wilkinson. Sterrett's difficulties with Wilkinson may have been more than purely personal. Sterrett to Evans, September 5, 1808, points out, along with his plea for money due him from Evans, that he owed "a balance to the United States which I Must pay next winter" (Nathaniel Evans and Family Papers). This debt may be related to Sterrett's arrest on unknown charges early in 1804. See James Wilkinson to the Secretary of War, January 24, 1803 [1804], TP, 9: 169.

55. James Sterrett's letters to Nathaniel Evans in 1808 and 1809 contain a number of references to his efforts to make ends meet as a result of the embargo. See, for example, Sterrett to Evans, May 13, 1809, in the Nathaniel Evans and Family Papers.

56. James Sterrett to Nathaniel Evans, October 31, 1805, tells of the partnership with John Clay. Sterrett to Evans, September 5, 1808, tells of being "nearly thro all my old commer-[c]ial bussiness [sic]" (ibid.).

57. Wilkinson, *Burr's Conspiracy Exposed,* 93. Sterrett also sought and won a seat on the city council, but the demands on his time resulting from his decision in the late summer of 1808 to reenter the business world kept him from fulfilling his public responsibilities. As a consequence, in December 1808, Dr. Louis Fortin was elected "to fill the vacancy occasioned" by Sterrett's absence (*Louisiana Gazette,* December 23, 1808, p. 2, c. 2). In the spring of 1809, a newspaper advertisement indicated that Sterrett's "counting room" was at No. 16 Bienville Street, where he would "attend to business in the Commission-Line," which was "confined chiefly to the purchase and sale of cotton" (*Louisiana Gazette,* May 23, 1809, p. 3, c. 4).

previous assignments to the Orleans Territory capital.[58] However, this did not limit his support of and participation in the social life that was much a part of New Orleans. Late in December 1809 a local businessman and wit described the Christmas season party given by Carmick: "The Dancing Campaign is opened. I was at a party last night where we had a brilliant display of beauty and good dancing, and what was Much to My taste, we had excellent eating and drinking. it was *L'Millitaire* given by Major Carmack [sic] of the Marine Corps."[59] No further report on Carmick's activities or community involvement appears until the British siege of New Orleans.

On December 28, 1814, the British moved to capitalize on the previous day's success. In that action the British had dislodged, set afire with hot shot, and sunk the USS *Carolina,* the schooner whose punishing cannonades and sniper fire had successfully blocked the British attack on the American "line Jackson" for several days.[60] The British maneuver on December 28 has been described as not an assault in the proper sense of that term, but a reconnaissance in force, a probing action to learn what the American strength might be and what they might do if they were attacked.[61] A part of the British reconnaissance consisted of a day-long barrage of the American breastwork with the latest British weapon, the Congreve rocket. Major André Lacarrière Latour, the principal engineer in the Seventh Military District of the United States Army and one of the participants in the battle of New Orleans, said the "British had great expectation from the effect of this weapon. . . . They hoped that its very noise would strike terror into us; but we soon grew accustomed to it, and thought it little formidable; for in the whole course of the campaign, the rockets only wounded ten men, and blew up two caissons." Latour went on to say the rocket was not very effective "against troops drawn up in line of battle, or behind ramparts."[62] For this reason most of the American forces took safe positions behind the high

58. *Whitney's New-Orleans Directory* for 1811 lists Carmick's residence "*à la caserne,* at the barracks." Thomas H. Whitney, *Whitney's New-Orleans Directory, and Louisiana & Mississippi Almanac for the Year 1811* (New Orleans: Printed for the Author, 1810), 12.

59. James Sterrett to Nathaniel Evans, December 30, 1809, Nathaniel Evans and Family Papers.

60. A. Lacarrière Latour, *Historical Memoir of the War in West Florida and Louisiana in 1814–1815. With an Atlas* (1816; reprint, with an introduction by Jane Lucas DeGrummond, Gainesville: University of Florida Press, 1964), appendix 26, pp. xlvii–xlix.

61. Wilburt S. Brown, *The Amphibious Campaign for West Florida and Louisiana, 1814–1815: A Critical Review of Strategy and Tactics at New Orleans* (University: University of Alabama Press, 1969), 117.

62. Latour, *Historical Memoir,* 121–2.

breastwork. However, one of the ten Americans wounded by a Congreve rocket during the barrage on December 28 was Daniel Carmick. He was hit while riding to deliver an order near the center of line Jackson. The rocket that hit Carmick "tore his horse to pieces" and wounded him in the arm and head.[63] No further description of the severity of either wound has been found. Some writers have said that Carmick died soon after being hit by the rocket, and the Marine Corps official records state that he died as a result of his wounds.[64] However, Major Carmick lived for nearly twenty months after being wounded.

In his report after the battle, Captain Daniel T. Patterson, who commanded the naval forces at New Orleans, praised Carmick for his promptness in responding to requests made of him and for the strong support he gave in furthering Patterson's objectives.[65] The U.S. Congress was also generous in its praise of the Marine Corps officers and noncommissioned officers who successfully defended New Orleans. They were recognized in a special resolution that singled Major Carmick out by name for his "high sense of . . . valor and good conduct."[66]

About the time that Congress passed the resolution recognizing Carmick and his fellow marines for their roles in the victory at New Orleans, the major married Marguerite Cowperthwaite, one of the daughters of Jacob and Charlotte O'Brien Cowperthwaite of New Orleans.[67] Daniel and Mar-

63. Edwin N. McClellan, "The Navy at the Battle of New Orleans," *United States Naval Institute Proceedings* 50, no. 262 (December 1924), 2055; and Charles B. Brooks, *The Siege of New Orleans* (Seattle: University of Washington Press, 1961), 188.

64. Collum, *History,* facing p. 58.

65. Ibid., 60. McClellan, "Navy at the Battle of New Orleans," 2041, 2043–45, 2047, points out that Commodore Patterson designed the battle plan used to defeat the British at New Orleans. His plan was based on his knowledge of the coastal terrain and waterways of West Florida and Louisiana.

66. McClellan, "Navy at the Battle of New Orleans," 2059.

67. There were several Cowperthwaite daughters, who were related to the O'Brien family through Mrs. Cowperthwaite. Henriette married George T. Ross. See the George T. Ross biographical sketch. James Sterrett married Charlotte O'Brien. James Sterrett to Nathaniel Evans, February 4, 1805, Nathaniel Evans and Family Papers. See also *Sacramental Records of the Roman Catholic Church of the Archdiocese of New Orleans, 1804–1806,* vol. 8, eds. Charles E. Nolan and Dorenda Dupont, trans. J. Edgar Bruns (New Orleans: Archdiocese of New Orleans, 1993), 305. Michael Reynolds, formerly a marine stationed in New Orleans, married Catherine Cowperthwaite. See the biographical sketch of George T. Ross, n. 51. Marguerite Cowperthwaite was named godmother to Guillaume Reynolds, the infant son of Catherine Cowperthwaite and Michael Reynolds, in 1813. Act 166, St. Mary's Church (Chartres Street), New Orleans, Register no. 1805–1830, folio 27. Some of the New Orleans records omit the

guerite were married in St. Mary's Catholic Church (Chartres Street) in New Orleans, on March 4, 1815. Friends of the couple who witnessed their marriage included George T. Ross, James Sterrett, Joseph McNeil, Robert Morrell, and H. C. Ross.[68] Given the fact that Carmick lived little more than nineteen months after his marriage, one can only wonder what kind of life the couple had. The newspaper notice of Carmick's death said he died "after a severe illness of four weeks," leaving "an amiable wife" and infant child.[69] The brief story went on to describe Carmick as "noble, generous and brave, . . . always respected for his correct conduct, as an officer and gentleman."[70]

---

last *e* in spelling *Cowperthwaite*. The authority for use of the *e* throughout this study is the Deposition of Marguerite Cowperthwaite Carmick, November 23, 1855.

68. Act 96, St. Mary's Church (Chartres St.), New Orleans, register M-1, folio 37. The H. C. Ross who is listed as a witness for the marriage may be Henriette Cowperthwaite Ross, the wife of George T. Ross and an older sister of Marguerite.

69. In her application for bounty land available to veterans under the September 28, 1850, act of Congress, Marguerite Cowperthwaite Carmick indicated she was then sixty-four years old, suggesting that the year of her birth was 1791. Deposition of Marguerite Cowperthwaite Carmick, November 23, 1855.

70. *Louisiana Gazette*, November 6, 1816, p. 2, c. 2.

SAMUEL FULTON

Samuel Fulton (1770–1827?) was the son of Thomas and Elizabeth Gambell (Gambrell) Fulton.[1] His association with the old Southwest began in 1790 at his mother's home, then Fayetteville, Guilford County, North Carolina, where he met Alexander McGillivray during the Creek Indian chief's journey to New York to meet President Washington.[2] The chance meeting with McGillivray appears to have encouraged Fulton's already active wanderlust. By 1791 he was in Pensacola, living with Captain John Lindar, who died later the same year. Fulton later said that his own republican political opinions made him unacceptable to the Spanish, so he left Pensacola before the end of 1791.[3] For part of the next two years, the North Carolinian traveled with Louis Leclerc de Milfort, brother-in-law of Alexander McGillivray and military leader of the Creek Indians.[4]

Fulton emerged from the Creek Indian territory in Knoxville in June 1793 to give a deposition on himself and his activities since leaving home

1. *Archives of the Spanish Government of West Florida*, vol. 12 (Baton Rouge: Survey of Federal Archives in Louisiana, 1937–40), 381 (hereinafter cited as *Spanish West Florida Papers* with volume and page range).

2. *American State Papers: Indian Affairs*, vol. 1 (Washington: Gales & Seaton, 1832), 463.

3. Ibid.

4. *Selections from the Draper Collection in the Possession of the State Historical Society of Wisconsin, to Elucidate the Proposed French Expedition under George Rogers Clark Against Louisiana, in the Years 1793–94*, vol. 1 (Washington, D.C.: Government Printing Office, 1897), 1063 n. 4. General Milfort does not mention Samuel Fulton in *Memoirs, or A Quick Glance at My Various Travels and Sojourn in the Creek Nation*, ed. and trans. Ben C. McCary (Kennesaw, Ga.: Continental Book, 1959).

in 1790.[5] The deposition apparently formed the basis of Fulton's rapport with William Blount, the North Carolina merchant and former member of the Continental Congress who was then governor of the Southwest Territory.[6] When Fulton left Knoxville, he carried letters of recommendation from Governor Blount to George Rogers Clark in Kentucky. Clark then employed Fulton as his assistant in the scheme being financed by France through Edmond Genet, the French minister plenipotentiary to the United States, to conquer Spanish territory in the trans-Appalachian West under Clark's leadership. Early the following year Clark commissioned Fulton a major in the French cavalry.[7] About a year later, the French promoted him to lieutenant colonel.[8]

Part of the time that Fulton held a commission in the French cavalry, he also held the rank of ensign in the U.S. infantry (May 12, 1794–November 1, 1796).[9] The appointment as ensign raises several questions: Did the U.S. officials involved know of Fulton's French commission? Was Fulton retained to function as a spy on the French for the United States? If the answer to these two questions is yes, who authorized Fulton's activities? Someone with authority in the national government must have known of and approved Fulton's appointment in the U.S. Army and his travels between the frontier West, Philadelphia, and New York in the United States, and Paris, France, in the years 1795–96. What parts William Blount and Secretary of War Henry Knox may have played in the appointment are not known. Fulton wrote Clark in April 1794 that he had refused a commission in the U.S. Army presented to him by Secretary Knox.[10] Apparently, Fulton later changed his mind and accepted the commission. Fulton's appointment as ensign is made even more curious because he received an honorable discharge without ever having served at a U.S. Army post. In an age noted for its penurious treatment of the military services, Fulton's service in the army was remarkable.

Before the date of his honorable discharge from the U.S. Army in No-

---

5. *American State Papers: Indian Affairs*, 1: 463.

6. On Blount, see William Masterson, *William Blount* (Baton Rouge: Louisiana State University Press, 1954).

7. *Selections from the Draper Collection*, 1: 1063–64.

8. Ibid., 1087, 1088, 1089.

9. Francis B. Heitman, *Historical Register and Dictionary of the United States Army from Its Organization September 29, 1789, to March 2, 1903*, vol. 1 (1903; Urbana: University of Illinois Press, 1965), 441.

10. *Selections from the Draper Collection*, 1: 1068.

vember 1796, Fulton made two trips to France. Both were made in an effort to collect his and Clark's claims against the French government for their leadership roles in the aborted plans to take Spanish territory. Although he was not successful in attaining his objective on either trip, Fulton did win minor concessions in other areas. On the first trip in 1794–95 he was promoted to lieutenant colonel (1795–99) in the French cavalry. At the same time, Clark was made a major general in the French service and the French government approved the proceedings between Genet and Clark.[11] Following his return to the United States in the summer of 1795, Fulton was sent by the French minister to the United States, Pierre Adét, to Amelia Island to report on the followers of Elijah Clark who had taken refuge on that strip of swamp and sand off the Florida coast when their part in the Genet project failed.[12] That winter while on his way from Florida to Kentucky to see George Rogers Clark, Fulton was seen on the road by John Chisholm, who figured prominently in the "Blount conspiracy" two years later. The garrulous Chisholm left the only known description of Fulton, saying that he was "a tall handsome man upwards of six feet high, well mounted and handsomely equipped in every particular, [who] appeared to be about twenty-five years of age."[13]

In the spring of 1796, Fulton made his second trip to France, this time carrying dispatches for Adét.[14] Although he continued to be unsuccessful in obtaining settlement of his and Clark's claims against the French government, Fulton refused appointment as a lieutenant in the 10th Infantry Regiment of the U.S. Army on January 8, 1799.[15] Perhaps his small successes with the French led him to believe that ultimately he would succeed in the larger matter. Yet, whenever the opportunity presented itself thereafter, Fulton, more transparently than before, attempted to turn his limited knowledge of U.S., French, and Spanish plans into personal gain. He may have

11. Ibid., 1087, 1088, 1089.

12. See Frederick Jackson Turner, "The Policy of France toward the Mississippi Valley in the Period of Washington and Adams," *American Historical Review* 10, no. 2 (January 1905), 270 n. 1.

13. Ibid.

14. Ibid.

15. See Charles K. Gardner, *A Dictionary of All Officers, Who Have Been Commissioned, or Have Been Appointed and Served, in the Army of the United States, Since the Inauguration of Their First President, in 1789, to the First of January, 1853 . . .* , 2nd ed. (1860; New York: D. Van Nostrand, 1965), 182.

realized that the French never intended to pay, but apparently never gave up hope or trying to obtain a settlement.[16]

Several years later Fulton reappeared in the Western Hemisphere as a captain in the mounted police that accompanied the French army of Victor Emmanuel Leclerc's expedition to reconquer Santo Domingo. In November 1802 the soldier of fortune wrote Secretary of State Madison, advising him that Leclerc's army ultimately was destined for Louisiana. Fulton also reminded Madison of their 1795 meeting in Philadelphia and renewed his offer to be of service.[17] Near the end of December 1802, Fulton was in New Orleans, where he wrote George Rogers Clark that he hoped to receive a land grant in Louisiana from the French government in lieu of salary for services rendered.[18] While in New Orleans, Samuel may have stayed with his two brothers, James and Alexander, who were in business there about the time the United States bought Louisiana from France.[19]

16. Ronald Dwight Smith, in *French Interests in Louisiana: From Choiseul to Napoleon* (Ann Arbor: University Microfilms, 1975), 167–70, confirms that the work of men like Clark and Fulton was part of a large and intricate French plan to restore French hegemony to the Mississippi Valley.

17. Irving Brant, *James Madison*, vol. 3 *James Madison, Secretary of State, 1800–1809* (Indianapolis: Bobbs-Merrill, 1953), 75.

18. *Selections from the Draper Collection*, 1: 945, 1101.

19. Hatch Dent to James H. McCulloch, July 14, 1804, in Clarence E. Carter, comp. and ed., *The Territorial Papers of the United States*, vol. 9, *The Territory of Orleans, 1803–1812* (Washington, D.C.: U.S. Government Printing Office, 1940), 267 (hereinafter cited as TP, with volume and page range). Alexander Fulton later was postmaster and coroner, as well as one of the founders of present-day Alexandria, Louisiana. See Register of Civil Appointments in the Territory of Orleans, February 13, 1806, and The Post Master General to Alexander Fulton, February 6, 1807, in ibid., 602 and 706, respectively; and G. P. Whittington, "Rapides Parish, Louisiana—A History," *Louisiana Historical Quarterly* 16, no. 2 (April 1933), 247–9, in which Fulton is identified as one of the appointees to office in the newly created Rapides County in June 1805. Alexander also represented Rapides in the territorial House of Representatives in 1807. During the debate on the Memorial to Congress critical of General James Wilkinson's conduct during the Burr conspiracy, Alexander Fulton opposed adoption of the memorial, which had been suggested by Speaker of the House John Watkins. *Debate in the House of Representatives of the Territory of Orleans on a Memorial to Congress, Respecting the Illegal Conduct of General Wilkinson* (New Orleans: Bradford & Anderson, 1807), 3, 15. Richard Claiborne, Governor Claiborne's cousin and at the time judge in Rapides Parish, characterized Alexander Fulton in 1811 as earlier having been a "Whiskey Rebel." See Richard Claiborne to John Graham, November 10, 1811, TP, 9: 953. A J[ames ?] Fulton was living in Feliciana in 1811. Inhabitants of the County of Feliciana to John Ballinger, 1811, enclosed in John Ballinger to the Secretary of State, December 26, 1811, TP, 9: 971.

Sometime in 1803, Fulton made Spanish West Florida his residence.[20] Apparently, the collapse of the Leclerc expedition, the acquisition of Louisiana by the United States, and Madison's refusal to assist Fulton caused him to do what his avowed republicanism had kept him from doing earlier: swear allegiance to the king of Spain. In a notice that he was one of the persons authorized to receive subscriptions to the New Orleans *Louisiana Gazette,* the July and August 1804 issues of that newspaper gave his address simply as Baton Rouge. Earlier in the spring of that year (May 9, 1804), Fulton was given the power of attorney by Mrs. Weizer Jones (Marie Tanner) for the sale of some Feliciana land to Edward Randolph.[21]

In Baton Rouge, Fulton actively supported the provincial government and settled into the life of the community. With the assistance of Armand Allard Duplantier, and George Dupassau, Fulton assembled, organized, and armed a force of 150 volunteers from the Amite and Comite Rivers area to search the Baton Rouge and Feliciana districts for the Kemper brothers and other perpetrators of the 1804 insurrection in Spanish West Florida.[22] It may have been this action that precipitated threats of assassination against his life and others in April 1805.[23] Later, Fulton officially was appointed (1808–11) adjutant general of the West Florida militia.[24] Although he participated in the economic life of the Baton Rouge community, the nature of his contributions is uncertain. He owned land adjacent to "Magnolia Mound," the plantation home of Armand Duplantier immediately south of Baton Rouge, but Fulton's business interests appear to have been chiefly of the middleman variety. This is suggested by what is known of his general activities, such as the land transaction for Mrs. Jones, and the notice of reward offered for the return of his large, newly repainted barge, which had

20. See Fulton to Jackson, September 20, 1814, in *Correspondence of Andrew Jackson,* ed. John Spencer Bassett, vol. 2 (Washington, D.C.: Carnegie Institution of Washington, 1927), 56, and the references that follow.

21. *Spanish West Florida Papers,* 12: 190.

22. Isaac J. Cox, *The West Florida Controversy, 1798–1813: A Study in American Diplomacy* (1918; Gloucester, Mass.: Peter Smith, 1967), 158.

23. An "Extract of a Letter from a Gentleman of Respectability in the District of Baton Rouge Dated April 22nd 1805" identifies Fulton, Carlos de Grand Pré, Pintardo, Murdock, Kneeland, the entire settlement at Bayou Tunica, and "several of the inhabitants high up on Thompsons Creak [*sic*]" as marked for assassination. *Official Letter Books of W. C. C. Claiborne, 1801–1816,* ed. Dunbar Rowland (1917; New York: AMS Press, 1972), 44–5 (hereinafter cited as CLB, with volume and page range).

24. To Henry Dearborn, June 15, 1806, ibid., 328–9.

been taken from its landing in Baton Rouge in the spring of 1805.[25] In 1809, Fulton, Philip Hickey, Joseph Sharp, and John Davenport recommended deepening the channels of Bayou Manchac and the Iberville River, and the construction of a canal to connect them with the Mississippi River. The objective was completion of the 1764–65 British proposal to open the interior of North America to the Gulf of Mexico via Lakes Maurepas and Pontchartrain, thus circumventing New Orleans.[26]

Much of the local influence that Fulton enjoyed appears to have stemmed from his two marriages as much as from his military experience and travels. Through his first marriage, to Mary Lintot Steer in 1804, Fulton acquired the acreage south of Baton Rouge adjacent to Magnolia Mound. Mrs. Steer was the daughter of William Bernard Lintot, the former commissary officer at English Manchac, and the widow of Samuel Steer, reputedly the wealthiest planter in the Baton Rouge District at the time of his death in the late winter or early spring of 1804.[27] Fulton's acquaintance with Mrs. Steer probably blossomed from his association with her as executor of the estate of Hubert Rowell. Rowell and Samuel Steer, who died within a few days of one another, had been business partners. In addition, Rowell's widow was Sarah Lintot, Mary Lintot Steer's sister.[28]

Less than four years after Fulton married the widow Steer, she died, leaving Fulton with her three children, all minors, from the marriage to Steer. In December 1807, shortly after her death, Armand Duplantier and George Mather, the testamentary executors of Samuel Steer's estate, petitioned to have Fulton return two thousand pesos to the estate.[29] Fulton opposed the petition, claiming that the money in question was willed to him by Mary Lintot as part of the dowry she brought with her into the marriage to Steer. Fulton was supported in his claim by Father Francis Lennan, the Catholic priest for the Baton Rouge area, and by Thomas Lilley and Sarah L. Rowell.[30] In the spring of 1810, Duplantier and Mather petitioned to have a date

25. *Louisiana Gazette*, May 17, 1805, p. 3, c. 4.

26. Cox, *West Florida Controversy*, 325–6. On the British scheme, see Philip Pittman, *The Present State of the European Settlements on the Mississippi* (Gainesville: University of Florida Press, 1973), xiv–xv, xxiii, xxiv, 26, 27–32, and illustration of the "Draught of the R. Iberville" facing p. 16.

27. *Spanish West Florida Papers*, 14: 61.

28. Ibid.

29. This is recorded in the later petition of 1810. See ibid., 18: 98.

30. Ibid., 99.

set when Fulton would have to place the three minor Steer heirs in possession of their rightful inheritance.[31]

The cause of the concern demonstrated by Duplantier and Mather is uncertain. Initially, it may have grown out of a sense of responsibility to the
Steer children, but appears to have been precipitated by Fulton's prosperity
and success in dealing with the aging commandant in Baton Rouge, Don
Carlos Luis Boucher de Grand-Pré. These developments are reflected in the
increase in Fulton's landholdings, which grew to several hundred acres after
his marriage to the widow Steer,[32] and in his marriage to Hélène Boucher
de Grand-Pré, a daughter of Don Carlos de Grand-Pré, almost a year after
the death of Mary Lintot Steer.[33]

Ironically, as Fulton attained importance on the fringe of government in
Spanish West Florida, that government was collapsing with the breakup of
the Spanish Empire. Recognizing this fact, Fulton wrote President Madison
in April 1810 to point out his position of authority in the Baton Rouge District of West Florida and to offer assistance if the United States wished to
take the province.[34] Subsequently, Fulton was active in the events that ended
Spanish control of West Florida. His house in Baton Rouge served as the
rendezvous at which the plans for the West Florida Rebellion were made.[35]
After the United States had taken the Spanish territory, Fulton took advantage of Claiborne's conciliatory policy toward the Spanish population to obtain a midshipman's appointment under U.S. Navy Commodore John Shaw
in New Orleans for one of Don Carlos de Grand-Pré's two surviving sons.
Fulton also received assurances from Claiborne that he would "remember
the other brother, and do all in my power to serve him."[36]

Increasingly little is heard of Samuel Fulton after the admission of Louisiana to the union of states. In November 1812 he and Thomas Lilley were
appointed commissioners to take depositions in the contested election be-

31. Ibid., 97–110, and ibid., 17: 316–9. See also Maurine T. Wilson and Jack Jackson,
Philip Nolan and Texas: Expeditions to the Unknown Land, 1791–1801 (Waco, Tex.: Texian
Press, 1987), 145–6 n. 2.

32. *American State Papers: Public Lands*, vol. 3 (Washington, D.C.: Gales & Seaton,
1834), 61.

33. *Spanish West Florida Papers*, 12: 381–4. Mary Lintot Steer died about January 12,
1808. Fulton married Hélène on December 12, 1808. *Louisiana Gazette*, December 13, 1808,
p. 2, c. 4.

34. Brant, *James Madison*, vol. 5, *James Madison, President, 1809–1812* (Indianapolis:
Bobbs-Merrill, 1956), 175.

35. Cox, *West Florida Controversy*, 324, 380.

36. To Col. Fulton, January 31, 1811, CLB, 5: 138.

tween Philip Hickey and Fulwar Skipwith.[37] Two years later, amid the rising
fear that the British were going to attack Louisiana, Fulton wrote Andrew
Jackson from New Orleans offering to serve the general in "any Capassity."
Although he pointed out his prior military service with the French and Spanish governments, and with the militia of the state of Louisiana, Fulton said
nothing about his service with the U.S. Army in the Southwest Territory
from 1794 to 1796. Fulton also attempted to align himself with Jackson in
the growing gap between the general and Governor Claiborne. In the opening paragraph of his letter Fulton noted the "total want of Confidence" by
all "Classes of people, in the Chief Magistrate of the State," and added that
he could not "Sit a Silent Spectator" to it.[38] Despite the attempt to ingratiate
himself with Jackson, Fulton did not obtain any special consideration from
the Tennessean. Extant records indicate that Fulton served as an enlisted
man in the Eighth Regiment of the First Division of the Louisiana Militia
in the defense of New Orleans.[39]

Finally, it is known that Fulton was a member of "La Loge l'Etoile Flam-
boyant, Numéro Dix" (Blazing Star Lodge, No. 10), the Free and Accepted
Masons, which was organized in Baton Rouge in 1817, and that he served
as justice of the peace in Baton Rouge.[40] He is believed to have died in 1827
in Baton Rouge, survived by his wife Hélène and their only child, Jose-
phine.[41]

37. *Journal of the Senate During the Second Session of the First Legislature of the State
of Louisiana* (New Orleans: Peter K. Wagner, 1813), 23.

38. Colonel Samuel Fulton to Jackson, September 20, 1814, in Bassett, *Correspondence
of Andrew Jackson,* 2: 56.

39. Powell A. Casey, *Louisiana in the War of 1812* (Baton Rouge: [by the author], 1963),
"Roster of Louisiana Troops in the War of 1812," xx.

40. With T. Larguier, P. Dubayle, T. de Bellievre, and P. Gautier, Fulton represented the
Blazing Star Lodge in the acquisition of lots two and three, square thirty-two south, Beauregard Town, Baton Rouge, December 26, 1818. Parish Judges Book G, entry 256 (p. 291), East
Baton Rouge Parish, Baton Rouge, Louisiana. The endpaper at the beginning of this volume
carries Fulton's signature as one of the justices of the peace who certified that the volume was
a record of notarial acts beginning on May 18, 1818.

41. Deposition of Philip Hickey and Louis Favrot with regard to the marriage of Samuel
Fulton and Hélène Boucher de Grand-Pré, August 11, 1828, Judges Book J–N, entry 368 (p.
299), East Baton Rouge Parish, Baton Rouge, Louisiana.

CASA CALVO

Sebastián Calvo de la Puerta y O'Farrill (sometimes spelled with an "e," O'Farrell), the Marqués de Casa Calvo (1754–May 20, 1820), knight of the Order of Santiago, brigadier of the royal armies, and colonel of the regular regiment of Havana, was born in Havana, Cuba, where his family had lived since the sixteenth century. The progenitor of the family was Martín Calvo de la Puerta, who was alcalde (mayor) of Havana and chief officer (1665) of the cavalry unit there. Casa Calvo's father, also named Sebastián, was the first Marqués de Casa Calvo, but died (1790) before receiving the title. He was a doctor of civil law.[1]

Casa Calvo entered the military service of Spain on April 1, 1763, at the age of nine as a cadet in the company of nobles and rose rapidly. By the age

1. Fermin Peraza Sarausa, "Casa Calvo, Marqués de," in *Diccionario Biografico Cubano* (Havana and Coral Gables, Fla.: Annuario Bibliografico Cubano, 1958), 9: 67–9 (entries 229, 234, 235; entry 235 deals with the Louisiana connected Casa Calvo); Jacobo de la Pezuela y Lobo, "Casa Calvo," *Diccionario Geografico, Estadistico, Historico, de la Isla de Cuba,* vol. 1 (Madrid: Mellado, 1863), 344; James A. Robertson, ed. and trans., *Louisiana Under the Rule of Spain, France and the United States, 1785–1807,* vol. 2 (1910–1911; Freeport, N.Y.: Books for Libraries Press, 1969), 42–4, 169 n. 176; and Jack D. L. Holmes, ed., *Documentos Ineditos para la Historia de la Luisiana, 1792–1810* (Madrid: J. Porrúa Turanzas, 1963), 371 n. 4. There is no biography of Casa Calvo. Miriam G. Reeves, in *The Governors of Louisiana,* 4th ed. (Gretna, La.: Pelican, 1985), 35–6, essentially updates Mrs. Eugene Soniat du Fossat, *Biographical Sketches of Louisiana's Governors* (New Orleans: World's Cotton Centennial Exposition, 1885), 20. These two studies and Raymond J. Martinez, *Pierre George Rousseau, Commanding General of the Galleys of the Mississippi* (New Orleans: Hope Publications, 1964), 96–7, are disappointing. Most of the materials for a much-needed biography of Casa Calvo are in Spanish archival depositories. No likeness of the marqués has been located.

of fifteen he was captain in the volunteer cavalry. Other promotions came equally early: lieutenant colonel, 1786; colonel, July 14, 1802. By the time he attained the rank of colonel, Casa Calvo had been a brevet brigadier general for eight years.[2] Subsequently, he was made *mariscal de campo* (lieutenant general). Following establishment of his residence in Madrid (1806), Casa Calvo was Napoleon's highest ranking lieutenant general in Spain, a distinction that came to him as a result of friendship with his kinsman, the minister of war, Count Gonzalo O'Farrill.[3]

Casa Calvo was no stranger to Louisiana, having come to the colony in 1769 with Governor Alexander O'Reilly, to whom Casa Calvo was doubly related by marriage.[4] The resentment of O'Reilly by Louisianians was extended to the teenaged Captain de la Puerta, first because of his close association with the unpopular O'Reilly, but also because he watched the executions of those Louisianians convicted of treason for their roles in the rebellion against Governor Antonio de Ulloa and Spanish rule of Louisiana in 1768.[5]

During the American Revolution Casa Calvo participated in the expeditions against Mobile (1780), Pensacola (1781), and New Providence, Nassau, The Bahamas (1782).[6] Later, he served in Santo Domingo and by his conduct there gained a reputation as a heartless and cruel man. While in command of the Spanish forces at Fort Dauphin, Santo Domingo (1793), Casa Calvo reportedly did nothing to protect the unarmed French settlers there who were attacked by the revolutionary followers of Toussaint l'Ouverture. As a result, 771 of the defenseless colonists were murdered. The following year (1794) Casa Calvo served on the front line in northern Santo Domingo, where the action was heaviest before Spain ceded the eastern part of the island to France.[7]

After the death of Governor Manuel Gayoso de Lemos in July 1799, Casa Calvo returned to Louisiana as interim military governor-general of the colony (September 18, 1799–June 15, 1801) until the aging Brigadier General Salcedo could arrive from the island of Tenerife to assume the gu-

---

2. Robertson, *Louisiana,* 2: 176; and Holmes, *Documentos Ineditos,* 371 n. 4.

3. Pezuela y Lobo, *Diccionario,* 1: 344.

4. O'Reilly married an aunt of Casa Calvo, perhaps while in command of the Spanish forces that reoccupied Havana after the failure of the British and colonial American expedition in 1762. A niece of Casa Calvo married O'Reilly's son. Robertson, *Louisiana,* 2: 43.

5. Ibid.

6. Holmes, *Documentos Ineditos,* 371 n. 4.

7. Ibid., and Robertson, *Louisiana,* 2: 43.

bernatorial duties. Perspective on Casa Calvo's management of affairs during this eighteen-month period was left by Daniel Clark, who wrote Secretary of State Timothy Pickering (November 18, 1799) that the Spanish official "hates application to business, is fond of company and amusement, affects to be frank and open in his manner, but is full of the consequences derived from the possession of rank and riches." Both Casa Calvo and the auditor, Nicolás Marie Vidal, Clark said, were dependent on the Secretary Don Manuel Andrés Lopez de Armesto, "who is famous for procrastination."[8] Several years later Pierre Clément de Laussat, colonial prefect and commissioner for France in the transfer of Louisiana to the United States, wrote that Casa Calvo gained a reputation as a "violent man who hated the French" during his governorship of Louisiana.[9] Both opinions appear to be rooted, at least in part, in the circumstances surrounding the retirement of Colonel Joseph Deville Degoutin Bellechasse from active military duty. Casa Calvo reportedly forced Bellechasse into an unfavorable retirement because he allowed Daniel Clark access to files containing the secret messages that Bellechasse carried from Governor Carondelet to General Wilkinson.[10] Perhaps because of his unpopularity in Louisiana and difficulties with Salcedo, Casa Calvo left Louisiana within twenty-four hours after Salcedo arrived.

Less than two years later, the haughty Casa Calvo returned as commissioner of the king of Spain for the transfer of Louisiana to France.[11] During the nearly three years he spent in Louisiana on this duty (May 10, 1803–February 15, 1806) Casa Calvo appears to have devoted his time to two projects. The first was undermining the confidence of Louisianians in the U.S. territorial government by threat, intrigue, and rumor. The second was promotion of a plan that called for the reconquest of former Spanish colonies in the Western Hemisphere through the use of Irish Catholic troops, priests, and immigrants. His intrigue may be conveniently dated from the publication of his statement in the *Moniteur de la Louisiane* newspaper on July 12, 1804, in which he insinuated that most Louisianians were still loyal to Spain and the former colony might some day be returned to Spain.[12]

8. Arthur Preston Whitaker, *The Mississippi Question, 1795–1803: A Study in Trade, Politics, and Diplomacy* (1934; Gloucester, Mass.: Peter Smith, 1962), 159.

9. Robertson, *Louisiana*, 2: 43.

10. Stanley Faye, ed., "Louis de Clouet's Memorial to the Spanish Government, December 7, 1814 (Conditions in Louisiana and Proposed Plan for Spanish Reconquest)," *Louisiana Historical Quarterly* 22, no. 3 (July 1939), 810–1.

11. Robertson, *Louisiana*, 2: 42–3, 169–70, n.

12. An Act for the Organization of Orleans Territory and the Louisiana District, March 26, 1804, Clarence E. Carter, comp. and ed., *The Territorial Papers of the United States*, vol.

Casa Calvo's idea for the restoration of colonial rule in Spanish America was not original. It first appeared in the United States as the concluding memorial in the volume titled *Political Essays; Relative to the War of the French Revolution* (Alexandria, Va., 1801) by the Irishman James Workman. Although Workman saw the conquest of Spanish America as British expansion, Casa Calvo saw it as a scheme to meet Spain's situation as it appeared from New Orleans in 1804–05.[13] Like Workman, Casa Calvo would have employed the Irish member of Parliament, Lord Moira, Francis Rawdon-Hastings, and Major General Sir John Moore to lead Irish soldiers in the reestablishment of Spain's splintering empire in the Western Hemisphere. The credentials of each man for such a role were noteworthy.

Moira demonstrated remarkable military ability during the American Revolution, receiving the praise of Cornwallis and being one of the few English generals to bring home an untarnished reputation from the conflict. In addition, Moira raised the Volunteers of Ireland corps, which distinguished itself on the battlefields of North America. Finally, Moira was well known as an advocate of emancipation for Catholics in Great Britain.[14]

Casa Calvo knew of, if he had not met, the tall and handsome Sir John Moore from his service under Sir Ralph Abercromby in the West Indies (1795–96). The then Brigadier General Moore was placed in command of the British forces charged with restoring order on St. Lucia. His success undoubtedly captured the admiration of Casa Calvo, who had not done as well on Santo Domingo. Moore won the respect and devotion of his men by living under the same conditions they endured in the field. Of greater importance, Moore restored order and security on the island under difficulties of every description in battling the lawless blacks who swarmed the woods.

9, *The Territory of Orleans, 1803–1812* (Washington, D.C.: U.S. Government Printing Office, 1940), 202 n. 91 (hereinafter cited as TP, with volume and page range).

13. Compare Casa Calvo to Miguel Cayetano Soler, Secretario de Estado y del Despacho Universal de Hacienda de España e Indias, March 20, 1805, *Archivo General de Indias, Papeles de Cuba,* legajo 179-B, which is forty pages long, with the original by James Workman in *Political Essays; Relative to the War of the French Revolution . . .* (Alexandria, Va.: Cottom & Stewart, 1801), 145–74, which is twenty-nine pages in length (hereinafter *Archivo General de Indias* will be abbreviated AGI). There are no folio numbers in the microfilm of *legajo* 179-B, which is owned by the author. Casa Calvo's *memoria,* which is a virtual duplication of Workman's proposal, may also be seen in AGI, *Sección V, Gobierno, Audiencia de Santo Domingo Sobre la Epoca España de Luisiana,* legajo 2600, folios 882–1040, reel 151, on deposit in Special Collections, Library, Loyola University, New Orleans.

14. *Dictionary of National Biography,* s.v. "Rawdon-Hastings, Francis, 1st Marquis of Hastings and 2nd Earl of Moira (1754–1826)."

Subsequently, when Moore was transferred to Ireland (1797–99), he transformed the unruly 51st Irish Regiment into a disciplined, first-class fighting unit. He was promoted to major general in 1798. Moore died at Corunna, Spain, stemming the French conquest of the Iberian Peninsula.[15]

Continuing with Workman's idea, Casa Calvo further proposed that the Irish soldiers employed in Spanish America be enlisted from Cork, Limerick, Galway, and Londonderry. These cities were then the most Catholic areas of Ireland. Limerick was very Spanish in its customs and appearance.[16] After the reconquests the soldiers were to be given farmland and tools to encourage settlement in the restored provinces. The king of Spain was to name even the local officials. Like Workman, Casa Calvo rounded out his proposal with the suggestion that the place to begin his project was Louisiana, which, he said, could be conquered from the Floridas with twenty-five hundred Spanish regulars and four or five thousand colonial troops. After the restoration of Louisiana to the empire, the conquering expedition was to move into the West Indies to take Santo Domingo and from there into South America, particularly Peru and Chile.[17] It was a grand design, worthy of Spain in another time, but in the early nineteenth century it was a project that Spain was incapable of mounting, although Casa Calvo attempted to launch the colonization portion of the scheme before he was forced to leave Louisiana in 1806.

Both Casa Calvo's projects depended on loyalty to Spain. Therefore, he began by requiring all military officers to sign a statement declaring whether they would remain in the service of the king of Spain. Their simple yes-or-no answer determined if they would receive a military pension. Because most of the local community leaders were militiamen, they were forced either to leave Louisiana or to decline to participate in establishing the new government. Unfortunately, little is known about the number of men affected by this requirement, but there is little reason to doubt that Casa Calvo exercised great influence over an unknown number of Louisianians through his manipulation of pension payments. There also is little reason to doubt that he controlled the pension funds. Claiborne revealed his awareness of the manipulation of the Spanish pensioners to Secretary Madison on April 25, 1805.[18] The following June 16, 1805, Claiborne notified Madison that two

15. See "Moore, Sir John (1761–1809)," ibid.

16. W. E. H. Lecky, *A History of Ireland in the Eighteenth Century* (Chicago: University of Chicago Press, 1972), 98–100.

17. Casa Calvo to Soler, March 20, 1805, AGI, *Papeles de Cuba, legajo* 179-B.

18. See Letter No. 203, To James Madison, April 21, 1805.

Spanish schooners had arrived in New Orleans from Veracruz consigned to the marqués. The two vessels brought with them "a large Sum in Silver," estimated to be "One Hundred thousand Dollars, . . . or much greater." The money, Claiborne reported, was "destined for the payment of the Pensions allowed to persons residing in Louisiana, and to meet the expences" Casa Calvo would incur as commissioner of limits.[19]

Fundamental to the success of both Casa Calvo's projects was the role of the Catholic Church. Although the evidence is circumstantial, there is little reason to doubt that Casa Calvo was the "grand counselor" of the church in Louisiana at this time.[20] Difficulties within the church first appeared in the spring of 1804 when the parishioners of the Catholic Church in Attakapas County almost came to blows over which priest would be their pastor, the appointee of Laussat or the previous (Spanish) appointee. There is no indication that Casa Calvo was involved in this quarrel, which brought Claiborne the reminder from Secretary Madison that such issues were to be resolved by the church parishioners and that no agency of the U.S. government was to involve itself in the settlement other than to maintain public order.[21] However, the marqués did involve himself in the quarrel between Father Antonio Sedella, known locally as Père Antoine, and Father Patrick Walsh over who was the pastor of St. Louis Cathedral and vicar-general of the Catholic Church in Louisiana. Casa Calvo sided with the Spanish Capuchin Sedella, who was a pensioner of the Spanish king. The intensity of the quarrel in New Orleans was relieved when Fr. Walsh died from the debilitating effects of yellow fever in August 1806. By then Casa Calvo was gone from the New Orleans scene, but the quarrel had involved Bishop John Carroll of Baltimore and might have involved Napoleon if the international situation in Europe had favored intervention.[22] A parishioner in New Orleans had appealed to Napoleon to appoint Fr. Sedella bishop of the Louisiana diocese.[23]

19. To James Madison, June 16, 1805, *Official Letter Books of W. C. C. Claiborne, 1801–1816*, ed. Dunbar Rowland, vol. 3 (1917; New York: AMS Press, 1972), 96.

20. Roger Baudier, *The Catholic Church in Louisiana* (1939; New Orleans: Louisiana Library Association, 1972), 258, 255–6, 260.

21. The President to the Secretary of State, July 5, 1804; The Secretary of State to Governor Claiborne, July 10, 1804, TP, 9: 259 and 260, respectively.

22. On the involvement of Archbishop Carroll, see Peter Guilday, *The Life and Times of John Carroll, Archbishop of Baltimore, 1735–1815* (1922; Westminster, Md.: Newman Press, 1954), 705–10.

23. On the attempt to involve Napoleonic France, see Letter No. 10, To Jean Baptiste Victor Castillon, October 8, 1804, n. 2.

While these tempests agitated segments of the population in New Orleans, Casa Calvo peppered Claiborne with various diplomatic and legal complaints. Claiborne sidestepped the diplomatic questions by referring them to Secretary of State Madison and reminded the marqués that neither of them had the authority to act in such matters.[24] The legal issues that Casa Calvo pressed Claiborne to settle involved suits brought prior to the transfer of Louisiana as well as more recent litigation. These matters could be resolved quickly, the wily marqués told the young governor, if he would accept the decisions of the *audiencia* (court) in Santo Domingo and the captain-general in Havana, and restore Spanish civil law in Louisiana.[25] Claiborne responded by telling Casa Calvo that Louisiana now was part of the United States and that U.S. law was supreme in the territory.[26]

Casa Calvo's activities created problems that demanded the attention not only of Governor Claiborne, but also of the territorial council and Spanish officials in adjacent West Florida and Texas. In New Orleans the offensive conduct of the marqués's personal guards on the street outside his residence precipitated a near riot in February 1804. The presence of the Spanish guards was further called to the attention of Governor Claiborne in December of that year by George T. Ross, who subsequently was appointed sheriff by Claiborne, and by resolution of George Pollock in the territorial council denouncing the guards as an insult to the United States.[27] The strain in the relationship between Casa Calvo and Vicente Folch y Juan, commandant of West Florida, was held in check by their mutual distaste for the activities of Juan Ventura Morales, intendant for West Florida. Folch shared Casa Calvo's views of Morales. The marqués reported that Morales's scandalous personal life was a source of embarrassment. More important, Morales's intrigue and land speculation in West Florida alarmed the government of the United States, and aroused the suspicions and fears of the Spanish in West Florida. In short, Morales was a disgusting and worrisome character with whom Casa Calvo no longer even corresponded.[28]

24. See Jared W. Bradley, "W. C. C. Claiborne and Spain: Foreign Affairs under Jefferson and Madison, 1801–1811, Part I, The Early Negotiations, 1801–1806," *Louisiana History* 12, no. 4 (fall 1971), 300, 303–6; and Letter No. 57, To Casa Calvo, November 18, 1804.

25. In addition to the material cited in n. 24, see also Letter No. 102, To James Madison, January 19, 1805.

26. See Letter No. 57, To Casa Calvo, November 18, 1804.

27. See Letter No. 75, From George T. Ross, December 6, 1804, and the references given there.

28. Casa Calvo to Soler, August 22, 1805, AGI, *Audiencia de Santo Domingo, legajo* 179-B. Greater detail on these points may be found in Bradley, "Claiborne and Spain, Part I,"

Despite the problems that his guards and Morales caused Casa Calvo, the marqués's popularity among the natives of New Orleans apparently remained high because of the support he received from Fr. Sedella, Bernard Marigny, and other important figures in the community. Evidence of Marigny's support appeared some years later. When the Faubourg Marigny, immediately below New Orleans, was planned, the extension of Royal Street in the Vieux Carré was named "Casa Calvo" in honor of the marqués.[29]

Whatever his hold on the people, Casa Calvo was not entirely a free agent, and this is nowhere more apparent than in his dealings with the Spanish officials in Texas. The marqués's interference in the governance of that province was opposed by the officials there as strongly as possible. It was their opposition that prevented John Minor, brother of Stephen Minor of Natchez, from mapping the rivers and coastal areas of Texas in the summer of 1805 and forced Casa Calvo to undertake this task in the fall of that year.[30] Significantly, the funds for this project did not come from the office of the intendant, partly because Morales exercised tight control over the purse strings and partly because of straitened finances of the Spanish along the Gulf Coast of North America. Casa Calvo obtained the money for this venture from José de Iturrigaray, viceroy of Mexico. The control Casa Calvo exercised over these funds is reflected in the account of their expenditures, which was kept by Juan Tala and Ramon Viguri. Both of these men were from the accounting office of the Army of Havana. Tala brought the money for the expedition from Veracruz.[31]

Casa Calvo said the purpose of the expedition through southern and western Louisiana and east Texas was to recover his health, which had been damaged by the fevers he suffered the previous month, and, if possible, to visit the site of the early mission and presidio of San Miguel de los Adaes on the Camino Real (royal highway) near Natchitoches in search of clues to the original boundaries of Louisiana. However, it is apparent that the expedition also was intended to promote Casa Calvo's career. It certainly

301–2. On Morales's personal life, see Jack D. L. Holmes, "*Dramatis Personae* in Spanish Louisiana," *Louisiana Studies* 6, no. 2 (summer 1967), 158–9.

29. See Charles R. Maduell, Jr., "New Orleans in 1810," *New Orleans Genesis* 14, no. 56 (September 1975), 426, 427 (citing "Plan de la Ville et des Faubourgs incorporés de la Nouvelle Orleans, A. D. Bell Map, 1811").

30. See Isaac J. Cox, "The Louisiana-Texas Frontier, II," *Southwestern Historical Quarterly* 17, no. 1 (July 1913), 40, and ibid., III, 146.

31. Morales to Casa Calvo, August 8, 1805, AGI, *Papeles de Cuba, legajo* 179-B, and Robertson, *Louisiana,* 2: 176.

was conceived as a kind of capstone to his strategy to reclaim as much of Louisiana as possible for Spain. The marqués's departure from New Orleans (October 17, 1805) looked more like a triumphal procession than a working expedition. He left in the Spanish river galley *La Vigilante,* once considered the best and fastest of the Spanish war vessels on the Mississippi, accompanied by the smaller *Del Fina* and a number of keel barges and lesser escort vessels. After he was gone, rumors began to fly in the frontier river town: Casa Calvo was going to take command of three thousand Spanish troops massed on the Texas border; he had gone to buy the alliance of Indians to use against Americans in the anticipated war with Spain; and he was sowing discontent among Louisianians.[32] When he arrived in Natchitoches in January 1806, Casa Calvo and his entourage dined and rested for several days at the home of Edward Murphy, Spanish spy, courier, and unofficial emissary for Spain in Natchitoches, before continuing on their expedition.[33]

One month after Casa Calvo left New Orleans, Secretary Madison instructed Governor Claiborne to expel the marqués and all other officials in New Orleans still in the service of the king of Spain, as soon as possible and without further discussion. It was now apparent that all hope for further negotiations with Spain over the Louisiana boundaries was ended.[34]

Claiborne, on receiving Madison's instructions, sent militia captain George T. Ross, now sheriff of New Orleans, to carry out Madison's orders. Ross and Major Moses Porter, who temporarily commanded Fort Claiborne at Natchitoches, both were given authority to use force to assure compliance with the secretary of state's instructions. Because Ross and his posse of Orleans Rangers looked for Casa Calvo on the road from Natchitoches and the marqués returned to New Orleans via the Red River, the two men missed one another. In reporting to Claiborne, Ross noted that Louisianians in the western part of the territory were alarmed by Casa Calvo's statements that most of Louisiana was to be returned to Spain. For months Claiborne had attributed this rumor to Casa Calvo, who had told Claiborne in April 1805 that Spain wished to establish the Mississippi River as the western

32. Jack D. L. Holmes, "The Marques de Casa-Calvo, Nicolas de Finiels, and the 1805 Spanish Expedition through East Texas and Louisiana," *Southwestern Historical Quarterly* 79, no. 3 (January 1966), 335. On the vessels *La Vigilante* and *Del Fina,* see Abraham P. Nasatir, *Spanish War Vessels on the Mississippi, 1792–1796* (New Haven, Conn.: Yale University Press, 1968), 38 n. 35, and 242 n. 4.

33. David LaVere, "Edward Murphy: Irish Entrepreneur in Spanish Natchitoches," *Louisiana History* 32, no. 4 (fall 1991), 388–9.

34. Bradley, "Claiborne and Spain, Part I," 306–7.

boundary of Louisiana in exchange for East and West Florida.[35] The corroboration now provided by Sheriff/Captain Ross in combination with other circumstances surrounding Casa Calvo's expedition—a confrontation between a Spanish patrol and an American force west of Natchitoches in January, the length of time the expedition was taking, and the report that Casa Calvo had not visited the Los Adaes site—convinced Claiborne of the marqués's treachery. Subsequently, Claiborne learned that Casa Calvo used the expedition as a screen to gather information for the location of fifteen hundred good Catholic families on the Trinity River under the guardianship of Fr. Juan Brady, the Irish priest serving the river parishes between Natchez and New Orleans.[36]

After his return to New Orleans on the evening of February 4, 1806, Casa Calvo questioned Claiborne's instructions, trying, as he had in October 1804, to ignore the order to leave the territory.[37] However, on February 8, Claiborne notified the marqués that he had until February 15 to leave and offered to assist his departure. On February 12 the governor gave the Spanish official his passport. Three days later Casa Calvo took passage on a lime scow headed for Pensacola. With him were his sixteen-year-old son, Ignacio, the chaplain who had accompanied the expedition to Texas, three servants, and two soldiers. What ordinarily was a few days sailing time became, in the lime scow, a journey of more than five weeks. Off the West Florida coast below the Mississippi Territory, the vessel was forced inland by a storm. At Pass Christian the marqués and his party took shelter in the cabin of a black family on shore for a week, waiting for the return of favorable weather. It was not until March 24 that the humiliated and enraged marqués arrived in Pensacola.[38]

Casa Calvo remained in Pensacola for approximately two months preparing his report on the Louisiana–East Texas expedition, which cost 117,200 pesos.[39] With regard to the Louisiana boundary, the marqués shifted the line from the Sabine River, which he believed was the true boundary in early 1804, to the Mermentau River, eight leagues farther to the east. He was strongly supported in his revised opinion by the French engineer on the expedition, Nicolás de Finiels. What Casa Calvo really wanted, how-

35. See Letter No. 197, To James Madison, April 21, 1805.
36. See Bradley, "Claiborne and Spain, Part I," 313 n. 46.
37. See Letter No. 13, To Casa Calvo, October 6, 1804.
38. Holmes, "Marques de Casa-Calvo," 337–8. See also Governor Claiborne to the Secretary of State, February 19, 1806, TP, 9: 603 n. 35.
39. Report dated February 28, 1805, AGI, *Papeles de Cuba, legajo* 179-B.

ever, was the return of all of Louisiana to Spain, and he asked for command of a strong military force to take the former colony from Claiborne and the United States. In appealing for a command to put "brakes on the insupportable arrogance of these Republicans," Casa Calvo revealed that he did not comprehend the declining power of Spain or the strength of the United States government. That government, he wrote, "remains unknown [to me], for truly I have been unable to discover which system governs it."[40]

Casa Calvo reached Havana sometime after May 23, 1806. He appears to have exercised the duties of captain-general, briefly replacing Salvadore Muro y Salazar, the Marqués de Someruelos.[41] Later in the year, Casa Calvo moved to Madrid and, under the influence of Count O'Farrill, joined the French party in support of Joseph Bonaparte as king of Spain. On the collapse of French influence in Spain, Casa Calvo was forced into exile (1813) in France. Because all his possessions and title were confiscated, he lived on the remittances that two daughters, Catalina and Maria Antonia, sent him from Havana. Casa Calvo died in Paris on May 20, 1820. Both his sons followed military careers in the service of Spain. Pedro Calvo de la Puerta y Peñalver attained the title Count Buenavista and the rank of colonel before his death from pneumonia in 1837. The younger son, Ignacio, lived in Paris with his father until the latter's death. When Spain extended amnesty to those who had supported the Bonaparte regime, Ignacio returned to Cuba and rose to the rank of colonel in the national militia of Havana before his death in 1856.[42]

40. Holmes, "Marques de Casa-Calvo," 331, 335, 338.

41. See Noel M. Loomis and Abraham P. Nasatir, *Pedro Vial and the Roads to Santa Fe* (Norman: University of Oklahoma Press, 1967), xii.

42. Pezuela y Lobo, *Diccionario*, 1: 344, and Sarausa, *Diccionario Biografico Cubano*, 9: 68 (entry 238), 69 (entry 241).

JUAN VENTURA MORALES

Juan Ventura Morales probably was the most unpopular Spanish official along the Gulf Coast in the late eighteenth and early nineteenth centuries, offending both his fellow Spanish officials and Americans because of his arrogant and dictatorial attitude.

Born in Málaga, Spain, in 1756, Morales began his service with the Spanish crown as an unpaid clerk in a tobacco customs house in Málaga in 1768. He came to Louisiana in 1777 as a clerk in the government of Bernardo de Gálvez, governor and captain-general of Louisiana.[1] Both the Gálvez and Morales families were from Málaga, and it is possible Morales owed his initial appointment in Louisiana to influential connections in Málaga. Morales began his service with Gálvez in 1779 in the clandestine delivery of funds to Oliver Pollock for use in financing the American Revolution in the West.[2]

Morales attracted the attention of his superiors after the departure of Gálvez from Louisiana through introduction "of the debit-and-credit method accounting" in Spanish colonial Louisiana. Morales introduced the modern methods of accounting first in the important Division of Immigration and Indian Friendship in 1782–83, and then in his skillful administration of funds for the army in February 1784.[3] His service in the important administrative post of intendant began with a temporary appointment on July 1,

1. Jack D. L. Holmes, *"Dramatis Personae* in Spanish Louisiana," *Louisiana Studies* 6, no. 2 (summer 1967), 155.

2. John Walton Caughey, *Bernardo de Gálvez in Louisiana, 1776–1783* (1934; Gretna, La.: Pelican, 1972), 99.

3. Holmes, *"Dramatis Personae,"* 156.

1784, and continued, with interruptions, until September 7, 1812. On the latter date Morales was suspended from office and charged with arson in the destruction of treasury records at Pensacola on October 24, 1811. Two years before he was exonerated of the arson charge (June 18, 1817), Morales was appointed intendant of Puerto Rico.[4]

Morales became active in local New Orleans politics about the time he received the interim appointment as intendant in Louisiana. He was elected *alcalde* (alderman) in 1783 and stood for the same post again in 1790, but was unanimously defeated by Don Andrés Almonester y Roxas. Morales won the seat in 1791 and 1792, but declined to serve the latter term because of the demands of his work for the colonial government of Louisiana. It was in these years that Morales's strong anti-American feelings developed, apparently as a reaction to the immigration and trade policies of governors Esteban Miró and François Luis Hector de Noyelles, Baron de Carondelet, who seemed to favor Americans at the expense of Spanish Louisiana and Spain. Morales's unbridled resentment of Americans and ambitious protection of royal interests often led him to interfere in matters that should have been left to others. This interference included restricting the commercial activities of William Panton, Leslie, and Forbes, the firm that supplied the Indians with trading goods; the prohibition of street repair work in New Orleans; the alteration of Spanish immigration policy; and the suspension, on the secret orders of King Carlos IV, of the right of deposit at New Orleans guaranteed to Americans by the Treaty of San Lorenzo (Pinckney's Treaty) in 1795.[5]

Heartily disliked because of his interfering arrogance, Morales also was disliked because of his objectionable personal behavior. Sebastián Calvo de la Puerta y O'Farrill, the Marqués de Casa Calvo, reported in 1804 that Morales had been beaten and kicked by a schoolmaster for theft. In the same letter the marqués also reported that Morales was being prosecuted for complicity in the poisoning of the husband of his alleged partner in adultery. At the time, Morales was married to the widow Marie Cataline Guesnon. Vicente Folch y Juan, commandant of West Florida, so objected to Morales that he refused to allow the intendant to establish his office in Pensacola until overruled by the secretary of the treasury for the Indies, Miguel

4. Arthur P. Whitaker, ed. and trans., *Documents Relating to the Commercial Policy of Spain in the Floridas, with Incidental Reference to Louisiana* (Deland, Fla.: Florida Historical Society, 1931), 244 n. 187.

5. Holmes, "*Dramatis Personae,*" 156; and Alexander DeConde, *This Affair of Louisiana* (New York: Charles Scribner's Sons, 1976), 120.

Cayetano Soler, and the captain-general, Salvadore Muro y Salazar, the Marqués de Someruelos.[6] Both Casa Calvo and Folch accused Morales of speculating in West Florida lands at the expense of the Spanish crown. This last accusation also was made by Governor Claiborne, who added in his reports to Secretary Madison that Morales promoted the land deals because they would hamper U.S. claims to the disputed territory.[7] Ultimately, Casa Calvo refused even to correspond with Morales. Folch prohibited any new surveys of land without his permission and refused to allow anyone to take possession of lands that had been sold since May 18, 1803, in the territory claimed by the United States and Spain.[8] Two years passed before Morales acquiesced to the agreements made by Folch.[9]

The insistence of Folch that Morales establish his intendancy in Mobile rather than Pensacola, the provincial capital of West Florida, was used by Morales to continue his residence in New Orleans. From his location in New Orleans, Morales continuously fomented opposition to Governor Claiborne and U.S. possession of Louisiana. Among his irritating and disrespectful actions toward Claiborne was the public statement that the U.S. governor had no authority to force the Spanish officials to leave Louisiana. Folch characterized this aspect of Morales's conduct as "indecorous."[10] Ultimately, Claiborne ordered Morales and his suite of support staff out of New Orleans.[11] Immediately on receipt of the order, Morales questioned Claiborne's authority for issuing it but requested authorization for establishment in New Orleans of an accredited agent of the Spanish government.[12] Sixteen days after receiving Morales's request a group of merchants in New Orleans petitioned Claiborne to allow location of an agent of the Spanish government in New Orleans for the "purpose of settling the remaining accounts of the Spanish Treasury" owed to businessmen of the ter-

6. Holmes, "*Dramatis Personae*," 157–8.

7. Jared W. Bradley, "W. C. C. Claiborne and Spain: Foreign Affairs under Jefferson and Madison, 1801–1811, Part I, The Early Negotiations, 1801–1806," *Louisiana History* 12, no. 4 (fall 1971), 300 and 301 n. 13.

8. Casa Calvo to Claiborne, August 8, 1805, *Archivo General de Indias, Papeles de Cuba, legajo* 1600, folio 345 (hereinafter *Archivo General de Indias* will be cited as AGI).

9. Morales to Casa Calvo, August 19, 1805, ibid., *legajo* 1600, folios 364–5.

10. Folch to Marqués de Someruelos, September 4, 1805, AGI, *Papeles de Cuba, legajo* 179-B. This microfilm is owned by the author. It contains no folio numbers.

11. [To Morales,] January 11, 1806, in *Official Letter Books of W. C. C. Claiborne, 1801–1816*, ed. Dunbar Rowland, vol. 3 (1917; New York: AMS Press, 1972), 238–9 (hereinafter cited as CLB, with volume and page numbers).

12. [To] Sir, January 12, 1806, ibid., 240.

ritory.[13] The thirty-one signatories of the petition included a cross section of Claiborne's friends and opponents, among them Eugene Dorsière, James Pitot, Evan Jones, and Paul Lanusse. After further questioning, Claiborne learned from Morales that the Spanish government owed between three and four hundred thousand dollars to various businessmen of the Orleans Territory. Claiborne also learned that a voucher for the amounts owed the Orleans Territory businesses had been transmitted to the viceroy of Mexico, who was to forward the amount due in cash for distribution. Morales stated if there was no Spanish agent to receive the money when it arrived, the only way the merchants could be paid was to travel to Pensacola, where his office was to be relocated. Under the circumstances, Claiborne arranged to issue a blank passport into which Morales was permitted to enter the name of the person he would authorize to receive and pay the businessmen in the Orleans Territory.[14]

The additional delays made it apparent that Morales would not, or could not, leave without further delay, whereupon Claiborne issued blanket passports for the departure of the intendant and his suite on the next departing ship from New Orleans.[15] When Claiborne issued the passports, four Spanish ships stood off the mouth of Bayou St. John to take on board Morales, his family of five, and fourteen slaves. In addition, Morales identified six of his office staff who were to accompany him to Pensacola and three men who were to accompany Gilberto Leonard to Baton Rouge. Leonard was Morales's accountant, or bookkeeper.[16] Despite Claiborne's pushing, the worrisome and obnoxious Morales did not leave New Orleans for Pensacola until February 1, 1806.[17]

13. Petition to Governor Claiborne by Merchants and Inhabitants of New Orleans, January [28,] 1806, in Clarence E. Carter, comp. and ed., *The Territorial Papers of the United States,* vol. 9, *The Territory of Orleans, 1803–1812* (Washington, D.C.: U.S. Government Printing Office, 1940) 578–9 (hereinafter cited as TP, with volume and page range).

14. To James Madison, January 28, 1806, CLB, 3: 251–2.

15. [To] Sir [Morales], January 27, 1806, ibid., 251. Copies of the passports for Morales and Don Gilberto Leonard, both dated January 27, 1806, precede Claiborne's letter to Morales. The two documents bear the heading By William C. C. Claiborne, Governor of the Territory of Orleans [internally dated], January 27, 1806, ibid., 250.

16. Morales's office appears to have been composed of ten persons. In addition, there were at least eight dependents and fourteen slaves to be moved from New Orleans to Pensacola and Baton Rouge. Juan Ventura Morales to Governor Claiborne, January 26, 1806, TP, 9: 577.

17. Morales advised his superior of the forced departure from New Orleans and arrival in Pensacola on the last day of February 1806. Morales to Miguel Cayetano Soler, February 28, 1806, AGI, *Sección V, Govierno. Audiencia de Santo Domingo, Sobre la Época Española de Luisiana, legajo* 2608, folio 140, reel 157, Special Collections, Library, Loyola University, New Orleans.

VICENTE FOLCH Y JUAN

The prickly Don Vicente Folch y Juan (March 8, 1754–November 8, 1829) was described by Governor William C. C. Claiborne as having "more temper than discretion, more genius than Judgment," and as being "far from conciliatory" in his conduct toward the United States.[1] Manuel Gayoso de Lemos, Folch's superior both as governor of Natchez and later as governor-general of Louisiana and West Florida, said that "Folch's arrogance, independence, and arbitrary actions were qualities not found in anyone who possesses the true spirit of order and military subordination."[2] Both characterizations are apt, but leave an incomplete picture of this proud, determined Spaniard from Catalonia.

Most information about Folch centers on his military career, particularly on the American frontier. However, despite his arrogance, Folch also was a man of social grace, charm, and ability. For example, the French Prefect Pierre Clément de Laussat described Folch as performing some "spirited dances" in New Orleans on the evening of November 30, 1803, following the transfer of Louisiana from Spain to France.[3] Little more than three years

---

1. Letter No. 178, To James Madison, March 30, 1805. Isaac J. Cox quotes from the copy of this letter in the Department of State files in *The West Florida Controversy, 1798–1813: A Study in American Diplomacy* (1918; Gloucester, Mass.: Peter Smith, 1967), 150. David Hart White provides the dates of Folch's birth and death in *Vicente Folch, Governor in Spanish Florida, 1787–1811* (Washington, D.C.: University Press of America, Inc., 1981), introduction [2].

2. White, *Vicente Folch*, 105.

3. Pierre Clément de Laussat, *Memoirs of My Life to My Son During the Years 1803 and After . . .* , trans. Sister Agnes-Josephine Pastwa, ed. Robert D. Bush (Baton Rouge: Louisiana State University Press, 1978), 81.

later, both General Wilkinson and Governor Claiborne turned to Folch for
assistance in defeating the Memorial to Congress that could have done irreparable harm to their careers.[4] In Wilkinson's words, he and Claiborne
knew that the men in "control [of] the legislative council" were "all friends"
of Folch.[5]

The deceit Folch practiced in defense of General James Wilkinson's espionage for Spain raises questions about information on Folch's life. An early
biographical sketch said that he served under Gálvez in the captures of Mobile and Pensacola.[6] The slender biography of Folch that appeared in recent
years accepted the earlier source as the basis for making the same statement.[7] Neither the published nor unpublished records of Folch's military
career document any service in North America before 1783.[8] Most important, Folch declared in February 1807 that he had "resided in these provinces of Louisiana and W. Florida, with little or no interruption, since the
14th of July, 1783 (when I came to New Orleans, at the pressing invitation
of my beloved uncle Don Estevan Miro)."[9] Although Folch concealed the
truth about Wilkinson's espionage for Spain, there was little for Folch to
gain from dissembling about the date of his own arrival in Louisiana.[10] Un-

4. The memorial was not passed, but was privately published as *Debate in the House of
Representatives of the Territory of Orleans on a Memorial to Congress, Respecting the Illegal
Conduct of General Wilkinson* (New Orleans: Bradford & Anderson, 1807), 15 (hereinafter
cited as Memorial to Congress).

5. [Arthur P. Whitaker, ed. and trans.,] "Documents. 5. An Interview of Governor Folch
with General Wilkinson, 1807," Folch to Someruelos, June 25, 1807, *American Historical Review* 10, no. 4 (July 1905), 839.

6. Jacobo de la Pezuela y Lobo, *Diccionario Geografico, Estadistico, Historico, de la Isla
de Cuba*, vol. 2 (Madrid: Mellado, 1863–66), 374.

7. White, *Vicente Folch*, introduction [3] cites Pezuela's sketch as the source for Folch's
military service.

8. Folch's unpublished military service record in the *Archivo General de Simancas. Sección de Guerra Moderna. Hojas de Servicias Militares de América, 1787–1799, legajo 7291,
cuaderno 1*, folio 33 reflects no such service, nor does Jack D. L. Holmes in *Honor and Fidelity:
The Louisiana Infantry Regiment and the Louisiana Militia Companies, 1766–1821* (Birmingham, Ala.: [Jack D. L. Holmes], 1965), 119–20, entry 120, nor Abraham Nasatir in *Spanish War Vessels on the Mississippi, 1792–1796* (New Haven: Yale University Press, 1968), 116
n. 59.

9. Folch to General James Wilkinson, Baton Rouge, February 10, 1807, in Daniel Clark,
Proofs of the Corruption of Gen. James Wilkinson (1809; New York: Arno Press, 1971), notes
p. 14.

10. The military service record of Folch in the *Archivo General de Simancas* reflects
Folch's service through his years with the Light Infantry of Catalonia and his promotion to
captain in the Louisiana Infantry Regiment (Regimento de Infantería de Luisiana) in November

less proof to the contrary is located, it seems unlikely that Folch saw service with Gálvez in the captures of Mobile and Pensacola.

Folch entered North America as most Spanish officials and settlers did, from Cuba, to which he had been ordered in 1780.[11] Born in Reus, in the province of Tarragona, near Barcelona, Spain, Folch began military service on April 23, 1771. Perhaps because of his youth—he was six weeks beyond his seventeenth birthday—and because he had studied mathematics in the Royal Military Academy in Barcelona, Folch was appointed a sublieutenant in the light infantry of Catalonia and assigned to practice as an engineer.[12] Prior to his assignment to Cuba, Folch participated in the siege of Melilla on the coast of North Africa in present-day Morocco, from December 28, 1774 to February 26, 1775. He also participated in the attack on Algiers on July 8, 1775, and, until he was ordered to Cuba, served in the campaign to blockade Gibraltar.[13] Whether Folch's service with the Cuban Infantry came at this time, or at the end of his military career, is not known, but it is known that one of his duties after arriving in Cuba was caring for hospitalized Spanish soldiers stationed in the West Indies.[14]

The half dozen documented occasions of Folch being on sick leave, sometimes for weeks or months, during his military service suggest that he may have been a patient on his arrival in Cuba. The first instance of Folch's sick leave was in 1791.[15] Less than two years later, from February through May 1793, he took approximately four months of sick leave. Folch took sick leave again in early 1794. In 1799 he apparently had to take sick leave twice, once in May and again in October. Folch temporarily relinquished his command responsibilities during these two illnesses to the engineering officer at

---

1786. Holmes, *Honor and Fidelity,* 119–20, entry 120, includes Folch's service record after leaving Louisiana and the Floridas. The length of Folch's service with the Light Infantry Regiment of Catalonia was 12 years, 9 months, and 7 days, suggesting that his transfer to the Louisiana Infantry occurred sometime in 1783. Holmes also lists 2 years, 4 months, and 8 days service with the Cuban Infantry, but gives no dates for this service.

11. *Archivo General de Simancas* says that Folch served in the blockade of Gibraltar until March 7, 1780, when he was ordered to Cuba.

12. White, *Vicente Folch,* introduction [2]. See also Nasatir, *Spanish War Vessels,* 116 n. 59.

13. *Archivo General de Simancas.* Holmes, *Honor and Fidelity,* 119, does not specify the date, only the month of March.

14. Holmes, *Honor and Fidelity,* 119, lists the service with the Cuban Infantry. White, *Vicente Folch,* introduction [3], tells of the hospital duty.

15. David H. White, "A View of Spanish West Florida: Selected Letters of Governor Juan Vicente Folch [*sic*]," *Florida Historical Quarterly* 56, no. 2 (October 1977), 139.

Pensacola, Francisco de Paula Gelabert.[16] Folch was so ill in the summer and fall of 1806 that he temporarily was relieved of his command in Pensacola by Lieutenant Colonel Carlos Howard.[17] Two years later, early in 1808, Folch was so ill that he ordered his son-in-law, Francisco Maximiliano St. Maxent, from Mobile to Pensacola to take temporary command of West Florida. On this occasion, Folch left Pensacola and went to New Orleans, taking with him the doctor of the Louisiana Regiment. Folch remained in New Orleans for several months, as he had in 1806.[18] Folch's illnesses may have been bouts with malaria, a disease endemic to the subtropical climate of the northern coast of the Gulf of Mexico. They also may have been mild cases of yellow fever, which also afflicted virtually all settlers along the shores of the Gulf of Mexico in the late eighteenth and nineteenth centuries. What is different is that Folch was granted extended convalescent leave, something that few Spanish soldiers received, or could afford. The extended stays in New Orleans in 1806 and 1808 also may have been lengthened so that Folch could watch unfolding political developments in Louisiana and the United States that could impact Spanish interests in the Floridas and Mexico.

Folch's assignment to Cuba heralded change in his life. Prior to the duty in Cuba, Folch's career was moribund. He had been a sublieutenant for more than twelve years and appeared to be going nowhere.[19] Real change began soon after transfer into the Louisiana Militia and owed much to his uncle, Estéban Miró, ranking colonel under Bernardo de Gálvez, the governor-general of Louisiana.[20] Miró succeeded Gálvez as governor in 1782 and remained in office until early in 1792.[21] On February 1, 1784, Folch was promoted to lieutenant.[22] In the same year, he married Maria de la Merced Bernardina Rodriguez Junco, daughter of Pedro Rodriguez Junco, a success-

---

16. White, *Vicente Folch,* 18, 19, 48, 71.

17. Cox, *West Florida Controversy,* 185, 187, 192, 195.

18. White, *Vicente Folch,* 90.

19. *Archivo General de Simancas,* and Holmes, *Honor and Fidelity,* 119.

20. Nasatir, *Spanish War Vessels,* 116 n. 59, points out the importance of Miró to Folch's career.

21. Caroline M. Burson says that Carondelet was named to succeed Miró on March 18, 1792, but the actual transfer of duties took place nine days later, March 27 (*The Stewardship of Don Esteban Miró, 1782–1792* [New Orleans: American Printing, 1940], 283). Total transfer of all duties was completed on December 30, 1792. Miró and his wife, the former Celeste Macarty of Louisiana, sailed for Havana and the Spanish court the following February. Ibid., 284.

22. *Archivo General de Simancas.*

ful merchant in Havana.[23] Twenty-one months later, on November 22, 1786, Folch was promoted to captain.[24] Approximately seven months after that, Folch sailed from Balize, near the mouth of the Mississippi River, to assume command of Mobile from Pierre Favrot as commandant on June 19, 1787.[25] Folch's next assignment (1793) was as commander of the naval expedition sent to chart the land and streams around present-day Tampa/St. Petersburg, Florida. This was followed by another nautical assignment, as commander (1794–95) of the Spanish war vessels on the Mississippi. Perhaps the most disliked duty Folch performed was as commandant of Fort San Fernando de las Barrancas de Margó (July 1795–September 1796). This duty, at the Chickasaw Bluffs overlooking the Mississippi River, was the site of present-day Memphis, Tennessee. However, it was Folch's five years as commandant of Mobile that determined the future direction of his career. This assignment led to his later commands in Spanish West Florida. His service as commandant of Pensacola from September 30, 1795, through March 30, 1804, and as governor of the province of West Florida, March 31, 1804, to May 11, 1811, assured that his name would be forever linked with the history of the Floridas.

In the assignment at Mobile, Folch was a key player for the Spanish in their control of the Indians in southeastern North America. His success is revealed in the relative peace enjoyed by the settlers around Mobile in Spanish West Florida. By comparison, the American settlers in Georgia and Tennessee were repeatedly subject to Indian attacks. Folch accomplished this feat in the 1780s and early 1790s with limited resources of manpower, money, and supplies.[26] The task was one that Folch repeatedly performed under increasingly difficult circumstances for the nearly quarter century of his life along the Gulf Coast of North America.

Although Folch's tour of duty at Mobile was an overall success, there were two unfortunate areas of conflict. On the professional level, Folch's

23. White, *Vicente Folch,* introduction [3].

24. The dates of Folch's promotions through the rank of captain may be found in *Archivo General de Simancas*. Holmes, *Honor and Fidelity,* 119, lists the dates of all of Folch's promotions.

25. Burson, *Stewardship of Don Esteban Miró,* 46, reports the date that Folch relieved Pierre Favrot. White, *Vicente Folch,* introduction [3], gives only the month Folch assumed command from Favrot.

26. White, *Vicente Folch,* 5, 13, 15 and the sources cited therein provide perspective on Folch's supply, money, and troop needs while in Mobile. White, "View of Spanish West Florida," 139 ff., provides perspective on the continual need for able-bodied and well-trained soldiers in the later assignment at Pensacola.

exchanges with Alexander McGillivray, the half-breed leader of the warlike Creek Indians, became so acrimonious that Miró instructed Folch to "never again write" McGillivray. Instead, Folch was to advise Miró and allow him to "do whatever seems best." The delay entailed in such a cumbersome procedure, Miró said, would "never be so harmful as that which McGillivray found so offensive . . . which could have the worst consequences." Near the end of this letter, in an almost fatherly tone, Miró told Folch that the order had been issued so that Folch would "not be the principal cause" of "some real controversy."[27]

The other area in which Folch suffered embarrassment while at Mobile was much more personal and painful. Knowledge of the incident is an aid to understanding much of Folch's later conduct, particularly after he assumed command at the isolated Barrancas de Margó post on the Mississippi River. In a long and difficult letter to Miró, his uncle and commanding officer, early in July 1788, Folch poured onto paper the story of how his wife had been forced into an affair during his absences from Mobile. The other man was a sublieutenant whom Folch had welcomed to Mobile as a brother when the young officer reported for duty and revealed that he had known members of Folch's family in Madrid. Perhaps because of his suspicious nature, Folch had difficulty in believing that his wife had not been seduced. Yet he declined to pursue the matter openly, he said, out of consideration for his sons and his honor. Folch did hold his wife under arrest until he felt assured there was no compliance on her part.[28] Although the affair was to prey on his mind long afterwards, Folch and his wife remained together until his death in 1829. Nonetheless, the experience, along with his awareness of Spain's decline as a world power, seemed to add to his gloomy and cynical outlook on life.

Just as Folch's years of command in Mobile foreshadowed a career in Spanish West Florida, these years also contributed to his negative opinions of Americans and the United States. Although he understood the language and political views of the nearby restless American settlers whom he was to prevent from encroaching on Spanish territory, Folch looked on them with dislike and foreboding. To him, they were a "rude and indolent" people, who would respond only to the power and might of the government of

27. John W. Caughey, *McGillivray of the Creeks* (1938; Norman: University of Oklahoma Press, 1959), 241, document 127. See also pp. 38–9 and document 80, p. 168, where McGillivray specifically objected to Folch's blaming him for inciting attacks on the settlers in the Mobile area. McGillivray blamed the unruly and warlike Alibamon Indians for the attacks.

28. White, *Vicente Folch*, 5–7.

Spain.[29] Folch's attitude derived in part from his experiences with disreputable Americans while in command at Mobile. Folch described some of them as "the scum of Georgia and the Carolinas."[30] One such American was the outlaw Charles Lucas, whom Folch captured and shipped to New Orleans under heavy guard with the warning that the man should be imprisoned in Havana or Mexico, where it would be very difficult to escape. Another outlaw identified in Folch's correspondence was a man named Lawrence—Folch called him "Larans"—who had left Georgia with a price on his head to settle among the Creek Indians. Even the two English-speaking men sent by Folch to capture Lawrence proved to be men without honor. According to McGillivray, they shot Lawrence as he stood by the side of Mrs. Charles Weatherford, McGillivray's sister and mother of Billy Weatherford, half-breed leader of a militant faction in the Creek War of 1813–14.[31]

Folch's dislike and distrust of Americans later figured prominently in his failure to maintain control over West Florida. Perhaps the greatest factor in shaping Folch's poor opinion of Americans was his first-hand knowledge of westerners, mostly Kentuckians, who were supposed to sever the trans-Appalachian territories from the union of states along the Atlantic seaboard and help Spain preserve its control over the heartland of North America. The best known of these traitors was General James Wilkinson, who had been a paid espionage agent of the Spanish since at least the late summer of 1789.[32] Although Wilkinson had been their tool for years, the Spanish never completely trusted him. Ultimately they came to believe that Wilkinson planned to lead an army from Fort Washington (Cincinnati) through Upper Louisiana to Texas, either to set up an empire of his own, or to acquire it for the British or the United States.[33] Indeed, much of Folch's attitude toward

29. Quoted from "Reflections on Louisiana," attributed to Vicente Folch by James A. Robertson, ed. and trans., *Louisiana Under the Rule of Spain, France, and the United States, 1785–1807*, vol. 2 (1910–1911; Freeport, N.Y.: Books for Libraries Press, 1969), 326.

30. White, *Vicente Folch*, 10.

31. Ibid., 9.

32. Arthur P. Whitaker, *The Spanish American Frontier, 1783–1795: The Westward Movement and the Spanish Retreat in the Mississippi Valley* (Boston: Houghton Mifflin, 1927), 117. See also James R. Jacobs, *Tarnished Warrior: Major-General James Wilkinson* (New York: Macmillan, 1938), 97.

33. Catherine Van Cortlandt Mathews, *Andrew Ellicott, His Life and Letters* (New York: Grafton Press, 1908), 160–3; Deposition of Samuel P. Moore, March 6, 1810, in James Wilkinson, *Memoirs of My Own Times*, vol. 2 (1816; New York: AMS Press, 1973), Appendix III; and Thomas P. Abernethy, *The South in the New Nation, 1789–1819* (Baton Rouge: Louisiana State University Press, 1961), 207, 269.

Americans appears to have been learned from his uncle, Miró, who was art-
fully led by Wilkinson to believe the United States would not survive because of the separatist attitudes along the American frontier, particularly in
Kentucky and Ohio.[34]

Miró's departure from Louisiana in 1792 brought a change in Folch's
duty assignments. Thereafter, they were not as good as the assignment at
Mobile until he was appointed commandant of Pensacola in 1796. Folch's
first assignment after Miró's departure came in August 1793 when he was
placed in charge of a naval expedition to explore and map the central west
coast of East Florida, the area known today as Tampa Bay–St. Petersburg.
The ultimate objective of the exploration and mapping expedition was to
establish a Spanish settlement at Tampa Bay. The duty was strenuous. Often
Folch was in mud up to his waist and water up to his neck, holding his
papers and instruments above his head. The soldiers in his command were
terrified of the Seminole Indians, who were noted for their hostility to Euro-
peans. Because he faced the constant threat of desertion on this remote duty
assignment, Folch reported that he kept a pistol on his subordinates in the
daylight hours and slept on the oars and rudder of the launch used to recon-
noiter the area as his headboard at night. Later, Folch proudly reported that
he had completed the difficult task in nine weeks.[35] This duty was followed
by several months' leave of absence in early 1794, presumably spent in Havana.[36]

Folch did not return to Spain at this time, as he had planned, because
the new governor-general of Louisiana, Don Francisco Luis Hector, Baron
de Carondelet de Noyelles, gave him a command in the fleet of river galleys
stationed at Balize, near the mouth of the Mississippi River.[37] Although the
galleys were not considered suitable for sailing on the open seas, Folch did
use them to guard the Spanish colonies from Louisiana eastward to Pensacola against French and English marauders. On two occasions he used the
galleys on extended patrols to Havana, perhaps to check on his wife and
children there.[38] Ambitious and hoping for a better-paying assignment, one
that would take him away from North America, Folch petitioned the Spanish court for a governorship in Yucatan on the southern shore of the Gulf

34. Abernethy, *South in the New Nation*, 48, 52, 54–60. See also Jacobs, *Tarnished Warrior*, 80–1, 88–94.

35. White, *Vicente Folch*, 19.

36. Ibid.

37. Nasatir, *Spanish War Vessels*, 116 n. 59; and White, *Vicente Folch*, 19.

38. Nasatir, *Spanish War Vessels*, 116 n. 59.

of Mexico. Instead, he was appointed commandant of the fort to be built at San Fernando de las Barrancas de Margó, the Chickasaw Bluffs.[39] The Spanish had taken possession of this site on May 30, 1795, after negotiations with the Chickasaw Indians.[40] The fort was intended as a bastion against the restless advance of American settlers and as a counterweight to the American Fort Massac constructed upriver at the confluence of the Ohio and Mississippi Rivers.[41] Folch's appointment was effective July 28, 1795, but he did not assume command at Barrancas de Margó from Elias Beauregard until September 17, 1795.[42]

The Fort San Fernando assignment also was a stressful one for Folch. Within days of his arrival, Folch's irascible temperament placed him at odds not only with his superior, Manuel Gayoso de Lemos, governor at Natchez, but also with all of his colleagues at Barrancas except one, the Frenchman Pedro Andrés Rousseau.[43] Rousseau, a native of Rochelle, France, who ultimately served the king of Spain for twenty-four years, liked Folch so well that he said he thought he could spend a lifetime with him without a single difficulty.[44] Gayoso, however, believed that Folch was extravagant and his whims unlimited. Folch wanted to reform all the workers at the post, lamented the chronic shortage of money, wanted chickens and young pigeons for his table, and craved comfortable lodgings.[45]

Two colleagues with whom Folch quarreled were Tomás Portell and Benjamin Fooy. Portell was commander at New Madrid, about forty or fifty leagues above Barrancas de Margó on the west bank of the Mississippi.[46] It

39. White, *Vicente Folch*, 20.

40. Nasatir, *Spanish War Vessels*, 253–4, 259–60.

41. Ibid., 105 n. 31, succinctly describes the Spanish reasons for establishment of the fort at Barrancas de Margó.

42. Ibid., 116 n. 59, and 279 n. 84 (the date Beauregard left Barrancas).

43. Ibid., 116 n. 59, points out the problems that Folch had in getting along with others. See also White, *Vicente Folch*, introduction [3], 21, 27. In the "Notes" section of Folch's military evaluation sheet printed in Holmes, *Honor and Fidelity*, 120, his conduct is characterized as "average."

44. Nasatir, *Spanish War Vessels*, 116 n. 59. White, *Vicente Folch*, 61, states that Rousseau was a native of Rochelle, France. Initially, Rousseau reported the men were happier under Folch than when Beauregard was commander.

45. Nasatir, *Spanish War Vessels*, 116 n. 59. White, *Vicente Folch*, 22, says that when Folch assumed command at Fort San Fernando there were no quarters for the officers, no kitchen, and no sentry houses.

46. Portell also was a native of Catalonia who had been sent with the expedition to Havana in 1780. Nasatir, *Spanish War Vessels*, 56 n. 65. See ibid., 105 n. 31, for the distance between New Madrid and Ft. San Fernando.

was through New Madrid that Folch received his commissary provisions and materials for constructing Fort San Fernando. The provisions frequently did not arrive on schedule and just as often were in poor condition. Folch accused Portell of diverting supplies intended for San Fernando to New Madrid, and once told Portell that if he received any more rotten provisions he would throw them in the river.[47] On at least one occasion, Fort San Fernando was left with only one day's supply of rations.[48] Fortunately, Folch was able to open a highly successful galley trade on the Mississippi River with American settlers, particularly those along the Cumberland River in Kentucky.[49]

Fooy, a native of Holland who had lived many years among the Choctaw Indians before settling in Natchez in 1788, was an experienced Indian trader and interpreter. His services were valuable to Gayoso in acquiring rights from the Chickasaw Indians to build Fort San Fernando.[50] Yet Folch found fault with him. However, he was not the only one to quarrel with Fooy, and he did fare better than his fellow officer, Don Manuel García y Muñiz, whom Fooy caused to be arrested.[51]

One of the more practicable objectives sought by Folch while commandant at Fort San Fernando was establishment of a permanent courier system of mail delivery, a subject that would claim his attention again when he was commander at Pensacola. What Folch wanted was a system so effective that dispatches from New Orleans could reach the most distant posts in Louisiana in twenty days.[52] Gayoso had made a similar proposal in late September 1794 to Governor-General Carondelet, but got no support for it, and there is no evidence Folch's proposal was acted on either.[53]

Underlying much of the friction between Folch and Gayoso was Folch's belief that Gayoso had not defined the duties of each officer under him. In certain areas, Gayoso had given Folch detailed instructions at the outset of his command, but in others Folch was left to proceed on his own without

47. White, *Vicente Folch,* 22–3.
48. Ibid., 23.
49. Ibid.
50. Nasatir, *Spanish War Vessels,* 254 n. 36.
51. Ibid., 126 n. 15, tells of the quarrel between García and Fooy. Ibid., 254 n. 36, tells of García's arrest. All these difficulties illustrate the tension and stress felt by the Spanish officials all along the Mississippi River frontier. The tension was relieved, but not abated, by the Treaty of San Lorenzo el Real, Pinckney's Treaty, 1795. See ibid., 13.
52. White, *Vicente Folch,* 27–8.
53. Jack D. L. Holmes, *Gayoso: The Life of a Spanish Governor in the Mississippi Valley, 1789–1799* (Baton Rouge: Louisiana State University Press, 1965), 48.

any guidance during the long intervals in which he heard nothing from Gayoso. Folch hesitated to take too much initiative for fear that he, like Elias Beauregard before him, might be dismissed for exceeding orders. As a consequence, the disagreements between Folch and Gayoso seemed to whirl out of control at times, spiraling up the chain of command to Carondelet as they quarreled about military duties, financial needs, and political issues.[54]

The origins of the friction between Folch and Gayoso, of course, were deeper than simply definitions of military duties. They essentially lay in the different personalities and experiences of the two men. Folch was proud in his inflexibility and always conscious of his own prestige.[55] Gayoso, by contrast, was more versatile, flexible, and moderate. He seemed to relish his life among Americans on the borderlands. Educated in England in his youth, Gayoso "retained in considerable degree the manners and customs of the English."[56] In addition, he was naturally gregarious, equally at home among the rough men on the frontier or in more courtly circles elsewhere. All these facets of Gayoso's personality and education made it easier for him to win the support and admiration of men on the frontier, particularly in the more polished society centered in Natchez. Similarly, these qualities made it easier for the inflexible Folch to find fault with Gayoso. Because Gayoso became governor-general of Louisiana after his assignment at Natchez, the difficult and unequal relationship for Folch ended only when Gayoso died suddenly on July 18, 1799.[57]

One other source of concern for Folch at this time may have been Carondelet's handling of the charge of favoritism made against Miró, who was governor and intendant when Folch was appointed commandant of Mobile. Miró approved a payment of three hundred pesos by the crown for a house for Folch and the land on which it stood within Fort Charlotte, as well as the purchase of land thirty leagues from Mobile in the name of the crown.

54. Ibid., 48, 52, 218.

55. White, *Vicente Folch,* introduction [3], says that in "many ways [Folch was] a typical Spanish officer."

56. Andrew Ellicott, *The Journal of Andrew Ellicott, Late Commissioner on Behalf of the United States . . . for Determining the Boundary Between the United States and the Possession of His Catholic Majesty* (1803; Chicago: Quadrangle Books, 1962), 215.

57. Holmes, *Gayoso,* 266, reports that the governor died from the effects of yellow fever. Gayoso may have died as a result of carrying too far the "convivialities" of the table, which he enjoyed with General James Wilkinson, particularly on the occasion of the general's last visit, as suggested by Charles Gayarré, *History of Louisiana: The Spanish Domination,* 4th ed., vol. 3 (1903; Gretna, La.: Pelican, 1965), 405.

Seven years after Miró's return to Spain and his death, the inquiry into these and other matters had not been resolved.[58]

The greatest problem for Folch may have been the time he had to brood about his frustrations. The work in building Fort San Fernando was slow and frequently delayed by a lack of materials, money, or both, which left Folch time to contemplate his own and Spain's predicament: the exposed position of Fort San Fernando on the frontier of the restless Americans; the lack of gifts with which to placate the wavering Indian allies; and the unsettled state of his marriage. In addition, as an ambitious officer, Folch's outlook on life was not improved by the oppressive heat and swarms of mosquitoes that hung over the Fort San Fernando site. Not even his promotion to lieutenant colonel on September 4, 1795, seemed to cheer Folch.[59]

It was during these months in 1795 that an ugly rumor was spread among the Spanish in the Mississippi Valley that Gayoso was keeping a mistress at New Madrid. A house supposedly was being built there for her by the masons who should have been working under Folch on Fort San Fernando.[60] Folch is believed to be the person who provided the gossipy intendant, Juan Ventura Morales, with the story, which eventually made its way to Carondelet.[61] This indiscretion may have been a reflection of Folch's concern about his own marriage as much as it was a lashing out in anger and frustration at Gayoso. It also is possible that Folch's remarks were foolishly and lightly offered in a weak effort to establish friendship. Whatever the intent, Folch lived to regret them. No official record of repercussions has been found, but, ultimately, Morales became Folch's bête noire. In December 1795, Folch's isolation seemed to close in on him when a visitor to Fort San Fernando brought news of the death of Miró. Folch's response to the message clearly reflects his morose and forlorn state of mind when he wrote Carondelet, saying, "I have lost the best of friends and I do not know where to turn."[62]

Folch's prospects did not improve with the passage of time. In the same month of December, Gayoso advised Folch he had received secret information the Americans planned to send an expedition against Fort San Fer-

58. Burson, *Stewardship of Don Esteban Miró,* 288, 294–5.

59. Holmes, *Honor and Fidelity,* 119.

60. One of Gayoso's instructions to Folch before he went to Fort San Fernando was to build as many buildings of brick as possible. Most of the fort was constructed of timber. White, *Vicente Folch,* 21.

61. Holmes, *Gayoso,* 123.

62. White, *Vicente Folch,* 23.

nando because they believed it was a usurpation of American territory.[63] Americans knew about the Treaty of San Lorenzo as early as the fall of 1795, but Folch and most of the other Spanish officials in the Mississippi Valley may not officially have learned of it until nearly mid-1796.[64]

The impact of the realization by Folch that Spanish control of the Mississippi River and Spanish claims to much of the vast North American continent were coming to an end can only be estimated. Although it would be 1798 before Spain actually quit the Mississippi Valley, Folch must have seen the futility of his efforts to stem the flow of Americans with Fort San Fernando. This probably only added to his gloom. As a consequence, when his able subordinate at Mobile, Joseph Deville Degoutin Bellechasse, arrived to relieve him at Fort San Fernando in June 1796, Folch turned the responsibility over to him and immediately left for New Orleans via the Mississippi River.[65]

In New Orleans, Folch relaxed in the company of his daughter, Irene, who had arrived from Havana sometime during the year 1796 to attend the school at Ursuline Convent.[66] Regardless of what Folch may have thought of his work at Fort San Fernando, Governor Carondelet was impressed and commended him for it. Soon after his return to New Orleans, Folch was assigned to command Pensacola.

Pensacola was the third most important Spanish post along the north shore of the Gulf of Mexico, exceeded in importance by the office of the governor-general in New Orleans and the office of governor at Natchez. The population of Pensacola in 1796 was approximately 650.[67] Folch's awareness of the importance of his new assignment, along with his recent promotion to lieutenant colonel, accounts in part for the preparations he made to assume this command. He spent several weeks in New Orleans buying household goods, slaves, and other items for his new assignment, suggesting that Folch intended to make a comfortable home for his wife and

---

63. Ibid., 28.

64. Writing to an unidentified subordinate on July 10, 1796, Carondelet said "I have not yet received any official news from the court [of Spain] concerning the treaty [of San Lorenzo], which we know nothing of but through the American gazettes." *American State Papers: Miscellaneous*, vol. 2 (Washington, D.C.: Gales & Seaton, 1834), 712. White, *Vicente Folch*, 29, says the Spanish received notification in April 1796.

65. Nasatir, *Spanish War Vessels*, 116 n. 59.

66. Holmes, *Gayoso*, 209.

67. Michael J. Curley, C.SS.R., *Church and State in the Spanish Floridas (1783–1822)* (Washington, D.C.: Catholic University Press of America, 1940), 258.

family. However, the observations of his good friend Joseph Xavier Pontalba, who accompanied Folch partway to the new post, confirm that
Folch's preparations were more likely an affirmation of his personality and
lifestyle than consideration of others. Writing of Folch, Pontalba said: "He
does not deny himself anything and I do not believe that he will improve
his affairs at Pensacola. He will come out of there as he did at Mobile without money, after having earned a great deal of it. . . . He takes with him the
household staff of a general and all sorts of provisions."[68] Folch assumed
command at Pensacola on September 30, 1795.[69] His official title at Pensacola was *commandante propietario,* but Folch's neighbors uniformly called
him "governor," and this was the title he used, even though he was not legally eligible to use it until he was appointed governor of West Florida in
1804.[70]

From the time he assumed command at Pensacola until he transferred
his authority as governor of West Florida to his son-in-law, Francisco Maximiliano de St. Maxent, in May 1811, Folch's time and attention were ab-
sorbed with an endless series of problems traceable directly to the crumbling
defenses of West Florida in the collapsing Spanish empire. He was forced to
fend off one potential enemy after another with inadequate numbers of
troops, who were invariably poorly trained;[71] forced to arm his troops with
weapons that were old, unreliable, or both;[72] and frequently had no money
to acquire proper supplies and arms. Indeed, on occasion, his troops went
without their pay.[73] The potential enemies remained the same: the Ameri-

68. White, *Vicente Folch,* 32.

69. Ibid. Even though Folch's domicile was Pensacola, he maintained a residence in New
Orleans and retained it after the transfer of Louisiana to the United States on December 20,
1803; Spanish troops also were garrisoned in New Orleans after the transfer. Hatch Dent to
James H. McCulloch, New Orleans, July 14, 1804, in Clarence E. Carter, comp. and ed., *The
Territorial Papers of the United States,* vol. 9, *The Territory of Orleans, 1803–1812* (Washington, D.C.: U.S. Government Printing Office, 1940), 266 (hereinafter cited as TP, with volume
and page range).

70. Cox, *West Florida Controversy,* 149 n. 16, tells of Folch's use of the title. White, *Vicente Folch,* 77 n. 22, confirms the date when Folch received the right to use the title "governor."

71. In the fall of 1798, Gayoso ordered a company of scouts that had been garrisoned at
Pensacola back to New Orleans. About the same time, Gayoso also ordered all the military
cadets at Pensacola to New Orleans to military school. Folch protested both losses, but was
overruled by the governor-general (White, *Vicente Folch,* 44–5).

72. Ibid., 47.

73. Folch's command always was in need of money. In February of 1805, the situation
was so desperate that Folch developed an elaborate plan for sending Don Manuel García to
Mexico City aboard the Mississippi River galley, *La Favorita,* to explain to the Viceroy the

cans, the Indians, and the British. It is no exaggeration to say that at times during the next sixteen years, Spain's position in the Floridas was so precarious that Folch literally found himself dependent on his potential enemies for survival—specifically the Americans, whom he particularly distrusted and disliked.

The first problem Folch faced as governor of Pensacola was the morale of his men. He sought to bolster their spirits by establishing procedures for capturing, trying, and punishing military deserters and other troublemakers.[74] While coping with this problem, Folch also learned it was necessary for him to give close attention to the defense not only of Pensacola, but also of settlements in nearby East Florida. This lesson was driven home when it became known that Tomás Portell, with whom Folch had clashed at New Madrid, had surrendered besieged Fort Apalachee on May 30, 1800, to William Augustus Bowles. Portell said he surrendered the installation because he feared that Bowles would not be able to restrain his Indian allies if Portell and his men were captured along with the fort. Although the fort was not part of Folch's command, he retook it a month later and garrisoned enough men and arms there to assure that the installation would not fall into the hands of Bowles or his followers again.[75]

Following this success, Folch sought appointment to head the troops sent to capture Bowles. However, the assignment was given to Lieutenant Colonel Zenon Trudeau of Louisiana, perhaps because most of the men in the command were Louisianians.[76] Thereafter, with a fair degree of success, Folch cooperated in preventing Bowles, or his followers, from retaking Apalachee and from using the rivers and harbors of northwestern Florida to resupply their marauding operations in the interior.[77] Folch was not present

---

"miserable state" of West Florida and how badly the *situado* silver was needed in the province (ibid., 79). In early 1809, Folch seized half of the *situado* designated for East Florida to pay the soldiers in his command their long overdue back pay (ibid., 94).

74. Ibid., 33–5.

75. Ibid., 54. Abraham Nasatir and Ernest R. Liljegren, in "Materials Relating to the History of the Mississippi Valley from the Minutes of the Spanish Supreme Council of State, 1787–1797," *Louisiana Historical Quarterly* 21, no. 1 (January 1938), 37 n. 75, point out that Portell was court-martialed and ultimately dismissed from the Spanish service as a result of his surrender of Apalachee.

76. In Folch's opinion the number of troops sent was inadequate and none of them had been trained to fight hostile Indians. In truth, the militiamen sent had received very little formal training. The command was composed of infantrymen from Louisiana and Mexico along with some mulatto militiamen from Louisiana (White, *Vicente Folch*, 54). Their commanding officer was Zenon Trudeau, a native of New Orleans and the former lieutenant-governor of Upper Louisiana, 1792–1799.

77. White, *Vicente Folch*, 57.

when Bowles finally was taken prisoner, but his older son, Estéban, was. At the request of his father, young Folch was present at the council meeting of the Indians in May 1803 when Bowles was captured at the "Hickory Ground," the ancient meeting place of the Creek Indians near present-day Wetumpka, Alabama. Bowles's capture had become possible because the Indians had tired of him and had begun to suspect he was turning from them toward the English.[78]

About the time events with Bowles reached their denouement, Louisiana and the Gulf Coast of North America were thrust into the international limelight. By the terms of the Treaty of San Ildefonso, signed on October 1, 1800, Spain ceded Louisiana back to France. Then, less than three years later, on May 2, 1803, in violation of his written pledge never to transfer Louisiana to a third power, Napoleon sold his new colonial possession to the United States.[79] The effect on Pensacola of the retrocession of Louisiana to France was not felt immediately. However, Folch eventually assumed the title and functions of government formerly exercised over West Florida by the governor-general of Louisiana.[80] West Florida now was a province in its own right and Folch was its governor, a fact that was made official on March 31, 1804.[81] At last, it seemed, Folch would receive the emoluments of office and support he needed to maintain himself and his country's image in North America. One of the indicators of Folch's new status was appointment of an *auditor de guerra,* a trained legal officer, to assist Folch in handling civil and criminal cases. Another was the personal secretary Folch was allowed to choose, also at the expense of the crown.[82]

Even before official notification of the retrocession of Louisiana to France, Folch saw an opportunity to curb the expansionist bent of the Americans and also to increase his influence. Americans believed the Louisiana Purchase included Mobile and the territory eastward to the Perdido River.[83] In support of this belief, the U.S. Congress passed the Mobile Act

78. Ibid., 64–6.

79. Thomas A. Bailey, *A Diplomatic History of the American People,* 7th ed. (New York: Appleton-Century-Crofts, 1964), 102–3, 108–10.

80. Folch did not receive official notice of the transfer until January 12, 1803 (White, *Vicente Folch,* 75).

81. Ibid., 77, particularly n. 22.

82. L. N. McAlister, "Pensacola during the Second Spanish Period," *Florida Historical Quarterly* 37, nos. 3 and 4 (January, April 1959), 306–7.

83. Dumas Malone, *Jefferson and His Time,* vol. 4, *Jefferson the President, First Term, 1801–1805* (Boston: Little, Brown, 1970), 303–9; and Cox, *West Florida Controversy,* 84–97.

on February 4, 1804, which extended American land claims to the Perdido River.[84] Folch responded to this threat by requesting that Captain-General Juan Manuel de Salcedo make available money to refurbish the defenses of his province, more troops to man them, and additional ships for Pensacola. Folch also pointed out to Salcedo the need for Pensacola to maintain close contact with Mobile on the west and Apalachee on the east to protect itself against the Americans and Indians. The Americans, Folch emphasized, were constantly making raids into West Florida, particularly in the Baton Rouge and Mobile districts.[85]

At the same time, Folch moved to link the settlements of his province along the northern shore of the Gulf of Mexico by building a military road. Folch had ordered construction on the road to begin in 1804, following his expedition to Baton Rouge in the fall of that year to quell the attempted insurrection by the Kemper brothers.[86] Perhaps the stickiest problem facing Folch was desertion, either from his own military service or from the United States Army. There was cooperation between Folch and the Americans in this matter, but in October 1805 it was necessary to reinforce the troops in Baton Rouge via the lakes, Bayou Manchac, and the road running from Manchac northward to the town.[87] By February 1809 the road from Baton Rouge to Pensacola was almost complete. Ironically, the man placed in command of the project was not Spanish, but an American, Joseph Collins, captain in the Fish River Dragoons from the Mobile District, Louisiana Militia.[88]

Folch also attempted to end Pensacola's isolation from New Orleans and Havana. He recommended that the mail from Havana be transported by the small river galleys, several of which now operated out of Pensacola harbor, first to Pensacola and then on to New Orleans. The galleys were to return to Pensacola with the responses from New Orleans, which then would be delivered to Havana. Folch's suggestion to use the river galleys for mail delivery reflected thought grounded in scientific knowledge and experience. It

---

84. The Secretary of the Treasury to Hore Browse Trist, February 27, 1804, TP, 9: 193; and *United States Statutes at Large, 6th–12th Congress, 1799–1813,* vol. 2, *Public Acts* (Boston: Little, Brown, 1850), 251–4.

85. White, *Vicente Folch,* 76–7.

86. Cox, *West Florida Controversy,* 161.

87. White, *Vicente Folch,* 82–3.

88. Ibid., 95. Holmes, *Honor and Fidelity,* 238, entry 848, provides the information on Collins's home district in Mobile. Cox, *West Florida Controversy,* 161, tells of Folch's initial efforts to get the road built from Baton Rouge to Mobile in 1804.

also represented another bid to accumulate power. The shallow-draft river vessels were to sail after three o'clock in the afternoon and to hug the shore, thus taking advantage of the gulf currents, the off-shore winds, and nightfall in their attempts to avoid privateers roaming the open waters of the Gulf of Mexico.[89] An important land link in the delivery of mail was Folch's proposal for a pony express system, complete with special riders and posts. What became of this suggestion is not known. It is clear, however, that Folch did not agree with Captain-General Salcedo's January 12, 1803, instructions that all the military personnel and others who wished to remain under Spain's rule should transfer to Havana.[90] In Folch's view, Pensacola, with its good harbor and supplies of food, particularly meat, should become the center of defense for Spain's remaining possessions in North America.[91]

A large part of the governmental establishment in New Orleans did transfer to Pensacola with the end of Spanish rule in Louisiana, but the move was slow. The population of Pensacola in 1810 was only about 1,000, approximately 350 greater than in 1796. Three years later, the population of the town had grown to 3,063. Most of the newcomers were French Creoles, Scots, and Irish.[92] Because there was very little industry in Pensacola, most of the residents were directly or indirectly dependent on the Spanish government. Clearly, many of the newcomers were former residents of Louisiana who did not want to settle in Havana, but who remembered the Spanish government's threat to cut off their pensions if they did not support the king of Spain.[93] Therefore, many of these Spanish subjects were afraid not to follow the power of the Spanish crown.[94]

One Louisiana government official who did not initially settle in Pensacola was the intendant, Juan Ventura Morales. He lingered in New Orleans until the end of January 1806, when the Orleans Territory governor, Wil-

---

89. White, *Vicente Folch,* 38, 40.

90. Ibid., 74, particularly n. 14, tells of Salcedo's order.

91. McAlister, "Pensacola during the Second Spanish Period," 305.

92. On the population figures for Pensacola, see Curley, *Church and State,* 258; and McAlister, "Pensacola during the Second Spanish Period," 307, 310.

93. On these threats, known to have been made by Casa Calvo, see the biographical sketches of Casa Calvo, Bellechasse, and Michel Cantrelle.

94. An indication of the economic and political hold the Spanish government had over its citizens who moved to Pensacola is reflected in the population loss experienced by the town after the departure of Vicente Folch as governor of West Florida, when it became clear that Spain could not hold Pensacola or protect its citizens. By 1816, the population had dropped to four hundred. McAlister, "Pensacola during the Second Spanish Period," 318.

liam C. C. Claiborne, forced him to leave the territory.[95] Morales initially stayed in New Orleans because Governor Folch found the intendant personally so objectionable that he refused to allow Morales to settle in Pensacola. Instead, Folch insisted that the intendant open his office in Mobile. Eventually, Folch was overruled by the secretary of the treasury, Miguel Cayetano Soler, and the captain-general, Salvatore Muro y Salazar, the Marqués de Someruelos. Then Morales, too, settled in Pensacola.[96]

Early in his term as governor of West Florida, Folch sought to strengthen the administration and defenses of the province. These efforts reflected national pride as much as Folch's human tendency to accumulate power. However, Folch's actions derived some of their energy from other sources. In part, his motivation was reinforced by secret advice from General James Wilkinson, who advised both Folch and Casa Calvo that Spain should hang onto the Floridas because they were the key to American commerce through the Gulf of Mexico.[97]

The acquisition of Louisiana by the United States established the strategic importance of Pensacola to Spain, but collapsing Spanish power increased the isolation and vulnerability of West Florida with each passing day. Initially, the center of problems was Baton Rouge, but as Spain's power waned the number and complexity of problems for Folch grew. Gradually, the focus of the problem of control shifted from Baton Rouge to Mobile and, eventually, to Pensacola itself.

The problems in the Baton Rouge district began with the Kemper brothers' attempts to lead a rebellion against Spanish rule.[98] After the Kempers were quashed in the fall of 1804, only the troublesome issue of trade through territory held by each country reared its potentially dangerous head: Spanish use of the Mississippi River through American territory and American use of the Tombigbee River through Spanish territory. In an attempt to resolve this matter, Governor Claiborne wrote Intendant Morales

95. Morales to Claiborne, January 30, 1806, *Archivo General de Indias. Sección V, Gobierno. Audiencia de Santo Domingo, Sobre la Época Española de Luisiana*, legajo 2608, folio 398, microfilm reel no. 155, Special Collections, Library, Loyola University, New Orleans.

96. Jack D. L. Holmes, *"Dramatis Personae* in Spanish Louisiana," *Louisiana Studies* 6, no. 2 (summer 1967), 157–8.

97. Jacobs, *Tarnished Warrior,* 205–6, points out that for this advice, given sometime in February–March 1804, Wilkinson was to have his pension from the Spanish increased to four thousand dollars annually, and the overdue payments, totaling nearly sixteen thousand dollars, were to be brought up to date.

98. Cox, *West Florida Controversy,* 151–66 and index references deal at length with the irrepressible Kemper brothers and their cohorts.

in October 1805 asking that the duties on American goods passing down the Tombigbee through Mobile be suspended. Morales refused, saying he could do nothing until he had consulted with Governor Folch.[99] The question of duties on American goods moving through Spanish territory languished in this limbo for some time because of Folch's distrust of the Americans[100] and because Folch, through his unrealistic assessment of Spanish power, initially believed he held the upper hand. This last point must be considered in the context of the international events unfolding in Europe.

In the summer of 1805 it still looked as though the power of the Spanish crown could not be challenged by the weak and disorganized United States.[101] More important, perhaps, in the fall of 1805 Folch felt flush with power. In October an additional 350 Spanish soldiers were assigned to West Florida, some of whom Folch parceled out to Baton Rouge and Mobile.[102] For the moment at least, it appeared the captain-general would give Folch the men and arms necessary to cope with the difficult situation facing Spain in West Florida.[103]

The Burr conspiracy began to unfold while the troublesome trade issue hung in suspension. When Folch first learned of it and of the expeditionary forces believed to be gathering in the Ohio and Mississippi river valleys, he appears to have honestly, but quite mistakenly, thought it would not involve West Florida. From his frontier knowledge of American resentment of the central government—reinforced by first-hand familiarity with the beliefs of westerners in general and General James Wilkinson in particular—Folch believed the reports signaled the separation of the states along the Atlantic seaboard from those in the trans-Appalachian West and the Louisiana Pur-

99. White, *Vicente Folch*, 83.

100. Carlos Martínez de Yrujo, the Marqués de Yrujo, diplomatic representative of Spain to the United States, reinforced Folch's suspicious fear of Americans about this time by advising him that the United States had recalled its Mediterranean squadron from Tripoli and suggested that the returning squadron might be used to attack Florida (White, *Vicente Folch*, 83–4).

101. Ibid., 82, relates Folch's mid-July report to José Iturrigaray, viceroy of New Spain, that a combined French and Spanish fleet of more than thirty-five ships had assembled in the West Indies on its way to battle the British fleet under Lord Nelson.

102. Folch also attempted to buy some French cannon still remaining in New Orleans. Although the French consul refused to sell them, he assured Folch the Americans would not get them either (ibid., 82–3; and Cox, *West Florida Controversy*, 173).

103. In January 1806, Folch began to map strategy for defending West Florida, assembling a war committee in Pensacola. A part of the committee's strategy included construction of gunboats at Mobile to repulse an enemy attack by sea (White, *Vicente Folch*, 84).

chase territory.[104] It was in this context that Folch's first thought was of a foreign policy that would protect Spanish interests and at the same time would not help the United States. The policy he settled on was strict neutrality.[105] Reflecting this siege mentality, Folch, on December 11, 1806, denied the request of Captain Thomas Swaine, the American commander at Fort Stoddert, for permission to take American troops across the West Florida border and Mobile Bay to New Orleans to confront the Burr expeditionary force believed to be approaching New Orleans. Folch advised Swaine, through Lieutenant Edmund P. Gaines, that he could not grant such permission until authorized by the captain-general in Havana. Folch also would not be swayed by Gaines's argument that Spain should join with the United States to dispel the published rumors that Spain was a willing accomplice in Burr's plans.[106]

Folch's refusal to grant permission for the Americans to move through West Florida, of course, was an obstructionist tactic, but it did not work. When Swaine heard nothing from Folch in two weeks, he ignored Folch's refusal and on January 2, 1807, the American troops moved out of Fort Stoddert, down the Tombigbee River, and across Mobile Bay. By the time Folch received notice of Swaine's intentions from Captain P. P. Schuyler, Second United States Infantry, it was too late for Folch to take any opposing action. Although Folch was furious with Swaine and all the Americans, there was little he could do. For this reason, and perhaps because the Americans did not tarry on their journey across Mobile Bay, Folch decided to ignore the incident.[107]

A few days after the American troops departed, Captain Swaine delivered to Folch another message from General Wilkinson along with a copy of the proclamation issued by President Jefferson outlawing Burr and describing his actions as treasonous. The message from Wilkinson advised Folch that

104. Adam Szászdi, "Governor Folch and the Burr Conspiracy," *Florida Historical Quarterly* 38, no. 3 (January 1960), 241–2. White, *Vicente Folch,* 85, says only that Folch thought the United States government sanctioned the Burr expedition.

Folch's belief that the union of the United States was coming apart is an echo of the opinion often expressed at this time by Daniel Clark. See To James Madison, November 18, 1806, in *Official Letter Books of W. C. C. Claiborne, 1801–1816,* ed. Dunbar Rowland, vol. 4 (1917; New York: AMS Press, 1972), 36 (hereinafter cited as CLB with volume and page range).

105. Szászdi, "Folch and the Burr Conspiracy," 243.

106. Ibid., 243–4.

107. Ibid., 244; and White, *Vicente Folch,* 86.

Burr and a band of his followers were approaching, and cautioned Folch to reinforce Baton Rouge because it, too, was to be attacked. Wilkinson also mentioned Burr's designs on Mexico.[108] Folch had learned earlier from Louis Brognier de Clouet—devotee of the Marqués de Casa Calvo, confidant of General Wilkinson, sometime business partner of Bellechasse, and lieutenant in the Louisiana Infantry Regiment of the Spanish army—that Burr's project was quite serious and its frustration very important. This information was made available to Folch after Wilkinson returned to New Orleans from Natchitoches on the evening of November 25 and before Folch left New Orleans to resume command at Pensacola.[109] These messages caused Folch to decide to transfer his headquarters from Mobile, where he had established them sometime in December, to Baton Rouge.

Folch's purpose in going to Baton Rouge, he advised Captain-General Someruelos on January 11, 1807, was to discover the intentions of Burr and his followers.[110] Several days before writing Someruelos, Folch realized the Burr conspiracy was a danger to Spain and its colonial possessions in North America. What information Folch may have received and from whom is not known, but on January 15, 1807, Folch wrote Morales that "three days ago" information had "come into my possession . . . [that] detailed [the] plan which the insurgents of Kentucky have formed against the King's domains."[111]

108. Szászdi, "Folch and the Burr Conspiracy," 244–5.

109. Cox, *West Florida Controversy*, 185, 187, 192, 194, 195. On de Clouet's military service with the Spanish, see *Archivo General de Simancas. Sección de Guerra Moderna. Hojas de Servicias Militares de América, 1787–1799, legajo 7291, cuaderno 3, Regimiento de Infantería de Luisiana. Diciembre 1796*, folio 61. De Clouet's full name was printed in the *Moniteur,* December 9, 1807, p. 3, c. 1.

110. *Moniteur,* December 9, 1807, p. 3, c. 1.

111. Cox, *West Florida Controversy,* 247. The information may have come from any one of several men: Jean-Batiste-Victor Castillon, who served as Spanish consul in New Orleans from March 4, 1806, to August 4, 1807; José Vidal, a former captain in the Spanish militia and New Orleans resident who served as Spanish consul from late in 1807 into early October 1809; or from Fr. Antonio Sedella, who served as a secret agent for the Spanish government for fifteen years, beginning about 1805. On their service, see Stanley Faye, "Consuls of Spain in New Orleans, 1804–1821," *Louisiana Historical Quarterly* 21, no. 3 (July 1938), 677–80. It is most likely Wilkinson supplied the information using one of these men, or Louis de Clouet, as courier. See Walter F. McCaleb, *The Aaron Burr Conspiracy and A New Light on Aaron Burr,* expanded ed. (1936; New York: Argosy-Antiquarian, 1966), 55–7. (The second part of this book, *A New Light on Aaron Burr,* is separately paginated. Therefore, references to this separate section will be cited as McCaleb, *Burr Conspiracy,* addendum, with page numbers.) Folch also received information on Americans, Burr in particular, from Yrujo (Cox, *West Florida Controversy,* 190).

This belated recognition of a fact that seemed obvious to many of his contemporaries raises the question, what caused Folch to change his mind about the Burr conspiracy and its objectives? It has been suggested that only one conclusion can be drawn from Folch's sudden shift in opinion: he received startling new information about the plans and activities of the Mexican Association of New Orleans.[112] The news most probably was Wilkinson's report to Folch on Lieutenant Colonel Constant Freeman's December 30, 1806, interview of Judge James Workman.[113] Throughout the Burr conspiracy, Wilkinson regularly corresponded with Folch. According to the West Florida governor, the general not only advised him of any new "information which he acquired, but also his intentions for the various exigencies in which he might find himself."[114] Wilkinson's objective, of course, was to collect more blackmail money from the Spanish.[115] Workman's interview by Colonel Freeman dealt at length with the history and origins of the Mexican Associates, or Association, also known as the Mexican Society or Mexican Club.[116]

The secretive Mexican Association is dealt with in greater detail in a separate essay in this appendix. However, it bears pointing out here that the Mexican Association was made up of many of the leading businessmen and governmental officials in the Territory of Orleans. With a few exceptions, what led to the formation of this group was their distrust of the uncooperative and antagonistic Spanish officials and soldiers who lingered in New Orleans beyond the grace period permitted under the terms of the Louisiana Purchase treaty.[117] The objective of the associates generally is thought to have been the conquest of New Spain (Mexico, which included present-day Texas) and West Florida, thereby putting an end to a feared invasion of the United States from those bordering Spanish possessions. However, this is

112. Szászdi, "Folch and the Burr Conspiracy," 245.

113. Freeman's interview of Workman was intended for General Wilkinson. The story of this key element in the Burr conspiracy is recounted in Samuel Wandell and Meade Minnigerode, *Aaron Burr, A Biography Written, in Large Part, from Original and Hitherto Unused Material*, vol. 2 (New York: G. P. Putnam's Sons, 1925), 124–7. See also the biographical sketch of James Workman in this appendix.

114. [Whitaker], "Interview of Governor Folch," 839.

115. Cox, *West Florida Controversy*, 194.

116. For the names of some of the known Associates see "The Mexican Associates/Association," in this appendix.

117. The ninety-day grace period ended on January 21, 1804. Hunter Miller, ed., *Treaties and Other International Acts of the United States of America*, vol. 2 (Washington, D.C.: U.S. Government Printing Office, 1931), 498, 502.

the distilled residue of a variety of diverse opinions held by the large, but uncertain, number of members.

The Marqués de Casa Calvo originally had been the observer of the Mexican Association in New Orleans, but after his expulsion from Louisiana by Governor Claiborne on February 15, 1806, Governor Folch took over the task. In the summer of 1805, Casa Calvo contemplated using Burr to advance his favorite project, the exchange of the Floridas for Louisiana and New Orleans. General Wilkinson had recommended Casa Calvo to Burr, but the former vice-president avoided the marqués and apparently spent most of his time with Judge James Workman, Daniel Clark, and other members of the Mexican Association.[118] Before his forced departure from Louisiana, Casa Calvo learned what he believed were the plans of the association: General Wilkinson was to lead an expedition against Mexico; a British fleet from Jamaica was to attack Pensacola; and Americans from Kentucky and the Ohio Valley were to seize Mobile and Baton Rouge in Spanish West Florida.[119] However, the piece of information that appears to have jarred Folch into action was the knowledge that the plan to conquer Mexico hinged on seizure of the Spanish artillery and ammunition stored at Mobile.[120]

Folch did not have enough troops or adequate fortifications to prevent loss of the artillery, which he knew the Americans needed and might easily take. As a consequence, Folch decided to send most of the artillery pieces, without the gunpowder, to Veracruz. The other arms and ammunition were collected at Mobile, where much of the merchandise used in the Indian trade was warehoused. One hundred and fifty troops and some of the artillery were ordered to Baton Rouge to assist in its defense. The troops and the artillery were readied to sail within twenty-four hours. Folch sailed for Baton Rouge immediately, but was forced to stop when he reached Pass Christian due to a ten-inch snowfall on January 17 and 18. It was here that

118. Cox, *West Florida Controversy,* 189.

119. With the exception of the Americans marching from Kentucky and the Ohio Valley, Casa Calvo's information sounds very much like James Workman's scheme for the conquest and emancipation of Spanish America published in Alexandria, Virginia, in 1801. See Workman, *Political Essays, Relative to the War of the French Revolution . . .* (Alexandria, Va.: Cottom & Stewart, 1801), 5–65. Workman's ideas are discussed in his biographical sketch. Casa Calvo was quite familiar with Workman's *Political Essays,* which was available to the public in New Orleans. See the Casa Calvo biographical sketch.

120. Szászdi, "Folch and the Burr Conspiracy," 245.

some of the troops caught up with him. The rest joined him later at Bayou Manchac.[121]

Folch received another letter from General Wilkinson while waiting at Pass Christian for the weather to improve. This letter, dated January 5, invited him to join in close cooperation with the Americans in resisting Burr. Wilkinson's letter prompted Folch to visit New Orleans. Folch did not trust Wilkinson and believed he could learn the latest developments about Burr and the Mexican Association plans in New Orleans. The ship carrying the West Florida governor and his staff arrived at daybreak on January 21 in Lake Pontchartrain off the military installation at Bayou St. John. Folch had the vessel anchor just beyond the range of the American cannons at the fort. From that vantage point he requested permission for himself and his staff to continue overland to Baton Rouge. Both General Wilkinson and Governor Claiborne refused Folch's request. The public was too agitated, they said, and the rumors that the Spanish were accomplices in Burr's scheme might be just the spark to set off a public disturbance.

This refusal angered Folch, as did the treatment he received at the hands of three representatives of Wilkinson and Claiborne who met him at Bayou St. John on the morning of January 22, 1807. The representatives insisted the meeting with Folch be held on the bridge over the bayou. Such an arrangement, Folch pointed out, was traditional between belligerents, but not between friendly nations. He also assured the Americans he would do his duty if Baton Rouge were attacked and that they could count on him to preserve peace in Louisiana. Because one of the American aides from Wilkinson and Claiborne did not understand English, Folch repeated all that he had said in French.[122] The four men then returned to their respective duty posts. The following day the Spanish convoy sailed on to Baton Rouge via Lakes Pontchartrain and Maurepas, and the Iberville River (Bayou Manchac), arriving on January 26, 1807.[123] Folch remained in Baton Rouge for several weeks. By the time the Burr conspiracy collapsed, Folch estimated his defensive preparations had cost him a "whole year's salary," by which he apparently meant budget, and he was going to have to "spend the next year's to finish" the current year.[124]

121. Ibid., 247–8.
122. This may have been Louis de Clouet, who Claiborne said in October 1804 "cannot speak a word of English." Governor Claiborne to the President, October 5, 1804, TP, 9: 308.
123. Szászdi, "Folch and the Burr Conspiracy," 248–9.
124. [Whitaker,] "Interview of Governor Folch," 838.

Folch sent a long report on the Mexican Association to Captain-General Someruelos in Havana before leaving Baton Rouge. The report, dated February 10, 1807, accepted General Wilkinson's assertion that the nebulous plans of Burr and those of the Mexican Association were one and the same. Folch also attributed the collapse of American plans to seize New Spain and West Florida chiefly to his own vigilance.[125] The evidence, however, continues to point to Folch as a peripheral figure also being swept along by all the events manipulated by General Wilkinson. Nonetheless, his February letter contains considerable first-hand knowledge of the *Comisio Revolucionario*, or the American Party, as he called the Mexican Association/Associates.

Folch believed the Mexican Associates in New Orleans were dependent on a similar group established in New York. The purpose of both, he advised Someruelos, had been to organize an insurrection in New Spain and at the same time to assemble a force to invade the province. The project later was modified, Folch said, to include the dismemberment of the United States with Kentucky, Tennessee, and Louisiana to be joined with the territory of New Spain and headed by Jefferson, Burr, or possibly someone from Mexico.[126]

One of the most interesting parts of Folch's letter to Someruelos described his attendance at a meeting of the Mexican Association in New Orleans. According to Folch, Wilkinson, and Claiborne, the association was a secret organization. Yet Folch refers to the meeting as a public affair, a banquet, which suggests that he may not be correct about who sponsored the meeting. The date of the function is unknown, but it most probably was sometime between Jefferson's war-like message to Congress in November 1805 and the fall of 1806, the period during which American feelings against the Spanish were running very high and the threat of war between the United States and Spain was at its greatest.[127] The occasion for the meeting appears to have been a Jeffersonian Republican banquet held to honor George Washington. Jefferson's followers had begun holding such functions in 1804, if not earlier, in an attempt to keep the first president's name from being irrevocably linked in the mind of the American public with the Federalists.[128] Regardless of the occasion, Folch said that during the meeting he

125. Szászdi, "Folch and the Burr Conspiracy," 249.

126. McCaleb, *Burr Conspiracy,* addendum, 90–1.

127. The occasion Folch described most probably took place in the summer or fall of 1806 when he was in New Orleans on extended sick leave.

128. Noble E. Cunningham, *The Jeffersonian Republicans in Power: Party Operations, 1801–1809* (Chapel Hill: University of North Carolina Press, 1963), 296–8. For a good example of how Claiborne continued this kind of harassment of Folch in 1808, see Jared W. Bradley,

was offered a bribe to join the association. In exchange for becoming a part of the Mexican Association's movement, he was to be made commander in chief of the army. Folch cagily avoided giving an answer to the proposition, saying he would have to know more about the plans before he could commit himself to support them.

The chief spokesman for the group, Folch reported, was Judge James Workman. Workman assured Folch that if he joined the movement, a large sum of money would be paid him, large enough to ensure his subsistence and keep his family the rest of their lives.[129] When the coterie seemed to be making no headway with the Spanish governor, Workman then suggested that West Florida easily could be seized and Folch taken prisoner. After that, as a "temporary *Realista*"—that is, a loyal Spanish subject—he could join the movement without "the dishonor of having lost the province which had been entrusted to him." When Folch still did not react favorably to any of the proposals, it was suggested that with him as their prisoner it would be quite easy to "put [him] . . . out of the way" so that he could not "injure" their cause. Folch did not name the person who described this grim circumstance, but presumably it was Workman. Folch did indicate that those present agreed to the proposition.[130]

The proposals advanced by Workman were so outrageous and preposterous that it is clear the judge and his friends were baiting and trying to unnerve the unpredictable and literal-minded West Florida governor. The whole incident sounds very much as though it may have originated in the fertile and playful mind of Lewis Kerr, aided and abetted by Workman. Although the military preparedness measures called for by Jefferson were inadequate, they would have served to encourage the boldness of Workman and some of his cohorts in the Mexican Association. Folch's responses reflect that he was aware Workman and his unnamed compatriots were playing what would be called today the game of "chicken" and that whoever "blinked," or gave in to the opposite side, would lose. The suggestion that Folch might be assassinated also points to the possible origins of Wilkinson's fear, echoed later by Claiborne, that they might be assassinated.[131]

"W. C. C. Claiborne and Spain: Foreign Affairs under Jefferson and Madison, 1801–1811, Part II, A Successful Expansion, 1807–1811," *Louisiana History* 13, no. 1 (winter 1972), 11–2.

129. McCaleb, *Burr Conspiracy,* addendum, 91–2.

130. Ibid., 92.

131. Wilkinson first publicly alluded to fears of assassination during his meeting with the members of the New Orleans Chamber of Commerce on December 6, 1806. Wandell and Minnigerode, *Aaron Burr,* 2: 131. Claiborne later issued a sworn statement of his concern about

Folch went on in his letter to Someruelos to say that because he had agreed to nothing, the Mexican Association "have postponed the bitter moment" when they were going to make good on their "treacherous propositions."[132]

The attendees that evening were not limited to those who later were identified as members of the Mexican Association. Folch reported that Governor Claiborne also was present at the banquet meeting heavily attended by the Mexican Associates. This fact suggests that the occasion was a Jeffersonian Republican banquet honoring George Washington. When toasts were offered, Claiborne joined in the harassment of Folch, ratcheting the pressure on the Spanish governor upward another notch with his toast for the successful outcome of the Francisco de Miranda expedition against Spain's loyal forces in rebellious Venezuela. There were other developments germane to the frustrated plans to seize West Florida and New Spain, but, Folch told Someruelos, "I cannot express [them] in writing." Clearly, the West Florida governor continued to conceal other aspects of the Burr conspiracy. Whatever these points were, Folch verbally recounted them to the trusted courier assigned to deliver the dispatch to Someruelos and charged him with the responsibility for reporting them orally to the captain-general.[133]

Why Folch waited for more than a year to report these events is unknown. It is possible the apparent end of the dangers from the Burr conspiracy triggered Folch's realization of the precariousness of his isolated circumstances in West Florida and the need to try to make his superiors in Havana fully aware of them. It also is likely that reports from New Orleans on the outcome of the first trials of Workman and Kerr for their purported roles in the Mexican Association's supposed plan to invade New Spain and West Florida elicited Folch's report to Someruelos as protective covering for himself against the revelations coming out of the trials.[134]

---

assassination during the Burr conspiracy. Nathan Schachner, *Aaron Burr, A Biography* (New York: Frederick A. Stokes, 1937), 367.

   132. McCaleb, *Burr Conspiracy,* addendum, 92.

   133. Ibid., 92–3.

   134. Folch would have received information on the trials from his own sources, if not from New Orleans newspapers, or other travelers arriving in Baton Rouge from New Orleans. The jury deliberating the verdict on Kerr and Workman was deadlocked for three or four days before being discharged. See the undated letter fragment that follows To Robert Williams, February 10, 1807, in CLB, 4: 119. Internal evidence in this long fragment suggests it probably was written by Claiborne on March 2, 1807. See James Workman, *The Trials of the Honb. James Workman, and Col. Lewis Kerr, Before the United States Court, for the Orleans District on a Charge of High Misdemeanor, in Planning and Setting on Foot, Within the United States, An Expedition for the Conquest and Emancipation of Mexico* (New Orleans: Bradford & An-

Governor Claiborne launched his counteroffensive against John Watkins and all those who opposed him in the territorial legislature on February 10, 1807, the same date that Folch made his report to Someruelos in Havana. Claiborne began his attack with a secret message to the legislature asking that the writ of habeas corpus be suspended. When the territorial house voted down this request on the recommendation of the territorial judges and lawyers in New Orleans, Claiborne and Wilkinson became so frightened that the Memorial to Congress denouncing them would be adopted they joined together to appeal to Folch for assistance to defeat it. As Wilkinson wrote Folch, he and Claiborne knew that " 'those who control the legislative council are all friends of yours, [and] I beg you to use your efforts to destroy this work, which is already very far advanced.' "[135] Although still smarting from the cold treatment he had received at the hands of the representatives of Claiborne and Wilkinson on the lakefront at Bayou St. John on January 22, Folch decided to return to Pensacola via New Orleans.

Folch later said the chief reason he decided to go to New Orleans was his belief that Claiborne and Wilkinson had been ordered by the president of the United States to "effect a reconciliation" with him as a redress for the hostile treatment Folch received at Bayou St. John. There was no foundation for this belief, but it is easy to understand why Folch may have thought it was true. When he reached the entrance to Lake Pontchartrain on his return journey to Pensacola, entry into the lake was prevented by contrary winds. While waiting for more favorable winds, Folch was visited by a schooner from New Orleans with "various persons sent by General Wilkinson, Governor Claiborne and other persons of position and distinction" from New Orleans "not only to greet me, but to induce me" to come to the territorial capital. Bellechasse was to have been one of the "persons of position and distinction," but "having felt indisposed at the moment of embarking, he commissioned in his stead Don Louis Declouet [sic]," who

---

derson, 1807), 176. According to the *Louisiana Gazette*, September 10, 1805, p. 1, c. 3, the mail stage left Vassault & Todd's hotel, New Orleans, every Tuesday at 6:00 A.M. and arrived at Manchac the next day at 5:00 P.M. The return schedule listed departure from Manchac on Sunday at 6:00 A.M. and arrival in New Orleans the following day, Monday, at 5:00 P.M.

In any event, news traveled with surprising speed between New Orleans and Baton Rouge at this time. For example, General Wilkinson did not say how he received the information, but within twenty-four hours after Folch left Baton Rouge on his return to Pensacola, Wilkinson claimed he had been informed of this fact. [Whitaker,] "Interview of Governor Folch," 839.

135. [Whitaker,] "Interview of Governor Folch," 839.

carried a special message to Bellechasse's former superior and friend. The
Bellechasse message urged Folch to come to New Orleans so as not to "produce a bad effect among the persons inclined to" the Spanish government.[136]

Folch's description of his arrival on the lakefront further delineates the
desperation of Wilkinson and Claiborne. Folch said that when he came in
sight of the bridge at Bayou St. John, a United States naval lieutenant asked
him to go ashore in the yacht under his command. This touch, obviously
arranged by Wilkinson, elicited from Folch the comment that "if the President himself had come to New Orleans they could not have given him a
better reception than the one I experienced."[137] The investment of time, energy, and taxpayer money by Wilkinson and Claiborne soon paid off. According to Folch, he succeeded in "obtaining at last the rejection of the
memorial so much feared by the general and the governor." However, the
task was not accomplished "without a great deal of trouble." Nonetheless,
Folch reported that both Wilkinson and Claiborne received the news with
"much satisfaction."[138] Not content with that success, a few days later Wilkinson sought Folch's assistance again, this time to promote passage by the
legislative council of two memorials, both of which approved the conduct
of Wilkinson and Claiborne during the Burr conspiracy. Folch lent his assistance to passage of these two items because, as he complacently said, he
thought he should do it "to show them that Spain could be useful to them
even in their own country."[139] By June 1807, Folch was back in Pensacola
with plenty of time to contemplate his prospects.

The realizations induced by the Burr conspiracy already had impinged
so strongly on Folch in the wake of those events that his desire to continue
as governor of West Florida was shaken. Writing to his friend General Antonio Samper in mid-April 1807, Folch displayed a clear understanding of the
untenable position he occupied. He was, Folch said, dependent on the captain-general, who lived almost two hundred leagues across the Gulf of Mexico and whose decisions could take weeks or even months to arrive.[140] If the
decisions were found to be ill-conceived, Folch pointed out, he was left with

136. Ibid., 837–8.
137. Ibid., 838.
138. Ibid., 839.
139. Ibid., 839–40.
140. Because of the British blockade maintained around Cuba, Folch had no way of communicating with the captain-general in Havana except through officers who disguised themselves as civilians and traveled on American passports aboard neutral ships from New Orleans.
Szászdi, "Folch and the Burr Conspiracy," 240.

the "difficult alternative of disobeying the Captain General or serving ill the King." The circumstances, Folch wrote, were "capital inconveniences which render this destination intolerable."[141] Folch, now a full colonel, was ready to move on to another assignment, but his request for a new duty station was denied.[142]

As a result of actions by both Spain and the United States, Folch's situation in West Florida seemed to spiral downward steadily after the Burr Conspiracy. Spain issued a royal order prohibiting American settlement in Spanish territory as a direct result of the Burr Conspiracy.[143] The revocation of an immigration policy that had begun with Miró simply added to the rising tensions along the U.S. border with West Florida. In many ways, the problems of West Florida mirrored those of the United States. Both the fledgling United States and the isolated Spanish province were dependent on foreign trade, West Florida more than the United States. A series of events, beginning with the adoption in December 1807 of the embargo by the U.S. Congress, contributed to the worsening situations of both the new nation and the Spanish province. All subsequent events stemmed directly or indirectly from the Napoleonic wars raging between Great Britain and France.

The embargo was intended to provide the United States with the power of economic coercion as a substitute for arms in the struggle to survive the war between Great Britain and France. The law permitted coastwise trade, provided the proper bond was posted by the merchants, but prohibited the export of any goods from the United States by sea or land. Ultimately, the embargo caused economic distress not only in New England, where objections to it precipitated the New England Confederation and nearly disrupted the union of states, but elsewhere. Florida, which had become dependent on food supplies from Americans, was equally hard-pressed. Folch believed the embargo was at least partially aimed at weakening Spanish Florida. Nonetheless, Spain's hold on the Floridas survived the embargo principally because of Folch's strong hand and dogged determination aided by widespread smuggling from American territory, and the reluctance of the United States to employ force to end Spanish control.[144]

The earliest and most troublesome problems originated in or near Baton Rouge and slowly rolled eastward toward Mobile.

141. Ibid., 241.
142. White, *Vicente Folch,* 102.
143. Ibid., 86–7.
144. Ibid., 89–90.

On July 21, 1808, crew members from an American gunboat anchored in the Iberville River south of Baton Rouge went ashore in Spanish territory and arrested an American deserter named Armstrong. The spirited accusations of Carlos de Grand-Pré, the commandant at Baton Rouge, brought about the release of Armstrong and the suspension of the American commander of the gunboat. At Baton Rouge again, in the fall of 1808, the settlers complained because they were not allowed to sell their very good crop of cotton or to receive trade goods destined for them from Europe because of the U.S. government embargo.[145] Then in December 1808 General Wilkinson was ordered to New Orleans with seven thousand troops in case of war with either Great Britain or France. Although Folch was wary of Wilkinson, the general visited not only Folch in Pensacola, but also the captain-general in Havana to give assurances there would be no American invasion.[146]

In January 1809, two Spanish schooners from Mobile were seized by the U.S. Army. The ships had been loading provisions on the banks of the Tensaw River when they were seized on the orders of Captain Edmond P. Gaines, the commander at Fort Stoddert, for allegedly taking on cargo above the West Florida boundary in violation of the American embargo. One vessel was released immediately because it was found to have no cargo. After a delay the other was released with an apology from Gaines, who explained that the boundary line had never been identified in the area because it was flooded when the boundary commission arrived there to do its work.[147]

On September 23, 1810, a band of rebels attacked the fort at Baton Rouge, killing two of the defenders and driving away the remainder of the small garrison. Subsequently, Folch learned the rebels had taken St. Helena and were marching east to the Pearl River with the intention of taking Mobile and Pensacola.[148] In November 1810, Reuben Kemper, one of the rebels who had attacked Baton Rouge in 1804, wrote the military commander of Mobile, Louis Pérez, saying that since the government of Spain had ceased to exist with its occupation by Napoleon, the citizens of West Florida had a right to freely choose their own government. If this was not permitted by the government at Pensacola, Kemper said, it would mean war. The American rebel added that if the officers at Mobile would join with his group,

145. Ibid., 92.
146. Ibid., 91.
147. Ibid., 94.
148. Ibid., 100.

they would be welcomed into the new government at the same rank and pay they enjoyed under the former government of Spain.[149]

At the same time, the incidence of robberies and assaults on settlers by marauding Indians increased. There was also a report from Diego Morphy, the Spanish consul in New Orleans, that an estimated eight hundred rebels were on their way to take both Mobile and Pensacola. These developments led Folch to seek assistance from the American commander of Fort Stoddert, Captain Edmund P. Gaines, and Governor David Holmes of Mississippi Territory. Folch asked these American officials to stop any rebels who attempted to come south against Mobile. Gaines replied that he could not legally provide assistance across the boundary line inside West Florida without authorization from his superiors.[150]

In December 1810, Folch fought a pitched battle with fewer than one hundred Americans under the command of Reuben Kemper. The American rebels had set up camp on the eastern shore of Mobile Bay and were threatening to attack Mobile. Folch attempted to contact the rebels twice, but failed each time. Then, on December 10, he surprised the rebels with a larger force of his own regulars and militia. Four rebels were killed, three were wounded, seven were captured, and the rest fled, thus ending for a while the threat to Mobile. In the same month the promotion to brigadier general requested by Folch arrived. This promotion revived his flagging spirits and encouraged him to request transfer to Spain to fight for his native country in the Peninsular War then raging. His request was denied.[151]

By the fall of 1810, Folch was threatened on all sides by a rising tide of filibusterers. His greatest worry was avoidance of a bloodbath at the hands of the rebels. With this as his leading concern, the harried Folch notified the captain-general in Havana that he proposed to enter into negotiations with the United States for establishment of a definitive boundary between Louisiana and Texas; placement of West Florida in the hands of the United States, pending the outcome of those negotiations; and if no boundary satisfactory to Spain could be established, Florida would then revert to Spain.[152] When Folch received no response from the captain-general on these proposals, he, on his own initiative, offered to turn West Florida over to the United States if help did not arrive before January 1, 1811. Perhaps because he had not

149. Ibid., 101.
150. Ibid., 100–1.
151. Ibid., 102.
152. McAlister, "Pensacola during the Second Spanish Period," 312–3.

heard anything from Someruelos, on January 8, 1811, Folch wrote the captain-general in Havana that the loss of West Florida was inevitable and described it as a "useless expense to Spain." Folch pleaded with Someruelos to do something for him, but he again asked for a transfer from Florida.[153]

Folch's proposal was exactly what the American government wanted. President Madison obtained from Congress an appropriation of $100,000 and the authority to use the armed services of the country to occupy both East and West Florida if they were delivered by the Spanish authorities, or to prevent the occupation of the territories by a third power. Two agents of the United States were sent to Pensacola to open negotiations with Folch, but by the time they arrived in March 1811, Folch's circumstances had changed. He had received some reinforcements and supplies in February. As a consequence, Folch withdrew his offer and determined to hold what was left of the Floridas for the Spanish crown.[154]

Someruelos now was angry with Folch. Not only did he reprimand Folch, he also reported him to their superiors in Madrid, accusing him of treason. Someruelos would not accept Folch's arguments that his offer to the Americans was a trick to gain time and that the weakness of his defenses and lack of manpower and supplies forced him to the decision. Despairing of his hopeless situation and determined to defend himself, Folch asked on April 3, 1811, to be relieved of his command. Little more than a month later, he transferred command of West Florida to his son-in-law, Maximiliano de St. Maxent, and sailed for Havana. That fall he busily prepared himself for his court martial, which took place in Spain. Folch did succeed in clearing himself of the charges of treason brought against him, but his reputation remained tarnished.

Folch returned to Cuba in November 1812 and was made second in command to the captain-general of Cuba. He held this position along with that of subinspector-general of the Army until he retired in 1822. In 1815, Folch was appointed by the king to the Royal and Military Order of San Hermanegildo. However, this honor carried no financial stipend. Perhaps because of his lifestyle, Folch's later years were filled with financial need. Part of his economic difficulties also stemmed from his unsuccessful attempts to obtain back salary due him and the pension he sought. After his death, a pension was granted to his wife.[155]

153. White, *Vicente Folch,* 103
154. McAlister, "Pensacola during the Second Spanish Period," 313.
155. White, *Vicente Folch,* 104–5, 109.

WILLIAM DONALDSON

William Donaldson (1773–November 27, 1813),[1] whose name was sometimes misspelled as Donelson, was described by Pierre Clément de Laussat,
the French prefect for the transfer of the Louisiana Purchase territory to the
United States, as being an American at the time Laussat appointed him to
the New Orleans *conseil de ville* (city council).[2] However, Governor Claiborne identified Donaldson as an Englishman by birth,[3] and a recent source
establishes that Donaldson was born in Scotland.[4]

Laussat further described Donaldson as a man "much-respected and

1. Aliens Reported by Secretary Dangerfield [August 25–September 1, 1812] listed William Donaldson's age as 39 years. Clarence E. Carter, comp. and ed., *The Territorial Papers
of the United States,* vol. 6, *The Territory of Mississippi, 1809–1817* (Washington, D.C.: U.S.
Government Printing Office, 1940), 309 (hereinafter cited as TP, 6 with page range). The 1812
aliens report also stated that Donaldson had "Applied to the prothonotary of Allegheny
County, Pena[.] to be naturalized in 1811." The date of Donaldson's death is provided by Sidney A. Marchand, *The Flight of a Century (1800–1900) in Ascension Parish, Louisiana* (Donaldsonville, La.: S. A. Marchand, 1936), 38.

2. Pierre Clément de Laussat, *Memoirs of My Life to My Son During the Years 1803 and
After . . . ,* trans. Sister Agnes-Josephine Pastwa, O.S.F., ed. Robert D. Bush (Baton Rouge:
Louisiana State University Press, 1978), 76.

3. Persons recommended by Governor Claiborne for members of the Legislative Council
of the Orleans Territory, enclosed in Joseph Briggs to the President, August 17, 1804, in Clarence E. Carter, comp. and ed., *The Territorial Papers of the United States,* vol. 9, *The Territory
of Orleans, 1803–1812* (Washington: U.S. Government Printing Office, 1940), 277 (hereinafter cited as TP, 9 with page range).

4. Glen Lee Greene, in *Masonry in Louisiana: A Sesquicentennial History, 1812–1962*
(New York: Exposition Press, 1962), 101, cites information from the records of the Perfect
Union Masonic Lodge, New Orleans, which reveals that Donaldson was born in Scotland.

much-loved."[5] Unfortunately, no information on the specific conduct that earned Donaldson the respect and love of his community has been found. Writing to Jefferson in August 1804, Claiborne said that Donaldson had been a merchant in New Orleans for "Several years," implying the Scotsman arrived in New Orleans in 1801.[6] The aliens report filed in 1812 by the Mississippi territorial secretary, Henry Dangerfield, stated that Donaldson had been in the United States for eight years.[7] Undoubtedly, Donaldson was appointed to the council because he spoke French fluently and, as Claiborne said of Donaldson, he was a merchant of "respectability and property."[8] The Mississippi aliens report also said that Donaldson traded "upon the [Mississippi] river between Pittsburgh and Natchez" and that he kept "a porter house at the last mentioned place."[9] Claiborne recommended Donaldson to Jefferson as a possible appointee to the territorial legislative council in 1804.[10]

Donaldson is best known in Louisiana history as the founder of Donaldsonville, the Louisiana town on the west bank of the Mississippi River below Baton Rouge that bears his name today. Donaldson acquired the property for the town site in February 1806 from the widow of Pierre A. Landry and commissioned Barthélémy Lafon soon thereafter to plat the town. Donaldson began advertising lots for sale in the town site in June 1806.[11] A village already on the site was known as "l'Ascension." In the early eighteenth century the site had been the location of a Chitimacha Indian village.[12] Donaldson apparently chose the site because of its location at the point where Bayou Lafourche, historically a distributary of the Mississippi when it is at flood stage, flows in a southwesterly direction away from the river.[13]

5. Laussat, *Memoirs of My Life,* 76.

6. Joseph Briggs to the President, August 17, 1804, TP, 9: 277.

7. Aliens Reported by Secretary Dangerfield [August 25–September 1, 1812], TP, 6: 309.

8. Claiborne characterized Donaldson's standing in the community and told of his command of French in Persons recommended by Governor Claiborne, TP, 9: 277.

9. Aliens Reported by Secretary Dangerfield [August 25–September 1, 1812], TP, 6: 309.

10. Ibid.

11. *Louisiana Gazette,* June 27, 1806, p. 3, c. 4. Other sales notices appeared in the *Moniteur,* October 22, 1806, p. 4, c. 4.

12. Sidney A. Marchand, Sr., "An Attempt to Re-Assemble the Old Settlers in Family Groups," *New Orleans Genesis* 3, no. 12 (September 1964), 358; and Sidney A. Marchand, *The Story of Ascension Parish, Louisiana* (Donaldsonville, La.: S. A. Marchand, 1931), 119.

13. See Philip D. Uzée, "Bayou Lafourche," in Edwin Adams Davis, ed., *The Rivers and Bayous of Louisiana* (Baton Rouge: Louisiana Education Research Association, 1968), 122, 124, 125 (map).

Before becoming involved with establishment of the town that would
bear his name, Donaldson spent much of his time in Ascension Parish at
Point Houmas, the property on the east bank of the Mississippi River being
developed with Edward D. Turner and others. At Point Houmas, Donaldson himself issued sales receipts in French.[14] In New Orleans, Donaldson
often was closely involved with shipping staples and building materials from
the port.[15] Successful pursuit of a variety of businesses prompted Donaldson's election to both the Louisiana Bank in New Orleans, on which he
served from 1805 through 1808, and the Louisiana Planter's Bank in Donaldsonville, on which he is known to have served in 1811.[16]

Donaldson's conscientious attention to his business responsibilities also
extended to his public obligations. Examination of the New Orleans city
council records reveal that although there seldom were enough members for
a quorum, Donaldson regularly attended the early meetings.[17] When election, rather than appointment, to the city council became law in 1805, Donaldson apparently did not stand for office, thereby ending his service on the
city council. However, the following year he sought election to the territorial house of representatives from Acadia, the Acadian Coast, present-day
St. James and Ascension parishes, above New Orleans, and won. During the
campaign for this office, Claiborne was a guest of the farmer, a man named
Barranger, who described Donaldson as the "perfect honest man."[18]

Donaldson, like many Americans with strong ties to the ancient Louisiana population, strongly supported Governor Claiborne in the Burr con-

14. Marchand, *Flight of a Century,* 19. In the long legal battle that developed over ownership of these New River lands, the claims of Donaldson and Scott were recommended for confirmation in 1809. See Henry W. Gautreau, Jr., *1830's Pre-Emption Entries on the Backlands
of New River, Louisiana, in Conflict with the Houmas Land Claim* ([Baton Rouge:] H. W.
Gautreau, 1995), 4, 6, 10–1.

15. For ship sailings associated with Donaldson's name, see notices in the *Louisiana Gazette,* April 26, 1805, p. 3, c. 4, and May 31, 1805, p. 3, c. 4.

16. Ordinance Providing for the Establishment of a Bank, March 12, 1804, in *Official
Letter Books of W. C. C. Claiborne, 1801–1816,* ed. Dunbar Rowland, vol. 2 (1917; New
York: AMS Press, 1972), 30; and Claiborne to the Secretary of State, January 13, 1804, TP,
9: 368. See also meeting and other bank notices in the *Louisiana Gazette,* January 11, and
December 10, 1805, pp. 3, cc. 4, respectively; January 7, 10, 1806, pp. 3, cc. 4 and 1, respec-
tively; January 6, 1807, p. 3, c. 2; and January 5, 1808, p. 3, c. 3, as well as B[arthélémy]
Lafon, *Annuaire Louisianais pour L'Année 1809* (New Orleans: By the Author, 1808), 201.

17. New Orleans Conseil de Ville: Proceedings of Council Meetings No. 1, book 1 (November 30, 1803–March 19, 1805). The minutes of the council meeting of February 8, 1804,
note the "absence of its members."

18. Governor Claiborne to the President, July 15, 1806, TP, 9: 674.

spiracy. His support was demonstrated in the house debate on whether to rescind or recommit the Memorial to Congress that was critical of both General Wilkinson and Governor Claiborne for their abuse of citizens' rights in the "reign of terror" in New Orleans during the several months from December 1806 into March 1807. The memorial had been suggested by John Watkins, Speaker, and drafted in committee after the legislature convened on January 12, 1807. Donaldson supported the initial motion by Colonel Alexander Fulton from Rapides and successful motion of John W. Gurley on the second day of debate to reject the memorial. Donaldson objected to the memorial being read because it was, he said, "fulsome to the ears of many in the house." When this move failed, Donaldson offered a motion to recommit it on the grounds that the memorial "was not confined to facts, and was vindictive."[19] Although this motion also was defeated, maneuvers outside of the house by Wilkinson and Claiborne with the support of Vicente Folch y Juan, the governor of Spanish West Florida, ultimately resulted in the defeat of the memorial sixty days after it had been introduced and approved.[20]

The parts played by Donaldson, John Gurley, and John Collins, representative from Opelousas, in the defeat of the memorial precipitated more harsh comments for the Claiborne administration and its supporters. Without naming anyone, John Watkins said that "before the discussion commenced, before the subject had been investigated, or even submitted to this committee," several house members had "actually pledged themselves to vote against it." Watkins went on to suggest there was a link between the decisions already made and discussions held "in the Coffee-House, or upon the banking table,"[21] this last reference possibly intended more for Donaldson than Gurley. On this point, Watkins's sharp barb went right to the heart of the matter when he asked, "how many persons are there in this busy city of ours, who do not stand now and then in need of assistance from the banks?"[22]

Among Donaldson's business enterprises was lumbering. In October 1807, he, with his business partner John Wren Scott (d. September 19,

19. *Debate in the House of Representatives of the Territory of Orleans on a Memorial to Congress, Respecting the Illegal Conduct of General Wilkinson* (New Orleans: Bradford & Anderson, 1807), 3, 9, 10.

20. Ibid., 29, 42.

21. Ibid., 37.

22. Ibid. Donaldson advertised lots for sale in his new town in the *Louisiana Gazette*, June 27, 1806, p. 3, c. 4, and the *Moniteur*, October 22, 1806, p. 4, c. 4.

1811), operated a steam-powered sawmill at Bayou Manchac.[23] The mill later was moved to Donaldson Town. Apparently it was the timber business that led Donaldson out of New Orleans and motivated him to found Donaldson Town, which became known as Donaldsonville soon after his death. Following his move to Ascension Parish in 1808, Donaldson began to urge that the territorial capital be located in his newly established town, even though it was not incorporated until March 25, 1813.[24] In an attempt to make the move attractive, Donaldson offered to donate the land on which the territorial capital would be built.[25] Despite his offer, it was not until the 1820s that the state government unsuccessfully attempted to locate outside of New Orleans in the town of Donaldsonville.[26]

William Donaldson's sense of public responsibility was inclusive. He was one of the seventeen founders of Christ Church, the first Protestant Episcopal church in Louisiana, in 1806.[27] Claiborne appointed him captain in the territorial militia on January 20, 1806.[28] It is possible that Donaldson was one of the large number of businessmen in New Orleans who would have supported a project to seize Mexico and other nearby Spanish colonial possessions. Support for this belief is drawn from Claiborne's statement in 1804 that Donaldson also was one of the men involved in land speculation in the Floridas.[29]

William Donaldson and James Lowrey Donaldson, who played a minor role in the Burr conspiracy, do not appear to have been related. James Lowrey Donaldson is variously referred to as James, James L., or Lowry Donaldson, but this Donaldson's surname was Lowrey. He changed it to Donaldson "for the reversion of an Estate."[30] Originally from the East

23. Announcement of the operation of the steam sawmill appeared in the *Louisiana Gazette,* October 23, 1807, p. 3, c. 4. See also Marchand, *Flight of a Century,* 22, 25, 28.

24. Marchand, *Flight of a Century,* 37.

25. Ibid., 24, 25, 37.

26. See the biographical sketch of Joseph Antoine Peytavin, pp. 585–6, for information on the later attempt to relocate the seat of government.

27. *Acts Passed at the Second Session of the Legislative Council of the Territory of Orleans, Begun and Held at the Principal, in the City of New Orleans, on Thursday the Twentieth Day of June, in the Year of Our Lord, One Thousand Eight Hundred and Five, and of the Independence of the United States the Twenty-Ninth* (New Orleans: James M. Bradford, 1805) 90; and also Georgia F. Taylor, "The Early History of the Episcopal Church in New Orleans, 1805–1840," *Louisiana Historical Quarterly* 22, no. 2 (April 1939), 433, 434–5.

28. Register of Appointments in the Militia of the Territory of Orleans, May 8, 1806, TP, 9: 632.

29. Governor Claiborne to the President, August 30, 1804, ibid., 284–5.

30. Ibid., 6: 115.

Coast, Lowrey Donaldson was one of the Louisiana Territory (Missouri) land commissioners appointed by General Wilkinson. He volunteered a deposition in support of Wilkinson's efforts to establish Burr as the leader of the parties in the states and territories of Ohio, Kentucky, Tennessee, Indiana, and Orleans who intended to dismember the union of states and establish an empire in Mexico.[31]

William Donaldson was survived only by his wife, Colgate Van Pradelles, daughter of Benedict F. Van Pradelles, land commissioner for the eastern district of the Orleans Territory.[32]

31. Thomas P. Abernethy, in *The Burr Conspiracy* (New York: Oxford University Press, 1954), 158, 175, tells of James Lowry [*sic*] Donaldson's written and oral reports to Wilkinson about stories he heard on his trip from Natchez to St. Louis during the nearly three months from October 15 to December 10, 1806. Most of James Lowrey Donaldson's information, according to his open court deposition, came from Wilkinson. The initial report was given to him in Natchez by a man identified only by the name of "Myers," who subsequently disappeared and could not be found. James L. Donaldson's deposition was given on January 26, 1807. It is reprinted in the *Louisiana Gazette,* March 20, 1807, p. 3, cc. 2 and 3, from the *National Intelligencer.* See also Royal Ornan Shreve, *The Finished Scoundrel. General James Wilkinson, Sometime Commander-in-Chief of the Army of the United States, Who Made Intrigue a Trade and Treason a Profession* (Indianapolis: Bobbs-Merrill, 1933), 174–5.

32. James Brown to the Secretary of the Treasury, October 30, 1805, and Benedict Van Pradelles to the Secretary of State, October 31, 1805 (TP, 9: 517 and 519, respectively), identify Van Pradelles's work and title for the U.S. government in the Orleans Territory.

ABRAHAM REDWOOD ELLERY

Abraham Redwood Ellery (May 22, 1773–November 1, 1820) was a native of Newport, Rhode Island.[1] He and his wife, the former Charlotte Weissenfels of New York, traveled from New York to Louisiana, arriving sometime in August 1803.[2] Ellery's initial purpose in going to Louisiana was to chart the Mississippi River for Alexander Hamilton. After arriving in New Orleans, Ellery moved up the Mississippi River to Deer Park, located on the west bank of the river in present-day Concordia Parish, Louisiana.[3] From there he began collecting and evaluating hydrographic information on the navigation of the river. In a letter to Hamilton (his former commander), El-

1. "Genealogy of the Redwood Family," *Genealogies of Rhode Island Families from Rhode Island Periodicals,* vol. 1 (Baltimore: Genealogical Publishing, 1983) 743. The date of death may be in error. The *Louisiana Gazette,* October 14, 1820, p. 2, c. 2, indicates that Abraham Ellery and one of his daughters, name not given, were among "a great number of people" who died as a result of a mysterious disease that struck the Bay St. Louis, Mississippi, community in the days before the report was received in New Orleans and published. Therefore, it appears that Ellery most probably died a few days before October 14, 1820. The same newspaper story reported that an urgent request arrived the day before the story appeared for two doctors to come immediately to the Mississippi Gulf Coast town.

2. Abraham R. Ellery to Alexander Hamilton, October 10, 1803, in *The Papers of Alexander Hamilton,* vol. 26, ed. Harold C. Syrett (New York: Columbia University Press, 1961–1987), 157 n. 1.

3. In his correspondence with Hamilton, Ellery consistently identifies Deer Park as being "near" the Mississippi Territory. See ibid., 157, and Ellery to Hamilton, January 7, 1804, ibid., 184. The location of Deer Park, about fifteen miles below Natchez on the west bank of the Mississippi, is provided in the *Directory of Louisiana Cities, Towns and Villages, 1971* (Baton Rouge: Louisiana Department of Public Works, 1971), 15.

lery stated that his objective was to reduce the information he assembled from various charts and studies to "one uniform scale." His goal was to place it "all in one large chart," which he hoped would be acceptable to Hamilton.[4]

Ellery's association with Hamilton began during his service as captain in the Sixteenth Regiment of Infantry in the Additional Army.[5] Ellery was appointed assistant adjutant general in May 1799 and ordered by the then adjutant general, William North, to communicate his acceptance to Alexander Hamilton.[6] George Washington was titular head of the army, but actual command of the Additional Army was in the hands of Hamilton.[7] Ellery's appointment made him first assistant to the adjutant general and de facto adjutant general in the absence of North.[8] In this capacity Ellery apparently worked very closely with Hamilton. More important, his work was well-regarded by North, who endorsed to Hamilton Ellery's request for a pay raise on December 12, 1799, saying, "You are better acquainted, Sir, than any one, [with] what Captn Ellery's duties have been, & . . . will be." North concluded his support for Ellery's request with the recommendation that "Ellerys [sic] extra pay should commence on the day he accepted the appointmt.[,] 26th May 1799, and that as his duty, so his emoluments should

4. Ellery to Hamilton, October 25, 1803, *Papers of Alexander Hamilton,* 27: 163. Hamilton's interest in the West beyond the Appalachians and in navigation of the Mississippi River is overshadowed by his accomplishments in establishing the nation and its economic credibility. However, as early as 1789, Hamilton was reliably reported to have said that the West must have the "right to navigate the Mississippi freely to the sea . . . *without it they will be lost to us*" (emphasis in the original). See the record of a "Conversation with George Beckwith," unofficial minister of Great Britain to the United States, New York, October 1789, in ibid., 7: 484. See also John C. Miller, *Alexander Hamilton, Portrait in Paradox* (New York: Harper & Brothers, 1959), 468.

5. The Additional Army, also known as the Provisional Army, was comprised of the ten thousand men who enlisted "for and during" the continuation of the undeclared war with France in 1799. Miller, *Alexander Hamilton,* 468. On Ellery's service, see Ellery to Hamilton, October 10, 1803, *Papers of Alexander Hamilton,* 27: 157 n. 1. Francis B. Heitman records that Ellery served approximately seventeen months in the Additional Army from January 8, 1799, to June 15, 1800. *Historical Register and Dictionary of the United States Army, from its Organization, December 29, 1789, to March 2, 1903* (1903; Urbana: University of Illinois Press, 1965), 401.

6. Ellery to Hamilton, May 14, 1799, *Papers of Alexander Hamilton,* 23: 118.

7. Miller, *Alexander Hamilton,* 476–7.

8. North's time apparently was greatly taken up with his additional duty as assistant inspector general. See William North to Alexander Hamilton, December 12, 1799, *Papers of Alexander Hamilton,* 24: 94.

be greater than those of an Aide de Camp and . . . those who are attached
to Majors, or Brigadiers General."[9]

The same date (October 25, 1803) that Ellery forwarded a completed
chart of the Mississippi River to Hamilton, he also notified Hamilton that
a number of other hydrographic charts were not complete because "Mr. E
who is my Hydrographer Genl. has been obliged to suspend his employment
in that line."[10] The departure of "Mr. E" apparently signaled the end of
Hamilton's hydrographic project for the Mississippi. On January 7, 1804,
Ellery advised Hamilton that he contemplated establishing himself in law in
New Orleans. He already had asked other friends in states along the Atlantic seaboard to write "letters of recommendation" in his behalf to Governor
Claiborne and now asked Hamilton to do the same.[11]

Ellery's decision to approach Claiborne for a position in the Orleans Territory is surprising in light of the opinions he expressed earlier to Hamilton
about Claiborne, who was then territorial governor of Mississippi. In October 1803, Ellery wrote Hamilton that it was "strongly conjectured" in the
Natchez area that Claiborne would be "appointed Governor of Louisiana,
or that part of it including New Orleans, either incorporated with this government, or as a distinct Territory." "These events," Ellery added, were
"contemplated with regret" because "neither his [Claiborne's] manners, dis-

9. North to Hamilton, December 12, 1799, ibid., 93–4. Abraham Ellery may have come
to the attention of Hamilton through his kinsman, William Ellery, collector of customs at Newport, Rhode Island. William Ellery was a veteran of the Revolutionary War, had been a member of the Continental Congress, and served as chief justice of the Rhode Island Supreme
Court. The friendly relations between Hamilton and William Ellery are suggested in their correspondence. See Hamilton to William Ellery, September 27, 1790, ibid., 7: 74. *Dictionary of
American Biography,* s.v. "Ellery, William," provides a useful sketch of his life.

10. Ellery to Hamilton, October 25, 1803, *Papers of Alexander Hamilton,* 26: 163. The
"Mr. E" referred to may have been either I. Elliot or J. B. Éliot. I. Elliot was the amateur hydrographer who discovered the Calcasieu River and the harbor site that became Lake Charles,
Louisiana. See James Pitot, *Observations on the Colony of Louisiana from 1796 to 1802,*
trans. Henry C. Pitot (Baton Rouge: Louisiana State University Press, 1979), 127. Further research suggests that the elusive "Mr. E" also could be the French cartographer J. B. Éliot whose
1783 map of the United States also included the West beyond the Mississippi River. He is believed to have been a liaison officer from the French army who served as an aide-de-camp to
George Washington during the American Revolution. See Walter W. Ristow, *American Maps
and Mapmakers: Commercial Cartography in the Nineteenth Century* (Detroit: Wayne State
University Press, 1985), 61–2. Whether J. B. Éliot is the James Elliott referenced in Jack D. L.
Holmes, "Joseph Piernas and a Proposed Settlement on the Calcasieu River, 1795," *McNeese
Review* 13 (1962), 65, is not known.

11. Ellery to Hamilton, January 7, 1804, *Papers of Alexander Hamilton,* 26: 184.

position, or talents qualify him for either of these situations; the simple circumstance of his ignorance of the French language & manners is no small
objection."[12]

Surviving correspondence indicates that Hamilton did not write Claiborne, but instead wrote General James Wilkinson in behalf of Ellery and
another American who settled in lower Louisiana early in the nineteenth
century, James Alexander. Wilkinson acknowledged receipt of Hamilton's
"Testimonials in favor" of Ellery and Alexander late in March 1804.[13] Ellery
apparently obtained a position in New Orleans before the year was out. By
early December 1804 he was serving as recorder in the territorial Superior
Court, perhaps under former New Yorker John B. Prevost, the only judge
on that court bench for months.[14] This may be where Ellery received his
legal training. In any event, the 1805 New Orleans city directory and census

12. Ellery to Hamilton, October 25, 1803, ibid., 165.

13. Wilkinson to Hamilton, New Orleans, March 26, 1804, ibid., 217. James Alexander
was the lawyer Wilkinson arrested at his home on December 19, 1806, and "conveyed through
the streets at noon-day under a strong escort of Dragoons . . . and committed to close confinement at head-quarters." Alexander was arrested because he, with the assistance of Edward
Livingston, was successful in obtaining a writ of habeas corpus from the Superior Court by
which he brought about the release of Samuel Swartout from his incarceration on a ship standing off the west bank of the Mississippi River at New Orleans. After his arrest, Alexander was
shipped to Baltimore with no money and only the clothing on his back. *Debate in the House
of Representatives of the Territory of Orleans on a Memorial to Congress, Respecting the Ille-
gal Conduct of General Wilkinson* (New Orleans: Bradford & Anderson Printers, 1807), 7;
Duplicate [Deposition of General James Wilkinson], December 26, 1807, in *Official Letter
Books of W. C. C. Claiborne, 1801–1816*, ed. Dunbar Rowland, vol. 4 (1917; New York:
AMS Press, 1972), 149, 153, 155 (hereinafter cited as CLB with volume and page numbers);
Walter F. McCaleb, *The Aaron Burr Conspiracy and A New Light on Aaron Burr* (1936;
New York: Argosy-Antiquarian, 1966), 184. Before Alexander's arrest, Wilkinson wrote
Claiborne a "confidential" note, saying that "Alexander must be taken up—indeed he
must—he said publicly at the Coffee House the other night, that if Br. [Burr] was a traitor I
was one also" (Confidential) [James Wilkinson To] Govr. Claiborne, December 16, 1806,
CLB, 4: 62. Almost two years later, Claiborne named Alexander, along with Dr. Eric Bollman,
former Judge James Workman, Lewis Kerr, and Auguste Davezac, as one of the "Society of
'Choice Spirits,' . . . distinguished for friendly dispositions towards the 'would be Emperor
[Burr].'" To James Madison (Private), March 17, 1808, CLB, 4: 167. François-Xavier Martin, in *The History of Louisiana, from the Earliest Period* ([1882; New Orleans: Pelican Publishing, 1963], 339–40), points out that Alexander was arrested at the time and date of Peter
Ogden's second arrest by Wilkinson. Alexander committed suicide on December 31, 1811,
for unknown reasons (*Louisiana Gazette,* January 2, 1812, p. 2, c. 3). The notice of Alexander's suicide characterized him as "a man of integrity, honour, and eminent professional talents." On the morning of his suicide, Alexander wrote a friend that he was "forced to commit
an act" that he condemned.

14. See Letter No. 69, From Robert [Abraham] R. Ellery, December 4, 1804.

lists his address as 27 Levee Street, the general area where most New Orleans lawyers had their offices at that time.[15] Sometime during the year
1805, Ellery was one of the twenty lawyers in New Orleans who signed a
petition to Congress requesting that the money appropriated for the salaries
of the two associate judges of the territorial Superior Court be paid to John
B. Prevost. The petitioners also asked that Prevost's annual salary, and the
salaries of other judges yet to be hired to preside on the territorial Superior
Court, be augmented by that amount annually thereafter.[16]

Ellery also participated in some of the community affairs in early New
Orleans while he actively pursued his career as a lawyer. In 1805 he was
identified as one of the seventeen founders of Christ Church, the first Protestant Episcopal Church established in New Orleans.[17] Following the organization of the church, he was elected a member of the vestry and served it
as minute clerk in 1805–06.[18] Thirteen years later, on February 5, 1818,
Ellery also was identified as one of the many founders of the Presbyterian
Church in New Orleans.[19]

Information on Ellery's activities is limited, but it seems clear that few

15. *New Orleans in 1805: A Directory and a Census, Together with Resolutions Authoriz-
ing Same, Now Printed for the First Time from the Original Manuscript,* ed. Charles L.
Thompson (New Orleans: Pelican Gallery, 1936), 22. The "'Premier Directory' de la Nouvelle
Orleans, 1807," in *Le Diamant* 1, no. 14 (May 1887), 45, lists Ellery as a lawyer. Four years
later Ellery is listed as *avocat* (lawyer) at 34 Douane, Custom House. Thomas H. Whitney,
Whitney's New-Orleans Directory and Louisiana & Mississippi Almanac for the Year 1811
(New Orleans: By the Author, 1810), 21.

16. Among the other lawyers listed as signers of the petition are Edward Livingston, Lewis
Kerr, James Alexander, James Brown, Pierre Derbigny, and Moreau Lislet. The petition is not
dated other than the endorsement date provided by the U.S. House of Representatives, December 31, 1805. See Petition to Congress by Lawyers of the Territory, no date, enclosed in James
Brown to Samuel Smith, November 28, 1805, in Clarence E. Carter, comp. and ed., *The Territorial Papers of the United States,* vol. 9, *The Territory of Orleans, 1803–1812* (Washington,
D.C.: U.S. Government Printing Office, 1940), 539–40.

17. *Acts Passed at the Second Session of the Legislative Council of the Territory of Orleans, Begun and Held at the Principal, in the City of New Orleans, on Thursday the Twentieth
Day of June, in the Year of Our Lord, One Thousand Eight Hundred and Five, and of the
Independence of the United States the Twenty-Ninth* (New Orleans: James M. Bradford,
1805), 90.

18. Georgia Fairbanks Taylor, "The Early History of the Episcopal Church in New Or-
leans, 1805–1840," *Louisiana Historical Quarterly* 22, no. 2 (April 1939), 439; and Philander
Chase, *Bishop Chase's Reminiscences: An Autobiography,* 2nd ed., vol. 1 (Boston: James B.
Dow, 1848), 58, 61.

19. Louis Moreau Lislet, comp., *A General Digest of the Acts of the Legislature of Louisiana: Passed from the Year 1804, to 1827, Inclusive, and in Force at the Last Period with an
Appendix and General Index,* vol. 1 (New Orleans: B. Levy, 1828), 164.

of them were supportive of the Jefferson administration or William C. C. Claiborne. For example, during the Burr conspiracy Ellery was a strong supporter of Aaron Burr and an outspoken opponent of General Wilkinson. Ellery has been described as one of the most vociferous in his opposition to the arrests of the men accused by Wilkinson of being Burr conspirators.[20] His critical approach to Claiborne's administration did not end with the squelching of the Mexican Association and Burr. In the fall of 1808, Ellery objected to the governor's naming of the public prosecutor. Ellery objected not to the person named, Benjamin Porter, but to the "right of nomination." That right, Ellery maintained, lay only within the authority of the territorial attorney general. The Orleans Parish Court upheld Ellery's contention, saying that the right to appoint the public prosecutor did not reside in the authority of the governor, but only with the office of the attorney general.[21] Several years later Ellery proved once more that he could be a stickler for the details of the law. In June 1811 one of the justices of the peace in Biloxi complained to the governor that Ellery demanded payment of a fifty-dollar fee from him if he wanted to continue serving as justice.[22] Claiborne asked acting Attorney General John Grymes to hear the poor man's "story thro' an Interpreter and advice [*sic*] him for the best." The governor acknowledged that what had been done was "not strictly Legal, [but] appears nonetheless to have been very just." Claiborne then added, "I often see instances of these poor people, being oppressed under Colour of Law, & Sincerely do I regret, that it is not in my power to furnish a Corrective." Claiborne concluded that it would "be well to gratify Mr. Ellery" and pay the fifty-dollar fee even though he strongly felt the charge was "indeed a heavy Tax on an honest act."[23]

Ellery also was a participant in the early legal maneuvering that led up to the protracted and bitter battle that ultimately established the paternity of Myra Clark Gaines. In the June 30, 1806, case named by Ellery *Zulime*

20. Thomas P. Abernethy, *The Burr Conspiracy* (New York: Oxford University Press, 1954), 182.

21. To William Thomson, Esqr., November 5, 1808, CLB, 4: 240.

22. This was the parish of Biloxi created within Feliciana County on January 4, 1811. Louisiana Historical Records Survey, *County-Parish Boundaries in Louisiana* (New Orleans: Department of Archives, Louisiana State University, 1939), 23 (entry 64). Feliciana County, created December 7, 1810, included the land lying below the boundary line of the Mississippi Territory from the Mississippi River on the west to the Perdido River on the east. Ibid., 23 (entry 62). Therefore, this was Biloxi, on the present-day Mississippi Gulf Coast.

23. To John Grymes, June 6, 1811, CLB, 5: 263–4.

Carriere v. *Jerome Desgrange,* he served as the "curator of Desgrange." Ellery accomplished several objectives with the case: he admitted nothing and
denied nothing for his client, while preserving the corpus of any estate Desgrange may have possessed, thereby enabling Zulime "to obtain a decree
annulling a void marriage which had never legally existed."[24] Ellery's pleas
"reveal by their very words that he was an able lawyer and alert to discover
every available defense."[25]

When the Supreme Court of the new state of Louisiana met for the first
time on March 2, 1813, Abraham Ellery was one of the seven lawyers present who pledged to discharge his duties as a councilor to the best of his
knowledge and ability. Administration of the oath to Ellery and the six other
men present marked the founding of the Louisiana Bar Association.[26]

24. Perry Scott Rader, "The Romance of American Courts: Gaines vs. New Orleans,"
Louisiana Historical Quarterly 27, no. 1 (January 1944), 107–9.

25. Ibid., 109.

26. The others present were Edward Livingston; his brother-in-law, Auguste Davezac;
François-Xavier Martin; George Prevost, one of the sons of John B. Prevost, the first territorial
Superior Court judge; John Randolph Grymes; and William Depeyster. Elizabeth Gaspard,
"The Rise of the Louisiana Bar: The Early Period, 1813–1839," *Louisiana History* 28, no. 2
(spring 1987), 183.

MAJOR RICHARD D. CLAIBORNE

The kinship of Major Richard Claiborne[1] (1757–1818) and Governor William C. C. Claiborne was characterized by the governor as "so remote that neither [of us] can trace it."[2] Why the governor said this is not clear. Perhaps he did not really know his cousin, who was eighteen years old when the future governor was born in 1775. It is more likely the governor said it to avoid embarrassment at seeking political preference for a relative who appears to have suffered straitened financial circumstances most of his adult life. A stronger reason may have been the major's embarrassing political views. About them, Governor Claiborne said only that Richard Claiborne "professes to be a Republican."[3]

The family of Claiborne descendants in eighteenth- and early-nineteenth-century Virginia was large but well known. For this reason, it is difficult to believe Governor Claiborne was not aware he and Major Claiborne were cousins. It also is difficult to believe because the fathers of Governor Clai-

1. Major Claiborne signed his name with the middle initial *D* shortly after beginning his military service during the American Revolution, but the initial has not been found with his name in other papers examined for writing this sketch. See "Letter of R. D. Claiborne, Deputy Quarter Master General at Estherton, Pennsylvania [now Coxtowne] to General Edward Hand, May 19, 1779," *Pennsylvania Magazine of History and Biography* 52 (1928): 174–5.

2. To James Monroe, August 1, 1813, in *Official Letter Books of W. C. C. Claiborne, 1801–1816*, ed. Dunbar Rowland, vol. 6 (1917; New York: AMS Press, 1972), 251 (hereinafter cited as CLB, with volume and page range). The *Index to the James Monroe Papers* (Washington, D.C.: U.S. Government Printing Office, 1963), does not list this letter among those in the Monroe Papers.

3. To Col. F. L. Claiborne (Private), September 11, 1808, CLB 4: 216.

borne and Major Claiborne were siblings. They were two of the seven sons of Thomas (1680–1732) and Anne Fox (1684–1733) Claiborne.

Richard was one of the fourteen children of Colonel Augustine (1721–May 3, 1787) and Mary Herbert Claiborne. Augustine Claiborne was a prominent figure in eighteenth-century Virginia. He served in the Virginia House of Burgesses and senate, and was prominent as a lawyer in Surry County with a large practice that extended into several counties. His wife, Mary Herbert, inherited a large landed estate with two hundred slaves and a block of houses in London, which reportedly sold for eighty thousand pounds sterling.[4]

William Charles Cole Claiborne was the son of the less prosperous and not as well-known William Claiborne (d. September 29, 1809). His mother was Mary Leigh. William and Mary Leigh Claiborne were the parents of four sons and one daughter.[5]

In addition to his ancestral connection to the Claibornes of Virginia, Richard Claiborne may have been a cousin of the governor's sister-in-law, Magdalene Hutchens. Magdalene was the wife of the governor's oldest brother, Ferdinand Leigh Claiborne, who lived at Natchez.[6]

Richard was well known before the American Revolution, having been elected to the Virginia House of Delegates to represent Brunswick County from 1775–1778 .[7] He gained the rank of major at the beginning of the American Revolution, serving as deputy quartermaster for Virginia in the Continental Army.[8] After the war Major Claiborne was employed in recon-

4. *Genealogies of Virginia Families from the Virginia Magazine of History and Biography,* vol. 2, *Claiborne-Fitzhugh* (Baltimore: Genealogical Publishing, 1981), 8 (entry 23).

5. Ibid., 9 (entry 32); and Dorothy Ford Wulfeck, *Marriages of Some Virginia Residents, 1607–1800,* vol. 1, *Surnames C-E* (Baltimore: Genealogical Publishing, 1986), 83.

6. Richard Claiborne to F. L. Claiborne, January 25, 1806, in Mrs. W. R. Buffington Papers, Southern Historical Collection, Wilson Library, University of North Carolina, Chapel Hill. The major's letter did not identify how they may have been related. He simply referred to Magdalene as "cousin." Magdalene was the daughter of Colonel Thomas Hutchens of Mississippi.

7. W. G. Stanard, "Abstracts of Virginia Land Patents," *Virginia Magazine of History and Biography* 1, no. 2 (October 1893), 323.

8. To James Monroe, August 1, 1813, CLB 6: 251; and John H. Gwathmey, *Historical Register of Virginians in the Revolution. Soldiers, Sailors, Marines, 1775–1783* (1938; Baltimore: Genealogical Publishing, 1987), 152. Major Claiborne's military record included service at Valley Forge and a campaign against the Indians in the Wyoming Valley of Pennsylvania under General John Sullivan in the spring of 1779. "Letter of R. D. Claiborne, May 19, 1779," 174–5. The quartermaster for Virginia, and Major Claiborne's superior, was Colonel Timothy Pickering.

ciling accounts with the assistant deputy quartermasters throughout Virginia. The major called on all assistants in 1783 to make "immediate returns . . . of all stores, horses, and other articles of public property issued" to officers of the Virginia line.[9]

The major's residence for the dozen years after 1783 is not known. It is possible that during this time he married his first wife, a Miss Heyward of South Carolina, and fathered his first son, James Heyward Claiborne.[10] The silence of the records on this marriage and the subsequent movement of Richard from the Atlantic coast to the old Southwest suggest a man searching for a new life while recovering from the loss of his wife, perhaps in the birth of their son.

A glimpse of Richard's movements is caught in 1794–95, when he served as secretary of the Columbianum Society in Philadelphia. This society attempted to establish "an association for the encouragement of the arts." Among those associated with this effort was the American artist Charles Wilson Peale, who had served under Washington during the American Revolution. The society ceased to exist in little over a year because some of the members advocated that students be allowed to draw from living models.[11]

Richard is next caught sight of in the District of Columbia in 1803. In July of that year he was identified by Robert Mills, then the twenty-year-old assistant to White House architect Benjamin Henry Latrobe, as being in Georgetown. Latrobe introduced Mills to the major on July 1. The following evening young Mills was on his way to dine with Secretary of State James Madison when he met Major Claiborne again. During this brief social exchange, the major informed Mills that the "'Floridas and Louisiana'" had been ceded to the United States by France.[12]

9. "Local Notices from the Virginia Gazette, Richmond, 1783," *Virginia Genealogist* 28, no. 3, whole number 111 (July–September 1984), 190.

10. *Genealogies of Virginia Families*, 2: 11 (entry 42). James apparently was reared in South Carolina by members of the Heyward family. He married Ann Kershaw of Charleston on December 20, 1822, but died without issue. Elizabeth Heyward Jervey, "Marriage and Death Notices from the City Gazette of Charleston, S.C.," *South Carolina Historical and Genealogical Magazine* 50, no. 2 (April 1949), 75, printed the notice of their marriage.

No public record of the marriage of Richard Claiborne to Miss Heyward has been found. Although a few counties compiled marriage records, South Carolina did not require public registration of marriages until early in the twentieth century. The established Church of England was expected to maintain such records. See Brent Howard Holcomb, *A Guide to South Carolina Genealogical Research and Records,* 3rd ed. (Columbia, S.C.: By the Author, 1998), 23.

11. "Notes," *Pennsylvania Magazine of History and Biography* 1, no. 2 (1877), 223.

12. Hennig Cohen, ed., "An Unpublished Diary by Robert Mills, 1803," *South Carolina Historical and Genealogical Magazine* 51, no. 4 (October 1950), 188.

The following year, 1804, Richard was in the Mississippi Territory serving as postmaster in the little town of Washington, which had been established by Governor Claiborne to be the territorial capital of Mississippi. The major appears to have served in this position for about a year. Before leaving it in April, he was asked by Postmaster General Gideon Granger to name his successor.[13] The major moved on to serve as clerk to the Board of Land Commissioners in Mississippi Territory in 1805.

It is possible the major may have obtained the positions as both postmaster and clerk to the land commission with the support of his cousin, William C. C. Claiborne, who had been appointed governor of Mississippi Territory by President Thomas Jefferson in 1801. Richard's service with the Board of Land Commissioners was described as "perfectly satisfactory."[14] The major's social circle in the Mississippi Territory appears to have been large. In March and April 1805 he joined others, including Governor Claiborne's wife, Eliza, in welcoming and entertaining Revolutionary War general George Matthews to Natchez.[15]

Evidence suggests that Major Claiborne's arrival in Louisiana coincided with his appointment as private secretary to Governor Claiborne in the spring of 1806. He held this office until October 17, 1807, when he was appointed clerk of the Superior Court for the First District of Orleans Territory.[16] During his year and a half as private secretary, Richard also evidently was preparing to become a lawyer. The appointment as clerk in the superior court seems to have completed his apprenticeship in law, which apparently began under Governor Claiborne. The major's service as clerk of the superior court in New Orleans was followed by his appointment as judge of Rapides Parish.[17]

Despite appearances, it is clear Governor Claiborne hired his kinsman

13. The Secretary of the Treasury to Richard Claiborne, January 18, 1804, and October 16, 1804, in Clarence E. Carter, comp. and ed., *The Territorial Papers of the United States*, vol. 5, *The Territory of Mississippi, 1798–1817* (Washington, D.C.: U.S. Government Printing Office, 1940), 314.

14. Ibid., 300–1, 341, respectively.

15. "Brevet Brigadier General George Mathews," *Pennsylvania Magazine of History and Biography* 44, no. 4 (1920), 343–4.

16. Civil Appointments, 1807, October 17, 1807, Richard Claiborne—Superior Court, for 1st District, CLB, 4: 146.

17. Civil Appointments, 1807, Clerks, October 17, ibid.; and Richard Claiborne to John Graham, November 10, 1811, in Clarence E. Carter, comp. and ed., *The Territorial Papers of the United States*, vol. 9, *The Territory of Orleans* (Washington, D.C.: U.S. Government Printing Office, 1940), 953 (hereinafter cited as TP, 9, with page range).

Richard Claiborne as private secretary because of his trustworthiness and honesty, not because of their family connections or Richard's political views. Regarding his work, the governor wrote the major in July 1806 from Attakapas saying: "I have abundant reason to be satisfied with your attention to the Duties of your office, and I pray you to be assured of my encreased [*sic*] confidence in your fidelity."[18] Richard apparently solicited the governor's opinion because of a complaint about fees charged by the governor's office for use of the public seal placed on documents emanating from the office.[19]

Governor Claiborne probably suffered the major's Federalist opinions mostly in silence, but those opinions evidently became well known during Richard's first term as judge in Rapides Parish. There the major came into conflict with Alexander Fulton, one of the founders of Alexandria, Louisiana, and a member of the territorial legislature. Richard Claiborne described Fulton as a fugitive rebel from the Whiskey Rebellion suppressed by Washington and Hamilton in Washington, Pennsylvania, in 1794.[20] Local political differences with Fulton and others in Rapides Parish who were inclined to Jeffersonian Republicanism led to Judge Claiborne's investigation by a local grand jury for "'oppression, extortion, & altering and mutilating records[']" in 1808.[21] Ultimately the major was cleared of any wrongdoing, but not before he was made to feel politically very uncomfortable in the parish.[22]

The major sought appointment as civil judge in neighboring Concordia Parish while waiting for the charges against him in Rapides Parish to be resolved. However, the governor advised against relocation and refused to appoint Richard to the judgeship in Concordia. The governor told Richard he would not be received with all the confidence he would be "entitled to" until the grand jury charges were resolved.[23] In a private letter to his brother Colonel Ferdinand Claiborne in Natchez, the governor said he would not send anyone to Concordia Parish "who in any manner would interfere in the elections, of the M[ississippi] Territory and particularly one who would do

18. To R. Claiborne, July 30, 1806, CLB, 3: 375.

19. See the governor's instructions to the major on how the charges for use of the seal were to be made. To R. Claiborne, May 31 and July 9, 1806, ibid., 322–3 and 358, respectively.

20. Richard Claiborne to John Graham, November 10, 1811, TP, 9: 953.

21. Ibid., 954.

22. Ibid.; and (Private) [To] Judge Claiborne, November 8, 1808, CLB, 4: 246–7.

23. (Private) [To] Judge Claiborne, November 8, 1808, ibid., 247.

so, in order to advance the cause of federalism."[24] As a consequence, Richard was reappointed as judge in Rapides Parish in 1811.[25]

Governor Claiborne sought appointment for Richard as U.S. marshal in Mobile from Secretary of State James Monroe in 1813. The major then was living in New Orleans. In the letter to Monroe, Governor Claiborne described the major as "now poor, dependent [sic] and in the vale of life;—But in the enjoyment of great activity of mind & body & fully competent."[26] Richard then was approximately fifty-six years old. The governor recommended his kinsman, saying, "I speak of him with no bias, but that which a knowledge of his integrity[,] his former faithful services, & his present dependent situation *has* excited." For unknown reasons, the major did not receive the appointment as a U.S. marshal.

Richard settled in New Orleans in 1812 and began practicing law after serving as judge in Rapides Parish. In the remaining years of his life, he apparently devoted his free time to refining the "hinge or duckfoot paddle" for use in propelling steamboats on the Mississippi River and its tributaries. In March 1818 the Louisiana legislature passed an act granting him the exclusive right to use his "collapsing paddle" within the limits of the state.[27]

Three letters written by Major Claiborne to William Miller of Rapides Parish during the years 1816–1818 provide insight into the major's activities shortly before his death. In one of the letters the major refers to a son. Other sources reveal the son was named Guilford Greene Claiborne. He was born to the major and his second wife, Catherine Ross, in 1812.[28] In the same October letter to Miller, the major displayed even more rigid adherence to Federalist beliefs than was apparent in his earlier life. Commenting

24. To Col. F. L. Claiborne, September 11, 1808, ibid., 216–7.

25. To Judge Claiborne, November 15, 1811, ibid., 5: 381–2.

26. To James Monroe, August 1, 1813, ibid., 6: 251.

27. Walter Pritchard, ed., "Three Letters of Richard Claiborne to William Miller, 1816–1818," *Louisiana Historical Quarterly* 16, no. 2 (April 1933), 732–3, 741.

28. Orleans Parish, Louisiana. Court of Probate, Succession and Probate Records, 1818–1819, vol. 3, 1819, Petition of Catherine T. Claiborne, widow of Richard Claiborne, May 19, 1819 (hereinafter cited as Petition of Catherine T. Claiborne). Richard Claiborne married the "amiable Miss Catherine Ross" on March 5, 1807. Elizabeth Heyward Jervey, "Marriage and Death Notices from the City-Gazett [sic] and Daily Advertiser," *South Carolina Historical and Genealogical Magazine* 30, no. 4 (October 1929), 252. See also "Newspaper Notices, Louisiana Gazette (New Orleans)," *Louisiana Genealogical Register* 5, no. 6 (December 1958), 42. The marriage notice published in this source indicates that all the Ross family were then living in New Orleans. The notice stated that Catherine was the daughter of General James Ross of New Orleans.

on the social and economic decline that he felt was evident in the nation after the War of 1812, the major wondered if it would be better "to instill into my son the doctrine of leggimacy [legitimacy]."[29] Legitimacy was the principle of dynastic succession introduced at the Congress of Vienna, 1814–15.[30]

Major Claiborne most probably died in 1818.[31] No notice of his death has been found, so it is not known whether his death was the result of a debilitating disease associated with the subtropical climate of New Orleans or some other cause.[32] There were cases of yellow fever in New Orleans in the summer of 1818, but those that occurred in the following year, 1819, were severe.[33] The major was survived by his older son in South Carolina, James Heyward Claiborne, his second wife Catherine, and their children Guilford Greene and Henrietta Elizabeth Claiborne (b. 1809).[34]

29. Pritchard, "Three Letters," 740.

30. See Jared W. Bradley, "Legitimacy," in *Handbook of World History*, ed. Joseph Dunner (New York: Philosophical Library, 1967), 513.

31. The Petition of Catherine T. Claiborne states only that her husband "hath died lately."

32. A death certificate for Richard Claiborne apparently never was filed, or if filed did not survive among the records of early nineteenth-century New Orleans. Orleans Parish, Louisiana, *Orleans Deaths Indices—Vital Records, 1804–1876*, reel ODI.001. State Archives and Records Service of Louisiana, Baton Rouge.

33. Jo Ann Carrigan, *The Saffron Scourge: A History of Yellow Fever in Louisiana, 1796–1905* (Lafayette: Center for Louisiana Studies, University of Southwestern Louisiana, 1994), 38.

34. The Petition of Catherine T. Claiborne identifies only her children from the marriage with Richard Claiborne.

EUGENE DORSIÈRE

Eugene Joris Dorsière (1761–December 17 or 18, 1809; sometimes spelled with a *c*, Dorcière, and occasionally Dorsier) was born in Valois, Switzerland, the son of Étienne Antoine Jorris [*sic*] Dorsière and Marie Josepha Joris. Like his father, Eugene had been an officer in the service of the King of Sardinia.[1]

Claiborne wrote Jefferson that Dorsière settled in Louisiana after service "with Reputation during the American War."[2] Before coming to Louisiana, Dorsière lived in Philadelphia, where he had been a dancing master, and in Illinois.[3] In the St. Louis Parish of Illinois, Dorsière met and married Marie Anne Nicolle, daughter of Étienne Nicolle and Angélique Gérard.[4] In New Orleans, Dorsière was a *liquoriste;* that is, he owned and operated a wholesale and retail liquor store located on the corner of South Levee (present Decatur) and Custom House (present Iberville) Streets.[5] Claiborne described

1. Joris Dorsière Will, Orleans Parish, Louisiana. Court of Probate, Record of Wills, Will Book, 1805–1817, vol. 1, 285; and Saint Louis Cathedral Funeral Register, 1803–1815, Act 511, 103b.

2. Governor Claiborne to the President, December 2, 1804, in Clarence E. Carter, comp. and ed., *The Territorial Papers of the United States,* vol. 9, *The Territory of Orleans, 1803–1812* (Washington, D.C.: U.S. Government Printing Office, 1940), 345 (hereinafter cited as TP, with volume and page range).

3. Characterization of New Orleans Residents, enclosed in James Wilkinson to the President, July 1, 1804, ibid., 255.

4. Marie Anne Nicolle Dorsière Will, Orleans Parish, Louisiana. Court of Probate, Record of Wills, Will Book, 1805–1832, vol. 4, 114–5.

5. *Louisiana Gazette,* May 1, 1807, p. 3, c. 4.

the business as a "handsome little property." It appears to have been a local landmark not only because of the nature of Dorsière's business in an age when New Orleanians mostly drank wine, but also because of its location near the juncture of the proposed Orleans Navigation Company canal with the Mississippi River.[6]

Dorsière was described by a contemporary, probably Daniel Clark, as "greatly overated [*sic*] . . . [and] destitute of influence," but the description does not accord with the facts.[7] Before his association with Claiborne, there is evidence that Dorsière was close to Daniel Clark. When Clark married Zulime Carrière Desgrange in Philadelphia in 1802, Dorsière stood as witness for Clark in the secret nuptial.[8]

Claiborne, like most of those acquainted with Dorsière, regarded him as a man of integrity and standing in the territory.[9] The governor praised the former Sardinian Army officer to President Jefferson as having "imbibed [his] principles of liberty . . . in his cradle." In short, Dorsière, like most of the men close to Claiborne in territorial Louisiana, was a Republican. Equally important, Claiborne saw Dorsière as "well informed[,] mild & energetick," and "possess'd with [a] sound & deliberate mind full of intergrity [*sic*]." Also quite important in Claiborne's opinion of Dorsière was that he was the "friend of Order & much attached to the welfare" of the Orleans Territory. Claiborne additionally described Dorsière as a man of "Upright & virtuous Morals."[10]

Evidence of Claiborne's reliance on Dorsière manifested itself early in the interim government period. The first post to which Claiborne appointed Dorsière was the territorial council in August 1804.[11] The governor next appointed Dorsière commander of the Orleans Volunteers. Dorsière apparently accepted the duties of this office about the time that Claiborne, in his efforts to avoid problems with Daniel Clark, called on the former Swiss citizen to organize the territorial militia in accordance with President Jeffer-

6. Governor Claiborne to the President, December 2, 1804, TP, 9: 345.

7. Characterization of New Orleans Residents, enclosed in James Wilkinson to the President, July 1, 1804, ibid., 255.

8. *Cases Argued and Adjudged in the Supreme Court of the United States, December Term, 1867*, reported by John William Wallace, vol. 6 (Washington: W. H. & O. H. Morrison, 1870), *Gaines v. New Orleans*, 682.

9. Characterization of New Orleans Residents, enclosed in James Wilkinson to the President, July 1, 1804, TP, 9: 249, 252.

10. Ibid., 252.

11. Letter No. 168, To James Madison, March 16, 1805.

son's instructions.[12] About this same time, Claiborne also named Dorsière judge on the Court of Common Pleas, the court created by the governor on December 30, 1803, as part of the interim government.[13] Dorsière remained as commander of the Orleans Volunteers until the summer of 1805 (August 11), when he was named commander of the Second Regiment of the reorganized territorial militia.[14] In the spring of 1805 (April 10), Dorsière also was appointed port warden.[15]

Further evidence of Claiborne's confidence in Dorsière is seen in his temporary appointment as commander of the First Regiment during the illness of Bellechasse in December 1806 and in the initial stages of the crisis precipitated by the Burr conspiracy. By this action, Dorsière became commander of the First Brigade of the territorial militia and, briefly, de facto commander of the militia.[16] Perhaps the two strongest indicators of Claiborne's trust in Dorsière are his election to the territorial House of Representatives in the wake of the Burr conspiracy in 1807 and his nomination as Speaker of the House on January 12, 1808. Dorsière was not elected Speaker, but his showing was creditable. Of the sixteen votes cast for the four nominees, Thomas Urquhart received seven, Dorsière four, Chevalier Lacroix three, and Joseph Villars two.[17] Moreover, the newspaper reports of the time reflect that Dorsière took an active part in the affairs of the house of representatives during his term.[18]

12. Governor Claiborne to the President, December 2, 1804, TP, 9: 345; and To Maj. Dorsier [*sic*], March 30, 1804, in *Official Letter Books of W. C. C. Claiborne, 1801–1816*, ed. Dunbar Rowland, vol. 2 (1917; New York: AMS Press, 1972) 71 (hereinafter cited as CLB, with volume and page range).

13. Characterization of New Orleans Residents, enclosed in James Wilkinson to the President, July 1, 1804; and A Register of Civil Appointments, June 30, 1805, Justices of the Peace (TP, 9: 254, 750, respectively). On establishment of the Court of Common Pleas, see To James Madison, January 2, 1804, and January 10, 1804, CLB, 1: 324–5, 329, respectively. The original ordinance from the State Department Territorial Papers is cited in Marietta M. LeBreton, *A History of the Territory of Orleans, 1803–1812* (Ann Arbor, Mich.: University Microfilms, 1973), 49 n. 61.

14. Register of Appointments in the Militia of the Territory of Orleans, Secretary John Graham to the Secretary of State, May 8, 1806 (TP, 9: 633), reflects that Dorsière was commissioned August 11, 1805.

15. Register of Civil Appointments in the Territory of Orleans, February 12, 1806, Wardens of the Port, ibid., 602; and *Louisiana Gazette*, August 2, 1805, p. 3, c. 4.

16. General Orders, December 24, 1806, and January 8, 1807, TP, 9: 713 and 716, respectively.

17. *Moniteur de la Louisiane*, January 13, 1808, p. 2, c. 3.

18. Ibid., February 24, 1808, p. 1, cc. 2–4; February 27, 1808, pp. 1–2, cc. 2–4; and March 9, 1808, pp. 1–2, cc. 1, 2–4.

Finally, the extant evidence suggests a closeness among Dorsière, Julien Poydras, and Claiborne that has largely gone unnoticed. Their closeness is implicit in the fact that Dorsière represented the Pointe Coupée district on the 1808–09 legislative council.[19] No evidence has been found that Dorsière ever lived in Pointe Coupée, but he apparently acquired property there sometime in the 1790s.[20]

After Dorsière's death, the street that led to his business-residence address retained his name, as it does today, apparently without official sanction by the city council.[21] Dorsière was survived by his wife, a brother named François, and his mother. The latter two lived in Switzerland.[22] The wills of both Eugene Dorsière and his wife state there were no children from their marriage. The funeral record of Dorsière gives his wife's name as Marie Anne Nicolle Les Bois to distinguish her from her sister, also named Marie, who lived with the Dorsières.[23] Marie Anne Nicolle Dorsière died in October 1826, by which time her husband's name was fixed on the street that bears it today.[24]

19. B[arthélémy]. Lafon, *Annuaire Louisianais pour L'Année 1809* (New Orleans: By the Author, 1808), 163.

20. LaVerne Thomas III, *Ledoux, A Pioneer Franco-American Family, with Detailed Sketches of Allied Families,* 1st ed. (New Orleans: Polyanthos, 1982), 89.

21. A search of New Orleans Conseil de Ville: Official Proceedings, No. 2, book 2 (January 14, 1809–December 26, 1810) and book 3 (January 12, 1811–November 7, 1812) City Archives, Louisiana Department, New Orleans Public Library established that in these years the city council never formally adopted Dorsière's name for the street that bears it today. The only references to the Dorsière property in these years occur on pp. 173, 174–5, and 177 of the first council minute book cited here. A cursory search of the council minute books into the year 1822 brought to light no information on when Dorsière Street may have been officially named. James S. Zacharie ("New Orleans—Its Old Streets and Places," *Publications of the Louisiana Historical Society* 2, Part 3 [February 1900], 70), states only that "Dorsière street, a small street near the Customhouse, [was] called after the Dorsière family who lived on that street in the 20's [sic]." Evidence of the general acceptance of the Dorsière name for the street where the former soldier lived and operated his business is suggested in an advertisement in the *Courier,* November 10, 1826, p. 3, c. 3.

22. Joris Dorsière Will, 285–6.

23. Saint Louis Cathedral Funeral Registers, 1803–1815, Act 511, 103b.

24. Marie Anne Nicolle Dorsière Will, 114–5.

WILLIAM FLOOD

William Flood (1775 ?–April 21, 1823) was one of five native-born American physicians living in New Orleans when the United States acquired Louisiana in 1803.[1] Born in Virginia, Flood settled in New Orleans in 1799 or 1800 and apparently began to practice medicine without a license. In response to a notice from the cabildo that this was illegal, the doctor presented himself in 1801 to be tested by a five-man commission, three of whom were doctors. Presumably, Flood passed the examination to be a surgeon and physician because he continued to practice medicine.[2]

Perspective on Flood as a doctor was left by Maunsel White. Shortly after arriving in New Orleans in August 1801, White was stricken with yellow fever. He credited his recovery from the dreaded disease to the cold water treatment prescribed by Dr. Flood and the assistance of a slave woman. The regimen of this treatment called for the patient to be placed in a bathtub and drenched repeatedly with cold water, then given a vigorous rubdown with dry towels and covered with blankets to induce perspiration.[3] This ex-

1. List of persons born within the limits of the United States residing at New Orleans, enclosed in Benjamin Morgan to Chandler Price, August 11, 1803, in Clarence E. Carter, comp. and ed., *The Territorial Papers of the United States,* vol. 9, *The Territory of Orleans, 1803–1812* (Washington, D.C.: U.S. Government Printing Office, 1940), 10 (hereinafter cited as TP, with page range).

2. John Duffy, ed., *The Rudolph Matas History of Medicine,* vol. 1 (Baton Rouge: Louisiana State University Press, 1958), 183.

3. Maunsel White, Esq., "The Olden Time in New-Orleans and the Yellow Fever," *De Bow's Commercial Review* 6, no. 2 (August 1848), 156–8.

treme treatment was not one subscribed to by the French and native Creole physicians, even though it was widely used in the early nineteenth century.[4]

The close association of Flood and Governor William Claiborne stemmed more from their political opinions than it did from their Virginia origins. Claiborne described Flood as a man with a "cool head and an honest heart who loves his Country, his Government and Laws."[5] Bernard Marigny graphically described Flood as a "Big fat" man, a "severe Republican, and an honest citizen."[6] The doctor held a number of medical, military, and political appointments in the territorial government. During the month of November 1803, Dr. Flood was one of the half-dozen Americans who gathered at George King's Coffee House to form the 180-man "Volunteer association" to protect the city against the feared unwillingness of the Spanish to surrender the Louisiana colony to Pierre Clément de Laussat, the French prefect sent to receive it. Flood also was one of the founding members of the association that patrolled the streets of New Orleans for three weeks until the American troops arrived in December for the transfer of Louisiana to the United States.[7] After the transfer and establishment of the territorial government, Flood was appointed to several offices: the first territorial council (December 22, 1804);[8] port physician (early in 1805 and again on April 21, 1809);[9] and major in the First Regiment of the territorial militia (April 20, 1805–December 1808).[10] Flood also was one of the incorporators

4. Duffy, *History of Medicine,* 1: 212, 278–9.

5. Governor Claiborne to the President, January 29, 1805, TP, 9: 386.

6. Bernard Marigny, "Reflections on the Campaign of General Andrew Jackson in Louisiana in 1814 and 1815," *Louisiana Historical Quarterly* 6, no. 1 (January 1923), 67.

7. [Arthur P. Whitaker, ed.,] "Despatches from the United States Consulate in New Orleans, 1801–1803, II," *American Historical Review* 33, no. 2 (January 1928), 356 n. 43.

8. Governor Claiborne to the President, January 29, 1805; Governor Claiborne to the Secretary of State, March 26, 1805, TP, 9: 386 and 426; and Letter No. 168, To James Madison, March 16, 1805.

9. Register of Civil Appointments in the Territory of Orleans, February 13, 1806, Physicians of Ports, and List of Civil and Military Officers, April 21, 1809, Physician of the Port of New Orleans, TP, 9: 601 and 836, respectively.

10. Register of Appointments in the Militia of the Territory of Orleans, May 8, 1806, enclosed in Secretary Graham to the Secretary of State, May 8, 1806, TP, 9: 632; To Paul Lanusse, December 17, 1808, in *Official Letter Books of W. C. C. Claiborne, 1801–1816,* ed. Dunbar Rowland (1917; New York: AMS Press, 1972), 273 (hereinafter cited as CLB with volume and page range); and *Louisiana Gazette,* August 2, 1805, p. 3, c. 4, and August 16, 1805, p. 2, c. 4.

of the New Orleans Library Society.[11] Following the acquisition of West Florida, Claiborne appointed Flood (January 5, 1811) as his personal representative to carry orders to the Bay St. Louis–Pascagoula area.[12]

During the Battle of New Orleans, Flood volunteered his professional services, serving on General Andrew Jackson's staff, without officially joining the Army Medical Department.[13] Flood appears to have suffered considerable economic loss as a result of the War of 1812. Surviving records indicate he was allowed compensation by the U.S. government for the destruction of a house and mill burned by the British on the west bank of the Mississippi River.[14] After the war Flood entered into business partnership with James Sterrett, formerly a captain in the U.S. Army, but then a resident of the Mississippi Territory.[15] Subsequently (1818), Flood joined with others to found the first Presbyterian Church established in the territory.[16]

Doctor Flood died of dysentery following a visit to his plantation below New Orleans early in the spring of 1823. The notice of his death said that Flood was about forty-eight years old and had lived in New Orleans for almost twenty-four years. He was survived by his wife, the former widow Lorrain, and three children, William, Henry, and Catherine Flood.[17]

11. *Acts Passed at the First Session of the Legislative Council, of the Territory of Orleans, Begun and Held at the Principal, in the City of New Orleans, On Monday the Third Day of December, in the Year of Our Lord, One Thousand Eight Hundred and Four, and of the Independence of the United States the Twenty-Ninth* (New Orleans: James M. Bradford, 1805), 322.

12. To Dr. William Flood, January 5, 1811, CLB, 5: 82–4.

13. Marigny, "Reflections," 67; and Mary C. Gillett, *The Army Medical Department, 1775–1818* (Washington, D.C.: Center of Military History, United States Army, 1981), 184.

14. Powell Casey, *Louisiana in the War of 1812* (Baton Rouge: [by the author,] 1963), 103, paragraph 3k.

15. *Louisiana Gazette*, October 15, 1815, p. 2, c. 1.

16. Louis Moreau Lislet, comp., *A General Digest of the Acts of the Legislature of Louisiana: Passed from the Year 1804, to 1827, Inclusive, and in Force at the Last Period with an Appendix and General Index*, vol. 1 (New Orleans: Benjamin Levy, 1828), 164.

17. *Louisiana Gazette*, April 23, 1823, p. 2, c. 1; Duffy, *History of Medicine*, 1: 307; and Orleans Parish, Louisiana. Court of Probate, Record of Wills, Will Book 3, 1817–1824, 362.

JOHN LYND

John Lynd (d. February 14, 1820) was the son of Joseph Lynd and Marie St. Claire (Sinclair?) of Tyrone County, Ireland.[1] When he came to Louisiana is not known. The uncertainty of his movements is compounded by the occasional spelling of his name with an *i* rather than a *y,* and by the fact that there was more than one John Lind along the Gulf Coast in the years from 1765 to 1832.

The name John Lind first appears in the history of Louisiana as that of a captain of a schooner operating between New Orleans and Mobile. In the fall of 1765, this Captain Lind was to have delivered the first installment of a total of 10,000 livres to be paid to Isaac Monsanto, who agreed to provision the British expedition that was to journey up the Mississippi River to take possession of the Illinois country under the terms of the Treaty of Paris, 1763.[2] Twenty-three years later, a "Juan Line" applied in Cadiz, Spain, for a license with trading privileges in New Orleans, New Spain (Mexico), and

---

1. St. Louis Cathedral, Orleans Parish, Louisiana, *Funeral Register, 1815–1830,* Act 2007. In this funeral record, Lynd's surname is spelled with an "i" rather than the usual "y." John Lynd is identified as a native of Ireland, "Many years Resident in Louisiana," in List of Civil and Military Officers, April 21, 1809, Notaries Public, in Clarence E. Carter, comp. and ed., *The Territorial Papers of the United States,* vol. 9, *The Territory of Orleans, 1803–1812* (Washington, D.C.: U.S. Government Printing Office, 1940), 837 (hereinafter cited as TP, with volume and page range). The *Louisiana Advertiser,* October 22, 1832, p. 3, c. 2, carries the death notice of a John Lind "in the prevailing epidemic."

2. Bertram W. Korn, *The Early Jews of New Orleans* (Waltham, Mass.: American Jewish Historical Society, 1969), 20–1.

the islands of the West Indies.[3] Although this name is spelled "Line" rather than Lind or Lynd, it is possible that Line and Captain John Lind were the same man. In his application for a trading license, Juan Line described himself as a native of France and demonstrated familiarity with Spanish possessions along the northern and western Gulf of Mexico, as well as in the Caribbean Sea. This does not appear to have been the John Lind who died of yellow fever on October 19, 1832, although extant information on both these men indicates they were natives of Alsace, France.[4]

The first record of John Lynd in the early territorial papers of Louisiana occurred with his appointment as notary on February 23, 1805.[5] His appointments to other positions of public responsibility and trust under the Claiborne administration appear to have helped Lynd to become the notary of choice for most settlers of English extraction in early territorial New Orleans.[6] Late in April 1805, Lynd was appointed justice of the peace, a position he held throughout the territorial period.[7] At the end of May 1805 he was appointed captain in the artillery company of the Orleans Volunteers.[8] It was in this capacity that he served as a member of the court martial that reprimanded Samuel B. Davis for conduct unbecoming an officer in October 1805.[9] Thereafter, except for occasional glimpses, little is known of the ac-

3. *Archivo General de Indias. Sección V, Gobierno. Audiencia de Santo Domingo Sobre la Época Española de Luisiana, legajo* 2587, folios 911–3, April 15, 1786, microfilm reel 150-E. Library, Special Collections, Loyola University, New Orleans (hereinafter cited as AGI, *Audiencia de Santo Domingo,* with folio number[s]).

4. On the possibility of his birth in Alsace, France, see AGI, *Audiencia de Santo Domingo,* folios 918–9. This John Lind may be the Alsace-born son of Martin Lind and Anne Marie Klin who married Christine Conrode, the daughter of Adam Conrode and Carvora Martin of Lorraine on November 19, 1721. See Alice D. Forsyth, "Extracts from St. Louis Cathedral Marriage Book 5 (1830–1834)," *Louisiana Genealogical Register* 21, no. 3 (September 1974), 228.

5. Register of Civil Appointments in the Territory of Orleans, February 13, 1806, Notary Publics, TP, 9: 601.

6. This general observation was offered by Sally K. Reeves, archivist in charge of the New Orleans Notarial Archives, and was confirmed by use of the archives by the author.

7. Register of Civil Appointments in the Territory of Orleans, Justices, February 13, 1806; A Register of Civil Appointments, June 30, 1807, Justices of the Peace; A List of Civil and Military Officers, April 21, 1809, Notaries Public; in TP, 9: 599, 750, and 837, respectively, reflects these appointments.

8. Register of Appointments in the Militia of the Territory of Orleans, May 8, 1806, Orleans Volunteers, ibid., 639, and "Premier 'Directory' de la Nouvelle-Orleans, 1807," in *Le Diamant* 1, no. 14 (May 1, 1887), 99.

9. A General Court Martial, October 19, 1805, TP, 9: 587.

tivities of Lynd until near the end of the territorial period. In 1811 he was appointed aide-de-camp to Governor Claiborne.[10] In May of the same year, the quiet, effective notarial work of Lynd was called to the attention of his peers when the governor specified that the form developed by Lynd to record proofs of citizenship was the form to be used by all notaries for such records.[11]

During the years between 1805 and 1811, when little is known of Lynd's activities, he apparently was busy building a reputation as a commission broker[12] and notary, studying law, and acquiring large landholdings. Lynd's first known appearance in his capacity as lawyer was in 1808 when he served not only as notary, but also as attorney in the bankruptcy proceedings for George Pollock.[13] Much of Lynd's income in these years was invested in land. In the summers of 1806 and 1808 he acquired patent rights to 45,159 arpents[14] in the Feliciana and Baton Rouge districts of Spanish West Florida.[15] The patents were issued by Juan Morales, the intendant for West Florida, and were among those strongly objected to by Governor Claiborne. Although the U.S. land commissioner recommended that the 13,134 arpents claimed under the patent of August 11, 1808, not be confirmed, Lynd's wife claimed part of the land until 1855. In that year the state legislature directed the state treasurer to pay Lynd's widow $1,407.42, the taxes paid on land in East Feliciana Parish from 1813 to 1827. In return, Lynd's widow was to relinquish all claim to the disputed land, which the state regarded as public domain.[16]

John Lynd was married twice. His first wife was Rosa Ramos, whom he

10. By William Charles Cole Claiborne, Governor of the Territory of Orleans [Appointment of Joseph Montegut, Senior, to the Council of Administration of the Charity Hospital of New Orleans], November 13, 1811, in *Official Letter Books of W. C. C. Claiborne, 1801–1816*, ed. Dunbar Rowland, vol. 5 (1917; New York: AMS Press, 1972), 376.

11. Circular to the Several Notaries Public, May 24, 1811, ibid., 254.

12. John Lynd is listed as a *courtier*, that is, broker, in the "Premier 'Directory' de la Nouvelle-Orleans," 45.

13. *George Pollock v. His Creditors*, Superior Court case no. 1503, March 5, 1808.

14. The size of an arpent in Louisiana varied, but the French Canadian arpent was equivalent to .84 acre. Using this as a standard, Lynd claimed title to approximately 37,933.56 acres in the Feliciana and Baton Rouge districts.

15. *American State Papers: Public Lands*, vol. 3 (Washington, D.C.: Gales & Seaton, 1834), 58, 61.

16. *Acts Passed by the Second Legislature of the State of Louisiana at Its Second Session, Held and Begun in the Town at Baton Rouge, on the 15th January, 1855* (New Orleans: Emile La Sere, 1855), 267, Act No. 218, "An Act for the Relief of Henrietta Blanc, Widow of John Lynd."

married on August 12, 1801.[17] No additional information about this marriage has been found. Lynd next married Henrietta Blanc, daughter of Antoine Louis Blanc, native of Marseilles, France, and Louise Gauvain of New Orleans, on January 23, 1808.[18] When Lynd died in 1820, age unknown, he was survived by his second wife and no other known heirs.

17. St. Louis Cathedral, Orleans Parish, Louisiana, Marriage Register 2 (1784–1806), Act 552, 138. The date of her death is unknown.

18. Saint Louis Cathedral, Orleans Parish, Louisiana, Marriage Register 3 (1806–1821), Act 71, 24. See also "Newspaper Notices, Louisiana Gazette (New Orleans)," *Louisiana Genealogical Register* 5, no. 6 (December 1958), 42.

CONSTANT FREEMAN

Constant Freeman (1757–February 27, 1824) should not be confused, as he sometimes is, with Thomas Freeman. Both men are associated with the lower Mississippi Valley. Thomas was born in Ireland, came to the United States in 1784, and was surveyor-general in the Mississippi Territory with deputies in Orleans Territory and that portion of West Florida acquired in 1810.[1]

Constant Freeman was from the state of Massachusetts. His military career began during the American Revolution when he entered the army as a first lieutenant in the Continental artillery (November 9, 1776). Almost two years later (October 1, 1778), he was promoted to captain, the rank he held when discharged (June 1783) after the formal conclusion of the Revolutionary War.[2]

Freeman apparently preferred military life, but on terms of his choosing. He declined a captaincy in the Second Infantry during the Indian warfare (March 1791) in the old Northwest Territory, but accepted appointment as

1. See *Dictionary of American Biography*, s.v. "Freeman, Thomas"; and The Governor of the Mississippi Territory to the Secretary of State, January 1, 1811, in Clarence E. Carter, comp. and ed., *The Territorial Papers of the United States*, vol. 9, *The Territory of Orleans, 1803–1812* (Washington, D.C.: U.S. Government Printing Office, 1940), 910, 913, and other index references in the Orleans Territory papers volume (hereinafter cited as TP, with volume and page range).

2. Francis B. Heitman, *Historical Register and Dictionary of the United States Army from Its Organization September 29, 1789, to March 2, 1903*, vol. 1 (1903; Urbana: University of Illinois Press, 1965), 435.

major in the First Corps of Artillerists and Engineers four years later (February 28, 1795). During the reduction in military forces initiated by the Jefferson administration, Freeman was promoted to lieutenant colonel (April 1, 1802). He was ordered to New Orleans (January 31, 1804) to replace General Wilkinson in command of U.S. troops there, arriving in early June.[3]

The choice of Freeman for the assignment in New Orleans appeared to achieve a happy combination of ability and experience. Freeman had first-hand knowledge of the lower Mississippi Valley and the Gulf Coast, spoke French, and practiced the Roman Catholic religion.[4] His knowledge of the lower Mississippi Valley stemmed from a visit there in 1798 during the occupation of Walnut Hills (also known as Nogales and Vicksburg) and Natchez. On that occasion he carried written instructions from General Wilkinson to Captain Isaac Guion, the officer in command of the American occupation forces. Then a major, Freeman spent nearly a week (March 7–13, 1798) in Natchez before journeying to New Orleans for passage to his ultimate destination, Georgia. When he left New Orleans (April 18), Freeman sailed for Pensacola via Lake Pontchartrain in the company of Lieutenant Colonel Carlos Howard, the Irish-born former commander of all Spanish military forces along the Mississippi River.[5]

Freeman began his duty in New Orleans in 1804 with the good will, even the praise, of Governor Claiborne. Within the year, however, the two men were in serious disagreement. The problems began with Freeman's refusal to move his family from the public building, formerly a school, intended for the district court. The friction intensified when the colonel refused the governor's request to increase the garrison at Fort St. John, located at the confluence of Bayou St. John with Lake Pontchartrain. Relations between the two men were further aggravated when Freeman would not comply with the city council's ordinance requiring property owners to pave the sidewalks

3. Ibid., 1: 435; To Henry Dearborn, June 9, 1804, in *Official Letter Books of W. C. C. Claiborne, 1801–1816*, ed. Dunbar Rowland, vol. 2 (1917; New York: AMS Press, 1972), 199; and Tommy Young, "The United States Army in the South, 1789–1835" (Ph.D. diss., Louisiana State University, 1973), 117.

4. The Secretary of War to Constant Freeman, April 23, 1804, TP, 9: 230; and Marietta Marie LeBreton, *A History of the Territory of Orleans, 1803–1812* (Ann Arbor, Mich.: University Microfilms, 1961), 81.

5. Isaac Guion, "Military Journal of Captain Isaac Guion, 1797–1799," in Dunbar Rowland, ed., *Annual Report of the Mississippi Department of Archives and History, 1908* (Nashville: Brandon Printing, 1909), 71, 73–4, 76, 77, 80, 81.

and repair the gutters on their property. Claiborne summarized matters for President Jefferson when he accused Freeman of lacking initiative.[6] The foundation for the charge was Freeman's demand that it was the territorial government's responsibility to find him suitable living quarters to replace those he was to vacate.[7]

After the assignment in New Orleans, Freeman was placed in command (June 1807) of Fort Claiborne, the military fortification built in northwest Louisiana at Natchitoches and named in honor of Governor Claiborne. Freeman remained at this frontier post until the spring of 1810, much of the time without his family and lamenting the fact that he was the oldest lieutenant colonel in the army. It was only after reassignment from Fort Claiborne that he was made brevet colonel (July 10, 1812). Three years later (June 15, 1815) he was honorably discharged from the army.[8] When he retired, Freeman sought and obtained employment with the national government. He was appointed (March 1816) fourth auditor in the Department of the Navy, Washington, D.C., where he remained until his death at age sixty-seven on February 27, 1824. Although he was married and had children, no surviving family members were identified in the notice of his death.[9]

6. James Brown to John Breckinridge, September 17, 1805; and Governor Claiborne to the President, May 19, 1807, TP, 9: 509, 735, respectively.

7. Young, "United States Army in the South," 123–9.

8. Marshall S. Miller, "The History of Fort Claiborne, Louisiana, 1804–1822" (master's thesis, Louisiana State University, 1969), 53–4, 84; and Heitman, *Historical Register,* 1: 435.

9. Heitman, *Historical Register,* 1: 435; and *Philadelphia National Intelligencer,* March 4, 1824, p. 4, c. 3.

EDWARD D. TURNER

Edward Demaresque Turner (17 ?–October 13, 1811) was described shortly after his death as "strictly the man of honour, probity, and integrity."[1] The notice of his death said that Turner, a native of Boston, Massachusetts, entered the United States Army "very young," and "served with much honour in the western army" during General Anthony Wayne's campaigns against the Indians.[2] His military record indicates that Turner was appointed ensign in the Second Infantry on March 4, 1791; lieutenant in July 1792; captain in November 1793; and major on November 19, 1794. During the reduction in force that occurred in April 1802 following the election of President Jefferson, Turner was retained in the army, accepting a reduction in grade from major to captain.[3] In 1803 he was commander of Fort Adams, Mississippi Territory, and was part of the military contingent that participated in the Louisiana Purchase transfer ceremonies in New Orleans on December 20 that year.[4]

Turner's assignment to command at Natchitoches was favored by Claiborne, but delayed because the Marqués de Casa Calvo refused to issue or-

1. *Louisiana Gazette*, October 16, 1811, p. 3, c. 3.

2. Ibid.

3. Charles K. Gardner, *A Dictionary of All Officers, Who Have Been Commissioned, or Have Been Appointed and Served, in the Army of the United States . . .*, 2nd ed. (1860; New York: D. Van Nostrand, 1965), 455.

4. To James Madison, November 18, 1803, in *Official Letter Books of W. C. C. Claiborne, 1801–1816*, ed. Dunbar Rowland, vol. 1 (1917; New York: AMS Press, 1972), 285 (hereinafter cited as CLB, with volume and page numbers); and Glenn Conrad, "Edward D. Turner: Soldier, Jurist, Planter, Patriot," *Louisiana History* 37, no. 2 (spring 1996), 218–9.

ders to the Spanish commandants at Natchitoches and Upper Louisiana to surrender their posts until after January 9, 1804. Turner left New Orleans sometime after his appointment (February 4, 1804) and arrived at Natchitoches April 26, 1804. It was under his command that Fort Claiborne was built at Natchitoches and named for Governor William C. C. Claiborne. In addition to his military duties at Natchitoches, Turner also was responsible for the administration of civil government in the Natchitoches District until June 1805, when John W. Alexander was appointed judge for the district. Turner resigned his army commission on November 20, 1805, and was appointed judge of the Natchitoches District on January 23, 1806, after Alexander resigned that position.[5] Turner left Natchitoches to become a sugar planter, settling on farmland "opposite the *Homas*," in Ascension Parish above New Orleans.[6] Soon after taking up residence in that parish, he was appointed parish judge of Ascension Parish (May 17, 1808; April 21, 1809). His last reappointment (June 27, 1811) was voided because of his death from yellow fever.[7]

Turner's wife, whose maiden name was Gray, also was from Boston, but was educated in England. She preceded him in death from yellow fever by one day (October 12, 1811). The Turners were survived by seven children, the eldest of whom was fourteen.[8]

5. To General James Wilkinson, October 10, 1805; To Coctr. [*sic*] John Sibley, October 30, 1805; [To Jno. C. Kerr,] November 14, 1805; in CLB, 3: 200, 218–9, and 232, respectively; and Register of Civil Appointments in the Territory of Orleans, February 13, 1806, Judges, in Clarence E. Carter, comp. and ed., *The Territorial Papers of the United States*, vol. 9, *The Territory of Orleans, 1803–1812* (Washington, D.C.: U.S. Government Printing Office, 1940), 598 (hereinafter cited as TP, with volume and page range).

6. *Louisiana Gazette*, October 16, 1811, p. 3, c. 3.

7. Register of Civil Appointments in the Territory of Orleans, February 13, 1806, Judges; Register of Civil Appointments, January 1–June 30, 1806, Judges; List of Civil and Military Officers, April 21, 1809, Parish Judges; Return of Civil Appointments made in the Territory of Orleans from the 1st Jany 1811 to the 31st Dec. of the same year, Judges; all in TP, 9: 598, 662, 835, 984, respectively; and Sidney A. Marchand, *The Story of Ascension Parish, Louisiana* (Donaldsonville, La.: S. A. Marchand, 1931), 174, 176.

8. *Louisiana Gazette*, October 16, 1811, p. 3, c. 3.

ABIMAEL Y. NICOLL

Abimael Youngs Nicoll (December 31, 1766–June 26, 1835) was born in Walkill, New York, the son of John Nicoll and Hannah Youngs. After graduation from Princeton University and the Medical College of the University of New York, Nicoll entered the U.S. Army with appointment as lieutenant in the artillery (March 4, 1791). Eighteen months later (October 4, 1792), he married Caroline Agnes Ledbetter, who was born in Yadkin River, North Carolina.[1]

Nicoll was promoted to captain (November 29, 1794) following the reorganization of the army in the 1790s and assigned to the First Corps of Artillerists and Engineers. He was among the officers retained during the reduction in force ordered by President Jefferson in the spring of 1802. After the United States took possession of Louisiana, Nicoll was ordered to New Orleans. While stationed there, he was promoted to major (December 12, 1804). Following the duty tour in New Orleans, Nicoll served as adjutant and inspector of the army (April 2, 1807), and inspector general with the rank of colonel (March 18, 1813). He resigned from the army on June 1, 1814, and moved to Savannah, Georgia. At his death Nicoll was survived by his wife and ten children.[2]

1. William L. Nicoll, *The Nicoll Family of Orange County New York* (New York: n.p., 1886), 37, 41–4.

2. Ibid., 41–4; Charles K. Gardner, *A Dictionary of All Officers, Who Have Been Commissioned, or Have Been Appointed and Served, in the Army of the United States . . .* , 2nd ed. (1860; New York: D. Van Nostrand, 1965), 39; and Francis B. Heitman, *Historical Register and Dictionary of the United States Army from Its Organization September 29, 1789, to March 2, 1903*, vol. 1 (1903; Urbana: University of Illinois Press, 1965), 748.

MICHEL CANTRELLE

Michel Bernard de Cantrelle (1750–October 24, 1814; sometimes spelled with an "i"—Cantrille—or without the last "e") was commandant of the Acadian Coast, the name given that area of settlement stretching along the Mississippi River above New Orleans in present-day St. James and Ascension Parishes.[1] Both his father, Jacques, and his brother-in-law, Nicholas Verret, preceded him in that post. The name subsequently given the Cantrelle home, "Cabanocey," came from a stream in nearby Lafourche Parish. The name, *cabanosé,* is a corruption of the Choctaw Indian word *kabahannossé,* and means Mallard's roost or duck's hut.[2]

1. Lillian C. Bourgeois, *Cabanocey: The History, Customs and Folklore of St. James Parish* (New Orleans: Pelican, 1957), 5, 183, 200.

The "Acadian Coast" was the second community above New Orleans on the east bank of the Mississippi River to take on an identity. It derived its name from the displaced Acadians from Nova Scotia who began to establish their homes here in the 1760s. The area today is known as St. James and Ascension parishes. Between this settled area and New Orleans was the older settled area, the "German Coast." The German Coast comprises St. Charles and St. John the Baptist parishes today. This two-parish land area derived its name from the earliest settlers, displaced German and Swiss immigrants who took on protective covering by gallicizing their names while still in France. J. Hanno Deiler, *The Settlement of the German Coast of Louisiana and the Creoles of German Descent* (1909; Baltimore: Genealogical Publishing, 1969), 11ff., tells of the German/Swiss origins of the settlers in Louisiana. "Coast" meant the natural levees bordering the Mississippi and not the backswamp. Ibid., 46–7. See also Fred B. Kniffen, *Louisiana: Its Land and People* (Baton Rouge: Louisiana State University Press, 1968), 7, 125 (map).

2. Bourgeois, *Cabanocey,* viii n. 2, 8–9, and 35. The last named page lists ten variants for the spelling of "Cabanocey." Bourgeois says (p. 8) the Cantrelles did not actually establish resi-

Universally revered, Michel Cantrelle appears to have embodied the kind of impartiality and honesty that Governor Claiborne hoped would develop throughout Louisiana to repudiate what he called the "calm [acceptance] of Despotism."[3] For example, Cantrelle once sentenced his son-in-law to thirty days in jail and fined him five hundred dollars for assault and battery.[4] Although Claiborne ultimately was successful in coaxing Cantrelle into limited government service, the Louisiana native initially declined appointment to the legislative council, giving as his reason distrust of his qualifications for such a high office.[5] However, Cantrelle did accept appointment as judge of the Acadian Coast, perhaps because the duties involved were simply a continuation of his function as commandant, a position he had held since 1775.[6]

Cantrelle's public stance illustrates the difficulties facing Claiborne in Louisiana. The commandant's self-deprecating modesty masks two factors that undoubtedly shaped his thinking and actions. One was his lack of command of the English language.[7] The other, more important factor was the rumor that all or part of Louisiana was to be returned to Spain. The man behind this rumor was the Marqués de Casa Calvo, whose presence in New Orleans cast an ominous shadow over many Louisianians because of the threats, intrigues, and rumors he fomented before Governor Claiborne finally ushered him out of the territory in February 1806.

Casa Calvo's threat to stop the pension of any militiaman who helped to establish the American government in Louisiana already had been given credence by the punishment meted Bellechasse. According to Louis de Clouet, Casa Calvo became angry with Bellechasse for his revelations to Daniel Clark about the conduct of General James Wilkinson.[8] Until it could

---

dence in St. James Parish until sometime near the end of 1764 or early 1765, when Michel was nearly fifteen years old.

3. This appears to be to be a quotation from Madison, but the exact source has not been identified.

4. Governor Claiborne to the President, July 15, 1805, in Clarence E. Carter, comp. and ed., *The Territorial Papers of the United States*, vol. 9, *The Territory of Orleans, 1803–1812* (Washington, D.C.: U.S. Government Printing Office, 1940), 673–4 (hereinafter cited as TP, with volume and page range).

5. Governor Claiborne to the President, November 19, 1804, ibid., 334.

6. Bourgeois, *Cabanocey,* 59, 200. Ibid., 89, states that John Watkins, serving as Governor Claiborne's confidential agent, persuaded Michel Cantrelle to continue in the commandant's post during his visit with Cantrelle in early 1804.

7. Characterization of New Orleans Residents, July 1, 1804, entry 88, enclosed in James Wilkinson to the President, July 1, 1804, TP, 9: 255.

8. See the biographical sketch of Bellechasse for the problems about his pension.

be established that the United States would retain Louisiana, or that Spain would regain its former colony, Michel Cantrelle prudently limited his endorsement of the U.S. government until his support, along with other prominent Louisianians, was solicited by Dr. John Watkins acting as the confidential agent of Governor Claiborne in February 1804.[9] Claiborne apparently suspected Casa Calvo was manipulating Spanish pensioners in Louisiana through intimidation, but lacked proof. On February 10, 1805, he wrote Secretary Madison that some Spanish officers "have been permitted to retire on half pay, and others I believe feel a strong desire to resign their Commissions and settle permanently in Louisiana." One such Spanish officer he named was the former intendant, Juan Ventura Morales.[10]

Although Cantrelle was a wealthy and respected planter, much was at stake for him if Spain regained control of Louisiana. He had more than thirty years of service in the colonial militia and Spanish Royal Army. Cantrelle had begun military service as a lieutenant in the Louisiana Infantry Regiment at age nineteen or twenty on February 12, 1770. He was promoted to captain on August 21, 1779. During the years of the American Revolution in the lower Mississippi Valley and along the northern shore of the Gulf of Mexico, Cantrelle saw service in the captures of Fort Bute (Manchac) and Baton Rouge, both in 1779, and Mobile in 1780. In the battles to take Fort Bute and Baton Rouge, Cantrelle was given command of four companies of Acadian Militia.[11] Entries in his military record state that Cantrelle was a man of "known valor; good application; capacity & conduct." During the attack on Mobile, his value to the Spanish government was demonstrated when he was breveted a lieutenant of the Spanish Royal Army (February 17, 1780) with the salary of that rank.[12]

In addition to the military claim that the Spanish could assert on him, Cantrelle's property holdings in Cabanocey included his home, a sugar mill, and a lumber mill. The discerning Laussat considered Cantrelle's plantation

9. Doctor Watkins' Report, February [March] 2, 1804, in *Official Letter Books of W. C. C. Claiborne, 1801–1816*, ed. Dunbar Rowland, vol. 2 (1917; New York: AMS Press, 1972), 4, references Watkins's visit with Cantrelle.

10. See Letter No. 134, To James Madison, February 10, 1805.

11. *Archivo General de Simancas. Sección de Guerra Moderna. Hojas de Servicias Militares de América, 1787–1799, legajo* 7291, *cuaderno* 2, folio 5, MSS 3124, microfilm 3124, Louisiana and Lower Mississippi Valley Collections, Louisiana State University Libraries.

12. Jack D. L. Holmes, *Honor and Fidelity: The Louisiana Infantry Regiment and the Louisiana Militia Companies, 1766–1821* (Birmingham, Ala.: By the author, 1965), 171–2 (entry 437).

"the finest and best arranged in Louisiana." The holdings, he said, were "among the most extensive of plantation lands," the whole irrigated by a bayou.[13] The thought that Cantrelle could lose his property, his position in the community, even his life, if Spain regained Louisiana and it was known that he had aided in the establishment of the American government, undoubtedly was not dismissed lightly by Cantrelle. He was well aware that such a thing had happened to well-known Louisianians in 1769.

When Cantrelle was eighteen years old, four Louisiana colonists were executed by General Alexander O'Reilly for rebelling against the newly arrived Spanish governor Antonio de Ulloa. Cantrelle probably remembered quite clearly the relief his father and mother's families felt when they escaped punishment at the hands of General O'Reilly. It was in Jacques Cantrelle's home that militia captains Judice Verret and Andrés Verret had held Colonel Gilbert Antoine de Saint Maxent captive, thereby precipitating the revolt against Ulloa.[14] Though essentially an onlooker, the role of a young man named de la Puerta, whose Casa Calvo title lay more than twenty years in the future, was remembered with repugnance. Captain de la Puerta, nephew of General O'Reilly, who ordered the executions, watched as the French settlers were executed by firing squad.[15]

Although Cantrelle never took a prominent role in establishing U.S. control of Louisiana, such as becoming a member of the territorial legislature, he was persuaded to continue serving as the local judge in St. James Parish,

13. Pierre Clément de Laussat, *Memoirs of My Life to My Son During the Year 1803 and After . . .*, trans. Sister Agnes-Josephine Pastwa, O.S.F.; ed. Robert D. Bush (Baton Rouge: Louisiana State University Press, 1978), 68. Like many of the early Louisiana plantations, the money crop originally grown at Cabanocey was indigo (Bourgeois, *Cabanocey*, 9, 35).

14. Deiler, *Settlement of the German Coast*, 43. See also Vicente R. Casado, *Primeros Años de Dominación Española en la Luisiana* (Madrid: Instituto Gonzalo Fernandez de Oviedo, 1942), 155.

15. John P. Moore, in *Revolt in Louisiana: The Spanish Occupation, 1766–1770* (Baton Rouge: Louisiana State University Press, 1976), 208, tells of the sentencing of ten men and the execution of four. A fifth man was sentenced to be executed, but died before his trial. Five men were given prison sentences ranging from six to ten years. Ibid., 209, states that the property of the convicted men was seized by the crown and sold at auction to pay debts to creditors, dowries, and any taxes owed to the state.

The public was reminded of the role that Casa Calvo played in the events of 1769 by Bellechasse in a letter to the New Orleans *Telegraphe* newspaper late in March 1805, a copy of which Governor Claiborne sent to Secretary Madison on April 1, 1805 (State Department Territorial Papers, Orleans Series, 1764–1813, reel 6, vol. 6, January 1, 1805–June 21, 1805; National Archives microcopy T260, folio 96. Louisiana Department, New Orleans Public Library).

thereby helping to provide political stability at the local level. Subsequently, Cantrelle was reappointed to the judgeship four times, May 15, 1805; June 30, 1807; April 21, 1809; and April 20, 1811. He served in this capacity until the new state constitution took effect in April 1812.[16] Cantrelle also served as register of the Acadian Coast, accepting appointment to this office in July 1806.[17] When the constitutional convention assembled in 1811, Cantrelle represented St. James Parish and was one of the five men chosen to draft the plan of the new state constitution.[18] In the convention, he was among those delegates who opposed annexation of the Florida parishes to the organizing state of Louisiana.[19]

Michel Cantrelle died on October 24, 1814, survived by his second wife, Madeleine Celeste Andry Cantrelle, and seven children.[20]

16. Register of Civil Appointments in the Territory of Orleans, Judges, February 13, 1806; A Register of Civil Appointments, June 30, 1807, Judges; List of Civil and Military Officers, April 21, 1809, Parish Judges; and Return of Civil Appointments made in the Territory of Orleans from the lst of January 1811 to the 31st of December of the same year; TP, 9: 598, 749, 835, 984, respectively.

17. John W. Gurley to the Secretary of the Treasury, July 24, 1806, ibid., 676–7.

18. Cecil Morgan, comp., *The First Constitution of the State of Louisiana* (Baton Rouge: Louisiana State University Press, 1975), 15.

19. Ibid., 31.

20. Sidney A. Marchand, *An Attempt to Re-Assemble the Old Settlers in Family Groups* (Baton Rouge: Claitor's, 1965), 27, entry 164, states that Cantrelle died on October 14, 1814. The date given in the text here, along with the information on Cantrelle's wives and children, may be found in Estelle M. Fortier Cochran, *The Fortier Family and Allied Families* (San Antonio: E. M. F. Cochran, 1963), 134. Cantrelle's first child, a daughter, was born to him and his first wife, Madeleine Croizet. Ibid.

JAMES CARRICK

James Carrick (?–August 7, 1808) was described by fellow businessman Benjamin Morgan in August 1803 as one of the few men then in New Orleans "worthy of confidence."[1] Morgan further identified Carrick three weeks later as one of the men in New Orleans who had been born in Great Britain.[2] Carrick, like his friend William Donaldson, was born in Scotland, at Keppen, near Glasgow.[3] Like Donaldson, Carrick also was an active Freemason, having been a founder of La Charité Lodge No. 2.[4] It is possible Morgan felt comfortable with Carrick because they were both businessmen of integrity. Two years later, when Carrick stood for election to the city council, he was described by Territorial Secretary John Graham as "Carrick the Merchant."[5]

Carrick lived about fifteen miles below New Orleans in the district centered around St. Bernard de Nueva Galvez Catholic Church (present-day St.

1. Benjamin Morgan to Chandler Price, August 11, 1803, in Clarence E. Carter, comp. and ed., *The Territorial Papers of the United States,* vol. 9, *The Territory of Orleans, 1803–1812* (Washington, D.C.: U.S. Government Printing Office, 1940), 8 (hereinafter cited as TP, with volume and page range).

2. List of persons born subjects of great Britain [*sic*] or of this colony now residing here, August 31, 1803, enclosed in Benjamin Morgan to Chandler Price, August 11, 1803, TP, 9: 10 (hereinafter cited as List of persons born subjects of great Britain, August 31, 1803).

3. Powell A. Casey, "Masonic Lodges in New Orleans," *New Orleans Genesis* 20, no. 77 (January 1981), 7, identifies the place of Carrick's birth, but no birth date has been found.

4. Ibid.

5. Secretary Graham to Governor Claiborne, September 16, 1805, TP, 9: 506.

Bernard Parish).[6] It is not known whether Benjamin Morgan called Governor Claiborne's attention to Carrick or if the governor met him as a result of Carrick's responsibilities as commandant of the St. Bernard District. These duties coincided with his fourteen months of service (June 6, 1804, to July 27, 1805) on the Municipal (city council).[7] Carrick also served as a member of the board of directors of the newly established Louisiana Bank beginning in January 1804, a position for which Benjamin Morgan had indicated Carrick was suitable in August 1803.[8] Late in the summer of 1804, he was one of several businessmen who endorsed William Brown for the office of collector of the port of New Orleans following the death of Hore Browse Trist.[9]

In 1805 Carrick requested Governor Claiborne's assistance in dealing with civil unrest related to the Catholic Church in his parish. Carrick's problems in St. Bernard were similar to those experienced by Lt. Henry Hopkins ten months earlier in Attakapas and Opelousas.[10] Both situations involved appointments of priests favored by one faction or another. The history of the Catholic Church in Louisiana is silent on the problems of St. Bernard de Nueva Galvez, but the trouble developed when the Irish-born Fr. Patrick Walsh, as acting vicar-general of the church in Louisiana, appointed the French secular priest Fr. Jean Marie Rochanson to the post in St. Bernard Parish. However, the priest who had been temporarily assigned there did not want to leave and was supported by Fr. Antonio de Sedella, *Père* Antoine. In addition, Sedella maintained that Walsh's claim to be vicar-general was illegal. Despite notification of the change in assignments, the interim priest met his replacement at the entrance of St. Bernard de Nueva Galvez. The result was a public commotion at the church door.[11] Because

6. *An Account of Louisiana, Being an Abstract of Documents, in the Offices of the Departments of State, and of the Treasury* (Philadelphia: John Conrad, November, 1803), 13.

7. "Biographies of the Mayors of New Orleans," comp. and ed. Works Project Administration (project 665-64-3-112, typescript; New Orleans, May 1939), 4.

8. List of persons born subjects of great Britain, August 31, 1803 (names identified with an asterisk); The President to the Secretary of State, April 17, 1804; and Governor Claiborne to the Secretary of State, January 13, 1804, all in TP, 9: 10–1, 224–5, and 368, respectively; and To James Madison, March 9, 1804, *Official Letter Books of W. C. C. Claiborne, 1801–1816*, ed. Dunbar Rowland, vol. 2 (1917; New York: AMS Press, 1972), 22–3.

9. John M. Gelston to the President, September 1, 1804, enclosing Recommendation of William Brown as Collector, TP, 9: 289–90.

10. See Roger Baudier, *The Catholic Church in Louisiana* (1939; Baton Rouge: Louisiana Library Association, 1972), 250–1.

11. Ibid., 252–3.

the parishioners began to choose sides in the matter, Carrick, as commandant of the parish, asked Governor Claiborne for assistance with the "disorderly conduct of one of the Priests in his Parish." Claiborne advised Carrick
to communicate the particulars of the problem to Judge John B. Prevost on
the territorial Superior Court, since that was the only source from which
the proper civil corrective measures could emanate.[12]

Carrick was not returned to office when he stood for reelection to the
Municipality in a crowded field in mid-September 1805. Harman B. Mc-
Carty was elected in his place.[13] Carrick died almost three years later, on
August 7, 1808.[14]

12. Governor Claiborne to Judge Prevost, March 23, 1805, TP, 9: 423. A few more details
of the incident may be found in James A. Robertson, ed. and trans., *Louisiana Under the Rule
of Spain, France, and the United States, 1785–1807*, vol. 2 (1910–1911; Freeport, N.Y.: Books
for Libraries Press, 1969), 283–4.

13. Secretary Graham to Governor Claiborne, September 16, 1805, TP, 9: 506, and "Biographies of the Mayors," 7.

14. *Louisiana Gazette*, August 9, 1808, p. 3, c. 4.

JOSEPH BOWMAR

Joseph Bowmar, a native of Tennessee and lieutenant in the U.S. infantry, was detached from his duties in New Orleans and ordered to the Ouachita Post in northeast Orleans Territory with a company of infantrymen sometime in March 1804.[1] Bowmar was ordered to take command of the Ouachita District, the site of present-day Monroe, Louisiana, and receive its archives and public papers from the Spanish commandant for both the French Republic and the U.S. government. Bowmar appears to have received instructions from both Governor Claiborne and French colonial prefect Pierre Clément de Laussat prior to setting out on his mission.[2]

The delay in taking possession of the frontier posts such as Ouachita arose, Claiborne advised Secretary of State Madison, "from an unwillingness to reduce our force in this City, until the greater part of the Spanish Troops had been withdrawn."[3] Given his firsthand knowledge of Spain's resentment over losing Louisiana, Governor Claiborne's concern for the safety and security of the Louisiana Purchase territory cannot be doubted.

1. Joseph Bowmar to Governor Claiborne, April 15, 1804, in Clarence E. Carter, comp. and ed., *The Territorial Papers of the United States*, vol. 9, *The Territory of Orleans, 1803–1812* (Washington: U.S. Government Printing Office, 1940), 223 (hereinafter cited as TP, with volume and page range). Bowmar's association with Tennessee is identified in Francis B. Heitman, *Historical Register and Dictionary of the United States Army from Its Organization September 29, 1789, to March 2, 1903*, vol. 1 (1903; Urbana: University of Illinois Press, 1965), 235.

2. Joseph Bowmar to Governor Claiborne, April 15, 1804, TP, 9: 223.

3. To James Madison, May 14, 1804, *Official Letter Books of W. C. C. Claiborne, 1801–1816*, ed. Dunbar Rowland, vol. 2 (1917; New York: AMS Press, 1972), 148.

At the time, Spain was regarded as one of the great world powers of Western Europe. The hollowness of the threat posed by the Spanish officials and soldiers scattered throughout Louisiana would not become apparent until later in the nineteenth century.

Other frontier posts that received military officers as commandants at this time were Natchitoches, Concordia, Opelousas, Attakapas, and Upper Louisiana. Military men were appointed to these positions of authority because these geographic areas were in danger of attack by Indians or other potential enemies of the United States.[4]

Bowmar reported his arrival in the district to Claiborne on April 15, 1804, saying there was no fortified place or public building of any kind. As a consequence, Bowmar immediately began preparations to build cabins to accommodate himself and the men under his command. In the same letter Bowmar estimated the heads of families in the area "not to exceed One hundred & fifty" and praised them for their "warm attachment to the Government of the United States."[5]

4. Marietta Marie LeBreton, *A History of the Territory of Orleans, 1803–1812* (Ann Arbor, Mich.: University Microfilms, 1973), 52–3; and Joseph T. Hatfield, *William Claiborne: Jeffersonian Centurion in the American Southwest* (Lafayette: University of Southwestern Louisiana, 1976), 126–7.

5. Joseph Bowmar to Governor Claiborne, April 15, 1804, TP, 9: 223–4.

ROBERT DOW

Doctor Robert Dow was the son of Robert Dow and Juana (Janet) Adie, or Adic, of Scotland.[1] In a deposition given on August 23, 1810, Dow stated that he arrived in New Orleans from the West Indies in September 1776 and began to practice medicine in 1778. He accepted appointment by Bernardo Gálvez, governor-general of Louisiana, as *médico* (physician) to the Royal Hospital in New Orleans the following year.[2]

A contemporary described Dow as "universally beloved," of "amiable disposition," urbane, and the "head of his profession."[3] The medical historian of Louisiana, Professor John Duffy, described Dow as "by far the most outstanding" of the English-speaking medical practitioners in New Orleans because he avoided extremism in his treatments.[4] Dow apparently never used bleeding, blistering, sweating, or vomiting, and only rarely used that mainstay of the medical profession, purging.[5] As a child, historian Charles Gayarré knew the doctor and recalled that Dow was "full of genial, exuberant kindness for all his fellow beings"; was of "a florid complexion" and

---

1. Saint Louis Cathedral Marriage Register, I (1777–1784), Act 212, 114.

2. General James Wilkinson, *Memoirs of My Own Times,* vol. 2 (1816; New York: AMS Press, 1973), appendix, CIX, unnumbered page.

3. Characterization of New Orleans Residents, enclosed in James Wilkinson to the President, July 1, 1804, entry 96, in Clarence E. Carter, comp. and ed., *The Territorial Papers of the United States,* vol. 9, *The Territory of Orleans, 1803–1812* (Washington, D.C.: U.S. Government Printing Office, 1940), 255 (hereinafter cited as TP with volume and page range).

4. John Duffy, ed., *The Rudolph Matas History of Medicine,* vol. 1 (Baton Rouge: Louisiana State University Press, 1958), 169.

5. Ibid., 145.

"convivial habits"; and was "aggressive in his mode of treatment, fond of stimulating nature when he found her too sluggish, and recommending a more generous diet than his French compeers generally did." Dow thought the climate of New Orleans was "malarial and debilitating, and had great faith in a luscious beef steak and a half bottle of port opportunely administered."[6] Because of his amiable disposition, Dow became a friend of Bernardo de Gálvez, who also believed in the tonic effect of port. According to Dow, Gálvez "made it a practice to retire when he was angry, and drink a bottle of Claret to compose his body and mind."[7]

Dow married Angélica Monsanto (September 9, 1781), daughter of Pedro David Rodriques Monsanto and Ester Levi. Angélica was the widow of George Urquhart, who died in 1779. Since there was no way for a Protestant to be married in Spanish Louisiana and Dow was the son of a Presbyterian minister, he and Angélica were married in St. Louis Cathedral.[8] Angélica and her family had come to New Orleans (circa 1757–58) from The Hague, The Netherlands, after two or three years' residence in Curaçao, The Netherlands West Indies. Originally, the Monsantos were Jewish. However, when Angélica married Dow, she, too, probably was Protestant, since her first husband also was Scottish and they were married in the Anglican Church in West Florida. There is no evidence the Monsantos made any effort to preserve their Jewish heritage after they and all Jews were expelled from Spanish Louisiana (1769–70) by Governor O'Reilly. Angélica eventually became a devoted member of the Episcopal Church and reared her two sons by her first husband, Thomas and David, as Christians.[9]

Angélica's quiet religious devotion probably stemmed from the influence of Dow as much as it did from within herself. The family recalls that Angélica cherished the Episcopal Book of Common Prayer that Dow gave her.[10] He was one of the incorporators of Christ Church, the first Protestant Episcopal Church in Louisiana, chartered (1805) by the territorial council.[11]

---

6. Ibid., 270.

7. George W. Corner, ed., *The Autobiography of Benjamin Rush: His "Travel through Life" Together with His Commonplace Book for 1789–1813* (Princeton, N.J.: Princeton University Press, 1948), 252–3.

8. *Saint Louis Cathedral Marriage Register,* 1 (1777–1784), Act 212, 114. Likenesses of both Angélica and Robert Dow may be found in Bertram W. Korn, *The Early Jews of New Orleans* (Waltham, Mass.: American Jewish Historical Society, 1969), following p. 208.

9. Korn, *Early Jews of New Orleans,* 9–18, 23–36, 40–1, 45–6, 50–3.

10. Ibid., 45.

11. *Acts Passed at the Second Session of the Legislative Council of the Territory of Orleans, Begun and Held at the Principal, in the City of New Orleans, on Thursday the Twentieth Day*

Dow served as senior warden of the church for eight years (1807–15) and was a close friend of Philander Chase, the first rector of Christ Church.[12] In 1818, Dow and his stepsons were among the founders of the Presbyterian Church in New Orleans.[13]

The warm and cheerful personalities of Angélica and Robert Dow were reflected in the gracious hospitality of their home, which was always open to guests. It was with the Dows that General James Wilkinson stayed in 1787 while on the first of his controversial visits to New Orleans. On that occasion Angélica and her younger son David became Wilkinson's "respectable, dear and honoured friends."[14] In his eulogy of Angélica years later, Wilkinson spoke of the hospitality that he and others had enjoyed at the Dow home: "A prominent and universally acknowledged trait of character which distinguished Madame Dow was her generous hospitality. She always spread a sumptuous table and health permitt[ing] every respectable stranger and a long list of the most distinguished inhabitants partook of the urbanity and good cheer of her home."[15]

Dow made several trips to Europe. The first was in 1785–86 on "urgent family business."[16] This journey apparently was undertaken by Dow in an effort to preclude loss of his position as physician to the Royal Hospital in New Orleans. When he reached Bordeaux, France, however, Dow learned that Stephen Forignet de Pellegrine, a surgeon of considerable skill, had been appointed to the post by a royal order of March 17, 1785.[17] Although Dow appealed directly to Count José de Gálvez, minister of the Indies and uncle and benefactor of Governor Gálvez, the doctor was denied appointment to the office. On his return to New Orleans, Dow was advised by Manuel

---

of June, in the Year of our Lord, One Thousand Eight Hundred and Five, and of the Independence of the United States the Twenty-Ninth (New Orleans: James M. Bradford, 1805), 88.

12. Georgia F. Taylor, "The Early History of the Episcopal Church in New Orleans, 1805–1840," *Louisiana Historical Quarterly* 22, no. 2 (April 1939), 449; and Leonard Huber and Guy F. Bernard, *To Glorious Immortality: The Rise and Fall of the Girod Street Cemetery, New Orleans' First Protestant Cemetery, 1822–1957* (New Orleans: Alblen Books, 1961), 36.

13. Louis Moreau Lislet, comp., *A General Digest of the Acts of the Legislature of Louisiana: Passed from the Year 1804, to 1827, Inclusive, and in Force at the Last Period with an Appendix and General Index,* vol. 1 (New Orleans: B. Levy, 1828), 163–4.

14. Korn, *Early Jews of New Orleans,* 52.

15. Ibid.

16. Ibid., 53.

17. Dow to [José de Gálvez ?], August 25, 1785, *Archivo General de Indias. Sección V, Gobierno. Audiencia de Santo Domingo Sobre la Época Española de Luisiana, legajo* 2587, folios 933–4, microfilm reel 150-E, Library, Special Collections, Loyola University, New Orleans.

Heras, the Spanish consul in Bordeaux, that the decision to appoint Pellegrine was irrevocable.[18]

Dow's second trip to Europe was begun in the first week of July 1800 and lasted into July 1802, if not longer. It was in the latter month and year that he wrote to Thomas Urquhart, who was in Bordeaux, expressing disappointment that Angélica was not to join him in France and happiness at the prospect of her being with him in England. From the phraseology of Dow's letter, it appears that he intended to establish their residence in France or England. For some reason Angélica did not join Dow in England either, and it was not until after her death that Dow left New Orleans.[19]

Dow also expressed concern in the July 1802 letter to Thomas Urquhart that the cession of Louisiana by Spain to France would adversely affect economic conditions in New Orleans. Whether Dow's correspondence home influenced James Pitot and Daniel Clark also to visit England and France about this same time is not known, nor is it known whether the three Louisianians saw one another while on their journeys. Like Pitot and Clark, Dow also called on the Pontalbas and Madame Miró, the former Celeste Macarty, who were living outside of Paris.[20]

After the United States acquired Louisiana, Dow sought to maintain a balance among his friendships with native Louisianians, the increasing numbers of Anglo-Americans who were settling in New Orleans, and his career.[21] The doctor's course is reflected in his refusal (1804) to serve on the territorial council and resignation (sometime in August 1804) from the Board of Health.[22] Dow's resignation from the Board of Health appears to have been precipitated by the appointment of Dr. Jean Baptist Casimiro Blanquet as director of Charity Hospital. The board objected to Blanquet's appointment on the grounds that he refused to take the medical licensing

18. Dow to Monseigneur de Gálvez, Minister of the Indies, August 25, 1785, ibid., folio 936; José de Gálvez to Dow, September 24, 1785, ibid., folio 937; and Manuel Heras to José de Gálvez, September 24, 1785, ibid., folio 939.

19. Korn, *Early Jews of New Orleans,* 53–4.

20. Ibid., 54.

21. For a different view, see Duffy, *History of Medicine,* 1: 312, who sees Dow as consistently aligning himself with the native Louisianians.

22. Ibid., 383–5. Claiborne apparently appointed Dow to this office shortly after it was created. See To the Mayor and Municipality of New Orleans, June 6, 1804, in *Official Letter Books of W. C. C. Claiborne, 1801–1816,* ed. Dunbar Rowland, vol. 2 (1917; New York: AMS Press, 1972), 194 (hereinafter cited as CLB with volume and page range). Dow's refusal to serve in the legislature may be seen in From Robert Dow, October 10, 1804, ibid., 374.

examination administered by the board.[23] Near the end of the territorial period, Dow accepted appointment (June 1, 1811) for one year to the Administrative Council of Charity Hospital.[24]

As Dow's conduct above indicates, his primary concern was medicine, but he and Angélica also demonstrated interest in cultural and educational developments. When the first professional theatrical company opened its stage in New Orleans, the Dows took a box.[25] The doctor's interest in the promotion of education manifested itself after the United States acquired Louisiana. When the territorial council provided for the establishment of the University of Orleans (April 19, 1805), Dow was named as one of the regents.[26] Dow also was one of the founders of the College of Orleans when it was established near the end of the territorial period.[27] The doctor also was a founder of the Société Médicale de la Nouvelle-Orléans, which was organized during the virulent outbreak of yellow fever in 1817 and chartered by the state legislature in 1818. He served as president of the society in 1822.[28]

Angélica died at the age of 72 (October 21, 1821) and was buried in the Girod Street Cemetery.[29] She was survived by Dow and her two sons by her first marriage.[30] Approximately two years later, Dow returned to England, where he was still living in 1840–41.[31]

23. Duffy, *History of Medicine,* 1: 385.

24. Return of Civil Appointments made in the Territory of Orleans from 1st Jany 1811 to 31st Dec, of the same year, enclosed in Secretary Robertson to the Secretary of State, Jany 18, 1812; and Members of the Council of Administration of the Charity Hospital of New-Orleans for 12 Months, TP, 9: 987; and Circular to Messrs. Felix Arnaud, Michael Fortier, Francis Caissergues, Richd. Butler, Robert Dow, J. D. Belchasse [*sic*], May 12, 1811, CLB, 5: 237.

25. René J. LeGardeur, Jr., *The First New Orleans Theatre, 1792–1803* (New Orleans: Leeward Books, 1963), 18.

26. *Acts Passed at the First Session of the Legislative Council, of the Territory of Orleans, Begun and Held at the Principal, in the City of New Orleans, on Monday the Third Day of December, in the Year of Our Lord, One Thousand Eight Hundred and Four, and of the Independence of the United States the Twenty-Ninth* (New Orleans: James M. Bradford, 1805), 306; and Memorial to Congress from the Regents of the University of Orleans, April 20, 1812, TP, 9: 1014.

27. Governor Claiborne to the President, March 25, 1805, TP, 9: 424 n. 6; Marietta Marie LeBreton, *A History of the Territory of Orleans, 1803–1812* (Ann Arbor, Mich.: University Microfilms, 1973), 290–300; and Duffy, *History of Medicine,* 1: 312–3.

28. Duffy, *History of Medicine,* 1: 488–91.

29. *Louisiana Courier,* October 22, 1821, p. 2, c. 1; and Huber and Bernard, *Girod Street Cemetery,* 20.

30. On the lives and careers of Thomas and David Urquhart, see the index references to them herein and in TP, 9.

31. Korn, *Early Jews of New Orleans,* 54.

JOSEPH PEYTAVIN

Joseph Antoine Peytavin (1749–February 18, 1835) was a minor figure, but one of the strong personalities in early Louisiana. The earliest record of Peytavin's presence in Louisiana is January 24, 1787, when he began acquiring property in what is now Ascension Parish.[1] By 1796 he had joined with Juan (Jean) Reynaud to form the New Orleans firm of Reynaud & Peytavin, which traded with Bordeaux, France, as well as ports in the United States and the West Indies.[2] Under the United States government Peytavin continued to prosper. In 1805 he was one of the founders of the Marine Insurance Company of New Orleans.[3] After William Donaldson founded Donaldson Town, later known as Donaldsonville, Reynaud & Peytavin opened a large mercantile business there. The store undoubtedly was opened in anticipation of business generated from the construction of a steam-powered sawmill at Donaldson Town by William Donaldson, and from the belief, promoted by Donaldson, Peytavin, and others, that the fledgling community would soon be the capital of territorial Louisiana. The bid to make Donaldson Town capital of Louisiana was not successful, and the Reynaud & Pey-

1. Sidney A. Marchand, *An Attempt to Re-Assemble the Old Settlers in Family Groups* (Baton Rouge: Claitor's Book Store, 1965), 85 (entry 554).

2. *Archivo General de Indias, Sección V, Gobierno. Audiencia de Santo Domingo Sobre la Época Española de Luisiana*, legajo 2668, folio 927, microfilm reel 221, Special Collections, Library, Loyola University, New Orleans.

3. *Acts Passed at the Second Session of the Legislative Council of the Territory of Orleans, Begun and Held at the Principal, in the City of New Orleans, on Thursday the Twentieth Day of June, in the Year of Our Lord, One Thousand Eight Hundred and Five, and of the Independence of the United States the Twenty-Ninth* (New Orleans: James M. Bradford, 1805), 102.

tavin business failed in March 1813, a victim of the economic depression brought on by the Napoleonic wars.[4]

Like many early Louisianians, Peytavin maintained a home in New Orleans and operated a plantation above the city immediately south of Donaldson Town.[5] Unfortunately, the business panic of 1819 contributed to Peytavin's loss of this property in 1822. The foreclosure suit filed in June of that year described the plantation as having a good stand of cane in the fields and well equipped to produce sugar.[6]

The idea of moving the state capital from New Orleans had never been forgotten, and when the legislature determined to move the state government to Donaldsonville in 1825, Peytavin, now seventy-three years old, signed a contract with the commissioners to build the new statehouse. Although he began construction of the building, it apparently was not completed to the satisfaction of the legislature because Peytavin was not paid in full for his work. Moreover, on January 6, 1831, several days after the second legislative session began in the Donaldsonville statehouse, the legislature adjourned to reconvene in New Orleans.[7]

Peytavin died at Donaldsonville on February 18, 1835. His funeral was held at Ascension Catholic Church.[8]

4. Claiborne to Madison, March 14, 1808, James Madison Papers, series I, General Correspondence and Related Items, 1723–1859, Presidential Papers microfilm no. 2974, reel no. 10, Troy H. Middleton Library, Louisiana State University Libraries; and Sidney A. Marchand, *The Flight of a Century (1800–1900) in Ascension Parish, Louisiana* (Donaldsonville: S. A. Marchand, 1936), 24, 37.

5. *New Orleans in 1805: A Directory and a Census, Together with Resolutions Authorizing Same, Now Printed for the First Time from the Original Manuscript* (1805; New Orleans: Pelican Gallery, 1936), 28, 76.

6. Marchand, *Flight of a Century,* 55–6.

7. *Journal of the House of Representatives of the State of Louisiana, Tenth Legislature, First Session* (New Orleans: John Gibson, 1831), 6, 7, 13. See also Marchand, *Flight of a Century,* 85–7, and Edwin Adams Davis, *Louisiana: A Narrative History,* 3rd ed. (Baton Rouge: Claitor's, 1971), 194.

8. Sidney A Marchand, Sr., "An Attempt to Re-Assemble the Old Settlers in Family Groups," *New Orleans Genesis* 4, no. 15 (June 1965), 266–7 (entry 554, Antoine Peytavin).

PIERRE BAILLY

Pierre Bailly[1] (sometimes misspelled "Bailey," as well as "Belly") was a free man of color who joined with fifty-five other free men of color (one of whom was his son, Pierre Bailly *fils*), to sign the January 1804 address to Governor Claiborne in which they offered their services and support for the United States government in Louisiana.[2]

Bailly, *père,* was a longtime resident of Louisiana and well known to the Spanish, having served as a sergeant second class in the New Orleans Mulatto Militia as early as 1792.[3] By the spring of 1795, Bailly had been promoted to lieutenant.[4] During the mid-1790s, Bailly also served as syndic (civil magistrate) of the first ward of the Iberville Coast.[5] Earlier in the decade, Bailly had expressed strong sympathy for the principles of the French Revolution and reportedly declared at one time that he and his companions were awaiting word from Santo Domingo to move against the Spanish officials in New Orleans. As a consequence, Governor Carondelet believed

1. Neither the dates of Bailly's birth nor death have been found.
2. Address from the Free People of Color, January 1804 [*sic*], Clarence E. Carter, comp. and ed., *The Territorial Papers of the United States*, vol. 9, *The Territory of Orleans, 1803–1812* (Washington, D.C.: U. S. Government Printing Office, 1940), 174–5 (hereinafter cited as TP, with volume and page range).
3. Jack D. L. Holmes, *Honor and Fidelity: The Louisiana Infantry Regiment and the Louisiana Militia Companies, 1766–1821* (Birmingham, Ala.: [Jack D. L. Holmes,] 1965), 233, entry 711.
4. Roland C. McConnell, *Negro Troops of Antebellum Louisiana: A History of the Battalion of Free Men of Color* (Baton Rouge: Louisiana State University Press, 1968), 27.
5. Holmes, *Honor and Fidelity,* 233, entry 711, states that Bailly was syndic in 1796.

Bailly "possessed diabolical ideas of freedom and equality" and had him arrested and tried. Following his trial, Bailly was sent to Havana on February 24, 1794, for confinement as a political prisoner until after the war. When released, Bailly was permitted to return to Louisiana.[6]

Bailly's resentment of the Spanish government stemmed from two unhappy experiences at their hands in the early 1790s. In one case, brought before the cabildo in 1790, Bailly sought damages from the government for the death of a slave whom he sent to work on a crevasse in the Mississippi River levee. The cabildo rejected his claim, saying the work had been assigned to Bailly and that the slave had died of natural causes, thereby exonerating the government of any responsibility in his death. In another instance Bailly sought to have the firewood belonging to someone else moved from the enclosed terrace built by Bailly on the batture[7] in front of his house. Governor Carondelet ruled against Bailly in this case on the grounds that the batture was held in common. An outgrowth of this suit additionally penalized Bailly. An enterprising individual, Bailly had permanently anchored a flatboat on the batture, from which he operated a store. Governor Carondelet ordered the flatboat removed or threatened to have it demolished.[8]

Claiborne's March 14, 1805, appointment of Bailly as judge (civil commandant) was confirmed by the territorial legislature on May 29, 1805.[9]

6. McConnell, *Negro Troops*, 28.

7. The batture was the alluvium of sand and clay gradually deposited by subsiding currents within the river channel on land fronting the Mississippi River. Through long-established custom, the batture was used as a place for anchorage and wharfage by riparian owners.

8. Ibid., 28–9.

9. See Letter No. 157, To Pierre Bailly, March 14, 1805, and Register of Civil Appointments in the Territory of Orleans, February 13, 1806, TP, 9: 598.

MUNICIPAL/CITY COUNCIL

Pierre Clément de Laussat, French colonial prefect and commissioner at the time of the Louisiana Purchase, replaced the cabildo, the Spanish governing body for the city of New Orleans, with the *conseil de ville,* city council, or "Municipal," as it was sometimes referred to in the early years of territorial Louisiana.

The reorganization and title change of city government were effective November 30, 1803, the date that Louisiana was officially transferred from Spain to France. Laussat considered creation of the Municipal Council the "dominant act" of his short-lived government. It was his intention that the Municipal should survive him and "hold its own" with the Americans after they took possession of Louisiana.[1] Governor Claiborne, faced with many responsibilities and with limited staff to assist him, continued the life of the Municipal after the transfer of Louisiana to the United States on December 20, 1803, and, in conjunction with the mayor and city council, handled most of the problems for New Orleans.[2]

The Municipal initially consisted of twelve council members, the mayor, and a recorder/secretary. Laussat selected his appointees to the Municipal from the merchant/planter class in and around New Orleans. They were Étienne de Boré, mayor; Pierre Derbigny, recorder-secretary; and council

---

1. Pierre Clément de Laussat, *Memoirs of My Life to My Son During the Years 1803 and After . . .,* trans. Sister Agnes-Josephine Pastwa, O.S.F., ed. Robert D. Bush (Baton Rouge: Louisiana State University Press, 1978), 75.

2. Letter No. 16, To James Madison, October 16, 1804; and Marietta Marie LeBreton, *A History of the Territory of Orleans, 1803–1812* (Ann Arbor, Mich.: University Microfilms, 1973), 187.

members Jean Noël Destréhan; Pierre Sauvé; Jacques Enould de Livaudais (*père*); Antoine Joseph Petit-Cavelier; Jacques Philippe Villeré; Evan Jones; Michael Fortier (*père*); William Donaldson; Joseph Faurie; Jean Pierre Allard (*fils*); Augustine Dominique Tureaud; and John Watkins.[3]

Not all of the Laussat appointees remained on the council after the transfer of Louisiana to the United States. The first to resign were Evan Jones and Pierre Sauvé. Sauvé was one of two assistants to Mayor Boré. The next to resign was Boré himself, who resigned as mayor on May 19, 1804, over political differences with the Jefferson administration. Claiborne appointed James Pitot mayor on June 2, 1804.[4]

The act to incorporate the city of New Orleans was passed by the legislative council on February 17, 1805. In the following month, the election was held to choose two council members from each of the seven wards created by the act.[5] Thus, by 1805 the Municipal had sixteen members: Le Breton Deschapelles; Jacques Livaudais, Sr.; Joseph A. Petit-Cavelier [*sic*]; Jacques Villeré; Michel Fortier, Sr.; William Donaldson; Joseph Faurie; Louis Allard, Jr.; A. D. Tureaud; John Watkins; Pierre Petit; William E. Hulings; James Carrick; Francis Joseph Le Breton D'Orgenois; Samuel Winter; and Thomas Porée.[6] Complaints of poor attendance at the meetings of the Municipal were frequent until after Governor Claiborne appointed John Watkins mayor in July 1805.[7] Stronger leadership and greater interest in the business of the council apparently began to cause better-attended meetings.

3. Laussat, *Memoirs of My Life,* 75–6.

4. See the biographical sketch of James Pitot.

5. Notice to the Citizens of New Orleans, February 25, 1805, in Clarence E. Carter, comp. and ed., *The Territorial Papers of the United States,* vol. 9, *The Territory of Orleans, 1803–1812* (Washington, D.C.: U.S. Government Printing Office, 1940), 398–404.

6. "Administrations of the Mayors of New Orleans, 1803–1936," comp. and ed. Works Project Administration (project 665-64-3-112, typescript; New Orleans, March 1940), 1.

7. See the biographical sketch of John Watkins.

MILITARY ASSOCIATION/ASSOCIATES

The earliest known reference to the "military association" occurs in the January 2, 1806, letter of John Graham, Orleans Territory secretary, to Secretary of State James Madison. In his letter Graham advised Madison that "the Mayor of the City and myself are endeavouring to draw all our countrymen into a military association for the defence of the city in case it should be attacked by the Spanish forces now on our Eastern or Western frontiers."[1] Graham reported that from the best accounts available to him there were "about three hundred and fifty men other than french, Spanish or natives" in New Orleans and its vicinity who could be relied on to help defend the city. The territorial secretary's estimate did not include the regular armed forces of the U.S. Army, Navy, or Marines stationed in New Orleans.[2] Graham went on in his letter to Madison to state that the association "would be put in no regular form until the return of the Governor."[3]

The military association proposed by Watkins and Graham is not heard of thereafter, not even in the crises of March and August 1806, when there was heightened concern for the security of New Orleans and all the Orleans Territory. It was in these months that Spanish troops had crossed the Sabine

1. Secretary Graham to the Secretary of State, January 2, 1805 [1806], in Clarence E. Carter, comp. and ed., *The Territorial Papers of the United States,* vol. 9, *The Territory of Orleans, 1803–1812* (Washington, D.C.: U.S. Government Printing Office, 1940), 555 (hereinafter cited as TP, with volume and page range). The date on the letter says 1805, but clearly should have been 1806, as indicated by Dr. Carter.

2. Ibid., 554.

3. Ibid., 555.

River to within seven miles of Natchitoches and there was considerable concern that New Orleans might be attacked from Mobile and Pensacola.[4]

During the latter scare, Claiborne, who was away from New Orleans on
the first leg of an intended visit to Tennessee, advised John Watkins, then
mayor of New Orleans, that Cowles Mead, the acting governor of the Mississippi Territory, would, if it became necessary, "detach to New Orleans,
such number of his militia, as may be in his power" to help defend the city.[5]
Nothing was said by Claiborne about alerting the "military association,"
which raises two questions: (1) How did Claiborne react to the concept of
the military association when Graham and/or Watkins presented it to him
early in 1806; and (2) did Claiborne implement their suggestion, or authorize its implementation? No record has been found that Claiborne objected
to the organization of the military association, but there also is no proof
that he endorsed it, or authorized anyone else to begin organizing it. However, there is evidence that he strongly supported the idea of a military resolution of the diplomatic conundrum along the Gulf of Mexico.

It is possible that on learning of the administration's plans for bolstering
the defenses of Louisiana, Claiborne dropped his call for the use of force
because of his knowledge of Jefferson's great reluctance to resort to arms.
It also is possible that Jefferson's secret requests to Congress in December
1805 to strengthen the defenses of the United States,[6] along with the support
of Watkins and Graham, encouraged Claiborne to try to nudge the president into taking action to end the tensions between Spain and the United
States in the old Southwest.

Midway through February 1806, Claiborne wrote Jefferson that he
would "indeed be gratified if an opportunity was offered me, to evince on
the Field, my devotion to the Interest and honor of my country" against
Spain.[7] Still smitten with the idea of success on the battlefield, as well as
vexed by the Spanish threat on Louisiana's boundaries and the territory's

---

4. The Spanish incursion near Natchitoches eventually was determined to number fewer
than seven hundred. Subsequently, the Spanish troops fell back to Bayou Pierre, which Claiborne described as about fifty-five or sixty miles west of Natchitoches. To Henry Dearborn,
August 28, 1806, *Official Letter Books of W. C. C. Claiborne, 1801–1816,* ed. Dunbar Rowland, vol. 3 (1917; New York: AMS Press, 1972), 388 (hereinafter cited as CLB, with volume
and page numbers).

5. [To] Dr. John Watkins, August 17, 1806, ibid., 378.

6. See Dumas Malone, *Jefferson and His Time,* vol. 5, *Jefferson the President, Second
Term, 1805–1809* (Boston: Little, Brown, 1974), 68–75, 241–3.

7. William C. C. Claiborne to the President of the United States, February 13, 1806, William C. C. Claiborne Collection, Historical Society of Pennsylvania.

vulnerability to attack from the Gulf of Mexico, Claiborne wrote Jefferson three times in March 1806 urging military action. On March 3 the governor wrote the president encouraging him to seize Baton Rouge and Mobile.[8] The frustrated governor wrote the president again on March 18, saying the only thing that would obtain respect for American rights in the old Southwest was force. The sooner this expedient was resorted to, Claiborne said, the better.[9] Eight days later, the governor once again wrote the president, saying that Mobile could be taken "without the loss of much blood" and that the Spanish on the Sabine River did not have the means "to do mischief."[10]

The reaction of Jefferson to Claiborne's pleas that force be used to seize Spanish territory along the U.S. border in the old Southwest is not known. There is no correspondence from the president to the governor dealing with the subject, thereby suggesting that Jefferson gave Claiborne's idea a cold shoulder. On the other hand, it is known that after March 26 Claiborne no longer urged the president to use force against the Spanish. Thereafter, the governor clearly adhered to the policy laid out by the president. This policy relied on the regulars of the U.S. Army, Navy, and Marines, along with the territorial militia, to provide for the defense of New Orleans and the Orleans Territory.

It also is possible that, on further thought, Claiborne fully embraced Jefferson's position because the idea he advanced sounded too much like the marshaling of men and resources headed by Daniel Clark for Laussat during the transition of governments from Spain to France to the United States in November 1803. During the transition from Spanish to French rule, the "Volunteer association" actually patrolled the streets of New Orleans for about three weeks.[11] Clark was Claiborne's most outspoken critic by 1806.

8. William C. C. Claiborne to The President, March 3, 1806, The Papers of Thomas Jefferson, 1651–1826, series 1, General Correspondence, Division of Manuscripts, Library of Congress, microfilm 4002, reel 35, Troy H. Middleton Library, Louisiana State University Libraries.

9. William C. C. Claiborne to the President, March 18, 1806, ibid. See also Jared W. Bradley, "W. C. C. Claiborne and Spain: Foreign Affairs under Jefferson and Madison, 1801–1811, Part I, The Early Negotiations, 1801–1806," *Louisiana History* 12, no. 4 (fall 1971), 311.

10. William C. C. Claiborne to the President, March 26, 1806, The Papers of Thomas Jefferson, 1651–1826, series 1, General Correspondence, microfilm 4002, reel 35.

11. Laussat refers to the Americans organizing themselves into companies and electing Clark as their captain. Pierre Clément de Laussat, *Memoirs of My Life to My Son During the Years 1803 and After. . .* , trans. Sister Agnes-Josephine Pastwa, ed. Robert D. Bush (Baton Rouge: Louisiana State University Press, 1978), 78. A slightly different perspective is provided by Charles Gayarré, *History of Louisiana*, 4th ed., vol. 3 (New Orleans: Pelican, 1965), 607,

Acceptance and implementation of an idea strikingly similar to one closely associated with Clark would have had the effect of building up Clark's image with Congress and the Jefferson administration when relations between Clark and Claiborne were entering their nadir. Most important, continued pursuit of a project not endorsed by President Jefferson could have cost Claiborne his job as governor of the Orleans Territory.

The refusal of Jefferson to support Claiborne's pitch for a military solution to the diplomatic tangle in the old Southwest raises two intriguing questions. Would Jefferson's support for organization of the military "association" or "associates" have made it difficult, if not impossible, for General Wilkinson to develop and spin his tale of the Burr conspiracy? This speculation in turn raises the question: would there have been an opportunity for either Burr or Wilkinson to have played any role on the national scene in 1806–07?

It appears in hindsight that the failure to organize the Volunteer Association early in 1806 later left the young governor of Orleans Territory with only one conclusion to be drawn from Wilkinson's tale of a conspiracy in New Orleans—that the group at the heart of the charge was the Mexican Association. The objectives of this group were well known to the governor. Indeed the surviving fragmentary evidence indicates that Claiborne supported the aims of the Mexican Association in a sub-rosa fashion. Given his documented efforts to persuade Jefferson to use military force to end U.S. entanglements with the Spanish in the old Southwest, it is unlikely that Claiborne had no knowledge of the rumored intent to use the Mexican Association to seize nearby Spanish colonial possessions. What neither the governor nor anyone else anticipated was Aaron Burr's desperation to return to a position of importance in the eyes of the American people—either as an elected official in the federal government or in some other capacity—or how close Burr's activities came to revealing the traitorous conduct of General Wilkinson.

It is true that both Watkins and Graham believed, in varying degrees,

---

613. Gayarré perhaps used an earlier edition of Laussat's memoirs and was closer in time to the events.

Daniel Clark's December 3, 1803, letter to Madison in which he tells of 180 American men and their friends who spontaneously decided to organize the "Volunteer association" in November 1803 because of their concern about Spanish hostility over the loss of Louisiana and public tension in New Orleans can be found in [Arthur P. Whitaker, ed.,] "Another Dispatch from the United States Consul in New Orleans," *American Historical Review* 38, no. 2 (January 1933), 291–2.

that the territorial militia could not successfully defend the territory. Watkins expressed his opinion on this and related points when he wrote his report on the insurrection plot of "Le Grand" to Secretary Graham in early September 1805. The report was addressed to Graham in the absence of Claiborne, who was on an inspection of the militia in Attakapas County.[12]

John Graham expressed even stronger views than Dr. Watkins about the weakness of the militia. Writing to Secretary of War Henry Dearborn on December 26, 1805, exactly one week before his January 2, 1806, letter to Secretary Madison, Graham said:

My own opinion is that it [the militia] is not, nor ever will be equal to the defence of the Territory. The climate, the nature of the country, which does not admit of a thick population, and above all, the number of negroes, will ever make this a feeble part of the Union, even if the Creoles should be tempted to shoulder their muskets and feel as Americans. In this city there are some volunteer corps which might, I believe, be depended upon, and no doubt, in case of an emergency, others might be raised, but these would consist of men who could not leave the city for any length of time.[13]

Beyond the similarity of their opinions on the uncertain dependability of the territorial militia, there is no evidence that either Graham or Watkins organized the Military Association, or the Mexican Association, with which it has been confused.

12. John Watkins to Secretary Graham, September 6, 1805, enclosed in Secretary Graham to the Secretary of State, September 8, 1805, TP, 9: 504.
13. Gayarré, *History of Louisiana*, 4: 91–2.

MEXICAN ASSOCIATION/ASSOCIATES

The Mexican Association, often linked with the Military Association, first was spoken of in 1806 during the Burr conspiracy. According to General James Wilkinson the Mexican Association was the linchpin in Aaron Burr's plans to dismember the Union, rob the bank in New Orleans, and, with the help of the British navy, set himself up as ruler of nearby Spanish colonial possessions (Mexico, which included present-day Texas, and both East and West Florida), the Louisiana Purchase lands, and unspecified portions of the trans-Appalachian West.[1]

It is possible the military association proposed on January 2, 1806, by John Watkins and John Graham, but apparently never organized, would have included many of the members of the surreptitious and loosely affiliated Mexican Association. Interestingly, John Watkins, sometimes referred to as president of the Mexican Association, described the group as "a club . . . called the Mexican society."[2] Vicente Folch y Juan, Spanish governor of West Florida, said in his February 10, 1807, letter to Captain-General Someruelos in Havana that the Mexican Association had been established "about two years ago," which meant that it probably coalesced during the war scare with Spain in 1805.[3] However, there is no evidence to link the

1. Thomas P. Abernethy, *The Burr Conspiracy* (New York: Oxford University Press, 1954), 150–2.

2. *Debate in the House of Representatives of the Territory of Orleans on a Memorial to Congress, Respecting the Illegal Conduct of General Wilkinson* (New Orleans: Bradford & Anderson, 1807), 24–5 (hereinafter cited as *Debate on a Memorial to Congress*).

3. Walter F. McCaleb, *The Aaron Burr Conspiracy and A New Light on Aaron Burr* (1936; New York: Argosy-Antiquarian, 1966), addendum, 90. (The second part of this book,

two organizations. Folch also said in his letter that the *comisio*, Folch's shorthand reference to the *comisio revolutionario*, his name for the American Party or Mexican Association, in New Orleans was "dependent on the one in New York."[4]

Harman Blennerhassett said the associates numbered three hundred. However, John Graham, secretary of the Orleans Territory, refuted Blennerhassett's statement and repeated his conviction that "no such organization existed."[5] Three hundred men was the number John Watkins said he and John Graham sought to organize in 1805 during the war scare with Spain, but no papers of that organization, or the Mexican Association, have been known to exist.[6] Therefore, the number of members of this group and their identities may never be established. Most of the members are believed to have been Americans.[7] Hence, Vicente Folch's reference to them as the "American Party."

The initiative for establishing the association apparently came from James Workman, then judge of the Orleans County Court (New Orleans), former secretary to the Orleans Territory legislative council, and prior to that, secretary to Governor Claiborne, as well as a lawyer, playwright, and political analyst.[8] Workman gave the fullest description of the purposes and aims of the group in his December 30, 1806, interview with Lieutenant Colonel Constant Freeman.[9] Other members were among the most important

---

A New Light on Aaron Burr, is separately paginated. Therefore, references to this separate section will be cited as McCaleb, *Burr Conspiracy,* addendum, with page numbers.)

4. Ibid.

5. Testimony of John Graham in the Trial of Aaron Burr, *American State Papers: Miscellaneous,* vol. 1 (Washington: Gales and Seaton, 1834), 528.

6. John Watkins referred to three hundred members in the Mexican Association in his testimony in the trial of Workman and Kerr in February 1807. See James Workman, *The Trials of the Honb. James Workman, and Col. Kerr, Before the United States Court, for the Orleans District on a Charge of High Misdemeanor, in Planning and Setting on Foot, Within the United States, An Expedition for the Conquest and Emancipation of Mexico* (New Orleans: Bradford & Anderson, 1807), 7.

7. Although contradictory on key points, Henry Adams, *History of the United States of America during the Second Administration of Thomas Jefferson* (New York: Charles Scribner's Sons, 1890), 1: 223, 227, continues to provide a point of departure for attempts to wrest reality from hearsay about the Mexican Association/Associates. McCaleb, *Burr Conspiracy,* addendum, 32 n. 6, prints Vicente Folch's February 10, 1807, letter to Captain-General Someruelos, which corroborates and supplements James Workman's description of the group to Lieutenant Colonel Freeman in December 1806.

8. See the biographical sketch of James Workman.

9. Samuel H. Wandell and Meade Minnigerode, *Aaron Burr, A Biography Written, in Large Part, from Original and Hitherto Unused Material,* vol. 2 (New York: G. P. Putnam's Sons, 1925), 124–7.

men in the Orleans Territory: John Watkins, former member of the legislative council, mayor of the City of New Orleans, speaker of the territorial house of representatives, a prominent doctor in New Orleans and port physician, and contributor to the *Transactions of the American Philosophical Society;*[10] Daniel Clark, recently elected Orleans Territory delegate to the U.S. Congress, former U.S. consul in New Orleans during the last few months of Spanish possession, and one of the wealthiest men in the Louisiana Purchase territory;[11] Lewis Kerr, U.S. marshal during the transfer of Louisiana to the United States, first sheriff of New Orleans, a lawyer trained in the King's Inns, Dublin, Ireland, and colonel on Governor Claiborne's staff;[12] and George T. Ross, who followed Lewis Kerr as sheriff of New Orleans, former U.S. Army officer in the occupation of New Orleans in 1803, captain in the Orleans Rangers of the Orleans Territory militia, and, like most of the men appointed to office by Claiborne, a part of the loose inner circle of early advisers of the governor.[13]

Other prominent Orleans Territory officials and residents of New Orleans identified as members of the Mexican Association were John B. Prevost, judge of the territorial Superior Court; two more judges, one named Old and the other named [Abimael?] Nicolle; Edward Livingston, an attorney and well-known opponent of Governor Claiborne; Father Rodriquez, pastor of the Catholic Church in St. Bernard County below New Orleans; and Major William Nott, aide-de-camp to Governor Claiborne.[14] Two other men who most probably were members of the Mexican Association were Abraham R. Ellery, former assistant adjutant general in the Additional Army working directly under Alexander Hamilton during the undeclared war with France, 1798–1800, sometime hydrographer on the Mississippi River for Hamilton, and a lawyer; and James Alexander, former resident of New Jersey and also a lawyer. Both Ellery and Alexander settled in Louisiana with recommendations from Hamilton and endorsements by General Wilkinson.[15] No list of the loose membership has been found or is known to have existed.

10. See the biographical sketch of John Watkins.

11. There is no book-length study of Daniel Clark, but a recent examination of the life and career of this manipulative and insecure businessman, which cites all the pertinent sources on his life, is Michael Wohl, "Not Yet Saint Nor Sinner: A Further Note on Daniel Clark," *Louisiana History* 24, no. 2 (spring 1983), 195–205.

12. See the biographical sketch of Lewis Kerr.

13. See the biographical sketch of George T. Ross.

14. Adam Szászdi, "Governor Folch and the Burr Conspiracy," *Florida Historical Quarterly* 38, no. 3 (January 1960), 245.

15. Additional information on James Alexander may be found in the biographical sketch of Abraham R. Ellery, n. 13.

Two characteristics distinguished the members of the Mexican Association in New Orleans. With a few exceptions, most of them were businessmen who disliked and distrusted the Spanish officials and soldiers who remained in New Orleans beyond the ninety-day grace period permitted by the treaty confirming acceptance of the transfer of Louisiana to the United States.[16] John Watkins said the Mexican Association—he called it the Mexican Society—grew out of the apprehension shared by "every man of sense" that the United States and Spain were about to go to war in 1805. The purpose of the society, Watkins said, was to collect "information relative to the population and force of the internal provinces of [New] Spain, which in the event of war, might be useful to the United States."[17] The term employed for the Spanish, usually as an epithet, by those opposed to continued Spanish presence in New Orleans was the *Dons*. Most of the association members strongly believed the lingering Spanish officials and their local sympathizers were the source of the recurring and unsettling rumor that the United States was going to return to Spain all of the Louisiana Purchase lands west of the Mississippi River.[18]

The beliefs of the Mexican Associates, as interpreted since the demise of the loose association, traditionally also have been the expansionist views identified with the history of the United States in the second quarter of the nineteenth century. Yet the roots of their ideas extended back into sixteenth-century England and were the same ideas that impelled Englishmen through the nineteenth century to take the lead in developing the British colonial empire. This most clearly is seen in the writings of Irish-born James Workman, who acknowledged that "emancipation of the Spanish provinces had been for many years his favorite object."[19]

Workman's views on Spanish rule are known not only from his play, *Lib-*

16. The ninety-day grace period ended on January 20, 1804. Hunter Miller, ed., *Treaties and Other International Acts of the United States of America,* vol. 2 (Washington, D.C.: U.S. Government Printing Office, 1931), 497, 508.

17. *Debate on a Memorial to Congress,* 25.

18. Secretary Graham to the Secretary of State, January 2, 1805 [1806]; Governor Claiborne to the Secretary of State, January 7, 1806; and George T. Ross to Governor Claiborne, February 11, 1806; all in Clarence E. Carter, comp. and ed., *The Territorial Papers of the United States,* vol. 9, *The Territory of Orleans, 1803–1812* (Washington, D.C.: U.S. Government Printing Office, 1940), 553, 557–8, and 581–2 (hereinafter cited as TP, with volume and page range); two letters by Governor Claiborne To James Madison, July 25, 1804, and January 12, 1806, in *Official Letter Books of W. C. C. Claiborne, 1801–1816,* ed. Dunbar Rowland, vol. 2 (1917; New York: AMS Press, 1972), 266–7, and vol. 3, 241–2, respectively; and Letters No. 78 and 197, To James Madison, December 11, 1804, and April 21, 1805.

19. Wandell and Minnigerode, *Aaron Burr,* 126.

erty in Louisiana, first performed in Charleston, South Carolina, in April 1804, but also from his 1801 political writings, which advocated the conquest and emancipation of Spanish America.[20] After settling in New Orleans in the spring of 1804, reportedly on the encouragement of John Watkins, Workman modified his views to meet the circumstances of Spain's collapsing empire and the situation the United States found itself facing on the eastern and western borders of the Orleans Territory in 1805 and 1806.

Perspective on Workman's role in shaping the thinking of the American community in early territorial New Orleans was revealed by Workman himself to Lieutenant Colonel Constant Freeman on December 30, 1806. The judge had gone to see Freeman, the commanding officer of all U.S. military forces in the Orleans Territory under the commanding general of the United States Army, General James Wilkinson, on a court martial matter.[21] During the meeting their conversation turned to the upset caused in the city by Wilkinson's extreme actions to combat what Wilkinson himself described as the conspiracy to dismember the Union. With Workman's permission Freeman made a record of the judge's remarks for the stated purpose of submitting them to General Wilkinson. Workman's statement revealed that the association's aims might be objected to by Jefferson, but that, aside from baiting and unnerving Vicente Folch, the governor of Spanish West Florida, the association was innocent of actively pursuing them.

Workman informed Freeman that he "had been one of the persons who had long contemplated a plan to emancipate Mexico from the Spanish Government." The plan was to raise an army "under the auspices of the United States," but to pay for it "at the expense of the adventurers." The objectives of the associates were to "take Baton Rouge and Mobile and then to march into the Spanish provinces west of the Mississippi." If they were successful in seizing the provinces bordering Orleans Territory on the west, the association members were then "to erect an independent government under the protection of the United States." In so "far as he knew," Workman said, "Colo. Burr had nothing whatever . . . to do in this project." Burr was "mentioned as a proper person to command," but so, too, were General Wilkinson and Jonathan Dayton, a Revolutionary War veteran, former U.S.

20. See James Workman's *Political Essays, Relative to the War of the French Revolution; viz. An Argument, Against Continuing the War, for the Subversion of the Republican Government of France . . . And a Memorial, Proposing a Plan, for the Conquest and Emancipation of Spanish America . . .* (Alexandria, Va.: Cottom & Stewart, 1801).

21. Wandell and Minnigerode, *Aaron Burr,* 2: 124.

senator, and prominent Federalist.[22] Secrecy was asked of the associates, Workman said, "not for any purposes . . . injurious to the interests of the United States," but to prevent the Spanish from learning their aims. When the plan was contemplated, Workman said, it was "supposed the United States would inevitably be involved in a war with Spain." With this thought in mind, the judge said, he continued to acquire "geographical information" that might "be useful in case his plan" was adopted.[23] Briefly, the association members thought that Francisco de Miranda would lead an invasion army with United States backing, but when the U.S. government disavowed any connection with Miranda, Workman said, "all conversation whatever in relation to the proposed conquest of Mexico ceased."[24]

A quite similar description of the Mexican society was given by John Watkins to Governor Claiborne. Watkins's conversation with Claiborne clearly must have been after Judge Workman's interview with Lieutenant Colonel Freeman. On his honor as a gentleman, Watkins assured Claiborne that the "society has ceased to exist for many months—that we had heard of Burr's plans, and that neither directly or indirectly did I ever hear from him or any other man upon earth, any propositions hostile to the interest of the United States, or any other nation with which we were at peace."[25]

Corroboration of some of Workman's statements is provided by a surprising source, Vicente Folch y Juan, Spanish governor of West Florida. In his February 10, 1807, letter to Captain-General Someruelos in Havana, Folch gave a reasonably accurate account of the development of the Mexican Association's plans to conquer the Spanish colonies adjoining the American-owned Orleans Territory. The worrisome Folch reported that he had been invited to a banquet meeting of what he called the *Comisio Revolucionario* (Revolutionary Commission), or the Mexican Association, in New Orleans. At this function, Folch reported, he was offered a bribe to join the

---

22. Ibid., 125, 126.

23. Ibid., 126. In September 1805, Daniel Clark made what he called a "large mercantile speculation" trip to Veracruz. James Wilkinson, *Memoirs of My Own Times,* vol. 2 (1816; New York: AMS Press, 1973), Appendix XXXIII. After his return to the United States, Clark gave to John Graham, Orleans Territory secretary, data that he had collected on the strength of the armed forces in Mexico, the garrisoned towns between Veracruz and Mexico City, the naval strength in Veracruz, and the general social unrest in New Spain. Daniel Clark, *Proofs of the Corruption of Gen. James Wilkinson and of His Connexion with Aaron Burr, with a Full Refutation of His Slanderous Allegations in Relation to the Principal Witness Against Him* (1809; New York: Arno Press, 1971), 103.

24. Wandell and Minnigerode, *Aaron Burr,* 2: 124–5, 127.

25. *Debate on a Memorial to Congress,* 25.

revolutionary movement taking shape in Mexico. In exchange for joining the *Comisio,* Folch was to be made commander in chief of the revolutionary army in Mexico.

Folch described Judge Workman as the chief spokesman of the group. Delaying his answer while attempting to dissemble, Folch said he could not give Workman an answer to his offer until he knew all about the plans. Workman would not reveal the plans, Folch said, for fear that Folch "would denounce them." Workman countered Folch's demand for full information by saying that he would not be able to resist the proposition because there was a large sum of money to be paid him, so large that it would keep him and his family the rest of their lives. Nonetheless, Folch was unswayed, whereupon Workman then pointed out that West Florida easily could be taken by the United States. Once that was accomplished and Folch made prisoner, Folch quoted Workman as saying, the same proposition could be offered, thereby enabling him to return to his country without being dishonored. When Folch did not accept this offer, he said, the *Comisio* voted to "put me out of the way so as not to injure the cause," but postponed the "bitter moment" when they would make "their treacherous propositions."[26] At this same banquet, Folch reported, he also was unhappy at the toast offered by Governor Claiborne. This toast, Folch said, called for the "happy success" of the Miranda expedition to Venezuela.[27]

Workman's conversation with Freeman occurred on the morning of December 30. That evening the judge paid Freeman another visit, during which Freeman repeated to him what he had reported to General Wilkinson that morning. The judge agreed to the essential "correctness" of the Freeman statement given to Wilkinson. Thereafter, both men talked freely about the subject of establishing an independent government in Mexico. In this conversation Workman said again that the "whole plan and its execution was to have depended on the approbation and concurrence of the United States." The judge reiterated that without the approval of the United States, "nothing was to have been undertaken." Before the meeting between the two men ended, Workman expressed the belief that the "United States would at some future day find it for their interest to carry into operation an expedition upon similar principles."[28]

Perhaps because the Mexican Associates came into existence in response

26. McCaleb, *Burr Conspiracy,* addendum, 91–2.
27. Ibid., 92.
28. Wandell and Minnigerode, *Aaron Burr,* 2: 125, 127.

to an invasion scare, few writers who have dealt with the group's intentions have seen them as a mixture of conflicting objectives. They have visualized the group as a servant of Aaron Burr, which, on the basis of the statements of Judge James Workman and Dr. John Watkins, the group's most important leaders, is not accurate.

Evidence supports the belief that many of the businessmen affiliated in this loose grouping had interests other than military conquest. Some wanted to establish Mexico as an independent state much like the nations that were making their appearance amidst the collapsing Spanish Empire in South America. Daniel Clark's "large mercantile speculation" trip to Veracruz in September 1805 was conceived as a business trip, but was expanded to include the gathering of strategic military information.[29]

Unfortunately, many of the lesser-known New Orleans businessmen did not come forward to support the business interests of the group after the Burr conspiracy was unleashed on the city and nation by General Wilkinson. These nameless small businessmen remained in the background, undoubtedly seeking to avoid attracting Wilkinson's wrath and power. In this context, it should be noted that the most recent research on the life of Philip Nolan, the earliest possible expansionist and Wilkinson's protégé, clearly indicates that Nolan's object was not conquest. He instead sought income from wild horses corralled in Texas for trade in New Orleans and elsewhere in the budding racehorse industry of the old Southwest. He certainly appealed to the avarice of the men who joined him on his last expedition into Texas in 1800.[30] Given the boyhood friendship of Philip Nolan and John Watkins, Nolan's image appears to have hovered over the Mexican Associates like a ghost.[31]

29. Clark, *Proofs of the Corruption of Gen. James Wilkinson*, 103. Wilkinson, *Memoirs of My Own Times*, vol. 2, Appendix XXXIII, generally supports Clark on this point.

30. See Maurine T. Wilson and Jack Jackson, *Philip Nolan and Texas: Expeditions to the Unknown Land, 1791–1801* (Waco, Tex.: Texian Press, 1987), 43.

31. Perspective on the impact of the life of Philip Nolan is provided in the biographical sketch of Dr. John Watkins.

FORT ST. PHILIP

Plans for a fort at Plaquemine were drawn in 1787–88 during the administration of Governor Miró by Joachim Peramas.[1] The installation was not built, however, until 1792–93, when then Governor Carondelet feared invasion by the French as well as the Americans. Carondelet ordered the fort to be built on the east bank of the Mississippi River about sixty miles below New Orleans and about eighteen miles above the first mouth of the river, where it makes almost a forty-five-degree turn to the east on its course to the Gulf of Mexico. Hence, the location was known as *Punta del Torno de Placcamin,* Point of the Plaquemine Turn.[2] The French had considered building a fortification on the site nearly fifty years earlier, but rejected it in favor of the location farther up the river at English Turn, where the ground was higher.[3]

Placcamin and its gallicized equivalent, *plaquemine,* which became the accepted spelling and pronunciation of the word in the English language of Americans, are derived from the Illinois Indian word *piakimin,* meaning persimmon.[4] Thus, at or near the site of Fort St. Philip, there originally must

---

1. Jack D. L. Holmes, Photographic Copies of 44 Louisiana Maps Made from Originals in the Archivo General de Indias, Seville, 1963, "No. 29, Joachim Peramas, *Plano del fuerte proyectado para la Punta del Torno de Placcamin, March 20, 1787.*"

2. Ibid., "No. 8, F. L. H. Carondelet, *Plano del Torno de Placcamin y sus cortornos, 17 enero 1792,*" and "No. 39, *Plano de Castillo de Sn. Felipe de Placcaminas y Fuerte Bourbon, 1795.*"

3. Bill Barron, *The Vaudreuil Papers: A Calendar and Index to the Personal and Private Records of Pierre de Rigaud de Vaudreuil, Royal Governor of the French Province of Louisiana, 1743–1753,* 1st ed. (New Orleans: Polyanthos, 1975), 227.

4. William A. Read, *Louisiana Place-Names of Indian Origin* (Baton Rouge: The University, 1927), 50, 51–2.

have been a grove of persimmon trees. Saint Philip, after whom the fortification was named, was one of the first chosen disciples of Christ. Philip
preached the Gospel in Eastern Europe and Phrygia before his crucifixion.[5]

In choosing to name the fortification St. Philip, Carondelet united several
significant elements in the history of Spain: its strong Catholic tradition; the
French and Spanish preferences for the name Philip; and the memory of the
reigns of Philip II (1556–98) and Philip V (1700–46) with that of Charles
III (1759–88). Charles III was the grandson of Philip V, the first Bourbon
ruler of Spain and the grandson of Louis XIV of France. Like Philip II two
hundred years before, Charles III is generally regarded as an effective administrator. Of the eighteenth-century Bourbon rulers of Spain, he undoubtedly was the most progressive and successful.[6]

Ironically, Fort St. Philip was built by men of French ancestry employed
by Spain as protection against suspected French plans to seize Louisiana.[7]
Gilbert Antoine de St. Maxent, a retired lieutenant colonel of the Spanish
infantry who was born in Lorraine, France, built the fort according to the
plans drawn by his nephew, Gilbert de Guillemard.[8] Because it was built at
that point where the land on both sides of the river ceased to be firm and
passable in the late eighteenth century, the fort could be approached only
from the river. Indeed, the fort itself stood on part of the moving swamp that
lay southward to the Gulf of Mexico. Immediately below the bastion lay the
meandering Bayou Mardi Gras, which supplied the water for the twelve-
foot-deep and twenty-foot-wide moat surrounding the brick structure.

French general Georges Victor Collot, who saw the fort from the river
in 1796, described it as looking like two long arms broken in the middle.
The parapets of the fort on the river side were eighteen feet thick. Although
they were built on pilings two feet in diameter and twenty feet long, and set
six inches apart, the massive weight of the parapets had caused them to settle three feet on the bayou side and two feet on the land side by the time of
Collot's visit. Inside the fort there were two barracks designed to house
three hundred men, including the commander, and a powder magazine.

5. See *Holy Bible*, Mark 3:18; John 1:43–48; John 6:5–7, Revised Standard Version (New
York: American Bible Society, 1980), on Philip's early discipleship. Acts 6 and 8:26–40 tell of
his preaching in Eastern Europe and south-central Turkey. The date of his death is unknown.

6. Hubert Herring, *A History of Latin America from the Beginnings to the Present*, 2nd
rev. ed. (New York: Alfred A. Knopf, 1965), 167–8.

7. Abraham P. Nasatir, *Spanish War Vessels on the Mississippi, 1792–1796* (New Haven,
Conn.: Yale University Press, 1968), 4–5, 74ff.

8. James Julian Coleman, Jr., *Gilbert Antoine de St. Maxent: The Spanish-Frenchman of
New Orleans* (New Orleans: Pelican, 1968), 112–3.

Entry to the fort was made along the low levee that extended from the moat opposite the northern face of the bastion for about three hundred *toises* (one *toise* equaled approximately one fathom, or six feet). A drawbridge built in the north wall of the fort opposite the low levee controlled access from that point. Between the low levee and the moat was a causeway made from the earth taken from the moat. Emplaced in the causeway at the base of the low levee was a palisade of stakes twelve feet high.[9]

By the time the United States acquired Louisiana and occupied Fort St. Philip late in December 1803, the fort had further deteriorated. Lieutenant Colonel Constant Freeman, who commanded U.S. troops in the Orleans Territory, advised General Wilkinson on October 11, 1805, that the fort must be repaired.[10] In his report to Congress on fortifications in the country on February 16, 1806, President Jefferson estimated that $25,000 would be needed to make repairs to the fortifications at New Orleans and its dependencies.[11] Congress did not appropriate any money for the repairs, however, because it did not have information on the particular needs of the fortifications. The necessary information reached Washington before the end of the year, apparently supplied by General Wilkinson. The following January 9, 1807, Secretary of War Henry Dearborn reported to Congress that it would take from $50,000 to $70,000 to make the improvements needed at the "old work at Placquemines," to establish a battery at English Turn and at the junction of Bayou St. John with Lake Pontchartrain, and to provide gunboat protection for New Orleans on the lake and the Mississippi River. Ten months later, Secretary Dearborn amended his report, adding that it would take about $60,000 to provide the sixteen gunboats needed at New Orleans.[12] Subsequently, Congress appropriated $80,373 for the fortifications in the New Orleans district.[13]

9. James A. Robertson, ed. and trans., *Louisiana Under the Rule of Spain, France, and the United States, 1785–1807*, vol. 1 (1910–1911; Freeport, N.Y.: Books for Libraries Press, 1969), 161. Collot's sketch of the fort is in Georges Henri Victor Collot, *A Journey in North America, Containing a Survey of the Countries Watered by the Mississippi, Ohio, Missouri and other Affluing Rivers* . . . (1826; 1924; Paris: A. Bertrand, 1974), Plate 36. See also Coleman, *Gilbert Antoine de St. Maxent*, "Plan of Fort St. Philip," between pp. 112 and 113.

10. Freeman's letter apparently has not survived, but it is referenced in one of the letters found in *Records of the Office of the Secretary of War. Letters Received, Unregistered Series, 1789–1860.* National Archives and Records Service, Record Group 107, microcopy 222, reel 2, 1805–1807, on deposit with the Troy H. Middleton Library, Louisiana State University Libraries.

11. *American State Papers: Military Affairs,* vol. 1 (Washington, D.C.: Gales & Seaton, 1832), 196.

12. Ibid., 204, 207, 222.

13. Ibid., 239.

By the summer of 1809 the sum spent on fortifications in the New Orleans district had grown to $91,769.17.[14] The cause of the increased district defense costs was revealed in Jefferson's message to Congress in January of that year. The condition of Fort St. Philip was so poor that a new fort had to be built.[15] A report later in 1809 establishes that the new fort was built on the site of the earlier structure. The new fort was an enclosed work of masonry and wood with two bastions, twenty cannons, a powder magazine, and barracks for one company.[16]

Despite these expenditures and improvements, Major William MacRae, commander of the New Orleans garrison, provided Secretary Dearborn with an estimate of additional work needed in the New Orleans district when he forwarded the plans of the newly completed Fort St. Philip on October 18, 1809.[17]

During the War of 1812, Fort St. Philip was a deterrent to British plans to attack Louisiana. Except for its barracks, the fort apparently was in good condition. Colonel MacRae advised Andrew Jackson on September 9, 1814, that the barracks in the fort were "very old and decayed, and might be easily fired by an enemy with shells and rockets." MacRae went on to state that the foundation had been laid for new barracks the previous winter, "but the work was suspended for want of funds."[18] Although the British did bombard the fort (January 9–18, 1815), they were unsuccessful in getting past the structure to relieve their troops attacking New Orleans.[19]

14. Ibid., 247.

15. Ibid., 236.

16. Ibid., 236, 246.

17. William MacRae to Secretary of War Dearborn, October 18, 1809, Records of the Office of the Secretary of War. Registers of Letters Received, 1800–1860, vol. 4, April 10, 1808–December 31, 1809, Alphabet Section M, entry 602, microcopy 221, reel 4, National Archives and Records Service, Record Group 107, on deposit with the Troy H. Middleton Library, Louisiana State University Libraries.

18. Lieutenant-Colonel William MacRae to Jackson, September 9, 1814, John Spencer Bassett, ed., *Correspondence of Andrew Jackson*, vol. 2 (Washington, D.C.: Carnegie Institution of Washington, 1927), 46.

19. Charles B. Brooks, *The Siege of New Orleans* (Seattle: University of Washington Press, 1961), 210, 212, 249, 254–7, 259–60; and Wilburt S. Brown, *The Amphibious Campaign for West Florida and Louisiana, 1814–1815: A Critical Review of Strategy and Tactics at New Orleans* (University: University of Alabama Press, 1969), 160.

BIBLIOGRAPHY

GUIDES TO SOURCES

American Library Directory, 1994–95. 14th ed. 2 vols. New Providence, N.J.: R. R. Bowker, 1994.

Arthur, Stanley C. *Index to the Archives of Spanish West Florida, 1782–1810*. New Orleans: Polyanthos, 1975.

———. *Index to the Dispatches of the Spanish Governors of Louisiana, 1766–1792*. New Orleans: Polyanthos, 1975.

Barron, Bill. *The Vaudreuil Papers: A Calendar and Index to the Personal and Private Records of Pierre de Rigaud de Vaudreuil, Royal Governor of the French Province of Louisiana, 1743–1753*. New Orleans: Polyanthos, 1975.

Beers, Henry Putney. *French and Spanish Records of Louisiana: A Bibliographical Guide to Archive and Manuscript Sources*. Baton Rouge: Louisiana State University Press, 1989.

Bertin, P. M., comp. *General Index to All Successions, Emancipations, Interdictions and Partition Proceedings Opened in the Parish of Orleans from the Year 1805, to the Year 1845*. New Orleans: P. O. Bertin, 1849.

Boling, Yvette Guillot, comp. *A Guide to Printed Sources for Genealogical and Historical Research in the Louisiana Parishes*. Baton Rouge: Land and Land, 1985.

———. *A Guide to Printed Sources for Genealogical and Historical Research in the Louisiana Parishes: Supplement*. Baton Rouge: Land and Land, 1992.

Brigham, Clarence S. *History and Bibliography of American Newspapers, 1690–1820*. 2 vols. 1947. Reprint, Westport, Conn.: Greenwood Press, 1976.

British Museum General Catalogue of Printed Books. Photolithographic edition to 1955. 263 vols. London: Trustees of the British Museum, 1961–66, vols. 14 and 122.

Congressional Information Service. *United States Serial Set Index.* Part I. *American State Papers and the 15th–34th Congresses, 1789–1857. Subject Index A–Z.* 2 vols. Washington, D.C.: Congressional Information Service, 1977.

Directory of Historical Organizations in the United States and Canada. Edited by Mary Bray Wheeler. 14th ed. Nashville: American Association for State and Local History, 1990.

Foote, Lucy, comp. *Bibliography of the Official Publications of Louisiana, 1803– 1934.* American Imprints Inventory No. 19. Baton Rouge: Works Project Administration, Historical Records Survey Program, 1942.

Guide to the National Archives of the United States. Washington, D.C.: National Archives and Records Service, General Services Administration, 1974.

Hamer, Philip M., ed. *A Guide to Archives and Manuscripts in the United States.* New Haven, Conn.: Yale University Press, 1961.

Hill, Roscoe R., ed. *Descriptive Catalogue of the Documents Relating to the History of the United States in the Papeles Procedentes de Cuba Deposited in the Archivo General de Indias at Seville.* Carnegie Institution of Washington, Papers of the Department of Historical Research, ed. J. Franklin Jameson, Publication 234. 1916; Washington: Carnegie Institution of Washington, 1965.

Jumonville, Florence. *Bibliography of New Orleans Imprints, 1764–1864.* New Orleans: Historic New Orleans Collection, 1989.

McDonald, Donna, comp. and ed. *Directory. Historical Societies and Agencies in the United States and Canada for 1973–74.* Nashville, Tenn.: American Association for State and Local History and Inforonics, 1972.

Newspapers in Microform, United States, 1948–1972. Washington, D.C.: Library of Congress, 1973.

Newspapers in Microform, United States, 1973–1977. Washington, D.C.: Library of Congress, 1978.

Owens, Kenneth E. *The Complete Cumulative Index to the Publications of the Louisiana Historical Society, 1895–1917.* Baton Rouge: Louisiana Library Association, 1984.

Peña y Camara, José de la, Ernest J. Burris, S.J., Charles E. O 'Neill, S.J, and Maria T. G. Fernandez. *Catalogo de Documentos del Archivo General de Indias, Sección V, Gobierno. Audiencia de Santo Domingo Sobre la Época Éspañola de Luisiana.* 2 vols. Madrid: Dirección General de Archivos y Bibliotecas, 1968.

Villeré, A. J., comp. *General Index of All Successions Opened in the Parish of Orleans, from the Year 1846 to the Month of August 1880.* New Orleans: [E. A. Peyroux] Press Job Print, 1881.

Wallach, Kate. *Bibliographical History of Louisiana Civil Law Sources: Roman, French and Spanish.* Baton Rouge: Louisiana State University Press, 1958.

Walne, Peter, ed. *A Guide to Manuscript Sources for the History of Latin America and the Caribbean in the British Isles.* London: Oxford University Press, 1973.

Weaks, Mabel Clare. *Calendar of the Kentucky Papers of the Draper Collection of*

Manuscripts. Publications of the State Historical Society of Wisconsin, Calendar Series, vol. 2. Madison: State Historical Society of Wisconsin, 1925.

PRIMARY SOURCES

MANUSCRIPTS IN THE NATIONAL ARCHIVES AND RECORDS SERVICE OF THE UNITED STATES

Card Register of Communications Sent and Received, 1798–1918, Entry 40, Daniel Carmick, USMC, Officer. Records of the United States Marine Corps, Historical Division. Record group 127. Photocopies owned by the author.

Daniel Carmick Pension Record. Records of the Veterans Administration. Record group 15. Navy and Old Army Branch, Military Archives Division. Photocopy owned by the author.

"General James Wilkinson's Order Book, December 31, 1796–March 8, 1808." Records of the U.S. Adjutant General's Office. Record group 94, microcopy M-654, reel 3. Troy H. Middleton Library, Louisiana State University Libraries.

Jackson, Andrew, Papers. Series I, General Correspondence and Related Items, 1775–1860, Presidential Papers microfilm no. 2725. Troy H. Middleton Library, Louisiana State University Libraries.

Madison, James, Papers. Presidential Papers microfilm no. 2974. Troy H. Middleton Library, Louisiana State University Libraries.

Registers of Letters Received, 1800–1860, Secretary of War. Record group 107, microcopy M-221. Troy H. Middleton Library, Louisiana State University Libraries.

Registers of Letters Received by the Secretary of War, Unregistered Series, 1789–1860. Record group 107, microcopy M-222. Troy H. Middleton Library, Louisiana State University Libraries.

State Department Territorial Papers, Orleans Series, 1764–1813, reel 6, vol. 6, January 1, 1805–June 21, 1805. National Archives microcopy T260, City Archives, Louisiana Department, New Orleans Public Library.

War of 1812. Bounty Land Warrant Applications. Records of the Veterans Administration. Record group 15. Daniel Carmick, BLWT-49626-160-55, Deposition of Marguerite Cowperthwaite Carmick, November 23, 1855, New Orleans. Photocopy owned by the author.

Williams, Henry E. "Biographical Sketch of Daniel Carmick, Major, USMC," rev. and ed. Ralph W. Donnelly. History and Museums Division, Department of the Navy. 1972; Washington, 1973 (typescript; photocopy owned by the author).

MANUSCRIPTS IN LOUISIANA DEPOSITORIES

Archivo General de Indias. Seville. Papeles de Cuba. Legajo 179-B (microfilm owned by the author).

————. *Legajos* 2366 and 2375. Louisiana and Lower Mississippi Valley Collections, Louisiana State University Libraries.

Archivo General de Indias. Sección V, Gobierno. Audiencia de Santo Domingo Sobre la Época Española de Luisiana. Special Collections, Library, Loyola University, New Orleans.

Archivo General de Simancas. Sección de Guerra Moderna. Hojas de Servicias Militares de América, 1787–1799. Legajos 7291 and 7292. MSS 3124, microfilm 3124. Louisiana and Lower Mississippi Valley Collections, Louisiana State University Libraries.

Denis-DeBuys Papers, 1789–1962. Folder 1, 1789–1848. Special Collections, Howard-Tilton Memorial Library, Tulane University.

Draper Manuscript Collection, Kentucky MSS, Draper MSS 15 cc. State Historical Society of Wisconsin. Troy H. Middleton Library, Louisiana State University. Microfilm 3074.

Evans, Nathaniel, and Family Papers. Louisiana and Lower Mississippi Valley Collections, Louisiana State University Libraries.

Governor's Office, American Documents, 1804–1814. City Archives, Louisiana Department, New Orleans Public Library.

Great Britain. Public Record Office. *Colonial Office Papers [Original Correspondence: America and West Indies.]* Series 5, vols. 574, 586, 587. Microfilm 1753, Louisiana and Lower Mississippi Valley Collections, Louisiana State University Libraries.

Haldimand Papers, 1769–1772, Sir Frederick. Louisiana and Lower Mississippi Valley Collections, Louisiana State University Libraries (Library of Congress microfilm 2964).

Jefferson, Thomas, The Papers of, 1651–1826. Series 1, General Correspondence and Related Materials. Troy H. Middleton Library, Louisiana State University (Division of Manuscripts, Library of Congress, microfilm 4002).

Jones, Evan, Letter. Miscellaneous Collections, Special Collections, Howard-Tilton Memorial Library, Tulane University.

Lafourche Parish Surveys, 1790–1803. Louisiana and Lower Mississippi Valley Collections, Louisiana State University Libraries.

McCall, Henry, Speech, 1899. Louisiana and Lower Mississippi Valley Collections, Louisiana State University Libraries.

Morgan, Dorsey & Company Account Book, 1818–1822. Special Collections, Howard-Tilton Memorial Library, Tulane University.

Morgan, General David Bannister, Papers. Special Collections, Howard-Tilton Memorial Library, Tulane University.

New Orleans Municipal Papers, box 1, 1770–1806, folder 13. Special Collections, Howard-Tilton Memorial Library, Tulane University.

Orleans Parish, Louisiana. *Orleans Deaths Indices—Vital Records, 1804–1876.* State Archives and Records Service of Louisiana, Baton Rouge. Microfilm ODI 001.

Rees, David, Papers. Special Collections, Howard-Tilton Memorial Library, Tulane University.

Seymour, William H., Papers. Folder 1, Louisiana and Lower Mississippi Valley Collections, Louisiana State University Libraries.

Taylor, Gertrude C. "Land Grants [map] Along the Teche, Part I, Port Barre to St. Martinville" (1979). Bluebonnet Regional Library, East Baton Rouge Parish Library, Baton Rouge.

MANUSCRIPTS IN OTHER DEPOSITORIES

"Admissions to the Inner Temple, 1505–1850." Edited by R. L. Lloyd. 4 vols. Typescript, 1950–1960. Archives of the Honourable Society of the Inner Temple, London.

Buffington, Mrs. W. R., Papers. Southern Historical Collection, Wilson Library, University of North Carolina, Chapel Hill. Microfilm M-1475.

Claiborne, John Francis Hamtramck, Papers, 1797–1884. Southern Historical Collection, Wilson Library, University of North Carolina, Chapel Hill. Microfilm M-151.

Claiborne, Magadalene H., Papers, 1813–1887. Southern Historical Collection, Wilson Library, University of North Carolina, Chapel Hill. Microfilm M-1475.

Claiborne, William C. C., Collection. Historical Society of Pennsylvania, Philadelphia. Photocopy owned by the author.

Cook, Lewis D. "Carmick of Salem, N.J., and of Philadelphia." Typescript (Philadelphia, 1949), Pennsylvania Historical Society.

Kerr, Lewis, to J. Carmichael-Smyth, January 31, 1832. Public Record Office, Colonial Office Papers, 23/86. London, England. Photocopy owned by the author.

Kirby, Ephraim, Papers. Rare Book, Manuscript, and Special Collections Library, Duke University, Durham, North Carolina. Microfilm owned by the author.

"Memorial of Lewis Kerr to be Admitted to the Degree of Barrister, Addressed to the Benchers of the Honourable Society of the Kings Inns, Dublin, 3rd November 1794." Kings Inns Library, Dublin (copy owned by the author).

Ross Family Papers. Lancaster County Historical Society, Lancaster, Pennsylvania. Photocopy owned by the author.

Rush, Benjamin Papers, vol. 19. Library Company of Philadelphia, Pennsylvania.

Smith, Uselima Clarks, Collection. William Jones Papers. Historical Society of Pennsylvania, Philadelphia. Photocopy owned by the author.

CHURCH RECORDS

Christ Church, Nassau, The Bahama Islands. Register of Baptisms, n.d. Register of Marriages, 1805–1828.

Sacramental Record of the Roman Catholic Church of the Archdiocese of New Or-

leans. Edited by Earl C. Woods and Charles E. Nolan. Translated by J. Edgar Bruns. Vols. 1–9. New Orleans: Archdiocese of New Orleans, 1987–1994.

St. James Episcopal Church, Lancaster, Pennsylvania. Rector's Record Book, n.d.

St. Louis Cathedral, Orleans Parish, Louisiana. Baptismal Registers, vols. 1 (1805–1838), 3–5 (1753–1766), 9 (1818–1822).

St. Louis Cathedral, Orleans Parish, Louisiana. Funeral Registers, 1803–1815; 1815–1830; 1831–.

St. Louis Cathedral, Orleans Parish, Louisiana. Marriage Book 2 (1784–1806).

Ursuline Convent Chapel. Baptismal Book 1 (1805–1838), Act 189, Baptism of Henriette Ross.

HISTORICAL RECORDS SURVEY, WORKS PROJECT ADMINISTRATION IN LOUISIANA

"Administrations of the Mayors of New Orleans, 1803–1936." Compiled and edited by Works Project Administration. Project 665-64-3-112. New Orleans, March 1940 (typescript).

Archives of the Spanish Government of West Florida. 18 vols. Baton Rouge: Survey of Federal Archives in Louisiana, 1937–40 (typescript).

"Biographies of the Mayors of New Orleans." Compiled and edited by Works Project Administration. Project 665-64-3-112. New Orleans, May 1939 (typescript).

French Document 47 and Spanish Documents 1240 and 1442, Translations. Louisiana State Museum Library MSS, New Orleans.

Governor's Office: American Documents, 1804–1814. City Archives, Louisiana Department, New Orleans Public Library.

Louisiana Historical Records Survey. *County-Parish Boundaries in Louisiana.* New Orleans: Department of Archives, Louisiana State University, 1939.

"Louisiana Military Data. Louisiana Militia, 1811–1814." Edited by P. L. Dupas. Jackson Barracks, La.: U.S. Works Project Administration, Louisiana, 1941 (typescript).

New Orleans Conseil de Ville. Messages from the Mayor, 1805–1836. Vol. 1, March 14, 1805–December 27, 1805; vol. 2, January 4, 1806–December 30, 1807; vol. 3, January 11, 1808–December 13, 1809; vol. 4, January 17, 1810–December 28, 1811. City Archives, Louisiana Department, New Orleans Public Library, New Orleans, Louisiana (translations).

New Orleans Conseil de Ville: Official Proceedings. No. 1, book 1 (November 30, 1803–March 29, 1805); book 2 (April 4, 1805–February 12, 1806); book 3 (February 15, 1806–July 1, 1807); No. 2, book 1 (July 6, 1807–December 28, 1808); book 2 (January 14, 1809–December 26, 1810); book 3 (January 12, 1811–November 7, 1812). Revised by A. Stetter. City Archives, Louisiana Department, New Orleans Public Library, New Orleans, Louisiana (typescripts by Civil Works Administration and the Federal Emergency Relief Administration of Louisiana, 1935–36).

St. Louis Cemetery Card File, Louisiana State Museum Library, New Orleans.

UNITED STATES GOVERNMENT PUBLICATIONS

American State Papers: Indian Affairs. Vol. 1. Washington, D.C.: Gales & Seaton, 1832.

American State Papers: Military Affairs. Vol. 1. Washington, D.C.: Gales & Seaton, 1832.

American State Papers: Miscellaneous. Vols. 1, 2. Washington, D.C.: Gales & Seaton, 1834.

American State Papers: Naval Affairs. Vol. 1. Washington, D.C.: Gales & Seaton, 1834.

American State Papers: Public Lands. Vols. 2, 3, 5, 6. Washington, D.C.: Gales & Seaton, 1834, 1860.

Annals of Congress: The Debates and Proceedings in the Congress of the United States, 1789–1824. 14th Cong., 1st sess. Washington, D.C.: Gales and Seaton, 1826; 2nd sess. Washington, D.C., Gales and Seaton, 1854.

Biographical Directory of the American Congress, 1774–1971. The Continental Congress, September 5, 1774, to October 21, 1788. The Congress of the United States from the First through the Ninety-First Congress, March 4, 1789, to January 3, 1971, Inclusive. (Senate Document 92-8, 92nd Congress, 1st sess.). Washington, D.C.: U.S. Government Printing Office, 1971.

Carter, Clarence E., comp. and ed. *The Territorial Papers of the United States,* vol. 9, *The Territory of Orleans, 1803–1812.* Washington, D.C.: U.S. Government Printing Office, 1940.

———. *The Territorial Papers of the United States,* vol. 5, *The Territory of Mississippi, 1798–1817.* Washington, D.C.: U.S. Government Printing Office, 1940.

———. *The Territorial Papers of the United States,* vol. 6, *The Territory of Mississippi, 1809–1817.* Washington, D.C.: U.S. Government Printing Office, 1940.

Cases Argued and Adjudged in the Supreme Court of the United States, December Term, 1867. Reported by John William Wallace. Vol. 6. Washington, D.C.: W. H. & O. H. Morrison, 1870.

Gillett, Mary C. *The Army Medical Department, 1775–1818.* Washington, D.C.: Center for Military History, United States Army, 1981.

Heitman, Francis B. *Historical Register and Dictionary of the United States Army from Its Organization September 29, 1789, to March 2, 1903.* 2 vols. 1903; Urbana: University of Illinois Press, 1965.

Journal of the Executive Proceedings of the Senate of the United States. 14th Cong., 2nd sess. Washington, D.C.: Duff Green, 1828.

Journal of the House of Representatives of the United States. 14th Cong., 2nd sess. Washington, D.C.: William A. Davis, 1816.

Miller, Hunter, ed. *Treaties and Other International Acts of the United States of America.* Vol. 2. Washington, D.C.: U.S. Government Printing Office, 1931.

Monroe, James. *Index to the James Monroe Papers.* Washington, D.C.: U.S. Government Printing Office, 1963.

Naval Documents Related to the Quasi-War Between the United States and France.
  Naval Operations, Including Diplomatic Background from February 1797–
  December 1801. 7 vols. Washington, D.C.: U.S. Government Printing Office,
  1935–38.
Naval Documents Related to the United States Wars with the Barbary Powers. Vol.
  2, Naval Operations Including Diplomatic Background from January 1802
  through August 1803. Washington, D.C.: U.S. Government Printing Office,
  1940.
Office of Naval Records and Library, Navy Department. Register of Officer Personnel United States Navy and Marine Corps and Ships' Data, 1801–1807. Washington, D.C.: U.S. Government Printing Office, 1945.
Richardson, James D., ed. A Compilation of the Messages and Papers of the Presidents, 1789–1897. Vol. 1. Washington, D.C.: U.S. Government Printing Office,
  1896.
Selections from the Draper Collection in the Possession of the State Historical Soci-
  ety of Wisconsin, to Elucidate the Proposed French Expedition under George
  Rogers Clark Against Louisiana, in the Years 1793–94. 2 vols. Washington,
  D.C.: U.S. Government Printing Office, 1897.
United States Statutes at Large, 6th–12th Congress, 1799–1813. Vol. 2. Public Acts
  Boston: Little, Brown, 1850.

PUBLICATIONS OF THE ORLEANS TERRITORY AND THE STATE OF LOUISIANA

Acts Passed at the First Session of the Legislative Council of the Territory of Orleans,
  Begun and Held at the Principal, in the City of New Orleans, On Monday the
  Third Day of December, in the Year of Our Lord, One Thousand Eight Hundred
  and Four, and of the Independence of the United States the Twenty-Ninth. New
  Orleans: James M. Bradford, 1805.
Acts Passed at the Second Session of the Legislative Council of the Territory of Or-
  leans, Begun and Held at the Principal, in the City of New Orleans, on Thursday
  the Twentieth Day of June, in the Year of Our Lord, One Thousand Eight Hun-
  dred and Five, and of the Independence of the United States the Twenty-Ninth.
  New Orleans: James M. Bradford, 1805.
Acts Passed at the First Session of the First Legislature of the Territory of Orleans
  Begun and Held in the City of New-Orleans, on the 25th Day of January, in the
  Year of Our Lord One Thousand Eight Hundred and Six, and of the Indepen-
  dence of the United States of America the Thirtieth. New Orleans: Bradford &
  Anderson, 1806.
Acts Passed at the Second Session of the First Legislature of the Territory of Orleans
  Begun and Held in the City of New-Orleans, on the 2nd Day of January, in the
  Year of Our Lord One Thousand Eight Hundred and Seven, and of the Indepen-

dence of the United States of America the Thirty-First. New Orleans: James M. Bradford, 1807.

Acts Passed by the Second Legislature of the State of Louisiana at Its Second Session, Held and Begun in the Town at Baton Rouge, on the 15th January, 1855. New Orleans: Emile La Sere, 1855.

Brown, James, and L. Moreau Lislet, comps. *A Digest of the Civil Laws Now in Force in the Territory of Orleans, with Alterations and Amendments to Its Present System of Government. By Authority.* New Orleans [Bradford & Anderson,] 1808.

A Digest of the Civil Laws Now in Force in the Territory of Orleans with Alterations and Amendments Adopted in Its Present System of Government. New Orleans: Bradford and Anderson, 1808.

Journal de la Convention D'Orléans de 1811–12. Pour L'Usage de la Convention de 1844. Jackson, La.: Jerome Bayon, August 3, 1844.

Journal of the House of Representatives of the State of Louisiana, Second Session, Third Legislature. New Orleans: J. C. de Romes, 1818.

Journal of the House of Representatives of the State of Louisiana, Tenth Legislature, First Session. New Orleans: John Gibson, 1831.

Journal of the House of Representatives of the State of Louisiana, Second Session, Tenth Legislature. New Orleans: John Gibson, 1832.

Journal of the House of Representatives of the State of Louisiana, Extra Session, Tenth Legislature. New Orleans: John Gibson, 1831.

Journal of the House of Representatives of the State of Louisiana, First Session, Eleventh Legislature. [New Orleans: Jerome Bayon 1833 ?] State Library of Louisiana, Baton Rouge. Microfilm L222, reel 1.

Journal of the Senate During the Second Session of the First Legislature of the State of Louisiana. New Orleans: Peter K. Wagner, 1813.

Kerr, Lewis. *An Exposition of the Criminal Laws of the Territory of Orleans: The Practice of the Courts of Criminal Jurisdiction, the Duties of Their Officers, with a Collection of Forms for the Use of Magistrates and Others.* New Orleans: Bradford & Anderson, 1806.

Moreau Lislet, L., trans. *Explication des Lois Criminelles du Territoire D'Orléans, Ainsi que de la Forme de Proceder des Tribunaux Criminels, des Devoirs de Leurs Officiers, avec un Recueil des Formules qui leur Sont Propres, a L'Usage des Magistrats et des Autres Citoyens.* New Orleans: Jean Renard, 1806.

Moreau Lislet, L., comp. *A General Digest of the Acts of the Legislature of Louisiana: Passed from the Year 1804, to 1827, Inclusive, and in Force at the Last Period with an Appendix and General Index.* 2 vols. New Orleans: B. Levy, 1828.

Orleans Deaths Indices—Vital Records, 1804–1876. Reel ODI 001. Archives and Record Service, State of Louisiana, Baton Rouge.

SUPERIOR COURT CASES OF THE ORLEANS TERRITORY

City Archives, Louisiana Department, New Orleans Public Library

No. 24, *Evan Jones v. Shaw et al.*, December 10, 1804
No. 50, *Government v. Le Grand Jean*, November 22, 1805
No. 1093, *The Mayor of New Orleans v. Samuel B. Davis*, February 2, 1805
No. 1228, *James Workman v. G. W. Morgan*, May 5 [1806?]
No. 1503, *George Pollock v. His Creditors*, March 5, 1808
No. 1643, *Thos. Hart, Jr., John S. Bartlett, and Nathaniel Cox v. Lewis Kerr*, May 27, 1808
No. 1748, *Thos. Hart, Jr., John S. Bartlett, and Nathaniel Cox v. Lewis Kerr*, August 1, 1808
No. 2139, *Evan Jones v. Isaac Briggs, John Ellis, William Dunbar, and F. L. Claiborne*, April 17, 1809

NOTARIAL RECORDS OF NEW ORLEANS

General Index, 1771–1833. J. B. Garic, L. Mazange, G. Rodriquez, Pedro & Philippe Pedesclaux, and L. T. Caire *étude*. Notarial Archives, New Orleans.
Gianelloni, Elizabeth Becker. *Love, Honor and Betrayal: The Notarial Acts of Estevan de Quiñones, 1778–1784.* [Baton Rouge] n.p., 1964.
———. *The Notarial Acts of Estevan de Quiñones, 1785–1786.* [Baton Rouge] n.p., 1966.
Notarial Acts of Narcise Broutin, January–December 1818. Notarial Archives, New Orleans.
Notarial Acts of Christoval DeArmas, January 1817–December 1818. Notarial Archives, New Orleans.
Notarial Acts of Michel DeArmas, January 1818–May 11, 1818. Notarial Archives, New Orleans.
Notarial Acts of Marc Lafitte, January–July 1818. Notarial Archives, New Orleans.
Notarial Acts of John Lynd, April 24, 1805, to December 31, 1812; and January–December 1818. Notarial Archives, New Orleans.
Notarial Acts of Phillippe Pedesclaux, 1818. Notarial Archives, New Orleans.
Notarial Acts of Pierre Pedesclaux, January–May 1801. Notarial Archives, New Orleans.
Notarial Acts of Carlile Pollock, vols. 1–3. February 1817–December 1821 [inclusive]. Notarial Archives, New Orleans.
Notarial Acts of Carlos Ximines, 1790–1805. Notarial Archives, New Orleans.

CIVIL PARISH AND COUNTY RECORDS

Abstracts of Wills and Administrations, Berks County, Pennsylvania, Will Book B, B-290 [497–8], Jacob Morgan Will, May 28, 1792 (photocopy owned by the author).

Caernarvon Township, Berks County, Pennsylvania, Tax Records, 1794 and 1795.

"Dublin Consistorial Office Marriage License Books, 1635–1825." Vol. 2, E–M, inclusive. Irish Records in the LDS Family History Library, Salt Lake City, Utah.

Philip Hickey and Louis Favrot Deposition, in re the Marriage of Samuel Fulton and Hélène Boucher de Grand-Pré, August 11, 1828. Judges Book J–N, September 15, 1826–January 16, 1830, Entry No. 368 (p. 299). East Baton Rouge Parish, Louisiana.

T. Larguier, P. Dubayle, T. de Bellievre, P. Gautier, and S. Fulton, representing Blazing Star Lodge No. 10, in the purchase of Lots 2 and 3, Square Thirty-two South, Beauregard Town, Baton Rouge, December 26, 1818. Parish Judges Book G, Entry No. 256 (p. 291). East Baton Rouge Parish, Louisiana.

Orleans Parish, Louisiana. Court of Probate, Record of Wills, Will Books, 1805–1837.

Orleans Parish, Louisiana. Court of Probate, Succession and Probate Records, 1818–1819.

Register of Wills, Book C 4, pp. 68–9. Nassau, The Bahama Islands. Lewis Kerr Will, March 26, 1829 (photocopy owned by the author).

Register of Wills, Orphans' Court Book, M-1–72, Lancaster, Pennsylvania. George Ross Will, May 28, 1816 (photocopy owned by the author).

John Watkins Will, December 10, 1799, Instrument No. 2267. St. Louis Archives, Missouri Historical Society, St. Louis, Missouri (photocopy owned by the author).

THESES AND DISSERTATIONS

Bittner, Robert E. "The Concert Life and Musical Stage in New Orleans up to the Construction of the French Opera House." Master's thesis, Louisiana State University, 1953.

Downs, Raymond H. "Public Lands and Private Claims in Louisiana, 1803–1820." Master's thesis, Louisiana State University, 1960.

Fox, Lawrence K. "The Political Career of James Brown." Master's thesis, Louisiana State University, 1946.

LeBreton, Marietta Marie. "A History of the Factory System Serving the Louisiana Indians, 1805–1825." Master's thesis, Louisiana State University, 1961.

———. *A History of the Territory of Orleans, 1803–1812.* Ann Arbor, Mich.: University Microfilms, 1973.

Liljegren, Ernest R. "Lieutenant-Colonel Carlos Howard and the International Rivalry for the Mississippi Valley, 1796–1798." Master's thesis, University of Southern California, 1939.

Lorio, Elaine C. "Place Names of Pointe Coupée Parish." Master's thesis, Louisiana State University, 1932.

Miller, Marshall S. "The History of Fort Claiborne, Louisiana, 1804–1822." Master's thesis, Louisiana State University, 1969.

Reynolds, Jack A. "Louisiana Place-Names of Romance Origin." Ph.D. diss., Louisiana State University, 1942.

Rose, Lisle A. *Prologue to Democracy: The Federalists in the South, 1789–1800.* Ann Arbor, Mich.: University Microfilms, 1972.

Rousey, Dennis Charles. *The New Orleans Police, 1805–1889: A Social History.* Ann Arbor, Mich.: University Microfilms, 1984.

Russell, Mary Flower Pugh. "The Life of Julien Poydras." Master's thesis, Louisiana State University, 1940.

Smith, Ronald Dwight. *French Interests in Louisiana: From Choiseul to Napoleon.* Ann Arbor, Mich.: University Microfilms, 1975.

Swick, Ronald Ray. *Harman Blennerhassett: An Irish Aristocrat on the American Frontier.* Ann Arbor, Mich.: University Microfilms International, 1995.

Uzée, Philip D. "The First Louisiana State Constitution: A Study of Its Origins." Master's thesis, Louisiana State University, 1938.

Witcher, Robert Campbell. "The Episcopal Church in Louisiana, 1805–1861." Ph.D. diss., Louisiana State University, 1969.

Young, Tommy. "The United States Army in the South, 1789–1835." Ph.D. diss., Louisiana State University, 1973.

NEWSPAPERS

Baton Rouge Advocate, September 6, 1994, *Directory '94,* Special Edition

Frankfort (Ky.) Western World, scattered issues: August 23, 1806–May 21, 1807

Lancaster (Pa.) Journal, June 7, 1816

Lexington Kentucky Gazette and General Advertiser, January 1, 1805–December 5, 1808

Nassau Royal Gazette and Bahama Advertiser (New Providence, The Bahamas Islands), October 18, 1834

New Orleans Bee, July 2, 1832–January 2, 1833; February 11, 1863; September 22, 1867; July 21, 1869

New Orleans Courier de la Louisiane, November 23, 1807–March 30, 1833

New Orleans Daily Picayune, October 24, 1829; October 29, 1848; March 27, 1856

New Orleans Louisiana Advertiser, October 18, 19, 22, 24, 1832

New Orleans Louisiana Gazette, July 24, 1804–March 30, 1810

New Orleans Louisiana Gazette and New Orleans Daily Advertiser, April 3, 1810–August 8, 1812

New Orleans Louisiana Gazette and New Orleans Mercantile Advertiser, April 4, 1815–May 24, 1817; October 14, 1820

New Orleans Moniteur de la Louisiane, August 14, 1802–December 31, 1811
New Orleans Télégraphe, December 17, 1803–April 18, 1812
New Orleans Union, December 20, 1803–November 28, 1804
New Orleans Weekly Delta, January 28, 1850
Niles' Weekly Register (Baltimore) October 22, 1814; February 14, 1815; February 15, 1815
Philadelphia National Intelligencer, March 4, 1824

DIRECTORIES

Burtchaell, George Dames, and Thomas Ulick Sadleir, eds. *Alumni Dublinenses: A Register of the Students, Graduates, Professors, and Provosts of Trinity College in the University of Dublin (1593–1860).* New ed. (with suppl.) Dublin: Alexander Thom, 1935.
The City and Country Calendar; or The Irish Court Registry for the Year . . . 1795. Dublin: N.p., 1795.
The City and Country Calendar; or The Irish Court Registry for the Year . . . 1796. Dublin: N.p., 1796.
The Irish Court Register, and the City and Country Calendar for the Year . . . 1797. Dublin: N.p., 1797.
Lafon, B[arthélémy]. *Annuaire Louisianais pour L'Année 1809.* New Orleans: By the Author, 1808.
———. *Calendrier de Commerce de la Nouvelle-Orléans, pour l'Année 1807.* New Orleans: Jean Renard, 1806 [*sic*].
New Orleans in 1805: A Directory and a Census, Together with Resolutions Authorizing Same, Now Printed for the First Time from the Original Manuscript. Edited by Charles L. Thompson. New Orleans: Pelican Gallery, 1936.
Paxton, John Adems. *The New Orleans Directory and Register; Containing the Names, Professions & Residences, of All the Heads of Families and Persons in Business, of the City Suburbs; Notes on New-Orleans; with Other Useful Information.* New Orleans: Printed for the author, 1822.
"Premier 'Directory' de la Nouvelle-Orléans, 1807," in *Le Diamant* 1, no. 14 (May 1, 1887), 43–6.
Sturgess, H. A. C., comp. *Register of Admissions to the Honourable Society of the Middle Temple from the Fifteenth Century to the Year 1944.* 3 vols. London: Butterworth, 1949.
Treble Almanac, 1798, Part 3, *The Dublin Directory for the Year 1798.* Dublin: William Wilson, 1798.
Whitney, Thomas H. *Whitney's New-Orleans Directory, and Louisiana & Mississippi Almanac for the Year 1811.* New Orleans: Printed for the Author, 1810.

SECONDARY SOURCES

BOOKS

Abernethy, Thomas P. *The Burr Conspiracy*. New York: Oxford University Press, 1954.

———. *From Frontier to Plantation in Tennessee: A Study in Frontier Democracy*. Chapel Hill: University of North Carolina Press, 1932.

———. *The South in the New Nation, 1789–1819*. Baton Rouge: Louisiana State University Press, 1961.

Adams, Henry. *History of the United States of America During the Second Administration of Thomas Jefferson*. Vol. 1. New York: Charles Scribner's Sons, 1890.

An Account of Louisiana, Being an Abstract of Documents, in the Offices of the Departments of State, and of the Treasury. Philadelphia: John Conrad, November, 1803.

Appendix to an Account of Louisiana Being an Abstract of Documents in the Offices of the Departments of State and of the Treasury. Philadelphia: John Conrad, November 1803.

Arsenault, Bona. *Histoire et Généalogie des Acadiens*. 2 vols. Quebec: Conseil de la vie Française en Amerique, 1965.

Arthur, Stanley Clisby. *Jean Lafitte, Gentleman Rover*. New Orleans: Harmonson, 1952.

Arthur, Stanley C., and George Campbell Huchet de Kernion. *Old Families of Louisiana*. 1931. Reprint, Baton Rouge: Claitor's, 1971.

Baker, Leonard. *John Marshall: A Life in Law*. New York: Macmillan, 1974.

Bassett, John Spencer, ed. *Correspondence of Andrew Jackson*. Vols. 2, 7. Washington, D.C.: Carnegie Institution of Washington, 1927, 1935.

Bates, Albert C., ed. *The Two Putnams: Israel and Rufus in the Havana Expedition 1762 and in the Mississippi River Expedition 1772–73 with Some Account of the Company of Military Adventurers*. Hartford: Connecticut Historical Society, 1931.

Baudier, Roger. *The Catholic Church in Louisiana*. 1939. Reprint, New Orleans: Louisiana Library Association, 1972.

Berkeley, Edmund, and Dorothy Smith Berkeley. *John Beckley, Zealous Partisan in a Nation Divided*. Philadelphia: American Philosophical Society, 1973.

Beveridge, Albert J. *Life of John Marshall*. 3 vols. Boston: Houghton Mifflin, 1916–1919.

Biddle, Charles. *Autobiography of Charles Biddle, Vice-President of the Supreme Executive Council of Pennsylvania, 1745–1821*. Philadelphia: E. Claxton, 1883.

Bodley, Temple. *George Rogers Clark. His Life and Public Services*. Boston: Houghton Mifflin, 1926.

Bourgeois, Lillian C. *Cabanocey: The History, Customs, and Folklore of St. James Parish*. New Orleans: Pelican, 1957.

Brady, Joseph P. *The Trial of Aaron Burr*. New York: Neal, 1913.

Brant, Irving. *James Madison*. 6 vols. Indianapolis: Bobbs-Merrill, 1941–61.

Brooks, Charles B. *The Seige of New Orleans*. Seattle: University of Washington Press, 1961.

Brown, Everett S., ed. *William Plummer's Memorandum of Proceedings in the United States Senate, 1803–1807*. New York: Macmillan, 1923.

Brown, Wilburt S. *The Amphibious Campaign for West Florida and Louisiana, 1814–1815: A Critical Review of Strategy and Tactics at New Orleans*. University: University of Alabama Press, 1969.

Burns, Annie Walker. *Historical Records of the Claiborne Family*. Jackson: Mississippi Department of Archives and History, n.d.

Burson, Caroline Maude. *The Stewardship of Don Estéban Miró, 1782–1792*. New Orleans: American Printing , 1940.

Caldwell, Stephen C. *A History of Banking in Louisiana*. Baton Rouge: Louisiana State University Press, 1935.

Carrigan, Jo Ann. *The Saffron Scourge: A History of Yellow Fever in Louisiana, 1796–1905*. Lafayette: Center for Louisiana Studies, University of Southwestern Louisiana, 1994.

Casey, Albert, comp. *Amite County, Mississippi, 1699–[1890]*. Vol. 4. *Environs*. Birmingham, Ala.: Amite County Historical Fund, 1969.

Casey, Powell A. *Louisiana at the Battle of New Orleans*. Battle of New Orleans Sesquicentennial Historical Booklets, no. 4. New Orleans: Louisiana Landmarks Society, 1965.

———. *Louisiana in the War of 1812*. Baton Rouge: [by the author,] 1963.

Caughey, John Walton. *Bernardo de Gálvez in Louisiana, 1776–1783*. 1934. Reprint, Gretna, La.: Pelican Publishing, 1972.

———. *McGillivray of the Creeks*. 1938; Norman: University of Oklahoma Press, 1959.

Chalfant, Ella. *A Goodly Heritage: Earliest Wills on an American Frontier*. Pittsburgh: University of Pittsburgh Press, 1955.

Chapelle, Howard I. *The History of the American Sailing Navy: The Ships and Their Development*. New York: Bonanza Books, 1949.

Churchill, W. A. *Watermarks in Paper in Holland, England, France, etc., in the XVII and XVIII Centuries and Their Interconnection*. 1935. Reprint, Nieuwkoop, The Netherlands: B. DeGraff, 1985.

Claiborne, J. F. H. *Mississippi, as a Province, Territory, and State, with Biographical Notices of Eminent Citizens*. 2nd ed. Baton Rouge: Louisiana State University Press, 1964.

Clark, Daniel. *Proofs of the Corruption of Gen. James Wilkinson, and of His Connexion with Aaron Burr, with a Full Refutation of His Slanderous Allegations in*

Relation to the Principal Witness Against Him. 1809. Reprint, New York: Arno Press, 1971.

Clark, John G. *New Orleans, 1718–1812: An Economic History.* Baton Rouge: Louisiana State University Press, 1970.

Clay, Henry. *Papers of Henry Clay.* Edited by James F. Hopkins. Vol. 1. Lexington: University of Kentucky Press, 1959.

Cleaves, Freeman. *Old Tippecanoe: William Henry Harrison and His Time.* New York: Charles Scribner's Sons, 1939.

Cochran, Estelle M. Fortier. *The Fortier Family and Allied Families.* San Antonio, Tex.: E. M. F. Cochran, 1963.

Coleman, James Julian, Jr. *Gilbert Antoine de St. Maxent: The Spanish-Frenchman of New Orleans.* New Orleans: Pelican, 1968.

Collot, Georges Henri Victor. *A Journey in North America, Containing a Survey of the Countries Watered by the Mississippi, Ohio, Missouri and other Affluing Rivers; with Exact Observations on the Course and Soundings of These Rivers; and on the Towns, Villages, Hamlets and Farms of that Part of the New-World; Followed by Philosophical, Political, Military and Commercial Remarks and by a Projected Line of Frontiers and General Limits, Illustrated by 36 Maps, Plans, Views and Divers Cuts.* 1826; 1924. Reprint, Paris: A. Bertrand, 1974.

Collum, Richard S. *History of the United States Marine Corps.* Philadelphia: L. R. Hamersly, 1890.

Coombs, J. J. *The Trial of Aaron Burr for High Treason, in the Circuit Court of the United States for the District of Virginia, Summer Term, 1807: Comprising all the Evidence and the Opinions of the Court upon All Motions Made in the Various Stages of the Case, with Abstracts of Arguments of Council; Compiled from Authentic Reports Made during the Progress of the Trial.* Washington, D.C.: W. H. & O. H. Morrison, 1864.

Corner, George W., ed. *The Autobiography of Benjamin Rush: His "Travel through Life" Together with His Commonplace Book for 1789–1813.* Princeton: Princeton University Press, 1948.

Cox, Isaac Joslin. *The West Florida Controversy, 1798–1813: A Study in American Diplomacy.* 1918. Reprint, Gloucester, Mass.: Peter Smith, 1967.

Craton, Michael. *A History of the Bahamas.* London: Collin, 1962.

———— and D. Gail Saunders. *Islanders in the Stream: A History of the Bahamian People.* Vol. 1, *From Aboriginal Times to the End of Slavery.* Athens: University of Georgia Press, 1992.

Cummins, Light Townsend, and Glen Jeansonne, eds. *A Guide to the History of Louisiana.* Westport, Conn.: Greenwood Press, 1982.

Cunningham, Noble E., Jr. *The Jeffersonian Republicans in Power: Party Operations, 1801–1809.* Chapel Hill: University of North Carolina Press, 1963.

Curley, Michael J., C.SS.R. *Church and State in the Spanish Floridas (1783–1822).* The Catholic University of America Studies in American Church History, 30. Washington, D.C.: Catholic University Press of America, 1940.

Dangerfield, George. *The Era of Good Feelings.* 1952. Reprint, New York: Harbinger Books, 1963.

Daniels, Jonathan. *Ordeal of Ambition: Jefferson, Hamilton, Burr.* Garden City, N.Y.: Doubleday, 1970.

Dargo, George. *Jefferson's Louisiana: Politics and the Clash of Legal Traditions.* Cambridge, Mass.: Harvard University Press, 1975.

Davis, Edwin Adams. *Louisiana: A Narrative History.* 3rd ed. Baton Rouge: Claitor's, 1971.

———. ed. *The Rivers and Bayous of Louisiana.* Baton Rouge: Louisiana Education Research Association, 1968.

Debate in the House of Representatives of the Territory of Orleans on a Memorial to Congress, Respecting the Illegal Conduct of General Wilkinson. New Orleans: Bradford & Anderson, 1807.

DeConde, Alexander. *This Affair of Louisiana.* New York: Charles Scribner's Sons, 1976.

DeGrummond, Jane Lucas. *The Baratarians and the Battle of New Orleans: With Biographical Sketches of the Veterans of the Battalion of Orleans, 1814–1815,* by Ronald R. Morazan. Baton Rouge: Legacy, 1979.

Deiler, J. Hanno. *The Settlement of the German Coast of Louisiana and the Creoles of German Descent.* 1909. Reprint with new Preface, Chronology, and Index by Jack Belsom, Baltimore: Genealogical Publishing, 1969.

Deléry, Simone de la Souchère. *Napoleon's Soldiers in America.* Gretna, La.: Pelican, 1972.

[Derbigny, Pierre Auguste Charles Bourisgay.] *Esquisse de la Situation Politique et Civil de la Louisiane depuis le 30 Novembre 1803 jusqu'à 1er Octobre 1804 par un Louisianais.* New Orleans: Belleurgey & Renard, 1804.

Doran, Michael F. *Atlas of County Boundary Changes in Virginia, 1634–1895.* Athens, Ga.: Iberian, 1987.

Duffy, John, ed. *The Rudolph Matas History of Medicine.* 2 vols. Baton Rouge: Louisiana State University Press, 1958, 1962.

Du Fossat, Mrs. Eugene Soniat. *Biographical Sketches of Louisiana's Governors.* New Orleans: World's Cotton Centennial Exposition, 1885.

Dunner, Joseph, ed. *Handbook of World History.* New York: Philosophical Library, 1967.

Elliot, D. O. *The Improvement of the Lower Mississippi River for Flood Control and Navigation.* 2 vols. Vicksburg, Miss.: U.S. Waterways Experiment Station, 1932.

Faulkner, Robert K. *The Jurisprudence of John Marshall.* Princeton, N.J.: Princeton University Press, 1968.

Finiels, Nicolas de. *An Account of Upper Louisiana.* Edited by Carl J. Ekberg and William E. Foley. Translated by Carl J. Ekberg. Columbia: University of Missouri Press, 1989.

"Vicente Folch." *Diccionario Geografico, Estadistico, Historico, de la Isla de Cuba.* Vol. 2. Madrid: Mellado, 1863.

Foote, Henry S. *The Bench and Bar of the South and Southwest.* St. Louis: Soule, Thomas & Wentworth, 1876.

Ford, Paul Leicester, ed. *The Writings of Thomas Jefferson.* 10 vols. New York: Putnam, 1892–99.

Forsyth, Alice Daly. *Louisiana Marriages: A Collection of Marriage Records from the St. Louis Cathedral in New Orleans During the Spanish Regime and the Early American Period, 1784–1806.* New Orleans: Polyanthos Press, 1977.

Fortier, Alcée. *A History of Louisiana.* Edited by Jo Ann Carrigan. Vols. 1, 2. Baton Rouge: Claitor's Book Store, 1966–72.

———. *Louisiana, Comprising Sketches of Parishes, Towns, Events, Institutions, and Persons, Arranged in Cyclopedic Form.* 3 vols. Madison, Wis.: Century Historical Association, 1914.

Friedman, Lawrence M. *A History of American Law.* New York: Simon and Schuster, 1973.

Gallatin, Albert. *The Writings of Albert Gallatin.* 2nd ed. Edited by Henry Adams. 3 vols. New York: Antiquarian Press, 1960.

Gardner, Charles K. *A Dictionary of All Officers, Who Have Been Commissioned, or Have Been Appointed and Served, in the Army of the United States, Since the Inauguration of Their First President, in 1789, to the First of January 1853,—With Every Commission of Each;—Including the Distinguished Officers of the Volunteers and Militia of the States, Who Have Served in Any Campaigne, or Conflict with an Enemy, Since that Date; and of the Navy and Marine Corps, Who Have Served with Land Forces: Indicating the Battle, in Which Every Such Officer Has Been Killed, or Wounded,—and the Special Words of Every Brevet Commission.* 2nd ed. (suppl.) 1860. New York: D. Van Nostrand, 1965.

Gaskell, Philip. *A New Introduction to Bibliography.* New York: Oxford University Press, 1972.

Gautreau, Henry W., Jr. *1830's Pre-Emption Entries on the Backlands of New River, Louisiana, in Conflict with the Houmas Land Claim.* [Baton Rouge:] H. W. Gautreau, 1995.

Gayarré, Charles. *History of Louisiana.* 4th ed. 4 vols. 1903. Reprint, Gretna, La.: Pelican, 1965.

Genealogies of Rhode Island Families from Rhode Island Periodicals. 2 vols. Baltimore: Genealogical Publishing, 1983.

Genealogies of Virginia Families from the Virginia Magazine of History and Biography. Vol. 2. Baltimore: Genealogical Publishing, 1981.

Gilson, Gordon. *Louisiana State Board of Health: The Formative Years.* New Orleans: n.p., 1967.

Glaister, Geoffrey Ashall. *Glaister's Glossary of the Book,* 2nd ed., rev. Berkeley: University of California Press, 1979.

Goins, Charles Robert, and John Michael Caldwell. *Historical Atlas of Louisiana.* Norman: University of Oklahoma Press, 1995.

Gracy, David B., II. *Moses Austin: His Life.* San Antonio, Tex.: Trinity University Press, 1987.

Green, Thomas M. *The Spanish Conspiracy: A Review of Early Spanish Movements in the Southwest; Containing Proofs of the Intrigues of James Wilkinson and John Brown; of the Complicity therewith of Judges Sebastian, Wallace, and Innes; the Early Struggles of Kentucky for Autonomy; the Intrigues of Sebastian in 1795–97 and the Legislative Investigation of His Corruption.* 1891. Reprint, Gloucester, Mass.: Peter Smith, 1967.

Greene, Glen Lee. *Masonry in Louisiana: A Sesquicentennial History, 1812–1962.* New York: Exposition Press, 1962.

Griffin, Charles C. *The United States and the Disruption of the Spanish Empire, 1810–1822: A Study of the Relations of the United States with Spain and with the Rebel Spanish Colonies.* 1937. Reprint, New York: Octagon Books, 1968.

Guilday, Peter. *The Life and Times of John Carroll, Archbishop of Baltimore, 1735–1815.* 1922. Reprint, Westminster, Md.: Newman Press, 1954.

Guion, Isaac. "Military Journal of Captain Isaac Guion, 1797–1799." In Dunbar Rowland, ed. *Annual Report of the Mississippi Department of Archives and History, 1908.* Nashville: Brandon Printing, 1909, 25–121.

Gwathmey, John H. *Historical Register of Virginians in the Revolution. Soldiers, Sailors, Marines, 1775–1783.* 1938. Reprint, Baltimore: Genealogical Publishing, 1987.

Haggard, J. Villasana. *Handbook for Translators of Spanish Historical Documents.* Austin: Archives Collection, University of Texas, 1941.

Hamilton, Alexander. *Papers of Alexander Hamilton.* Edited by Harold C. Syrett. Vols. 7, 23, 24, 26, 27. New York: Columbia University, 1961–87.

Hamilton, Peter J. *Colonial Mobile: An Historical Study, Largely from Original Sources, of Alabama-Tombigbee Basin from the Discovery of Mobile Bay in 1519 until the Demolition of Fort Charlotte in 1821.* Rev. ed. Boston: Houghton Mifflin, 1910.

Hammond, Bray. *Banks and Politics in America from the Revolution to the Civil War.* Princeton, N.J.: Princeton University Press, 1957.

Harlow, Ralph V. *The History of Legislative Methods in the Period Before 1855.* Yale Historical Publications Miscellany, 5. New Haven, Conn.: Yale University Press, 1917.

Harmon, Nolan B. *The Famous Case of Myra Clark Gaines.* Baton Rouge: Louisiana State University Press, 1946.

Hart, Freeman H. *The Valley of Virginia in the American Revolution, 1763–1789.* Chapel Hill: University of North Carolina Press, 1942.

Hatcher, William B. *Edward Livingston: Jeffersonian Republican and Jacksonian Democrat.* University: Louisiana State University Press, 1940.

Hatfield, Joseph T. *William Claiborne: Jeffersonian Centurion in the American Southwest.* Lafayette: University of Southwestern Louisiana, 1976.

Hayden, Horace E. *Pollock Genealogy: A Biographical Sketch of Oliver Pollock, Esq., of Carlisle, Pennsylvania, United States Commercial Agent at New Orleans and Havana, 1776–1784. With Genealogical Notes of His Descendants.* 1883. Reprint, Harrisburg, Pa.: Lane S. Hart, 1976.

Hébert, Reverend Donald J. *Southwest Louisiana Records. Church and Civil Records of Settlers, 1756–1810.* Eunice, La.: Reverend Donald J. Hébert, 1974.

Heinl, Robert D., Jr. *Soldiers of the Sea: The United States Marine Corps, 1775–1962.* Annapolis, Md.: United States Naval Institute, 1962.

Herring, Hubert. *A History of Latin America from the Beginnings to the Present.* 2nd ed., rev. New York: Alfred A. Knopf, 1965.

Holcomb, Brent Howard. *A Guide to South Carolina Genealogical Research and Records.* 3rd ed. Columbia, S.C.: By the Author, 1998.

Holmes, Jack D. L. *Gayoso: The Life of a Spanish Governor in the Mississippi Valley, 1789–1799.* Baton Rouge: Louisiana State University Press, 1965.

———. *Honor and Fidelity: The Louisiana Infantry Regiment and the Louisiana Militia Companies, 1766–1821.* Birmingham, Ala.: By the author, 1965.

———. Photographic Copies of 44 Louisiana Maps Made from Originals in the Archivo General de Indias, Seville, 1963.

———, ed. *Documentos Ineditos para la Historia de la Luisiana, 1792–1810.* Madrid: J. Porrúa Turanzas, 1963.

Holy Bible. Rev. stand. vers. New York: American Bible Society, 1980.

Honeyman, A. Van Doren, ed. *Documents Relating to the Colonial History of the State of New Jersey.* First series, 32. *Calendar of New Jersey Wills, Administrations, etc.* Vol. 3, *1751–1760.* Somerville, N.J.: Unionist-Gazette Association of Printers, 1924.

Houck, Louis. *A History of Missouri From the Earliest Explorations and Settlements Until the Admission of the State into the Union.* 3 vols. Chicago: R. R. Donnelley & Sons, 1908.

———, ed. and trans. *The Spanish Regime in Missouri; A Collection of Papers and Documents Relating to Upper Louisiana Principally within the Present Limits of Missouri during the Dominion of Spain, from the Archives of the Indies at Seville, etc., Translated from the Original Spanish into English, and Including also Some Papers Concerning the Supposed Grant to Col. George Morgan at the Mouth of the Ohio, Found in the Congressional Library.* 1909. Reprint, New York: Arno Press, 1971.

Howard, Clinton N. *The British Development of West Florida, 1763–1769.* University of California Publications in History, 34. Berkeley: University of California Press, 1934.

Huber, Leonard, and Guy F. Bernard. *To Glorious Immortality: The Rise and Fall of the Girod Street Cemetery, New Orleans' First Protestant Cemetery, 1822–1957.* New Orleans: Alblen Books, 1961.

Jackson, Jack. *Los Mesteños. Spanish Ranching in Texas, 1721–1821.* College Station: Texas A & M University Press, 1986.

Jacobs, James Ripley. *Tarnished Warrior: Major-General James Wilkinson.* New York: Macmillan, 1938.

James, James A. *Oliver Pollock: The Life and Times of an Unknown Patriot.* New York: D. Appleton-Century, 1937.

———. *The Life of George Rogers Clark.* Chicago: University of Chicago Press, 1928.

Jefferson, Thomas. *The Writings of Thomas Jefferson.* Edited by Andrew A. Lipscomb and Albert Ellery Bergh. 20 vols. Washington, D.C.: Thomas Jefferson Memorial Association of the United States, 1905–1907.

Johnson, Cecil. *British West Florida, 1763–1783.* New Haven: Yale University Press, 1943.

Jones, Wilbur D. *"Prosperity" Robinson: The Life of Viscount Goderich, 1782–1859.* New York: St. Martin's Press, 1967.

Jordan, John W., ed. *Colonial and Revolutionary Families of Pennsylvania.* 3 vols. 1911. Reprint, Baltimore: Genealogical Publishing, 1978.

Kendall, John S. *The Golden Age of New Orleans Theater.* Baton Rouge: Louisiana State University Press, 1952.

Kerr, Lewis. *An Exposition of the Criminal Laws of the Territory of Orleans; The Practice of the Courts of Criminal Jurisdiction, the Duties of Their Officers, with a Collection of Forms for the Use of Magistrates and Others.* New Orleans: John Mowry, 1806.

Kincaid, Lawrence, ed. *Spain in the Mississippi Valley, 1765–1794, Part I, The Revolutionary Period, 1765–81. American Historical Association Annual Report, 1945.* Washington, D.C.: U.S. Government Printing Office, 1946.

Kniffen, Fred B. *Louisiana: Its Land and People.* Baton Rouge: Louisiana State University Press, 1968.

Konkle, Burton A. *Thomas Willing and the First American Financial System.* Philadelphia: University of Pennsylvania Press, 1937.

Korn, Bertram W. *The Early Jews of New Orleans.* Waltham, Mass.: American Jewish Historical Society, 1969.

Laffite, Jean. *The Journal of Jean Laffite: The Privateer-Patriot's Own Story.* Translated by John A. Laffite. New York: Vantage Press, 1958.

Latour, A. Lacarrière. *Historical Memoir of the War in West Florida and Louisiana in 1814–1815. With an Atlas.* 1816. Reprint, Gainesville: University of Florida Press, 1964.

Laussat, Pierre Clément de. *Memoirs of My Life to My Son During the Years 1803 and After, Which I Spent in Public Service in Louisiana as Commissioner of the French Government for the Retrocession to France of that Colony and for Its Transfer to the United States.* Translated by Sister Agnes-Josephine Pastwa, O.S.F. Edited by Robert D. Bush. Baton Rouge: Louisiana State University Press, 1978.

Lecky, W. E. H. *A History of Ireland in the Eighteenth Century.* Abridged. Chicago: University of Chicago Press, 1972.

LeGardeur, René J., Jr. *The First New Orleans Theatre, 1792–1803.* New Orleans: Leeward Books, 1963.

Lewis, Charles L. *Famous American Marines: An Account of the Corps: The Exploits of Officers and Men on Land, by Air and Sea from the Decks of the "Bonhomme Richard" to the Summit of Mount Suribachi.* Boston: L. C. Page, 1950.

Lomask, Milton. *Aaron Burr: The Conspiracy and Years of Exile, 1805–1836.* 2 vols. New York: Farrar, Straus, & Giroux, 1982.

Loomis, Noel M., and Abraham P. Nasatir. *Pedro Vial and the Roads to Santa Fé.* Norman: University of Oklahoma Press, 1967.

Low, Sidney A., and F. S. Pulling, eds. *The Dictionary of English History.* Rev. ed. London: Cassell, 1904.

McCaleb, Walter F. *The Aaron Burr Conspiracy and A New Light on Aaron Burr.* 1936. Reprint, New York: Argosy-Antiquarian, 1966.

McDermott, John Francis, ed. *Frenchmen and French Ways in the Mississippi Valley.* Urbana: University of Illinois Press, 1969.

———. *The Spanish in the Mississippi Valley, 1762–1804.* Urbana: University of Illinois Press, 1974.

McMurtrie, Douglas C. *Early Printing in New Orleans, 1764–1810.* New Orleans: Searcy & Pfaff, 1929.

Madison, James. *Letters and Other Writings of James Madison, Fourth President of the United States.* 4 vols. Philadelphia: J. B. Lippincott, 1865.

Maduell, Charles R., Jr. *New Orleans Marriage Contracts, 1804–1820. Abstracted from the Notarial Archives of New Orleans.* New Orleans: Polyanthos Press, 1977.

———. *Marriage Contracts, Wills and Testaments of the Spanish Colonial Period in New Orleans, 1775–1804.* New Orleans: Charles R. Maduell, 1969.

Malone, Dumas. *Jefferson and His Time.* Vols. 4, 5. Boston: Little, Brown, 1970, 1974.

Marchand, Sidney A. *Across the Years: [Donaldsonville and Ascension Parish].* Donaldsonville, La.: S. A. Marchand, 1949.

———. *An Attempt to Re-Assemble the Old Settlers in Family Groups.* Baton Rouge: Claitor's Book Store, 1965.

———. *The Flight of a Century (1800–1900) in Ascension Parish, Louisiana.* Donaldsonville, La.: S. A. Marchand, 1936.

———. *The Story of Ascension Parish, Louisiana.* Donaldsonville, La.: S. A. Marchand, 1931.

Martin, François-Xavier. *The History of Louisiana, from the Earliest Period.* 1882; New Orleans: Pelican, 1963.

Martinez, Raymond J. *Pierre George Rousseau, Commanding General of the Galleys of the Mississippi.* New Orleans: Hope Publications, 1964.

Masterson, William. *William Blount.* Baton Rouge: Louisiana State University Press, 1954.

Mathews, Catherine Van Cortlandt. *Andrew Ellicott, His Life and Letters.* New York: Grafton Press, 1908.

Meade, Robert D. *Judah P. Benjamin: Confederate Statesman.* New York: Macmillan, 1943.

Milfort, General [Louis le Clerc de]. *Memoirs, or A Quick Glance at My Various Travels and Sojourn in the Creek Nation.* Edited and translated by Ben C. McCary. Kennesaw, Ga.: Continental Books, 1959.

Miller, John C. *Alexander Hamilton, Portrait in Paradox.* New York: Harper & Brothers, 1959.

Mims, Sam. *Trail of the Pack Peddler.* Homer, La.: Guardian-Journal, 1968.

Monette, John W. *History of the Discovery and Settlement of the Valley of the Mississippi, by the Three Great Powers, Spain, France, and Great Britain, and Subsequent Occupation, Settlement and Extension of Civil Government by the United States, Until the Year 1846.* 1846. Reprint (2 vols. in 1), New York: Arno Press, 1971.

Moore, John Preston. *Revolt in Louisiana: The Spanish Occupation, 1766–1770.* Baton Rouge: Louisiana State University Press, 1976.

Morgan, Cecil, comp. *The First Constitution of the State of Louisiana.* Baton Rouge: Louisiana State University Press, 1975.

Morris, Robert. *Papers of Robert Morris, 1781–1784.* Edited by James E. Ferguson. Pittsburgh: University of Pittsburgh Press, 1973–1995.

Nasatir, Abraham P. *Spanish War Vessels on the Mississippi, 1792–1796.* Yale Western Americana Series, 18. New Haven, Conn.: Yale University Press, 1968.

Nelson, William, ed. *Documents Relating to the Colonial History of the State of New Jersey, 23. Calender of New Jersey Wills.* Vol. 1, *1670–1730* Paterson, N.J.: Press Printing and Publishing, 1901.

Nicoll, William L. *The Nicoll Family of Orange County New York.* New York: n.p., 1886.

Official Letter Books of W. C. C. Claiborne, 1801–1816. Edited by Dunbar Rowland. 6 vols. 1917. Reprint, New York: AMS Press, 1972.

Oglesby, Richard Edward. *Manuel Lisa and the Opening of the Missouri Fur Trade.* Norman: University of Oklahoma Press, 1963.

O'Neill, Charles E. *Church and State in French Colonial Louisiana: Policy and Politics to 1732.* New Haven, Conn.: Yale University Press, 1966.

Palmer, Frederick. *Clark of the Ohio: A Life of George Rogers Clark.* New York: Dodd, Mead, 1930.

Pezuela y Lobo, Jacobo de la. "Casa Calvo." *Diccionario Geografico, Estadistico, Historico, de la Isla de Cuba.* Vol. 2. Madrid: Mellado, 1863.

Philbrick, Francis S. *The Rise of the West, 1754–1830.* New York: Harper & Row, 1966.

Pickett, Albert J. *History of Alabama and Incidentally of Georgia and Mississippi, from the Earliest Period*. 1850. Reprint, New York: Arno Press, 1971.

Pitot, Henry C. *James Pitot (1761–1831): A Documentary Study*. New Orleans: Bocage Books, 1968.

Pitot, James. *Observations on the Colony of Louisiana from 1796 to 1802*. Translated by Henry C. Pitot. Baton Rouge: Louisiana State University Press, 1979.

Pittman, Philip. *The Present State of the European Settlements on the Mississippi*. Bicentennial Floridiana Facsimile Series. Gainesville: University of Florida Press, 1973.

Plumb, J. H. *England in the Eighteenth Century (1714–1815)*. Middlesex, Eng.: Penguin Books, 1950.

Read, William A. *Louisiana Place-Names of Indian Origin*. Baton Rouge: The University, 1927.

Record of Pennsylvania Marriages, Prior to 1810. 2 vols. Baltimore: Genealogical Publishing, 1987.

Reeves, Miriam G. *The Governors of Louisiana*. 4th ed. Gretna, La.: Pelican, 1985.

Reid, John, and John H. Eaton, *The Life of Andrew Jackson*. Southern Historical Publications No. 19. Edited by Frank L. Owsley, Jr. University: University of Alabama Press, 1974.

Remini, Robert V. *Andrew Jackson and the Course of American Empire, 1767–1821*. New York: Harper & Row, 1977.

Ristow, Walter W. *American Maps and Mapmakers: Commercial Cartography in the Nineteenth Century*. Detroit: Wayne State University Press, 1985.

Roberts, Matt T., and Don Etherington. *Bookbinding and the Conservation of Books: A Dictionary of Descriptive Terminology*. Washington, D.C.: Library of Congress, 1982.

Robertson, James A., ed. and trans. *Louisiana Under the Rule of Spain, France and the United States, 1785–1807*. 2 vols. 1910–1911. Reprint, Freeport, N.Y.: Books for Libraries Press, 1969.

Rodriquez Casado, Vicente. *Primeros Años de Dominación Española en la Luiziana*. Madrid: Consejo Superior de Investigaciones Cientificas, Instituto Gonzalo Fernandez de Oviedo, 1942.

Rose, Lisle A. *Prologue to Democracy: The Federalists in the South, 1789–1800*. Lexington: University of Kentucky Press, 1968.

Rowland, Dunbar. *Courts, Judges and Lawyers of Mississippi, 1798–1935*. Jackson, Miss.: Hederman Brothers, 1935.

———, ed. *Mississippi, Comprising Sketches of Towns, Events, Institutions, and Persons, Arranged in Cyclopedic Form*. 4 vols. Atlanta: Southern Historical Publishing Association, 1907.

Safford, William. *The Blennerhassett Papers, Embodying the Private Journal of Harman Blennerhassett, and the Hitherto Unpublished Correspondence of Burr, Alston, Comfort Tyler, Devereaux, Dayton, Adair, Miro, Emmett, Theodosia Burr*

Alston, Mrs. *Blennerhasset, and Others, Their Contemporaries; Developing the Purposes and Aims of Those Engaged in the Attempted Wilkinson and Burr Revolution; Embracing the First Account of the "Spanish Association of Kentucky," and a Memoir of Blennerhassett.* Cincinnati: Moore, Wilstach, Keys, 1861.

————. *The Life of Blennerhassett, Comprising an Authentic Narrative of the Burr Expedition: and Containing Many Additional Facts Not Heretofore Published.* Chillicothe, Ohio: Ely, Allen & Looker, 1850.

Salley, A. S., Jr., comp. and ed. *Marriage Notices in [the] Charleston Courier, 1803–1808.* Columbia: State Company for the Historical Commission of South Carolina, 1919.

Sarausa, Fermin Peraza. "Casa Calvo, Marqués de," *Diccionario Biografico Cubano.* Vol. 9. Havana: Anuario Bibliografico Cubano, 1958.

Sargent, Winthrop. *Papers in Relation to the Official Conduct of Governour Sargent.* Boston: Thomas & Andrews, 1801.

Schachner, Nathan. *Aaron Burr, A Biography.* New York: Frederick A. Stokes, 1937.

Schleifer, James T. *The Making of Tocqueville's Democracy in America.* Chapel Hill: University of North Carolina Press, 1980.

Schuon, Karl. *The United States Marine Corps Biographical Dictionary: The Corps' Fighting Men, What They Did, Where They Served.* New York: Watt, 1963.

Schweikart, Larry. *Banking in the American South from the Age of Jackson to Reconstruction.* Baton Rouge: Louisiana State University Press, 1987.

Scott, Kenneth, and Janet R. Clarke. *Abstracts from the Pennsylvania Gazette, 1748–1755.* Baltimore: Genealogical Publishing, 1977.

Shreve, Royal Ornan. *The Finished Scoundrel. General James Wilkinson, Sometime Commander-in-Chief of the Army of the United States, Who Made Intrigue a Trade and Treason a Profession.* Indianapolis: Bobbs-Merrill, 1933.

Siebert, Wilbur H. *The Legacy of the American Revolution to the British West Indies and Bahamas.* Columbus: Ohio State University, 1913.

Stark, James H. *Stark's History and Guide to the Bahama Islands . . . Including Their History, Inhabitants, Climate, Agriculture, Geology, Government and Resources.* Boston: Stark, 1891.

Stephenson, Wendell Holmes. *Alexander Porter: Whig Planter of Old Louisiana.* Baton Rouge: Louisiana State University Press, 1934.

Stutesman, John Hale. *Some Watkins Families of Virginia and Their Kin: Abbott, Anderson, Bass, Clay, Cox, Farrar, Hancock, Hundley, Montague, Moseley, Randolph, Walthall, Wooldridge.* Baltimore, Md.: Gateway Press, 1989.

Texada, David Ker. *Alejandro O'Reilly and the New Orleans Rebels.* The University of Southwestern Louisiana History Series, no. 2. Lafayette: University of Southwestern Louisiana, 1970.

Thomas, LaVerne, III. *Ledoux, A Pioneer Franco-American Family, with Detailed Sketches of Allied Families.* New Orleans: Polyanthos, 1982.

Trabue, Daniel. *Westward into Kentucky: The Narrative of Daniel Trabue.* Edited by Chester Raymond Young. Lexington: University Press of Kentucky, 1981.

Tregle, Joseph G., Jr. "The Antebellum Period." In *A Guide to the History of Louisiana.* Edited by Light Townsend Cummins and Glen Jeansonne. Westport, Conn.: Greenwood Press, 1982.

Trevelyan, George M. *History of England.* Vol. 3, *From Utrecht to Modern Times: The Industrial Revolution and the Transition to Democracy.* Garden City, N.Y.: Doubleday Anchor Books, 1952.

Turner, Frederick J. *The Significance of the Frontier in American History.* 1894. Reprint, Ann Arbor, Mich.: University Microfilms, 1966.

Vella, Christina. *Intimate Enemies: The Two Worlds of the Baroness de Pontalba.* Baton Rouge: Louisiana State University Press, 1997.

Villers du Terrage, Marc de, Baron. *Les Dernières Années de la Louisiane Française. Le Chevalier de Kerlérec, D'Abbadie-Aubry, Laussat.* Paris: E. Guilmoto, 1904.

Wandell, Samuel H., and Meade Minnigerode. *Aaron Burr, a Biography Written, in Large Part, from Original and Hitherto Unused Material.* 2 vols. New York: G. P. Putnam's Sons, 1925.

Whitaker, Arthur Preston. *The Mississippi Question, 1795–1803: A Study in Trade, Politics, and Diplomacy.* 1934. Reprint, Gloucester, Mass.: Peter Smith, 1962.

———. *The Spanish American Frontier, 1783–1795: The Westward Movement and the Spanish Retreat in the Mississippi Valley.* Boston: Houghton Mifflin, 1927.

———, ed. and trans. *Documents Relating to the Commercial Policy of Spain in the Floridas, with Incidental Reference to Louisiana.* Publications of the Florida Historical Society, No. 10. Deland: Florida Historical Society, 1931.

Whitaker, John Smith. *Sketches of Life and Character in Louisiana: The Portraits Selected Principally from the Bench and Bar.* New Orleans: Ferguson & Crosby, 1847.

White, David Hart. *Vicente Folch, Governor in Spanish Florida, 1787–1811.* Washington, D.C.: University Press of America, 1981.

Wilkinson, James. *Burr's Conspiracy Exposed; and General Wilkinson Vindicated Against the Slanders of His Enemies on That Important Occasion.* [Washington City: Printed for the Author,] 1811.

———. *Memoirs of My Own Times.* 3 vols. 1816. Reprint, New York: AMS Press, 1973.

Wilson, Maurine T., and Jack Jackson. *Philip Nolan and Texas: Expeditions to the Unknown Land, 1791–1801.* Waco, Tex.: Texian Press, 1987.

Wilson, Samuel, Jr. *The Vieux Carré, New Orleans: Its Plan, Its Growth, Its Architecture.* New Orleans: Bureau of Governmental Research, 1968.

Workman, James. *Brief of the Case of Caricaburu, Arieta & Company, Merchants of the Havana, Appellants in the Following Suits: First the Josefa Segunda, Her Tackle, Cagro [sic] &c versus the United States. Second . . . Caricaburu, Arieta & Company versus the Josefa Segunda, Her Tackle, Cargo, and the 152 Negroe*

Slaves. Now Pending in the Supreme Court of the United States for the Louisiana District. New Orleans: Benjamin Hanna, 1820.

[———.] *Case of Mr. Workman on a Rule for An Alleged Contempt of the Superior Court of the Territory of Orleans.* Philadelphia: William Fry [1809].

———. *Defence of the Orleans Navigation Company, Before the Supreme Court; in the Suit Instituted Against Them by Scire Facias, Pursuant to a Resolution of the Legislature of the State of Louisiana.* New Orleans: Benjamin Levy, 1822.

———. *Essays and Letters on Various Political Subjects.* 2nd American ed. New York: I. Riley, 1809.

———. *A Letter to the Respectable Citizens, Inhabitants of the County of Orleans, Together with Several Letters to His Excellency Governor Claiborne, And Other Documents Relative to the Extraordinary Measures Lately Pursued in this Territory.* New Orleans: Bradford & Anderson, 1807.

———. *Political Essays Relative to the War of the French Revolution; viz. An Argument, Against Continuing the War, for the Subversion of the Republican Government of France: A Letter to the Duke of Portland, Being an Answer to the Two Letters of the Late Right Honourable Edmund Burke, Against Treating for Peace with the French Republic: And a Memorial, Proposing a Plan, for the Conquest and Emancipation of Spanish America, by Means which Would Promote the Tranquility of Ireland.* Alexandria, Va.: Cottom & Stewart, 1801.

———. *The Trials of the Honb. James Workman, and Col. Lewis Kerr, Before the United States Court, for the Orleans District on a Charge of High Misdemeanor, in Planning and Setting on Foot, Within the United States, An Expedition for the Conquest and Emancipation of Mexico.* New Orleans: Bradford & Anderson, 1807.

Wulfeck, Dorothy Ford. *Marriages of Some Virginia Residents, 1607–1800.* Vol. 1. *Surnames C–E.* Baltimore: Genealogical Publishing, 1986.

Zink, Frances P. *Julien Poydras: Statesman, Philanthropist, Educator.* Southwestern Studies, Humanities Series, No. 1. Lafayette: University of Southwestern Louisiana, 1968.

ARTICLES

Barnard, Ella Kent. "Isaac Briggs, 1763–1825." *Maryland Historical Magazine* 7, no. 4 (December 1912): 409–19.

Baudier, Roger. "Sanitation in New Orleans." *The Southern Plumber* 9, no. 3 (October 1930): 11–4.

———. "Sanitation in New Orleans." *The Southern Plumber* 9, no. 4 (November 1930): 13–6.

———. "Sanitation in New Orleans." *The Southern Plumber* 9, no. 5 (December 1930): 9–12.

Billings, Warren M. "A Neglected Treatise: Lewis Kerr's Exposition and the Making of Criminal Law in Louisiana." *Louisiana History* 38, no. 3 (summer 1997): 261–86.

Bradley, Jared W. "William C. C. Claiborne, the Old Southwest and the Development of American Indian Policy." *Tennessee Historical Quarterly* 33, no. 3 (fall 1974): 265–78.

———. "W. C. C. Claiborne and Spain: Foreign Affairs under Jefferson and Madison, 1801–1811, Part I, The Early Negotiations, 1801–1806." *Louisiana History* 12, no. 4 (fall 1971): 297–314.

———. "W. C. C. Claiborne and Spain: Foreign Affairs under Jefferson and Madison, 1801–1811, Part II, A Successful Expansion, 1807–1811." *Louisiana History* 13, no. 1 (winter 1972): 5–26.

"Brevet Brigadier General George Mathews." *Pennsylvania Magazine of History and Biography* 44, no. 4 (1920), 343–4.

Casey, Powell A. "Masonic Lodges in New Orleans." *New Orleans Genesis* 20, no. 77 (January 1981), 1–20.

"Celebration of the Louisiana Centennial." *Publications of the Louisiana Historical Society* 6 (1912).

Cohen, Hennig, ed. "An Unpublished Diary by Robert Mills, 1803." *South Carolina Historical and Genealogical Magazine* 51, no. 4 (October 1950), 187–94.

Conrad, Glenn. "Edward D. Turner: Soldier, Jurist, Planter, Patriot." *Louisiana History* 37, no. 2 (spring 1996): 217–25.

Couch, R. Randall. "William Charles Cole Claiborne: An Historiographical Review." *Louisiana History* 36, no. 4 (fall 1995): 453–65.

Cox, Isaac J. "General Wilkinson and His Later Intrigues with the Spaniards." *American Historical Review* 19, no. 4 (July 1914): 794–812.

———. "Hispanic-American Phases of the Burr Conspiracy." *Hispanic-American Historical Review* 12, no. 2 (May 1932): 145–75.

———. "The Louisiana-Texas Frontier, I." *Quarterly of the Texas State Historical Association* 10, no. 1 (July 1906): 1–75.

———. "The Louisiana-Texas Frontier, II." *Southwestern Historical Quarterly* 17, no. 1 (July 1913): 1–42.

———. "The Louisiana-Texas Frontier, III." *Southwestern Historical Quarterly* 17, no. 2 (October 1913): 140–87.

———. "Western Reaction to the Burr Conspiracy." *Illinois Historical Society Transactions* (1928), 73–87.

H. H. C. [Heloise H. Crozat]. "When Knighthood Was in Flower." *Louisiana Historical Quarterly* 1, no. 4 (April 1918): 367–71.

Dainow, Joseph. "Moreau Lislet's Notes on Sources of Louisiana Civil Code of 1808." *Louisiana Law Review* 19, no. 1 (December 1958): 43–51.

DeGrummond, Jane Lucas. "Cayetana Susana Bosque y Fanqui, 'A Notable Woman.'" *Louisiana History* 23, no. 3 (summer 1982): 277–94.

DeVille, Winston. "Some Louisiana Land Claims." *Louisiana Genealogocial and Historical Register* 16, no. 2 (June 1969): 126–7.

Din, Gilbert C. "The Irish Mission to West Florida." *Louisiana History* 12, no. 4 (fall 1971): 315–34.

Downs, Randolph C. "Indian Affairs in the Southwest Territory, 1790–1796." *Tennessee Historical Magazine* 2nd ser., 3, no. 4 (January 1937): 240–68.

"Faithful Picture of the Political Situation of New Orleans at the Close of the Last and the Beginning of the Present Year, 1807." Edited by James E. Winston. *Louisiana Historical Quarterly* 11, no. 3 (July 1928): 359–433.

Faulkner, Robert K. "John Marshall and the Burr Trial." *Journal of American History* 53, no. 2 (September 1966): 247–58.

Faye, Stanley. "Consuls of Spain in New Orleans, 1804–1821." *Louisiana Historical Quarterly* 21, no. 3 (July 1938): 677–84.

———, ed. "Louis de Clouet's Memorial to the Spanish Government, December 7, 1814 (Conditions in Louisiana and Proposed Plan for Spanish Reconquest." *Louisiana Historical Quarterly* 22, no. 3 (July 1939): 795–818.

———, ed. "The Schism of 1805 in New Orleans." *Louisiana Historical Quarterly* 22, no. 1 (January 1939): 98–141.

Forsyth, Alice D. "Extracts from St. Louis Cathedral Marriage Book 5 (1830–1834)," *Louisiana Genealogical Register* 21, no. 3 (September 1974): 223–38.

Forsyth, Hewitt L., and various contributors. "Tombstone Inscriptions from New Orleans Cemeteries." *New Orleans Genesis* 1, [no. 2] (March 1962), 184–97.

Fournier, Melva Mae Guerin, and Jess Bergeron. "The Pollock and McDonnell Family." *Terrebonne Life Lines* 6, no. 2 (summer 1987): 60–7.

Franklin, Mitchell. "The Eighteenth *Brumaire* in Louisiana: Talleyrand and the Spanish Medieval Legal System of 1806." *Tulane Law Review* 16, no. 4 (June 1942): 514–61.

———. "An Important Document in the History of American, Roman and Civil Law: The de la Vergne Manuscript." *Tulane Law Review* 23, no. 1 (December 1958): 35–42.

———. "The Place of Thomas Jefferson in the Expulsion of Spanish Medieval Law from Louisiana." *Tulane Law Review* 14, no. 3 (April 1942): 319–38.

Freeman, Arthur. "The Early Career of Pierre Soulé." *Louisiana Historical Quarterly* 25, no. 4 (October 1942): 971–1127.

Gaspard, Elizabeth. "The Rise of the Louisiana Bar: The Early Period, 1813–1839." *Louisiana History* 28, no. 2 (spring 1987): 183–97.

Gilmore, William E. "General Joseph Kerr." *Ohio Archaeological and Historical Publications* 12 (1903), 164–7.

Groner, Julius, and Robert R. Rea. "John Ellis, King's Agent, and West Florida." *Florida Historical Quarterly* 66, no. 4 (April 1988): 385–98.

Hale, E. E. "The Real Philip Nolan." *Publications of the Mississippi Historical Society* 4 (1902), 281–329.

Harlan, Louis R., "Public Career of William Berkeley Lewis." *Tennessee Historical Quarterly* 7, no. 1 (March 1948): 3–37.

Hayden, Horace E. "Pollock Genealogy: A Biographical Sketch of Oliver Pollock,

Esq., of Carlisle, Pennsylvania, United States Commercial Agent at New Orleans and Havana." *New Orleans Genesis* 15, no. 57 (January 1976): 1–10.

Hemperley, Marion R., comp. "Federal Naturalization Oaths, Charleston, South Carolina, 1790–1860." *South Carolina Historical Magazine* 66, no. 1 (January 1965): 218–28.

Holmes, Jack D. L. "Andres Almonester y Rozas: Saint or Scoundrel?" *Louisiana Studies* 7, no. 1 (spring 1968): 47–64.

———. "*Dramatis Personae* in Spanish Louisiana." *Louisiana Studies* 6, no. 2 (summer 1967): 149–85.

———. "Joseph Piernas and a Proposed Settlement on the Calcasieu River, 1795." *McNeese Review* 13 (1962): 59–80.

———. "The Marques de Casa-Calvo, Nicolas de Finiels, and the 1805 Spanish Expedition through East Texas and Louisiana." *Southwestern Historical Quarterly* 79, no. 3 (January 1966): 324–39.

———. "Three Early Memphis Commandants: Beauregard, Deville Degoutin, and Folch." *West Tennessee Historical Society Papers* 18 (1964): 5–38.

James, Mrs. Fred O. (Thelma Coignard). "Index to French & Spanish Translations of Original Documents." *New Orleans Genesis* 3, no. 11 (June 1964), 197–206.

———. "Index to French & Spanish Translations of Original Documents." *New Orleans Genesis* 3, no. 12 (September 1964), 327–40.

James, James A. "Oliver Pollock, Financier of the Revolution in the West." *Mississippi Valley Historical Review* 16, no. 1 (June 1929): 67–80.

Jervey, Elizabeth Heyward. "Marriage and Death Notices from the City-Gazett [*sic*] and Daily Advertiser." *South Carolina Historical and Genealogical Magazine* 30, no. 4 (October 1929), 241–54.

———. "Marriage and Death Notices from the City Gazette of Charleston, S.C." *South Carolina Historical and Genealogical Magazine* 50, no. 2 (October 1949), 71–6.

Johnson, Jerah. "Dr. John Watkins, New Orleans' Lost Mayor." *Louisiana History* 36, no. 2 (spring 1995): 187–96.

Kendall, John S. "According to the Code." *Louisiana Historical Quarterly* 23, no. 1 (January 1940): 141–61.

———. "The Huntsmen of Black Ivory." *Louisiana Historical Quarterly* 24, no. 1 (January 1941): 9–34.

———. "The Pontalba Buildings." *Louisiana Historical Quarterly* 19, no. 1 (January 1936): 119–49.

"Kentucky State Papers. Excerpts from Executive Journal No. 1, Governor Isaac Shelby." *Register of the Kentucky Historical Society* 27, no. 81 (September 1929): 587–94.

King, George H. S. "Will of George Hudson of Hanover County, Virginia." *Virginia Magazine of History and Biography* 66, no. 1 (January 1958): 85–7.

King, Grace. "The Real Philip Nolan." *Publications of the Louisiana Historical Society* 10 (1918), 87–112.

LaChance, Paul F. "The 1809 Immigration of Saint-Domingue Refugees to New Orleans: Reception, Integration and Impact." *Louisiana History* 29, no. 2 (spring 1988): 109–41.

Lafargue, André. "Pierre Clément Laussat: An Intimate Portrait." *Louisiana Historical Quarterly* 24, no. 1 (January 1941): 5–8.

LaVere, David. "Edward Murphy: Irish Entrepreneur in Spanish Natchitoches." *Louisiana History* 32, no. 4 (fall 1991): 371–91.

LeBreton, Dagmar R., and Mitchell Franklin. "Bench and Bar: A Late Letter by Edward Livingston on the Criminal Code of Louisiana." *Tulane Law Review* 17, no. 2 (November 1942): 283–7.

"Letter of R. D. Claiborne, Deputy Quarter Master General at Estherton, Pennsylvania [now Coxtowne] to General Edward Hand, May 19, 1779." *Pennsylvania Magazine of History and Biography* 52 (1928), 174–5.

"Local Notices from the Virginia Gazette, Richmond, 1783." *Virginia Genealogist* 28, no. 3, whole number 111 (July–September 1984), 187–96.

Lynch, John. "British Policy and Spanish America, 1783–1808." *Journal of Latin American Studies* 1, Part I (May 1969): 1–30.

McAlister, L. N. "Pensacola during the Second Spanish Period." *Florida Historical Quarterly* 37, nos. 3 and 4 (January–April 1959): 281–327.

McClellan, Edwin N. "The Navy at the Battle of New Orleans." *United States Naval Institute Proceedings* 50, no. 262 (December 1924), 2041–60.

McCutcheon, Roger P. "Libraries in New Orleans, 1771–1833." *Louisiana Historical Quarterly* 20, no. 1 (January 1937): 152–8.

Maduell, Charles R., Jr. "New Orleans in 1810." *New Orleans Genesis* 14, no. 56 (September 1975): 425–8.

Marchand, Sidney A., Sr. "An Attempt to Re-Assemble the Old Settlers in Family Groups." *New Orleans Genesis* 3, no. 11 (June 1964): 207–21.

———. "An Attempt to Re-Assemble the Old Settlers in Family Groups." *New Orleans Genesis* 3, no. 12 (September 1964): 345–59.

———. "An Attempt to Re-Assemble the Old Settlers in Family Groups." *New Orleans Genesis* 4, no. 15 (June 1965): 256–71.

Marigny, Bernard. "Reflections on the Campaign of General Andrew Jackson in Louisiana in 1814 and 1815." *Louisiana Historical Quarterly* 6, no. 1 (January 1923): 61–85.

"Memoirs of Micah Taul." *Register of the Kentucky Historical Society* 27, no. 79 (January 1929): 343–80.

Morazan, Ronald. "The Cabildo of Spanish New Orleans, 1769–1803: The Collapse of Local Government." *Louisiana Studies* 12, no. 4 (winter 1973): 591–605.

Nasatir, Abraham P., and Ernest R. Liljegren. "Materials Relating to the History of the Mississippi Valley from the Minutes of the Spanish Supreme Council of State, 1787–1797." *Louisiana Historical Quarterly* 21, no. 1 (January 1938): 5–75.

"Newspaper Notices, Louisiana Gazette (New Orleans)." *Louisiana Genealogical Register* 4 [5], no. 5 (October 1958): 34.

"Newspaper Notices, Louisiana Gazette (New Orleans)." *Louisiana Genealogical Register* 5, no. 6 (December 1958): 42.

"Notes." *Pennsylvania Magazine of History and Biography* 1, no. 2 (1877), 223.

Padgett, James A., ed. "The Difficulties of Andrew Jackson in New Orleans Including His Later Dispute with Fulwar Skipwith, as Shown by the Documents." *Louisiana Historical Quarterly* 21, no. 2 (April 1938), 367–419.

————. "The Letters of Doctor Samuel Brown to President Jefferson and James Brown." *Register of the Kentucky Historical Society* 35, no. 110 (January 1937): 1–28.

————. "The Letters of Doctor Samuel Brown to President Jefferson and James Brown." *Register of the Kentucky Historical Society* 35, no. 111 (April 1937): 99–130.

Pascal, Robert A. "A Recent Discovery: A Copy of the 'Digest of the Civil Laws' of 1808 with Marginal Source References in Moreau Lislet's Hand." *Louisiana Law Review* 26, no. 1 (December 1965): 25–7.

Pritchard, Walter. "Selecting a Governor for the Territory of Orleans." *Louisiana Historical Quarterly* 31, no. 1 (April 1948): 269–393.

————, ed. "Three Letters of Richard Claiborne to William Miller, 1816–1818." *Louisiana Historical Quarterly* 24, no. 3 (July 1941): 729–43.

"Queries." *Pennsylvania Magazine of History and Biography* 50, no. 1 (1926): 94.

Rader, Perry Scott. "The Romance of American Courts: Gaines vs. New Orleans." *Louisiana Historical Quarterly* 27, no. 1 (January 1944), 1–322.

Sawitzky, William. "The American Work of Benjamin West." *Pennsylvania Magazine of History and Biography* 62, no. 4 (October 1938): 433–62.

Seilhamer, George O. " 'Old Mother Cumberland.' " *Pennsylvania Magazine of History and Biography* 24, no. 1 (1900), 17–47.

Stanard, W. G. "Abstracts of Virginia Land Patents." *Virginia Magazine of History and Biography* 1, no. 2 (October 1893), 310–24.

Stone, Ferdinand. "The Civil Code of 1808 for the Territory of Orleans." *Tulane Law Review* 33, no. 1 (December 1958): 1–6.

Szászdi, Adam. "Governor Folch and the Burr Conspiracy." *Florida Historical Quarterly* 38, no. 3 (January 1960): 239–51.

Taylor, Georgia Fairbanks. "The Early History of the Episcopal Church in New Orleans, 1805–1840." *Louisiana Historical Quarterly* 22, no. 2 (April 1939): 428–78.

Tregle, Joseph G., Jr. "Louisiana and the Tariff of 1816–1846." *Louisiana Historical Quarterly* 25, no. 1 (January 1942): 24–148.

Turner, Frederick Jackson. "The Policy of France toward the Mississippi Valley in the Period of Washington and Adams." *American Historical Review* 10, no. 2 (January 1905): 249–78.

Vogel, Robert C. "The Patterson and Ross Raid on Barataria, September 1814."
    Louisiana History 33, no. 2 (spring 1992): 157–70.
Watson, Charles S. "A Denunciation on the Stage of Spanish Rule: James Work-
    man's 'Liberty in Louisiana' (1804)." *Louisiana History* 11, no. 3 (summer
    1970): 245–58.
———. "Stephen Cullen Carpenter, First Drama Critic of the Charleston *Courier*."
    South Carolina Historical Magazine 69, no. 4 (October 1968): 243–52.
[Whitaker, Arthur P., ed.] "Despatches from the United States Consulate in New
    Orleans, 1801–1803, I." *American Historical Review* 32, no. 4 (July 1927):
    801–24.
[———.] "Despatches from the United States Consulate in New Orleans, 1801–
    1803 II." *American Historical Review* 33, no. 2 (January 1928): 331–59.
[———.] "Another Dispatch from the United States Consulate in New Orleans."
    American Historical Review 38, no. 2 (January 1933): 291–5.
———, ed. and trans.] "Documents. 5. An Interview of Governor Folch with Gen-
    eral Wilkinson, 1807." *American Historical Review* 10, no. 4 (July 1905):
    832–40.
White, David H. "A View of Spanish West Florida: Selected Letters of Governor
    Juan Vicente Folch [*sic*]." *Florida Historical Quarterly* 56, no. 2 (October 1977):
    138–47.
White, Maunsel. "The Olden Time in New-Orleans and the Yellow Fever." *De
    Bow's Commercial Review* 6, no. 2 (August 1848): 156–8.
Whittington, G. P. "Rapides Parish, Louisiana—A History." *Louisiana Historical
    Quarterly* 16, no. 2 (April 1933): 235–55.
Wilson, Samuel, Jr. "An Architectural History of the Royal Hospital and the Ursu-
    line Convent of New Orleans." *Louisiana Historical Quarterly* 29, no. 3 (July
    1946): 559–659.
Wohl, Michael. "Not Yet Saint Nor Sinner: A Further Note on Daniel Clark." *Loui-
    siana History* 24, no. 2 (spring 1983): 195–205.
Wood, Minter. "Life in New Orleans in the Spanish Period." *Louisiana Historical
    Quarterly* 22, no. 1 (January 1939): 642–709.
Zacharie, James S. "New Orleans—Its Old Streets and Places." *Publications of the
    Louisiana Historical Society* 2, Part 3 (February 1900): 45–88.

RESEARCH CORRESPONDENCE TO AUTHOR

Jennifer Ambrose, research services librarian, Historical Society of Pennsylvania,
    Philadelphia, January 26, February 14, 1996
Jonathan N. Armstrong, librarian, King's Inns Library, Dublin, Ireland, April 6,
    1998
Adrian Blunt, deputy librarian, Honourable Society of the Inner Temple, Library,
    London, April 8, 1998
W. W. Bream, librarian, Honourable Society of the Inner Temple, Library, London,
    February 11, 1977

Joanne J. Brooks, Virginia Historical Society, Richmond, June 20, 1995

Kenneth S. Carlson, reference archivist, Rhode Island State Archives, Providence, June 10, 1995, July 22, 1998

Jo Currie, assistant librarian, Special Collections, Edinburgh University Library, May 12, 1995

Rita Dockery, assistant manuscripts librarian, American Philosophical Society, Philadelphia, January 16, 1996

William R. Erwin Jr., senior reference librarian, Rare Book, Manuscript, and Special Collections Library, Duke University, Durham, N.C., January 16, 1996, April 1, July 28, 1998

Clark Evans, reference specialist, Rare Book and Special Collections Division, Library of Congress, Washington, D.C., April 17, 1996

Susan S. Fint, Frankfort, Ky., January 22, 1996 (postmarked)

Alice D. Forsyth, archivist, St. Louis Cathedral, New Orleans, February 9, 1976

Florence I. Gallagher, Lancaster County Historical Society, Lancaster, Pa., May 6, 1975 [1976]

Susan S. Koelble, Southampton, Pa., November 5, December 17, 1996

John Ward Willson Loose, secretary, Lancaster County (Pa.) Bicentennial Commission, December 24, 1975

William C. Luebke, Virginia State Library and Archives, Richmond, June 26, 1995

Wilbur E. Meneray, assistant university librarian for special collections, Howard-Tilton Memorial Library, Tulane University, New Orleans, April 24, 1998

Robert D. Mills, assistant librarian, Kings Inns Library, Dublin, Ireland, February 1, 1977

Dennis Northcott, assistant archivist, Missouri Historical Society, St. Louis, July 26, 1995, August 8, 1995 (postmarked)

Mrs. Henry (Mary) Z. Pain, London, July 28, August 22, September 5, October 17, 1976

Robert E. Parkin, Genealogical Research & Productions, St. Louis, August 8, 21, 1995

Suzanne Porter, curator, History of Medicine Collection, Duke University Medical Center, Durham, N.C., February 8, 1996

Martin Reuss, senior historian, Department of the Army, U.S. Army Corps of Engineers, Office of History, October 12, 1995

D. Gail Saunders, archivist, Public Records Office, Nassau, Bahamas, November 10, 1976

————, director, Public Records Office, Nassau, Bahamas, May 23, 1995

Faye Simkin, executive officer, Local History and Genealogy, New York Public Library, November 14, 1977

Elizabeth Wills, staff genealogist, Kentucky Historical Society, Frankfort, September 9, 1995

John Wood, Reader Services Department, Public Record Office, London, June 29, 1995

INDEX